The Burfor

A study in minor town government

R. H. Gretton

Alpha Editions

This edition published in 2019

ISBN : 9789353806217

Design and Setting By
Alpha Editions
email - alphaedis@gmail.com

THE
BURFORD
RECORDS

A Study in

Minor Town Government

By R. H. Gretton, M.A., M.B.E.

OXFORD

AT THE CLARENDON PRESS

MCMXX

THIS BOOK IS DEDICATED TO
MY WIFE
In love and gratitude for her unfailing
encouragement and help and in
commemoration of
our home at
BURFORD

Printed in England
At the Oxford University Press

PREFATORY NOTE

My thanks are due to many whose kindness has contributed to the making of this book. In the first place, I have to thank Mrs. Cheatle, who, by allowing me access to the portion of the Burford Records in her possession, gave the first impulse towards what has become a considerable undertaking. Secondly, I express my thanks to the Burford Charity Trustees for the long study I was permitted to make of the Records in their keeping. In this connexion I gladly acknowledge my indebtedness to Mr. E. J. Horniman, who not only provided the monetary guarantee required by the Trustees for the safety of their documents, but has, throughout my work, given me that peculiarly valuable kind of encouragement—an ever-ready interest in the details of my investigations. To the President and Fellows of Brasenose College, Oxford, my thanks are due for permission to print extracts from the series of leases of property in Burford formerly held by the College, which the kindness of the Bursar of the College enabled me to consult, and from which I have gathered some of the earliest facts, hitherto unknown, in the history of the Corporation of Burford.

The Rev. W. C. Emeris, M.A., Vicar of Burford and Rural Dean, has added to many incidental kindnesses the writing of much of the chapter on the parish church of Burford, thus giving to my book in that respect an authority which no one else could have given it. I am sincerely grateful to him for the generosity with which he has allowed me to make use of his knowledge in this and other points of Burford history.

PREFATORY NOTE

To the skill of my brother-in-law, Mr. David Crichton, M.A., and of Mr. Frederick Hall, Controller of the Oxford University Press, I owe the admirable series of photographs of Burford buildings; and to Mr. H. E. Conway the view of Burford, from a painting by him, which appears as the frontispiece.

I am under a great obligation to the Rev. A. J. Carlyle, Litt.D., Fellow of University College, who devoted much of his valuable time to reading the book in manuscript, made fruitful suggestions as to the arrangement of the matter, and was kind enough to stand sponsor for it to the authorities of the University Press.

Finally, though it would be impossible here to express an adequate gratitude for the generous help my wife has afforded at every stage of the book's progress, it would be equally impossible to make no mention of it. Without her constant aid, her wise and patient criticism, and her love and knowledge of Burford and the Cotswolds, the work would never have been done.

R. H. GRETTON.

CONTENTS

PART I

HISTORY OF THE CORPORATION OF BURFORD

PART II

STUDIES IN THE HISTORY OF BURFORD

PART III

CALENDAR OF THE RECORDS

CONTENTS

LIST OF PLATES

NOTE ON THE FRONTISPIECE TO PART III

THE following description of the Maces and Seals of the ancient Corporation of Burford is extracted from *Corporation Plate and Insignia of Office*, by L. Jewitt, F.S.A., and E. H. St. John Hope, F.S.A. (ii. 258).

The earlier of the maces is of silver, and measures thirteen and three-sixteenths inches in length. It has a plain slender shaft (with an iron core) to which are affixed, just below the centre, five wavy flanges with moulded edges and enclosing strap-work scrolls. Just below the head is a moulded ring, and at the bottom is a flat button engraved, seal fashion, with a lion rampant. The head, which is supported by a calix of sixteen petals, is globular in form and surmounted by a coronet of ten crosses and as many fleur-de-lis, resting on a bold cable moulding. On the flat top, within a quatrefoil, are the royal arms, *France and England quarterly* ; originally enamelled. This interesting mace is probably of sixteenth-century date, but the lion on the button looks later.

The other mace is two feet nine inches and five-eighths long, and also of silver. It is of the usual late type with crowned head surmounted by the orb and cross, but the design of the shaft is somewhat unusual. The head, which is supported by four slender brackets, is handsomely wrought with four frosted oval panels, with ornate leafwork between, containing the usual royal badges, viz. the rose, thistle, fleur-de-lis, and harp, severally crowned. The crown surmounting the head has a delicately worked coronet, and jewelled arches depressed in the centre so as to touch the cap beneath, which bears in relief the royal arms and supporters in use from 1714 to 1801, with the arms of Burford, *a lion rampant* below. The shaft consists of (i) a short plain section with the brackets below the mace-head ; (ii) a long section, with slight medial band and two panelled terminal bosses, ornamented throughout with a bold leaf pattern arranged as a spiral band ; below this again is (iii) the handle or grip, at first plain, then wrought with leaves, and gradually swelling out towards the foot-knop, which is also chased with leafwork. The mace bears the leopard's head and lion passant gardant of the London hall-marks, but no date letter, and for the maker, I W, with a rose above, for John Wisdome (entered 1720). The maker's mark is twice struck, and similarly repeated under the head. The mace not improbably dates from George the Second's charter of 1742.

The common seal, of silver, is of the unusual form of a pointed oval, two and one-eighth inches long. The device is a boldly engraved lion rampant, facing to the sinister (probably by inadvertence on the part of the engraver), with the marginal legend ✠ SIGILL' COMMUNE . BURGENSIUM . DE . BUREFORD. On either side of the lion are the two centres from which the curved sides and lines of the seal were struck. On the back is a loop for suspension, from which three long leaf-like branches diverge and extend over the seal.   Date *circa* 1250.

The other seal, which is attached to the silver one by a plaited leather thong, has probably been used as a counter-seal. It is a pointed oval, one and three-eighths of an inch long, and of latten, with a small loop at the top. The device represents a clerk in amice and girded alb kneeling under a trefoiled arch surmounted by a half-length figure of Our Lady and Child. Legend ✠ AVE MARIA GRĀ PLENA DN̄S TECUM.

It should be remarked that in the reference to ' George the Second's charter ' the authors of the above description had been misled by a faulty list of the town charters. No charter was ever obtained at such a date ; the document mistaken for a charter of 1742 is really a writ under the Great Seal.

It may also be remarked that the smaller seal has sometimes been described as the ' Priory seal '. In view of the device it bears it is much more probable, to say the least, that it was the seal of the Gild, which was dedicated to the Blessed Virgin. This also would account for its having been kept attached by a thong to the Town seal, since the Gild and the Corporation are indistinguishable. The Priory seal would, on the contrary, have been very unlikely to be preserved in that particular way. Moreover, the dedication of the Priory was to St. John the Evangelist ; and the legend on its seal would almost certainly have been in the common form—Sigillum Hospitalis Sti. Iohannis de Burford—or something of that kind.

LIST OF SUBSCRIBERS

The Duke of Marlborough, K.G., Blenheim Palace, Woodstock.
Beatrice, Countess of Portsmouth, Hurstbourne Park, Whitchurch, Hants.
The Viscount Dillon, M.A., D.C.L., Ditchley, Enstone.
The Bishop of Ripon.
Colonel Lord Gorell, O.B.E., M.C., Buckingham Gate, London, S.W. 1.
Lord Moreton, D.L., Sarsden House, Churchill.
Lord Redesdale, Asthall Manor, Oxon.
Lord Sherborne, Sherborne House, Glos.
Lord Wyfold, Wyfold Court, Reading.
Hon. Lady Barrington, The Old Lodge, Wimbledon.
Sir W. H. Hadow, D.Mus., Vice-Chancellor of the University of Sheffield,
  . Eccleshall Grange, Sheffield.
Sir Robert Hudson, G.B.E., Dean's Yard, Westminster.
Sir Francis Hyett, Painswick House, Stroud.
Sir Sidney Lee, D.Litt., LL.D., 108a Lexham Gardens, South Kensington.
Sir Theodore Morison, K.C.S.I., K.C.I.E., Principal of Armstrong College,
  Newcastle-on-Tyne.
Sir William Osler, Bart., F.R.S. (the late), Norham Gardens, Oxford.
Sir Walter Raleigh, D.Litt., Ferry Hinksey, Oxford.
Sir Michael Sadler, C.B., Vice-Chancellor of the University of Leeds.
Sir John Simon, K.C.V.O., K.C., 59 Cadogan Gardens, London, S.W.
Admiral Sir Edmund Slade, K.C.I.E., 128 Church Street, Kensington.
Sir R. Sothern-Holland, Westwell Manor, Burford.
Sir Herbert Warren, K.C.V.O., D.C.L., President of Magdalen College
  Oxford.
Colonel Sir Rhys Williams, M.P., 6 Charles Street, Mayfair.
The Dean of Canterbury, D.D., The Deanery, Canterbury.
The Dean of Norwich, D.D. (the late).

Robert Akers, Esq., The Manor, Black Bourton, Oxon.
All Souls College, Oxford.

Balliol College, Oxford.
Messrs. Banks & Co. (two copies), The Imperial Library, Cheltenham.
Harrison Barrow, Esq., J.P., Wellington Road, Edgbaston.
Walter Barrow, Esq., Ampton Road, Edgbaston.
Mrs. Alice Baxter, Northcliff, Alderley Edge, Cheshire.
Birmingham Friends' Book Society.
Messrs. Blackwell (six copies), Broad Street, Oxford.
W. C. Braithwaite, Esq., LL.B., Castle House, Banbury.
Brasenose College, Oxford.
E. D. St. John Brooks, Esq., M.A., Wickham Road, Sutton, Surrey.
Mrs. Byrne Bryce, Littleham, Burford.
Col. John Buchan, M.A., Elsfield Manor, Oxon.
Major Butler, J.P., Alvescot Lodge, Oxon.

Mrs. Barrow Cadbury, Wheeleys Road, Edgbaston.
Miss Campbell, Burford.
Miss Carbutt, The Forum Club, Grosvenor Place, S.W.
C. T. Cheatle, Esq., M.R.C.S., Burford.
The Community of the Resurrection, Mirfield, Yorks.
H. E. Conway, Esq., Burford.

Christopher Cookson, Esq., M.A., Magdalen College, Oxford.
Messrs. Cornish Bros., New Street, Birmingham.
C. W. Cottrell-Dormer, Esq., J.P., D.L., Rousham, Oxon.
David Crichton, Esq., M.A. (two copies), St. Mary's, York.
Miss Vida M. S. Crichton, Somerville College, Oxford.
Stafford Cripps, Esq., Essex Court, The Temple.
Mrs. Cull, Lucerne Chambers, Kensington.
Henry Curtis, Esq., B.Sc., M.D., F.R.C.S., Harley Street, London, W.

Rev. F. N. Davies, D.Litt., Rowner Rectory, Gosport.
S. H. Davies, Esq., D.Sc., New Earswick, York.
W. F. Drummond, Esq., Fulbrook, Burford.
Thomas Duckworth, Esq., Victoria Institute, Worcester.

Edward C. Early, Esq., Sunnyside, Witney.
Charles East, Esq., J.P., Burford.
Frederick Elder, Esq., Antrim Mansions, Hampstead, N.W. 3.
C. Ellis, Esq., Butter Hill House, Dorking.
Rev. William C. Emeris, M.A. (four copies), The Vicarage, Burford.
The Misses Emeris, The Vicarage, Burford.
Mrs. Agnes Evans, Byways, Yarnton, Oxon.
Exeter College, Oxford.

J. Meade Falkner, Esq., M.A. (five copies), The Divinity House, Durham
Professor C. H. Firth, Northmoor Road, Oxford.
W. R. Foster, Esq., The Granville, Ilfracombe.
W. Warde Fowler, Esq., D.Litt., Kingham, Oxon.
G. H. Fox, Esq., Wodehouse Place, Falmouth.
H. Sanderson Furniss, Esq., M.A., Ruskin College, Oxford.

W. G. Garne, Esq., Burford.
J. S. Gayner, Esq., M.D., New Earswick, York.
Gloucester Public Library.
A. D. Godley, Esq., D.Litt., Magdalen College, Oxford.
G. P. Gooch, Esq., M.A., South Villa, Campden Hill Road, W.
R. Goodenough, Esq., Filkins Old Hall, Lechlade.
R. H. Gretton, Esq., M.A., M.B.E. (seven copies), Calendars, Burford.
Messrs. Groves & Sons, Milton-under-Wychwood, Oxon.
Miss Imogen Guiney, Amberley, Glos.

J. G. Hailing, Esq., Cheltenham.
Alexander N. Hall, Esq., O.B.E., Barton Abbey, Oxon.
G. R. Hambidge, Esq., Burford.
H. D. Harben, Esq., M.A., Grosvenor Street, London, W. 1.
St. Hilda's Hall, Oxford.
Mrs. F. Hinde, The Prebendal House, Shipton-under-Wychwood.
S. M. Hodgkins, Esq., Burford.
R. Holland-Martin, Esq., C.B., F.S.A., Overbury Court, Tewkesbury.
George Hookham, Esq., M.A., Furze Hill, Broadway.
E. J. Horniman, Esq., J.P. (twelve copies), Burford Priory, Oxon.
Rev. C. H. Bickerton Hudson, Holyrood, Oxford.
Lt.-Col. A. R. Hurst, D.S.O., Little Barrington, Oxon.

Mrs. Ivimy, Waynes Close, Burford.

J. de M. Johnson, Esq., M.A., The Clarendon Press, Oxford.
J. E. A. Jolliffe, Esq., M.A., Keble College, Oxford.
Messrs. Jones & Evans, 77 Queen Street, Cheapside, E.C.

Keble College, Oxford.
Philip Kenway, Esq., Highdown Wood, Godalming.
Commander W. R. W. Kettlewell, R.N. (five copies), Burford.

Hugh M. Last, Esq., M.A., St. John's College, Oxford.
Aubrey T. Laurence, Esq., 13 Norfolk Terrace, Hyde Park, W. 2.
J. W. Leitch, Esq., Somerville, Edgerton, Huddersfield.
R .E. Lenthall , Esq., C.E., Newport Islands, Co. Gaspé, P. of Quebec, Canada.
Miss Wolseley Lewis, Barrington, Burford.
H. T. Ley, Esq., 17 Curzon Road, Muswell Hill, N.
Philip Lockwood, Esq., St. Werburgh St., Chester.
London Library.
T. Loveday, Esq., Williamscote, Banbury.
T. Lyon, Esq., Cheltenham.

Compton Mackenzie, Esq., B.A., Casa Solitaria, Capri.
Magdalen College, Oxford.
Manchester University, Manchester.
P. E. Matheson, Esq., M.A., 1 Savile Road, Oxford.
F. W. P. Mathews, Esq., J.P. (2 copies), Fifield, Oxon.
Thomas McCulloch, Esq., Woodfield House, Lockwood, Huddersfield.
Merton College, Oxford.
Mitchell Library, Glasgow.
W. J. Monk, Esq., Burford.
J. B. Morell, Esq., Burton Croft, York.
Miss May Morris, Kelmscott Manor, Lechlade.
Charles Campbell Murdoch, Esq., M.A., M.C. (two copies), Burford.
Mrs. Murdoch, Burford.

New College, Oxford.
J. H. B. Noble, Esq., Ardinglass, Scotland.
Edwin Norton, Esq., 2 Queen's Court, Hagley Road, Birmingham.

Rev. W. T. Oldfield, M.A., Shipton-under-Wychwood, Oxon.
Professor Sir C. W. C. Oman, F.S.A., LL.D., M.P., All Souls College, Oxford.
A. S. Owen, Esq , M.A., Keble College, Oxford.
H. E. Owen, Esq., c/o The Lamb, Burford.
Oxford Public Library.

Messrs. Packer (three copies), Burford.
Messrs. Parker (two copies), Broad Street, Oxford.
Messrs. Patrick & Page, 12 Collingwood St., Newcastle-on-Tyne.
A. E. Peake, Esq., M.R.C.S., Burford.
Rev. S. Spencer Pearce, M.A., The Vicarage, Combe, Oxon.
Mrs. E. Hope Percival, Burford.
Mrs. Phillip Percival, Uley, Stroud.
Rev. L. R. Phelps, M.A., Provost of Oriel College. Oxford.
H. F. Piggott, Esq., M.A., Burford.
S. E. Pollok, Esq., 20 Augustus Road, Edgbaston, Birmingham.
H. G. Powell, Esq., jun., Wokingham, Bucks.
Rees Price, Esq., F.S.A. Scot., Bannits, Broadway, Worcestershire.
Public Record Office, Chancery Lane, W.C.

A. L. Radford, Esq., Bradninch Manor, Devon.
Messrs. Hugh Rees, 5 Regent St., S.W.
Lt.-Col. Fairfax Rhodes.
L. Rice-Oxley, Esq., M.A., 5 Prince of Wales Terrace, Kensington.
T. H. Riches, Esq., M.A., Kitwells, Shenley, Herts.
Charles Roberts, Esq., M.A., 10 Holland Park, W.

Rev. W. Fothergill Robinson, The Vicarage, Bloxham.
Rothamsted Experimental Station Library, Harpenden.

Captain A. E. W. Salt, War Office School of Education, The Hutments, Newmarket.
Rev. H. E. Salter, M.A., Dry Sandford, Abingdon.
C. Samuda, Esq., J.P., Bruern Abbey, Oxon.
R. H. Schuster, Esq., Church Bank, Bowden, Manchester.
C. P. Scott, Esq., M.A., J.P., Fallowfield, Manchester.
Mrs. R. A. Scott, Williamstrip, Glos.
Mrs. Basil de Sélincourt, Kingham, Oxon.
Sheffield Public Library.
Mrs. Arthur Sidgwick, Woodstock Road, Oxford.
Miss C. A. Skeel, D.Litt., F.R.H.S., Well Road, Hampstead, N.W. 3.
Miss Skinner, Burford.
J. Charnock Smith, Esq., Lloyd's Bank, Handsworth, Birmingham.
Miss H. E. Snelling, The Public Hall, Tonbridge.
The Rev. Father Sole, Chipping Norton.
Somerville College, Oxford.
Christopher Stone, Esq., M.A., Field House, Horsham.
P. S. Stott, Esq., Stanton Manor, Broadway.
L. R. Strangeways, Esq., Grammar School, Bury, Lancs.
Charles Sturge, Esq., M.A., Summerhill, Sunderland.
Frank Sturge, Esq. (three copies), Wrexham, N. Wales.
Charles F. Sylvester, Esq., Branksome, Godalming.
Lt.-Col. G. Sylvester, Tonbridge, Kent.
Percy Sylvester, Esq., Hilperton, Nr. Trowbridge, Wilts.

R. H. Tawney, Esq., M.A., Balliol College, Oxford.
Trinity College, Oxford.

G. E. Underhill, Esq., M.A., Magdalen College, Oxford.

The Rev. H. C. Wace, M.A., Brasenose College, Oxford.
The Rev. W. H. Kirwan Ward, M.A., Asthall Vicarage, Oxon.
Vernon Watney, Esq., M.A., J.P., Cornbury Park, Oxon.
H. E. H. Way, Esq., M.A., Milton-under-Wychwood, Oxon.
Professor C. C. J. Webb, Magdalen College, Oxford.
J. Wells, Esq., Warden of Wadham College, Oxford.
D. J. Wilson, Esq., 40 Albemarle St., W.
W. Page Wood, Esq., 114 Sternhold Avenue, Streatham Hill, S.W.
Worcester College, Oxford.
E. H. Wyatt, Esq., Burford.
P. S. Wyatt, Esq., Burford.

York Public Library.

PART I

HISTORY OF THE CORPORATION OF
BURFORD

INTRODUCTION

THE study of the development of town government and
municipal structure in England is of necessity founded chiefly
on the history of the large and important towns, partly because
the processes of their growth are comparatively coherent and
easy to follow, partly for the reason that their records are
more ample and more readily available. But the history of
a small town may, nevertheless, have its contribution to
make ; its very failures may help towards a truer understanding of both the potentialities and the limitations of
borough charters.

The history of the ancient Corporation of Burford certainly
has light to throw upon the relation between a manorial
borough and its lord. It shows at once how far such a borough
could proceed, in favourable circumstances, towards an
apparent independence, and how precarious was its liberty.
Owing to the fact that for some centuries after its first enfranchisement Burford was an outlying and insignificant
member of the Honour of Gloucester, and that even tenants
for life were men of great possessions and resided elsewhere,
the original Gild Merchant attained by degrees a position
which during the sixteenth century was in practice indistinguishable from that of a completely chartered town. Yet as
soon as a lord of the manor put that position to the test of the
law it collapsed. The reason for the collapse provides the
first sidelight upon the study of municipal institutions which
Burford has to offer. It is the truth that the keystone of town
charters is to be found in the fee-farm. For a hundred years
certainly, and probably for longer than that, the burgesses of

Burford administered the Borough Court, the markets, and the fairs, maintained a gallows and pillory, made by-laws and punished by fines and imprisonment any breaches of the by-laws. Nor were the burgesses passing beyond the bounds of what the charters had allowed to be done in Burford. But when the exercise of these franchises was questioned by a lord of the manor it was clear that they belonged not to the men of Burford as such, but to them as the men of a manorial lord. Unless, therefore, they were in recognizable allegiance to a lord they had no claim to the privileges ; and that recognizable allegiance had to be expressed by payment of a rent. In other words, the clauses of charters may contain everything neces-sary for the passing of town affairs into the hands of people of the town ; but if they do not contain a definite farm of the town they are an extension of the privileges of the lord of the manor and not really an enfranchisement of the town.

Another conclusion to be drawn from the history of Burford is that the use of the words ' enfranchisement ' and ' liberties ' should be carefully restricted, as we have already learned to restrict the use of the words ' corporation ' and ' corporate body '. To the modern mind, accustomed to the idea of self-government in our great towns, it is almost impossible to use the words ' franchises ' or ' liberties ' without an accompany-ing conception of a policy of local independence and local responsibility. No such conception is ever to be traced in the proceedings of the burgesses of Burford. Their emergence as a corporate body is purely accidental, the result of a series of administrative needs that had to be met, and opportunities that offered themselves to be taken. At the period of their highest development they show no concern for the internal well-being of the town ; the bailiffs, the wardsmen, and the constables are answerable to the lord of the manor at the Court Leet, not to the burgesses in the Borough Court. There is no association of the general body of inhabitants in the government of the town ; the Corporation remained a self-electing Gild, devoid of public responsibility. Their own inter-pretation of their charters, and the functions they exercised in that interpretation, will be much better understood by keeping always to the front the idea of 'privileges', and avoiding altogether the idea of 'liberty'.

This is not to say, of course, that in the more highly developed towns there was the same total lack of a deliberate policy of independence. But it serves as a useful warning that even in the case of those towns the word 'enfranchisement' should be used with caution, and must be justified by proof. Charters, Professor Maitland remarked, do not create communities. It might be added that they do not necessarily enfranchise communities. They often merely confer privileges for the enrichment of the lord, which might in certain circumstances be perverted to the enrichment of some of the members of the community.

Another theory of Maitland's will be found to be well illustrated in the following pages. He was fond of maintaining that the growth and survival of a 'personality' in a town depended largely upon the existence of 'a revenue which is not going to be divided amongst the townsfolk'. This in Burford was provided by the Charity Lands. From an early date the burgesses found themselves in control of property held for public purposes ; and on at least two occasions when the Corporation appeared to be in danger of extinction, it was this control which secured its continuance.

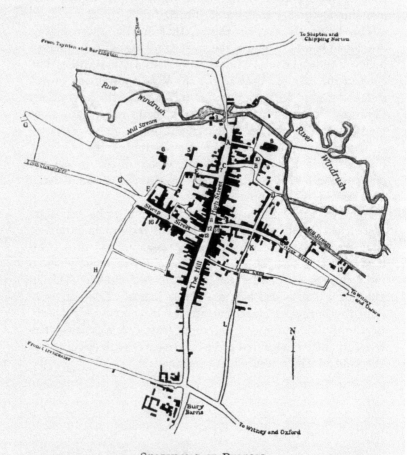

SKETCH-MAP OF BURFORD

A, Lawrence Lane. B, Church Green. C, Church Lane. D, Gildenford.
E, Priory Lane (formerly St. John's Street). F, Priory Lane. G, Line of
ancient road to Cirencester and Gloucester. H, Tanner's Lane. J, Formerly
Lavington Lane. K, Batt's Lane (later called Pytt's Lane). L, Barns
Lane.

1, Bury Orchard. 2, The Bridge. 3, The Town Mills. 4, The Vicarage.
5, The Rectory. 6, The Priory. 7, The Bear Inn. 8, The Church. 9, The
Almshouse. 10, The Grammar School. 11, Formerly the George Inn.
12, Formerly the Crown (Novum Hospitium Angulare). 13, The Tolsey.
14, The Bull. 15, The Mill in Witney Street. 16, Formerly the Culverclose.

CHAPTER I

THE ORIGINS OF THE TOWN

§ 1

THE original grant of liberties to Burford is of remarkably early date. It provides, indeed, the earliest dated instance of the establishment of a Gild Merchant. For the first charter is in the name of Robert FitzHamon,[1] and must therefore have been granted between 1088, the year in which Burford, with other possessions in Oxfordshire and Gloucestershire, came into his hands, and 1107, the year in which he died.

The grant was not of a Gild Merchant alone. It included also the liberties customary in the setting up of a borough, namely, the right to hold houses and lands at a money rent instead of by service, the right to sell or otherwise dispose of property and to devise property by will without obligation to the lord of the manor, the right to hold a market, and other ' free customs '—in this case the free customs of the men of Oxford.

The community to which this grant was made was small and purely agricultural. In the Domesday Survey, which is so near in date to FitzHamon's charter that its evidence on this point may be taken without modification, the entry relating to Burford is as follows :

Albericus Comes tenuit de terra episcopi Bureford Ibi sunt viii hide Terra xx carucarum Nunc in dominico iiii carucae et iii servi et xxii villani et xviii bordarii habent xii carucas Ibi ii molini de xxv solidis et xxv acrae prati Pastura i leu in longitudine et in latitudine Valuit xvi libras modo xiii libras.

Nothing is indicated here beyond a village community of a usual Domesday type, and of a size that could give it no special place among the villages of the hundred or the shire. Of other

---

[1] Chancery Misc. (P. R. O.), Certificates of Gilds, bundle 45, no. 388. The Certificate will be found transcribed in full *infra*, Part III, p. 301.

villages in the same hundred, Stanton Harcourt, for instance, was larger, and Bampton, with its four mills, fisheries, saltings, and market, was more than six times as valuable.

§ 2

The bestowal of liberties upon a community so small and devoid of any special resources demands some explanation. What motive and what intention directed the alteration of its status ? An answer to this question is perhaps to be found in the history of the lordship of the manor at this period.

In 1088 Robert FitzHamon,[1] in reward for his support of William Rufus against the rebellion of Bishop Odo, received a large gift of lands formerly held by the Bishop, and among them the manor of Burford. He incorporated it into the Honour of Gloucester—the most valuable part of his new possessions—and it remained for some centuries a manor of that Honour.

In this way Burford, from having been in all probability the principal seat of a manorial lord,[2] became an outlying dependency of a lord with far more important places in which to reside.[3] As a source of supplies in kind it was insignificant.[4] There might easily therefore be every inclination on the part of a lord reviewing his new territories to make the place a source of monetary revenue by erecting in it a market which would pay him tolls and a court which would collect fees. He would be the more likely to do this, since otherwise the inhabitants of this portion of his territories, remote from markets subject to him, would frequent the markets of other manors and be adding to the revenue of other lords.

[1] Hamon was lord of Corbeille in Normandy. Atkins's *Gloucestershire* (2nd ed.), p. 45.

[2] The mansion here was, at any rate, more than twice as large as Earl Aubrey's two other mansions. See Part II, p. 158.

[3] He certainly had, besides Gloucester Castle, a residence at Tewkesbury ; a charter of the Abbey there mentions 'curiam cum domibus que fuerunt proprie Roberti filii Hamonis' : Charter Rolls, 28 Edward I, m. 1.

[4] No manorial accounts of the place are available for so early a date ; but in 1295 accounts of the Honour of Gloucester show that whereas the produce of the manor of Tewkesbury, for instance, amounted to 115 qrs. 5 bushels of wheat and 202 qrs. 3 bushels of oats, the produce of the manor of Burford amounted to 23 qrs. and 65 qrs. 3 bushels respectively. P. R. O., Min. Accts., 1109, 7.

It is difficult to find any other explanation than this of the grant of the first charter. The motive cannot have been given by the inhabitants of the place. It is, no doubt, possible that in the years following the Norman settlement the situation of Burford upon what was to be for centuries the main route from South Wales and Gloucester to Oxford, and by Oxford to London, had brought into the place new inhabitants. The number of Welsh names found among the population at a later date is evidence of the passage of merchants and tradesmen along this route from the west, and traffic of that kind may have begun to affect Burford before the end of the eleventh century. It is also possible that these travellers, coming from places already large and flourishing, such as Gloucester and Tewkesbury, may have discerned in this situation an opportunity for trading-profits. But it is not possible to suppose that in the twenty years between the date of Domesday and the year 1107, during which the first charter must have been granted, the village had become so profoundly modified in character as to make a movement towards market privileges and liberties. It is more reasonable to regard the grant of liberties as an act by the lord of the manor in development of his estate ; and that explanation will be found to accord with such knowledge as we have of the effects of the charters upon the life of the place during the earliest period of their operation.

§ 3

This period is conveniently set for us by the fact that in the middle of the fourteenth century we come to the beginning of the records preserved in the town, so that it is natural to make the first stage in the town's history run from its enfranchisement to that date. Moreover, this division coincides so clearly with a distinct grouping into which the town charters fall that it becomes a real, and not merely a convenient division.

The first six of the documents coming under this head may properly be called charters, four of them emanating from lords of the manor and two from the Crown.[1] The remainder are Letters Patent of Confirmation, obtained by the town from

[1] See Part III, p. 298.

the Chancery at the beginning of every new reign, with the exception of two, from the accession of Edward III to that of James I.[1]

One effect of this grouping of the charters is to show markedly that the town had in its earliest period no conception of burghal liberties or of the tenure of a borough in independence of a manorial lord. The two royal charters do not tell against this view. For it is clear from their phrasing that neither was really granted to the town. They were obtained from Henry II by William, Earl of Gloucester, and are confirmations of his rights and privileges with special clauses relating to Burford. They are not, therefore, royal charters to Burford in the strict sense of the term, but are royal confirmations of manorial grants, belonging to a period before the Chancery had developed the system of Letters Patent of Inspeximus.

The significance of this fact becomes more striking when we observe that these are the only royal documents of our first period. In other words, the reigns of Richard I and John— a singularly active time in the securing of privileges and liberties by English towns—are wholly unrepresented in our series. The manorial history of Burford makes this blank particularly noticeable. For John's marriage with Isabella, daughter of Earl William of Gloucester, brought him, among the territories assigned to him by Richard in 1189, the Honour of Gloucester. He was thus lord of the manor of Burford, and he retained the manor for seven years after his accession. It might have been expected that this special association with the Crown, at the very time when the granting of borough charters had been discovered to be a source of revenue, and was therefore being expanded and elaborated beyond any point hitherto reached, would have offered an opportunity which the men of Burford could hardly miss. Yet they made no attempt to take advantage of it, either for clearer definition of their liberties, or for effecting the passage—easy to them

---

[1] The two exceptions are the reigns of Edward V and Richard III. Not all the Letters Patent are now extant, but there is evidence that those now missing from the series were duly obtained at the time.

when their manorial lord was also the king—from subjection to a mesne lord to direct responsibility under the Crown.

It is, no doubt, necessary to remember that, as the Chancery developed the contents and phraseology of borough charters, the fees due to the Exchequer would also be developed, and Burford must have been far from wealthy. Yet a place like Godmanchester, no less immature than Burford as a commercial centre, rose to the obtaining of quite an important charter from King John.[1] The idea of such a degree of independence, rather than the means of obtaining it, must have been lacking.

This conclusion is emphasized by the character of the last charter of our first group. It is in the name of Richard de Clare, and is therefore to be dated between 1230 and 1262.[2] He grants to the burgesses of Burford ' eas libertates et liberas consuetudines quas habent a predecessoribus nostris comitibus Gloucestriae '. There is no suggestion here of the town's privileges having passed in any sense beyond what previous Earls of Gloucester had granted, or beyond what Richard de Clare could grant in the exercise of a mesne lord's powers. It is clear that the charters of Henry II had not been intended as an enhancement of the previous charters by privileges which the Crown alone could bestow upon a town, and equally clear that they had not been interpreted by the burgesses in any such way.

This persistence in their original status may be held to support strongly the view that the motive for the town's enfranchisement resided wholly on the side of the lord, and not at all on that of the inhabitants. So complete a detachment from the general movement of English boroughs during the late twelfth and early thirteenth centuries towards more precise definition of liberties and more detailed and authoritative charters could hardly have been shown by a community with any conception of burghal independence. It is, however, quite comprehensible on the theory that the grants of privileges were, so to speak, imposed on the town from without, by the lord of the manor for his own purposes, and were in origin unrelated to aspirations of the inhabitants.

[1] Webb, *English Local Government, Manor and Borough*, i. 181.
[2] P. R. O., Inq. P. M., Hen. III, file 27, no. 5. m. 41.

§ 4

An examination of the terms of the charters will be found to lead to the same conclusion. They are throughout vague and rudimentary; and they contain, with the single exception of the establishment of a Gild Merchant, no organizing or structural clauses at all.

Three of the six are but confirmations in general terms of existing liberties, and refer to 'liberties and free customs' without specifying them. Another, the charter of Earl William of Gloucester, is an express repetition of the original charter of Robert FitzHamon. Thus, of effective charters, there only remain two—that of FitzHamon and one of the charters of Henry II.

The franchises conveyed in the former are as follows:

Ut unusquisque domum et terram et omnem pecuniam suam possit vendere et in vadimonio ponere et de filio et filia vel uxore et de quolibet alio absque ipsius domini requisicione heredem faciat et gildam et consuetudines quas habent Burgenses de Oxenford in Gildam mercatorum et quicunque ad mercatum venire volunt veniant et in ipso mercato habeant licenciam emendi quecunque volunt preter lanam et corea nisi homines ipsius ville.[1]

The charter of Henry II is as follows:

H Rex Angliae et Dux Normanniae et Aquitaniae et Comes Andegaviae Episcopo Lincolnensi et Iusticiariis et vice-comitibus et omnibus ballivis suis de Oxenfordscira salutem Mando vobis et firmiter precipio quod homines Willelmi comitis Gloecestriae de Boreford et de Mora sint ita bene et in pace et quieti de omnibus querelis et ita teneant omnes terras suas et omnia tenementa sua cum sak et soc et tol et theam et infanghenethef et cum omnibus aliis libertatibus et liberis consuetudinibus suis sicut melius et liberius tenuerunt tempore Regis H avi mei Testibus Reginaldo comite Cornubiae et Umfredo de Bohun dapifero et Warenno filio Geroldi comite apud Norhampton.

These documents give us the setting up first of burgage tenure with the right of testamentary disposition, a Gild

---

[1] The charter is imperfect on the Gild Certificates, but enough remains to show that the charter of Earl William which follows it was a verbal repetition.

Merchant, and a market with a ban of wool and hides to the inhabitants; to which were added by the later document two jurisdictional privileges—freedom from external pleas,[1] and cognizance of minor offences under the phrase ' sak et soc et tol et theam et infanghenethef '.[2]

Now these franchises would not strike us, in relation to any period up to the end of the reign of Henry II, as inadequate for an enfranchised community, nor the phrases conveying them as unusually vague. When, however, we find them existing unmodified in the fourteenth century, at which time they have to stand, as vehicles of burghal liberties, beside the charters wherein other boroughs had laid their foundations firmly during the reigns of Richard and John and then built up systematic constitutions under succeeding sovereigns, their limited nature becomes very apparent. The privileges obtained are seen to be insignificant beside those that might have been obtained. The holding of the borough at farm, the return of writs, the right to appoint a reeve or other chief officer, the right to appoint coroners, freedom from the Hundred and Shire Courts with the right to appear before the Justices in Eyre by twelve representatives of the town—none of these privileges, so generally sought by the boroughs of the time, find place in the Burford charters.

Thus from another direction we come to the same view of the motive for the charters. If it had resided in the inhabi-

---

[1] This must, I think, be the purport of the phrase *sint ita bene et in pace et quieti de omnibus querelis*. Liberty from external pleas was usually granted in more exact terms (Ballard, *Borough Charters*, pp. 115–21); but if the phrase does not bear this meaning it is difficult to give it any interpretation. It must be remembered that Mr. Ballard's instances are mostly of a period when the phraseology of charters had been rather more highly developed.

[2] I do not agree with Mr. Ballard in reading this phrase as a grant to the inhabitants as individuals, for the following reasons : (i) There is nothing in the form of the phrase to differentiate it from that used in many other charters in which it is found in exactly the same conjunction with house and land tenure. (ii) The parallel Mr. Ballard draws with a grant to ' the 19 burgesses of Warwick with their 19 masures ' is not to the point, since there is no question here of a grant to a limited number of burgesses ; the charter is addressed to the men of Burford. (iii) The evidence for the early existence here of a Borough Court makes it quite unnecessary to give any unusual interpretation to the phrase, since its customary application is not out of accord with facts.

tants there must have been some modification of the contents and phraseology of the grants, since that motive, during a period of active burghal development, could hardly have remained stationary. If, on the other hand, the motive resided in the lord of the manor, there would be less need for modification. His object being to convert a place compara-tively useless to him in its agricultural activities into a source of monetary revenue, he would be under no necessity to provide more than the minimum of executive machinery for that purpose. The singular absence of detail in the charter of Richard de Clare, and the apparent sufficiency of its general reference to the grants of previous Earls, may be taken as the final proof that this is the true interpretation of the whole group of charters.

§ 5

Of the nature of the executive which in fact came into being under the charters we are but scantily informed during this first period. I have been able to find only five references which distinctly indicate the beginnings of incorporation. Two are in a grant and quit-claim of *circa* 1250 ; the execution of the deed is ratified by the use of ' commune sigillum de Bureford ' ; and the list of witnesses closes with the words ' et curia burgen-cium de bureford '.[1] The third is in an indenture of lease dated 1264 between the Abbey of Cold Norton and Walter Adgar of Burford, in which the tenant binds himself to certain cove-nants concerning repairs, &c.,

et ad ista predicta fideliter observanda suponit se et omnia catalla sua mobilia et immobilia sub pena dimidie marce solvende dictis priori et canonicis et ballivis de bureford.[2]

The fourth occurs in the Hundred Rolls in an entry concerning lands at Nether Worton held by John Giffard of Brimpsfield :

Idem Iohannes tenet de Comite Glov'nie de feodo de Bureford redditu xs. et secta curiae de iii septimanis in iii septimanas de Bereford pro omni servicio.[3]

---

[1] Muniments of Brasenose College, Oxford : Burford Leases, 1.
[2] B. N. C. Mun. : Burford Leases, 3.
[3] *Hundred Rolls* (ed. 1818), ii. 842.

The fifth is in an Inquisition Post Mortem concerning the lands of Gilbert de Clare in 1314, in which the following entry occurs among his possessions at Burford :

Et sunt ibi xiii burgenses qui reddunt per annum xiiis. vid. ad iiii terminos videlicet ad festum nativitatis beati Iohannis Baptiste Beati Michaelis Beati Thome Apostoli et festum palmarum equis porcionibus.[1]

This evidence, though not great in quantity, is at any rate fairly precise. It establishes the existence, first, of a Common Seal at an early date ; secondly, of a Borough Court of the regular three-weekly type ; thirdly, of Bailiffs of the town ; and fourthly, of a limited body of inhabitants discharging some kind of fixed rental.

The reference to the common seal is especially interesting.[2] For it speaks, not of the common seal of the Burgesses, but of the common seal *of Burford*. We can already discern the presence of that idea of the town's personality—of the town as something other than the mere sum of its inhabitants— which Maitland finds so elusive in the early history of boroughs.

In the Court of the Burgesses and the thirteen Burgesses mentioned as a body, we can equally discern a repository for this idea—a group of men in which the town's personality was beginning to be seen as residing. In other words, there was already a kind of Corporation formed inside the general body of enfranchised inhabitants. This is not a direct corollary of the charters. So far as they go, they only incorporate the town in the very rudimentary sense of combining into a privileged community the whole of the inhabitants without exception. The charter of FitzHamon conveys ' omnibus meis hominibus de Burford ' the right to have a Gild Merchant. Even in the middle of the thirteenth century a literal application of the words would not have been impossible. There were hardly more than a hundred

---

[1] Inq. P. M. (P. R. O.), Edw. II, file 42.
[2] The ancient Common Seal still extant, and now in the possession of Mrs. Cheatle, is quite possibly the very one here referred to. The late Sir William Hope dated it at *circa* 1250 (Ll. Jewitt and St. John Hope, *Corporation Plate*, ii. 258).

free inhabitants to share in the privileges of the Gild.[1] But as those privileges—the right to pre-emption in the market, the exclusive right to sell by retail in the town, and so on— were very real advantages, there would be a tendency quite early to limit the membership, whether by imposing an entrance fee or by demanding some qualification for entrance.

Whether the Curia Burgensium was at this date (as we know it was later) co-extensive with the limited Gild we have no evidence to show. But since this was a body acting officially and using a common seal, and since the only body that had been called into existence by the charters was the Gild, the two may be, provisionally at least, identified.[2] It is at any rate clear that a concentration of the town's personality, capable of becoming later an incorporation of that personality, had taken place. For the description ' burgensis ' is beginning to have a limited application. It was ultimately to be the official title of a member of the Corporation ; and even in the thirteenth century it was ceasing to be used at Burford in the general sense for any holder of a burgage tenement. The description for these tenants in documents of the thirteenth and fourteenth centuries is ' liberi tenentes ' ; they appear so in all the Inquisitions Post Mortem of that period. Hence a reference to thirteen people as ' burgenses ', occurring as it does in a document of that very class, must be a deliberate designation by a formal title. The particular number of men thus designated is not without significance. The Burford Corporation, when it emerges fully constituted, was composed with more or less regularity of two Bailiffs, an Alderman, and ten Burgesses. The number was not very strictly held, and in the sixteenth century was slightly exceeded. But the variation was never very great. It can hardly be a mere coincidence that the mention of certain men in 1314 under a description not applied generally to the townsmen should give us a number closely corresponding with the number of the Corporation at later periods.

---

[1] See, e.g., Inq. P. M. (P. R. O.), Edw. I, file 91, no. 2.
[2] This point is discussed at greater length *infra*, pp. 24–6.

There is thus enough evidence to establish the important
fact that the Curia Burgensium, whether co-extensive with
the Gild or not, was certainly not co-extensive with the
population of the enfranchised area. This constitutes the
vital step in the history of a borough at which a limited
number of the inhabitants begin, by the use of a common
seal which can be described as the seal *of the town*, to act
as the town.

We may have a glimpse of a chief officer of this body in
an Inquisition of 1294, when one of the jurors was Robertus
le Maior.[1] The head of the established Corporation of a later
date was always called the Alderman. But titles of borough
officials during the thirteenth century were not very rigidly
employed ; and the chief officer of Burford may occasionally
have been called the Mayor.

We may have also a glimpse of a minor official called the
Marshal. One William le Maryschal or le Mareschal de
Bureford appears in various documents.[2] He was constantly
present on the juries of Inquisitions ; yet his assessment in
the Lay Subsidies is a small one. He may, therefore, have
served on the juries by reason of an official position ; and
he may have been the officer whose title later on was that
of Seneschal or Steward.

The reference to the Bailiffs shows that they were commonly
regarded as officers of the town. But there is another reference
to them within the first period which provides a warning of
the limits within which even so distinctly formed a Corporation has to be considered. In the Close Roll for 1301 there
is a case of replevin of land forfeited by default ' before the
bailiffs of Ralph de Monte Hermeri and Joan his wife, in
their Court of Burford '.[3] The position of the Bailiffs was
equivocal throughout the history of the town, owing to the
manner of their appointment. The custom was for the
Burgesses to nominate four men annually to the steward

---

[1] Inq. P. M. (P. R. O.), Edw. I, file 77, no. 3.
[2] Inq. P. M., Edw. I, file 91, no. 2 ; Edw. II, file 42 ; Inq. A. Q. D.,
file 145 ; Lay Subsidies, Oxfordsh. 161, 8 and 9.
[3] Cal. Close Rolls, Edw. I (1296–1302), p. 491. Ralph de Monthermer
held the manor at this time as guardian of the young Gilbert de Clare.

of the lord of the manor, who thereupon selected two of them to be Bailiffs.[1] Naturally, as the corporate life of the town strengthened, the Bailiffs became more and more identified with the Corporation. But at this early date it is clear that they could still be regarded as manorial officers.

The same warning applies also to our estimate of the Borough Court. Not only does the reference just quoted speak of it as the Court of the lord of the manor, but the reference from the Hundred Rolls quoted earlier shows that in practice it was used for manorial purposes, since it was in this Court that John Giffard owed suit for his holding. Quite evidently the charters, in the view of the lord of the manor, had been designed to alter merely the function, and not the status of Burford. Just as the Court Leet and the Homage of a village were his, and yet acted as a kind of self-government for the village, so the Borough Court and the Burgesses, however much they were beginning to incorporate the town, were his. They were different in kind, because the function of a town in producing a monetary revenue required different machinery—a more frequently sitting and more authoritative Court and a more concentrated executive—from that of a place producing only agricultural supplies. But in theory (if one may for the moment speak as if theory on such a point could have existed) they were the same.

§ 6

This accounts for the state of things we find when we turn from the embryo Corporation itself to the question of what it administered—the scope and nature of its functions. For of town affairs, as such, there is no trace at all; everything seems to be the affair of the lord of the manor .

There were three heads under which the place would produce revenue: (i) The burgage rents; (ii) The market, mills, &c.; (iii) The Court. Of course, in every borough these sources of revenue were in some sense the affair of the

---

[1] There is no record of the appointment of bailiffs at this period; but as the later form bears such signs of the manorial system it may safely be read back to early times.

overlord, whether the charter proceeded from a private individual or from the Crown. For the fee-farm was a payment in consideration of the loss of these profits by the lord as a result of handing over to the borough the whole of its internal affairs. But in Burford they were directly, and not indirectly, the affair of the lord ; the evidence of Inquisitions during this first period goes to show that under all three heads the revenue was paid in detail to the lord of the manor. The town was never held at farm.

There is, indeed, one instance of the use of the phrase ' firma burgi '. An Account of Escheats of 1231 includes the following :

Oxonia. Et de vii*li*. vii*s*. x*d*. et obolo de firma forinseca de Bureford de hoc anno et termino S Michaelis anni precedentis Et de liiii*s*. iiii*d*. de firma burgi molendini et fori Et de c & v*s*. de operationibus parvis ad firmam.[1]

The ' firma burgi ' here may possibly be the same item as the 13*s*. 6*d*. paid by the thirteen Burgesses in 1314 ; it must at any rate have been a small sum, since the total of this rent and the rents of the mill and market only amounted to 54*s*. 4*d*. Possibly also the same item may be traced in an Inquisition of 1337, in which Eleanor, wife of Hugh le Despenser, who was then in possession of the manor, appears seised

de octodecim solidis uno denario uno obolo et uno quadrante Redditus assisi per annum de quibusdam liberis tenentibus in Bureford.[2]

This small sum can hardly be a true ' firma burgi '. Moreover, the details given in other Inquisitions make it perfectly clear that the town was not held at farm. In 1297 there is an entry of

cv liberi tenentes qui reddunt per annum xx*li*. xiii*s*. v*d*. ad quatuor anni terminos . . . est ibi quoddam mercatum quod valet per annum simul cum feria stallagio et tolneto cervisie ibidem xii*li*. . . . est apud Upton quoddam molendinum aquaticum quod valet per annum lx*s*. . . . placita et perquisita curiae et visus ibidem valent per annum xx*s*.[3]

---

[1] Min. Accts. (P. R. O.), bundle 1117, no. 13.
[2] Inq. P. M. (P. R. O.), Edw. III, file 51.
[3] Inq. P. M. (P. R. O.), Edw. I, file 91.

In 1304 the entries are as follows :

Sunt in eadem villa cum hameletto predicto xxx*libr.* vi*d.* de quodam redditu per annum, . . . tolloneum dicte ville valet per annum xi*libr.* xviii*s.* Et est ibi unum molendinum ad predictam villam pertinens quod valet per annum lx*s.* . . . placita et perquisita curie valent per annum xxv*s.* vi*d.*[1]

In 1314 the entry relating to the thirteen Burgesses is the only mention of town rents ; other profits appear thus :

Et quoddam mercatum per annum per diem Sabbatis cuius proficuum valet una cum Nundinis ibidem die Nativitatis beati Iohannis Baptiste existentibus valent (*sic*) per annum x*li.* Et placita et perquisita curie eiusdem ville valent per annum lx*s.*

In the Inquisition of 1337 which gives the rental already mentioned to Eleanor le Despenser, the market toll is put at 50*s.*, the fair on St. John's Day at 26*s.* 8*d.*, the view of frank-pledge at 3*s.* 4*d.*, and the Court pleas at 13*s.* 4*d.*

From these documents it is evident that no branch of the town's activities was in the hands of the Corporation except as agent for the lord of the manor. There is, however, one document coming within this period which did raise for a short time a revenue to be paid to, and administered by, men of the town without responsibility to the lord of the manor. In 1322, the bridge over the river having fallen into disrepair, Edward II issued at the instance of Hugh le Despenser Letters Patent addressed ' probis hominibus de Bureford ', granting them the right to levy tolls for a period of three years upon all merchandise passing over the bridge for sale.[2]

After the warnings which other references have given against assuming at this stage too much ' personality ' or corporate entity in the character of the town, this grant may be used as a corrective on the other side. The Letters Patent are addressed to ' the men of Burford ', in the general formula employed in the charters. But it is obvious that the business arising under the grant must have been transacted by some smaller body than the inhabitants at large. It must have

[1] Inq. P. M. (P. R. O.), Edw. I, file 128.
[2] Pat. Rolls, 16 Edw. II, ps. 2, m. 1.

devolved upon the limited group of Burgesses. Moreover,
the grant may, without undue conjecture, be regarded as
rendered possible only by a generally accepted recognition
of this group as embodying, in however rudimentary a
degree, the town. Otherwise it would almost certainly have
been made to the lord of the manor. It is important to note,
too, that the grant must have accelerated the tendencies
towards incorporation of the town in this body. The collection and expenditure of a revenue not derived from the
townsfolk, and not payable to the lord, would make the
position of the group of Burgesses less purely domestic, so
to speak, than it had hitherto been ; and, since their responsibility under the Letters Patent, for the proper disposal of
the money accruing and for the observance of the time limit
of the grant, was to the Crown direct, they would be by so
much removed from the manorial supremacy.

Another corrective of our estimate of the Burgesses'
position is to be found in the Hundred Rolls. The town there
appears as claiming the important liberty of the return of
writs : ' Qui eciam alii a Rege clamant habere returnum
brevium et alias libertates, etc.' [1] In one way the claim
need not be taken very seriously. It was put forward after
the close of the long reign of Henry III, when the country
was full of encroachments upon the rights of the Crown ; it
appears in the Rolls only in the course of the Extractum
Inquisicionum specially made for the use of the Justices,
concerning liberties unwarrantably assumed ; [2] there is no
record of any attempt to uphold it in the Quo Warranto
proceedings which followed the Inquisitions, and no trace
at any time of the appointment of coroners in Burford.

The validity of the claim, therefore, need not concern us.
The fact of its having been made is the point of interest.
No clause in the charters would justify it for a moment.
Therefore the fact of its having been made means that the

---

[1] *Hundred Rolls* (ed. of 1818), ii. 37.

[2] Curiously enough, Burford appears in the Rolls only in this Extractum ;
it is absent from the fuller Inquisitions of 7 Edw. I. This is unfortunate,
since it deprives us of the detailed information about the status of the
inhabitants which is available for other Oxfordshire towns.

burghal consciousness was strong enough to conceive of rights as belonging automatically to the place as a borough. The corporate entity of the Burgesses was sufficiently marked to cause them to act, upon occasion, in the same way as bodies which were by charter incorporations of towns.

That is, in reality, the formula upon which the whole evolution of the Burford Corporation proceeded.

CHAPTER II

THE GROWTH OF CORPORATE RESPONSIBILITY:
1350–1500

§ 1

THE opening of the series of Burford Records preserved in the town itself, which has already been noted as marking the second period of its history, is of importance from more than one aspect. Obviously it may be expected to provide more ample information about the character of the burgensic body. But it may also be regarded as an indication of a new spirit at work in the life and affairs of the town.

That new spirit must, it is true, be but cautiously interpreted. It is not to be seen wholly as marking the advance in a conception of town government and the purport of incorporation. For only a very small portion of the existing Records can be called strictly municipal records, and of that portion not one item belongs to the period now under consideration. Two fragments of a book covering parts of the years 1596, 1597, and 1598 are all that survive to represent the work of the Borough Court. The only volume that could . be classed as a Minute Book or Memorandum Book of the Corporation is a thin volume of the sixteenth century, which contains a number of entries of meetings and resolutions of the Corporation, records the names of Bailiffs during the greater part of the century, and preserves some notes on the mode of election and the duties of certain officials. But it is, throughout, a note book rather than a systematic Minute Book. A roll of 1605 records the Rules of the Fellowship of Burgesses, with the signatures of all the Burgesses from that date down to the extinction of the Corporation in 1861. A copy of a judgement of the Court of Exchequer in 1620 concerning the town's liberties, and a mass of papers relating to a Royal Commission in 1738 and a subsequent Chancery suit, may be added to the list.

With these exceptions, practically all the Records, amounting to over four hundred documents and some thirty volumes of accounts and memoranda kept during the seventeenth, eighteenth, and nineteenth centuries, are concerned with the administration of certain public properties, chiefly for charitable purposes. Indirectly a good deal of knowledge of the constitution and methods of the Corporation is to be derived from these sources ; but in character they are nearer to the churchwardens' accounts of a village than to the muniments of a town.

This fact gives us the principal reason for the beginning of a systematic preservation of records in the town. We have to find this, not in a new sense of corporate unity and continuity, but simply in the responsibilities arising from the foundation of a number of charities. We are now in the most prosperous period of the Cotswold country—the great period of the English wool trade. At Burford, as elsewhere, much of this wealth was given to the service of religion—the building and adornment of the church, the foundation and endowment of chantry chapels, and the relief of the poor. Some of these funds came directly to the Gild as such, for the maintenance of its chapel and priest and the welfare of its members. Indirectly a partial responsibility for almost all the funds would tend to be laid upon the same body, partly because its continuity would secure the trusts, and partly for the reason that in a small community the men of wealth and standing who would naturally be sought as the guardians of trusts would inevitably be members of the Gild.

But while the nature of the Records compels us to see in this the principal reason for their preservation, there is another consideration which permits us not to be content with it as the only reason, and to discern also traces of a new conception of the borough and burghal life. It is to be found in that grouping of the charters, which marks, quite as distinctly as the preservation of records, the difference between the first and second periods of the town's history. The second group of charters has two outstanding features which distinguish it from the first; the series of Letters

PLATE I. FIFTEENTH-CENTURY ARCH

FORMERLY IN AN END WALL OF THE MASON'S ARMS, WITNEY STREET

Patent of Confirmation, of which it is composed, is homogeneous, and it is continuous. The Letters Patent of Edward III, obtained in 1351, are followed in the series by similar Confirmations purchased from the Chanceries of Richard II, Henry IV, Henry V, Henry VI, Edward IV, and Henry VII.[1] Thus only the reign of Richard III is omitted, since we need not consider the brief reign of Edward V. The corpus of the Letters Patent is the same throughout ; each document in turn recites as its substantive portion the two charters of Henry II.

It is not too much to deduce from these two features of the series an advance in the clearness, though not in the scope, of the burgensic body's conception of its position. We have left behind that indeterminate outlook which had returned from the first Royal confirmations to a belated manorial confirmation ; and had also allowed the town to remain outside the vigorous movement of the boroughs in general during the thirteenth century. Even yet there is no sign of mistrust of the sufficiency of the existing grants. Recital of the charters of Henry II bestowed no more than the set of franchises examined in the previous chapter. But the making of a different kind of effort to render them secure and to maintain them constantly means that the burgensic body was regarding itself in a new light, even if it continued to regard its functions in the old light.

§ 2

The existence of this body as a distinct entity formed within the general body of inhabitants, and enjoying the description ' Burgess ' as a title, is established beyond doubt very soon after the opening of our second period. In a conveyance of 1367 Robert le Cotelir is described as ' Senior Burgensis de Boreford ', a formula which would have had next to no meaning unless the Burgesses were an official group. In seventy-five conveyances dated before the end

---

[1] I am here dealing only with the period up to the end of the fifteenth century. Similar Confirmations were obtained from the Chanceries of Henry VIII, Mary, Edward VI, Elizabeth, and James I ; but the Letters Patent of Elizabeth have been lost.

of the fifteenth century only five cases of the application of
the description ' Burgensis ' are to be found ; and in seven
cases in which the property conveyed is specifically written
down as a burgage the owners are not described as ' Burgensis '.

In view of this limited use of the word the evidence of
the phraseology of the Letters Patent becomes conclusive.
Those of Richard II confirm the existing liberties ' hominibus
et Burgensibus de Bureford . . . prout iidem homines et
Burgenses libertatibus et consuetudinibus predictis rationabiliter uti et gaudere consueverunt '. This duality of address
is not found in any earlier charter, and implies that there was
now in the town some recognizable recipient of liberties other
than the whole body of inhabitants. The Letters Patent
of Henry IV move a step further in making the Confirmation
' hominibus et Burgensibus de Bureford et successoribus suis
. . . prout iidem homines et Burgenses et antecessores sui
libertatibus et consuetudinibus ', &c. A formal entry of
successors and predecessors is not usual in documents of
the Chancery except in relation to an official body possessing
legal permanence. Finally, a charter of Henry VII, bestowing
a fair upon the town in addition to the one already belonging
to the lord of the manor, is granted ' dilectis ligeis nostris
Ballivis Burgensibus et inhabitantibus ville nostre de Bourford '.
Short of specific incorporation, these documents go as far as is
possible in recognizing a definite official status in the Burgesses.

The identification of the Burgensic body with the Gild
also passes now beyond doubt. One of the difficulties of
identification in the first period is that nowhere, except in
the early charters, is there any mention of the Gild in documents of the period. The reason may be that in documents
originating outside the town itself, as was the case with all
the documents upon which we have to rely for that period,[1]
the official group was naturally recognized rather by its
function—that is to say, as a Court and as discharging the
duties of a borough, as a Curia and Burgenses—than by its

---

[1] This is obviously the case with the Crown and manorial documents ;
the only other documents, the Brasenose leases, would be much more
likely to be drawn up by the officials of the Abbey of Cold Norton than
by any one in the small community of Burford.

constituting principle, that is to say, as a Gild. When, however, we come to documents originating inside the town, references to the burgensic body are much more likely to bear traces of its primary form ; more especially when the contents are concerned with religious and charitable bequests.

The use of the term ' Gild ' is, in fact, frequent ; and fortunately in several instances in such conjunction with the word ' Burgesses ', or with borough matters, as to leave no reasonable doubt of identity. A lease of 1404 is granted by persons specifically described as officers of the Gild, the rent is to be received by the Proctors of the Gild, and the tenant is to be allowed to cut wood for the repair of the house ' with the advice and consent of the Gild '. But the lease is made ' with the assent of all the Burgesses of the town '.[1] Now the Gild can have been under no necessity to consult the wishes of the general body of the inhabitants or burgage tenants ; nor, if the advice of ' the Gild ' (not merely the officers of the Gild) were sufficient for the cutting of timber, can any one outside the Gild have had any legal interest in the lease. Consequently the provision of the assent of ' all the Burgesses of the town ' must mean that the Burgesses were co-extensive with the Gild.

Almost equally strong is the evidence of a phrase in the bequest of the Novum Hospitium Angulare in 1422[2] to Thomas Spycer with reversion to church purposes. Here reference is made to ' capella beate marie in eodem cimeterio que est burgi '. The Chapel of Blessed Mary was the Gild Chapel. This method of describing it shows clearly that the ' burgus ' as an entity was regarded as synonymous with the Gild.

In the lease of 1404, quoted above, one of the officers mentioned is ' Senescallus Gilde '. In a lease of 1465 an officer is described as ' Seneschal of Burford '.[3] There is no evidence of the existence at any time of two Seneschals ; so that apparently an officer could be equally well described as an officer of the Gild or as an officer of the town.

---

[1] Burford Records, bundle CC, S 4.
[2] Burford Records, bundle A, CH 5.
[3] Burford Records, bundle A, CH 16.

Evidence of a rather different kind is provided by a conveyance of the Fifteen Lands dated 1382.[1] This piece of property was held on trust for the purpose of relieving the burden upon the town when a tax of tenths or fifteenths was levied. That would be business of the town at large, and no charge is made upon the rents, in this or any other document concerning the trust, for religious or Gild purposes. Yet the conveyance is made by the two heads of the Gild ' consensu fratrum nostrorum dicte Gilde '.

It is true that, unless the later Corporation of Burford could be definitely classed as of the Gild type, this evidence might still leave room for the view that there were really two bodies growing up—a Gild and a Court of Burgesses, only identified by the accidental circumstance that in a small town the same group of leading men would tend to form both bodies. But since the Corporation at its highest development bears all the characteristics of a Gild—being a close, self-electing body, with an Alderman as its head, discommoning members for breach of its rules, and describing itself formally as a Fellowship of Burgesses—the evidence just given is enough to establish the identification as essential and not merely accidental.

§ 3

For our knowledge of the organization and constitution of the burgensic body at this period we are forced, in the absence of any early custumals or records of the proceedings of the Gild or the Court, to rely upon such casual information as is given by the ancient conveyances and leases.

There is as yet no instance of the use of the term ' Alderman ' or of any other term singling out an individual as head of the Burgesses. The only hint of any position of leadership in the Gild is to be found in three references to persons described as ' Seniors '. In 1367 Robert le Cotelir is called ' Senior Burgensis de Boreford ' ;[2] in 1382 John Wenryche and Thomas Spycer are described as ' Senior Gilde Borfordie ' and ' Senior

---

[1] Burford Records, bundle BB, T 1.
[2] Brasenose Muniments : Burford Leases, 4.

dicte Gilde' respectively ; [1] in 1404 Thomas Spycer again is
described as 'Gilde Senior'.[2] But this was hardly the title
of a chief officer. At later dates, after the establishment of an
Alderman as head of the Corporation, there are still references
to the Seniors ; for instance, in the Rules of 1605 the Burgesses are bidden to ' give reverence and place to the Senyors
and elder brethren according to the oulde and Auncyente
custome of this said Brotherhoode '. The title and status of
a Senior evidently did not pass into that of the Alderman ;
and therefore he cannot have been in the same sense head of
the Corporation. Probably the system was simply that, in
order to meet the practical requirements of having certain
people to keep the Common Box, to take the lead at meetings
of the Burgesses, and to act in any matter touching the
dignity or internal well-being of their company, two at least
of the older members were regarded and spoken of as Seniors,
and exercised in that way a kind of authority.

This would account for the small number of references to
the Seniors. If they had held a more formal headship, there
would have been more numerous instances of use of the title
in documents, partly for the extra validity conferred thereby
upon the transaction, partly as a supplementary dating of the
deed. Neither purpose would be effectively served by the
mention of a position which was little more than an arrangement of convenience, and would by its very nature be held for
long by the same men.

The truth is that the Bailiffs were the real heads of the
town. For they presided in the Borough Court; and thus
discharged the duties which are of the essence of the chief
officer of a town—those of a chief magistrate. They are the

[1] Burford Records, bundle BB, T 1.
[2] Burford Records, bundle DD, S 4. It is the form of this last reference
which justifies the reading of the word Senior in the other cases as a title
in conjunction with the words Burgensis or Gilde, and not in conjunction
with the name of the man in each case as a distinction from another
person of the same name but younger. In any event the former reading
would be the more probable, since the distinction between an elder and
a younger man is usually only made when the younger is intended to be
understood, the word Junior being added. But all doubt is set at rest
by this occurrence of the word Senior after the word Gilde, and not after
the man's name.

only officers who make any appearance among the charters :
that of Henry VII already quoted is a grant ' Ballivis Burgensibus et inhabitantibus de Bourford '. A letter from Warwick
the King-maker, during his lordship of the manor, is addressed
to ' the Bailiffs and Burgesses '. This was, in fact, throughout
the whole career of the Corporation the normal description in
use. It may be added that the position of the Bailiffs comes
out in less deliberate ways in the Records. They are the only
officers of whom a systematic list was ever kept ; from 1504
to 1861 the list, with a few intervals, is complete. It is significant, too, that the earliest list appears in a Memorandum
Book the keeping of which began in 1554. That is to say, at
the time of the highest development of the Corporation some
trouble was taken to go back over a period of fifty years to
recover the names of Bailiffs ; but nothing of the kind was
attempted for the Aldermen.

To minor officials very few references are to be found. There
were Proctors or Pronotours, who discharged the duties of the
Chamberlains of a later date in receiving and sometimes also
in disposing of the rents of property held for public purposes.[1]
A single instance occurs of the mention of Chamberlains as
such.[2] There was also a Serjeant.[3] But the most important
of the minor officials was evidently the Seneschal or Steward.
The earliest reference to this office is in 1404, when it was held
by Henry Coteler ; [4] and as Robert le Cotelir had been Senior
Burgess in 1367 it is clear that the post of Seneschal was not
below the dignity of the more important families of the town.
Still more remarkable is a reference of 1465 in which Sir Robert
Harecourte appears as Seneschal.[5] But that remains the sole
instance of the holding of the office by a man of rank.

§ 4

While we are thus rather more definitely informed of the
nature of the body of Burgesses, and officials of the town,

---

[1] See, for instance, Burford Records, bundle CC, S 4 ; and Brasenose
Muniments : Burford Leases, 11.
[2] Burford Records, bundle BB, T 2.
[3] Burford Records, bundle A, CH 18.
[4] Burford Records, bundle CC, S 4.
[5] Burford Records, bundle A, CH 16.

we remain almost completely in the dark as to their public functions. No book of record, or fragment of such a book, survives to reveal to us the Burgesses at their periodical meetings or at the sittings of the Court.

We have to be content with being able to see that they must have had such functions, and were steadily leaving behind the status of a Gild and approximating to that of a Borough authority. Evidence of this advance is provided by two features in the organization of the town. The first is the absence throughout this period of an Alderman. If the Gild influence had been the guiding principle, a period of such length, especially when coinciding with a notable increase in wealth, could not have passed without a single reference to the characteristic chief officer of a Gild. When we find that, on the contrary, the tendency was clearly towards regarding the Bailiffs, the characteristic Borough chief officers, as at the head of the Burgesses, the reasonable conclusion is that the latter were more occupied in Borough affairs than in purely Gild affairs.

The second feature is the increasing formality of this conjunction of the Bailiffs and Burgesses. In our first period the position of the Bailiffs was seen to be at the best equivocal, and on occasion capable of being treated as wholly manorial. Some trace of this uncertainty may be discerned in the fact that not until 1435 do the names of Bailiffs appear upon leases or conveyances of the town or charity lands. There may have been a reluctance to admit to participation in such business officers whose association with it might have been used by some lord of the manor as an acknowledgement of a right of interference on his part. But as the fifteenth century progresses, the participation of the Bailiffs becomes more and more frequent. When to this kind of conjunction is added that of the charter of Henry VII and the letter of the Earl of Warwick, it may be concluded that the Bailiffs on their side were tending to find their authority rather in their headship of the Borough than in their connexion with the lord of the manor.

We have two sidelights of another kind upon the position which the Burgesses were coming to occupy in the town.

One is given by the subject of Warwick's letter. There had been in Burford from an early date a small foundation of a religious nature, the Hospital of St. John the Evangelist. Among the few references to it are two concerning the appointment of a new Master of the Hospital. In 1327 an entry in the Close Rolls records the admission to the Mastership of Robert le Glasiere, one of the brethren, the presentation of Robert being made on this occasion by the brethren to the King, ' by reason of the lands of Hugh le Despenser and Eleanor his wife being in the King's hands '.[1] Again, in 1389 the Crown appointed one of the Royal clerks, also at a time when the manor was in the hands of the King, under the attainder of Thomas le Despenser.[2] One other record of presentation has been found ; but on these two alone the patronage can be attributed to the lord of the manor, and to no one else. Yet the letter from the Earl of Warwick preserved among the Burford Records, requests of the Bailiffs and Burgesses that they will allow him the next presentation.[3] In itself the patronage can have had no importance ; the Hospital was of little value and no influence. All that is interesting is the indication that the right to the patronage had evidently been neglected during the fifteenth century by those to whom it belonged, and that in these circumstances the position of the Burgesses was such that they stepped in and assumed it without question.

The other sidelight is given by the bequest of one Thomas Pole or Poole, citizen and tailor of London, in 1500. He gave two messuages, a close and dovecot, and twenty-two acres in the common fields, to be put in feoffment to the Burgesses with the intent that after a small weekly dole to the poor in the Almshouse the rents should be bestowed for the good continuance of the fraternity, especially by the provision of funds for paying the Chancery fees for the confirmation of the charters, and thereafter for any purpose thought by the Burgesses to be for the common good of the town.[4] Now in

[1] Cal. Pat. Rolls, Edw. III (1327–30), p. 195.
[2] Cal. Pat. Rolls, Ric. II (1388–92), p. 156.
[3] Burford Records, bundle GG, A 1.
[4] Burford Records, bundle EE, P 18.

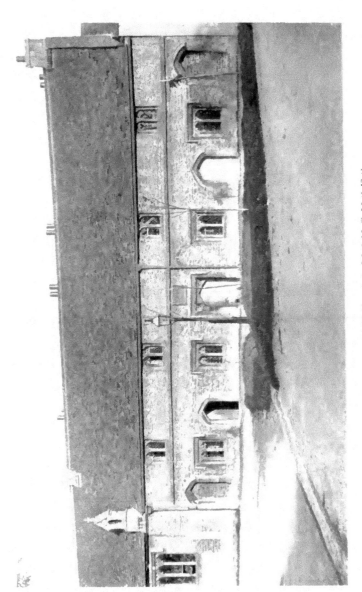

PLATE II. THE ALMSHOUSES

one sense this bequest seems to differ very little from trusts which the Burgesses were already administering. But there is just enough difference in the special concern for the charters and in the recognition of the Burgesses' discretion as to the common good of the town to separate this from the old Gild bequests and trusts, and to make of it rather more of a Borough trust.

But when the utmost has been extracted from the documents available for this period, the result is still vague and formless. The most that can be said is that the dimly descried group of Burgesses of our first period has undergone just enough definition of outline and modification of character to prepare the way in some degree for that display of authority which the ampler records of the next century will reveal. Although the only public activity of the Burgesses of which we have so far any record is no more than the administration of public property, and of that property only one item, the Fifteen Lands (with the addition at the very end of the period of Poole's Lands), can be regarded as other than the old charitable work of a Gild, yet the burghal character of the body has been strengthening and the Gild character weakening. Slight as the indications may be, the most has to be made of them, since otherwise the developments of the next century would be so startling as to be almost incapable of explanation.

CHAPTER III

THE CORPORATION AT ITS ZENITH : 1500–1600

§ 1

At the very outset of the sixteenth century, and on the most superficial survey of the Records, a distinct change is apparent. Not only are the documents far more numerous, but they also begin to include Records of a class not found in previous centuries, and at the same time the Records of a less important class, such as those which have hitherto been the sole sources of information, are so much changed both in content and form as almost to take rank with true Borough records.

The second of these points is obviously the most significant. But the other two are not without weight. An increase in the number of documents preserved means that the duties which had first dictated the keeping of muniments had become more systematic and more continuous ; and this in turn means that the body in charge of the duties had become aware in a new way of its own continuity and corporate responsibility. This is, in fact, put beyond doubt by the third feature of this new period in the Records—the change in their content and form.

There were by this time four classes of property held in trust. Firstly, there were lands and tenements given to the Church ; secondly, lands and tenements belonging to the Gild ; thirdly, the Fifteen Lands held for the relief of the burden of taxation ; and fourthly, Poole's Lands. It is remarkable that in every one of these classes we come during the early part of the sixteenth century upon a document containing a specific declaration of the nature of the trust. This cannot be an accidental circumstance. It must imply that in each case, as it became necessary to re-convey the property owing to the death of previous feoffees, opportunity was taken to put the trust upon record. For Church and Gild property this was done in 1502, 1508, 1512, 1537, and 1538 ; for the Fifteen Lands in 1546; and for Poole's Lands in 1502 and 1530. Moreover, in each case, while the body of the conveyance is still in Latin, the declaration of the ' intent ' of the conveyance is written in English. The nature of the trust was therefore being declared to the public, and was not stated for legal purposes.

So much for the change of content ; the change in form is slighter but not to be missed. More care is taken to record the official standing of new feoffees. This begins to be traceable towards the end of the preceding century; but it is a constant feature of the feoffments of the sixteenth century—so constant that it may almost be said to have been a rule that Burgess-ship should be a qualification for appointment as a feoffee. There is also a very marked tendency to enlarge the numbers of the men put in charge of the properties. Towards the end of the century the bodies of feoffees become almost unwieldy; but quite at the beginning they show a departure from the old practice of being content with the nomination of two or three men. Many of the fifteenth-century documents might, so far as the form goes, be private conveyances in the ordinary processes of sale. It is, indeed, difficult in some instances to be quite sure of the stage at which the property actually passed to public uses. No document of the sixteenth century is open to any such doubt ; the public nature of those con-nected with the town or charity lands is fully apparent.

The inferences to be drawn from these new qualities in documents of the older class are such that, although Records of the regular Borough type do not occur till after the middle of the century, we need not, in our view of the corporate body and its work, be at pains to distinguish between stages in this period. We can take the century as a whole, since, even if the facts are actually drawn from documents of the latter half, there is none which could not reasonably be predicated of such a body as the other documents allow us, though in less detail, to perceive.

§ 2

The Corporation, reaching now the full development of its type, consisted of an Alderman, a Steward, and a number of

D

Burgesses, usually fourteen or fifteen.[1] The Alderman seems
to have held office for life, or until he resigned, and not to have
been an annually elected chief officer. Six men are to be found
described in various documents as Alderman in the course of
the century: Peter Eynesdale in 1530 and 1537, Richard
Manyngton in 1540 and 1553, Simon Wisdom in ten years
at short intervals between 1559 and 1581, Richard Chadwell
in 1586 and 1589, William Symonds in 1596, and Richard
Merywether in 1598 and 1599.[2] Now it is true that the mention
of any one man in two separate years as Alderman need not
mean that he held office all the time between those years ;
two documents might happen to coincide with two entirely
distinct tenures of an annual office by, let us say, Peter Eynesdale. But it is rather too much to suppose that the same
coincidence should occur in the cases of three other Aldermen
in the same century ; and altogether too much to suppose
that it could have happened ten times in the case of Simon
Wisdom. In no instance does the name of any other holder
of the office interpose between two mentions of the same man
as Alderman. The facts accord with no view except that
the Alderman was not annually elected, but held office continuously. Thus he is revealed as rather a Gild official than
a Borough officer, and the Corporation is seen at its highest
point as deriving its organization from the original Gild
Merchant.

The Steward—probably the official who has previously
appeared as the Marshal and the Seneschal—was the second
officer of the Corporation, and he also seems to have held
office indefinitely. This case is not so clear as that of the
Alderman, because there are not so many consecutive references to the same holder of the office. Richard Hans in 1540,
Simon Wisdom in 1553, Edmund Sylvester in 1566, occur only
in these single instances as Stewards. John Hans, however,
is described as Steward on six occasions between 1568 and
1581, again without the interposition of any other name during

---

[1] The account of the Corporation is mostly derived from the Memorandum Book : see Part III, p. 410.

[2] For references for these dates see the list of Aldermen, Part II, p. 102.

PLATE III. SIMON WISDOM'S TENEMENTS, NEAR THE BRIDGE

ON THE LEFT THE LATE 17TH-CENTURY FRONT OF THE VICARAGE

that period ; and Symon Symons, who was Steward in 1598 and 1599, held the post also in 1605.[1] Naturally the Steward-ship would be less likely to be held for life than the chief dignity of the Corporation. For one thing, the Steward might rise to the higher rank ; three of the Stewards of the sixteenth century did so rise. Failing that, he would be more likely to resign after some years an office which involved as much attention to duty as that of the Alderman, but was less highly regarded. There is enough evidence to lead to the opinion that at any rate he was not, any more than the Alderman, annually elected.

Minor officers of whom we have record are the town clerk, the serjeant, the constables, and the wardsmen. The town clerk's duties were mainly at the Borough Court. The one reference to the appointment of a new clerk does not make clear who appointed him, but the form of it implies that it was the Corporation. He received an annual fee of 13s. 4d. from the Bailiffs and took the ' profits of the Courts ' ; [2] he also made an income out of such business as the drawing up of feoffments for the town and charity lands. The serjeant also was a town's officer, being paid by the Corporation.[3]

The constables and the wardsmen, on the other hand, retained much of the character of manorial officials. The manner of appointment of the constables was that four ' honest inhabiters ' were nominated by the Burgesses to the steward of the lord of the manor at the annual law-day, and he selected two to serve for the following year. The duties of the wardsmen, of whom there were four, were to bring in writing to the Steward at the annual law-day a statement of the ' deffawtys' committed during the year in their respec-tive wards.[4] Thus neither constables nor wardsmen were true Borough officers.

There is only one reference to ale-tasters and clerks of the market.[5] They were apparently not quite the subordinate

---

[1] See the list of Stewards, Part II, p. 103.
[2] Memorandum Book, fol. 9 rev.   [3] Memorandum Book, *passim.*
[4] Memorandum Book, fol. 38.
[5] Borough Court Book, fol. 19 ; and Burford Records, bundle EE, P 23.

officials that they were apt to be in other towns. The names of one of the ale-tasters and one of the clerks of the market in 1596 are found on the list of Burgesses in 1599. The single reference to them records a swearing-in by the Bailiffs at the Borough Court, which would make them Borough officials and not manorial.

The general body of Burgesses retained, as strongly as its chief officers, the marks of its Gild origin. It was constituted by close election within the body, and new members paid an entrance fee of 20s.[1] There was a rota of seniority, since in one case the new Burgess ' in consideracyon of his towardnes was placed in Senyoryte next to John Lymme then beyng one of the Baylyffes of the towne '.[2] The chief object of the rota may have been to secure that the responsibility of taking the office of Bailiff was properly laid upon each Burgess in turn. But it also conferred a certain dignity and right to precedence on public occasions.

§ 3

This account of the Corporation differs mainly in positiveness of statement from those which can be put together out of the documents of earlier periods. The constitution of the Burgess body has been made clearer by the greater mass and improved character of the sixteenth-century Records. When we come to deal with the Bailiffs, on the other hand, the striking feature is not the more extended view of their function, but the complete change in the nature of their relation to the town on the one side and the lord of the manor on the other.

The formal mode of their appointment remained the same. The record of the Court held at Burford in 1546, when the manor was in the hands of the Crown, contains the entry :

And thereon the bailiffs aforesaid came and placed their offices in the hands of the King on which the Seneschal of the King elected in their places Robert Payne and William Hewys to perform the duties in the proper way and to perform them for one year and they took oath.[3]

---

[1] Memorandum Book, fol. 3 rev., 23, 32 rev.

[2] Ibid., fol. 32 rev.

[3] Court Rolls (P. R. O.), Portf. 197, no. 15. This is, unfortunately, the only Burford Court Roll I have been able to find.

But the significance of the formal appointment must by this time have become entirely obscured. Throughout the sixteenth century the Bailiffs' office appears to be wholly identified with the interests of the Burgesses, and their duty to be owed to the town alone. This fact can be traced both directly in the tenor and phrasing of certain documents, and indirectly in the nature of transactions with which the Bailiffs were—rather remarkably—associated.

The charter of Henry VII granting a second annual fair in Burford has already been quoted. It may be referred to again, although it actually belongs to the fifteenth century, because of its bearing upon this altered situation of the Bailiffs. The fair was granted to ' the Bailiffs, Burgesses, and Inhabitants ' of Burford, without any reservation to the lord of the manor, and the profits of the fair, together with the profits and fines of a Court of Pie Powder, are specifically given to them. The earlier fair belonged to the lord of the manor.[1] Considering how jealously the right to a fair was guarded, it is not likely that, if the Bailiffs could in any serious degree be identified with the interests of the lord of the manor, the town would have risked associating them with a fair of their own ; since there would have been, in that case, a danger of the lord laying some claim through his officials to an interest in the fair.

Even more striking evidence is afforded by the entries of fines inflicted for refusing the office of Bailiff. In the Memorandum Book under date 1561 the following occurs :

yt ys agreyd by the consent of all the bretherne that Rychard Dawby schall pay for his fyne for Reffusyng the baylyffe weke thys last yere xs. upon the condicion that he schalle not Reffuse the same the next yere or otherwyse to pay the whole sum wyche ys xls.[2]

Now in the case of an office to which the appointment was made by the lord's Steward the fines for refusing the office should certainly have been adjudged by and paid to the Steward, according to the usual manorial custom. When we find them being inflicted by the Corporation, it is a fair con-

---

[1] See, e. g., *Cal. Charter Rolls*, vol. iii, p. 453.
[2] See Part III, p. 412.

clusion that the Bailiffs had ceased to be regarded as manorial officers, and that the lord of the manor was, if not consenting to, at any rate not contesting, their change of status.

As indirect evidence of the change three references are worth quoting. One is in a conveyance of the Bridge Lands in 1571, made by ' Ballivis Libertatis ville de Burford '.[1] ' Bailiffs of the Liberty ' is a phrase customarily employed of towns possessing the most complete kind of enfranchisement ; and its use here, even though it has no parallel among the Records, implies that the manorial allegiance had become in practice obsolete. It may also be remarked in passing that this view of the Bailiffs holding the Bridge Lands, one of the Burgesses' trusts, shows that there was no longer any tendency to keep them aloof from the Corporation's affairs in mistrust of their divided obligations.

Much the same deduction may be drawn from the fact that on one occasion, in 1561, the office of Bailiff was actually held in conjunction with that of Alderman. True, it is noted that ' Thys presydent hadd never byn seen beffore that any affter beyng electyd Alderman to have the office any more of the Bayliffe '.[2] But that it could have happened once is significant enough, since the combination of the offices would certainly have been avoided by the Burgesses of an earlier date.

But the most striking piece of indirect evidence is given by the first recorded instance of the expulsion of a Burgess from the Fellowship. It is of the year 1591, and the discommoning order is signed first by the Steward of the Fellowship and secondly by the Bailiffs. No doubt the Bailiffs were members of the Fellowship, and would as such be entitled to take part in the expulsion of one of their number. But that they signed as Bailiffs implies that they regarded their official standing as an authority within and of the Fellowship.

§ 4

Of this body of the Bailiffs, Alderman, and Burgesses acting as a town authority the ampler documents of our present

---

[1] Burford Records, bundle C, B 10.
[2] See Part III, p. 415.

period give us for the first time an adequate view. In that capacity they had their corporate existence in the Borough Court, which, like all Borough Courts, was at once a judicial and an executive instrument.

As a court of law[1] it had cognizance of civil actions involving sums of money less than 40s.,[2] and of criminal cases as a court of first instance. Of the civil cases the greater proportion were actions for debt, but there were also actions for detention of goods and for valuation of goods of which the price had been disputed. The Court could inflict fines for non-appearance, and could issue distraints for the non-payment either of fines or of debts for which judgement had been given. A small fee could be charged for the adjournment of an action at the request of either party to it, but on the other hand there are many entries of adjournments without the payment of a fee. The Court could also award costs in its judgement and distrain for the payment of them.

Actions are frequently entered by or against persons not of the town, and sometimes not of the immediate neighbourhood. There are cases of litigants from as far away as Wiltshire and Berkshire and the more distant parts of Gloucestershire. In several instances both litigants were non-residents. Presumably in all these cases the matter of dispute had arisen in the town, either at the market or the fairs, or, as in one case at least, in connexion with the administration of the goods of a deceased resident.

It is not possible to make out with any clearness from our Records what differences of standing before the Court applied to residents and non-residents respectively. In many cases sureties are entered, sometimes for one of the parties, sometimes for both; but no system can be deduced from the entries. It does seem to be clear that, as was to be expected, no Burgess ever had to provide a surety. It would also be expected that on the other hand every non-resident should appear by surety, since the Court would require a security

---

[1] A transcript of the fragments of the Borough Court Book, from which every fact in this account is taken, will be found in Part III, p. 522.
[2] See Part III, p. 375.

in cases in which it obviously would be unable to issue
distraint. There are, indeed, very few cases of non-residents
appearing without sureties, and in several of these the matter
in dispute was settled out of hand, by agreement between
the parties. It may perhaps be concluded that the rule was
that non-residents should appear with sureties, but that the
rule was often waived where the Court had to do no more
than recognize an agreed settlement. The standing of
residents who were not Burgesses is even more hazy. On
the whole they seem to have been able to appear without
sureties, but there are many cases of residents providing
sureties, and one in which a resident litigant did so, while the
other party, a non-resident, did not. It may be added that
any resident might act as surety. From one entry recording
that a defendant, non-resident, had not paid the fee of the
Court, 'nor for the second Court', it might be supposed that
non-residents had this further difference of standing—that
they had to pay fees for the hearing of their cases, whereas
a resident would have a right of free entrance to the Court.
But there is no other reference bearing on this point. Fees
can hardly have been chargeable in any case arising from the
market or fairs, since it was of the essence of the being of
such a Court to be available for such cases. The case in
which a fee is mentioned was between two residents in
neighbouring villages concerning a debt; the rule may have
been that the Court could be appealed to by non-residents
in matters not arising within the town when it suited their
convenience to make use of a Court near at hand, but in
such matters payment of a fee was exacted.

The criminal cases recorded are very few. There are two
charges of assault, or 'bloodshed', each of which ended in
the taking of bail to keep the peace. One case of petty
larceny occurs, the prisoner, a woman, being expelled from
the town by the Court on pain of a whipping if she should
be brought before the Court again. There is also a case of
trespass. The single case of a more serious nature is a charge
of sheep-stealing; the end of it is not clear, but apparently
the defendant was held to bail, presumably for the Assize.

In this Court the Alderman, Steward, and Burgesses sat with the Bailiffs. But it may be doubted whether their presence was vital to the composition of the Court. The Court Book speaks frequently of judgements of ' the Court ', adjournments granted by ' the Court ', and evidence given to ' the Court '. On the other hand it speaks also of judgements of the Bailiffs ; and in view of references of an earlier date it would seem safer to regard the Bailiffs rather as judges sitting with assessors than as presiding members of a homogeneous body.

The Bailiffs were certainly in judicial matters the executive of the town. The oath for the Steward of the Fellowship charges him to ' assiste the Baylyffs of this towne in the execucon of their office to see Justice mynystered '. They were responsible for the stocks and pillory. It was to the Bailiffs' custody that prisoners sentenced at Assizes in Burford were committed by the Judges.

Of the Court as a burghal executive, on the other hand, the Bailiffs were in no way predominant members. Assessments for Crown Subsidies, whether of Tenths and Fifteenths or special Subsidies for military purposes, as well as assessments charged upon the town for robberies committed and assessments for purely internal affairs such as the repair of the church and the keeping of a poor child, were levied by Burgesses acting without the Bailiffs. It may also be noted that when, in 1557, there was a desire for recording deeds of sale of houses in the town, the record appears not in the Court Book but in the Burgesses' Memorandum Book.

§ 5

Thus the ampler Records of the sixteenth century enable us to be positive about certain aspects of the development of town life in Burford which have up to this period been rather dimly discernible. That it was in some degree a conscious development may be gathered from a curious entry in the Memorandum Book. It puts on record a definition drawn up by contemporary lawyers of the phrase ' sac and soc and toll and theam and infangenthef ' in the first charter of

Henry II. This entry must mean that the Burgesses were taking a new kind of interest in the scope of authority that might be claimed under their charters ; they wanted to know exactly what legal powers the phrase conferred.

Now conscious questioning by a corporate body of its position is very rare in the history of town government in England. Powers were exercised as the opportunity or the need arose ; and the distinctions that modern criticism can draw between one and another aspect of burghal unity have no historical reality. It becomes necessary therefore to find some reason for this manifestation by the Burgesses of Burford of a new interest in their constitution ; and a reason can be suggested.

Their existence as a body had originally been determined by the erection under the earliest charters of a Gild ; and their continued corporate entity had been assured much more by the administration of Gild affairs than by their association with a Court of which the essence resided in the Bailiffs. In the middle of the sixteenth century—just before the date of the significant entry in the Memorandum Book— the course of national events suddenly interrupted this channel of continuity.

The first of those sequels of the Reformation which so much affected local life in England, namely the Dissolution of the Monasteries, need concern us here very little. The Hospital of St. John the Evangelist, the sole religious foundation in Burford, was, as has already been said, only a small institution, possessing no more property in the town than a house or two and some closes of land. The Master surrendered the foundation,[1] and it was granted in 1544 to Edmund Harman, one of the King's Barber Surgeons.[2] He also obtained in 1546 a grant of the Rectory of Burford, the one other piece of monastic property here, which had belonged to the Abbey of Keynsham.[3] But these grants had no effect upon the town, for the passage of ecclesiastical property into lay hands did not mean here the advent of a new lord

---

[1] Augm. Court Proc. (P. R. O.), 13, 10.
[2] Particulars for Grants (P. R. O.), 541.   [3] Ibid., 542.

of the manor. The Priory had never had any manorial rights in Burford.. Even when Harman, a few years later, added to his possessions some manorial rights, the town remained unaffected. His lease was only of the agricultural portion of the manor, which had always been outside the scope of the charters,[1] and he was never lord of the town. The Dissolution therefore brought no disturbance to the Corporation.

But another Act of confiscation followed which must have given it a severe shock. This was the Act of Edward VI, dissolving the Gilds and Chantries and alienating their possessions to the Crown. The Fellowship of the Alderman, Steward, and Burgesses had indeed passed in practice far enough beyond the limitations of its Gild origin, however clear the Gild type remained in its constitution, to escape absolute extinction. It was not now a Gild within the meaning of the Act—a body existing solely for mutual benevolence, the maintenance of a chapel, and the observance of obits. Yet there was hardly a single piece of its property which was not held, so to speak, on Gild terms, that is to say, which did not impose upon the Fellowship, as a condition of holding the property, the duty of observing an anniversary, of paying a priest for the saying of memorial Masses, or at the least of making some annual payment for the upkeep of lights or other accessories of church services classed by this Act as superstitious. Even Poole's Lands, given as they were for the benefit of the Corporation and the maintenance of its charters, were subject to a direction that the people in the Almshouse, who were to be the recipients of a small weekly dole, should pray for the souls of Thomas Poole and his wife ; and that apparently unimportant phrase was enough to vitiate the obviously secular intentions of the testator and bring his bequest under the Act.

The result was that the Burgesses found themselves stripped of all that property, the administration of which had

---

[1] Misc. Bks. Land Revenue (P. R. O.), vol. 189, fol. 88. The actual date of the lease has not been filled in, but it is entered as of the reign of Edward VI.

provided them with their most continuous public activity and their strongest impulse towards cohesion. The process appears to have been a gradual one. For a considerable time after the passing of the Act some of the properties continued to be administered by the Burgesses; a few were successfully defended against the claims of the Crown's officers, and one or two pieces were never brought to question.[1] But on the whole the effects of the Act were sweeping, and during the latter half of the sixteenth century the Records show an almost complete blank in that series of leases and enfeoffments which previously provided our chief material for knowledge of the borough system.

Here, then, is a very natural explanation of the sudden appearance in the Memorandum Book of a definition of the jurisdiction conferred by the sac and soc phrase. The entry is not dated, but from its position in the book it must have been made after 1560, and it was between 1560 and 1570 that the alienation of the charity lands became most stringent. The Burgesses, finding that nothing was left to them as a Gild to administer, had a new concern for that other sphere in which their entity subsisted, the work of the Borough Court.

This entry does just allow us to go so far as to discern in the Burgesses a consciousness of two distinct spheres of activity, and a deliberate turning from one to the other. But the distinction can hardly be made before it is obliterated again; the turning from one sphere to the other had been merely by force of circumstances, and the Burgesses set themselves to correct the circumstances. It would appear to a modern mind that, so long as the Borough Court remained secure, the town's corporate vitality was ensured; and, indeed, that any circumstances which tended to concentrate the existence of the Burgess body rather in the Court than in charity administration were for the good of the town and required no correction. But the slight distinction which the Burgesses evidently made did not amount to any perception of such differences. They were incapable of perceiving the

[1] Part III, p. 373.

constitutional distinction between themselves as adminis-
trators of town lands and themselves as members of the
Borough Court. All their functions were to them upon the
same plane of corporateness, if the phrase may be allowed,
and none of them could be lost with equanimity.

It is necessary therefore to pursue further the history of
the charity lands. In detail it is rather obscure. No document gives a list of the property at the moment of confiscation; we have to derive our knowledge of what happened
from the grants of confiscated estate made to individuals by
the Crown, and from some proceedings of the Court of
Exchequer,[1] until in the year 1599 the town Records become
again our source of information after the recovery by purchase of most of the lost lands and tenements. The documents in the Public Record Office are confusing, and it is
almost impossible to identify all the various pieces of property
at all the stages. But a rough outline of events can be given.

The bulk of the property passed into the hands of private
individuals having previously no connexion with Burford,
who may be said in modern phrase to have taken it as
a speculation. The first of these, Richard Venables, sold
eight lots to a Burford man, which thus became private
property and ceased to serve charitable purposes. Venables
obtained his grant in 1549 at twenty-five years' purchase.
He evidently let the speculation drop, for several of his
properties appear, together with others not previously
granted, in the next speculation, when in 1563 two men
named Smith and Devyse obtained a sixty-years' lease from
the Crown. They seem to have sold none of the property,
but again to have let their speculation drop, since after
twenty-seven years of their lease had run the property was
granted to two other men named Typper and Dawe.

Meanwhile, in 1567, proceedings were taken in the Court
of Exchequer concerning a few houses and pieces of land
which had escaped confiscation. They were claimed by the
Crown, but without success, and remained in the hands of
local feoffees. Some of these were put to a use calculated

[1] See Part III, pp. 373, 647.

to protect them against further claims by the Crown, being made part of the foundation endowment of the Grammar School in 1571. Other portions, in spite of the verdict of the Court of Exchequer, were included by Typper and Dawe in their application for lands and passed into their possession.

The final stage in these transactions was reached in 1598, when the Burgesses recovered nearly all the old charity lands by purchase from Typper and Dawe. In each group of the charities the series of leases and conveyances, interrupted at the middle of the century, begins again in 1599 with a conveyance by two of the prominent Burgesses, Richard Merywether and Toby Dallam, to certain other Burgesses, the conveyance being made by Merywether and Dallam 'in discharge of the trust and confidence reposed in them by their fellows'. This phrase is explained by an entry in one of the Corporation Account Books, in which a list of the charity lands dated 1600 is prefaced by the statement that the lands and tenements had been purchased by Simon Green, Richard Merywether, and Toby Dallam 'whoe were putt in trust for the purchase thereof Amountinge to the some of fower score pounds'. The Burgesses had clearly subscribed for the repurchase of the properties.

They proceeded at once to re-establish the charities in a way which shows considerable business ability. The property must all have been in a very bad condition. Even in 1563 most of it is described as ruinous; and although Smith and Devyse obtained their grant on easy terms upon an undertaking to effect the necessary repairs, it is certain from later documents that neither they nor Typper and Dawe did more than the minimum required to keep the houses standing. The Burgesses dealt with this state of affairs by leasing the houses, not directly and singly to the occupiers, but in groups to prominent Burgesses. These leases were for long periods, eighty or ninety years, at small rentals, the lessees undertaking repairs. In each case the old leases obtained from the Crown grantees were surrendered, and a fine paid for the new lease, these fines amounting in all to about £100.

By these measures the property was placed in the hands of individuals who could afford to lay out capital on putting the houses into good condition and take interest on their money in the rents received from their sub-tenants. The rents received for the charities from the chief lessees were indeed small ; but this was at any rate better than the total suspension of the charities for the preceding fifty years, and better also than leasing the houses, for the sake of immediate rents, to single occupiers in whose hands they would soon fall into a condition in which they would become untenantable and produce no rent.

Now in every aspect this re-establishment of the ancient charities is also a deliberate recovery of ground on the part of the Burgess body. There was, to begin with, no particular reason for re-establishing the charities at all. They had, through no fault of the Burgesses, practically ceased to exist, and there is no evidence of any feeling against the conversion of charity lands into private property in the cases in which that happened. The men who found the money for the purchase from Typper and Dawe might just as well have regarded the transaction as a private investment on their own behalf. Or again, granted that they had some charitable intention, they might have founded the charities anew in their own names instead of merely carrying on the old foundations. They followed neither of these lines, but carried the business through simply as a public duty falling upon them as Burgesses.

This, at the close of a century in which they had attained to the complete exercise of functions which we should now recognize as a sufficient expression of corporate borough life, is significant. It means that the Burgesses were incapable of differentiating between one kind of function and another. To them everything which they did or had done as a Burgess body was necessary to their continued existence as a body. The point is important because of its corollary—that of the true borough liberties the Burgesses had a very imperfect appreciation. Unable to distinguish between one kind of function and another, they failed to distinguish between their status in exercising one and their status in exercising the other. Because they were, as the Burgess body, the undoubted authority in the matter of the Charity lands, they assumed that their position in any other duties discharged by them as Burgesses was on the same plane.

It never occurred to them, therefore, to question the efficacy of their charters. They continued throughout the sixteenth century to obtain from the Chancery Letters Patent of Confirmation, which neither expanded the rudimentary charters of Henry II nor in any way gave definition or validity to the corporate constitution. Events were soon to occur which reveal the true character of the apparently great developments of this century.

CHAPTER IV

THE LOSS OF THE FRANCHISES: 1600-1700

§ 1

THAT the Burgesses themselves were at this time quite unconscious of any uncertainty in their position is well seen in one of the first documents to confront us among the Burford Records of the seventeenth century. A large vellum roll dated January 1605/6 contains ' The Auncyente Ordynaunces Rules Constytucions and customes of the Corporacion and Fellowshippe of the Burgesses of this Towne and Burroughe of Burfford'.[1] It is the only extant custumal of the town; and although it contains references to earlier enactments of rules and ordinances, there is no reason to suppose that these had ever been reduced into a written constitution in some custumal now lost. The Roll of 1605/6 nowhere speaks of any previous document of the same kind, and nowhere quotes an ancient rule; it only mentions in general terms that there had been such rules.

The first thing, therefore, to be noticed about the Roll is that the Burgesses of Burford were singularly late in providing themselves with a written constitution. From this we may deduce that they had also been late in taking upon themselves the exercise of any considerable public duties. The need for such rules as are here inscribed would only become apparent as the Burgesses became more and more a public body whose proceedings affected the general mass of inhabitants outside the limits of their Fellowship. Practically this must mean that, while we need not think of all the developments of the sixteenth century as sudden or unexplained by tendencies of earlier date, it was not until

---

[1] This roll has been printed in full by the Historical MSS. Commission (*Various Collections*, vol. i, 1901, p. 34), and is therefore not reprinted in the present work.

that century that the Burgesses approximated effectively to a town incorporation.

Detailed examination of the Roll shows that they never did more than approximate. The ordinances are not those of a town corporate forming an entity of the realm and responsible to the laws of the realm directly. They are the rules of a body regarding itself as assistant to the chief officers of the borough in the maintenance of peace and order and the administration of law; its relation to the Crown subsisting in the fact that these officers were officials of the Crown—'the Prynce's chiefe officers of this saide Towne' (Article 2). The body is a close one, self-electing (Article 20), and its members are responsible to no one but fellow-members for the discharge of their duties (Articles 7, 16, 17, 18); punishment for breach of the Rules is inflicted by the Fellowship, and fines and fees are paid into a common fund disposable for purposes of the Fellowship (Article 18). The Gild tradition is very strongly present; as for instance in Article 6, forbidding members to 'procure or ingrosse or cause to be procured or ingrossed' from other members houses, lands, or anything 'that ys parte or parcell of their lyvinge'; in Articles 8 and 9 concerning the relief of poor and aged members of the Fellowship and the attendance of members at the funeral of one of their number; and in Articles 10 and 20 providing for reform of the 'great charges' which had fallen upon the Bailiffs and Burgesses at their election in feasting the brethren.

At no point do the Burgesses show themselves as responsible to the townspeople, or as exercising functions on their behalf. The elected officers are responsible to the Fellowship, and modifications of their duties, whether concerning the Fellowship alone or affecting such public matters as the market and tolls, may be made upon the vote of the Fellowship (Article 11). None of the Rules applies to any inhabitant of the borough other than members of the Fellowship, and no control of the borough is contemplated except in administration of the common law by the Crown's officers.

§ 2

Now it is precisely in the fact that the chief officers of the borough are thus spoken of as the Crown's officers that we are to look for the clue to the Burgesses' view of their position. For the Roll of 1605/6 is at once a correct interpretation of the charters, as it professes to be (Article 1), and a completely mistaken deduction from them. The constitution of the Gild was right and proper; but when the chief officers of the town were described as ' the Prynce's chiefe officers ' the Burgesses were being misled by the Crown's tenure of the manor into supposing that their position was as independent of intermediate lordship as a fully chartered borough held at fee-farm from the Crown.

In order to understand the blow which was now to fall upon the place, it is necessary to summarize briefly the past relations between the town and the manorial lords who had owned it. From the time when it became an appanage of the Honour of Gloucester, Burford had been an unimportant item in the possessions of a succession of great lords, none of whom had ever resided in, or even near, the place. From the first Earls of Gloucester it had passed to the De Clares, then to the Despensers, and from them to the Earls of Warwick. Though the agricultural part of the manor had often been in the hands of tenants, the town had nearly always remained in the direct holding of the chief lord; and even when, for a short period, a tenant for life had held the town, he also was a man of considerable possessions, John Giffard of Brimpsfield, who did not reside in the place and had no close relations with it.[1]

The inevitable result of these conditions was that, as the Burgesses, advancing in importance and capability, began to take more share in the affairs of the town, they would be confronted by no very strict assertion of the manorial supremacy. Constantly associated with the work of the Borough Court and with the supervision of the market, they would tend gradually, and perhaps even unconsciously, to regard

[1] For more detailed information about the descent of the manor see Part II, p. 82.

these as their own Court and market. The way in which the interests of the Bailiffs came to be identified with the town rather than with the lord of the manor is a very distinct sign of this tendency. When, at the end of the fifteenth century, the manor passed into the hands of the Crown, the process of encroachment on the manorial rights must have been much accelerated. The Records of the century show that in almost every department the Burgesses were in effective occupation of what did not belong to them. The Bailiffs excused from office pay their fine to the Burgesses. The Borough Court profits are allotted to the clerk of the Court as his remuneration. The Burgesses let the stalls in the market and fix the market tolls. They even went so far, in one curious instance, as to deal with the waste inside the town, levying fines on the inhabitants of Sheep Street for the sheep pens erected on the open spaces before their houses.[1] Not one of the sources of burghal profit had been held at a rent from the lord ; the proceeds had, as we have seen, been paid direct to him. The only conclusion to be drawn from the sixteenth-century Records is that, under a remote and weakening manorial control, this money had begun to find its way into the common box of the Burgesses.

Now when a town in these circumstances happened, by the accidental conditions of the tenure of the manor, to have its chief officers appointed by the Crown, it was natural that the Burgesses should fall into the belief that they were as other boroughs responsible to the Crown and forget their manorial status. They could not possibly have the constitutional knowledge to distinguish between the appearance and the reality. Events were now to bring it home to them in a disastrous manner.

In 1601 the Crown alienated the town and manor of Burford by sale to Sir John Fortescue, for a long period Chancellor of the Exchequer under Queen Elizabeth. This transaction had no more immediate effect upon the place than the ancient lordships had had, and for the same reason. Fortescue was a very rich man, whose chief seat was at Saldan in Buckingham-

[1] See Part III, p. 416.

shire; and since there was no manorial mansion at Burford he probably did not concern himself much with the town. With him, however, the long disjunction of Burford and its lords ended. His executors sold the town and manor in 1617 to Sir Lawrence Tanfield, who was already resident at Burford, being described in the deed of sale as ' of the Priory near Burford '.[1]

Thus at a late date, and by an accidental combination of tenures, the Dissolution of the Monasteries was to have here the same effect as it had immediately and directly elsewhere —the introduction of a new lord. Harman had never resided at the Priory, probably because the old religious building must have been poor and insignificant, and he could not, or did not care to, spend money on the erection of a mansion; nor had he ever obtained the lordship of the town. Tanfield, rich enough to build a great house and to add to his importance by acquiring the lordship of the town, became the first resident lord of the manor Burford had had since the Norman Conquest.[2]

In any case such a change would necessarily have brought about some difficulties in a town whose Burgesses had acquired the exercise of their functions so largely by default of the manorial control. But it was peculiarly unfortunate for Burford that the change came with a man like Tanfield. Corrupt and avaricious in his public life, he was grasping and overbearing as a territorial lord. In his other manor of Great Tew he seized upon lands and rights to which his tenants' title was not in dispute. He was not likely to spare the rights of Burgesses whose position was, to say the least, open to very serious question.

§ 3

Within two years of his purchase of the lordship of the town and manor of Burford the Burgesses, in the persons of six of their number, were put on their defence in the Court of Exchequer by a writ of *Quo Warranto* on the charge of

[1] Priory Deeds.
[2] For a further account of Tanfield and his origins see Chap. XI (Part II, p. 268).

usurping certain liberties and privileges to which they had no title. Tanfield's name appears nowhere in the record of the case. The proceedings were instituted on information lodged by the Attorney-General, Sir Henry Yelverton. But there can be little doubt that Tanfield had set the case in motion. To begin with, there was no particular reason why the Burgesses' position should be called in question just at this time, except that a new lord had entered upon the manor, and manorial dues had been usurped by the Burgesses. Secondly, there is evidence in connexion with his other manor that this new lord was very far from being complaisant or mild in his holding of a manor ; a petition of the inhabitants of Great Tew to the House of Lords complains that he had interfered with common rights there, had enclosed pieces of tenants' lands, stopped rights of way, and so on.[1] It may be that the petition is not wholly to be relied on, but it could not have been made without some reasonable grievance behind it ; and even if Tanfield had been within his rights, the petition shows—what is enough for our present purpose— that he sharply exacted his rights. In other words, he would have been likely to assert his rights in Burford, and to institute proceedings such as those which took place. Thirdly, local tradition has always pointed to Tanfield as the cause of the town's loss of liberties ; this would be unimportant if it were not that the proceedings against the Burgesses were such as would be instituted by the lord of the manor, and that this lord of the manor was precisely the kind of man to institute them.

The reason why his name does not appear in the record of the case is obvious. He was, as Chief Baron of the Exchequer, the presiding judge in the Court before which the case came. It began on June 17, 1620 (Trinity Term, 18 James I), and judgement on the various points was given by degrees, the final points receiving judgement a year later, on June 16, 1621. A transcript of the judgements is among the Burford Records.[2] It sets forth that, on an information lodged by the

---

[1] J. A. R. Marriott, *Life and Times of Lucius Cary*, p. 48.
[2] Burford Records, bundle MM, Part III, pp. 374–85.

Attorney-General, William Taylor, William Bartholomew, Simon Simons, Leonard Mills, Thomas Silvester, and John Hunt, and other inhabitants of the town and borough of Burford were charged with exercising without warrant or royal grant the following liberties, privileges and franchises :

   i. The holding of a weekly market on Saturdays ;

  ii. The holding of two annual fairs, viz. one on the feast of St. John the Baptist and one on the feast of the Exaltation of the Holy Cross, or Holyrood Day ;

 iii. The taking of picage and stallage at the market and fairs and the exercising of other jurisdictions therein ;

 iv. The levying of toll on goods exposed for sale and on all live stock brought for sale and the converting of this toll to the use of the defendants ;

  v. The right to felons' goods and chattels ;

 vi. The right to waifs and strays ;

 vii. The right to appoint a Seneschal of the town ;

viii. The right to appoint a Deputy Alderman ;

 ix. The right to remove officials from their offices ;]

  x. The right to hold a Borough Court every three weeks, and to convert to the use of the defendants all profits of the Court ;

 xi. The right to try in that Court all cases involving a sum of less than 40s., to administer oaths in the hearing of cases and to examine witnesses on oath ;

 xii. The right to make statutes and by-laws and to fine or imprison persons for breaches thereof ;

xiii. The right to put persons on oath to keep the by-laws.

Now if we set against this list the list of privileges which Tanfield had bought from Fortescue and Fortescue from the Crown, as set out in the deeds of sale and in the Letters Patent which Tanfield obtained from James I in confirmation of his purchase, the reason for these proceedings of *Quo Warranto* is quite clear. The privileges thus alienated by the Crown to the new lords of the manor included, with the manor and borough, the market and the fair of St. John the Baptist with their stallage and tolls, the Stewardship of the borough with the profits of the Courts, and the right to waifs and strays and felons' goods. Clearly the Crown had regarded itself as owning these privileges and profits by right of the manor, and Tanfield, in view of his purchase deed and

Letters Patent, cannot be blamed for bringing to question the Burgesses' occupation of them.

Some of the impeached privileges were not defended at all by the Burgesses. The right to appoint a Deputy Alderman, the power to administer oaths to witnesses in the Borough Court and to examine them on oath, the right to imprison for breaches of the by-laws, and the right to put persons upon oath to keep the by-laws were abandoned. Whether they were only accidentally omitted from the pleadings for the defence, or whether they were deliberately given up, does not appear. Judgement was forthwith pronounced, seizing these privileges into the hands of the Crown and inhibiting the defendants from exercising them.

On the other points the defence was twofold, consisting first of the import of the Letters Patent of Edward III, and secondly of the plea that the Bailiffs, Alderman, and Burgesses had exercised these franchises from time of which the memory of man ran not to the contrary. In other words, the privileges were claimed partly by grant and partly by prescription.

The plea of prescription was referred to a jury. The privileges claimed on this ground were the Saturday market, the two fairs, and the tolls and stallage of the market and fairs. It is obvious that this plea could not hold water. Documents have been quoted in previous chapters which show clearly that market profits and tolls at Burford were reckoned among the revenues of the lords of the manor; [1] and the fair of St. John the Baptist, besides appearing at early dates among those revenues, had been specifically regranted to Hugh le Despenser.[2] A curious point is that the fair of Holyrood Day was not separately defended in the pleadings. In spite of the fact that this fair had been distinctly granted to the Bailiffs, Alderman, and Burgesses by charter,[3] that charter was not put in evidence, and the two fairs were dealt with on the same basis. It may be that the defendants perceived that to produce a separate charter for one fair would react unfavourably upon their claim to

[1] See p. 17.   [2] See Part III, p. 572.   [3] See p. 24.

the other fair and the market, and decided that all these sources of profit must stand or fall together.

Stand they could not. The Burgesses had certainly not owned these profits time out of mind, and the jury gave a verdict to that effect. The Court gave judgement upon the verdict, and these privileges in turn were seized into the hands of the Crown and the Burgesses were inhibited from the enjoyment of them.

The plea of the charter of Edward III was dealt with by the Court itself. The judgement as recorded is not what would nowadays be called a reasoned judgement, and there-fore we do not know on what ground this plea was held invalid by the lawyers of the time. But that it was so held can hardly surprise us. No attempt had ever been made by the Burgesses to obtain a charter which should amplify or render more precise the rudimentary phrases of the first grants from the Crown—the two charters of Henry II. These gave the burgage tenure, set up a market, authorized the establishment of a Gild ; and one of them included the sac and soc clause. No charter the Burgesses had ever obtained conferred any other franchise ; throughout the whole series the sole effective portion of each document is a recital of the grants of Henry II; and it was upon the first Royal confirma-tion of 'them that the defence relied. It was bound to fail, because no clause gave the town to be held by the Burgesses, and no clause conferred upon them any right except as men of a manor. In Henry II's first charter they are ' homines Willelmi comitis Gloecestrie de Boreford ', and in the second they are ' liberi Burgenses ville comitis Willelmi de Bureford '.

The flaw in the legal position of Burford is very clearly shown by a certain letter from the Corporation of Oxford, which is among the Burford Records.[1] It is dated 25 Sep-tember, 18 James I (1620), and is a certificate under the Common Seal of Oxford concerning the right of the Mayor and Commonalty of that city to waifs and strays, felons' goods, picage, stallage, and tallage. The Bailiffs, Alderman, and Burgesses of Burford had applied to be certified on these points, according to the usage customary between

---

[1] Burford Records, bundle PP, no. 4.

towns when one had been expressly granted in charters the free customs of another, as was the case here. The Mayor and Commonalty of Oxford replied that they had the rights in question ' as part of that wee hould by fee farme and for which wee pay the same '.[1] In that passage lies the whole difference between the position of Oxford and that of Burford. The Burgesses of Burford had never paid any rent for the sources of profit which they had taken into their hands, and obviously therefore had no right to them.

On considerations presumably of this kind the Court held invalid the plea of charter with regard to the remaining privileges—the right to waifs and strays, the right to elect a Seneschal or Steward, the right to hold a Borough Court, the making of ordinances and by-laws and to impose fines for breach thereof. Judgement was given seizing these franchises also into the hands of the Crown, and inhibiting the Burgesses from the enjoyment of them.

The disaster was complete; but it enables us to see the meaning of the advance in burghal activity during the sixteenth century and the comparative lack of any such activity in the previous century. It had arisen partly from the universal decay of the manorial system after the Wars of the Roses, and partly from the particular circumstances at Burford which had put the manor into the hands of the Crown. The Burgesses, finding themselves acting as a Court and managing a market and fairs without being called to account by any one for the revenues, and then observing that their chief officers were appointed by the Crown, had passed—quite probably without any deliberate intentions of encroachment—into the belief that their position was the same as that of other boroughs which in appearance presented the same conditions. They omitted to notice that in those boroughs the privileges were accompanied by responsibilities—that boroughs under the Crown owed duties to the Crown and paid for their franchises.

[1] Evidently this certificate was applied for in connexion with the *Quo Warranto* proceedings; the date of it is between the date of the Attorney-General's information and the date of the first hearing of the defence.

The mistake cost them dear. From this time forth Burford has not even the shadow of likeness to the great boroughs. The long series of Letters Patent from the Crown confirming liberties comes to an end with those issued by the Chancery of James I. There are no more Borough Court Books, and no Memorandum Books of any importance.

§ 4

One thing, indeed, survived the disaster, and that was the Corporation itself. Nothing had passed to prevent the con-tinued existence of a body under the title of the Alderman and Burgesses of Burford. But that existence would probably not have been as long as it actually was, and certainly not as important, if the Burgesses of the sixteenth century had not, by that curious stroke of foresight, taken pains to recover into their hands the ancient Charity Lands. In the control of them the Burgesses had work that held them together and gave them still, in a much modified sense, a public position.

Even this remaining fragment of authority was now to be challenged. In 1628 a Royal Commission, appointed under the Elizabethan Act ' concerning the MisImployment of Lands heretofore given to Charitable Uses ', held an inquiry at Burford, and made decrees which were intended to destroy the supremacy of the Burgesses in the management of the charities.

Again, although no motive for the appointment of the Commission appears on the existing records, it is not difficult to discover the reason for the proceedings. This is to be found in the form which the recovery of the Charity Lands had taken. They had been purchased from two men who had obtained a grant of them from the Crown. Now of course the Crown did not grant confiscated lands for nothing, and the Letters Patent of the grant to Typper and Dawe reserved certain quit-rents to the Crown. The same rents were reserved in the deeds of sale to the Burgesses who made the purchase. But the payments to the Exchequer had not been kept up ; a document of 1631 shows that they had ceased in

1603.[1] It is hardly to be supposed that the Officials of the Exchequer would allow this state of things to continue for long without an explanation; and it seems, from certain passages in the Commission's decrees, that the Burgesses in reply had questioned the validity of the transactions with Typper and Dawe, pleading that the lands had been wrongfully confiscated and ought never to have been in the hands of the Crown or consequently in the possession of Typper and Dawe. This plea would require investigation, and provides us with a sufficient reason for the appointment of the Commission.

At the same time, the Commission's decrees are so plainly unfriendly to the Burgesses that there may have been also some element of criticism of their control at work to bring about an inquiry. Tanfield had died in 1625. But Lady Tanfield, who was certainly almost as energetic as her husband in the controversies with the tenants of Great Tew, and therefore probably took her share in all that had taken place at Burford, lived until 1628. She may have brought influence to bear upon the Exchequer which caused the Commission to have in mind other considerations than those of the unpaid quit-rents alone, when the inquiry began.

The Decrees, at any rate, are a drastic reconstitution of the charitable trusts over the heads of the Burgesses and a termination of the Burgesses' complete control. Briefly, the Decrees are as follows: The Commissioners first lay it down that the lands under investigation were anciently given upon trust for certain purposes, which they set forth specifically, ordering that for the future the rents shall be used for those purposes alone; secondly, they find that in nearly every case the rents then being received were inadequate, and they order the cancelling of all the long leases granted after the recovery of the lands, with instructions that for the future no leases shall be granted for a longer period than twenty-one years or for rents lower than those which in each instance the Commissioners proceed to fix; thirdly, they find that Typper and Dawe had obtained their Letters

[1] Burford Records, bundle K, nos. 2 and 3.

Patent by fraud, the lands not being justly subject to confiscation, and the ancient status of the charities is thereby restored ; fourthly, the Commissioners appoint a new body of trustees, including a number of members of county families from the immediate neighbourhood with a limited representation from among the Burgesses.

Of actual misuse of the charities the Commissioners have little to say. One house, the capital messuage of which the rental was a main part of the support of the Almshouse, had been sold outright—a transaction which was, of course, forthwith declared void. Otherwise there is no accusation of technically illegal proceedings. There is only the general implication, alike in the raising of rents and in the cancelling of existing leases and in the appointment of trustees of a new character to lessen the Burgesses' control, that the Corporation had not discharged its duty faithfully, but had taken advantage of the disturbed and equivocal position of the Charity Lands under various Tudor Acts of Parliament to bring into its absolute power property in which it should never have had more than a trust interest.

The cancelling of the transactions with Typper and Dawe is at the root of the whole of the Decrees, and was for the Corporation the vital portion of them. While those transactions remained valid, the rentals received were not altogether unsatisfactory and the long leases had a good reason, for, as we have seen, they were based upon a perfectly comprehensible and not unenlightened policy of paying for the repurchase and placing the property in the hands of responsible men with some inducement to them to repair the houses and keep them well tenanted. If, on the other hand, the property was still subject to the old forms of trust, and had never legally passed out of them, then the Burgesses were to blame for not contesting the fraud of Typper and Dawe, and for the state of disrepair into which their acquiescence had allowed the houses to fall.

Again, if the transactions remained valid, the Commissioners would have been acting in a very high-handed way in appointing a fresh body of trustees and deliberately infusing into it so

large a proportion of men outside the Burgess body and even
outside the town. Indeed, they might have been acting *ultra
vires*. But once the lands were restored to their ancient basis,
the Commissioners could quite properly make any arrangements they chose for the future administration.

Thus in this matter, as in the *Quo Warranto* proceedings,
the Burgesses had brought trouble upon their own heads. If
the proper manorial payments had been made to Tanfield,
they might have gone on sitting in the Borough Court and
otherwise conducting affairs. If the Crown had continued to
receive the quit-rents of the recovered Charity Lands—a total
sum, after all, of no more than 19s. 2d. a year—the Royal
Commission of 1628 might never have been appointed. We
need not suppose that it was from greed or parsimony that the
payments in either case were withheld. The feeling in the
minds of the Burgesses may very well have been rather one of
objection to acknowledgement of a higher authority, and of
desire to act in complete independence. But that does not
render the results of their attitude less disastrous.

§ 5

The circumstances of the time tended to obscure, a few
years later, the effects both of the judgement of 1620–1 and
the Decrees of 1628. In general the Civil War has left but the
slightest traces on the Burford Records. The place was indeed
the scene of a skirmish or two, and of Cromwell's famous
handling of the Levellers, so that the register of burials has
not escaped the marks of the time. But there are no signs of
internal confusion or interruption of the town's life. Two
reasons may be assigned for this. One is that the loss of
borough privileges would remove any necessity for public
decisions of policy or public action in support of either side.
The other is that the town was by that time in the hands of
a lord of the manor whose official position would quite sufficiently shelter it from the need for decision. Lord Falkland,
who had inherited the town and manor with the Priory by his
father's marriage with the daughter of Sir Lawrence and Lady
Tanfield, sold them in 1637 to William Lenthall, Speaker of

the Long Parliament.[1] His influence, from all we know of him, would be of a kind to keep the town passive and opportunist in its attitude.

Indirectly, however, the Civil War must have affected one important part of the Decrees of 1628—the part which set up the new body of Trustees. That would in any case have been extremely likely to become a dead letter. It was all very well to appoint county gentry as Trustees ; but in practice the actual business of the charities would soon fall back, when the novelty had worn off, into the hands of the resident members of the body, and since those residents would naturally, as men of standing in the town, be Burgesses, the Corporation would in fact recover its control. When events followed which must have sufficiently occupied the minds of the county gentry, if only on the question of how to secure their own property and persons, they would be less and less inclined to spare attention for the affairs of Burford.

Consequently, although the names of the external Trustees appear with all due formality upon the leases of charity pro- perty, the detailed management, the reception and disposal of the rents, reverted to the Corporation. The proof of this is to be found in the Account Books of the seventeenth century. There is one of general charity accounts in which the entries run from 1602 to 1658 ; another containing entries from 1656 to 1737 ; and a book of school accounts from 1644 to 1735. The whole tenor of the entries is that of management by the Corporation. No record appears of a decision being taken by any meeting of persons other than members of the Corpora- tion ; and the accounts are rendered by the Bailiffs to the Burgesses.

The obscuring of the effects of the judgement of 1620–1 came in a different and rather more direct manner. Preserved in company with the series of Letters Patent of Confirmation among the Burford Records are two documents under the Great Seal of the Commonwealth, which did restore some jurisdiction in the town, though not to the town as such. They are commissions issued, the first in 1649 and the second

---

[1] Priory Deeds.

in 1659 after Richard Cromwell had succeeded to the Protec-
torate, appointing the Bailiffs and Seneschal and two of the
ancientest Burgesses of Burford to be Justices of the Peace
for the town, in company with William Lenthall (and later
John Lenthall, his son, also), and to be responsible for the
affairs of the town. This, of course, did not restore the lost
corporate jurisdiction nor re-establish the Borough Court.
But it gave some semblance of the old activities and the old
dignity to the Burgess body, and rendered less obvious the
stripping away of their former authority.

§ 6

The latter part of the seventeenth century, while it was in
one respect the beginning of a new era for Burford, brought
no revival of burghal functions. In material prosperity the
town advanced considerably. The convenience of its position,
for the Burford Races, inaugurated early in this century,
brought Charles II here more than once, filled the inns with
the Court and its hangers-on, and let loose at such times a
flood of carelessly spent money. Meanwhile, the posting
system was coming into being ; and the situation of Burford,
eighteen miles from Oxford on one of the great roads to the
West—the main road to Gloucester and South Wales—made
it the inevitable place for breaking a journey. The rise of the
tanning and saddlery trades, in place of the old subsidiary
occupations of the wool trade, and still more the rise of malting,
are plain indications of the new life of the town.

But the new life had no power to restore the old conditions.
Indeed, even if the Burgesses had been minded to challenge at
this date the judgement of 1620–1 they would have been ill-
advised to make the attempt. The Crown's mistrust of the
loyalty of the towns, and the new policy of strengthening the
Royal executive, were causing havoc in the sphere of borough
liberties. Charters that were of the most ancient authenticity,
and valid in law for every item of the jurisdiction exercised
under them, had to be fought for, and re-established by fresh
grants jealously circumscribed. Short work would certainly
have been made of any claim to the erection of liberties on

PLATE IV. ARCHWAY FORMERLY OF
THE GEORGE INN

charters against which a court of justice had already pronounced.

Thus the close of the century following upon the highest development of the Corporation of Burford sees it but a shadow of its former self. The Bailiffs, Aldermen, and Burgesses are still, indeed, the heirs of a certain unity and of a title. It is noteworthy, moreover, that most of the gifts of money for charitable purposes (for loans to tradesmen, for apprenticing youths, and so on), which were frequent during the seventeenth century, were made to the Bailiffs and Burgesses as a body. They could still stand in lesser degree for the community ; and a Burford man could still feel, in making his will, that his town had an enduring entity to which he could commit his charitable intentions. He could not discern, as we can to-day, the state of constitutional insignificance to which the Corporation had been reduced; nor was the effect of that insignificance, in weakening the Burgesses' self-respect and sense of responsibility, so apparent as it was soon to become.

CHAPTER V

THE DECLINE OF THE CORPORATION, AND ITS LAST STAGES

§ 1

IT is a Corporation sadly changed in character that confronts us when we next obtain a clear view of its activities. Once again we owe this view to a combination of the proceedings of a Royal Commission and a case in the High Court ; and once again the lord of the manor is seen setting the proceedings in motion. On this occasion, however, the ground of the action taken had nothing to do with manorial rights. No functions remained to the Corporation, or had been recovered by them, which could provide a starting-point for a repetition of the controversy with Tanfield. The proceedings of the eighteenth century concerned the town charities alone ; and the Burgesses of the time are revealed to us, not in the comparative dignity of defending, however hopelessly, a claim to burghal privileges, but simply on their trial for mismanagement of trust funds and petty misdemeanours.

The prime mover in the action taken was Mr. John Lenthall;[1] and he seems to have been impelled to the course he took by discovering that a charity fund established by Speaker Lenthall, his grandfather, was in a thoroughly unsatisfactory condition. In 1737 he brought before a vestry meeting a proposal to petition for a Royal Commission to investigate the Burford charities, and it was agreed that petition should be made by the churchwardens and the overseers of the poor.[2] Lenthall and some others of the principal persons engaged

---

[1] That Lenthall was the chief instigator of the proceedings is clear, first from a copy in one of the Corporation Account Books of a letter addressed to him by the Burgesses (Tolsey Coll., Acct. Bks., no. 2), and secondly from the fact that in the law-suit which followed he was made principal respondent. That the Lenthall charity was his reason for interfering is rendered probable by the fact that this charity, though one of the last to be established, was the first to be investigated.

[2] Burford Records, bundle L, no. 10.

came to an agreement as to the costs of the petition, and the affair was placed in the hands of a solicitor.

The Corporation on its side decided to fight. Various fragments of correspondence surviving among the Burford Records show clearly enough the mood of the Burgesses. They were indignant rather than apprehensive, though they display some anxiety to keep abreast of any steps taken by the other side during the necessary preliminaries. At the same time these letters give us our first revelation of the depths to which the Corporation was falling. To begin with, the Burgesses were not united; two or three of them were on Lenthall's side. Meetings of the two parties were being held in separate inns, each meeting claiming to act as a meeting of the whole Corporation. Then again, so slack had the Burgesses become that they had not at this period either an Alderman or a Steward— an irregularity which permitted either party to call its colloguings a meeting of the Corporation, since one party meeting without proper officers could claim no greater authority than another meeting without officers. The Bailiffs, it is true, were on the side opposed to Lenthall—a curious fact, since it shows how completely these officials had become members of the Corporation, in spite of their formal appointment by the lord of the manor.[1] But the Bailiffs had not, strictly speaking, authority within the Corporation, so that their presence gave no real validity to the meetings they attended.

§ 2

A Royal Commission was appointed, and sat in 1738. Two copies of its decrees are in the Burford Records, and a transcript in full will be found elsewhere.[2] The upshot of its proceedings was briefly as follows : it found that the Bailiffs and Burgesses had usurped the sole management of funds in which other persons should have been conjoined with them ; that they had mismanaged funds, in some cases having lost money by loans improperly made to members of their own body in an unsound financial position, in others having used money for

---

[1] They were still so appointed ; see Part III, p. 389.
[2] See Part III, p. 391.

purposes for which it had not been intended, in others again having omitted to put the money to any uses at all ; that they had allowed charity property to fall into a scandalous state of disrepair, even where provision had specifically been made for the upkeep of the property ; that they had allowed gross neglect at the Grammar School, so that the Master was drawing the whole income without any supervision of expenditure, and was neither doing any work himself nor appointing an usher. Moreover, when the Commission was appointed the Burgesses had done all they could to delay its proceedings and to withhold evidence ; and there was more than a suspicion that they had altered their books before producing them, and had made away with documents.

Upon these findings the Commission based certain Orders. Lost money was to be refunded ; damages were to be paid, in some cases by the Bailiffs and Burgesses as a body, in other cases by individuals for particular default ; [1] the disposition of certain charity rents was altered, a moiety of the rents of Poole's Lands, for instance, being ordered to be paid to the Vicar ; and in almost every case the absolute control of the Bailiffs and Burgesses was to cease, and the charities to be managed either by the Bailiffs and churchwardens or by the Burgesses and churchwardens, the overseers of the poor being included in some instances. Finally, stricter arrangements were to be made for the annual rendering of accounts ; a schedule of all documents in the possession of the Corporation was to be made, to prevent any attempt at suppression in the future ; and a fresh body of Trustees was nominated, much on the lines of the body nominated by the Commission of 1628, with the object of bringing in country gentlemen and others of the neighbourhood likely to modify the exclusively town element.

These Orders were drastic indeed, and on the face of them threatened to put a final end to the ancient Corporation of Burford. If the control of the charity lands departed from it,

---

[1] Notably by Griffiths, the schoolmaster ; and by one Underwood, a Burgess, who, having the administration of a periodical gift of 40s. to maidservants, had on one occasion only paid it on condition that the recipient spent 20s. in his shop.

then everything was gone which could hold it together or give it importance.

That the Burgesses perceived this themselves is clear from the attitude they now assumed, an attitude very different from that in which the Decrees of the Commission of 1628 had been accepted. The Burgesses of that date had made no appeal. The Burgesses of 1738, thus severely condemned, determined to challenge the Commission's Orders, and instituted a suit in the Court of Chancery by petition to the Lord Chancellor—The Bailiffs and Burgesses of Burford, Exceptants *v.* Lenthall and others, Respondents. Of this suit, as of the Commission, there is very ample information in the Burford Records. Several copies of the Lord Chancellor's judgement are extant, and also—what is far more valuable—two large portions of copies of the pleadings and depositions on either side. The two portions are not in the same handwriting ; one would appear to be the copy for the use of the Exceptants, and the other that for the use of the Respondents. But it happens that they supplement one another almost exactly, so that for all practical purposes we have a complete set of the pleadings.[1]

The case came on for hearing in 1742. The line taken by the Exceptants may be said to have been in general a denial of the power of the Commission to make the Orders to which exception was being taken, firstly because some of them overrode Decrees of the Commission of 1628 ; secondly because some of them altered dispositions properly made by various testators in wills duly proved ; thirdly because it was *ultra vires* for the Commission to order restitution of money, and still more so for it to order payment of damages and costs. The main answer of the Respondents was that the Commission had in no case acted beyond its powers ; and that the usurpation of control by the Bailiffs and Burgesses was on the evidence so indefensible, and their management of the funds so incompetent, if not fraudulent, that fresh dispositions were very necessary. In one or two matters the Exceptants

[1] For the judgement see Part III, p. 486 ; and for a summary of the pleadings, Part III, pp. 398 and 509.

pleaded that they had been condemned as a body for acts committed by individuals and not corporately. For the rest the pleadings are a mass of flat assertion and counter-assertion. Here and there glimpses are given of the hostility to the lord of the manor which had survived from the days of Tanfield ; one of the objections raised by the Exceptants to the conjoining with them of the churchwardens is that the churchwardens for the town were always ' under the influence of the lord of the manor ', and that to appoint them would be equivalent to giving the lord of the manor a power of interference in purely town affairs.

Judgement was delivered in May 1743. It was a complete triumph on points of law for the Bailiffs and Burgesses. On nearly every issue they raised the Lord Chancellor decided in their favour. Their strong card was evidently the plea that the Royal Commission had no power to vary the Decrees of a previous Royal Commission. This gave them most of their points ; and their plea as to the Commission's power to order the payment of damages and costs gave them other points which had perhaps been particularly disturbing to them. They were, indeed, compelled to make good certain losses of money, though in lesser degree than the Commission had ordered. In their objection to the inclusion of the churchwardens they had their way by pleading the earlier Decrees ; and they also carried their point against the nomination of a fresh body of Trustees. This did not, it is true, technically leave the Burgesses in absolute control ; the previous Decrees had joined with them certain country gentlemen. But, as we have seen, that body had become inanimate ; all detailed control was in the hands of the Burgesses. By carrying their point that under the Decrees of 1628 the only way to appoint new Trustees was by feoffment made by the existing Trustees they secured themselves against any introduction of new members other than such as they agreed to.

§ 3

Thus the Corporation found itself with a stronger hold than ever upon that source of a public income, which had always been the heart of its corporate existence, and for the past hundred years had constituted its sole common activity. We may remark here how firmly that hold had been re-established against the obvious intentions of the Decrees of 1628. For if we ask ourselves by what right the Bailiffs and Burgesses as such instituted the law-suit of 1742 we can find no sufficient answer in their legal position with regard to the charity property. The Commission had certainly named the Bailiffs and Burgesses in its Orders ; and wherever they were condemned in damages and costs, it was, no doubt, open to them to appeal. But by what right did they contest the Commission's Orders as to the future management of the trusts or the appointment of a new body of Trustees ? If any one had taken action on those points, it should have been the official body of Trustees as appointed by the Commission of 1628. The Bailiffs and Burgesses do not even make the pretence of acting in that name ; they appear throughout in their own title. No clearer evidence could be desired of the completeness with which the Corporation had succeeded in making the charity property a Corporation property, held indeed for the good of the public, but held by them as a Corporation, not as members of a body of Trustees ; and nothing could more clearly show the importance this gave them than the fact that nobody, even in the course of the law-suit, seems to have questioned their right to carry that assumption into the Courts.

It is evident that to them the core of the triumph they won in 1743 was not so much the liberation from the monetary damages as the establishment of their power of control. Some of the surviving copies of the judgement, which seem to have been written out by individual Burgesses in the enthusiasm of victory, contain an index-summary of the charities ; and these indexes reiterate the declaration, ' the management of this charity remains in the Bailiffs and Burgesses ', or some such phrase. The supremacy which the Burgesses had acquired at the end of the sixteenth century by the repurchase of the charity lands, had lost by the Commission of 1628, and had since been regaining by quiet usurpation, was now theirs by a legal judgement. No wonder that, long as the judgement is, they enjoyed writing it out patiently in little books to tell those which should come after.

Apparently it mattered not at all to them that morally, on the charge of misuse of funds and misappropriation of moneys, they made the poorest kind of defence, and that their victory was won almost entirely on technical points of law. It was, perhaps, inevitable that in the minds of Lenthall and those who acted with him the rottenness of the charity administration should have been held to proceed wholly from the unchecked authority of the Bailiffs and Burgesses, so that the one aspect of the question could not be dealt with except by attacking the other. But this had the unfortunate result of causing any attempt at reform to depend upon fresh dispositions of responsibility, which involved conflict with existing Decrees of a Royal Commission. By concentration on that weak spot the Burgesses evaded the moral condemnation.

But it remains on record for any one who peruses the pleadings and depositions. These leave no doubt of the carelessness, incompetence, smug favouritism, and in more than one case the dishonesty, of the management of the charity property. Trust money was lent by the Burgesses to other Burgesses whom they must have known to be in financial difficulties, and no security was taken in spite of specific directions to that end ; appointments of aged widows to the Almshouses depended upon getting into the Burgesses' good graces ; materials to be distributed under charitable bequests were purchased from Burgesses ; the rents of houses were taken and no money spent on repairs, even when repairs had been made a first charge upon the charity. The case of the Grammar School is the worst of all, because it must have been patent to the whole town that the Master was doing no work at all, and that the children were being left untaught and undisciplined.

§ 4

In fact, the moment at which the Corporation is seen with its remaining hold upon public life more secure than at any previous period in its history is not the height, but the very depth of its existence. It was not appointing its ancient officers ; it was disunited and quarrelsome ; it was composed of petty tradesmen, who held their meetings at various inns, and passed rules which are those of a drinking club rather than a Corporation.[1]

Yet the Burgesses had not wholly lost the memory of their former status as a borough. There are signs that shortly before the date of the Royal Commission of 1738 they contemplated a movement to recover the privileges which the sixteenth-century Burgesses had exercised. Among the Burford Records is an Indenture of Agreement made in 1728 between the Bailiffs of the year, the Alderman, the Chamberlain, and six of the Burgesses, of the one part, and Richard Griffiths of the other part. It sets forth that the lords of the manor had ' by pretence of a judgement in the Court of Exchequer seized upon the profits of the markets ' ; that this judgement had been obtained only against certain Bailiffs and Burgesses in their private capacity ; that no execution was ever taken, and the franchises had not been seized into the King's hands, but the lord of the manor had used the judgement in order to possess himself of the franchises by intimidating the Burgesses. In these circumstances the Bailiffs had been advised to sue out a writ of error to reverse the judgement. For this purpose the rents of Poole's Lands, given to be used for the confirmation of charters and other objects in furtherance of the well-being of the Corporation, might properly be employed. But as these rents amounted only to £25 a year, the present Indenture of Agreement was made, to the effect that Richard Griffiths was to receive this sum of £25 a year on trust, and if necessary a capital sum of £10 apiece from each of the other parties to the agreement, in order to set proceedings on foot ; and meanwhile an effort was to be made to mortgage Poole's Lands, with the intent of raising the sum required for carrying on the proceedings.[2]

Plainly to be taken in conjunction with this Agreement are two small pieces of paper containing notes on the franchises anciently exercised ; these fragments are dated 1727.

---

[1] See, e. g., Burford Records, bundle RR.   [2] Part III, pp. 390-1.

Now the Agreement was based on a thorough misapprehension of the situation. The Burgesses could never comprehend that the association of the town of Burford with the Crown was not the proper constitutional relation of a borough held at fee-farm and thereby authorized to elect its chief officers and manage its own affairs, but the merely accidental relation arising from the passage of the manor into the hands of the Crown. Consequently, they had never grasped the fact that when the Crown disposed of the town and manor to a purchaser, it disposed also of all the privileges which went with the town. The lord of the manor was in enjoyment of the profits of the markets, not by pretence of the judgement, but by simple purchase; the judgement only corrected the mistake which the original purchaser had made in not assuring himself that the vendor was in effective possession of the property sold. Whether it is true or not that the judgement had never been put in execution, we have no means of knowing. That process would in any case have been a mere formality, and such a lawyer as Tanfield is not likely to have omitted it. The probability is that the Burgesses were misled by the phrase ' seized into the hands of the Crown '. Seeing that the privileges were not, in point of fact, in the hands of the Crown, they very likely assumed that the judgement had not been carried into execution. They did not realize that already the privileges had been sold by the Crown to another holder, so that execution would not bring the Crown back into possession of the town, but would only secure the title of Tanfield.

Even apart from this fundamental misapprehension the movement cannot be taken seriously. Richard Griffiths, who was chosen to be the repository of the funds, was the schoolmaster who was ten years later to be exposed as having converted to his own use the whole income of the school, while performing none of the duties. His position in that matter was so bad that he avoided appearing before the Commission, and ' did privately withdraw himself from Burford and conceal himself in London until after the Return or Close of the said Commission '.[1] Before the suit of 1742 was brought

[1] See Part III, p. 399.

he seems to have become feeble-minded. If he was to occupy
a position of responsibility in the attempt to recover the
borough privileges, the proposal cannot have been launched
with much wisdom. It was probably little more than a piece
of pot-house pompousness, set on foot by one of the inn-
frequenting groups of Burgesses.

At any rate it went no further. For one thing, the attack
made by Lenthall and his associates gave the Burgesses
enough to think about, and certainly enough opportunity to
spend what money they had at their disposal, in defending
their position without attempting to improve it. When that
trouble was safely over, they probably felt that their new
security in control of the charities sufficed for their sense of
their own importance, No other movement was ever made for
more exalted functions.

§ 5

With this incident, therefore, the history of the Corporation
of Burford comes, in one sense, to an end. But the body of the
Bailiffs and Burgesses still survived, and the record of its
existence must be carried further, though it can be hardly
more than a record of increasing decay.

In another hundred years (with such regularity did the
Corporation fall into sloughs of mismanagement) a public
inquiry had again become necessary. A Report of the Charity
Commissioners of 1822 reveals the Burgesses to us yet once
more neglecting their property, losing the rents, and allowing
some of their own members to misuse trust property for their
private profit.

As one after another the charities come under review the
report of the Commissioners is almost monotonously the same.
With few exceptions the houses were in disrepair—one was
actually a mere heap of rubbish—and the rents heavily in
arrear. From 1805 to 1814 the office of clerk to the feoffees
was held in conjunction with the office of treasurer to the
Corporation, by one Waters. ' During that period no account
was ever delivered by him to the feoffees ; and upon his death
no papers were found from which any account could be made

out '; or, as another reference puts it, ' he died suddenly in 1814, having made no entry whatever of any receipts or disbursements during the whole of the time he held that situation.'

In several instances the Lord Chancellor's judgement of 1743 had been evaded. While relieving the Bailiffs and Burgesses of the heaviest parts of the payments ordered by the Commission, the judgement did direct the refunding of certain sums of money. These, it was found, had never been refunded.

Five years later the muddle, into which the Burgesses had allowed their business to fall, came to a head in a manner almost ludicrous, though in the end it was to the good of the charity property that the situation which arose in 1827 was so extreme as to require the intervention of the law.[1] Among the laxities to which the Commission of 1822 had drawn attention (but in vain) was this : that the body of Feoffees, or Trustees, which by the constitution of the Trusts should never have sunk below six in number without the making of a new feoffment appointing fresh members, had actually dwindled to one old man, the Hon. and Rev. Francis Knollis, Vicar of Burford. In 1826 he died, and died intestate, without having appointed any new Trustees. Apparently no attempt had been made to get him to appoint any, until about a year before his death, and he was by that time too feeble and too forgetful to carry the matter through.

The position, then, was this extraordinary one : the whole of the charity property, Mr. Francis Knollis having been the sole surviving feoffee, had passed by his intestacy to his heir-at-law, the Rev. James Knollis, Vicar of Penn, Buckinghamshire ; and no one could tell what now became of the title to the ownership of the property. Mr. James Knollis could hardly treat the charity lands as his private possession ; but on the other hand the tenants might refuse to pay rent at all, since he was certainly not a feoffee under the constitution of the charities. Fortunately for the town he was a straightforward man, and his one desire was to rid himself of the

[1] Burford Records, bundle N, no. 1.

embarrassment by handing over the property to a new body of Trustees. Had it been otherwise, long and costly processes of law might have been necessary to recover the title. But, even with all his willingness, the matter was not so simple as it looked. The constitution of the trusts made no provision for the appointment of new Trustees by the heir of a surviving feoffee—naturally enough, since every care had been taken, as far as direct instructions could go, that the matter should never come to such a pass.

Had the difficulty arisen a few years earlier, there could have been no course except to lay an information before the Attorney-General, and move him to proceed—a most expensive business. But an Act of Parliament had recently been passed, under which it was possible to rectify the situation by petition to the Master of the Rolls. This was done; a draft list of new feoffees was by his order submitted to one of the Masters in Chancery, and from him authority was obtained for the transfer of the property to them.

In the correspondence concerning the difficulty there are many proofs of the carelessness still vitiating the management of the charities. In a statement of the case to be submitted to counsel it is remarked that ' a leading member of the Corporation ', one Tuckwell, was tenant of a large part of the charity property, and was at this time at least seven years in arrear with the rents, owing some £400. All the other tenants were more or less in arrear. It was known, too, that the defaulters, ' especially Tuckwell ', were watching for any legal flaw in the transfer, to take advantage of it in order to escape payment of their arrears.

The whole affair was very much in the spirit of the preceding century. With the rents so heavily in arrear every duty of the Corporation in regard to the charities must have been neglected, the property ruinous, the school inefficient, the poor unrelieved. Tradition was even maintained to the point of finding one of the chief defaulters a member of the Corporation.

§ 6

For the brief remainder of its career the Burford Corporation has next to no history, but what there is is decent. Public opinion was beginning to improve, and the Municipal Corporations Act of 1835 is a sign of the dawning conviction that the national life was getting no good from small unrepresentative bodies ranking as Corporations.

It is, of course, unlikely that so slack and incompetent a management of business as was revealed by the Commissioners' Report of 1822 would be other than a reflexion of the managing body. The Corporation which in 1738 had rendered an inquiry necessary was disunited, petty in outlook, poor in self-respect. The Corporation of 1822 was practically moribund. The Commissioners record that, though there was an Alderman again, there was no Steward, and there were only three Burgesses; no meeting had then been held for six or seven years.

It never really revived. The management of the charities, after the absurd muddle of 1826–7, was firmly vested in a proper body of Trustees, and the Corporation was at last in the subordinate place to which the Commission of 1628 had unsuccessfully attempted to reduce it. For a quarter of a century yet the title of the Bailiffs, Alderman, and Burgesses of Burford remained to represent one of those wizened little survivals which so curiously took rank as Corporations alike with the vigorous ancient bodies that had early been subjected to the healthy discipline of public responsibility, and with the great modern Town Councils, which were the expression of a new element in the nation's history—the huge industrial concentrations of population.

The end of the Burford Corporation came in 1861. Even the manner of its abolition has some of that accidental quality which had marked its whole career. The Act of Parliament which extinguished it is not an Act primarily concerning the Corporation, or identified with its name. The ancient title, with nearly eight hundred years of history behind it, does not appear on the index of the Public Statutes. In 1861 was passed ‘ An Act for confirming a Scheme of the Charity Com-

missioners for certain Charities in the Town and Parish of
Burford in the County of Oxford '.   In a single clause the Act
confirms the Scheme ' as the same is set out in the Schedule
to this Act '.   Of this Schedule the first sentence is : ' The
existing Corporation of the alderman, steward, bailiffs, and
burgesses of the Borough of Burford is hereby dissolved.'

Surely the depth of insignificance—to be abolished by a
Schedule.

PART II

STUDIES IN THE HISTORY OF BURFORD

CHAPTER VI

THE LORDSHIP OF THE MANOR AND TOWN OF BURFORD

THE history of the lordship of the manor and town of Burford is to be seen at large in the list of those who held it. Little in the shape of personal detail need be added to the bare list, for the names entered there over a period of six hundred years have their places in the history of England.

Robert of Gloucester, Queen Matilda's champion against Stephen; John, King of England; the De Clares—always among the leaders of the feudal barons, whether in the days of that Gilbert de Clare who was one of the barons of the Great Charter, the later Gilbert, ' the Red ', who was with Simon de Montfort in the Provisions of Oxford, or the last Gilbert who fell at Bannockburn; the Despensers, from Hugh the King's favourite to Thomas, shamefully beheaded by Henry IV; Henry Beauchamp, the friend and companion of the young Henry VI; Warwick the King-maker; and then, at a later period, following upon a long tenure of the manor by the Crown, Fortescue, Tanfield, Lucius Lord Falkland, and William Lenthall—names such as these require no comment here.

All that need perhaps be said is that for the first time an attempt has been made to trace the entire descent of the lordship, leaving no step in the succession unaccounted for; and also to give documentary authority, not merely for the tenure by each individual of territories known to have included Burford, but for his actual tenure of Burford itself. This authority is lacking in only one instance in the ensuing

list. The most interesting addition to the known lords of
Burford is certainly Robert of Gloucester. This was due to
recognizing as granted by him a charter occupying an obscure
place on the Burford Gild Certificate. Owing to its brevity
and omission of specific grant of liberties it was placed by the
Burgesses, who made the Certificate, out of its due order. But
the style with which it opens is the unique style of Robert of
Gloucester, so that the document is unimpeachable evidence
of his lordship ; curt and abrupt, reduced to the smallest
possible limits in phrasing, it may well be characteristic of the
man. It is interesting also to have established King John's
tenure of Burford ; and on the lesser plane of picturesque
associations to have inserted the names of Edward, son of the
Duke of Clarence, executed on charges of complicity with
Perkin Warbeck, and of that skilful but unpleasant personage,
John Dudley, Duke of Northumberland.

It is, of course, to its connexion with the territories of one
of the greatest of feudal Honours that Burford owes the
remarkably distinguished list of its lords. The Honour of
Gloucester was the chief item in the lands granted to Fitz-
Hamon by William Rufus ; and the history of Burford shows
that the former possessions of the Bishop of Bayeux in this
extreme western portion of Oxfordshire were attached by
FitzHamon, no doubt as a measure of administrative convenience, to his Gloucester territories, to which, indeed, in spite
of county divisions, they have natural affinity. It would
appear, also, that in some subdivision of the territories
Burford, together with Fairford and one or two other places,
was grouped with Tewkesbury at an early date. Certain
writs of King John concerning the place are addressed, not
to the Sheriff of Oxfordshire, but to William de La Faleise,
who was Keeper of the manor of Tewkesbury ; and in an
early account of escheats (1232–3), when the Honour was held
by the Crown as guardian during the minority of Richard
de Clare, the revenues of the manor of Burford are definitely
allotted in the main ' ad partem de Theokbiri '.

Thus Tewkesbury may be regarded as, in some sense, a

mother-place to Burford ; and with more than slight stirrings
of loyalty the Burford man may stand in the great Abbey
Church there, beholding the tombs of those to whom his
predecessors owed allegiance.   He may turn his eyes to the
beautiful little chantry on the north side of the chancel, where
were laid, ' wrapped in fine diaper ', the bones of him who first
gave Burford men their liberties and their Gild ; and he may
see, wrought upon the tiles in the floor of the chantry, the
rampant lion which from that day to this Burford has borne
as arms.   Beneath the chancel floor the dust of the de Clares
is mingled with the dust of royalty.   Close by the chantry of
FitzHamon, Hugh le Despenser, son of Edward II's favourite,
lies at his mailed length ; and opposite him, on the south side
of the chancel, Edward le Despenser kneels in the shadows on
the roof of his chantry, facing towards the altar in his age-long
prayer.

Splendid as is the roll of the Burford lords, it has not on that
account been the easier to trace and establish in detail. A
princely territory like the Honour of Gloucester is not likely
to show the placid succession of lords through long periods
that minor possessions enjoyed. Its holders were always, from
the nature of the case, men so near to the throne and the
Blood Royal that in disturbed times their lands were constantly being forfeited, and regranted by the Crown.

The first difficulty of this kind, though but a slight one, is
the uncertainty about the date at which King John actually
entered the lordship. When he married Isabella, one of the
daughters and co-heirs of William, Earl of Gloucester, he was
already in possession of such vast territories that Henry II
appears to have hesitated about allowing the Gloucester lordship also to pass into his hands. But at any rate some part of
it, including Burford, had been recognized as his by the time
of Richard's accession.

Thereafter, for some two hundred years, the position of the
manor of Burford is clear enough. It followed in turn each of
the lines of descent through Earl William's three daughters.
King John, after his divorce from Isabella, granted it to

Amaury, Count of Evreux, who was the son of Mabel, the eldest daughter, and after his death to William de Cantilupe, who married his widow. From him (if he ever actually held it, for the grant to him is curiously worded) the manor of Burford passed, with other Gloucester territories, to the de Clares, in virtue of Richard de Clare's marriage to Amice, the other daughter of Earl William.

In their hands Burford remained until the death of the last Gilbert de Clare at Bannockburn in 1314. He left three sisters, all of whom were married, Eleanor to Hugh le Despenser, Margaret to Piers Gaveston, and Elizabeth to John de Burgh. After Gilbert's death these three men seem to have made a division of his estates among themselves. Appended to the Inquisition Post Mortem (Edward II, File 42) is a sheaf of writs to the Sheriffs of various counties, bidding them eject these three from castles and lordships of which they had taken possession. They had not waited to see whether a posthumous heir might be born. The Sheriffs' returns to these writs display no little helplessness; they virtually confess themselves unable to carry out the evictions. We may conclude, in the case of Burford at any rate, that they ultimately succeeded, from the evidence of the Lay Subsidy of 1316, which places at the head of the list for Burford the name of Isabella de Clare, Gilbert's aunt; her possession of the place, on a grant by her brother, Gilbert the Red, must have been restored. Moreover, we have the evidence of the formal grant to Hugh le Despenser and his wife in 1322 as proof that they had not previously been in possession.

The death of Thomas le Despenser in 1399 brings us to the next uncertainty. By his attainder his lands must have been forfeited. The fact that a lease of the site and agricultural lands of the manor to a tenant was made in 1428 by the Crown, and that an account of escheats of 1435-6 speaks of Burford as having been held by Thomas, last Lord le Despenser, on the day of his death, without any mention of a subsequent holder of the manor, can hardly mean anything except that Burford was for all this time in the hands of the Crown. Yet it must soon after this have been restored to the Despenser heirs, because Isabel, the daughter of Thomas le Despenser, who brought the Gloucester territory by marriage to the Beauchamps and then to the Nevilles, appears as seized of the manor of Burford in 1439.

The fate of Burford at the next escheat of the territory, after the death of the King-maker, is clear enough, and is set out in the list which follows. But another period of some uncertainty occurs in the middle of the sixteenth century. Upon an exchange of lands between Edward VI and John Dudley, Earl of Warwick, in 1549, the latter acquired, perhaps in order to give colour to his title, then still new, the old ' Warwick's lands ' in Burford. Yet in 1552 the town and manor were again in the hands of Edward VI, there having been another exchange.[1] A further complication is introduced later by references in the Burford Corporation Books to Sir Edward Unton as holding courts of the manor, and by a statement in one of the Priory Deeds of Sale that he held the manor in right of his wife Anne, Countess of Warwick, for term of her life. This Countess of Warwick was the widow of the Duke of Northumberland's son, who died so soon after his release from the Tower, on his pardon for complicity in the Lady Jane Grey plot. Either there must have been yet another exchange, subsequent to 1552, or the manor, as once having been held by John Dudley, was granted for the maintenance of his son's widow.

Nor is it only the exalted station of the lords of Burford which produces obscurities in the history of the manor. Another cause, almost equally fruitful of difficulty, is the division that was created by the erection of a chartered community within the manor. There is, indeed, nothing in the charters themselves to create division. They bestow liberties upon ' the men of Burford ' in general ; and no document of an early date suggests that the term ' Burford ' was of limited application in regard to the whole feudal unit. Yet by the end of the thirteenth century the manor clearly comprises

[1] According to a Survey taken in that year, transcribed *infra*, Part III, p. 624.

three members, the Burgus of Burford, and the hamlets of
Signett and Upton. The question of how this partition came
about may be more conveniently discussed in a later Chapter
on the Topography of Burford. For our present purpose it
is enough to point out that the manor had become thus
divided. Consequently it is necessary to establish very carefully the exact holding of any person mentioned in connexion
with the tenure of the manor. When the division first appears
in our Records there is no uncertainty. A tenant, John
Giffard, held by sub-infeudation, at a service of one knight's
fee, £20 of rent of the town of Burford to himself and his heirs,
with the rest of the town for his life only, and the hamlet of
Signett, which was outside the burghal system. The chief lord
retained only the hamlet of Upton, also outside the burghal
system, and the remaining value of the town above £20 of rent
after the lifetime of John Giffard. But even this does not
exhaust the subdivisions, for the family of de Fanencourt held
some portion of the town by service of half a knight's fee.

Without a clear understanding of these circumstances the
history of the manor in Edward II's reign would be very
puzzling ; for the simultaneous holdings of Hugh le Despenser
and Isabella de Clare would be inexplicable. But in the light
of the Inquisitions of 1295 and 1299 they can be reduced to
order. Gilbert the Red, ninth Earl, it appears from the
Patent Roll of 1 Edward III (pt. I, m. 13), had given the
manor of Burford to his sister Isabella. Now in view of the
sub-infeudation to John Giffard this can only mean that he
gave her the hamlet of Upton ; and this is also proved by
the Inquisition Post Mortem of the last Gilbert de Clare (1314),
in which he appears as holding only that portion of the town's
value which had reverted to the chief lord on the death of
John Giffard the elder, and not (as his father had done) the
hamlet of Upton. Isabella married Maurice de Berkeley,
whose estates were forfeited on the accession of Edward III ;
but his wife received a special regrant of ' the manor of
Burford without the town ', on the ground that she had always
held this land herself by her brother's grant, and had not
enfeoffed any other person. Hugh le Despenser's holding had

come about by another and earlier forfeiture, the estates of John Giffard the younger being escheated. This brought the town of Burford into the hands of the Crown ; and Eleanor, Hugh le Despenser's wife, being already, as one of the co-heirs of the last Gilbert de Clare, in possession of that part of the town's value above John Giffard's £20 of rent, the whole was combined in the grant to le Despenser.

Possibilities of confusion in the earlier centuries are much increased by the use of the name ' Burford ' to describe sometimes the complete feudal unit including the town, sometimes the town alone, and sometimes the agricultural portion alone. Thus, although the land held at farm by Robert Atkyns in 1428 was entirely in the hamlets of Signett and Upton, it is described as the manor of Burford. Hence, too, the mistake that has been made in supposing that Edmund Harman, some hundred years later, obtained the lordship of the manor. He only obtained the agricultural portion for a term of years, the lordship remaining in the Crown.

This kind of confusion disappears about the middle of the sixteenth century, when the burghal and the agricultural portion received different names. In the Edwardian Survey the latter is entered as ' the manor of Bury Barns '; and thereafter the name of ' Burford ' belongs distinctively to the town.

But by that time we approach the end of obscurities from another direction. The Letters Patent by which Queen Elizabeth disposed of the manor and town to Sir John Fortescue, her Chancellor of the Exchequer and Sub-Treasurer, leave some remnant of the old duality in clauses reserving certain leases of the Bury Barns land. But when Sir Lawrence Tanfield acquired the property from Fortescue's heirs, he seems to have extinguished, by purchase, this divided tenure, and from henceforth the whole of the manor and town passes as a single manorial property. So it remained until William John Lenthall, under the load of mortgage incumbrance that had accumulated by 1820, broke it up by selling the farm of Bury Barns and some other pieces of the estate to various purchasers, before he finally sold the Priory and the Manor to Charles Greenaway of Barrington Grove, in 1828.

Mr. Charles Greenaway, who was M.P. for Leominster, married Charlotte Sophia, daughter of Mr. Robert Hurst, of Horsham Park, Sussex, but had no children. He had, however, a niece, the daughter of his sister Mary, who had married Mr. Edward Youde of Plas Madoc, Denbigh. Mr. Greenaway died in 1859, and the estate was for some time in Chancery. Mrs. Greenaway died in 1875, and the niece, Miss Mary Jane Youde, succeeded to the property. With her death, in 1892, the Greenaway line came to an end, and the property and lordship of the manor passed to Mrs. Greenaway's family— the Hursts of Horsham Park—with whom the lordship of the manor now remains.

CHIEF LORDS AND TENANTS OF THE MANOR AND TOWN OF BURFORD

Lords of the Manor and Town of Burford.	Tenants of the Manor.	Notes and Authorities.
1085 Odo, Bishop of Bayeux	Earl Alberic	According to the Domesday Survey.
1088 Robert Fitz-Hamon	—	From the fact that he granted the first charter to Burford, it is clear that Burford had been part of the lands of the Bishop of Bayeux granted to Fitz-Hamon by William Rufus in return for his support of the King against the Bishop's rebellion. From this time till 1400 the manor of Burford formed part of the Honour of Gloucester.
1107 Robert of Gloucester, natural son of Henry I	—	Obtained the Honour of Gloucester by his marriage with Mabel, one of the daughters of Robert Fitz-Hamon. Granted the second charter to Burford.
1147 William, Earl of Gloucester	—	Succeeded on the death of Robert, his father. Granted the third charter, and obtained from Henry II the first Royal Confirmations.
(1183 The Crown)	—	The Honour of Gloucester was held by the Crown for some years after the death

Lords of the Manor and Town of Burford.	Tenants of the Manor.	Notes and Authorities.
		of Earl William. Presumably Burford passed with the rest of the Honour, but the place is not specifically mentioned in the rentals of the Honour on the Pipe Rolls of Henry II.
1189 circa John, afterwards King of England	—	Pipe Rolls, 2 & 3 John. John married Isabella, one of the daughters of Earl William. At this date he obtained from King Richard some of the lands of the Honour, and probably Burford among them, since the place does not appear upon the Pipe Rolls of Richard's reign, but does appear on those of King John.
1206 Amaury, Count of Evreux	—	P. R. O. Close Roll 7 John, m. 8. John granted him, besides the Manor, the rental and tallage of the Town.
1214 Geoffrey de Mandeville	—	P. R. O. Close Roll 16 John. Granted on his marriage to Isabella of Gloucester, whom the King had divorced after his accession. He received with her the whole Honour of Gloucester, except the castle and town of Bristol, and the town of Campden.
1216 William de Cantilupe	—	P. R. O. Close Roll 18 John. A grant of the manor of Burford by itself 'nisi dominus Rex alii illud contulit'.
(1217 Gilbert de Clare, 7th Earl of Gloucester)	—	According to the Dictionary of National Biography he succeeded, in right of his wife Amice, one of the daughters of Earl William, to the Honour of Gloucester on the death of her sister Isabella. There is no document actually recording his tenure of Burford.
1230 Richard de Clare, 8th Earl of Gloucester	—	P. R. O. Inq. P. M. Hen. III, file 27, no. 5, m. 41. Granted a charter

Lords of the Manor and Town of Burford.	Tenants of the Manor.	Notes and Authorities.
		to Burford, the last received from the manorial lord.
	Geoffrey de Fanencourte	Held part of the manor by service of half a knight's fee. See Inq. P. M. just quoted.
1262 Gilbert de Clare, 9th Earl of Gloucester	John Giffard of Brimpsfield	P. R. O. Inq. P. M. Edw. I, file 77. The tenant at this time held nearly all the town and manor, the town by service of one knight's fee, and part of the manor, excluding Geoffrey de Fanencourte's holding, by a quarter of a knight's fee. The lord of the manor retained only the hamlet of Upton.
1295 Joan, widow of Gilbert de Clare, daughter of Edward I	—	P. R. O. Inq. P. M. Edw. I, file 128. Held by her during her son's minority.
	1299 John Giffard, son of the preceding	P. R. O. Inq. P. M. Edw. III, file 5.
1305 Ralph de Monthermer	—	P. R. O. Pat. Rolls, 33 Edw. I, ps. 2, m. 1. He was guardian of the young Gilbert de Clare, whose mother he had married. See also Close Rolls, 29 Edw. I, m. 10 d.
1312 Gilbert de Clare, 10th Earl of Gloucester	—	P. R. O. Inq. P. M. Edw. II, file 42.
1316 Isabella de Clare	—	P. R. O. Lay Subsidies Oxfordshire, 161.8; 161.9. She was one of the sisters of Gilbert, 9th Earl; see Inq. P. M. last quoted.
1322 Hugh le Despenser, and Eleanor de Clare, his wife	—	P. R. O. Charter Rolls, 16 Edw. II, m. 6. By the attainder of John Giffard, the town of Burford had fallen into the King's hands in April 1322; he granted it to Hugh le Despenser in July. Eleanor was one of the sisters of Gilbert, 10th Earl.
	1327 Isabella de Clare	P. R. O. Close Rolls, 1 Edw. III, ps. 1, m. 13.

Lords of the Manor and Town of Burford.	Tenants of the Manor.	Notes and Authorities.
		The holding of John Giffard having been escheated by his disloyalty, the remainder of the manor was escheated by the disloyalty of Maurice de Berkeley, whom Isabella de Clare had married. But a special regrant was made to her of the manor excluding the town.
1328 Eleanor, widow of Hugh le Despenser	—	P. R. O. Close Roll, 2 Edw. III, m. 30. Burford was specially granted to her, as the King did not consider it consonant with justice that her lands should be swept into the forfeiture of her husband's lands.
1337 Hugh le Despenser, son of the preceding	—	P. R. O. Inq. P. M. Edw. III, file 51.
1359 Edward le Despenser	—	P. R. O. Inq. A. Q. D. Edw. III, file 259.
1375 Thomas le Despenser	—	P. R. O. Min. Accts. 1122.13.
	1387 Hugh, Earl of Stafford	Cal. Inq. P. M., vol. iii, p. 85. Held half a knight's fee, as heir of the Fanencourts (see Cal. Inq. P. M., vol. iii, p. 251).
(1399) The Crown	—	P. R. O. Min. Accts. 957.10. This account, of the year 1435/6, refers to the town and manor as having been held by Thomas, last Lord Despenser, at the time of his death, but makes no reference to any other holder since then. Evidently, therefore, Burford had not passed with the other Despenser lands to the son and daughter of Thomas le Despenser.
	1420 Robert Atkyns	P. R. O. Min. Accts. 957.10. He had a lease from the Crown for three lives, his own, and those of his wife and his son.
1439 Isabel, Countess of Warwick	—	Cal. Pat. Rolls, Hen. VI, 1436–1441, p. 359. Isabel,

Lords of the Manor and Town of Burford.	Tenants of the Manor.	Notes and Authorities.
		Countess of Warwick, was the daughter of Thomas le Despenser. Apparently the manor of Burford had been restored to her as heiress of the Despenser lands.
1439 Henry Beauchamp, Duke of Warwick	—	P. R. O. Inq. P. M. 24 Hen. VI, no. 43. He succeeded to his mother's estates, and Burford is entered among his possessions on the Inquisition.
1446 Lady Anne, daughter of the preceding	—	Cal. Pat. Rolls, Hen. VI, 1441–1446, p. 434. John Norreys, King's Esquire of the Body, was appointed Steward of the Despenser lands, during the minority of the Duke's heir.
1449 Richard Neville, Earl of Warwick, 'The King-maker'	—	By his marriage with the Lady Anne Beauchamp, sister of the Duke of Warwick, he succeeded to the estates on the death of the Duke's daughter. His possession of Burford is proved by two documents in the Burford Records, bundle GG, nos. A1 and A4, the date of the latter being 1456, and that of the former between 1461 and 1471.
	1460 Humfrey, Duke of Buckingham	Cal. Inq. P. M., vol. iv, p. 290. Held half a knight's fee as heir of W. de Fanencourt.
(1471 The Crown)		After the death of the King-maker his estates were escheated to the Crown, and Edward IV divided them between his brothers, the Duke of Clarence and Richard, Duke of Gloucester (afterwards Richard III), who had married the two daughters of the King-maker. The Tewkesbury lands fell to the Duke of Clarence, and it is clear from the succeeding entries that Burford thus came into his hands,

Lords of the Manor and Town of Burford.	Tenants of the Manor.	Notes and Authorities.
		though no document actually records his possession of the place.
1479 Edward, son of the Duke of Clarence	—	Cal. Pat. Rolls, Edw. IV & V and Richard III, 1476–1485, p. 157. Records the appointment of William Noreys to the stewardship of the manor of Burford pending the minority of the son of the Duke of Clarence.
1487 The Crown	—	P. R. O. Ancient Deeds. A. 11056. A feoffment by Anne, Countess of Warwick, conveying to Henry VII all the castles, manors, lordships, &c., of the Warwick lands.
1489 Anne, Countess of Warwick (widow of the King-maker)	—	Cal. Pat. Rolls, Hen. VII, 1485–1494, p. 298. A grant to her for life of the manors and lordships of Tewkesbury, Burford, and others.
1493 The Crown	—	Cal. Pat. Rolls, Hen. VII, 1485–1494, p. 405. Appointment of Robert Harcourt, Esquire, to the stewardship of various manors, including Burford, 'which are in the King's hands by the death of Anne, Countess of Warwick.'
	1547 (?) Edmund Harman	P. R. O. Misc. Bks. Land Rev., vol. 189, fol. 88. The regnal year of Harman's lease is not filled in, but it must have been before 1549, since the lease was granted by the Crown, and in 1549 the manor of Burford passed out of the Crown's hands for some years. But it cannot have been earlier than 1547, since the date of the lease gives the reign as of Edward VI.
1549 John, Earl of Warwick	—	P. R. O. Augm. Off. Deeds of Purchase and Exchange, G. 12. The town and manor of Burford

Lords of the Manor and Town of Burford.	Tenants of the Manor.	Notes and Authorities.
		granted to Warwick in exchange for certain other lands.
1552 The Crown	—	P. R. O. Misc. Bks. Land Rev., vol. 189, fol. 85a. By another exchange Burford had again become Crown property.
	Sir Edward Unton, in right of his wife Anne, Countess of Warwick, for term of her life	
	1577 John (or Thomas) Moore, Thomas Cooke, and Margaret Curteis	Priory Deeds.
	1598 Richard Bell, of Gray's Inn, London	Priory Deeds.
1601 Sir John Fortescue, Chancellor & Sub-Treasurer of the Exchequer	—	Priory Deeds. He acquired the town and manor by purchase from the Crown.
1617 Sir Lawrence Tanfield, Lord Chief Baron of the Exchequer	—	Priory Deeds. By purchase from the heirs of Sir John Fortescue.
1625 Lady Tanfield	—	On the death of her husband. See Part III, p. 389.
1629 Lucius Cary, Viscount Falkland	—	By succession, his mother having been the daughter of Sir Lawrence and Lady Tanfield. The estates of Burford and Great Tew were settled upon Lord Falkland by Tanfield, after Lady Tanfield's life.
1637 William Lenthall, Speaker of the House of Commons	—	Priory Deeds. By purchase from Lord Falkland.
1662 Sir John Lenthall	—	Son of William Lenthall. See the Will of the latter, 28 July 1662.
1681 William Lenthall	—	On the death intestate of Sir John Lenthall, in Nov. 1681.

Lords of the Manor and Town of Burford.	Tenants of the Manor.	Notes and Authorities.
1686 John Lenthall	—	Under the Will, dated 4 Sept. 1686, of his father William Lenthall, died 1686.
1763 William Lenthall	—	Under the Will, dated 24 April 1762, of his father John Lenthall, died April 1763. Settled Burford estates on his brother and his brother's heirs.
1781 John Lenthall	—	Brother of the preceding. Succeeded under the Will, dated 22 April 1781, of William Lenthall, died October 1781.
1783 John Lenthall	—	Son of the preceding. Succeeded, on the death of his father, under the Will of William Lenthall.
1820 William John Lenthall	—	Son of the preceding. Succeeded, on his father's death in Nov. 1820, under the Will of William Lenthall.
1828 Charles Greenaway	—	Son of Giles Greenaway, of Gloucester, who had purchased the manor of Little Barrington late in the eighteenth century.
1859 Charlotte Sophia Greenaway	—	Widow of the preceding. Succeeded on the death of her husband, 25 November 1859.
1875 Mary Jane Youde	—	Niece of Mr. Charles Greenaway. Succeeded on the death of Mrs. Greenaway, 28 March 1875.
1892 Robert Henry Hurst	—	Of Horsham Park, Sussex. Nephew of Mrs. Charlotte Sophia Greenaway.
1905 Lt. Col. Arthur Reginald Hurst, D.S.O.	—	Of Horsham Park and Barrington Grove. Son of the preceding.

CHAPTER VII

OFFICERS OF THE TOWN, THE GILD, AND THE CORPORATION

THE first mention of Bailiffs of Burford occurs in 1263 in a conveyance preserved among the muniments of Brasenose College, Oxford. But in that instance the officers are not named. The earliest mention of a Bailiff by name is of the year 1285, and is found in a document preserved at the Public Record Office. Various documents among the Burford Records give the names of Bailiffs at intervals during the fifteenth century. No systematic record of them was kept until the sixteenth century, when a complete list of the Bailiffs from 1509 to 1587 was entered in one of the Memorandum Books of the Corporation. From that date until 1651 we have to depend again upon occasional entries in Account Books, leases of the Charity Lands, &c. After 1651 another systematic list becomes available.

From these various sources the following list has been compiled :

BAILIFFS OF BURFORD

1285	John le Fraunceys	P. R. O. Assize Roll 710, m. 43
1399	Henry Coteller Thomas Grene	P. R. O. Min. Accts. 1122, 13
1435	William Coteler Richard Lavynton	Burf. Rec. CH 7
1438	William Coteler Richard Lavynton	Burf. Rec. CH 8
1445	William Coteler Richard Lavynton	Burf. Rec. CH 10
1458	Henry Byschop John Pynnock, junior	Burf. Rec. CH 12
1460	John Pynnock, junior Robert Coburle	Burf. Rec. CH 14
1464	John Granger John Lavyngton	Burf. Rec. CH 15

1466	John Pynnock, junior	Burf. Rec. B 2
	John Grove	
1472	John Pynnock, junior	Burf. Rec. CH 18
	John Granger	
1481	John Pynnock	Burf. Rec. B 3
	Robert Leveriche	
1489	Thomas Bishop	Burf. Rec. S 9
	John Boterell	
1491	William Fludyate	Burf. Rec. CH 23
	Richard Brame	
1493	John Tanner	Burf. Rec. P 11
	Thomas Dodde	B. N. C. Burf. Leases 17

From this date till the year 1587 the dates given are the years in which the Bailiffs took office, in September of each year. It is therefore to be remembered that they were in office during the greater part of the year following.

1508	Richard Brame	1522	Richard Hannes
	Thomas Staunton		John Sharppe
1509	William Brisse	1523	Richard Hannes
	Peter Enysdale		John Sharppe
1510	John Bisshope	1524	John Busbye
	William Floudyate		William Hodgis
1511	Thomas Staunton	1525	Richard Hannes
	William Burrell		William Hodgis
1512	Thomas Staunton	1526	Peter Enysdale
	William Burrell		William Smythe
1513	Robert Ryleye	1527	John Sharp
	John Hill		John Busbye
1514	Peter Enysdale	1528	Richard Hannes
	Robert Rylye		William Hodgis
1515	Thomas Staunton	1529	John Sharpe
	John Harrys		David Tailor
1516	Robert Osmonde	1530	Richard Hannes
	Robert Payne, senior		John Strange
1517	Thomas Pinnock	1531	William Hodgis
	Peter Enysdale		Robert Jonson
1518	John Harris	1532	John Sharp
	Robert Ryleye		Thomas Tomson
1519	Robert Payne	1533	Richard Hannes
	Richard Hannes		William Hodgis
1520	Peter Enysdale	1534	Robert Jonson
	Nicholas Clerk		Thomas Richards
1521	Nicholas Clerck	1535	John Sharpe
	John Frankeleyn		John Jones

1536	John Jones	1555	Thomas Faller
	Thomas Tomson		Richard Charleye
1537	William Hodgis	1556	William Hewis
	Robert Payne		Thomas Freers
1538	James Grene	1557	Edmunde Sylvester
	Symon Wisdome		Thomas Heynes[1]
1539	John Sharpe	1558	John Floyde[2]
	William Hewis		Richard Dawbe
1540	Richard Hannes	1559	Robert Bruton
	John Lamberd		John Smythear
1541	John Sharpe	1560	John Hans
	John Jones		Rychard Chawrley
1542	Simon Wisdome	1561	Symon Wysdom
	William Hewis		Thomas Fryeres
1543	William Hodgis	1562	Edmunde Sylvester
	Robert Enysdale		Thomas Heynes
1544	Richard Hannes	1563	William Hewes
	James Grene		Richard Dawbe
1545	Richard Monington	1564	John Floyde
	Simon Wisdom		Water Molener
1546	Robert Payne	1565	John Hans
	William Hewis		Richard Chawrley
1547	Robert Enysdale	1566	Thomas Fryeres
	William Roberts		Thomas Fetyplace
1548	Richard Hannes	1567	Symon Wysdom
	Thomas Faller		Rychard Renolles
1549	Richard Hodgis	1568	William Symons
	Robert Brewton		William Pertrysche
1550	Simon Wisdome	1569	William Symons
	John Floid		John Jenkyns
1551	William Hewis	1570	Rycharde Dawbe
	Edmond Silvester		Edmunde Sylvester
1552	William Roberts	1571	Benydict Fawler
	Thomas Prikyvaunce		Thomas Hewes
1553	Robert Brewton	1572	John Hannes
	John Smithear		John Wyllyames[3]
1554	Simon Wisdome	1573	Rycharde Chadwell
	John Hannes		Rycharde Reynoldes

[1] Note appended to this entry : 'the same year deceasd Mr Monyngton being then alderman. The same year Symon Wisdom elected alderman'.
[2] Note preceding this entry : 'by Mr Edward Unton in the ryght of my Lady of Warrewyke'.
[3] Note appended to this entry : 'Md the vth day of November Ano 1572 Thomas Fryers on of the burges of burfford decessyd and yeldyd hys body to the erthe and hys sowle to god that gave yt / god send him a yoyfful Resurreccyon Amen'.

1574	William Symons	1581	Richard Chadwell
	William Sylvester		Robert Silvester
1575	John Jhenkins	1582	Rychard Reynolds
	Roberte Silvester		Thomas Silvester
1576	Wyllyam Partrydge	1583	William Symonds
	Edmond Sylvester		Symon Greene
1577	Richard Reynuld	1584	Robert Silvester [1]
	Thomas Hewes		Symon Symons
1578	Richard Chadwell	1585	Rychard Chadwell
	Richard Dalbie the		Rychard Dalbye
	elder	1586	William Symonds, tan-
1579	William Symonds		ner
	Robert Silvester		John Lyme, shewmaker
1580	John Lymme	1587	John Wylliams
	John Wylliams		Symon Symons

The list in the Corporation Memorandum Book ends here. A few years of the interval before other lists become available can be filled up as follows, from certain documents :

1589	Richard Dalby	Burf. Rec. CH 29
	Richard Meryweather	
1596	John Roffe	Burgess Court Book, fol. 13
	Raphe Wisdom	
1597	Simon Simons	Burgess Court Book, fol. 19
	Richard Merywether	
1599	John Roffe	Burf. Rec. S 27
	John Yate	
1607	Richard Merywether	Burf. Rec. S 32
	Toby Dallam	
1620	William Taylor	Burf. Rec. S 40
	William Bartholomew	
	the elder	
1627	Thomas Silvester	
	Richard Taylor	

From the year 1630 an almost complete list can be compiled from various Account Books, Assessment Books, &c. In this list, as in the earlier one, the date given is the year in which the Bailiffs took office.

1630	David Hewes	1632	John Clerk
	Paul Silvester		Nathaniel Noble
1631	William Bartholomew,	1633	Thomas Silvester
	sen.		Symon Warde
	Edmond Serrell		

[1] Note preceding this entry : 'for Mr Henry Umpton'.

1634	William Bartholomew Richard Taylor	1657.	John Hughes Stephen Smythe
1635	John Taylor Richard Syndrie	1658	David Hughes John Knight
1636	David Hughes George Watkins	1659	Richard Bartholomew Paul Silvester
1637	John Clarke Edmund Serrell	1660	John Jordan Leonard Mills
1638	Thomas Silvester Paul Silvester	1661	Richard Haynes Thomas Hughes
1639	William Bartholomew Symon Ward	1662	Thomas Matthews John Widdowes
1640	Richard Taylor Richard Sindrye	1663	Richard Hayter John Payton
1641	David Hughes George Watkins	1664	John Hughes Paul Silvester
1642	Symon Ward Edmund Serrell	1665	Stephen Smith Thomas Castle
	[No mention of Bailiffs for the years 1643 and 1644.]	1666	David Hughes John Knight
1645	Edward Fettiplace, Esquire. Symon Ward	1667	Paul Silvester Richard Haynes
1646	Thomas Silvester Richard Syndry	1668	Thomas Matthews Thomas Hughes
1647	William Bartholomew Leonard Yate	1669	John Widdowes John Payton
1648	John Hunt Thomas Silvester, jun.	1670	Stephen Smith Paul Silvester
1649	Edward Serrell Henry Hayter	1671	Thomas Castle Richard Bartholomew
1650	John Hughes Stephen Smyth	1672	John Knight John Ward
1651	David Hughes John Knight	1673	Paul Silvester Thomas Silvester
1652	John Jordan Paul Silvester	1674	Richard Haynes Edmund Heming
1653	Richard Sindrey Richard Haynes	1675	Thomas Mathewes John Collier
1654	Richard Hayter Robert Yate	1676	Thomas Hughes Richard George
1655	Edmund Serrell Thomas Matthews	1677	Paul Silvester, jun. David Hughes
1656	John Hunt Thomas Silvester	1678	Thomas Castle John Payton
		1679	Richard Bartholomew John Price

1680	Francis Kible	1703	John Haynes
	Thomas Silvester		William Bowles
1681	John Collier	1704	Paul Silvester
	John Winsmore		Edward Saunders
1682	Richard George	1705	Dennis Cosins
	Robert Aston		Edward Saunders
1683	Paul Silvester	1706	John Castle
	Stephen Matthews		William Bowles
1684	John Payton	1707	William Ford
	William Taylor		Paul Silvester
1685	Thomas Castle	1708	John Castle
	William Rogers		Dennis Cosens
1686	John Price	1709	William Bowles
	John Haines		Richard Whithall
1687	John Collier	1710	Paul Silvester
	John Winsmore		George Hart
1688	Thomas Silvester	1711	John Castle
	John Castle		William Taish
1689	Richard George	1712	Dennis Cosens
	Robert Aston		William Castle
1690	John Haines	1713	William Bowles
	George Hart		Robert Taylor
1691	John Collier	1714	Paul Silvester
	Simon Partridge		William Taylor
1692	John Winsmore	1715	George Hart
	William Taylor		(*No second name recorded.*)
1693	Robert Aston	1716	Richard Whitehall
	Samuel Wyatt		Matthew Underwood
1694	John Castle	1717	John Castle
	William Ford		William Castle
1695	Richard George	1718	Dennis Cosens
	Dennis Cosens		Robert Taylor
1696	John Haynes	1719	William Bowles
	John Linsey		Paul Silvester
1697	George Hart	1720	Paul Silvester
	Simon Partridge		Henry Taish
1698	Samuel Wyatt	1721	George Hart
	William Bowles		John Cooke
1699	John Castle	1722	Richard Whitehall
	William Ford		Matthew Underwood
1700	John Haynes	1723	William Castle
	Dennis Cosens		Robert Taylor
1701	Paul Silvester	1724	William Bowles
	Edward Saunders		Paul Silvester
1702	John Castle	1725	Thomas Hunt
	William Ford		John Green

1726	Matthew Underwood	1758	William Upston
	Paul Silvester		Thomas Silvester
1727	Richard Whitehall	1759	Paul Silvester
	James Partridge		Thomas Silvester
1728	William Bowles	1760	William Upston
	Robert Taylor		Thomas Sylvester
1729	Matthew Underwood	1761	Paul Sylvester
	John Green		Edward Ansell
1730	Robert Taylor	1762	Thomas Sylvester
	Paul Silvester		Edward Ansell
1731	George Hart	1763	Paul Sylvester
	Richard Whitehall		William Upston
1732	Robert Taylor	1764	William Upston
	Matthew Underwood		Thomas Sylvester
1733	George Hart	1765	Thomas Sylvester
	John Green		Edward Ansell
1734	Richard Whitehall	1766	William Upston
	Matthew Underwood		Edward Ansell
1735	Paul Silvester	1767	William Upston
	John Green		Edward Ansell
1736	George Hart	1768	William Upston
	Matthew Underwood		Edward Ansell
1737	Paul Silvester	1769	William Upston
	Thomas Ansell		Edward Ansell
1738	Matthew Underwood	1770	William Upston
	George Hart		Edward Ansell
1748	Paul Silvester	1771	William Upston
	John Green		William Boulter
1749	William Chapman	1772	William Boulter
	John Collier		Absalom Monk
1750	Paul Silvester	1773	William Chapman
	John Green		William Boulter
1751	John Collier	1774	William Chapman
	John Castle		William Boulter
1752	Paul Silvester	1775	William Chapman
	John Green		William Chavasse
1753	William Upston	1776	William Chapman
	John Collier		James Monk
1754	William Upston	1777	William Chavasse
	John Collier		John Kempster
1755	Paul Silvester	1778	William Chapman
	John Green		William Chavasse
1756	William Upston	1779	William Chapman
	Thomas Silvester		John Arkell
1757	Paul Silvester	1780	William Chapman
	William Chapman		William Chavasse

1781	William Chapman	1795	William Boulter
	Edward Ansell		Pye Chavasse
1782	William Chavasse	1796	William Turner
	John Kempster		Richard Tuckwell
1787	William Boulter	1797	William Turner
	James Monk		Pye Chavasse
1788	Thomas Silvester	1798	Pye Chavasse
	William Chavasse		William Turner
1789	William Boulter	1799	Pye Chavasse
	John Arkell		William Turner
1790	William Boulter	1800	Benjamin Waters
	James Monk		John Tuckwell
1791	William Boulter	1801	Benjamin Waters
	William Chavasse		Pye Chavasse
1792	Edward Ansell	1802	John Tuckwell
	John Arkell		Benjamin Waters
1793	William Chavasse	1840	William Ackerman
	Pye Chavasse		William Tuckwell
1794	John Arkell	1841	William Ackerman
	William Turner		William Tuckwell

From the year 1846 William Ackerman held office alone as Bailiff until the Corporation was dissolved.

No mention can be found of any member of the Corporation described as ' Alderman ' before 1530. Yet it is difficult to imagine that neither the Gild nor the Corporation had a Chief Officer ; and therefore, as occasional references are found to Burgesses described as ' Seniors ', it has been assumed that they may be included in the following list of the Chief Officers. No systematic list of the holders of the Aldermanship was ever kept ; and the only possible list is a fragmentary one, made up from various references in the Burford Records.

ALDERMEN OF BURFORD
Seniors

1367	Robert le Cotelir		Thomas Spicer
1382	John Wenryche	1404	Thomas Spicer

Aldermen

1530	Peter Eynesdale	1540	Richard Manyngton
1537	Peter Annysdale	1553	Richard Monyngton

1559	Simon Wisdom	1589	Richard Chadwell
1566	Simon Wisdom	1596	William Symonds
1568	Simon Wisdom	1598	Richard Merywether
1570	Simon Wisdom	1599	Richard Merywether
1571	Simon Wisdom	1605	Richard Merywether
1573	Simon Wisdom	1608	Richard Merywether
1574	Simon Wisdom	1620	Symon Symons
1579	Simon Wisdom	1725	Charles Perrott
1580	Simon Wisdom	1728	Charles Perrott
1581	Simon Wisdom	1792	Charles Fettiplace
1586	Richard Chadwell	1828	Thomas Cheatle

The earliest mention of an official with the title of Steward is of the year 1537. But in the case of this office there is less difficulty in recognizing it under earlier names. The 'Seneschal' mentioned occasionally during the fifteenth century was certainly the officer later called the Steward. It also seems certain that occasional references both of early and of late periods to a 'Chamberlain' indicate the same officer. Again, we have no systematic record of the holders of the post, and can only compile a fragmentary list.

STEWARDS

1404	Henry Coteler, Seneschal	1492	John Hyll
1465	Sir Robert Harcourt, Seneschal		William Bowdelare Chamberlains

Stewards

1537	Richard Hannys	1581	John Hans
1540	Richard Hans	1589	William Symons
1553	Simon Wisdom	1591	William Symons
1566	Edmund Sylvester	1596	Symon Grene
1568	John Hannes, senior	1598	Symon Symons
1570	John Hannes	1599	Symon Symons
1571	John Hans	1605	Symon Symons
1573	John Hans	1620	William Webbe
1579	John Hans	1728	George Hart, Chamberlain

CHAPTER VIII

THE CHURCH OF ST. JOHN THE BAPTIST, BURFORD

By the Rev. William C. Emeris, Vicar of Burford

WITH SOME HISTORICAL NOTES ON CHURCH AFFAIRS IN BURFORD

By R. H. Gretton

A CHURCH must have existed in Burford from early times ; but of an Anglo-Saxon or early Norman structure nothing now remains, unless a fragment is to be seen in the doorway, within the church, leading to the tower steps.

The outline of the history of the present building would seem to be as follows :

(i) A church, consisting of nave, tower, and short chancel, was built towards the close of the twelfth century. Of this building there remain the west wall and west door, and the tower. One other small fragment may be seen, built into the north wall of the Tanfield chapel ; and in the room over the porch there are two stones, which have formed part of a Norman doorway, perhaps the south door of the original church.

(ii) In the thirteenth century the chancel was lengthened, arches were opened in the north and south walls of the tower, and the transepts were built. A south aisle must also have been erected.

(iii) A hundred years later the chapel of St. Thomas of Canterbury was built west of the south transept, with a crypt beneath. The font is of this period.

(iv) Towards the close of the fourteenth century a great work of reconstruction began. It may be said that for a hundred and twenty years work of building or decoration was going on in the church ; and at the close of this period the church had reached the size and shape which we now see. A sacristy was built to the north of the sanctuary, in which the original altar still remains, a new nave with north and south aisles was erected, the tower was raised and a spire added,[1] and the beautiful porch arose. Then, however, the Norman tower showed signs of weakness under the additional weight that had been put upon it. In order to save it, reinforcing work had to be done, the nature of which is perfectly evident to-day. The north and south arches opening from the tower space into the transepts were partially filled up, lower and narrower arches appearing under the original ones; the north transept was shortened and strengthened with thrusts and buttresses, and the north wall of the chancel was widened and so arranged as to form a support; several of the small arches within the tower above the main arches were blocked up. The slightly distorted curve of these main arches, and certain signs of old cracks in the walls above, remain to show what danger the tower had been in. At about the same time as this building was taking place, the north wall of the north transept was prolonged eastwards to form a chapel north of the chancel. Later a south chancel chapel was built, and a new east window inserted in the chancel.

(v) There remains to mention one other feature of the church, which was not from the first an integral part of the structure. In the thirteenth century the Gild Merchant of Burford built a chapel, dedicated to the Blessed Virgin Mary, in the churchyard, close to the south-west corner of the church, but detached from it. The separate position of the chapel is evident in one document of the Burford Records, a convey-ance of property by one William More, of Henley-on-Thames, to Thomas Spicer, with certain remainders to the church of Burford. Remainder to the Gild chapel is also included, and it is described as ' capella beate marie *in eodem cimeterio* que est burgi '. This specific description of the chapel as ' in the churchyard ' proves that it was not at that date (1422) a part of the church. In the fifteenth century this chapel was lengthened towards the east, so as to reach the great south porch; it was shortened at the west end, and was opened to

---

[1] The will of John Cakebred of Burford helps to date this work; he bequeathed ' campanili nostro emendando xs '. See Part III, p. 420.

the south aisle by an arcade. On its enlargement, it was re-dedicated as the great chapel of St. Mary and St. Anne. As it stands the chapel bears signs of its two distinct stages of existence. The south door, now blocked, with a defaced crucifix above it, and the windows and door, also now blocked, in the north wall, are relics of the original Gild chapel. It is just possible that the remains of the window to be seen at the junction of the north wall with the west wall of the main building, at a lower level and of somewhat later date than the other windows in the north wall, may mark for us, if it was a kind of low side window, the position of the altar in the original chapel.

The extension of the chapel into the church fabric coincides interestingly with the period at which the Gild of Burford was rising to importance, and was assuming authority over various church funds.

It is interesting also in another way, because the detached position of the first chapel has produced a curious irregularity in the ground plan of the church. The two buildings were not oriented on quite parallel axes, with the result that the Gild chapel, when lengthened eastwards, entered the main building at a distinct slant.

Of the original arrangements within the church and of the decoration which adorned it some idea can be formed from hints which the present building supplies, and from documents which have survived.

We see the blocked doorway which led out upon the rood loft, and this marks the position of the great rood at the western tower arch, and doubtless of some form of screen beneath it. There are unmistakeable traces of another screen under the eastern tower arch.

Probably the altar in St. Peter's chapel was connected with the rood screen. The present dedication is modern. Of the general structure of this chapel, which is such an unusual and interesting feature of the church, it is impossible to speak with certainty. The stone canopy must undoubtedly have belonged to a mediaeval altar; but the woodwork, according to the accepted view, was erected by Sir Lawrence Tanfield

PLATE V. BURFORD CHURCH
INTERIOR
SHOWING MEDIAEVAL CHAPEL PARCLOSE AND PULPIT

to form a priory pew, a use which the canopied enclosure served for some two centuries. In support of this view it is pointed out that the woodwork does not fit on properly to the stone canopy, and conceals some remains of decoration on the upper face of the stonework. However, the most recent authoritative opinion regards the wooden canopy as also part of the original chapel, though of later date than the stone canopy.

The screens dividing the north and south chancel chapels from the chancel are original ; but that dividing the Tanfield chapel from the north transept is a medley of mediaeval and Jacobean work ; it was placed there by Lady Tanfield. The screen of St. Thomas's chapel is mainly original, and still preserves much of its colouring. About the beginning of the eighteenth century this chapel was reserved for the attendance of members of the Corporation at divine service, and called the Burgesses' Aisle ; portions of the screen have been cut out, apparently for their convenience, and fresh pieces have had to be inserted.

The pulpit also is original mediaeval work, but in this case the colour has been revived.

Of the colour decoration of the walls traces are to be found in the south transept and in St. Thomas's chapel, and in the Tanfield chapel there is a very interesting recess in which the decoration still lingers. Patches of colour on the stonework in the nave suggest how much was lost through the disastrous removal of the plaster in early stages of the nineteenth-century restoration ; and it is on record that there was a figure of St. Christopher on the wall near the pulpit.[1]

Of other features of the mediaeval church, evidence is provided by the will of Henry Bisshoppe, dated October 28, 1478, which is among the Burford Records. In this document a chapel of St. Katherine is specially mentioned, perhaps the chapel in which the Tanfield monument stands ; the matrix of a brass which may have been Henry Bisshoppe's is in this chapel. He bequeathed one pair of vestments for celebrating Mass particularly at the altar of that chapel.

[1] Stated by the Rev. John Fisher, in his *History of Burford*, p. 29.

But what we chiefly owe to his will is a knowledge of the altar lights anciently in the church. He left bequests for the maintenance of many of them, naming those of the Holy Cross, the Holy Trinity, St. Katherine, St. Mary and St. Anne in ' the chapel ', St. John, St. Stephen, St. Clement, St. Thomas, the light called Sidelight, the light called Torchlight, and the light of All Souls. The situation of some of these can, of course, be identified.

Five years earlier John Pynnok, senior, had made bequests to the high altar, and for the repair of that altar and every other altar in the church ; but unfortunately he does not say how many these were, nor give their dedications.

Of ancient glass such fragments as survive are to be seen in the upper lights of the east and west windows, and in the north window of the north transept.[1]

Some few pieces in the west window are *in situ*. The figures and angels would seem to have come from tracery lights. Among the figures the following saints have been identified : the Blessed Virgin Mary, St. Barbara, St. Margaret, St. Mary Magdalen, a female saint holding a book in her left hand, perhaps St. Katherine, and St. George piercing the dragon with a spear held in both hands, and wearing armour of *circa* 1480. It would appear that the angels belonged to a series representing the Nine Orders ; they may have been in the clerestory windows in the nave, and the female saints in the windows of the Lady Chapel. Of a set of symbols of the Evangelists, that of St. Luke is in the west window and that of St. Matthew in the east. Some small letters of an inscription in the west window read ' How a manne ma wedde ', and suggest that there was also a series representing the Seven Sacraments. Other fragments give interesting types of canopies, and parts of a figure of an archbishop, fully vested, with the pallium, perhaps St. Thomas of Canterbury.

In the east window there are rounds with the Jesus and the Mary monograms, *in situ*. We see also St. Christopher, and

---

[1] The account here given of the surviving fragments of ancient glass is from notes compiled by Mr. G. McN. Rushworth, by whose kind permission this use is made of them.

two angels of the Annunciation. At the top of one light is a head of fourteenth-century character, but all the other fragments are of fifteenth-century glass. However, in the cusped head of one of the central lights there is the merchant's mark of some donor (inverted), and it corresponds exactly with the mark used by Simon Wisdom on his seal. As is remarked elsewhere, there is no evidence of any one of this name, or of the name of Wisdom at all, in any of the Burford Records, before the well-known Simon Wisdom, who figures so largely in the town's history. As he was living till about 1582 or 1583, he can hardly have been concerned in the erection of fifteenth-century windows; and this fragment must almost certainly have come from some later window given by him.

The collection and placing of the fragments in the east and west windows was done in 1826.[1] When the lower lights of the west window were filled with modern glass in 1874 one head under a canopy was removed, and this is now in the north window of the north transept; it represents St. James of Compostella, with a cockle shell on his hat. Other fragments found in the church have been placed in the centre of this window. The piece bearing the arms of St. Edward the Confessor and the glass in the tracery lights were given to the church in 1911.

Of the monuments in the church, the oldest, and the only one which preserves the memory of a mediaeval citizen of Burford, is the beautiful bracket brass beneath the rood, from which John Spicer, with his wife Alys, still speaks to us.[2] He died in 1437, and the rood beneath which his body was laid had been his gift to the church, together with one of the windows :

> The wiche rode soler in this chirche
> Upon my cost I dede do wirche
> Wt a lamp birnyng bright
> To worschip god both day & nyght
> And a gabul wyndow dede do make
> In helth of soule and for Crist sake.

---

[1] In the course of the changes made by the Rev. Alexander Dallas, referred to later.

[2] During the work on the church in 1826-7 this brass was discovered a foot below the flooring of that time ; this, no doubt, accounts for its preservation.

This window we can perhaps identify by connecting it with the question of the dedication of St. Thomas's chapel, which is of particular interest, because St. Thomas of Canterbury is not a saint usually commemorated in the churches of this part of England. It would seem likely that the chapel was given by some one who had a peculiar attachment to the saint. Now the document concerning Thomas Spicer, which has already been referred to in connexion with the Lady Chapel, makes very special provision for the upkeep of ' the light which is before the altar of the said Thomas Spycer in the parish church '; that light is to take precedence of every other purpose in the ultimate disposal of his money. In view of this fact, and in view also of the curiously personal description of the altar, it is evident that ' the altar of Thomas Spycer ' was in some rather unusual way connected with his name. Thus it is at least permissible to conjecture that he may have built the chapel of St. Thomas of Canterbury as to his name-saint. If so, perhaps John Spicer's gable window is the one in this chapel, and is his contribution to his relative's work.

Another mediaeval citizen, and obviously a greater than John Spicer, has left the fine decorated altar-tomb in the south transept. The tomb originally bore another bracket brass, of exactly the same type as John Spicer's, with the two figures kneeling at the foot of an elevated bracket ; but every scrap of metal has now disappeared, except one small fragment of the inscription round the edge, bearing the name ' Willelmus '. We are not, however, without other clues. Sir Richard Lee, the Herald, who visited and made notes in so many of the churches of Oxfordshire in 1574,[1] records ' a fair tomb of marble ', which must almost certainly have been this one, since we have knowledge of no other tomb in the church at that date to which the description would apply. It was even then ' defaced ', but it had not been completely stripped, for Lee records three coats of arms upon it.[2] From the fact that he

[1] Printed in the *Visitations of Oxfordshire* (Harleian Socy. Pubns., vol. v).
[2] The visitor in 1660 (see p. 116) appears to note this same monument : ' In another Chappell on the same ' (the south) ' side, a grey marble monument. The arms on it not discernable.'

gives the tinctures, it would seem probable that these coats were not in the now empty matrices of shields on the top of the tomb (for arms in brass were seldom, if ever, tinctured), but were on some of the shields held by angels round the body of the tomb. The arms recorded were: (1) Gules a lion rampant guardant or, impaling a merchant's mark ; (2) argent three stumps of trees couped and eradicated sable, impaling argent a maunch sable; (3) quarterly first and fourth argent three stumps of trees couped and eradicated sable, second and third argent a maunch sable.

Unfortunately these clues, taken in conjunction with such indication of date as the style of the tomb affords, do not suffice to identify the person buried beneath. The character of the brass, as seen from the matrices, together with the general style of the tomb, would date it somewhere between 1370 and 1450. The first of the three coats of arms given above is proof that the man commemorated was a Burford merchant. The impaling and quartering of the Hastings device (the maunch) shows that one of this family married one of the Hastings family. But the link which the other device might be expected to supply is missing. The tree stumps cannot be connected with any Burford family. But for the shield bearing the Burford lion and the merchant's mark we should, indeed, hardly have looked among Burford men for the person here commemorated. Not only is the stonework elaborate, but the surviving fragment of metal is a piece of unusually fine and delicate engraving.

The tomb has been popularly associated with the family of John Leggare, because he ' decorated ' the window of this transept—as an inscription in an unaccustomed place, the outside moulding of the window, informs us—for the welfare of the souls of his father and mother. Leggare was a Burford man, who appears in the Records once as feoffee of the church lands in 1487, and later as the founder of an obit. But there is nothing to suggest that he would have been of such position as to erect so elaborate a monument, and it is, moreover, unlikely that, if he did, his petition for prayers for the souls of his parents would have appeared on the outside of the window ;

he would have placed it upon the tomb, if the William buried there were his father.

The following extracts from early Burford wills at Somerset House, kindly taken by Mr. Michael W. Hughes, add several interesting details to our knowledge of Burford church in the Middle Ages, and afford one or two important identifications. For instance, from the will of John Pynnok, 1486, the chapel of the Holy Trinity can be placed. We know from the notes of Sir Richard Lee in 1574 that the arms of Pynnok, with the date 1485, were in the chapel containing the brass of John Pynnok, senior, 1474, and that this was the south chancel chapel. This, therefore, was the chapel of the Holy Trinity, and it was rebuilt by Pynnok. Hence we may perhaps further conclude that St. Katherine's chapel, which evidently ranked equal in importance with that of the Holy Trinity in the minds of Burford men, was the north chancel chapel, in which the Tanfield tomb now stands.

Other points made clear are : (i) that there was in the Lady Chapel a separate altar of St. Anne ; (ii) that there was a cross or rood in the churchyard. We also have the very interesting addition of St. Roch to the list of known lights in the church.

Will of William Bery alias Glover of Burford (P. C. C. 40 Horne). Dated 8 Nov. 1499.

. . . my bodie to be buried in the churchyarde of saynte John Baptiste of Burford a foresaid, Moreover I bequethe to the mother church of Lyncoln vi*d.* Also I bequethe to the high Aulter of Seynte John Baptiste of Burford a foresaid in recompense for tithes forgotten vi*s.* viii*d.* Also . . . I bequethe to the Bellis of the same church xii*d.* . . . . Also I bequethe to the Church of Burford v*s.* to the makyng of surples.

(Proved at Lambeth 5 Feb. 1499/1500.)

Will of Richard Bysshop of Burford (P. C. C. 5 Bennett). Dated 17 March 1507/8.

. . . Body to be buryed by my wif before thymage of our lady in the burgeysis chapell. Item to the church of Lincoln iiii*d.* Item to the said chapell where my wif lyeth xx*s.* Item to the Trynite chapell in the same church xx*s.* Item to seynt Kateryn chapell beyng there vi*s.* viii*d.*

(Proved at Lambeth 10 Oct. 1508.)

Will of Richard Brame of Burford (P. C. C. 36 Bennett). Dated 17 Dec. 1510.

. . . corpus meum in capella et (*sic*) divine virginis Marie de Burford sepeliendum. Item lego Cathedrali ecclesie Lincoln vi*d*. Item summo altari sancti Iohannis Baptiste de Burforde xii*d*. Item lego cuilibet lumini computabili predicte ecclesie vi*d*. Item ad edificationem gilde sancti Thome xl*s*. si ante obitum meum non contingat me solvere. . . .

(Proved 12 Feb. 1510/11.)

Will of William Stodam (P. C. C. 23 Stokton). Dated 15 July 1461.

. . . corpus meum sepeliendum in cimiterio ecclesie sancti Iohannis Baptiste de Burford. Item lego matrici ecclesie de Lincoln iiis. iiii*d*. . . . lego lumini sancti Stephani vi*s*. viii*d*. Item lego lumini sancte Katerine xii*d*. Item lego summe Cruci vocate Rode solar' iii*s*. iiii*d*. Item lego lumini sancte Trinitatis xx*d*. Item lego reparacioni dicte ecclesie de Burford v*li*.

(Proved at Lambeth 30 July 1461.)

Will of William Bysshop of Burford (P. C. C. 14 Logge). Dated 3 April 1485.

. . . corpusque meum in ecclesia parochiali sancti Iohannis de Burford lego tumulandum. Item lego matrici ecclesie Lincolniensi iiis. iiii*d*. Item lego ecclesie parochiali de Burford v*li*. sterlingorum. Item ad reparacionem cuiuslibet luminis computabilis in ecclesia de Burford v*s*. Item lego cuilibet presbitero celebranti in dicta ecclesia in die sepulture mee xii*d*. Item lego ad distribuendum inter pauperes et egenos die sepulture mee v*li*. et in die trigintali v*li*. ac in die anniversali v*li*. . . . Item lego sacerdotibus celebrantibus pro anima mea & animabus omnium fidelium defunctorum in ecclesia de Burford xl*li*. sterl. videlicet cuilibet sacerdoti per annum integrum celebranti x marcas sterl. . . .

Witnesses—Dominus Robertus Elys artium baccalaureus & confessor meus Magister Ioh. Pryttewell artium magister.

(Proved at Knoll 3 Oct. 1485.)

Will of John Pynnok of Burford (P. C. C. 4 Milles). Dated 8 Nov. 1486.

. . . . corpus sepeliendum in capella sancte Trinitatis sumptibus meis noviter edificata eidem ecclesie de Burford annexa. . . . Item lumini Beate Marie in capella ibidem xx*d*. Item lego ad sustentacionem dicte capelle secundum provisionem fratrum meorum Burgensium dicte ville xiii*s*. iiii*d*.

(Proved at Lambeth 20 Oct. 1486.)

Will of Thomas Poole citizen and tailor of London (P. C. C.
1 Moone). Dated 4 April 1500.

. . . (Bequest of lands in Burford and Fulbrook) [1] . . . Wife
to have lands, &c., that were Sir Thomas Blount's in Idbury
and elsewhere, she finding ' a preeste to singe for my soule in
the church of Burford aforesaid atte the auter of saint Anne
in our Lady Chapell there. . . .'

(Proved at Lambeth 21 May 1500.)

Will of Henry Stodham of Borford (P. C. C. 4 Moone). Dated
27 May 1500.

. . . corpus . . . sepeliendum in Nova Capella beate Marie
ecclesie parochialis de Borford. . . . Item lego campanis
eiusdem ecclesie vi*d*. . . .

(Proved at Lambeth 24 August 1500.)

Will of William Janyvere of Burford (P. C. C. 19 Blamyr).
Dated 15 September 1502.

. . . Item lego lumini sancte Crucis in cimiterio xii*d*. Item
lumini sancti Rochi in dicta ecclesia xii*d*. Item lego ad
reparacionem dicte ecclesie xx*s*. Item lego ad reparacionem
librorum et vestimentorum in dicta ecclesia xx*s*. Item ad
reparacionem campanarum in dicta ecclesia xx*s*. Item lego
ad sustentacionem capelle beate Marie virginis gilde Burgensium secundum provisionem fratrum meorum burgensium
eiusdem xx*s*. . . .

(Proved at Lambeth 26 Sept. 1502.)

Will of Robert Janyns of Burford (P. C. C. 11 Adeane). Dated
1501.

. . . Also I biqueth to our Lady Chapell of Burfford a stondyng cuppe covered & gilte for to make a chalys therewith to
continue in the said Chapell as long as it will endure. . . . [2]

(Proved at Lambeth 9 Oct. 1506.)

Will of John Busby of Burford (P. C. C. 20 Jankyn). Dated
7 June 1530.

. . . to be buried within the chapell of saint Katerine on
the ryght syde wher my wif was buryed. And I will hav
a stone of marble upon me after my beryall.[3] Item I bequethe

---

[1] See Part III, p. 336.

[2] Robert Janyns's directions for his chalice were soon defeated, if this
was the chalice of silver parcel gilt taken by the Surveyor of Colleges and
Chantries in 1555-6 (P. R. O. Land Revenue—Church Goods—E 117,-
bundle 13). The chalice, a silver Pax, and two sets of vestments, one of
red damask for festivals, were entered as received from the wardens of
the Gild of Our Lady.

[3] This may identify for us one of the stones in the north chancel chapel
from which the brasses have been stripped.

to my ghostly father Sr Nicholas Swinnerton xx*s*.   Item
I bequethe to every prest longyng to this church that is to say
maister priour iii*s*. iiii*d*.   Sr Thomas Taylour iii*s*. iiii*d*.
Sr Robert Thyrby iii*s*. iiii*d*.   Sr Thomas Schelton iii*s*. iiii*d*.
Sr Robert Walker iii*s*. iiii*d*. . . . . a preeste to syng for me a hole
yere the which shalbe frier Robert Stevenson that shall have
for his wage viii markes. . . .

(Proved at Lambeth 22 Oct. 1530.)

The monuments of the sixteenth century are not such as
add beauty to the church.   There are none belonging to the
first half of the century, the earliest being the Harman monument of 1569, which is dull and uninspired in workmanship.
The most curious feature of it is the introduction of figures of
Red Indians.   The other tombs of this century are all of one
type, and it is a type which can hardly be called beautiful.
It may be described as a half-altar tomb placed against the
wall, decorated in front with strap-work and panels for
inscription, and with a rising back-piece carved with detached
devices—merchants' marks, stars or starfish, &c.   These tombs
begin with that of Edmund Sylvester, who died in 1568, and
most of them are tombs of that family.   One, in the south
chancel chapel, commemorating Richard Rainoldes, who was
Bailiff at the time of Queen Elizabeth's visit in 1574, bears
the quaint and touching words : ' I go to sleepe before you
& wee shall wake togeather '.

To the seventeenth century belong a brass of 1624 in the
Lady Chapel to John Osbaldeston and his wife (a branch of
this Chadlington family had some property here) ; monuments to Richard Sindrey and John Warren, which show
better craftsmanship in stone, and come from the same hand
as the great mantelpiece at the Priory ; and the Bartholomew
monuments in the south chancel chapel, notable for their good
lettering (which is a partially redeeming feature of some of the
later Sylvester monuments).   Two brasses of this period
which still remain on tombs in the churchyard may also be
mentioned ; one to John Hunt, mercer, of 1608, and one of
1651 to Elizabeth White, who ' willingly and peaceably
exchanged her vile enjoyments here for those rich, precious
and unspeakable '.   In St. Thomas's Chapel is a half-length

figure monument of John Harris, 1674, in painted stone, good of its kind ; it was the Burford Burgesses' acknowledgement of his generous bequest to the charities of the town where he was born. Good lettering again distinguishes the stone in the south transept to the memory of the murdered John Pryor ; [1] but it is with difficulty that we decipher the inscription over the sacristy door to ' Mr. Nathaniel Brooks Gent. a truly honest man ' (1695).[2]

The principal monument, however, of this century is of course the ornate erection by the ' noble and verteous lady ' Tanfield to her most honoured husband ' in memory of his vertues and her sorrows '. It is a fine example of its kind ; for while parts of the canopy decoration, such as the cherubs' heads and carved bosses, have a rather stuck-on appearance, the modelling of the symbolical figures placed on the capitals of the pillars is fine and delicate, and the carving of the recumbent effigies is full of character. The introduction of the small figures kneeling at the heads and feet of the effigies—the Tanfields' daughter who married the first Lord Falkland, and their grandson, the famous Falkland—adds much charm to the monument. It may perhaps be added that the long Latin inscription at the foot of the monument, though rather obscure in meaning, seems to betray some disappointment on Lady Tanfield's part that her husband had not been interred in a more notable spot—Westminster Abbey, we may presume.

It used to be thought that this monument was the work of Nicholas Stone ; but it is now known definitely that he did not design it.

It is interesting, after this view of the existing monuments, to refer to the accounts of the church given first by Sir Richard Lee in 1574, and secondly by an antiquarian visitor in 1660.[3] They show, for one thing, how comparatively little we have lost since the sixteenth century.

[1] See Chapter XI, p. 282.
[2] Mr. Brooks lived in a house between the Almshouse and the church-yard, where the Church Schools now stand. See Part III, p. 364.
[3] Brit. Mus. Harl. MSS. 4170. Printed in *The Topographer*, vol. ii (1790), pp. 349–53.

Sir Richard Lee is chiefly concerned with coats of arms in the glass of the windows and on escutcheons in the stonework of the building. But he mentions, as we have seen, the tomb in the south transept; and he also describes the Harman monument. The only other tomb he enters on his notes is lost: ' On a graveston Pynnok as before[1] impaling a lion rampant guardant (untinctured) Over it written John Pynnok marcator and Elein his wife mcccclxxiv '.

Another lost Pynnok monument is recorded by the 1660 visitor thus : ' Nigh hence on a brasse on the ground Hic jacet Johes Pinnock primogenitus Thome Pinnock gentleman quondam societa– de Greisiñe qui quidem Johes obiit v die Augusti MCCCCLXXXX cujus etc '. The matrix of this brass remains.

This visitor identifies for us the monument in the north-east corner of the south chancel chapel, now without a name, though the mark of the brass plate is still visible. The inscription copied in 1660 ran : ' Here lyeth the body of George Symmons Gent. sometime dwelling in the house near the bridge foot, being a good benefactor to the poore people of this towne and departed this life the xxvii day of January 1590 God be praysed for him '. The house here mentioned is the one George Symons calls ' my now dwelling house called cobhall ' in the will by which he left it to the poor of Burford. The entrance arch to the courtyard can be seen in the wall between the Vicarage and the river.

A tomb has disappeared from the Tanfield chapel; the 1660 visitor, after describing the Tanfield monument, proceeds : ' On an old raised monument of stone in this chappell this at the feet

Obitus Thome Frieri Burfordiae epitaphius, qui

vita excessit 5° Novembris anno dni 1572 ';

and he adds some Latin verses from the monument chiefly remarkable for containing a hexameter with seven feet.[2]

' In the north ile of the church ', the visitor says, ' 2 proportions ', or, as we should now say, effigies. Both of these have

---

[1] He has just entered the Pynnok coat of arms from the glass in one of the windows.

[2] Thomas Freer appears frequently in the Burford Records; he was one of the original feoffees of the Grammar School lands.

disappeared ; but perhaps two large stone fragments preserved in the room over the porch may be relics of them. One piece is the half of a tilting helmet, such as is customarily found supporting the head of an armed figure on a tomb ; the other piece, though it is difficult to recognize what it has been, may be the haunches of a dog or lion placed at the feet of an effigy. The lack in Burford history of resident lords of the manor, or other men likely to have armed effigies, makes these fragments the more interesting. Possibly one of them may have been on a monument to Robert Harcourt, seneschal of the town in 1465, and also seneschal here for the King-maker.

Finally, the 1660 visitor mentions the altar tomb in the north-west corner of the Lady Chapel bearing the Barber Surgeons' arms, but even then the name on it had been lost.

Comment on the monuments would be incomplete without a remark on the extraordinary fact that, with the exception of a tablet erected within the last few years to a descendant of the family, who died in Australia in 1894, there is not a single memorial to any of the Lenthalls in the church. More than twenty of them lie buried here,[1] including six who were lords of the town and manor ; and to no one of them is there any monument. Speaker Lenthall, it is true, left particular instructions that he was not to be commemorated in any such way ; his burial place was to have no mark, save ' at the utmost a plain stone with this inscription only, "Vermis sum" '. Even that stone is no longer to be seen ; it appears to have been broken accidentally during some repairing of the church. His son John died at Besselsleigh, and was buried there. But five succeeding owners of the Priory estate lie in Burford church, each of whom might have been expected to leave some memorial behind him.

The coats of arms recorded by Sir Richard Lee, several of which appear also in Symonds's Notes of 1644 and the Notes of the visitor of 1660, have many points of interest. Most of them have a traceable connexion with the history of Burford ; and they may in some instances help to date portions of the

[1] According to the Burials Register in the church.

fabric. The coats of de Clare, Despenser, and Beauchamp, as lords of the manor, appeared frequently. The Stafford coat, which the 1660 visitor records, was due to the sub-infeudations of the manor ; Hugh, Earl of Stafford, held in 1387, by right of his descent, the half knight's fee originally held in Burford by the de Fanencourts. The visitor enters this coat as ' in the chappell on the south side ' in one of the windows. ' The chapel' in the sixteenth- and seventeenth-century Notes nearly always seems to mean the Lady Chapel. But in this case the visitor has just been describing the tombs in the Lady Chapel, and must obviously be referring to another part when he recommences ' in the chapel on the south side '. As he goes on immediately to the nameless monument in the south transept, it would seem certain that in this case he is speaking of the chapel of St. Thomas of Canterbury ; and the presence of the Stafford coat there would not be inconsistent with the other indications of the date of that chapel.

Lee, on the other hand, only speaks of one ' chapel ', and it may therefore be taken that the following coats he records were in the Lady Chapel.

Skochens in the top of the chapel :
    Quarterly 1st and 4th a Fess checky between 6 cross crosslets 2nd and 3rd two bends (untinctured)
    Or three chevronels gules (Clare)
    Gules a fess or between six cross crosslets or
    Quarterly 1st and 4th argent 2nd and 3rd argent a fret sable over all a bend sable (Despenser)
    Twelve roundels a canton ermine
    Gules three padlocks or

Where these escutcheons were placed does not now appear ; they may have been on bosses of the roof, and have been lost when, in the late eighteenth century, this roof was in grievous decay. At any rate, the presence among these coats of the Beauchamp coat—the fess and cross crosslets—would imply that the part of the building where it appeared is of a date subsequent to 1439, when the manor passed by marriage to the Beauchamp family. As Symonds records ' in the southe yle of the south-west yle where the 2 Bayliffs etc sit '—clearly the old Gild chapel and present Lady Chapel—the Beauchamp coat with the de Clare coat, it becomes more likely that Lee also was referring to this part of the church.

Lee records in one of the windows the following coats : Parted per saltire sable and gules on a fess or between three lions' heads erased argent three roses azure seeded or in base a cross crosslet of the last ; and the same coat impaling argent a saltire azure between four woodpeckers proper (Woodward) —' Over it written John Pynnok and iii wyfes mcccclxxxv.' Symonds gives these as ' in a southe windowe and southe yle of the church '.

Symonds also records the coats of arms on seven of the eight shields held by angels just below the battlements of the great south porch ; and with his help, though the shields are now much ravaged by weather, six are still just decipherable. On the extreme left is the bear and ragged staff ; next it is a strange charge of a lion passant on the point of a sword in pale, hilt downwards ; and next that the coat with three padlocks, already noted in the Lady Chapel, which was the coat of Sydenham of Tichmersh, one of whom married a Lovel of Minster Lovell,[1] and may have given money to the building of the porch. The fourth shield Symonds does not figure, and it almost looks now as if it had always been blank. The fifth has the three leopards of England ; the sixth, the cross fleury and martlets of Edward the Confessor, not now decipherable ; the seventh, the three crowns of St. Edmund the King ; and the eighth, so far destroyed now that hardly even the shield itself is left, bore the three chevronels of de Clare.

The interesting point about these shields is that they include the device of the Nevilles, the bear and ragged staff, but do not include the Beauchamp coat which was in the Lady Chapel. Now the town and manor passed from the Beauchamps to the Nevilles by the marriage of Lady Anne Beauchamp to the King-maker in 1449. The lengthening of the old Gild chapel and the building of the south porch which it was made to adjoin must have both been part of a single plan. But the fact that

---

[1] Lee records in Minster Lovell church a coat on which the Lovel arms impale the arms of Sydenham of Tichmersh.

PLATE VI. BURFORD CHURCH

SOUTH TRANSEPTAL CHAPELS, SOUTH PORCH AND LADY CHAPEL.

the Beauchamp arms without the Neville device were in the chapel, and the Neville device without the Beauchamp arms is on the porch, shows that the chapel was finished before the building of the porch had reached its last stages. We also thus have proof that the whole plan belongs to the middle years of the fifteenth century.

Of the interior arrangements of the church during the seventeenth and eighteenth centuries we have little knowledge. Symonds records in his Notes that Essex quartered his army in the church on June 6, 1643, and ' used it with the greatest incivillity ', in especial tearing down the pennons and flags hanging over the Tanfield monument and wearing them as scarves. But of any extensive and systematic destruction by Puritans we have no record. Since Lee mentions so few coats of arms as existing in windows in 1574 we may take it that the painted windows had shared the fate of the altars and lights in the days of the Reformation.

In the seventeenth century a gallery was erected at the west end of the church ; and it was probably in consequence of this that the Burgesses moved out of their original chapel and converted the chapel of St. Thomas of Canterbury into the Corporation pew. The new gallery would very likely obstruct the view from the Lady Chapel. They can hardly have made the change before the end of the seventeenth century, because the monument erected by the Burgesses to John Harris in 1674, now in St. Thomas's Chapel, used to be in the Lady Chapel, and it would almost certainly have been placed by them in their own portion of the church.

In 1826 considerable changes took place, of which we have unusually exact record. The Rev. Alexander Dallas was at that time curate-in-charge, the vicar (the Rev. William Birch) being non-resident. Mr. Dallas had been an officer in the Army, and had fought in the Peninsular War ; and he carried his military energy into his church work. He was a reformer of abuses in the town charities, and he repaired and re-pewed the church with zeal, if not with knowledge.

The result of his alterations is preserved for us not only in a ground plan, dated 1827, now in the room over the porch, but still more vividly in an exact and beautifully made model of the church, which is kept in the same place.[1] The western gallery, being then decayed, was removed, and another put up in the north aisle. The font was moved to a position near the Harman monument. The pulpit, much exalted, was placed at the west end of the nave, facing east, and the pews were set to face westwards.

These peculiar arrangements disappeared forty years later, when, unfortunately, the organ was removed from the position it had hitherto occupied, on what had been the Rood loft. Some of the work done at this time is to be deplored; but the fabric of the church was badly in need of attention. The Rev. J. H. Burgess was vicar when the work was taken in hand; and on his resignation the Rev. W. A. Cass carried it on with zeal until the greater part of the necessary repairs had been completed. The modern glass, by Kempe, in the western windows and the windows of the north aisle was put in during Mr. Cass's time, with the exception of one in the north aisle which is in memory of him.

Since his death, the roofs of the porch, the Lady Chapel, and the Tanfield Chapel have been repaired and re-leaded, and the Tanfield monument strengthened. Generous friends of the church have given the window, by Whall, in the south transept; and have erected the Reredos in the Lady Chapel, of Campden stone, and re-floored the same chapel with local stone, recovering from beneath the former floor several memorial slabs and two matrices of brasses, which are placed at the west end near the door.

A list of the vicars of Burford, made as accurate as is possible at present, is appended. A curious feature of it is the large number of appointments during the sixteenth century—no fewer than eleven men succeeded one another in the vicarage in the course of a hundred years. They were, as a rule, after the time of Thomas Cade,[2] non-resident. The vicars of the

---

[1] It was the work of a Mr. Mann, who was clerk to Mr. J. S. Price, a solicitor practising in Burford at that time.

[2] There is every reason to regard Cade as having been resident. But in the Clerical Subsidy List for the Diocese of Leicester in 1526 (edited by

seventeenth century, on the contrary, were few in number, and three of them were certainly resident, though John Thorpe actually lived at Fulbrook. Neither Hill nor Glynn deserves to be remembered very gratefully, as a later note will show, though it must be admitted that they seem on the whole to have kept the Registers with care. Their successor, however, John Thorpe, stands out as one of the best of Burford vicars— upright, honourable, and faithful to his charge. Unhappily he was succeeded by one of the worst of the vicars, John Eykyn, who, though presented by the churchwardens in 1704 for all kinds of scandalous behaviour and neglect of duty,[1] not only remained vicar till his death in 1734, but even acquired in 1718 a plurality, the Rectory of Farmington near Northleach. It would appear, however, that he had to leave Burford ; for his handwriting disappears from Burford Registers after August 1706, and there follow various handwritings at intervals of several years, no doubt those of curates in charge. After Eykyn's presentation to Farmington he must, indeed, have resided there entirely, for the Registers there are in his handwriting from May 1719 to May 1734. He is buried with the wife whom, according to the Burford churchwardens, he treated so scandalously, in Farmington church.[2]

Very few monuments to vicars have been preserved in the church. Possibly some vanished brasses may have marked the graves of mediaeval vicars ; but in view of the constant changes in Elizabethan times we cannot be surprised that the vicars of that period have left no memorials. We might, how-

the Rev. H. E. Salter, Oxford Historical Society, 1913, pp. 259 and 260) deduction is allowed from the stipend of Cade, as vicar, for a curate, Nicholas Swynerton. Mr. Salter is of opinion that such a deduction was only allowed when the incumbent was doing ecclesiastical work elsewhere or was studying at the University ; and that the word 'curatus', here applied to Swynerton, always implied 'curate-in-charge'. The curate of Fulbrook, William Wryters, is separately entered. Cade was not yet Master of the Hospital. Therefore it would appear, if Mr. Salter's view admits of no exceptions, that Cade must at this time have been non-resident. It may however be noted that his predecessor also had employed a curate ; one of the witnesses to Agnes Stodam's gift to the church in 1512 (see Part III, p. 321) was 'William Calaway Curate of Burford'.

[1] See Part III, p. 479.

[2] For information respecting Eykyn's tenure of Farmington I am indebted to the Rev. Leonard Wilkinson, Rector of Farmington.

ever, have expected tablets to Philip Hill and Christopher Glynn. John Thorpe's monument, recording also his grief at the early death of two promising sons, is in Fulbrook church. The Right Hon. and Rev. Charles Knollis, 'Earl of Banbury', who was vicar 1747–71, is commemorated by a tablet in Burford church, and the inscription, which tells us that it was erected by his two youngest sons, preserves the memory of his son and successor, Francis Knollis. The connexion of the Rev. Alexander Dallas with the church is perpetuated by a very plain tablet in the north-west corner of the north transept recording the brief life of an infant child of his ; a tablet to his own memory is to be seen in St. Patrick's Cathedral, Dublin.

THE VICARS OF BURFORD

The following list has been compiled from the Lincoln Rolls and Registers, and from the Oxford Diocesan Register after the creation of the See of Oxford, with the addition from other sources of some names not found in the Registers. There is every reason to suppose that, with the exception of a gap in the thirteenth century caused by the loss of one of the Lincoln Rolls, the list is complete. The year of institution is still lacking in a few instances ; but dates obtained in these cases from other sources are such as to render it at least probable that no intermediate names are missing.

Grateful acknowledgement of assistance given in the compiling of this list is due to Mr. A. Hamilton Thompson, who very kindly searched the Lincoln muniments, and, besides supplying several fresh names, provided the dates of the institution of some men, whose tenure of the vicarage had, indeed, been known, but without those specific dates which of course can alone establish the due succession of the vicars. Equal acknowledgement is due to the Rev. S. S. Pearce, Vicar of Combe, Oxon., whose unrivalled acquaintance with the sources of information on this subject in the sixteenth and seventeenth centuries has added many names to the list. Thanks are also due to Mr. Michael W. Hughes and Mr. Harry Paintin for additional references and information.

Date of Institution.	Name.	Patron.	Authorities and Notes.
	(?) William	—	Mentioned in 1199 as 'Clericus de Bureford'. Rotuli Curiae Regis, 1 John.
1214	Matthew de Cygon	The Crown	Pat. Roll, 16 John. Presented by the Crown, owing to the abbacy of Keynsham being vacant at the time and in the King's hands.
1227	William of Bitton, sub-deacon	Abbot & Convent of Keynsham	Rotuli Hugonis de Welles (Lanc. & York Soc.), ii. 28.
1247	Richard of Tewkesbury, chaplain	,,	Rotuli Roberti Grosseteste (Lanc. & York Soc.) 489. Also mentioned as Vicar in 1268; Assize Roll, 52 Hen. III.

(Bishop Lexington's Roll no longer exists. Bishop Gravesend's Rolls (1256–80) record no institution to Burford.)

	Adam (of Belee)	—	No institution recorded. 'Adam' is mentioned as Vicar of Burford in 1297: Close Roll, 25 Edw. I. The rest of his name is added from the next entry, which confirms his possession of the vicarage.
1307	Robert, called Brown of Orcheston, chaplain	Abbot & Convent of Keynsham	Linc. Reg. ii (Dalderby), folio 152. Presented on the death of Adam of Belee.
1325 22 Sept.	Robert de la Lee, chaplain	,,	Linc. Reg. iv (Burghersh), folio 252d. Presented on the death of Robert, called Brown.
	John Waryn	,,	No institution recorded in the Lincoln Registers. In 1326 an exchange of benefices is recorded between him and Robert de la Lee: Patent Roll, 19 Edw. II.
	Roger of Thornham	—	Pat. Roll, 18 Edw. III. No institution is recorded in the Lincoln Registers, but he is mentioned in this Patent Roll as Vicar in 1344, and the next entry affords clear evidence of his possession of the vicarage.
1348/9 9 Feb.	Walter Whityng, priest	Abbot & Convent of Keynsham	Linc. Reg. ix (Gynewell), folio 241d. Presented on the death of Roger of Thornham. Also mentioned

Date of Institution.	Name.	Patron.	Authorities and Notes.
			as Vicar in 1355: Pat. Roll, 29 Edw. III.
1361 6 Oct.	Geoffrey of Causton, priest	Abbot & Convent of Keynsham	Linc. Reg. ix (Gynewell), folio 277d. Also mentioned as Vicar in 1384 in the Burford Records (bundle CC, S. 2) in a grant by him to Thomas Causton 'cognato meo'.
	Henry of Norfolk	—	Pat. Roll, 20 Richard II.
1397	Geoffrey Walker	The Pope	'Licence for Geoffrey Walker alias Ludlowe to accept the Vicarage of the Parish Church of Burford in the Diocese of Lincoln, void by the death of Henry de Norfolk, to which he has been provided by the Pope, who has commanded that he be inducted therein by the Abbots of Oseney and Rewley and Richard Velde, Canon of St. Mary's, Lincoln: notwithstanding the statute of provisors of the thirteenth year.' No record of the institution of either of these two is to be found in the Lincoln Registers.
	Walter Eymer	—	Pat. Roll, 3 Hen. IV. Mentioned in this Roll as Vicar in 1402, and his possession of the Vicarage is confirmed by the next entry.
1403/4 17 Jan.	William Ingelby	Abbot & Convent of Keynsham	Linc. Reg. xiii (Beaufort), folio 331. Presented on exchange of the Vicarage of Bitton, Glos., with Walter Eymer. Also mentioned in the Burford Records as Vicar in 1429 (bundle CC, S. 6).
	Thomas Redeman	—	No institution recorded in the Lincoln Registers, but see the next entry.
1433/4 16 Feb.	Thomas Send	Abbot & Convent of Keynsham	Linc. Reg. xvii (Gray), folio 61d. Presented on exchange of the church of Leckhampstead, Bucks., with Thomas Redeman.

Date of Institution.	Name.	Patron.	Authorities and Notes.
1453 16 Oct.	William Creek, priest	Abbot & Convent of Keynsham	Linc. Reg. xx (Chedworth), folio 229d. Presented on exchange of the church of Taynton, Oxon., with Thomas Sende.
1457 30 Oct.	Thomas Mayow, priest	,,	Linc. Reg. xx (Chedworth), folio 234. Presented on the resignation of William Creke. Was Master of the Hospital of St. John the Evangelist, Burford, in 1448–9. Mentioned as Vicar in 1472 in the Burford Records (bundle A, CH. 18).
1473/4 22 March (? 5 Feb.)	John Meteve, chaplain	,,	Linc. Reg. xxi (Rotherham), folio 80d. Presented on the death of Thomas Mayow.
1473/4 5 Feb. (? 22 Mar.)	Christopher Seintlo, deacon	,,	Linc. Reg. xxi (Rotherham), folio 80. Presented on the death of John Meteve. This entry and the previous one appear to have been transposed by error in the Registers.
	Thomas Pollard	—	No institution recorded in the Lincoln Registers. Mentioned as Vicar in 1478 in the Burford Records (bundle KK, W 2). Consecrated Bishop at Rome in 1447. Bishop of Down, 1450. Later acting Suffragan Bishop of Lincoln.
1480 14 June	Richard Chaunceler	Abbot & Convent of Keynsham	Linc. Reg. xxi (Rotherham), folio 90. Presented on the death of Thomas Pollard. Mentioned as Vicar in 1489 in the Burford Records (bundle CC, S. 9).
1515 4 April	Thomas Cade, priest	Edward, Duke of Buckingham, Earl of Hereford, Stafford, and Northampton	Linc. Reg. xxv (Atwater), folio 44. The presentation for this turn granted to the Duke of Buckingham by the Abbot and Convent of Keynsham on the death of Richard Chaunceler. Cade was also Master of the Hospital at the time of its surrender to the Crown in 1538.

Date of Institution.	Name.	Patron.	Authorities and Notes.
1542 16 May	Anthony Barker, clerk	The Crown	Linc. Reg. xxvii (Longland), folio 199. Presented on the death of the last incumbent. C.C.C., Oxon., 1517. Fellow 1519. Held several other livings. Canon of Lincoln, 1540, and of Windsor, 1541.
1551 12 Dec.	Robert Webster, or Webstare	Edward Sandys	Oxfd. Dioc. Reg. His Will is a very detailed and curious document. Oxon. Prov. Wills 1.5, p. 123. Resigned.
1557 Aug.	Thomas Pitcher	Sir Edward Unton and Anne, Countess of Warwick	Oxfd. Dioc. Reg.
1558	John Rodlay	,,	Oxon. Prov. Wills 1.4, p. 284. Parker Register, Lambeth. A Benedictine monk of this name graduated as B.D. at Oxford, 1514.
1571 3 Sept.	Robert Temple	,,	Parker Reg. Lambeth iii, p. 55. Demy, Magd. Oxon., 1560. Canon, Bristol. Preb., St. Paul's. He would not pay compositions due to the Crown as the benefice was a subject of dispute. The Crown claimed the patronage and appointed William Masters. Resigned.
1571/2 30 Jan.	William Masters	The Crown	Parker Reg. Lambeth iii, p. 55. A friend of John Foxe. Vicar of Shipton-under-Wychwood.
1578 3 Dec.	Bartholomew Chamberleyne	,,	Grindal's Register, p. 357. Scholar, Trin. Coll., Oxon. Held many preferments. Resigned.
1586 3 Nov.	Richard Hopkins	,,	Oxford Clergy Certificate, 1593. St. Albans Hall, Oxon. B.A., 1573. Vicar of Shipton-under-Wychwood, where he died.
1593/4 17 March	Barnard Robinson	,,	Whitgift's Register ii, p. 191. B.A. Queen's Coll., Oxon., 1582. B.D. 1591. Canon of Carlisle, 1612. Resigned.

Date of Institution.	Name.	Patron.	Authorities and Notes.
1600 9 June	Thomas Colfe	The Crown	Whitgift's Reg. iii, p. 171. B.A. Broadgate Hall, Oxon., 1581.
1611 29 June	Philip Hill	Douglas Davys, Gent.	Oxfd. Dioc. Reg. The Bishop of Oxford here first mentioned as Patron. He granted the right of presentation to Douglas Davys for that occasion. Philip Hill was much under the influence of Sir L. Tanfield, who secured for him the benefice of Eaton Hastings, Berks. Died 1634.
1635	Anthony Andrewes	Bishop of Oxford	Comp. Books iii. 1, 10 Car. I. Resigned.
1636 1 April	Richard Turner	,,	Comp. Books iii. 1. Buried at Oxford. Parochial Reg., B. V. Mary, Oxford.
1637 28 March	Christopher Glynn	,,	Oxfd. Dioc. Reg. St. John's Coll., Oxon., 1615. Master of the Grammar School. Protected by William Lenthall, the Speaker. He held the benefice without interruption until 1668/9. Became blind 1665.
1668	John Thorpe	,,	Oxfd. Dioc. Reg. A native of Burford. New Inn Hall, Oxon., 1657. Chorister Magd. Coll., Oxon., 1659/60. Curate of Burford, 1665. Lived at Fulbrook.
1701	John Eykyn	,,	Oxfd. Dioc. Reg. Pemb. Coll., Oxon., 1692. Vicar of Farmington, Glos., 1718.
1734	Francis Potter	,,	Oxfd. Dioc. Reg. Lincoln Coll., Oxon., 1702.
1746	Francis Webber	,,	Oxfd. Dioc. Reg.
1747 20 Oct.	The Right Hon. Charles Knollis, Earl of Banbury	,,	Oxfd. Dioc. Reg. B.A. Ch. Ch., Oxon., 1725. Vicar of Blackbourton 1731/2 until his death in 1771.
1771 11 April	The Hon. Francis Knollis	,,	Oxfd. Dioc. Reg. Son of the last Vicar. Born at Blackbourton 1743. Magdalen Hall, Oxon., 1771. Rector of Eastleach Martin, Glos.

Date of Institution.	Name.	Patron.	Authorities and Notes.
1826	William Birch	Bishop of Oxford	Oxfd. Dioc. Reg. Non-resident. Resigned 1836.
1836	Edward Philip Cooper	,,	Oxfd. Dioc. Reg. St. John's Coll., Oxon. Founder's Kin Fellow 1812–25. B.D. 1825. Resigned 1850. Died 1864.
1850	James Gerald Joyce	,,	Oxfd. Dioc. Reg. Magdalen Hall, Oxon., 1843. Resigned 1855. Rector of Strathfieldsaye, Hants, to his death in 1878.
1855	Daniel Ward Goddard	,,	Oxfd. Dioc. Reg. Exeter Coll., Oxon. B.A., 1833. Resigned 1860. Vicar of Holwell, Oxon., to his death in 1884.
1860	John Hugh Burgess	,,	Oxfd. Dioc. Reg. Resigned 1871. Vicar of Blewbury, Berks., to his death in 1890.
1871	William Anthony Cass	,,	Oxfd. Dioc. Reg. Curate Horbury, 1854–61. Vicar of St. Michael's, Wakefield, Yorks., 1861–71. Died Dec. 31, 1906.
1907	William Charles Emeris	,,	Oxfd. Dioc. Reg. New Coll., Oxon. B.A., 1886. Vicar of Taynton, Oxon., and Great Barrington, Glos., 1896.

SOME HISTORICAL NOTES ON CHURCH AFFAIRS IN BURFORD

The Alleged Synod at Burford

The earliest recorded event of ecclesiastical history connected with Burford is, unfortunately, of doubtful authenticity. A synod is said to have been held here in A. D. 685; but the sole ground of support for the statement is a charter of questionable genuineness in the Register of Malmesbury Abbey. The terms of the charter are as follows:

‘Ea que secundum timorem et amorem domini religiosa largitionis devotione difficiuntur, quamvis solus sermo sufficeret, tamen pro incerta futurorum temporum conditione scriptis publicis et documentorum gestis sunt confirmanda. Quapropter ego Berhtuualdus regnante domino rex pro remedio animae meae et indulgentia commissorum criminum aliquam terram conferre largirique Aldelmo abbati decreveram id est illam de orientali plaga fluminis cuius vocabulum est Temis iuxta vadum qui appellatur Sumerford xl cassatos ea scilicet definitione ut omni servitute saecularium potestatum portio terrae illius perpetualiter sit libera ad serviendum necessitatibus monachorum deo servientium in monasterio quod nominatur Maeldubesburg. Et ut firmius ac tenacius haec devotio in perpetuum roboretur etiam precellentissimum monarchum Aethelredum regem ad testimonium axivimus cuius consensu et confirmatione haec munificentia acta est. Si quis contra hanc donationem venire temptaverit aut tyrannica fretus potestate violenter invaserit sciat se in tremendo cunctorum examine coram Christo rationem redditurum. Actum publice in synodo iuxta vadum Berghford mense Iulio tricesimo die eiusdem Indictione xiii[a] anno ab incarnatione domini sexcentesimo xxxv.’[1]

Dr. Stubbs, when entering this charter in the third volume of *Councils and Ecclesiastical Documents*,[2] adds the comment that it is ‘a questionable charter’, and does not transcribe

---

[1] Brit. Mus. MS. Laud 417, fol. 1; Kemble's *Codex Diplomaticus Aevi Saxonici*, vol. i, p. 30; *Registrum Malmesburiense* (Rolls Series, 1879), vol. i, p. 279. Kemble notes that l must have dropped out of the date before xxxv, in order to reconcile the calendar date with the Indiction and also with the presence of the personages named.

[2] *Councils and Ecclesiastical Documents*, Haddon and Stubbs, vol. iii, p. 169.

it. Dr. Plummer, in a note in his edition of Bede's *Ecclesiastical History*, referring to William of Malmesbury's *Life of St. Aldhelm*, says : ' The rest of Malmesbury's work is largely made up of extracts from Aldhelm's letters, and Malmesbury charters, most of the latter being of very doubtful authenticity.'

Thus the single record of the alleged synod at Burford is under suspicion, to say the least, both from one of the greatest modern authorities on charters in general and also from one of the greatest modern authorities on ecclesiastical charters in particular. It is pertinent, therefore, to remark first, that Burford was not a place likely to be chosen for the meeting of a synod, being remote from any important centre of the ecclesiastical life of the time ; and secondly, that at this period of hatred and hostility between Wessex and Mercia it was improbable, on the face of it, that Berhtwaldus, a vicegerent of the royal power in Mercia, and Ethelred, King of Mercia, would be concerned in a gift of land to the great churchman of Wessex, Aldhelm.

Yet the synod has always had an appearance of great authenticity in the modern accounts given of it, for they are amplified with detail of discussion at this alleged synod. They go on to relate, in connexion with the gift to Aldhelm, the historic facts of a controversy about the date of Easter, as to which the British Church was in error. But this connexion has sprung from a confusion of two distinct synods, for which Camden, in his *Britannia*, must be held responsible. He writes in his account of Burford :

Here was held a council 682 by the Kings Etheldred and Berthwald, at which Aldhelm, Abbot of Malmesbury, afterwards Bishop of Shirburn, being present, was commanded to write against the error of the British Church in the observance of Easter (Bede, *Eccl. Hist.* v. 18). Spelman calls this a Mercian Synod, and dates it 705, without fixing any place, or the exact time ; whereas both are evident from Malmesbury (*De Pontif.* v) and the leiger book of that Abbey.[1]

Now Bede's *Ecclesiastical History* in this connexion mentions no place. The passage reads as follows :

[1] Camden, *Britannia*, 2nd edition (London 1806), vol. ii, p. 3.

Denique Aldhelmus cum erat adhuc presbyter et Abbas monasterii quod Maildulfi urbem nominant, scripsit, iubente Synodo suae gentis, librum egregium adversus errorem Britonum, quo vel Pascha suo tempore celebrant, vel alia perplura ecclesiasticae castitati et paci contraria gerunt. Multosque eorum, qui Occidentalibus Saxonibus subditi erant Britones, ad Catholicam Dominici. Paschae celebrationem huius lectione perduxit.[1]

Faricius, in his Life of Aldhelm, dates this synod with some care. His version is :

Regnante Anglorum rege Osredo anno Dominicae Incarnationis septingentesimo sexto, quidam Britonum nomine tenus praesules haeretizabant de Paschali termino et de aliis pluribus ecclesiasticae orthodoxitatis institutionibus. Quare Saxonum Orientalis (*sic*) plagae sancta synodus venerabilem Aldhelmum abbatem, et adhuc tantum presbyterum (nondum enim sanctus vita et moribus in ordine ponebatur pontificum) pro sanctitatis suae reverentia rogavit librum componere egregium, quo maligna quae tunc supra modum pullulabat haeresis Britonum destrueretur.[2]

Apart from this fixing of the date of the synod concerning Easter there are two points to note in these references. Firstly, if at this synod Aldhelm had received a gift of land, it is unlikely that Bede, with his admiration for Aldhelm and his concern for the details of Aldhelm's life, would not have known of it, and thus fixed the scene of the synod. Secondly (and more significantly), both Bede and Faricius speak of the synod as a synod of the Wessex people.[3] This could not conceivably have taken place in what was at that time Mercian territory. It is quite clear that the synod concerning Easter cannot be identified with the occasion on which the alleged gift of land to Aldhelm was made.

This confusion of two separate events, in which Camden has been followed by all who have since written of Burford, being cleared away, there remains no authority for the supposed synod at Burford except the Malmesbury charter ; and that is hardly good enough to rely upon.

[1] Bede, *Eccl. Hist.* v. 19 (Cambridge, Folio, p. 436).
[2] Faricius, *Vita Aldhelmi*, cap. 2 (Ed. Giles, pp. 362–3), quoted in Haddon and Stubbs, op. cit., vol. iii, p. 268.
[3] Faricius's reference to 'Saxonum *Orientalis* plagae' is evidently a mistake for *Occidentalis*.

The Rectory and Vicarage

It will therefore be safer to regard Church history in Burford, apart from that which is inscribed in the structure of the Parish Church, as beginning with the gift of the Rectory of Burford and the chapelry of Fulbrook to the Abbey of Keynsham by William, Earl of Gloucester, the founder of the Abbey. In the charter granted to the Abbey by Gilbert de Clare, confirming gifts made by Earl William, occurs the following clause :

Concessi etiam et confirmavi dictis canonicis ad susten-tationem suam quantum ad advocatum et dominum fundi pertinet omnes ecclesias quas W comes avus meus eisdem canonicis concessit scilicet in Bristoll ecclesiam S. Mariae et S. Werburgae et ecclesiam S. Sepulchri et ecclesiam S. Iohannis Baptistae in Bureford cum capella de Fulebrook et omnibus aliis pertinenciis suis. . . .' [1]

The foundation of Keynsham Abbey took place between 1167 and 1172 ; and we have therefore to give the same dates to the acquisition by Keynsham of the Rectory and advowson of Burford. Perhaps we may ascribe to the influence of these new patrons the building of that Norman church of which such considerable portions have survived.

A certain amount of land would, of course, go with the church—the rectorial and vicarial glebe of later times—and a portion of this land must have been the ground upon which the Rectory and Vicarage were built. The Vicarage is first mentioned in the Burford Records in 1384 in a grant of certain houses standing between the Vicarage and the river Windrush.[2] No rectory house is mentioned at anything like so early a date by that specific name. But in the *Taxatio Ecclesiastica* of *circa* 1291 the Abbot of Keynsham is entered for an annual rent of 3s. in Burford as his temporality, apart from the Rectorial revenues ; and the same rent appears in a Clerical Subsidy of 1450–1.[3] Some grants among the Burford Records dated 1435 and 1445, concerning a house standing next to the Vicarage on one side, describe it as being bounded on the other

---

[1] Pat. Roll, 3 Edw. I, p. 1, m. 30, a recital and confirmation of Gilbert de Clare's charter : see also Dugdale, *Mon. Angl.*, vi. 452.
[2] See Part III, p. 317.   [3] See Part III, p. 599.

side by ' a house of the Abbot of Keynsham '.[1] It is possible that this was the earliest Rectory house, leased to tenants (since there was no resident Rector) and standing, like the Vicarage, in the High Street, upon the front edge, so to speak, of the church land in this part of Burford, the ground behind being left open meadow, as the ground behind the Vicarage is to-day.

No other mention of the Rectory occurs until the year 1546, when Edmund Harman obtained a grant of this portion of the possessions of Keynsham. It was at that time in the tenancy of Thomas Baylie, who had obtained in 1532 a lease from the Abbey for ninety years at an annual rent of £10.[2] This lease would, of course, include all the glebe and temporalities of the Rectory, the advowson remaining in the hands of the Abbey; the size of the rent shows that more than a house was being leased. At the same time, there certainly must have been a house; for the Memoranda upon Harman's grant speak of ' the said parsonage ', and of ' the trees growing about the scytuacion of the saide parsonage '; and since ' the hedgs inclosing the gleybe lands ' are mentioned separately, it is quite clear that ' the parsonage ' was a house with grounds around it.

It may by this time have been on the site of the present Rectory house, for although the main frontage of the existing building is of a period much later than this, there is older work in the back wing of the house, and also in the wing at the north end.

When Harman obtained the Rectory the lease to Baylie had apparently ceased to be valid, or else it was surrendered, for Harman made a new lease to Thomas Smyth ' generosus ', for a term of sixty years, at the enhanced rent of £15, an annual payment of 20s. to the Crown being reserved. In the following year, 1547, Harman made an exchange of lands with the College of Fotheringhay, and the Rectory passed into the possession of the College. In 1584, the College having ceased to exist, a new grant of the Rectory was obtained by Mary, Edmund Harman's daughter, for the term of three lives—her

[1] See Part III, pp. 422, 426.
[2] Bodl. MSS., Rawlinson B 419 (131). Baylie was a clothier, of Trowbridge, Wilts.

own, that of her husband, William Johnson, and that of their son, Harman Johnson.[1] It appears from the terms of this last grant that the lease to Thomas Smyth still held good, and had not been disturbed by the exchange of 1547.

Meanwhile the advowson had become in some curious way detached from the tenure of the Rectory. It had passed with the Rectory to the Crown upon the surrender of Keynsham Abbey, for the presentation in 1542 was made by the Crown. It was also included in the grant to Harman, and must have gone to the College of Fotheringhay in the exchange, for the Edward Sandys, 'generosus', who presented to the Vicarage in 1551, cannot be traced as having any connexion with Burford, and must have presented by some right derived from the College. But then occur three presentations, in 1555, 1558, and 1571 by Sir Edward Unton and his wife, Anne, Countess of Warwick, who held for her life the lordship of the town and manor.[2] How these two came to be exercising the patronage does not appear. But the result was that, when, upon the Countess of Warwick's death, the lordship reverted to the Crown, the advowson reverted with it, and presentations continued to be made by the Crown, even after the grant of the Rectory to Mary Johnson.

In 1611 the patronage appears for the first time in the hands of the Bishop of Oxford, where it has since rested continuously. But the Rectory remained separated from the advowson, and was being leased out by the Crown, the three lives of Mary Johnson's grant having evidently expired. In 1613 it was in the hands of two men named Reginald Edwards and Humfry Repington; in 1618 Sir Lawrence Tanfield was in possession; and after his death it came into the hands of Robert Veysey of Chimney.[3] While it is possible that Harman Johnson may have lived in the Rectory house, it is clear that these others merely held the Rectory for the sake of the rents to be derived from the glebe. Edwards and Repington appear in no local documents; Tanfield had his fine new house at the Priory; and when Robert Veysey died in 1634, there was nothing to be valued in the Rectory house except

[1] See Part III, p. 653. [2] See *supra*, p. 84.
[3] See Part III, pp. 666, 667.

PLATE VII. THE RECTORY

a few odds and ends put away in a chest, and ' in the chamber
over the hall ' ; he had houses at Ducklington, Bradwell, and
Taynton, as well as the house at Chimney, where he principally
lived. He would appear only to have rented the Rectory
house, for the Book of Church Officers shows that the lay
rectorship was held by Lady Tanfield after her husband's
death, and then by Lord Falkland, since the appointment of
Rector's churchwardens continues in their names. The
same evidence shows that the rectorship went with the
other Priory possessions to Lenthall ; but for some reason
he took other steps later on to confirm his possession of it.
Whitelocke records, on May 4, 1649 : ' An Act passed for
settling the rectory and glebe lands of Burford upon a
member.'[1] It remained in Lenthall hands for more than
a century, and ultimately became reunited to the advowson,
for in 1741 it was in the possession of the Bishop of Oxford,
having become part of the endowment of the bishopric.
He leased it in that year to Elizabeth Clarke Pryor, widow ·
of John Pryor—probably grandson of the John Pryor who
was murdered in the Priory garden. The lease which she
obtained was for three lives, and was prolonged, as appears
by an endorsement, for four lives more.[2]

Unfortunately there is no means of identifying the builder
of the Rectory house. It is a finer piece of building than we
should be inclined, on the evidence of the Priory structure, to
attribute to any Lenthall, being a beautiful example of a type
described in the succeeding chapter, distinguished by carefully finished ashlar work uninterrupted by ornament, high
sash-window openings framed with a broad shallow moulding,
and a great simplicity of outline. The later Pryor connexion
just makes possible the conjecture that the murdered John
Pryor may have built this house, and lived in it. He was
probably, as William Lenthall's agent and the trustee under
his will, a man of some means. We know also that he had
some interest in the Rectory, for an entry in John Thorpe's
' Booke for the Vicaridge Rights ' describes how Thorpe on
one occasion, being at the house of a Mrs. Matthews with
John Pryor, had seen the latter take away a terrier of the

· [1] Whitelocke's *Memorials* (1853), iii. 29.   [2] See Part III, p. 405.

Rectorial glebe written upon parchment. However, that is not enough to make more than guess-work of the idea that John Pryor may have built the present house.

The Vicarage, we may conclude from the earliest extant reference to it, has from the first occupied its present site. Of the existing building the oldest portion is in the wing furthest removed from the street, the ground-floor room of which is of the sixteenth century. To whom the addition of the charming street façade, of the year 1672, is due is not known. John Thorpe, the vicar of that date, was certainly a man of means, and might have built it ; but as he lived in Fulbrook it is at least equally possible that the building was done by some tenant to whom he had let the Vicarage. In the nineteenth century the central part of the house was rebuilt, in the time of Mr. Cooper.

The Glebe Lands

The history of the glebe lands of Burford is rather a disgraceful one. The secularization of the Rectorial glebe is, indeed, no different here from what it was in the hundreds of parishes of which the Rectories were held by monastic foundations, and were made sources of profit to the Crown after the Dissolution by sale or lease to lay impropriators.

But the Vicarial glebe, which had escaped this fate, was subject in Burford, in the succeeding century, to manipulations which, though not in the truest sense more scandalous, were certainly more mean and underhand. The annual value of the Vicarage is entered on the Clerical Subsidies of the fifteenth century at £6 13s. 4d., which, though not a large sum, even when all allowances have been made for the different value of money, nevertheless represents a sufficiency of glebe land, in addition to the small tithes. Unfortunately the two Vicars of Burford in the early seventeenth century, Philip Hill and Christopher Glynn, seem to have been little more than creatures of the lords of the manor ; and they allowed Tanfield and Speaker Lenthall to obtain complete possession of the glebe in exchange for comfortable payments during their own lives.

We have what is virtually contemporary evidence of these

transactions. Glynn's successor was a man of a very different type, John Thorpe, who by every record or indication that he has left must have been a straightforward, painstaking man. Preserved now among the registers is a little quarto book, bound in limp vellum and inscribed on the cover: 'Burford Booke for the Vicaridge Rights'.[1] It contains John Thorpe's notes, made chiefly between 1674 and 1680, on the existing vicarial tithes and a little glebe, and also the story of what had happened to the rest of the glebe. Thorpe had the story in the main from Mr. Benjamin Griffin, who was at that time 'Minister of Barrington Magna', and had been the usher at Burford Grammar School in Christopher Glynn's time. His account was that sixty or seventy years before the date at which John Thorpe was writing there had been 'an Agreement Between the Bishop, the Parson, & the vicar of Burford, about stateing every mans Right'. There could hardly have been any real uncertainty as to the respective glebes, but this nominal reason for the 'agreement [2] is in the next few sentences revealed as a mere blind. 'It was agreed that the Parson (who was Tanfeild) should pay the vicar 80£ per Ann. for his maintenance & the parson should take all the vicars dues, whereupon some have told mee, as one Robert Hayter shoemaker they Remember the Ld Tanfeilds servants gather (*sic*) for their master the very Easter offerings.' There would have been no great harm in .this arrangement, though of course it was unwise and impolitic of a. vicar, for the sake of the convenience of an outright annual cash payment, to allow a layman to enforce the tithes. But Tanfield had other plans as well.

In a short time the Powerfull Lord persuades ye Vicar to Let him keep these 4 yards of Glebe called the vicars Lands & to take for the vicaridge all the other profitts here but Tanfeild during Hill the vicars Life would make up the Losse of these Lands procuring for him Eaton [2] a Living of a 100£ per Ann. besides this place &c. & after many years Mr. Christopher Glin enters who rec^d Advantages from Mr. Wm Lenthall above 40£ a year.

[1] This book was recovered from private possession by Mr. William J. Monk, whose *History of Burford* has been so well known to visitors for many years, and was by him restored to its place among the Church archives.   [2] Eaton Hastings, Berks.

In other words, Philip Hill having been made comfortable for his lifetime, Christopher Glynn agreed to follow the same course, without regard to the interests of later Vicars. They exchanged the permanent possessions of the vicarage for what was only a personal arrangement with themselves. John Thorpe, coming into the vicarage, found practically no glebe left, except what lay in Fulbrook ; and, as he says, ' so many years and alterations being past and no script of anything left mee by the vicars precedent I am wholly at a Losse what to doe '. He was not without evidence of a kind. Apart from Mr. Griffin's story there was the fact of four yard lands (nearly 200 acres) being called ' Vicars lands ', held ' with a more than ordinary number of sheep commons ', and tithe-free—all of which Thorpe duly records. He had an idea of searching ' Lincolne Records ', in order to discover the true conditions of the glebe in earlier times. But whether he ever did so or not, he has no more researches to enter in his book.

Thorpe's successor, John Eykyn, was certainly not a man to interest himself in the vicar's legal rights. So more ' years and alterations ' went past ; and the glebe which Tanfield had so meanly acquired, and Speaker Lenthall hardly less meanly retained, was lost for good. In the Enclosure Award of 1797 no allotment for Vicarial glebe appears at all.

The Rectorial glebe, returning to the hands of the Bishop of Oxford after the expiry of the prolonged lease of the Rectory to the Pryor family, was ultimately handed over to the Ecclesiastical Commissioners, who now make from the proceeds an allowance for the payment of a curate.

The Churchwardens

At the earliest date at which churchwardens are mentioned in the Burford Records, and for several hundred years afterwards, they were four in number. They appear, in the first regular lists of the parish officers, which begin in 1613, as holding office thus : one for the Rector, one for the Vicar, and two for the township, *pro villa*.

Upon the origin of this rather unusual custom we have very little light. In the course of the controversy of 1738-43,

over the administration of the charities, there was some discussion of the position of the four churchwardens. The
Royal Commission of 1738 had ordained that in several
charities with which the churchwardens had then no concern
they should be joined with the Bailiffs and Burgesses. The
latter took exception to these orders, largely on the ground
that the two churchwardens for the township were generally
under the influence of the lord of the manor, and did not
fairly represent the mind of the people. But the two interesting points put forward by the Bailiffs and Burgesses were
these—first, that the Rector's churchwarden certainly ought
to have no voice in the town charities, because the Rector's
nomination was on behalf of 'the outward tythings' of Upton
and Signett; and, secondly, that, strictly, one of the township
churchwardens was the representative of the Corporation.

The respondents in the case, while not contesting the
former point, denied entirely that the Bailiffs and Burgesses
had ever enjoyed the right of electing a churchwarden of
their own. Yet no alternative explanation of the existence of
two wardens for the township was offered. If the representative of 'the outward tythings' had been one of these
two, the system would have been comprehensible; but no
attempt was made to maintain that position. It may, in
fact, have been the truth; for it seems unlikely that the
Rector would have any special reason to nominate the warden
for those tythings. It is more probable that originally his
warden fulfilled the normal duty of representing the owner
of the chancel of the church; the Rectory being impropriate,
a Vicar's warden also had been elected; and, as happened
elsewhere, the township being in two distinct portions,
parishioners' wardens were elected for each. But when the
Rectory passed to lay hands, and had been held for some time
by men who were also lords of the manor, with their chief
interests in Upton and Signett, the most natural explanation
of their nomination of a warden, in the minds of men who had
no knowledge of the original system, was that this warden
was the Upton and Signett warden. Then, in order to account
for the two parishioners' wardens, the theory of a Corporation
warden was invented.

Another explanation is, however, just possible. In mediaeval times, when the Gild Chapel and the Church were separate structures, each had its own 'proctors' or wardens, responsible for the fabric, the ornaments and plate. It may be that, when the chapel became an integral part of the church, the separate responsibility was continued, one of the two Gild proctors acting in conjunction with one of the two church proctors. In other words, the Bailiffs and Burgesses may have had a sound tradition at the back of their claim; and in that case the theory of a warden for Upton and Signett was really the invention. In support of this it may be remarked that at no point in the existing church records is there any entry of a warden as elected or nominated for the outward tythings.

The normal entries throughout the seventeenth century are : one churchwarden *pro rectore*, one *pro vicario*, and two *pro villa*. But this regularity in the formula is not attained for some time. When Sir Lawrence Tanfield held the Rectory, the Rector's warden is usually entered as 'for my lord being parson', or, in his later years, simply 'for my lord'. In 1626/7 the entry is 'for the Lady Tanfield', and in 1628/9 'for my lady'. This personal formula continues to be used for some years in the entries of a warden 'for Sir Lucius Cary', but gives place in 1630 to one more official in character, but quite unjustifiable, 'pro domino Burgi'; it was not as lord of the town, but as Rector, that Lord Falkland exercised this nomination. It is interesting to observe that in 1638 the words *domino Burgi* have been erased, and *Rectore* substituted. We observe the accuracy of the legal mind of William Lenthall, whose first nomination this was. Hereafter *pro Rectore* is the invariable form.

The two parishioners' wardens are entered for the first twenty years after 1613 as 'for the parish'. This is strong evidence against the later theory that the 'outward tythings' were represented by the Rector's warden; for Upton and Signett were certainly part of the ecclesiastical parish of Burford, and wardens 'for the parish' must have represented the hamlets as well as the town. In one year, 1635, at the time when the Rector's warden was being entered as *pro domino Burgi*, the parish wardens are entered as *pro Burgo*, an equally unjustifiable form, since the *Burgus* excluded part of the parish. It only occurs once, and may have been due to carelessness; or we may perhaps see in it a hint of the theory that Upton and Signett were represented through the Rectorial warden. After this date the use of the form *pro villa* is uninterrupted.

The custom of four churchwardens continued until the year 1871. For many years the office of Rector's warden had been served by Mr. C. F. A. Faulkner, of Bury Barns. He died in 1870; and in the minutes of the Easter Vestry meeting of 1871 the following passage occurs: 'In consequence of the death of Mr. Allen Faulkner and the Ecclesiastical Commissioners, the present Rectors, not having nominated any successor to him as Churchwarden on their part the appointment to this remains in abeyance.'

So it remains to the present day. The parishioners still elect two wardens, and the Vicar nominates one. But no Rector's warden has been nominated since 1871.

The Parish Registers

The Parish Registers of Burford now extant begin in the year 1612, when Philip Hill was Vicar. They appear to have been for the most part carefully kept, without intermission. The only signs of the disturbance of the Civil War in this respect are contained in the Register Book of the Church Officers. Under the date 1642 in that volume occurs the following entry: 'The three churchwardens Richard Veysey, Symon Ward and Henry Hayter being churchwardens the yeare past were continued in the office by the vicar and parishioners for the yeare by reason the government of the church at this time was unsettled.' The Rector, Speaker Lenthall, had nominated a churchwarden as usual. After the next year's date, this note is made: 'There hath beene noe choice made of Churchwardens by reason of troublesome tymes since the 4th day of Aprill 1642 untill the 20th of Aprill 1647.' But meanwhile the Register of Baptisms, Marriages, and Burials shows but slight interruptions.

The Reformation in Burford

The history of Burford in connexion with the Reformation
is curious and rather puzzling. The town has no recorded
place in the Marian persecutions or on the roll of the
Protestant martyrs. Yet at an earlier date it was certainly
a centre for the Wycliffites of the neighbourhood, and a resort
for those who strove for the possession of the Scriptures in
their native tongue. When John Longland, Bishop of
Lincoln, made his investigations of heresy in the diocese in
1521, a number of Burford people were informed upon, and
there must have been some reason for the selection of the
town as one of the places of public penance for offenders.
But it must, of course, be added that Longland's heresy
hunt was regarded even at the time as a pursuit of trifles,
and it does not follow that persons accused before his commissioners were very passionate reformers (indeed the charges
in most of the Burford cases border on the ludicrously petty) ;
so that Burford's prominence in those investigations does not
necessarily imply a zeal and conviction that would have
made it prominent under Mary. In point of fact, all the
persons charged in 1521 recanted.

The leaders of the group were John Edmunds, a Burford
tailor, with his wife, and John Harris and his wife, of Upton.
It was in their houses that meetings were most frequently
held. Others who were denounced were Robert Burges and
his wife, John Boyes and his brother (' a Monk of Burford '),
Edmunds's daughter Agnes, Edward Red, who is described as
' Schoolmaster of Burford ', Eleanor Higges, John Through,
of the Priory, Roger Dods, Thomas Reiley, Thomas Clemson
who was servant to ' the Prior of Burford ', Joan Taylor
(servant to John Harris), and the brother of Burges's wife.
The meetings they held were attended by people from as far
away as West Hendred, Ginge near Wantage, and Steventon ;
and also by some from Witney, Clanfield, Standlake, Asthall,
and Lechlade.[1] They met sometimes to hear books read to
them—' a book called W. Thorpe ' (either, we may presume,

[1] John Hakker of London came occasionally, and sold them some of
the books in English which they possessed.

the account of his trial written by William Thorpe, the Wycliffite, or his ' Short Testament of his Faith '), ' a book speaking of the Plagues of Pharaoh ', ' a Book called Nicodemus's Gospel ', in which was ' the story of the destruction of Jerusalem ', ' the Book of the Exposition of the Apocalypse ', and ' a book called the *King of Beeme* '. One reading of this kind took place at Harris's house after the marriage of Burges and his wife. At other times they met to hear Joan Edmunds or Alice Colins, whose husband was an Asthall man, recite passages of Scripture, such as the Eight Beatitudes, the Epistles of St. Peter and St. James, and the first chapter of the Gospel of St. John ; or the Seven Works of Mercy, the Seven Deadly Sins, the Five Wits bodily and ghostly, and other such things.

. All this appeared in accusation against them, together with apparently insignificant charges, such as that they discussed the Apocalypse and the matter of opening the Book with the seven clasps, the seven lean and seven fat oxen, and John the Baptist's foretelling of the One that should come after him ' whose buckle of his shooe he was not worthy to undoe '. Charges of this kind may have had reference to particular tenets of the Lollards. More comprehensible are various charges of speaking against pilgrimages and worship of saints ; in this connexion we see John Edmunds as a man of ideals ahead of his time : ' This John Edmunds . . . talking with the said Baker of Pilgrimage, bad him go offer his money to the Image of God. When the other asked, What that was ? he said that the Image of God was the poor people, blind and lame.' Against Eleanor Higges there was a charge of saying she should ' burn the Sacrament in an oven '. But that is the single charge of anything inconsistent with a simple piety and religious spirit. Edmunds and John Colins both gave evidence against their fellows and denounced others.

It must be remembered, in considering the apparent triviality of some of the accusations, that the real charge in all the cases was, of course, an attempted independence of the priest's authority, a discussion of spiritual and religious matters not at that time within the competence of the laity, and the holding of religious gatherings in private. The individual accusations are no more than specific instances of what went on at these gatherings, and are evidence rather than charges in the strict sense.

Although all the accused abjured, and many of them gave information, all seem to have been punished; and there is enough to indicate that the punishment was not light. The penances enjoined were of the usual kind. Offenders were to be branded on the cheek, to keep fasts as ordered, and recant all their errors upon the Gospels. They were also to appear in the market-place of Burford, and at certain other towns, on the market-day, to go three times about the market and stand a quarter of an hour on the steps of the market cross, each with a faggot on the shoulder; and on an appointed Sunday to carry faggots in this way in procession and kneel with them on the steps of the High Altar all the time of High Mass. The more drastic part of the punishment has been less noticed. All were committed as prisoners to some monastery or convent, and as a rule to one distant from the offender's home. What this involved may be read between the lines of one of the Bishop's letters, committing a prisoner to Eynsham Abbey. The prisoner is to be put to perpetual penance; no lodging need be provided for him, and his food is to be such as the Abbey usually gives in alms to the poor; if he can do any work useful to the monastery he may have his diet improved as the Abbot sees fit, but he is not to leave the precincts of the Abbey except for his public penance on the appointed days. This kind of committal order in the hands of a severe Abbot must have inflicted a great deal of suffering.

CHAPTER IX

THE TOPOGRAPHY AND POPULATION OF BURFORD

THE position, and with it the date, of the original settlement of inhabitants on the site of Burford, may be deduced from certain marked characteristics of this region of the Cotswolds.

The high ground above the town is part of one of those spurs of the hill-range which, descending from its bold northwestward rampart, form the watersheds of the northern tributaries of the Upper Thames. Between each pair of these streams—between the Churn and the Coln, the Coln and the Windrush, the Windrush and the Evenlode, the Evenlode and the Cherwell—irregular hilly ridges lead down to the great Thames valley.

Now the earliest remains of human habitation, the earthworks of prehistoric man, throughout the Cotswold region have one distinct feature. They are numerous upon the loftier north-westward side ; and a few are found advancing, as it were, down the spurs between the rivers. But in every case (save for one isolated instance between the Evenlode and the Cherwell) there is a complete absence of earthworks as the spurs approach the Thames. This is not difficult to understand if the distribution of earthworks on the Cotswolds be regarded in conjunction with their distribution on the hill-ranges of Wiltshire and Berkshire. It then becomes clear that the people who constructed these works, keeping, as they always did, to high ground, discovered that the southwestward trend of the main Cotswold range formed a natural way of avoiding the Thames valley with its swamps and forests. It turned the head-waters of that river, and led between them and the head-waters of the Wiltshire Avon to the southern hills, to Avebury and Stonehenge.

The site of Burford lay off the ground thus traversed.

The nearest earthworks are Windrush Camp, some four and a half miles to the west, and the camp near Aldsworth, to the south-west. The line given by these two shows that the current of that early life, whether coming from Hailes and Roel Gate Camps straight down the watershed by Norbury Camp, or crossing the upper watersheds from the direction of the Rollright Stones by way of Maugersbury and Idbury Camps, avoided the falling ground of the lower Windrush valley, and turned south-westwards to cross to the southern hills by Poulton Camp (Ranbury Ring) and Bury Hill Camp.

This evidence of the earthworks is confirmed by a remarkable difference in the situation of the villages on either side of the line thus drawn. North-west of it lie Stow, Great Rissington, Clapton, Farmington, Aldsworth, Turkdean, and so on—all of them villages on the hills. South-east of it, where the spurs begin to fall, lie the Barringtons, Taynton, Burford, Swinbrook, Asthall, Minster Lovell, Witney—all of them valley settlements.

It may, therefore, be concluded that the original inhabiting of the site of Burford was of comparatively late date, not earlier than the Bronze Age. Small round barrows are the oldest signs of population along the lower Windrush. Neolithic flint implements have, indeed, been found at Burford, but only in insignificant quantity ; and they are for the most part the lesser implements, like arrow-heads, such as would be carried for hunting expeditions, which would of course go far afield from the general lines of movement and habitation. They are not enough to disturb the conclusion to be drawn from the very clear differences between the northern and southern portions of this watershed—the earthworks and hill villages of the former, the barrows and river-side villages of the latter.

Yet there is one fact which suggests that within the area of what was to be later the manor and the parish of Burford there may be a trace of a still earlier settlement. A clue to the *burh*, which usually offers an indication of the site of an original settlement, may be found, for the town of Burford,

in Bury Orchard, a piece of ground near the Church, and lying
in an angle of the river, exactly where the heart of a valley
settlement might be looked for. But, if we are to take this
clue, we can hardly neglect another name, that of Bury Barns,
a farm at the top of the hill.

In the curious, and often baffling, divisions of the manor
between various tenants at later times, after the erection of
the borough, two hamlets remained outside the chartered community, that of Upton, near the river, and that of Signett,
on the hill not far from Bury Barns. No doubt these two
hamlets, as they exist to-day, take their origin from those
inhabitants of the feudal manor who, unable or unwilling
to enter the burghal status under the charters of Burford,
remained on the old terms of tenure of their land ; and
gradually formed settlements, the position of which was
naturally dictated by convenience of access to the common
fields and meadows.

But it is also possible that, if the name Bury Barns marks
the site of a hill-top *burh*, another fact should be taken into
consideration. Upton and Signett, though members of the
ecclesiastical parish of Burford, form a distinct civil parish.
Therefore they may represent, not merely a late partition of
the inhabitants of the manor, but also a prehistoric settlement which, as being on the hill-top, may be regarded as
older than the earliest settlement on the site of the town of
Burford.

But again, this conjecture, like the occasional discovery of
flint implements, does not affect the conclusion with regard
to this latter settlement, that such considerations as can be
advanced concerning its probable date do not tend to make it
earlier than the Bronze Age.

Of the Roman occupation only slight traces have been
recorded here. In 1814 a stone coffin was found, during the
making of the present lower road from Upton to Little
Barrington,[1] about a mile to the west of Burford. Unfortunately the discovery was made before the days of .

---

[1] One of the roads ordered to be made in the course of the Upton
Enclosure Award ; see Part III, p. 704.

modern scientific excavation; and we know no more of it than is to be found in a communication made at the time by the Hon. and Rev. Francis Knollis, then Vicar of Burford :

On Monday the 21st of November, 1814, some workmen repairing a road on the estate of John Lenthall, Esq., on the West of Burford and about a mile from the town, discovered a large stone coffin about 3 feet below the surface of the earth, containing the skeleton of a human body. The coffin was covered by a lid of stone, exactly fitted to it, with a rim or ledge, upon which a cement of reddish colour had been introduced, so as to entirely shut out the air ; and the more effectually to secure the purpose, the sides of the lid were covered with blue clay, brought from some distance, no clay being found near this spot. The bones appeared extended as the body lay—most of them entire, the large ones quite so— and are firm and perfect ; the skull is also unimpaired, and the teeth not in the least decayed, but fixed in each jaw unimpaired. The only thing in the coffin besides the bones, and some particles of a dusty substance, were a number of small iron studs, the heads rounded, and appear to have been fixed in a substance similar to leather, some of the points being near an inch in length ; they were set very close together, and might perhaps have been worn as a defence, not unlike a Roman Lorica. There was no weapon of any kind, or any inscription to be found. The coffin is formed of an entire block of freestone, which is found in quarries not far distant. It is neatly worked, both in the excavation and on the outside. The cavity is 6 feet in length, 21 inches deep at the head, 16 inches at the feet, gradually declining ; the breadth over the breast is 2 feet 2 inches, and at the feet contracted to 4 inches. The whole height from the ground (excluding the lid or cover, about 5 inches thick) is 2 feet 11 inches. The right side is quite straight, but the left curved. It was fixed in the ground with the feet almost pointing due south. The field where it was discovered is open, and no house or burial ground is supposed to be near it. The coffin weighs .16 cwt. The perfect state, from the exclusion of the air, in which the bones are preserved renders it a matter of great curiosity to form a reasonable judgement.

It used to be popularly supposed that this coffin, which is now in the churchyard, was a relic of the battle here in A.D. 752 between the Mercians and the West Saxons. But

Mr. Reginald Smith, of the British Museum, upon seeing the coffin, pronounced it Roman. Of the fate of the contents of the coffin nothing is now known.

It is remarkable that no other Roman remains, except a few coins, should have been found at Burford. For Akeman Street must have passed, at its nearest point, not much more than a couple of miles to the south-east of the town; and both at Asthall, about four miles distant, where Akeman Street crosses the river, and at Widford, only a mile and a half distant, there are considerable signs of Roman settlement. But in both these cases the Romans had sites on the other side of the river with a southward-facing aspect. Burford, on its northward-facing slope, would offer a less attractive position.

The developments of the early settlement may be discerned, as we approach the Anglo-Saxon period, from the place-name which it then acquired. Evidently the ford over the river had come into use; and that, in turn, means that new lines of movement were being followed. During the Roman occupation, with Akeman Street crossing the river four miles to the east,[1] and the Fosse Way marching over the high ground above the head-waters some ten miles to the west, Burford had remained off the main currents of movement. The fact that it was now named from the ford shows that a new channel of communication was in use. Since it provided a straight way from the northern and north-eastern Cotswolds to the upper—and easier—crossings of the Thames, it must have been a frequented route.

To this situation Burford owes its place in Anglo-Saxon records. One of the references to it at this period is of such doubtful authenticity that it had better be left out of account —the one, namely, which alleges the holding of a Synod here in A.D. 685.[2] The other reference, however, is open to no such doubt. It is the account in the Anglo-Saxon Chronicle of a battle fought here in A.D. 752.

[1] After crossing the river it approaches much nearer to Burford.
[2] The authenticity of the reference is discussed in connexion with the ecclesiastical history of Burford : chapter viii, pp. 131-3.

In this year Cuthred King of the West Saxons in the twelfth year of his reign fought at Burford against Aethelbald King of the Mercians and put him to flight.[1]

Later chroniclers expand this brief statement with some picturesqueness of detail. The version in Richard of Cirencester, which is almost word for word identical with that in Matthew of Paris, is as follows :

Hathellardo rege Occidentalium Saxonum defuncto, regnavit pro eo frater eius Cuthredus quindecim annis. Hic vero Cuthredus adversus Ethelbaldum regem Merciorum et Britones iugi exercitio victorias adipiscens non minimum sudoris consumpsit. Nam Cuthredus praedictus cum regis Merciorum Ethelbaldi superbas exactiones et insolentias ferre non posset, occurrit ei hostiliter apud Beoreforde, ubi praelium gravissimum dicti reges commiserunt. Ethelbaldus vero, praecedente Ethelmo cum vexillo eius, in quo erat aureus draco depictus, acriter ruit in hostes, sed vexillifer regis Cuthredi in hostilem vexilliferum lanceam dirigens perforavit eum. Unde clamore elato pars Cuthredi regis valde confortata est. Tonitruum ergo belli et sonitus ictuum clamoresque hinc inde cadentium terribiliter personarunt. Spes enim mutuo victoriae certa memoria fugae nulla. Sed Deus tandem qui superbis resistit et humilibus dat gratiam, Ethelbaldum in fugam compulit, et laeta Cuthredo victoria provenit.[2]

Henry of Huntingdon expands the account a little more :

Cudredus decimo tertio anno, cum iam regis Edelbaldi superbas exactiones et insolentiam ferre non posset, occurrit ei cum legionibus vexillatis apud Bereford, omni spe vivendi postposita libertati. Adduxit autem secum Edelhun praedictum consulem, iam sibi concordem, cuius viribus fretus et consilio, belli discrimen ingredi potuit. Edelbaldus vero rex regum cum Mercensibus Centenses adduxerat, Orientalesque Saxones et Anglos, copiasque multiplices. Aciebus igitur dispositis cum in directum tendentes appropinquarent, Edelhun praecedens Westsexenses, regis insigne draconem scilicet aureum gerens, transforavit vexilliferum hostilem.

---

[1] *The Anglo-Saxon Chronicle* (Rolls Series, 1861), pp. 80, 81. Her Cuthred Westseaxna cyning gefeaht þy xii geare his rices aet Beorhforde wið Aethelbald Myrcna cyning hine geflymde. (Brit. Mus. MS. Cott. Tiber. B. iv.)

[2] *Ricardi de Cirencestria Speculum Historiale de gestis Regum Angliae* (Rolls Series, 1863), vol. i, 239; cf. *Matthaei Parisiensis Chronica Maiora* (Rolls Series, 1872), vol. i, p. 341.

Unde clamore orto, pars Cudredi valde confortata est ; statimque acies sibi invicem offenderunt. Ergo tonitruum belli, scilicet offensionis armorum et sonitus ictuum clamorisque cadentium, terribiliter exarsit, bellum maximum et inaestimabile incipitur : quod vel Mercenses, vel eos Westsexe, usque in longam posteritatem vincenti supponeret. Videres igitur acies loricis crispantes, galeis acutas, lanceis hirsutas, vexillis depictas, auro resplendentes, parvo tempore sanguine perfusas, lanceis cassas, ruina dissipatas, cerebris asperas, visu horrendas. Congregantes autem se ad vexilla utrinque procaces et fortissimi, gladiis et securibus Amazonicis rem agentes, acies aciebus funeste irruebant. Memoria fugae nulla, spes victoriae utrinque certa : Mercenses superbiae tumor invitabat, Westsexas servitutis horror accendebat. At ubicunque consul praedictus aciebus se infigebat, via ruinarum patebat, dum securis eius timendissima, modo fulminis, corpora findebat et arma. Rex fortissimus autem Edelbaldus quacunque ruebat, strages hostilis fiebat, dum gladio eius invictissimo essent arma pro veste, ossa pro carne. Cum igitur, quasi duo ignes diversis in partibus impositi obstantia quaecunque consumerent, contigit ut sibi obviam rex et consul venirent. Uterque vero alteri terribilis corpore infrenduit, dextram excussit, se in armis collegit, et ictibus immensis arma obstantissima pares lacessunt. Deus autem, qui superbis resistit, a quo robur fortitudo et magnanimitas procedit, gratiae suae regi Edelbaldo terminum posuit, animoque regis confidentiam solitam dempsit. Cum igitur nec animum suum nec vires ipse recognosceret, pugnantibus adhuc suis, a Domino omnipotenti territus, fugam primus incepit. Nec ab hac die usque ad mortis suae tempora prosperum aliquid ei Deus permisit.[1]

It is clear from these accounts that Burford lay upon a well-known and customary line of the travelling of that period. Neither army was at Burford to begin with ; they were moving towards one another, when they met here, and the line of march must, from their use of it at this juncture, have been one of the best to take in moving from Wessex into Mercia, or from Mercia into Wessex.

The name of Battle Edge, by which a piece of land on the slope of the hill west of the town is known, is supposed to mark the site of the battle ; and Camden relates that in his

---

[1] *Henrici Archdiaconi Huntendunensis Historia Anglorum* (Rolls Series, 1879), p. 121.

day the Burford people used to ' make up a dragon and giant, and carry them about in procession ' on Midsummer Eve,[1] in allusion to the standard borne (whether on Ethelbald's side or on Cuthred's, for the Chroniclers do not agree upon this point [2]) in the fight.

On the strength of the records of this event, the derivation of the place-name of Burford has usually been given as Beorh-Ford, the Hill-Ford. In effect, this derivation depends on the Anglo-Saxon Chronicle alone. The later Chroniclers must have copied from that the form of the name, since at the period at which they.were writing that form is never found in documents. The various MSS. of the Anglo-Saxon Chronicle give the name as ' Beorgeforda ' (C.C.C. Camb.), ' Beorh-forda ' (Bodl. Laud 636; Brit. Mus. Cott. Tiber. A. 6, and B. 1), and ' Beorhforde ' (Brit. Mus. Cott. Tiber. B. 4).

It may be difficult, in the face of this authority, to suggest any other derivation. Yet the later forms of the place-name are all against this one. In Domesday it appears as ' Bure-ford ' ; and that remains throughout the three succeeding centuries the almost invariable form, with occasional instances of the present form of ' Burford '. Now the Anglo-Saxon ' Beorh- ' could not possibly modify naturally into ' Bure- '. The pronunciation of that word—and it is on the pronuncia-tion of words, in those days of little writing, that our judgement must depend—would be more or less like our pronunciation of the word ' bear '. This would modify into ' Bere- ', and ultimately produce, as in actual instances it has produced, a place-name ' Barford '. Amid many hundred written examples of the name of Burford the form ' Bereford ' only occurs twice, and it never occurs at all in documents of local origin.

It is, therefore, not altogether a gratuitous complication of a subject at best obscure to offer an alternative derivation

---

[1] Camden, *Britannia* (2nd edition, London 1806), vol. ii, p. 3.

[2] Richard of Cirencester and Matthew of Paris say that ' Ethelmus ' carried the banner of Ethelbald, which was a golden dragon. Henry of Huntingdon says that Edelhun, a ' consul ' of Cuthred's, who had pre-viously, according to the paragraph preceding the one quoted, been in revolt against Cuthred, bore in this battle Cuthred's standard, a golden dragon.

of the name from 'Burh-Ford', the ford with defensive enclosure. This would modify quite naturally into 'Bureford', and ultimately produce 'Burford'. The local dialect word which represents to this day the Anglo-Saxon 'Burh'—namely, 'Burry', meaning 'Sheltered' or 'Protected'[1]—gives us precisely the pronunciation which would account for 'Bureford'. It is, of course, necessary, if this derivation is to be put forward, to suggest some reason for the appearance of the place as 'Beorhforda' in the Chronicle. But, bearing in mind the rarity of the written word in those times, and considering that the author of the Chronicle would no doubt have heard that the fighting took place on a hill above the river, it is not fantastic to suppose that his version was his own version, created to meet the need for a written form, and not that current in speech among the people of the place itself. All the evidence, as written documents increase in number, goes to show that in their minds it was from the *burhs* that the settlement took its name.

Derived in this way, it would be a far more distinctive name than the other derivation would give. Beorh-Ford would not be distinctive at all. Any ford over the Windrush from Minster Lovell upwards would be quite equally a Hill-Ford, both in the approach to it and in the passage up from it. But if, as the names of Bury Orchard and Bury Barns have already suggested, there were near this ford two *burhs*, the settlement at such a point might easily be distinguished by the name of the Burh-Ford.

The natural situation would certainly lead us to accept without surprise the existence of two *burhs*. For while the new trackways of the Anglo-Saxon period had made the ford a point requiring defence, the older way down the crest of the watershed remained, and would surely afford a reason for another defensive enclosure protecting a settlement situated, during the long struggles between Wessex and Mercia, upon very debatable ground. If there was such a work, Bury Barns, standing just at the point where the

---

[1] e. g. 'a nice burry spot', meaning a spot protected from the wind. The word is in use still in Gloucestershire and the Cotswold region.

crest road and the road from the ford meet on the way to
the Thames, is exactly where it might be expected to be placed.
Bury Orchard, in its turn, occupies the most obvious ground
for defending the ford (presuming that the latter was near
the line of the present bridge), since it lies in a salient angle
formed by the course of the river, from which the ford could
be effectively enfiladed. In neither place are there any
surviving traces of a *burh*; unless the noticeably square outline of some fields at Bury Barns, marked, moreover, along
part of their sides by a narrow strip of rough ground carrying
a belt of trees, be indication of an old defensive enclosure.

The small community recorded in Domesday was settled
beside the river *burh*. This would be almost certain from
the existence of the ancient church on the river's bank, the
town mills a little higher up the stream, and the fact that, at
the earliest dates at which grants of houses begin to define
the situation of them, they are found to be more or less
near the river. But it is rendered quite certain when we
observe that the town of Burford, as we shall have occasion
to remark later, was for a long period confined to the lower
portion of the ground it covers to-day. FitzHamon's charter
having been granted at some date within twenty years of
Domesday, it is evident that the situation of the town it
ultimately created must locate for us the Domesday community.

For their arable land, however, those who settled here had
had to go to some distance. Close at hand they had only
ground with a northward aspect. But at the top of the hill
they found land with a good sunny aspect, sloping slightly
towards the south as far as the Shil Brook, which was in the
end to become, for a great part of its length, the boundary
of the common field on that side, and of the ecclesiastical
parish of Burford. Here, then, they cultivated their crops,
using the ground that lay on both sides of the way leading
over the hill to the Thames at Lechlade. This way made
a natural division of the land into two parts, an East Field
and a West Field; and throughout the history of Burford
the common field cultivation remained on a two-field basis.

As time went on, and more land was needed, parts of the northward-facing slope adjoining to the original fields were put under cultivation. But these were reckoned as belonging to either the East or the West Field.[1]

Thus the situation of the community here accords well with certain observed characteristics of the villages of this part of Oxfordshire. Dr. Warde Fowler, in his masterly piece of village history, *Kingham Old and New*,[2] writes: ' It is characteristic, not only of Kingham, but of almost all the villages round us, that the church stands at one extremity, while the houses straggle away in one or two streets towards the land which before the enclosures was the " open field ". In the *hams* and *tons* of the valley, the church is usually at the end nearest the river, and the village has grown out in the direction of the slopes where the arable of the farms is for the most part situated.'

But, of course, that growth is of a later date. The Domesday community, comprising, apart from the demesne *servi*, some forty households, would find ample space on the level ground near the church. If it reached out at all, it would be more likely to have stretched along the level towards the valuable hay meadows, which lay to the east beside the river in the direction of the present Witney road. Grants of houses in Witney Street are found, in fact, as early as those of houses elsewhere in the town.

The river-side *burh* thus proving to be the one that dictated the site of the town, what was the destiny at this period of the hill-top *burh*? The answer is that, by all the evidence, it became the enclosure of the manor house. The history of the Burford manor house is obscure; and it is a singular fact that no house at the present day retains the tradition of being the manor house, nor for the past four hundred years does any document conveying the manor lands and the manorial rights mention a house. Its former situation, however, is not open to doubt.

Domesday places at Burford a *mansio* of considerable size.

---

[1] See, e. g., the schedule of arable lands, Part III, pp. 353-5.
[2] *Kingham Old and New*, by W. Warde Fowler, D.Litt. (Oxford 1913), p. 8.

Among the houses of manorial lords recorded at the opening of the Oxfordshire Survey is one here belonging to Earl Alberic. The entry reads:

Ad terras quas tenuit Albericus comes pertinent i ecclesia et iii mansiones Harum ii iacent ad ecclesiam S Marie reddentes xxviii denarios et tertia iacet ad Bureford reddens v solidos.

Now although it is impossible to arrive at any exact estimate of the comparative importance in the shire of this *mansio*, owing to the fact that the *mansiones* of most of the chief lords are entered simply by the total numbers and total value, not by the value of each separately, yet it is not difficult to deduce from the nature of those totals that the Burford *mansio* was at any rate one of the largest in the county.

It is, therefore, the more curious that the early Inquisitions Post Mortem, in the thirteenth century, make no mention of a house as among the possessions of the manor. Nor does any early Account Roll (though one for the years 1235–9 gives expenses of the manor for three successive years) record any payment for work done, either in repairs or new building, on the manor house. It is not until 1344, in connexion with the settlement of the manor made by the Hugh le Despenser of that date, that a house is again mentioned, the *capitale messuagium* then being entered at an annual value of 2s.

That is a considerable decline from the 5s. of Domesday. But, indeed, the circumstances of the manor would lead us to expect a decline. The great men who held it in chief, with their large territories and their castles, would never need for their own use the house of this small and remote manor. The thirteenth-century tenant by sub-infeudation, John Giffard, was also a man of wide possessions, from the Cotswolds to the Welsh Border, and would be as little likely to need a house here. It may well have sunk to being no more than a residence for the steward of the manor. That some life, at any rate, went on in it we may conclude from one small indication in the Account Roll of 1235–9, an entry of money spent on leeks and cabbages and salt *ad potagium famulorum*.[1]

[1] Part III, p. 607.

These *famuli* must have been the house servants of the manor house.

Such as it was, it stood at Bury Barns. Fairly good evidence of this is given by a couple of references in the Burford Records. In the Lay Subsidy list of 1316 is a Iohannes ad Aulam ; and in the list of 1326–7, which distinguishes between the three members of the manor, Iohannes atte Halle appears among the Signett assessments.[1] More definite is the entry in the Edwardian Survey of a close called ' Hawllecrofte iacentem prope Burybarnes '.[2] But the final proof is to be drawn from the later history of the manor. When at length the agricultural portion begins to be entered in documents under a name of its own, to distinguish it from the chartered borough, the name given to it was ' the manor of Bury Barns alias Burford '.[3] Obviously that name would not be chosen at random ; it would almost certainly represent the seat of the manorial court to which the tenants of this portion owed suit ; and thus it might be advanced by itself as proof of the site of the manor house. The matter is put beyond doubt by the Deeds of Sale of the town and manor in the seventeenth century. Tanfield, Falkland, and the Lenthalls were lords of the manor. But the only manorial property conveyed in these Deeds, besides the lordship of the town, is Bury Barns. That must, therefore, on all these grounds, have been the old manor house, occupying the position of the hill-top *burh*.

Little use though its lords may have made of it, it had kings of England under its roof more than once in these early centuries. The first Royal visitor of whom we have record is Stephen, who tested at Burford two charters to the Monastery of Gloucester.[4] His visit may best be dated between 1147 and 1150. For, considering the relations between Stephen and Robert of Gloucester, it is not very likely that a grant to Gloucester by the former would have been made before

[1] Part III, pp. 594, 596. [2] Part III, p. 631.
[3] Part III, p. 624.
[4] *History and Cartulary of the Monastery of St. Peter of Gloucester* (Rolls Series, 1865), vol. ii, pp. 108, 176. The two charters have the same witnesses, so there is no reason to suppose that Stephen was here more than once.

Robert's death in 1147; nor, it may be added, very likely that before that event Stephen would have been staying on one of Robert's manors, when there was the royal domain of Wychwood close at hand.

The next king whom we know to have been here was King John. Whether he was ever here during the early years of his reign, when he actually held the manor, cannot be said. It is difficult to think that he was not, coming so often as he did to Oxford, where he seems to have been particularly fond of spending Christmas. But the only definite record of his being here occurs quite at the end of his life. It was on September 2, 1216, on his way from Cirencester, where he had been the day before, to Oxford; and he only stayed for a single night. That was little more than a month before his death; and it can hardly have been a joyous Court that the Burford folk saw gathered then round the bitter King.

Before the century closed another king visited the place, Edward I. A writ of his is dated here 1291; and he too was only here for a single night. It may be added here that Edward III was in Burford in 1329, and Richard II in 1399.[1]

Of the topography of Burford during the two centuries after Domesday we have very little information. The two mills can be placed. In the sixteenth century there is a grant by the Crown of 'two corn mills built under one roof called Burford Mills'; and we find later that mills near the bridge were called the Port Mills.[2] That name is enough to justify the conclusion that these were the mills of Domesday; and there need be no hesitation in identifying them with the two mills under one roof of the sixteenth-century grant.

We know also that the Hospital was in existence before 1226;[3] and can thus identify another occupied site. But the references during these centuries to houses do not specify their situation. At some date before 1107 two houses here were given to the Abbey of Tewkesbury by 'Ralph the Priest'; and at some date before 1205 two burgages were

[1] Pat. Roll, Rich. II, 1399, ps. II, m. 18.
[2] Part III, pp. 504.   [3] Part III, p. 568.

given to Bruern Abbey by a man with an extraordinary name,
' ex dono Lowinilapis.'.[1] Both the abbeys must have sold
these houses, since neither of them held property in Burford
at the time of the Dissolution ; and thus we are deprived of
any chance of identifying the houses.

In 1200 two messuages and a half are mentioned in a case
brought by ' Willelmus Clericus de Bureford ' and Richard
son of Simon against William of Upton and his wife Paulina,
concerning a division of property.[2] In 1193 it appears from
another partition of property that Thomas de Langley, who
was Warden of Wychwood Forest, held five messuages in the
town.

The single identification that can be made during this
period is of a house granted to the Priory of Cold Norton
circa 1250.[3] From later grants, and from the fact that it
ultimately became one of the houses held here by Brasenose
College, the house can be placed at the southern corner of
Lawrence Lane and the High Street, on the site of what was
later the King's Head Inn.[4]

Although that is the only scrap of topographical detail
among these references, the others are not without some
interest. The half-messuage, for instance, is an indication
of increasing population ; it shows that the original buildings
of the burghal tenants were beginning to be subdivided, in
order to accommodate new inhabitants unable to pay a full
burgage rent.

It is interesting also to observe that, even at this early date,
one effect of the granting of charters, and of the consequent
tenure of houses at a money rent with right of disposal by
will, was the accumulation of house property as a form of
wealth. Ralph the Priest had two houses ; William the cleric
and the other parties in 1199 dispute about two and a half
houses, which must have been a single holding, since there
is question of division between two parties ; Thomas de
Langley held five. Evidently the burgage tenure was already
producing a class of landlords, holding several of the

---

[1] Part III, p. 571.
[2] Part III, p. 566.
[3] Part III, p. 668.
[4] Part III, pp. 670–72.

M

messuages at the small burgage rent, and sub-letting them to occupiers.

This deduction becomes of some importance in connexion with estimating the population of the town at later dates in these two centuries. The first facts that we have to rely on, after the date of Domesday, are contained in the Inquisition Post Mortem of 1299. In this the 'free tenants' are entered as numbering 105. But if the burgages were in some instances grouped in single ownerships, this figure may need some modification before reckoning from it the probable total population. However, a reference of later date shows that the precaution is hardly necessary. The Survey of 6 Edward VI gives at that date only 124 full burgages in the town. There would certainly not be more than this in 1299. The conclusion therefore must be either that the accumulation of several burgages in single hands had not proceeded far; or that in this Inquisition it is of no account, the 'free tenants' being the occupiers. In the latter case, which is the more likely, the population of the town in 1299 may be put at about 500.[1]

That was not the total population of the manor, for the hamlets of Signett and Upton appear separately. In the former there were twelve villeins holding a full virgate, and three holding a half virgate, which gives fifteen households and some seventy-five inhabitants. They already held at a money rent in lieu of services, the rent for a full virgate, entered as twenty acres, being 12s. 6¾d., and for a half virgate of ten acres 6s. 3¼d. At Upton there were eight customary tenants, which would add forty persons to the total population, the whole manor of Burford thus containing by estimation about 600 people. The customary tenants of Upton were still on the old terms of tenure. A money value of their services is, indeed, entered, but in such a manner as to leave it more probable that they were not yet actually in the position of paying a money rent.

[1] The increase in the number of burgages between 1299 and 1552 may seem very small. But it has to be remembered that by the latter date there had been much subdivision of burgage tenements to accommodate the increasing population.

Evidence of the state of the population for the next two
hundred years is very scanty. The Lay Subsidy Rolls for
1316 and 1326-7 give lists of the persons assessed here to the
tax; but no later Rolls give similar lists until the Subsidy of
1524. At the same time another source of information is
removed by the fact that in 1344 Hugh le Despenser and in
1459 Isabella, Countess of Warwick, made settlements of the
manor of Burford (among other of their lands) to feoffees in
trust for their heirs, so that Inquisitions Post Mortem no
longer give details of the manor. Consequently from 1344
until well into the sixteenth century practically no estimate
of the population can be made.

Hence we are unable to see with any certainty the effects
in Burford of that event which is so terribly important in
relation to the population of England at this period, namely,
the Black Death. All that we have to go upon points to the
rather strange conclusion that some such heavy blow as fell
on the rest of the country in 1348 had fallen here some time
before 1344. In the Inquisition of that year concerning Hugh
le Despenser's request for licence to alienate the manor to
trustees for his heirs the total rental of the ' liberi et nativi
tenentes ' of the manor is entered at £14 10s. Now if we put
together the rents of the borough tenants and those of the
agricultural hamlets entered in earlier Inquisitions, we find
that in 1295-9 they amounted to £35 0s. 11¾d., and in 1307
to £37 1s. 0d. The same extraordinary decline is visible if we
take the total value of all the assets of the manor. In 1261
these amounted to £61 19s. 1d.; in 1295-9 to £55 16s. 0¾d.;
in 1307 to £62 16s. 2d.; and in 1344 to no more than
£19 16s. 4d.

Such evidence as can be gathered from the totals of Lay
Subsidies is very similar in effect. The total of a Subsidy of
a twentieth in 1326-7 was £11 8s. 9d.; the total of a Subsidy
of a tenth and a fifteenth, which should have produced at
least three times as much, in 1347 was only £19 12s. 4d.
Again, the decline occurs before the date of the Black Death.
No conclusion seems to be possible except that Burford had
been ravaged by some epidemic before 1344—perhaps a minor

incursion of the same plague. When the culminating horror came, the place suffered again. A tenth and fifteenth in 1383-4 produced only £14 1s. 4d., or £5 10s. less than even in 1347, though thirty-five years had intervened for recovery from the plague.

A few points of general interest arise from an analysis of the Subsidy Lists of 1316 and 1326-7. In the latter case separate lists are given for Burford, Upton, and Signett. The earlier list makes no distinction of this kind; but, by comparison with the later one, we find that it contains 37 Burford names, 13 Upton names, and 8 Signett names. In 1326-7 there are 48 names under Burford, 20 under Upton, and 14 under Signett.[1]

It is evident that the later figures are the more instructive ; the increase under each heading shows that there had been a stricter enumeration for assessment, and therefore a better representation of the population. Taking those figures, then, the first thing that strikes us is the increase in the population of Upton. Instead of the eight tenants of 1295 (seven in 1307), there are now twenty men of substance. This is an interesting reflection of the changes in the manorial system which were making the tenure of land less onerous, especially the substitution of money rents for services. Signett, where money rents were in operation in 1299, shows no increase in 1326-7. Upton, where the tenants were on the old service tenure in 1295 and 1307, has, since the latter date, trebled its population ; the change to money rents must have taken place there. The inducement to live in the town, which the burghal tenure offered, had disappeared.

Two other conclusions which emerge from the lists are, first, that even leaving the burghal tenants at the same number as in 1299, less than half of them were of sufficient substance to be taxed on their movable goods ; and secondly, that comparison of the amounts paid by individuals in the town and in the two hamlets shows that the people of the borough were on much the same level of assessments as the people of the agricultural settlements. These facts, in con-

[1] Part III, pp. 594-5.

junction with an inability to deduce any increase of the town population, can only mean that the Market and Gild privileges had not as yet brought much prosperity to the town.

This deduction, bearing in mind the circumstances of the time, becomes of importance in any attempt to reconstruct the general life of Burford in the fourteenth and fifteenth centuries. For we are already well into the famous Cotswold wool period; yet the Subsidy lists show us no individual or individuals of outstanding wealth. There are certain levels of assessment, to which the inhabitants of substance conform, to such a degree that regular classification would not be impossible; and all would come into one or the other class. No one is markedly better off than others who could be ranked as of the same assessment class.

The truth is, as this would lead us to expect, that the more magnificent aspect of the Cotswold trade, the wholesale dealing of the woolmen, is seen but rarely in the Burford Records. It appears occasionally, as in the licence granted in 1273 to Lambert le Fraunccis to export twenty sacks of wool; and in the Chancery cases arising out of the deals in which John Pynnok and Thomas Stanton were concerned at the end of the fifteenth century. But they are usually small affairs; Pynnok's was a matter of £92, Stanton's of £68.[1]

The business of Burford was rather in occupations subsidiary to the wool trade. These are constantly met with, as in the mention of drapers in 1250,[2] 1375,[3] and 1404,[4] a shearman in 1461,[5] tailors in 1316 and 1327,[6] dyers and weavers, and an individual described as ' le Napper ',[7] which probably indicates the occupation otherwise known as fulling—the raising of the nap on cloth. Moreover, wealthier men, when described, are clothiers, dealers in the manufactured product, not woolmen.

No reason can be given for this, unless it be that the situation of the town on a river, convenient for washing and dyeing cloth and for the erection of fulling-mills, inclined the inhabitants to woollen manufacture rather than to the production

[1] Part III, p. 616.   [2] p. 668.   [3] p. 317.   [4] p. 665.
[5] p. 670.   [6] p. 596.   [7] p. 594.

of the raw article. It is, of course, possible—and indeed likely, in view of the adornment of the Church—that some of the richer citizens of the fifteenth century, of whose occupations we have no record, were more or less regular woolmen. But Burford has no one to reckon among the great Staplers.

Thus we must see the place as engaged in woollen manufacturers and general trade. Of its mercantile life we can gather a very fair picture from the Records. Tradesmen whose occupations are mentioned (other than those just given) are a tanner,[1] some bakers,[2] a brewer,[3] an ironmonger,[4] a glover,[5] a slater,[6] some spicers (or, as we should now say, grocers),[7] butchers,[8] chandlers,[9] a cook-shop keeper,[10] and a nail-maker.[11] The description ' merchant ', which is applied to several townsmen late in the fifteenth century, needs to be interpreted with some caution.[12] In one instance a man is described as ' merchant alias mercer ', which shows that the term does not necessarily imply any very large business dealings.

But the best idea of the trade of the place is to be derived from the Letters Patent of Edward II, establishing the Bridge tolls in 1322.[13] All sorts of live stock came to market, horses, cattle, pigs, sheep, and goats ; hides of horses and oxen both fresh and tanned, fleeces of sheep, skins of goats, of deer of several kinds, of rabbits, hares, foxes, rats, and squirrels ; fresh and salt meat and bacon ; fresh and salt salmon, mullets, conger eels and fresh-water eels, stock-fish (or salt cod), and— an interesting item—' fish of Aberdeen ', which, mentioned as it is in conjunction with stock-fish, shows that red herrings were an Aberdeen export six hundred years ago. Various kinds of woven stuffs came in for sale, as samite, diaper, and baudekyn cloth, silk fabrics with and without gold embroidery, linen, and cloths of Galway and worsted. Wine and cider are mentioned, oil, honey, cheese, butter, salt, peas and beans; as also verdigris and certain unguents. Iron, lead, copper and tin, horse-shoes, cart-wheel tires, large and small nails, and

---

[1] Part III, p. 323.   [2] p. 338.   [3] p. 419.   [4] p. 613.
[5] p. 347.   [6] p. 316.   [7] p. 312.   [8] p. 321.
[9] p. 325.   [10] p. 332.   [11] p. 312.   [12] p. 426.
[13] p. 436.

brazing materials were to be had in the market; and so were wood, coal, turf, and faggots.

When increasing use and more careful preservation of written documents begin to reveal more of the topography of Burford, the extent of the town becomes apparent. Until well into the sixteenth century it did not reach up the steeper part of the hill. It formed, roughly speaking, a square between the river on the north and the line of Sheep Street and Witney Street on the south, the Priory on the west and the further end of Witney Street on the east. For thus limiting the mediaeval Burford there are several reasons. One is that no documents of this period refer to any houses in what is now the upper part of the town. Moreover, when houses in that direction do begin to occur, in the later six-teenth century, they are described as lying, not in the High Street simply, but as ' in the High Street on the hill ', or some-times merely ' on the hill '.[1] Clearly, therefore, they were in a place which, not having been hitherto commonly mentioned in documents, had to be specially defined. Finally, it is to be noticed that more than once the early descriptions of houses employ a form of phrase which could not have arisen if the town had had its present shape. A grant of 1413 speaks of a house standing about where the Grammar School stands to-day as being ' in the eastern part of Burford '.[2] A house in that position could only be described to-day as in the northern part. But in a town not of greater extent from north to south than from east to west, the part near the Church would be the eastern part. Similarly there are descriptions of houses near the Priory, which we should equally regard as in the northern area of the town, as ' in the western part '. The High Street then divided the place into halves.

Within this square, the plan of the streets was exactly as it is to-day. The High Street, Witney Street, Sheep Street, and both the lanes leading to the Church are mentioned. The modern names of these two lanes, however, are not

---

[1] This distinction still survives. Burford people usually speak of ' the hill ' as something different from the High Street.

[2] Part III, p. 360.

found. They are called, as a rule, the upper lane, and the lower lane, leading to the Church. But the latter has, in one deed of 1493, the queer name of Bordemwetlane—queer, but, on a superficial view, probably descriptive of its normal condition. References to Church Green and Guildenford Lane are frequent. The street leading to the Priory was called St. John's Street; and Priory Lane, which has now extended its name to this street, was only the narrow way leading up behind the present Lamb Inn. Both sides of Sheep Street and both sides of Witney Street were built upon, but not to the full length of the modern streets in either case. The end of Sheep Street on the south side is described in the sixteenth century as newly built upon ;[1] and a description of some premises in Witney Street in 1423 as situated in ' le Newelond '[2] implies that at that date fresh ground was being occupied there.

Grants of houses at this time so invariably specify their situation that a rather more detailed picture can be attempted. The Vicarage stood where it does now, since an early deed concerning houses on the site of Cob Hall speaks of them as standing between the Vicarage and the river. A little higher up was a house belonging to the Abbey of Keynsham, and somewhere near the corner of the road leading to the Priory was a forge. On the opposite side of the High Street, the ground between the two lanes to the Church was occupied by a group of houses and gardens, a small pasture-close, and a stable. The corner house on Lawrence Lane was the one already mentioned as belonging to the Priory of Cold Norton. Next to it in Lawrence Lane were a house and garden belonging to Thomas Spicer, and then came the pasture-close with the stable at its edge, curving round by the churchyard much as the Grammar School site curves round to-day. At the Grammar School corner stood another house, and next to it in Church Lane a cottage and a bake-house. Between this and the High Street came a garden with another house. On the other side of Church Lane was a garden, as there is to-day, and a large house towards the High Street

<hr>

[1] Part III, p. 342.   [2] Part III, p. 669.

PLATE VIII. FIFTEENTH-CENTURY ARCH
HIGH STREET (W. SIDE)

LEADING TO A ROW OF COTTAGES CALLED THE COLLEGE

end called Broadgates. The site of the Almshouses, until their erection, was open, consisting of two pasture-closes; but there was a house on the site of the present Church School next the churchyard, the tenement of one John Bavork, from whom the site was for a long time known as ' Bavorks '.

Returning to the High Street, the first spot above Church Lane on the eastern side which we can determine is the Cock Row, not far below the Witney Street corner; it has now been cleared away, but a gap in the line of houses shows where it was. At the upper corner of Witney Street the house on the turning and the house next to it, now the Bull, are mentioned. On the other side of the High Street the most easily identified house is the Novum Hospitium Angulare, which stood at the Sheep Street corner on ground now occupied by two houses.[1] The only shop of the period definitely mentioned as such was beside the George archway, on the south of it. Lower down on that side, behind the houses in the angle formed by the High Street and the road to the Priory, lay an open space called Salmon's Close.

In Witney Street two houses east of the Bull back gate, in one of which a fifteenth-century doorway could quite lately be seen, are mentioned. So is the barn opposite that back gate, which stood then, as it does now, at the corner of an opening from the street; at that time, however, the opening led through into the High Street by way of the Cock Row. The further end of the street gave upon small enclosed fields, much as it does to-day.

In Sheep Street the Gild of the town had a tenement, standing apparently in rather extensive grounds, about the middle of the south side of the street. At the further end on that side the street was open to a pasture-close with a dove-cot on it, which gave it the name of the Culverhey. The site of the present Bank house was occupied by a house with a garden, which, judging by later mentions of it, must have been a good-sized messuage.

---

[1] As some attempt has been made to identify this inn with the Lamb, it may be as well to remark that the site is described beyond all possibility of question in the Records. See CH 5, Part III, p. 421.

Several closes and garden grounds not attached to houses are mentioned. The area of mediaeval Burford would easily accommodate all the houses we need allow for, and yet leave space for a good many open plots. At present there are within the limits given some one hundred and seventy houses, and a great deal of garden space behind them; so that one hundred and twenty burgages or so would not have crowded the ground. But many of the closes were on the steep hill above the inhabited space. On the west side of the hill they belonged chiefly to the demesne land of the manor;[1] but on the east side also was a succession of small enclosures reaching out along the slopes as far as the houses reached in Witney Street, and these would account for a good many of the pasture-closes mentioned.

The manor house, standing at the top of this open rise of the hill, comes at last more definitely into Burford history in 1428. In that year the demesne was leased at farm to Robert Atkyns for three lives, a tenancy that would run through a great part of the rest of the century. There is, of course, no certainty that this was the first tenant occupation of the place, but it is the first of which we have record. Atkyns held the whole of the manor land; and we may attribute conjecturally to this date the fine cruciform barn still existing at Bury Barns; it has all the characteristics of a fifteenth-century structure of this class. It is possible also that some remains of old building at the back of the present dwelling-house are of this period; and if so, it will hardly be too much to suggest that Atkyns's tenancy marks a new stage in the history of the manorial domain, the lands being no longer kept in hand under the management of a steward, but leased out in a way which would be very likely to cause the buildings to be improved for the tenant's residence.

The town of Burford, thus planned, would have presented not only a smaller, but also a much humbler, appearance than the town of to-day. For the houses up to the end of the fifteenth century must have been very largely of wooden

[1] See Part III, p. 334.

construction. In some cases there would be a lower storey of stone, with an upper storey of timber and plaster. But the majority must have been built throughout of wattle and daub between timber uprights based on a low plinth of two or three courses of stonework. The extent to which timber entered into house-building here, even as late as the fifteenth century, is shown by a clause in the lease of a house in Witney Street, dated 1404, by which the tenant is allowed, subject to the advice of the lessors, to cut down trees on the premises for repairing the house.[1] But it is shown more conclusively by the fact that there is no mention of quarries in any of the manorial documents until 1435. There cannot, therefore, have been any considerable demand for building-stone until, at any rate, the latter part of the fourteenth century; if there had been, quarries, as a valuable manorial asset, would have been sought for in a stone country like this, and opened at an earlier date.

Three are entered on the manorial Account Roll of 1435–6.[2] One was a freestone quarry called Whiteladies Quarry; the two others, of slating stone, were called Sterte Quarry and Le Wort Quarry. All three appear again in the Survey of 6 Edward VI, the first as Whichelate Quarry, Sterte under the same name, and the third as ' le Slatte quarry lying in Signett '. With this information they can all be identified. The ground called Sturt is in the extreme south-east part of Burford parish, and the site of an old quarry can be seen there. The only old freestone quarry in the place is the one now called Upton Quarry, which later supplied stone for the building of Christ Church, Oxford, and for the rebuilding of St. Paul's Cathedral in London. The reference to the remaining quarry as lying in Signett identifies Le Wort as the old quarry pit on the east of the Lechlade road about a mile from the town.

The fact that the only freestone quarry was at later dates supplying stone for great buildings elsewhere is proof that it had not been very heavily worked for building in Burford. This supports the view that, even when stone began to be

---

more freely used, it was not as a rule employed above the ground-floor storey, the upper parts of the houses being still of timber with wattle and daub filling.[1]

That would account for a certain architectural incongruity which must have puzzled many observers in Burford, namely, the existence of fine old pointed archways in what are now insignificant positions. These, it has been remarked by a distinguished architect, are the entrance doorways of the larger type of burgage houses here.[2] Nowadays they open only into narrow yards, or else into little alleys of cottages; while nothing in the buildings in which they are set is of an impressive character. The explanation, given the nature of the original houses, is not difficult to provide. The archways stood in the centre of the house frontages, with living rooms on either side and above, and led through the buildings to the gardens, closes, barns, wool-sheds, and workshops of their owners. Now, as increasing population necessitated division of the burgage tenements, a house of this kind offered itself peculiarly to the purpose. The entrances under the archway to either side of the original house would instantly facilitate division into two separate dwellings. At the same time ease of access through the archway to ground at the back would facilitate the building of rows of cottages there, on the courtyard or close. Once the tenement had been thus dealt with, the timber and plaster upper storey would, in later times when stone was more freely used, be very easily destroyed, and very likely to be destroyed, to make way for new ideas and a more complete partition of the building. It can be seen in this way how nothing of the original structure would remain except the arch ; and how, by the very nature of the case, the arch would survive amid a number of small houses having nothing in common with its own character.

These entries, then, together with the few remaining

[1] This in turn gives yet another proof that the mediaeval town lay within the limits we have set for it. A great number of houses there, though plastered surfaces disguise the construction, have the upper stories of this ancient character ; whereas only two or three houses on the hill arè so built.

[2] *Old Cottages, Farmhouses, &c., in the Cotswold District,* by W. G. Davie and E. G. Dawber (London 1905), p. 62.

PLATE IX. EARLY SEVENTEENTH-CENTURY
HOUSE IN HIGH STREET

THE CELLAR SHOWN ON P. 182 IS UNDER THE HOUSE ON THE LEFT

specimens of timber and wattle work in ground-floor storeys,[1] are some of the oldest survivals of domestic architecture which can be definitely indicated in Burford. Others of the same type, escaping the first subdivisions only to be more radically altered and rebuilt later on, must have perished without leaving even an archway. But, as these would be the most important houses of the town, they cannot have been very numerous. The smaller burgage house, such as the one in the High Street of which we have the dimensions in 1403 [2]— 20 feet long and 23 feet deep—would not have room for this kind of arched entrance.

One other architectural feature of Burford may be noted in connexion with the documents of this period. A grant of 1404 gives the dimensions of a shop in the High Street.[3] It was 17½ feet long, 7 feet broad, and 7 feet high. The curiously shallow depth, taken in conjunction with the separate sale of the shop, without a tenement, indicates that the shop cannot have been an entirely separate structure, and yet was not part of a house proper. But being sold thus it must have had some permanence of building. If, as seems therefore likely, it was a kind of lean-to erection against the front of a house, it may be suggested that the stone-slated pent-houses, which are a feature of several frontages in the High Street, represent the very early Burford shops. Most of them are now more or less disguised by the throwing out under them of bay-windows to the ground-floor rooms of the houses behind them. But the dimensions of one or two which remain partly open can be seen at a glance to correspond fairly well with those recorded in the grant of 1404. Originally they would be mere shelters on wooden uprights, just wide enough to protect a counter for the display of a tradesman's goods, the mediaeval house being so badly lighted that it would be necessary to bring the goods out of doors on a market day.

These glimpses of the ancient town can be completed

---

[1] For instance, a piece in a side passage by Riverside House, and a piece in the courtyard of a house in Sheep Street, occupied by the author.
[2] Part III, p. 333.   [3] Part III, p. 333.

from the documents with some information as to the common
arable fields. A terrier of the Rectory and glebe lands in
1501[1] gives indications which allow us to delimit roughly
the extent of the fields at the end of the fourteenth century;
and also to see how widely cultivation had expanded by that
time. The Inquisition of 1299 enters as manorial tenants
twelve virgaters and three half-virgaters, and puts the
virgate at twenty acres.[2] In 1300, therefore, the extent of
the East and West Fields would be about 270 acres each;
which implies that the Fields barely reached to Signett on
the south, and did not reach beyond the Shilton road on the
east and the Westwell road on the west. By 1500 most, if
not all, of the land within the parish boundaries south of the
Witney–Northleach road was under cultivation, and the open
fields had thus reached almost their fullest extent. For
furlongs are recorded abutting upon Westwell Way, upon
White Hill and a hedge near there, and upon both sides of
Bampton Way.[3] Now White Hill and the hedge take us
quite to the eastern boundary of the parish. Bampton Way
cannot be the modern Bampton road, which is altogether
outside the parish, but must be the footpath from Signett
across to the Shilton road and thence into the Bampton road
near Stonelands; the reference to both sides of it gives us
as our southern limit the Shil Brook, again the parish
boundary. The western limit is not so clear. The only
furlongs naming the Westwell road lay east of it. But it is
curious that the terrier speaks of furlongs on this side of
the common lands as lying in 'the East-West field', not

---

[1] John Thorpe records in 'The Book of the Vicaridge Rights' (see
p. 137) that on a certain occasion he saw John Pryor carry off from a house
in Burford a terrier of the Rectory lands. Can this be the identical
terrier? Thorpe says he thinks it was written by Symon Randolph,
Town Clerk at that time; and if so obviously this is not the one. But
Thorpe may have been mistaken, and the fact that this terrier is now in
the Bodleian Library with other diocesan documents suggests that it
passed into the Bishop's hands with the rest of the Rectory property. It
is a tempting addition that the family of Pryor were certainly living in
the early eighteenth century in the Rectory house. The terrier will be
found transcribed in full on pp. 673–680.

[2] See Part III, p. 582.

[3] See the maps of the fields on pp. 194 and 227.

the West Field '. It may be conjectured from this formula
that the fields did· by this time extend beyond the Westwell
road, and that, as this road made so marked a division, the
West Field had come to be regarded as in two parts, of which
the older portion (in which Rectory and glebe lands would be
likely to lie) was called, for the sake of clearness, the ' eastern
west field '. If that is so, the Burford Fields on this side also
had reached their full extent;[1] though not the parish boundary,
Upton Fields intervening in that direction. At the White
Hill end it is doubtful whether any land had yet been taken
into cultivation north of the road along the ridge ; the only
named furlongs abutting on this road lay south of it ; but
at the other end the Fields stretched across this road and
already came down to the end of Sheep Street. It may be
added that the terrier shows that the manor demesne was by
the East Field, between the present Lechlade and Shilton
roads ; the Lechlade road was at this time known as Dean-
acre (or Denacre or Dynacre) Way.

In the East Field we have nineteen furlongs named : Hen
furlong, Brodhedden furlong, Bampton Way furlong, the
furlong over Bampton Way, Coppedslade furlong, Bellam (or
Beldam) furlong, Ridgway furlong, Esterhen furlong, Westerhen
furlong, Offley furlong, Sawnfyfe furlong, Whitston furlong,
Comfast furlong, Down furlong, Hedsondye furlong, Stertwell
furlong, Uphed furlong, Hiot, and Monsty furlong.   In the
West Field twenty are named : Cheyney furlong, Clay furlong,
Denacre furlong, Cleyt furlong, Westwell Way East furlong,
Long furlong, Middle furlong, North furlong, Fuldenslade,
the Worthy, Old Hill furlong, the Gorse, Fulden Hill furlong,
Hillslade, Short furlong, Brighthill furlong, Ridgway furlong,
Ferny furlong, Whitslade furlong, and Elerstub furlong.[2]

---

[1] It may also be remarked that one of the named furlongs is ' Westwell
Way East furlong ', which suggests that there was a ' Westwell Way West
furlong '.

[2] Mr. St. Clair Baddeley has kindly suggested explanations of some of
these curious names. ' Brodhedden ' may, he thinks, be ' Broad Headland ', and ' Hedsondye ', ' Sandy Headland '. ' Fulden ' may be ' Foul
Deane ', a muddy hollow. ' Coppedslade ' is explained by· its abutting
upon ' Copped Cross ', a ridged cross-roads, perhaps the point where the
path to Bampton crosses the Shilton road on a rise of ground. ' Hiot '

Upton had its own arable fields farther to the west. They
appear to have lain at this time in a square of which the
eastern boundary was a roadway turning out of the Witney–
Northleach road a little to the east of the Cirencester turning
and running straight towards Westwell, and the western
boundary was the boundary of Burford Parish, while the
southern boundary corresponded with the line through
Signett and the northern was the Witney–Northleach road.
This square is divided into two triangular halves by the
Cirencester road running diagonally across it; and each
half contained about 250 acres at the Enclosure. This,
while more than enough to accommodate the seven virgaters
and one half-virgater of 1307, is too little for the twenty
inhabitants of Upton on the Lay Subsidy of 1326–7.[1] We
must therefore suppose that in this case the land on the
northward face of the hill, across the Witney–Northleach
road and towards the lower road to Little Barrington, which
was included in Upton Fields at the time of the Enclosure,
had already been taken into cultivation to accommodate
the new tenants brought to Upton by the substitution of
money rents for services. That gives a total area, at the
Enclosure, of over 800 acres; which, at twenty acres to the
virgate, would exactly correspond to the holdings of twenty
virgaters.[2]

The common hay meadow is only referred to during this

may be ' High Yate ', a furlong near a gate on a rise of ground, or ' Hey
Gate ', the gate in a hedge. ' Monsty ' may be ' mossy '. ' Uphed ' may
again be named from the headland, and be ' Upper Headland '. ' Cleyt '
may mean clayey (Mr. Baddeley compares the dialect word ' clitty ',
for ground that cakes); but it is odd that there should have been a ' Clay '
furlong also. ' The Worthy ' is clearly named from ' Worth ', a farm or
dwelling, which would perhaps place this furlong near Signett. ' Stertwell '
is placed by the surviving name of Sturt Farm; the meaning, a tail or
tongue of land, implies an outlying piece of ground. ' Elerstub ' I take to
be ' Elder-tree Stump '.

[1] It must, of course, be borne in mind that a virgate of twenty acres
means twenty acres in each Field, one field being fallowed each year.
Thus forty acres has to be allowed for each holding. The same allowance
has to be made in calculating the extent of the Burford Fields.

[2] In the 1552 Survey the two Upton Fields are not, as in the Burford
Fields, an East and a West Field, but a North and a South Field. This
agrees with the natural divisions by old roads, both in the case of the
small original square and the larger later area.

period as 'commune pratum', without any name; but it can be seen, by comparing early gifts of meadow land to the Church with later lists of the Church lands, that the meadow was that known later as High Mead. It has already been described as lying to the east of the town, along the line of the Witney road close to the river. It was a lot meadow of the usual type, since a gift of meadow land in 1396 contains the phrase 'sicut per sortem acciderit'; and a grant of two half-acres in 1422 has the more specific phrase 'sicut in sorte Abbatis et sorte de Whitemeyes acciderit'.[1] These phrases need, perhaps, some explanation.

Hay meadows were of great value in the mediaeval manor. They were not possessed by every community, being dependent upon the neighbourhood of a river. It has been calculated that, on an average, meadow land was reckoned at from six to ten times the value of arable; and the Survey of 1552 shows that at Burford a single acre of meadow was the equivalent holding for a virgate of twenty acres of arable. Consequently the meadow and the arable were controlled by the early communities in quite different ways. In the arable a man held his various acre strips permanently; a strip he once acquired was always his. But for the meadow, since it was so valuable, a system was devised whereby the strips might change hands every year, so that each in turn might have his chance of getting the crop from the better parts, and no one would be permanently confined to the poorer parts. This was achieved by an annual casting of lots. But again, if the lots had been cast once for the whole of each man's holding, sufficient variation might not be secured. Therefore the hay land was divided into a certain number of meads, three, four, or more, and the lots were cast in each portion. Thus a right to an acre means, not a single acre, but an acre each time the lots were cast. In the Burford meadow there seem to have been four such divisions, so that an acre in this case would mean four acres.

Hence a man's holding in the meadow was not like his holding in the arable, a definite piece of ground to be described

----

[1] See Part III, p. 421.

N

by its position ; it was only a right to so much ground, which might be in one spot one year and in quite a different spot the next year. Obviously, however, it would soon become necessary for a man owning rights in the meadow to be able to describe them in some definite way for documentary purposes when he wished to sell his land, for instance. To meet this requirement the lots were named. In one case in which these ancient customs are still in operation, the old lots are cast with small balls of some hard wood—holly or box—on each of which a name is written, and every man's holding is known by one of those names.[1] Each time the ball with that name comes out of the bag, he receives his acre or half-acre of ground for that year's mowing. Thus he is able, if he wishes to describe his meadow rights for purposes of sale, to say that he owns an acre or a half-acre of So-and-So, using the name on the ball. The gift of meadow land to Burford Church in 1422 shows that precisely this system was in use here ; the donor describes his gift by the names of the lots.[2]

Of the men of mediaeval Burford there are a few who come down to us as more than shadows. We have, for instance, our first glimpse of the men of authority in John Wenryche and Thomas Spicer, who drew up the Gild Certificate in 1382 and were frequently in demand for the witnessing of grants and taking charge of trusts. Then there is the company of men who have writ their names large in the glories of Burford Church, and have been more fitly commemorated in another chapter—the Spicers, Leggare, Bishop, and Pynnok. Pynnok we may know better than most of them, because his will which has come down among the Records contains more domestic detail than the will, also among the Records, of Henry Bishop. It is in one sense, perhaps, disappointing ; for, in comparison with wills of the same period in other towns, it betrays the fact that the more important Burford Burgess was less well off than men of his class elsewhere. His house-

---

[1] I have described the lot-meadow customs in this case in the *Economic Journal*, vol. xx, no. 77, and vol. xxii, no. 85.

[2] For the later names of the lots at Burford, and the meadow customs in the eighteenth century, see Part III, pp. 408–9.

hold gear—tables and chests, sheets and blankets, brass pans and cooking vessels, brewing plant, wooden platters, tin and silver spoons, warming stoves, and so on—is of a fair level of comfort for the time. But his personal gear is very modest—a saddle and bridle, a ' poll-ax ' and a sword, for his journeyings ; a dyed girdle or two, a cloak or two and some pieces of amber. One phrase in the will casts an interesting sidelight on the life of the good-sized burgage houses. A certain chest is among the bequests, and is described as ' stantem in camera que vocatur Hardyngs chamber '. This curious name was difficult to account for until an entry in the Eynsham Cartulary illuminated it. In the list of expenses for the year 1471 appears : ' Et in diversis pannis lineis emptis de Iohanne Hardyng de Burefford xxs. vid.' [1] Now Hardyng is not a name found among those constantly asso-ciated with Pynnok in the Burford Records ; yet we should have expected to find it if he was a Burford man. It may be conjectured that the name ' Hardyngs chamber ' is a strange little indication of a system of partnership. Burford men owning good-sized houses may have kept a room for the use of merchants and traders coming to the town from elsewhere, who may thus have acquired a sufficient status to avail themselves of the privileges of Burford residents in the market, and may in turn have provided for their Burford hosts similar privileges in their own towns.

More vividly human even than those of Pynnok's will are some of the touches to be found in the early files of the Chancery. There we meet persons like John Sclatter and John Stowe, whom we might otherwise have taken for unexceptionable fellows, going ' with force of arms ' to the house of John Dyer and carrying off in one encounter a horse, in another a mixed lot of goods, and in yet another a maid servant whom they detained for a year and a half—an epic feud. There is much human nature too in the complaint of John Hatter that he could not obtain justice against Thomas Alys and John Irnemonger, who had assaulted him

---

[1] *Cartulary of the Abbey of Eynsham*, edited by the Rev. H. E. Salter (Oxford Hist. Soc. 1908), vol. ii, p. lxxxvii.

and his wife, because Alys and Irnemonger were on such good terms with the Sheriff and Deputy-Sheriff of the county. Again, Pynnok's gifts to the Church are laid open to some criticism by the fact that he had a debt of £80 outstanding, which his pious generosity rendered him unable to meet.[1]

But a wider horizon has to be added to our picture to include some solid men of Burford before we leave our account of the Middle Ages. The inscription, now lost, on the tomb of John Pynnok who died in 1480[2] records him as ' eldest son of Thomas Pinnock gentleman formerly of the Society of Gray's Inn ' ; which shows that the family had ideas and associations beyond Burford and its wool industries. John Stowe, again, was of sufficient consequence to marry a Berkshire heiress ; indeed, it is through him that the well-known family of Eyston of East Hendred obtained that manor and estate. John Stowe had married Maud de Arches, heiress of the Turberville estates at East Hendred. His daughter, Isabel, married John Eyston, and as her father's heir brought the estates with her. The Stowe arms—argent a chevron gules between three crows proper, beaked and legged or— are still quartered by the Eystons.[3] Yet another of our citizens must have had a life more interesting than any of these. The Bill of Attainder passed in 1485 by Henry VII's first Parliament, against Richard III and his adherents, which opens with the resounding names of John Duke of Norfolk and Thomas Earl of Surrey, ends with the name of William Brampton of Burford. The name of Brampton is found at intervals in our Records from the late fourteenth century onwards, the first William Brampton being sometimes described as ' of Oxford '. He seems to have been followed by a Thomas Brampton, and then by this William of the Attainder who is often to be seen in Burford annals going about his business as a mercer and dealing with house property. There is nothing to show how he became involved in affairs of State and in such high company. Seven years

---

[1] Part III, p. 614.

[2] Not the Pynnock just previously mentioned, for the will of that Pynnock is dated 1473 and he died in 1474 ; see p. 117.

[3] See *Visitations of Berkshire*. Harl. Soc. Publications, vol. lvi (1907).

after his death the Act of Attainder, so far as it concerned himself and his heirs, was reversed on the petition of his sister and heir, then the wife of Hugh Johnson, a Burford man.[1] This, however, did not restore all the property Brampton had forfeited : he had owned the George Inn, and this had been granted by Henry VII to one of his household—John Basket, and after Basket's death Henry VIII granted it to William Gower, one of his Grooms of the Chamber.[2] Brampton appears to have been the only person who ever brought Burford into the perilous eminence of an Act of Attainder.

Signs of increasing wealth in the place are frequent in the Records throughout a great part of the fifteenth century. Some are direct, such as the gifts to the Church and the Gild, the foundation of the Almshouses, and the institution of Charities for the poor. Another indication is the constant traffic in house property, with a general tendency towards the acquisition of houses by Burford residents from owners living elsewhere.[3] A part of the apparent enrichment should be attributed, doubtless, to the easier command of currency rather than to actual advance in wealth. Nevertheless, a certain increase in material prosperity is, at this time, to be seen in the town.

The aspect of the place was beginning to change, from the freer use of stone in domestic building, this improvement being dictated in the main by sheer necessity. The early timber building would not be very durable, especially if neglected ; and the number of references in sixteenth-century Records to houses in decay shows that a considerable amount of rebuilding must now have become necessary. It would be helped forward, also, by the more vigorous working of the freestone quarry, as its value had become apparent, and by the influence of the skilled masons at work on the Church in this period of its enlargement and adornment.

Certain remains of the domestic building of this time— the latter half of the fifteenth century—are not open to the

---

[1] *Rot. Parl.*, vol. vi, pp. 276, 454.   [2] See Part III, p. 653.
[3] See the Early Chancery Proceedings *passim*, as well as Deeds and Grants in the Burford Records.

casual visitor of to-day. Behind many a comparatively
uninteresting Burford frontage—tucked away in back courts
or surviving incongruously in later pieces of building—is
a considerable number of archways and window openings of
early date ; and one of the most curious features of Burford,

for the inquiring mind, is the manner in which its houses,
when seen from their backs, reveal a quite different architectural history from that which their frontages suggested.

Of fifteenth-century survivals three examples may be
particularly noted. One is the arch with ball-flower ornament
to be seen in the back wall of the forge of Messrs. Howse
and Son, on the west side of the High Street. This house has

a fine arched passage-way from the street. The second is
a stone-vaulted cellar with a central pillar of stone under
London House—a noble and interesting piece of domestic
building. The third, and much the most important specimen,
is the cottage beside the Bull Inn back gate, and next to
the Mason's Arms. Here, incorporated now in the party wall,
is a row of four pointed arches, rising from what might be
termed large and strong mullions rather than pillars (they
are not circular or square, but narrow and deep uprights

shaped like window mullions), the row continuing through
the back wall of the cottage room, and appearing again by
the staircase behind the room.[1]   Along the row of arches,
at the level of the spring of the arch from the ' mullions ',
runs a wide shelf of stone, dividing the series of arches into
a series of upper and lower recesses. In the outer wall of the
cottage at the back are two pointed arches joined together
at right angles to one another and springing from the same
pillar at their junction, one arch a trifle larger than the other.[2]
In an outhouse entered through one of these arches is yet
a third arch, with remains of a billet-pattern in the moulding.

[1] The arches are interrupted by a chimney-breast.   See Plate X.
[2] Illustrated on p. 182.

This same house was the one that, until recent years, had a fifteenth-century chimney above it: the chimney rose in fact above the very wall in which the extraordinary row of arches survives, and a curious little stone bracket is now just below where the chimney used to stand. At the other end of the block of building of which the cottage forms a part is a piece of very ancient structure in which was a pointed archway, deeply moulded, with Decorated carving above it.[1]

It is natural, perhaps, that remains such as these, and the vaulted cellar, should be popularly explained as relics of 'chapels', or associated with the Priory, in the belief that pointed arches must be, in some way, ecclesiastical. But such belief is groundless; and, in the case of the many-arched cottage, it can be demonstrated to be wrong; for this house adjoining the Bull back gate can be identified in the Records of Burford as far back as 1500. It is practically certain, too, that the house given to the Church by John Pinnock in 1473 stood close by. And in neither of these cases do the early deeds make any mention of chapels or of buildings of an ecclesiastical character. Nor, indeed, is any such explanation required. A rich burgess, building his house of stone in the later part of the fifteenth century, might well construct such a cellar as the one beneath London House or adorn his dwelling with the Witney Street arches—arches which were a normal feature of building work of the time. Exactly what purpose the row of arches with deep shelves was made to serve may not be easy to determine, but that they belonged to a domestic building all the available evidence goes to show. Of the general architectural style that the new ideas in building developed at this time we have happily one or two almost complete examples left. Means of recognizing the type is afforded us by the ability to date the Almshouse structure.[2] Bishop obtained his licence to erect it in 1456, and his will, made in 1478, contains no provision for the building, which must therefore have been finished by that date. Although, as a tablet on the building records, it was to some extent rebuilt in 1828, it obviously retains most of its original

[1] This wall collapsed in July 1919. See Plate I.   [2] See Plate II.

PLATE X. CELLAR UNDER LONDON HOUSE
HIGH STREET

features. Of these the principal ones are narrow doorways with a pointed arch ; square-headed windows divided by stonework into more than one light [1] ; a flat frontage ; and a long, unbroken roof-line.

If we look at the house standing near by, at the southern corner of Church Lane and the High Street, it is easy to see in it precisely the kind of domestic building which would result from carrying out in the early Tudor period, on a rather ampler scale and with the modifications arising in an interval of twenty or thirty years, the architectural type visible in the Almshouse. The flat frontage, the unbroken roof-line, the square-headed windows, are immediately recognizable, though · the doorway shows a later date of building and some of the windows have been mutilated by alterations. But the whole building is loftier, showing a greater height allotted to each storey ; dormers in the roof give it a third storey ; and the windows, while taller and wider, are also much plainer, and of a more strictly domestic order. It can hardly be doubted, comparing this structure with the other, that this house gives us very distinctly the new type of stone-built burgage at its best, [2] perhaps some thirty or forty years later than the Almshouse.

From it we can recognize, especially by looking at upper storeys, which have suffered less than the ground floors reconstructed for shop premises, several houses of the period, of differing sizes. They may all be dated within a space of about a hundred years, that being the period during which the style lasted. As we can date its origin, so we can fix the time at which it gave way to another type. In the latter part of the sixteenth century houses were built by Simon Wisdom, who recorded the date in some cases on tablets let into the walls. Thus we know that the tenement by the bridge, which

---

[1] The Decorated character of these windows lends colour to the suggestion that the masons at work on the church had their influence on the new era of building in the town. The square-headed doorway which is now the main entrance to the Almshouse is obviously of rather later date.

[2] The preservation of this house is due to Mr. E. J. Horniman. It was on the verge of irretrievable ruin when he bought it, and carried out the admirably directed repairs which have saved it in all its characteristic dignity. By the clearing away of a modern structure at one end the original proportions of the house have been most happily revealed.

so charmingly closes the view down the High Street, is of the year 1576.[1] It shows one development in particular from the type we have been considering, so marked as to constitute a new style. The windows of the uppermost floor are not set back in the roof as dormers, but are brought out to the line of the frontage in bold gables rising nearly as high as the ridge-line of the roof. The result is that the roof-line no longer strikes the eye as straight and rigid; it is in effect broken by the tall gables rising in front of it and carrying their ridges back to it; moreover, the long gutters or valleys at the junction of these gables with the roof break the upper structure into bays. The type at its best is a worthy successor to the earlier Tudor type, plain yet dignified, not concerned with ornament, but achieving distinction by its varied lines and proportions.

Again, as in the previous case, the dating of an example enables us to recognize the work of this period elsewhere in the town. In general the square-headed doorways and windows persist; but in a few cases where a larger entrance was required (as at the George Inn) a depressed arch is found. One building in Sheep Street is interesting, as the single instance in Burford in which modification of the type becomes reminiscent of a building style seen in Chipping Campden and other Cotswold towns; the frontage line, instead of being flat, is carried out in two bays rising to the line of the eaves.[2]

The great increase in stone building would by itself have made a very striking difference in the outward aspect of Burford. But to it must be added the advance of the town up the hill. This appears to have taken place only in the latter half of the sixteenth century. No house on the hill displays the characteristics of the early Tudor type of domestic building; but there are several, including one at the very top on the west side, which can be assigned at a glance to the Elizabethan type. Moreover, it is not until about 1570 that we have documentary references to houses on the hill. Even then the town did not there present the continuous lines of house-fronts that the older streets must have presented. Descriptions

[1] See Plate III.   [2] See Plate XIV.

of houses on the hill frequently give, as the boundary on one side or the other, 'the land' of some other owner, not another tenement; so that clearly many open spaces were left.

Otherwise the ground-plan of the town remained as we have seen it in the preceding period. All the principal streets appear under the same names, with the addition that now the name of Church Lane is found. Curiously enough, the lower lane to the church is not mentioned at all on the Survey of 1552. The explanation probably is (as we might easily suppose from the look of the lane to-day) that at the date of the Survey there were no houses there to be recorded among the town tenements. The ground had, in our view of the place during the fourteenth and fifteenth centuries, been mostly gardens and closes, with a fringe of houses at the corners of the High Street and towards Church Green and the upper lane. What tenements there were in the lower lane may very likely have been but a few small and ancient dwellings of the twelfth and thirteenth centuries surviving from the Domesday settlement near the *Burh*. They would by this time have disappeared; so that the only houses to be entered on the Survey would be in such positions that they would be entered as either in the High Street or in Church Lane. The latter name included, for the purposes of this document, Church Green, since the Almshouses are described as in Church Lane.

We can, however, add to our ground-plan two by-ways not previously mentioned. The lane leading out of Witney Street opposite Gildenford Lane appears as Batts Lane. The continuation of it up the hill to the top road seems to be indicated by the entry on the Survey of a certain way which the tenants of Holwell have the right to use for taking their sheep to the water at Gildenford; no other lane in Burford would be so likely to have had this purpose.

It may be added that the first mention of the Tolsey by that name occurs in 1561. There is no previous reference to the actual building in which the Bailiffs had held the Borough Court; but the Tolsey, even as it stands to-day after much repair and reconstruction, retains enough ancient building to show that, although this is the first occurrence of the name in the Records, it was applied to the old Court House. Proof, if any were needed, of the truth of the tradition that it consisted of an upper storey carried on pillars is provided by an entry in 1579 of a payment for repairing ' the pillars and stairs ' of the Tolsey.[1] Yet the substructure must have been to some extent enclosed towards the back, for there is a lease, dated 1580, of a shop ' adjoining to the Tolsey and lying next to Sheep Street '.[2] It is unlikely that this shop would have stood on ône side or the other, where the openings from Sheep Street led round, leaving the Tolsey as a kind of island. The more probable situation would be at the back ; and in fact no traces of old pillars can be seen in as much of the back wall as is now visible.

This was the Burford—a bright and prosperous little Burford with its fresh stone buildings, and green with its closes and garden grounds—which Queen Elizabeth saw when she paid the visit recorded with so much satisfaction in the Corporation Memorandum Book.[3] She came, as the record shows, from Langley, being there doubtless on a visit to the old royal hunting lodge, since she was not at that time on one of her famous Progresses through her kingdom ; and she received the ' purse of gold ' (in this case containing twenty angels) which was the form wherein her subjects were expected to display their gratification at sight of her.

It appears that she must have been here again at a later date, though of this we have no local record. In September 1592 she was making a Progress, and having come from London by way of Newbury, Ramsbury, and Cirencester, she was entertained for some days at Sudeley Castle.[4] Thence she went to Woodstock, and so to Oxford. Now Lord Burghley's diary of èvents in that month includes the following entries : [5]

Sep. 9. The Q. cam to Sudley Castell.
Sep. 14. To Shyrborn, Dottons houss. Teyntonbre. (sic).
Sep. 15. At Burford.
Sep. 16. To Wytney.

[1] Part III, p. 412.   [2] Part III, p. 400.   [3] Part III, p. 415.
[4] *Progresses of Queen Elizabeth*, by John Nichols, vol. iii, p. 129.
[5] *Hatfield House Papers* (Hist. MSS. Com. 1915), Part XIII, p. 466.

Burghley was in attendance on the Queen, and his use of a different form—'I went' or 'I came'—in later entries implies that the entries quoted refer to movements of the Queen. Moreover, from Sherborne to Woodstock the Queen's way would naturally take her through Burford. A particular point of interest is that the form 'At Burford', taken in conjunction with the sequence of dates, makes it fairly clear that on this occasion the Queen actually stayed the night here. It is difficult to think where she can have been lodged, unless we may assume that already Lawrence Tanfield's new house on the Priory site was at the disposal of a royal visitor.

The extension of the town up the hill is as much enlargement as we need look for ; the population, even at this stage of the town's prosperity, did not call for any great multiplication of dwellings. From all the indications that can be used for making an estimate it would appear that until, at any rate, the end of the century the total population was under a thousand. The earliest fact of much service for our purpose is to be found in the Chantry Certificate of 1547.[1] On this the number of 'howselyng people'—or, as we should now say, communicant members of the Church of England—is entered as 544. In estimating from this figure several points must be borne in mind.[2] The first is that at that date the age of Confirmation and First Communion was much lower than at present ; next, there was no other church than the Church of England ; thirdly, it was a serious matter of misdemeanour to be notably lax in attending Divine Service, or to fail to attend the statutory minimum of Communions ; and fourthly, the tendency of those who furnished returns for the Certificate would naturally be to enter the highest possible figures of Church membership. On all these grounds the 'howselyng people' must be taken as representing a proportion of the

[1] Part III, p. 643.
[2] There seems to be no authoritative pronouncement as to the proportion which the number of these 'howselyng people' may reasonably be held to bear to the total population. I have proceeded on certain considerations which are set out above ; and the fact that the figures thus arrived at tally well with those derived from calculations on quite a different basis does give validity to those considerations.

population out of all relation to modern standards. Every one over the age of twelve or so would be included. Therefore, if we follow the reasonable course of taking the figure as standing for about two-thirds of the inhabitants of all ages, we should arrive at a total population of some 825 souls.

This is fairly accordant with such calculations as can be made from the Edwardian Survey of the manor and town. That document gives us upon analysis one hundred and forty households in the town, made up of twelve holdings of a burgage and a half, one of a burgage and a quarter, eighty-four single burgages, forty-two half-burgages, and one quarter-burgage. On this basis the town population should have been about 700.[1] To this must be added the population of Upton and Signett, since, as the one Church of Burford served all three members of the parish, the hamlets must have been included in the reckoning of the ' howselyng people '. The Survey gives, for Upton and Signett, ten messuages. But from the *Domesday of Enclosures*[2] it is plain that several tenements existed on a single messuage; in one case there were four, in another, though no figure is given, the value entered shows that there were more than this. Supposing that we allow for thirty tenements altogether on the ten messuages (which is not too much, seeing that in 1326–7 the number of households in the hamlets was 33) we shall add 150 to the town inhabitants, and arrive at a total population of 850, which is near enough to the estimate based on the number of ' howselyng people ' five years earlier. To give a margin for the greater crowding of the time, and for other circumstances, we may put the number in round figures at 900.[3]

[1] Analysis of the town Survey is difficult, since it is not always clear when mixed holdings of complete and half burgages ought to be reckoned as one household. In a few instances there is a possibility that as many as two and a half burgages were thus combined into one tenement. But the figures given above may be taken as approximately representing the conditions.

[2] Vol. i, p. 344.

[3] It has been supposed, from a misquoted reference, that the population in the sixteenth century must have been much larger than this. The reference upon which such calculations have been based will be found in Part III, p. 655, in a letter from Thomas Cade, Vicar of Burford, to Thomas Cromwell. The statement there made that the clothier Tucker

Forty years later there is evidence that a long time of comparative peace and plenty had again enlarged the population. An assessment list for the Lay Subsidy of 1596 contains 120 names. Now the list for 1524 shows only 78 names. The advance must not be attributed wholly to a proportionate increase of population ; it would be due in great measure to a more widely spread ability to pay the small sums taxed, of which the majority are sixpence or less. If we consider that the number of inhabitants had increased by one-third, that is the utmost allowance that need be made to explain the figures of 1596 ; and we shall thus conclude that by the end of the century the population had risen to some 1200.

There is indication now of very much more marked differences in wealth than we were able to find in the previous period. The richest man of whom we have record is one John Busbyne or Busbye, assessed at £200 in goods and paying £10 to the Subsidies. For so rich a man, he appears singularly little in our Records. He served as Bailiff in 1524 and 1527, ; but is not found holding any other office, not even that of a Feoffee of Charity Lands. After 1527 the name is not seen again except in the entry on the Survey of 1552 of one Richard Busby of Islington as holding a burgage in High Street and a close in Batts Lane.

Apart from him, however, there is a small group of men ranking by themselves in the assessments—William Hodges at £80, Richard Smyth at £50, Peter Eynesdale, Thomas Teysdale, and John Lambert at £40. Next to them come ten men assessed at between £10 and £20. Thirty-seven assessments are between £3 and £10, and twenty-eight under £3.

This gives us a classification which may usefully be compared with the rough classification of the burgage holders.

employed 500 persons has been misquoted as a statement that he employed 500 persons *at Burford*, and it has been argued from this that, if 500 persons were employed by one man, the total population must have been very large. But it is not stated that he employed 500 at Burford. On the contrary, it is explicitly stated that he sent much of his work to Abingdon and Stroud.

The figures do not exactly correspond, but they are interestingly parallel. We have fifteen men of comfortable substance on the Subsidy—five whom we might call 'forty-pound men', and ten whom we might call 'twenty-pound men'— and thirteen holders of tenements. comprising more than a single burgage. We have sixty-five men on the Subsidy who may be taken as the general run of tradesmen and craftsmen in the town, and eighty-four holdings of a single burgage. Finally, it may be noted from the number of servants taxed as such on their wages, that ten households in the town kept these men-servants.

In other words, the improved, more systematic civic life of Burford in the sixteenth century can now be seen as a reflection of its attainment at last to the natural and obvious characteristics of a market and manufacturing town. The old equality between the town residents and those of the hamlets has disappeared. Only one man in the hamlets is assessed at anything like the higher town figures, and his assessment is but £20. That is to say, the richest group in the town is now beyond all comparison with the agricultural tenants, and even the second group comes out as essentially of the town. Moreover, the gap between these two groups implies that better brains and energy were going into the town's trade, and reaping the results; while at the same time stimulating a competitive spirit, which has its effect in the existence of the small group between the richest men and the mass of the tradesmen.

A fair idea of the general spread of the prosperity accompanying the particular successes thus traceable can be derived from the one Muster Roll for Burford. Forty-seven men are entered as of substance to equip themselves or their substitutes as archers, and forty-one to do the same as billmen. It is useful to compare this with the Witney Muster Roll of the same date. Throughout the Lay Subsidy lists Witney is entered for higher sums than Burford. Yet its Muster Roll shows a smaller total—70 as against 88—and still more significantly shows only twenty-seven men to provide archers. The deduction from this is that, although

Witney may have had men of greater individual wealth, whose taxes would make the Subsidy totals larger than those of Burford, there was in Burford a much greater number of men of moderate substance, and the general level of trading prosperity was higher.

It happens that less can be said about the actual trades pursued here during the sixteenth century than could be said about those of the earlier period. The occupations of persons mentioned in grants and leases are not so often inserted ; and no such illuminating document as the grant of the Bridge tolls occurs to assist us. But all the trades previously mentioned can be found recorded, while the saddlers, who were soon to make their trade famous here, begin to appear. It is also clear, from the fines in the Court Rolls of 1547 and 1549, that business was becoming good enough to lead to the setting up of permanent shops for victuals, instead of the trade being confined to market days. Several bakers, butchers, fishmongers, and vintners were carrying on trade apart from the market. It is also clear from the same Rolls that Burford was already the town of inns which it so markedly was later on. Alehouse keepers, inn keepers, brewers, and keepers of hostelries are rather numerous ; and the grant of the George Inn to servants of the Royal Household implies that an inn here must have been worth possessing. That the George was at this time the chief inn may be gathered from the fact that it is the only inn mentioned by name in the Survey of 1552. Others recorded in various town grants and leases were the Bull (in the same position as the Bull of to-day, since its back gate on Witney Street is mentioned), the Crown (which was the old Novum Hospitium Angulare at the northern corner of Sheep Street and the High Street), the Angel (apparently next to the Bull at the corner of Witney Street), and the Bear.

The mills had increased in number. Besides the two called Burford Mills there were now a corn-mill at Upton and a fulling mill in Burford. The latter may be taken to be the one at the end of Witney Street, at the present day the electric light works. At any rate the Survey places a mill there, in the description of a close as lying ' in Witneystret iuxta le Walkemylle '. All four mills were leased by the Crown in 1521 to another servant of the Royal Household, Thomas Wildyng, a Yeoman of the Ewery; in 1538, upon

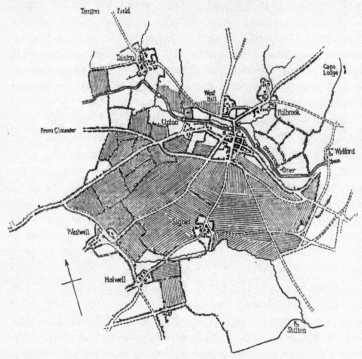

MAP OF BURFORD IN 1793, SHOWING THE OPEN FIELD CULTIVATION.
From the map engraved by Davis of Lewknor.

Wildyng's death, John Jones, a Burford man, took over the lease. In 1545 Edmund Harman bought them; the fulling mill he sold later to Edmond Silvester.[1]

Further analysis of the Edwardian Survey shows how complete was that separate development of the town, apart from the hamlets, which the Lay Subsidies indicate. It is on the Survey that the hamlets appear for the first time with

[1] Part III, p. 657.

the distinct title of ' The Manor of Bury Barns '. The details under that head have several interesting features.

Firstly, we can see how the new ideas of farming, which were giving rise to so many complaints in the political satires of the time, had here replaced the old system. At our last view of the hamlets in 1299 and 1307 the old order was, of course, still undisturbed ; twelve tenants in Signett held a full virgate, and three a half-virgate ; in Upton there were seven virgaters and one half-virgater. Thus in the two there were twenty-three tenants with twenty-one virgates. In 1552 the holdings are almost doubled in extent, but the tenants number less than half ; there are ten tenants with thirty-five virgates. Four of the tenants are still small cultivators, two holding a virgate and two a half-virgate. Of the rest one man holds seven virgates with two messuages, three hold four virgates each, one has three and a half virgates, and two have three virgates each. Here, on a small scale, is precisely that gathering of the farm land into a few hands which was one of the great economic perils and problems of the time. It was inevitable, no doubt ; as capital increased, and commercial ideas improved, the power to make money out of the land was bound to have its way. The change would be seen comparatively early in manors like this, which included a borough ; the prosperity of the tradesmen would provide capital for engrossing the land on the skirts of the town. Nor is Burford devoid of the evil which followed upon this engrossing. Two cases here of destruction of tenements on the agricultural messuages appear in the *Domesday of Enclosures*, the local instances of another inevitable process in the creation of large farms, namely, the expulsion from tenements, which had now lost their old fixed relation to the virgates, of those who had become labourers for a wage instead of independent virgate-holders.[1] The man who held four virgates did not need for himself the four tenements they had once supported ; he wanted a single, and better, house, and the tenements disappeared to make way for it, leaving the occupiers to find cottages as best they could.

[1] *Domesday of Enclosures*, i. 344.

The number of virgate tenants entered on the Survey leaves us in no doubt that by this time any portions of the later common fields, which may have been uncultivated in 1500, were in use. The portion north of the ridge road near White Hill must have been broken up, and the small detached portion near Holwell;[1] and the fields must have been much as they were at the time of the Enclosure. At that date the Burford and Signett Fields stretched from the eastern boundary of the parish beyond White Hill to the junction with Upton Fields on the west, and from the Shil Brook on the south to the Witney–Northleach road on the north, taking in also a portion beyond this road on the White Hill slope. This area and Upton Fields both north and south of the Witney–Northleach road contained together, at the dates of the Enclosure Awards, 1,955 acres. For the thirty-five virgates of the tenants of 1552, together with the six virgates held in demesne and six and a half virgates held by tenants in the town we require, on the Survey's allowance of twenty-four acres to the virgate, 2,280 acres.[2] These, however, were customary acres, not the modern surveyed acres, and the apparent discrepancy need not disturb us. At the same time, this virgate total can hardly be accommodated unless by the middle of the sixteenth century the common fields had already attained their full extent.

This reveals the interesting fact that the arable land held by the borough inhabitants was not now common field land at all. In earlier days the townsmen had held in the fields side by side with the people of the hamlets. In 1552 not only is it impossible to find room, at the extreme extent of the fields, for more than the hamlet tenants, but the entries concerning the town holdings are of so distinct a form that they clearly have nothing to do with the common field. They are in no case complete virgates or fractions of virgates; they are all of an arbitrary number of acres. They carry no

---

[1] See the maps on pp. 194, 227.

[2] It may perhaps be remarked again that the virgate area as entered on documents has to be doubled in order to give the true extent. Half the common field was fallowed each year, so that a virgate holding has to mean a virgate in each field alternately.

commonable rights ; and the tenant has only a single cropping of them in the year. As it happens, two residents in the town did hold in the common fields, and the difference is at once apparent ; for in their cases the virgate measurements apply, nothing is said about a single cropping, and it is specifically recorded that they have common with the tenants of the manor of Bury Barns, and owe suit to that court for this land. These entries, put beside the others concerning arable land held with town tenements, prove beyond question that the arable of the townsmen was not in the common fields.

We need not be at a loss to discern where it was. The map which represents the Enclosure Award shows several stretches of old enclosures. One lies on the hill-side immediately east of the town, its name, the Leasowes, indicating old enclosure. Another is found at Sturt, in the southeastern extremity of the parish ; another beyond Signett towards Westwell, again at the extremity of the parish. Roughly speaking these areas contain about 520 modern acres. The arable land entered to town tenants in the Survey amounts to 789 acres. The discrepancy between the modern and the old customary acre is here rather larger than in the case of the common fields ; but it is likely that in enclosures the acre was often overestimated. At any rate, with these old enclosures before us, we may conclude that the town arable was, as might be expected, situated in such places on the edges of the common fields as the virgate holders had left outside their cultivated area.

The meadow holdings of borough and hamlets had become equally distinct. In the earlier days town and agricultural tenants alike had held in High Mead, the riverside meadow east of the town. But the 1552 Survey shows that the meadow west of the town had become equally important, and it was here, in Veronhill and Wyldmore Meads,[1] that the hamlet tenants held their meadow. It is remarkable that in this matter the town tenants retained the older land, and

[1] The modern name of Fernhill Copse places these meads for us along the riverside at Upton.

were not reduced to taking what the virgaters left. But of course meadow is on a very different footing from arable in this respect—that old arable has a value accruing to it from past cultivation and manuring; whereas one meadow, in days when no manure was given to such land, was no better than another as well situated in relation to the river. The reason why the virgaters moved from High Mead may well be that, when the demesne portion was taken out of it, the remainder, while corresponding closely to the virgate holdings of 1299–1307, was too small for the requirements of the more numerous virgaters of 1552. The town holdings of meadow amount in the Survey to 21 acres, which, with the demesne meadow here of seven acres and one or two small enclosed portions, make up the thirty acres of High Mead. But the hamlet tenants required 41½ acres, and evidently moved to the western meadows to find them. High Mead, thus left to the town tenants, reveals the change in the arbitrary character of the holdings there. The virgaters maintain in their meads the strict relation of one acre of meadow to a virgate. Among the town tenants we find men with 143 and 110 acres of arable possessed of only one acre and one and a half acres respectively of meadow, while a man with only 44 acres of arable has 5½ acres of meadow.

The processes of divergent development on the part of the town and the hamlets must, of course, have been gradual. But the Survey of 1552 enables us to see them as practically complete, and we can understand better how the necessity had arisen for providing separate names for two such distinct kinds of community. We may indicate the change (speaking now not historically, but loosely) by saying that the old mediaeval manor of Burford, consisting of a territory with a privileged community living on part of it, has disappeared, and in its place there is a town with farm lands around it. Town and farm land are, indeed, still joint members of a single lordship; but from henceforth their histories run in quite separate directions.

The story of the hamlets becomes ever more meagre. The tenancy of the manor domain we can follow through nearly the whole of the century. It was leased by the Crown to one William Gittyns or Gittons in 1526 for a term of 21 years. In 1542 Thomas Edgare obtained a similar lease to commence on the expiry of Gittyns's tenancy. But he can never have taken this up, because at just about the time when Gittyns's term was expiring Edmund Harman took a lease for three lives. He may perhaps have farmed the land himself, since the Survey of 1552 mentions no sub-tenant. Upon his death the Crown leased the manor lands to three joint tenants, John (or Thomas) Moore, Thomas Cooke, and Margaret Curteis, for 21 years ; and at the end of that time to Richard Bell, who presumably did sub-let the land, for he is himself described as of Gray's Inn, London.

The house at Bury Barns was still in a real sense the manor house ; the Courts of which we have record in 1547 and 1549 must have been held in it. But the fact that its occupiers were not owners of the manorial rights must have tended to weaken the association of those rights with this house, and so have prepared the way for that entire loss of the manor house tradition which was inevitable, when new lords of the manor, the first resident owners of the rights, established themselves in a mansion built on the site of the Hospital.

The history of the town, on the other hand, becomes more ample and more interesting. Many circumstances, as the History of the Corporation has shown, combined to make it so ; but no one who studies the Records can fail to notice the mark upon the age made by two or three individuals— a mark so strong as to produce the impression that without them no material circumstances would have availed to make this century quite what it was in Burford.

Foremost among them all is Simon Wisdom. We first meet the name in 1530, when in the course of the Bishop of Lincoln's investigations of heresy in his diocese

Simon Wisdom of Burford was charged in judgment for having 3 books in English, one was the Gospels in English, another was the Psalter, the third was the summ of Holy Scripture in English.

He abjured, and no penance or punishment is recorded in the case.[1]

In 1538 a Simon Wisdom was Collector of the Lay Subsidy for the Hundreds of Bampton and Chadlington;[2] and in the same year the name appears among the Burford Burgesses. There is no earlier trace of the name of Wisdom in Burford, and it would appear likely that Simon came of a family of substance[3] living elsewhere, and settled himself here. He must have lived to a good age, for he was certainly alive in 1581. There is no need to assume that we have to deal with a father and son of the same name. For if the notable Simon Wisdom was old enough to become a Burgess in 1538 (and no other of the name appears later, so that this must be our Simon) he would not be too young to have been charged in 1530. The absence of any penance implies the likelihood that it was a case against a quite young man or even a lad.

In 1539 he was tenant of some of the Priory lands situated at Great Rissington, and in 1553 he was Steward of the Burgesses. From that time on he must have devoted himself to the town, being Alderman of the Gild for no less than twenty-two years, and serving more than once as Bailiff. To him we owe the only Memorandum Book of the Corporation, which is largely written with his own hand. That he had a particular taste for system and organization may be seen not only from his draft in this book of the oath to be taken by the Steward of the Corporation, but still more in the Rules and Constitutions composed by him for the conduct of the Grammar School. The great part he took in the foundation of the School is related elsewhere, in the Introduction to the School Records. He also established a small Almshouse, and benefited the town by rebuilding much of the dilapidated charity property. He was a man of several occupations; he is described on occasions both as a clothier and a mercer; but in 1547 and 1549 he is found

---

[1] Foxe's *Acts and Monuments* (edition of 1684), ii. 196.

[2] See Part III, p. 606.

[3] Apart from other considerations, these ' books in English ' were out of the reach of poor men. An English Bible would cost at least 20s. See *Acts and Monuments*, ii. 37.

PLATE XI. TURRET AT BACK OF ONE OF
SIMON WISDOM'S HOUSES ON THE HILL

acting as a fish merchant, and in 1552 he held so much arable
land that he may have been a farmer as well, especially as
he describes himself sometimes as ' yeoman '. Building must
have had a peculiar attraction for him ; no man has left his
name or his device on so many houses in the town. It is
a singular fact that, after all he did for Burford, there should
be no record of his burial-place, nor any sort of memorial to
him. He died about 1585, apparently unmarried ; no lease
or conveyance of any of his numerous bits of property
mentions a wife. One Raphe Wisdom, perhaps a nephew,
carried on the name for some time in Burford ; it lasted
longer in the family of a brother, Thomas Wisdom, at Shipton.

No figure can quite be placed beside Simon Wisdom's
for interest. Yet Peter Eynesdale, the first who actually
bears the title of Alderman in the Records, and who brought
the Gild through the rather perilous period of the Reformation, deserves to be mentioned. He was energetic in charge
of Church and Charity Lands. At the other end of the
century, Richard Merywether stands out as the one successor
to Simon Wisdom who appears to have had something like
his vigour and capacity. He was the leading spirit in the
recovery of the confiscated Charity Lands in 1595 ; and the
Roll of the Burgess Rules and Customs was drawn up while
he was Alderman, therefore probably upon his suggestion
and advice.

Of the attitude and the inclinations of Burford men during
the Civil War we have no knowledge. If feelings ran high
on one side or the other, nothing has come down to us which
reveals them. It is unfortunate that, so soon after the sixteenth-century Memorandum Book was filled, should have
come the dispute with Sir Lawrence Tanfield and the extinction of all the duties that would have made the keeping of
another Memorandum Book likely; and equally unfortunate
that this disaster should in its turn have been followed so
soon by the Royal Commission's reconstitution of the
charities. Resentful, we may well imagine, perhaps also
rather bewildered by what had befallen them and the com-

parative insignificance to which they were reduced, the Burgesses never again attempted to keep even those casual records which the habits of Simon Wisdom preserved for us through thirty years of the sixteenth century. Even before disaster fell upon the Burgesses, that kind of record had become very fragmentary. It had not been entirely dropped ; in 1600 some one, apparently Symon Symons, then Steward of the Burgesses, drew up a statement as to the recovery by the town of the confiscated Charity Lands. This is precisely the kind of thing that might have had its place in a new Memorandum Book. But it stands alone, bound up now as the first few leaves of an Account Book.

There is thus no section of the Records in which we can look for light upon the townsfolk's feelings in the Civil War. We can indeed be sure of one or two Royalists ; the Calendar of the Committee for the Advance of Money enters three sums from Burford. Leonard Yates lent £40, David Hughes 14 guineas, and Thomas Silvester £77, and the contributions of Yates and Silvester are, for their position, large. On the other hand it is to be observed that there are but three loans, and there were at least a score of men in Burford whose circumstances were no humbler than those of Yates and Hughes. For the rest we have only isolated facts which show Burford at times in the track of war. The town first saw fighting on New Year's Eve of 1642/3.[1] On December 30, 1642, Sir John Byron had been ordered to proceed with his whole regiment to Burford, to convoy two cartloads of ammunition for the Marquis of Hertford, who was expected at Stow on the following day. On reaching Burford, Byron made inquiries about the Parliament forces at Cirencester, and we may perhaps catch a glimpse of the townsmen's sympathies in the fact that he could ' get no satisfaction ' from them. But the position of Burford, near enough to Oxford to be drawn into trouble, yet not near enough to be occupied permanently by either side, may well have inclined the inhabitants to caution, and we need not conclude from

[1] The best account of this affair is to be found in *Mercurius Aulicus*, under date January 1st, 1643.

this incident that the place was Parliamentarian in feeling.
Byron sent a patrol out towards Cirencester, and they, after
approaching to within a mile and a half of that town, brought
back word that there were not above five hundred dragoons
there.   The next day, a Saturday, passed quietly until seven
o'clock at night, when another patrol from the Cirencester
road came in with news that about two miles from Burford
they had met four dragoons, who, on encountering them,
had ridden back so fast that they could not be captured.
Byron at once ordered one of his captains to take forty men
along the Cirencester road, and warned the whole regiment
to be in readiness at the sound of the trumpet.   He then
went up the hill to post sentries, apparently at the cross
roads by Bury Barns.   Coming back into the town he found
that half of the party ordered to the Cirencester road had
not yet started; but before he could give any other orders
muskets began to go off; the Parliamentarians were in the
town.   Byron's first care was to secure the Bridge with a
' competent ' party of horse under his Lieutenant-Colonel,
to avoid being cut off from Lord Hertford, and to dispatch
the ammunition at once with a small guard of thirty men.
It is doubtful whether the Parliamentarians knew of Byron's
business, and were intending to intercept the ammunition.
If so, they were late in attacking, for, since Hertford was
expected at Stow that day, the chances would be that the
convoy would have been on its way to him before they
reached Burford.   The more reasonable conjecture to make
is that, without knowing the cause of Byron's presence, the
troops at Cirencester had heard of the patrols on the road,
and had therefore come up to reconnoitre, and to attack if
the chance offered.   But in any case Byron's precautions
were good.   Having thus secured the Bridge, he returned to
the town, to find the firing coming from the direction of the
White Hart, ' an Inne in the utmost part of the Towne,
from whence a lane leadeth to the Market Crosse '.   This
would place the skirmish that ensued in Witney Street, not
only from the fact that an inn of that name survived in
Witney Street till modern times, but also because it is not

likely that, with the look-out that was being kept towards the Cirencester road, the attack could have come so suddenly from the Sheep Street side. It is more probable that the four troopers who had been observed had, on riding back to the main body, given warning that that approach to the town was watched, and the force had thereupon struck across country from the Cirencester road eastwards, so as to make a surprise attack from the other side. Byron was, in fact, being taken in the rear. But it was not a serious affair. Byron found his men being driven out of Witney Street, and seeing the danger of allowing the enemy to hold the centre of the town he rallied his men, charged in with his sword, having no other weapon, and in spite of some firing from the back of the enemy forced the Parliamentarians down Witney Street again to the inn. Here he received a wound in the face from a halberd, and finding himself ill supported (most of his troops, misunderstanding his orders, had remained about the Market Cross to secure the centre of the town) he returned to bring up more forces. But the fight in the dark was really over. When Captain Apsley tackled the inn once again the enemy were already escaping by the back door, although the one loss on Byron's side happened at this moment, a trooper being killed as he entered the inn. The Parliamentarians were pursued for six miles; but the darkness and the lack of a moon saved them.

The parish registers contain a record of the skirmish, which reveals in an interesting way the losses on either side. One man, ' slain in Burford ', was buried on January 1, and six soldiers, also ' slain in Burford ', on the 2nd. But as the name of the single interment is given, and the other entry only records ' six soldiers ', we may conclude that the one was the loss on Byron's side, his comrades being there to give his name, and the others were the casualties left by the Parliamentarians, and therefore nameless. There appear to have been two deaths from wounds; on January 10 Thomas Tunkes, ' slaine wth the shot of musket ', was buried, and on January 15 William Bolton, ' slaine in Like manner '. On the 8th had been buried ' a soldier dying of sicknes '.

Soldiers must have been about Burford early in the following year, though there are no accounts of any fighting. Andrew Royer, 'a ffrench Leiftenant slaine in Burford', was buried on February 17, 1643/4; and on March 12 'Bryan Roy an Irishman & soldier'.

Later in that year the town was within an ace of being the scene of what might have proved a most important battle. It was at Burford that Charles called the first real halt on that famous march, when he had slipped out of Oxford by night between the armies of Essex at Bletchingdon and Waller at Newbridge; he and his personal troop rested at the Priory,[1] and his army about the town, from the afternoon until nine o'clock at night, when they moved out again, reaching Bourton-on-the-Water by midnight. This was on June 4, 1644. Waller, getting first news of what had happened, sent some horse up so quickly that they found a few Royalists still in the town; but Essex was not here in pursuit till June 6. So there was no battle, and Essex, finding himself so far behind, stayed a few days, quartering his troops in the Church, while he summoned his principal officers to a council of war. It must have been at this time that his troopers took the banners over the Tanfield tomb for scarfs.

The result of Essex's deliberations was such that Charles was able to return to Oxford, and a fortnight later the King was back in Burford, staying the night at the George,[2] and going to Church to hear a sermon next morning before resuming his march. Four thousand troops and fifteen pieces of cannon, which he had left in Oxford and Abingdon, were sent to rejoin him in Burford. Again our one local record of this event may be an entry in the Register stating that 'William Callis of ffilkins a wounded man and lyeing under y[e] chirurgeons hand at Burford dyed, and was buried y[e] 4th of July'.

In November of the same year Prince Rupert was here, being joined at Burford by General Gerard with his forces.[3] He came to the town on November 1. On this occasion our

---

[1] Symonds's *Diary* (Camden Society, 74), p. 8.   [2] *Ibid.*, p. 15.
[3] *English Historical Review*, vol. xiii, p. 729.

Registers seem to indicate some rowdiness and indiscipline. There are two entries: 'Thomas Williams a Trooper slaine by his fellow soldier with shott of a Pistoll and buried the 24th day of Novemb.'; and 'Lewis Davies a serjeant of a ffoote company under Generall Gerrard dyed of a wound given him by a Captaine & was buried ye 29th of Novemb.'

Three more entries reveal to us the presence of soldiery in the town from time to time. 'John Hethewood a soldier belonging to Sr Marmaduke Langdale dyed of hurt received from a fellow soldier and was Buried ye 30th of ffebruar' (1644-5); 'George Rowley an officer in Prince Rupert his Army dyeing of a wound receaved was buried ye eight of May'; and 'John Bullocke Farrier in the Lord Goreings army shott by his fellow soldier buried eodem die'. The two latter entries can be connected with the fact that Prince Rupert and Prince Maurice were in Burford with a thousand foot and a thousand horse on May 3rd.[1] It may be remarked that our Registers add one more to the proofs that the use of churches for billeting troops was not confined to one side in the war; there are entries of payments for 'takeing downe the wall for the carryinge of straw into the Church for the souldiers', and 'for makeing cleane the church when the souldiers went away'. These can only refer to the Royalist troops. An entry of a payment for ringing the bells 'for the Prince' must also refer to this visit. Rupert was here again this year, on September 14, but that was not an occasion on which he would have been gratified by the ringing of bells. The entry in the diary of his marches reads: 'Our convoye left us. Layd downe armes.'[2] He was on his way from Cirencester to Oxford, where on the 17th he was relieved of his command on instructions from the Lords by letter from the King, and his regiments were cashiered.

Of what the townspeople thought of all these things—the hasty marches, the to and fro of captains, the dead men in the streets—we know nothing. We cannot tell how many of them had their sympathies with Lord Falkland, whom they had so often seen among them, knowing not how a few pages

---

[1] Dugdale's *Diary*.   [2] *English Historical Review*, loc. cit.

of great literature were to make him a better known figure of the Civil War than many men of more forceful character. It is likely, however, that they found their guide in the new owner of the Priory, and were well content to make under Speaker Lenthall's wing the transition from one régime to the other.

The part which Burford played in one critical episode of that other régime—the famous scene of the execution here of the ' Levellers ' and the suppression of the mutiny of 1649 in the Parliamentary army—offers so many points of detailed interest that it is treated in a separate chapter.

Of those other aspects of Burford history, the character of the town, the number of people it contained, their occupations and conditions, which we have followed through previous centuries, we are not left in the seventeenth century without information.

Upon the size of the town, to begin with, much light is thrown by two Burgage Rent Rolls, for the years 1652 and 1685, which somehow found their way into the Corporation Records. They differ in one respect from the Survey of 1552. In the latter document the burgage holdings are given simply as totals, without specification of the particular tenements; a man is entered as holding ' eight burgages in High Street and Witney Street ', or ' three burgages in High Street '. Consequently the probable population had to be estimated on the total number of burgages. The two Burgage Rent Rolls are drawn up on a much more informative system. Each tenement is entered separately, with its situation mentioned; and—still more usefully—the number of occupiers is given. Thus we can base calculations on a recorded number of households, not on a number only conjecturally derived from a total of burgages; and we can also discover the number of households existing in each street.

The Rolls are so near in point of time and in their main statistics that it would not much matter which of them were used for calculation. The 1652 Roll enters 128 tenements and the 1685 Roll 127 tenements. The latter is, for practical reasons, the more convenient for our purpose; because the former, evidently in use for several years, has so many erasures and corrections in the names of occupiers that it is a confusing document to analyse.

Taking the 1685 Roll, then, it appears on a superficial glance that the numbers of households in each street are singularly near the totals of to-day. On the east side of the High Street there were 55 households; to-day there is actually the same number; on the west side there were 45 as against 51 to-day. On the north side of Sheep Street there were 9 as against 8 to-day, and on the south side 14 as against 20. On the north side of Witney Street there were 17 as against 25, and on the south side 8 as against 10. In Priory Lane and St. John's Street together there were 9, as against 16 in the modern Priory Lane, which covers the ground of both the older names. On Church Green there were exactly the same number of separate buildings as to-day, namely a house next the churchyard, the Almshouse, and a house at the Gildenford end of the Almshouse. Church Lane is a difficult point, because to-day almost the whole of it on both sides is School building; in 1685 there were seven households here. A few households are entered in Gildenford Lane, but the number is not specified; as they were all in the hands of John Castle, who later on gave six houses in the Lane for the purposes of an Almshouse, we may perhaps conclude that this would be the number of his tenements here on the 1685 Roll.

Now it is at first sight curious that the numbers of the separate houses should so nearly correspond with those of the present day. True, there has been no considerable increase of population. But general ideas of the closer quarters and more cramped way of living in the earlier period would lead us to expect that the houses nowadays would be more numerous, even if the population were much the same. The answer to this difficulty may be found on a little further analysis. To begin with, the apparent correspondence of the High Street figures needs modification. Several cottages lying back from the Street, like the row up an alley below the Post Office, would be entered under the burgage rent of the tenement on the back premises of which they had been constructed, and so would appear under the head of the High Street. Similarly some cottages which we should now describe as lying on the north side of Priory Lane, at the back of the Falkland Hall, would for the same reason appear in 1685 as High Street households. Again, no entries are made for Lawrence Lane, though there are houses there obviously older than the date of this Roll ; they must have been classed with the High Street tenement behind which they stood. This is the first consideration which makes it necessary to subtract from the High Street totals of 1685. Another is that, although for general comparison we combined in the earlier figures the High Street and the Hill, it is also requisite to separate them for a proper view of the conditions then and now. In 1685 there were only ten houses on the Hill, five on the east, four on the west, and one not assigned on the Roll to either side. It is not quite easy, owing to lack of any definite indication of where the High Street ceased and the Hill began, to provide any corresponding figures from the town of to-day ; but, roughly speaking, we may take it that where there were only ten houses in 1685 there are now about forty.

Adding to these considerations the fact that the modern figures give us five more houses in Sheep Street, ten more in Witney Street, and a number in Gildenford Lane, with perhaps two or three more in Priory Lane, we can see where the real change has been, behind the apparent similarity of the figures. Improved ideas of comfort and privacy have expanded the town outwards from an overcrowded central space to the side streets and the Hill. The High Street below the Witney Street and Sheep Street turnings must have been in 1685 a mixture of some rather large houses with huddled cottages between and behind them. Taking the total population of the town, on a basis of 180 households, as about 900, we find some 460, or rather more than half, living in that area.

It follows that we cannot yet picture the town as having attained quite its modern form. The Hill was as yet chiefly

P

open ground with a few houses scattered up it; and there were some clear spaces on the south side of Sheep Street, and on the north side of Witney Street towards the river.

It is not possible to say exactly where the larger houses broke the frontage lines of the streets. On the east side of the High Street there were several. One, which paid burgage rent at the highest rate recorded on these Rolls, namely 9s., appears to have occupied the site of the present Wesleyan Chapel. Another, which paid 6s., probably stood just above this one. Three others on that side paid together 16s. Higher up on the same side a large house stood at the corner of the modern Swan Lane, its ground running back alongside the lane. It has a particular interest, because it is associated with the family of Warren Hastings. A document of 1648 shows that the ownership was partly vested in ' George Hastings of Dalford in the County of Worcester '.[1] When the messuage ceased, at some time between the two dates of these Rolls, to be a single residence, and was divided between three occupiers, one of them was Hercules Hastings.[2]

On the west side of the High Street there were fewer large houses. One mansion paid 6s., and another, held with some arable land, 8s. 8d.

In Sheep Street the largest house stood about in the middle of the south side. It appears from various indications to be the one formerly held by the Gild, with rather ample ground about it; and to have occupied the ground now covered by three houses and several gardens.

A few small details can be added to our mental picture of the town. Opposite the Tolsey stood the High Cross; it was, of course, standing there in earlier times, but the first actual mention of it is not before 1608. The base of it, dug up during a re-making of the roadway, now stands behind the Tolsey railing in Sheep Street. On the east side of the High Street was a forge known as ' Middle Forge'; it stood just below the Witney Street corner; on the west side was a pump.

---

[1] Part III, p. 462.
[2] He was a clockmaker, some of his productions being still in existence. One is in the possession of Mr. John Lane.

Indications such as those which have assisted us in dating the buildings of earlier periods are not lacking in the later part of the seventeenth century. It is not, however, easy to assign definitely to the first half of this century any of our buildings. The most that can be said is that there are considerations which might assign to that time the building of the beautiful three-gabled, barge-boarded house on the west side of High Street, opposite the end of Sheep Street. Obviously this frontage involved a much freer use of glass for the windows of the upper storey than did the late sixteenth-century type. Yet as late as 1608 ' the glass in the windows ' was valuable enough in Burford to be separately scheduled in the sale of quite a large house.[1] Therefore the frontage which has just been mentioned should probably be regarded as not earlier than 1625.

Of an early type of Jacobean structure we need hardly expect to find many examples. So much rebuilding had been done—so many substantial stone houses erected—in the Elizabethan period. Yet of course necessity is not the only cause of new building; it may equally be dictated by changing taste backed by easier means. When we find, as we shall shortly be finding, among the inhabitants of Burford a distinctly new kind of resident, we may, therefore, be prepared for the appearance also of a new kind of domestic architecture. Some houses bearing an inscribed date, which allow us to date others by their resemblance, prove that the latter half of the seventeenth century was almost as active a building period as the latter half of the previous century had been.

The front of the Vicarage towards the High Street bears the date 1672; a house in Sheep Street is inscribed 1696; and with these we may place the house at Kit's Quarries built, according to a stone let into the wall, by Christopher Kempster in 1698. In these three, different as they are in general outline, we can discern certain common characteristics. They have stone fronts of more carefully worked ashlar than the earlier houses had, extremely well fitted and pointed. The window openings are plain with a broad shallow moulding

[1] Part III. pp. 402–3.

outlining them, and are tall in proportion to their width ; they are very distinctly designed for sash windows. The whole effect is of a smoother, more refined style, with a tendency to rectangular outline and to a great restraint in taste.

Two houses almost opposite the Vicarage, obviously built at one time and included under one roof-line—perhaps for economy in labour—display the same characteristics ; and so does a house higher up the street on the same side, a little above the Wesleyan Chapel.

We may without much hesitation assign to about this period the building on the south side of Witney Street now called the Great House. It has the same kind of window opening, varied with pleasing circles in the uppermost storey and oval lights for the cellar ; and the same good ashlar stonework. Other decorative details, such as the large pine-cone ornaments, the pedimented frontage and the castellated turrets, are not unsuitable to so high a façade. This may perhaps be the building which appears for the first time on the Burgage Rent Roll of 1685 as part of Mr. Robert Glyn's land—' a new tenement on the south side of Witney Street in the possession of the said Robert Glyn '.

There is reason, too, for classing among our late Jacobean buildings the present frontage of the Bull. In the Burford Records is a lease of the Bull to Edmund Heminge, dated October 13, 1658. The house is described as ' now in his tenure ', but the new lease is not to begin until October 18, 1661, and then the rent is to be raised from £6 a year to £14 a year, with an increased chief rent to the lord of the manor which the lessee covenants to pay. The post-dating of the new lease has one obvious explanation ; the existing lease of the premises, granted in 1630, was not due to expire before 1661. But there are some facts which require further explanation. Heminge was already in possession, and had no need to anticipate by so long a time the end of his tenure. The new lease imposes a very heavy advance of rent, which is the more striking because, after the Commission of 1628 had fixed the fair rents for the charity properties, the practice of the Burgesses was to maintain them at the same figures,

PLATE XII. THE GREAT HOUSE

even when, in justice to the charities, they ought to have been advanced to keep pace with increasing wealth. An explanation which would meet these facts, and would at the same time be not discordant with the style of the Bull frontage, is that the interval of three years prescribed in Heminge's new lease may very likely have been arranged to allow for the rebuilding of the inn, after which it would, of course, be rented more highly.

This opens the way to an interesting conjecture. The Bull frontage is remarkable as being the single instance of a considerable use of brick in Burford architecture[1]—a very successful use of it, for the structure is in no way displeasing, though so uncompromising a departure from the natural building material of the district. But why should brick have been used at all? The answer may be found in certain circumstances of Burford life at this time. The current of road traffic and travellers, which was later to become its chief business, was beginning to flow into the town. A project for rebuilding the Bull may easily have arisen from the idea that more than one good inn might profitably be kept here, and that a rival to the George might stand a good chance of success. If so, it may not be straining the point too far to suggest that the unusual recourse to brick may have been due to a deliberate intention to be striking, and even, considering the great beauty and distinction which brick building attained in later Jacobean architecture, to be fashionable and up to date. In other words, the one brick façade in Burford may be an early instance of the use of advertisement.

That new element in the population, to the presence of which we may attribute the building activities of this period, is singled out on the Burgage Rent Rolls by a curious little distinguishing mark. A certain number of the chief tenants are entered with the title ' Mr.', an obvious indication that they were persons of consequence. It is clear from the use of this title that Mr. Highlord, Mr. John Jordan, Mr. Robert Glyn, Mr. Heylin, Mr. Templer, Mr. William Elstone, Mr. Robert Pleydall, Mr. Robert Veysey, ranked as of a

[1] See Plate XIII.

different station even from men like the Bartholomews, the Taylors, the Silvesters, the Webbes, and so on, who, though there can have been little difference in wealth, are not endowed with any formal title. A group of residents is thus seen growing up in the town somewhere between the few who were, in those more accurate days, entitled to be addressed as 'Esquire'—like the Lenthalls or the Duttons—and the traditional Burgess families. It is the beginning of an upper middle class in Burford, to be increased in time by the physicians, like John Castle, and the lawyers, like the Randolphs.

We can discern some families of the townsfolk on the way from one classification to the other. Though the Burgage Rent Rolls do not explicitly recognize their status, the Bartholomews, some of the Silvesters, and a few more are in some documents described as 'gentlemen'; and in such cases as the references to 'William Webbe the younger, of Clifford's Inn, London, gentleman, son of William Webbe, of Burford, yeoman', and 'William Hunt, of New College, in the University of Oxford, gentleman, son of John Hunt, of Burford, mercer', the process of rising in the world was evidently being assisted by departure from the town.

But the distinct position of the group of residents to whose names the title 'Mr.' is prefixed is for the moment sharply defined, and even emphasized, by the fact that none of them ever appears among the Burgesses. There can have been no great social distinction to account for this. Mr. Highlord's ancestry, within two or three generations, took him back to London tradesmen;[1] Mr. John Jordan, though a man of property who ultimately became lord of a manor (that of Black Bourton),[2] was at this time Steward to the Lenthalls, and several of his name were in trade in Burford. Such men can hardly have held their heads higher than the Bartholomews, who were Burgesses. The only conclusion open to us is that the new group ranked essentially as men of comfortable means and leisured independence, and were for that reason outside the circle of the tradespeople.

[1] See Part III, p. 474.   [2] See Part III, p. 470.

They are our representatives of a class that was, of course, increasing greatly in numbers all over England. A better understanding of the principles of currency, combined with the enormous addition to the stock of precious metals which the discoveries and conquests of the sixteenth century had brought about, had spread through innumerable channels of domestic trade the prosperity accruing from the expansion of foreign mercantile adventure. At the same time improved education, the multiplication of books, and an advancing standard of comfort were adding attractiveness to the leisure thus rendered possible. Men not of noble or gentle birth could, if they chose, find for themselves in social life a pleasant place which neither shackled them to affairs nor involved them in aping their betters.

In most towns the mild sophistication of life which this new class was producing must have been evident at this period. In Burford it may well have been hastened by the fact that the situation of the town in relation to the routes of travel, which has already been seen to have so much importance in our history, was again about to become an active factor in its development. The ridge of hill above the town south-east of the Windrush valley lies along the shortest practicable route from Oxford to Cheltenham, on the way to Gloucester and the crossing of the Severn into Wales. There is one curious little sign in the Burford Records of the traffic along this route, namely, the frequent occurrence of Welsh names in grants and leases of the sixteenth century. John Griffith, Hugh Owen, Griffith Jones, William Hughes, John Lloyd, William Roberts, John Jones, John Williams, Owen Thomas, John Lyme alias Jenkins, David Hewes alias Lloyd, George Watkyns, Evans Lloyd, Griffith Lewis—all these are found among the Burford residents of that century, and some of them became Burgesses. This striking incursion of Welsh names is enough to show that the road which was ultimately to be one of the great coach roads of England, the road between London and South Wales by way of Gloucester, was even then much in use.

As yet, however, the road just at this point was not of

first-rate importance. Direct traffic from London to Gloucester followed a line south of the Thames, crossing the river at
Lechlade.[1] But at that period, before the development of
the through coaching systems, the wide difference between
a main road and a by-road, a coach road and a posting road,
had not arisen. The posting system was all that had been
organized ; and that Burford had already taken its place in
that system is sufficiently indicated by the fact that so early
as 1685 there is a reference to ' the postmaster ' at Burford.[2]
The town's main activity as a posting station came, not
from the Oxford–Cheltenham–Gloucester route, which was
later to be its chief artery of life, but from its situation on
the road to Stow-on-the-Wold, a junction line between the
southern and midland through routes.

One other point of difference between the roads of this
and later periods may also be noted. The normal way from
Oxford to Burford did not at this time lie through Botley
and Eynsham to Witney, but took the less direct course by
Bladon, Long Handborough, and the northern side of
Eynsham Park. That was the direction taken by Charles I
on his night march out of Oxford ; and he would hardly have
taken it if there had been a good road through Eynsham,
since this latter route would have kept him farther away
from Essex at Bletchingdon, while bringing him very little
nearer to Waller at Newbridge. But a more significant proof
of the old lie of the road, because one connected with an
ordinary journey and uncomplicated by considerations of
tactics, is the fact that Charles II, returning from the races
at Burford, and hawking on the way home, finally entered
his coach at Campsfield, which is upon the road between
Oxford and Bladon.[3]

Burford Races can claim a very early place in the records
of organized race-meetings. The history of the sport, as we
know it now in England, may be said to have begun with
James I. Horses have been raced against each other, of

---

[1] See Ogilby's *Britannia Depicta*.
[2] *Ormonde Papers* (Hist. MSS. Com.), New Series, vol. vii, p. 410.
[3] *Ormonde Papers*, New Series, vol. v, p. 619.

course, since men first learned to ride them; and races arranged more or less on the moment were constantly taking place at English fairs and festivities. But not until the reign of James I do we come upon race-meetings as a pastime, or upon challenge trophies (usually in those days gold or silver bells) held for a year and then raced for again on the same course. Races of this kind date from 1603 at York, and 1609 on the Roodee at Chester; while subscription purses are first mentioned in 1613.[1]

Hence a record of racing at Burford in 1620 gives the town an early place in the annals of the sport. The parish registers contain the following entry, among the burials:

1620/1. Robt Tedden a stranger stabde wth a knife at the George by one Potley at the race buried ult. Januarie.

And in 1626:

William Backster gent. sometyme of Norfolk and in that sheir borne and now belonging to the Lord Morden was slaine at the George the next daie after the race and buried the 6 of November.

Since it was without doubt the personal passion of James I for the sport that brought horse-racing into fashion in English life, it seems not far-fetched to conjecture that on his visit to Sir Lawrence Tanfield in 1603[2] he may have perceived that Burford Downs would form an excellent Course, and may have helped to establish the meeting. That, from the first, it was a fully organized meeting we may conclude from the form of the Register entries and the use of the term ' the race '.

Racing continued at Burford under the Commonwealth. The following entry is of the year 1654:

William Howard servant to Mr. Rowland Lacy received a wound at the race and died thereof and was buried the 10 day of Aprill.

In 1680/1 the race for the King's Plate was transferred from Newmarket to Burford.[3] Charles II was at Oxford that

---

[1] *Encycl. Brit.*, article on ' Horse-racing '.   [2] See chap. xi, p. 271.
[3] *Ormonde Papers*, New Series, vol. v, p. 618.

year, and he came over to witness the races on March 17, being received by the Bailiffs and Burgesses and conducted by them to the Priory, where he dined before proceeding to ' the large plain adjoyning ' for the races. The company at the meeting, Anthony Wood tells us, was larger than at any time on Newmarket Heath ;[1] but, on the other hand, the racing, according to one of the Duke of Ormonde's correspondents, was inferior. The King agreed in this verdict ; but he liked the hawking here better than at Newmarket. He had some sport of that kind before the races ; when he arrived at Burford his famous huntsman, Will Chiffinch, met him ' with his little devil black beagles and his hawks ; but to show his Majesty's partiality to the latter, though the former brought their new started hare into his view, he cried let them go and went a-hawking '. The country was evidently as good a hare country then as it is now.

In spite of the Royal opinion Burford Races were to continue for over a century longer. This meeting that Charles II attended was a spring one ; Register entries already quoted show that a meeting was held in November ; and an entry of the year 1630—' Mr. William Clarke, servant to the Lord Grey, killed by a fall from his horse at the race meeting June 8 '—gives us a summer meeting also.

Burford racing was discontinued at the beginning of the nineteenth century. The site of the Course can be identified still by remains of some buildings in a small wood, close to the road on the way from Burford to Bibury, about a mile before Aldsworth. These buildings are obviously remains of a grand-stand and stables.

Races to which the King came, races which attracted a larger company of rank and fashion than Newmarket, must have meant busy days in the town, the inns full, the streets alive with comings and goings. Whether this was quite salutary for Burford is another question. It may have had an ill effect in flooding the place with easily earned money, and introducing a certain parasitic habit, likely to sap the steadiness of trade. It is significant that the industry

[1] Wood, *Life and Times* (Oxfd. Hist. Soc.), vol. ii, p. 529.

specially noted by Dr. Plot as characteristic of Burford in 1675 was malting. Inns begin to appear in the Records in astonishing numbers. Besides the old signs of the George, the Bull, the Bear, the Angel, and the Crown, we find the Greyhound (then at the corner of what is now Swan Lane), the Swan (which occupied Cob Hall between the Vicarage and the river), the King's Arms, the Mermaid, the Three Goats' Heads, the Blackamoor's Head, the Three Cups, the Black Boy, the Talbot, the White Hart. No doubt they all did a good trade; but we may entertain the suspicion that Burford's activities at this time were often more in the nature of bustle than genuine business.

There was, indeed, one trade here as important as malting; the Burford saddlers had a great reputation. The first glimpse of this may perhaps be found in the letter, previously quoted, from Thomas Cade to Thomas Cromwell, recommending as a suitable applicant for a lease of some Crown property a Burford clothier named Tucker. Cade clinches recommendations of various kinds by the promise: ' And he schall gyf yow xx^{ti}li. to by yow a sadell.'[1] It is not said that the saddle should be a Burford one; but the choice of this particular article for the offering may well mean that it was beginning to be the town's best product. It certainly was so in 1663, when three saddles were presented to Charles II and the Duke of York, at a cost of £21; in 1680/1, when Charles was given another, which, Anthony Wood says, was a finer present than Oxford had made to the King;[2] and in 1695, when two were given to William III, which he ordered to be reserved for his own personal use. The tanners, curriers, smiths, and collar-makers, whom we find also among the tradesmen of the time, reveal a general harness-making industry such as would naturally flourish in a posting town.

But though the Burford saddlers for a time rivalled in reputation (and in more belligerent ways) the Witney blanket-makers, Burford never devoted itself in the same degree as

[1] See Part III, p. 656.
[2] Wood, *Life and Times* (Oxfd. Hist. Soc.), vol. ii, p. 529.

Witney to one staple trade. Broadweavers, fullers, a felt-maker kept the more ancient occupations alive to some extent. Masons, joiners, carpenters, and a brazier got their living from the taste for improved housing and the command of easier incomes.

For the rest, the trade of the town tended more and more towards general shop-keeping. This is to be expected both from the posting traffic through the place, and from the demands of that leisured class which we have seen appearing among the inhabitants. Mercers, haberdashers, tailors, bakers, and so on are as common among the Burgesses as are tanners. Barber surgeons, a physician, and an apothecary or two had found it worth while to set up in business. But the most interesting sign of the rising social outlook of Burford is that there was already a bookseller's shop.

In fact, the doubt whether this was really Burford's most prosperous time is suggested rather by the quality of its trade than by the volume of it, which in a miscellaneous way must have been larger than ever. It sufficed to maintain Burgesses like Leonard Mills, Simon Simons, the Silvesters, John Hannes, in big comfortable houses; to establish the Bartholomews in the manor house on Westhall Hill; and to send the scions of the Webbes, the Hunts, and the Jordans forth into the world as gentlemen. In these families we discern the successors of what might be called the ' forty-pound group ' of Tudor times; and in the Sessions, the Serrells, the Taylors, the Yates, and so on we can equally discern the ' twenty-pound group '. It is difficult, after the view we have had of these men in their public capacity as a rather discredited Corporation, to observe them without bias in their capacity as tradesmen. But in so far as they can thus be seen, they show no sign in their business of the blight that had fallen upon them in larger affairs.

This is the period when, in Burford as elsewhere, trade was assisted by the use of a local currency—the trades-men's tokens. There are nine known Burford tokens, as follows :

1. Obv.   ✿ A ✿ BURFORD TOKEN 1669 ✿ ✿ ✿
   Rev.   B. B. .   on either side of a lion rampant.
   Value—One farthing.

2. Obv.   ☆ Thomas ◊ MATHEWES ◊ At (round a
   chained bear)
   Rev.   THE BEARE IN BURFORD (around the

   device ₒMₒ
   TₒE).

   Value—One farthing.   Date
   between 1658 and 1669.

3. Obv.   AT THE 3 SHUGER LOVES (around three sugar
   loaves)
   Rev.   ☆ IN BURFORT □ 1653 (around E ✿ C).

4. Obv.   ✿ LEONARD MILLS . AT (around a wagon
   and team)
   Rev.   ✿ BURFORD. WAGONNER (around L.M.
   1669).

   Value—one farthing.

5. Obv.   ◊ JOHN ◊ SINDRIY ◊ (around a shield of the
   Grocers' Arms)

   Rev.   ☆ OF ◊ BURFORD ◊ 1653 (around ◊S◊
   I◊E).

   Value—one farthing.

6. Obv.   ☆ IOH PAYTON CLOTHYER (around a talbot
   passant)

   ☆ IN. BURFORD. 1666 (around ☆P☆
   I☆S).

7. Obv.   ◊ IOHN ◊ PAYTON—HIS HALFPENY
   Rev.   OF BURFORD 1669 (around I. P. and a merchant's mark).

8. Obv.   AT. THE. GEORGE (round a George and Dragon)
   IN BURFORD (around R. A. V.).
   Value—one farthing.

9. Obv.   CHARLES YATE (around three gates)
   OF BURFORD 1664 (around C. H. Y.).

Of the eighteenth century our Records have very little to tell beyond the range of the controversy that arose in 1738 and was prolonged till 1743 over the administration of the charities. That has been fully discussed elsewhere.

Richard Rawlinson was here in 1717, in the course of collecting the notes which were to have been the foundation of his projected *History of Oxfordshire*. But his manuscript tells us little. He devoted himself chiefly to the monumental inscriptions in the Church, using largely the notes of the 1660 visitor; incidentally he mentions that the inscription by John Leggare outside the south transept window[1] had then been re-cut ' by Mr. Silvester '.[2] He makes, however, one important statement. ' In 1645 ', he writes, ' Sir Wm Waller demolished the Cross, which stood upon eight pillars was the third for beauty in England, the vase stands now on a neighbours house near adjoining.'[3] This would appear to refer to the Tolsey. The date 1645 is perhaps a mistake for 1644, in June of which year Waller was here for several days ;[4] it may be suggested that the few Royalist soldiers he caught in the town had attempted to hold the Tolsey, and so brought about this demolition.

Rawlinson also records the holding of the Assizes at Burford in 1636, on account of the plague then raging in Oxford ; and he adds that the condemned persons, three men and a boy, ' all of the name of Thomas ', were hanged on Battle Edge. One of the bodies was dissected by Mr. William Taylor, and Rawlinson saw the skeleton, then in the possession of Mr. Taylor's grandson, a surgeon, of Burford.

From every point of view little is to be expected of this period in the way of notable additions to the town's buildings. Yet there is a type of house which is probably to be attributed to the early eighteenth century. The best specimen is the fine tall-windowed façade opposite the Tolsey. We cannot date it with the accuracy which has been possible in the case of types of other periods ; but the great height of the windows and the character of the woodwork in them are enough to give an approximate date. The marked feature of

---

[1] See p. 111.   [2] Bodl. MSS. Rawl. B. 400 B, fol. 21.
[3] Bod. MSS. Rawl. B. 400 F, fol. 220.   [4] See p. 205.

the style is that the frontage is carried up to a more or less emphatic parapet, throwing the roof back into a position of minor importance. This feature had, indeed, found a place earlier in some houses; the façade of the Vicarage and that of the Great House display it. But both of these are cases in which the parapet is an ornate detail of a decoratively treated frontage. They are not quite on the same level as the cases in which the parapet is the governing characteristic of the design of small façades, as in the present Post Office, or a house, lower down on the opposite side of the High Street, in the block between Church Lane and Lawrence Lane, or, on a rather bigger scale, the house on the south side of Sheep Street to which the sign of the Greyhound was removed in the eighteenth century. Several houses on the Hill are also of this type.

Apart from these recognizable structures, this period must be responsible for a great deal of entirely featureless building, which filled the gaps in the street frontage lines, and so allowed a little more elbow-room to the population. For two maps of the end of the century make it quite clear that by that time the streets had come to present virtually the unbroken appearance that we have to-day. One is the map engraved by Davis of Lewknor in 1797, but based on surveys made in 1793; and the other is the map of 1823, drawn, as there is reason to conclude, from the Enclosure Award Map of 1795. Neither is on a large scale; yet the scale is sufficient to have shown any considerable gaps in the street lines, and none are to be seen. We may therefore take it that much of the building work of the century was given to squeezing in, between existing houses, cottages and small houses to accommodate the larger population of the time. For the first of the modern census returns, made in 1801, shows that by the end of the eighteenth century there were not less than 1,500 persons in the town.

Probably the chief part of the increase in population occurred in the last quarter of the century, with the advent of the great days of coach travelling. Until the middle of the century Burford was relying on its trade as a posting station. Even the 1749 edition of Ogilby represents the through road to Gloucester as still passing south of the

Thames; and in a Road Improvement Act of 1751 the route in which the Bailiffs of Burford are officially interested is one that leads in the old way by Campsfield. But a change was by this time close at hand. In 1761 a coach began running from Burford to London by way of Witney; the enterprise was undertaken by Thomas Castell.

Thus was opened the road along which the remunerative traffic of the next sixty or seventy years was to pour through Burford. It is probable that better methods of road-making, combined with better drainage of the fields, had rendered practicable all the year round the rather low-lying stretch between Oxford and Eynsham. This was all that had been needed to bring the Gloucester, South Wales, and Hereford traffic down from London by way of the Chilterns, Oxford, Burford, and Cheltenham, instead of by the roads south of the Thames, which would be served by the Bath and south-western coaches. In the fierce competition that was now beginning the new route offered an ample prospect of profit.

Burford's interest in the coach traffic was even greater than might appear at first sight to the traveller of to-day; for the modern main road really passes the town by, keeping to the ridge of the hill. But during the longer part of the coaching period there was no proper road along the ridge at this point; there was only a farm track serving for the work on the arable fields. The main road, directly it entered the parish of Burford at the eastern boundary, left the ridge and turned down White Hill, to come right into the town by way of Witney Street. It left the town again by way of Sheep Street, at the end of which it took a turn down through the Priory woods, towards the river, to rise steeply from the farther corner of the woods up past Upton quarries to the top of the hill once more, not far from the western boundary of the parish. Of this curious deflection towards the river the traces can still be seen. Inside the modern wall of the Priory grounds just beyond the Lamb Inn there runs a short length of the older wall, going off at a slant inwards; and beyond the woods the deep indentation of the old road in the hollow is perfectly plain.

PLATE XIII. THE BULL

For a long while, even after Palmer's reforms of the coaching system and the great speeding-up that he effected, the coaches continued to come thus into the heart of the town; and the business they brought must have been considerable. True, the coaches probably did not make any long stop here; Witney seems to have been the stage for changing horses, and the passengers would take their chief meals either at Oxford or at Cheltenham. Much the most profitable business in Burford must have been done with those who came in from the country-side to catch the through coaches here. That often involved a stay of more than one night, for coaches might come in fully loaded and unable to take more passengers; there was then nothing to be done but wait until a later coach came in with a vacant seat. Moreover, the posting business, though no longer the chief trade, must still have been valuable.

It has been calculated that in the best time Burford saw no fewer than forty coaches passing up and down in the course of the twenty-four hours. From the reminiscences of an old coaching guard on this route we know the names of some of the 'fliers', and can calculate the hours at which they passed Burford.[1] About 9.30 in the morning the Magnet from Cheltenham would arrive, on its way to Oxford, and just behind it came the Berkeley Hunt, a green coach, working the same route. At 11 the Regulator from Gloucester would rattle in, and with it, or on its heels, the Retaliator, also from Gloucester. At 1 o'clock the Mazeppa from Hereford and its rival on the same road, the Rapid, would appear; and soon after they had gone the down Magnet and the down Berkeley Hunt would be roaring up the narrow end of Witney Street. Later in the afternoon the down Regulator, Retaliator, Mazeppa, and Rapid were due; and by 7 o'clock the first of the night coaches, the Champion from Hereford, came through, followed about 10.30 by the Paul Pry from Aberystwyth. At 12.30 a.m. the down Champion, and soon afterwards the down Paul Pry, would be waking the echoes. Last of all in the small hours came the Gloucester

[1] *Collectanea* (Oxfd. Hist. Soc.), vol. iv, pp. 274 sqq.

Royal Mail, the up coach at 1.30 a.m. and the down at 4.30 a.m.

Thus, without counting the less important coaches and those working only short distances, eighteen of the through ' fliers ' were seen here every day. The rows of hooks that are yet visible in the beams under the archways of the George and the Bull must always have been laden then with joints of beef, hams and hares and partridges ; and the yards that are now so quiet can never have been without the clatter of the stable hands and the gossip of the post-boys.

What this constant touch with the world might mean to the more leisured class of Burford resident is seen in the correspondence between the ladies who lived in the Great House towards the end of the eighteenth century and their brother, ' Daddy ' Crisp, the friend of Fanny Burney. The story of Mrs. Gast and her sister has been told by Dr. Hutton,[1] and all that need be said here is that it makes an interesting addition to the rather meagre picture of Burford life in general during this period.

Meanwhile the outward aspect of the place underwent the last of the great changes that made it as it is now. The enclosure of the old common arable lands swept away the open fields, and put in their place the walled fields and pastures of the modern landscape. This occurred here at a rather early date, the Upton fields being enclosed in 1773 and the Burford fields in 1795. Analysis of the Awards provides us with the explanation of this. In Burford Fields, out of some 1,100 acres enclosed, only about 300 went to independent farmers. John Lenthall and the Impropriator of the Rectorial tithes received the rest. We can perceive only two farms which were not held on tenancy from these two persons. One was White Hill farm, held by Mrs. Mary Legg, of which the farm-house was not the one now called by that name, but the one in the valley by the Widford road ; and the other was apparently worked in partnership by two men named Finch and a Mrs. Tebbut. Some ten others are named in the Award, but only for insignificant allotments of two or three

[1] *Burford Papers*, by W. H. Hutton, D.D., now Dean of Winchester.

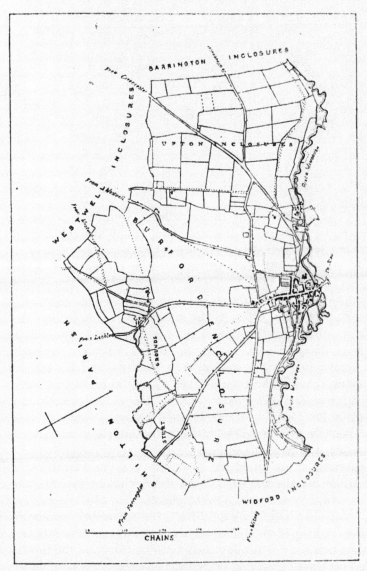

MAP OF THE BURFORD ENCLOSURE AWARD.
From a copy, preserved in the Tolsey at Burford, of the original Map.

acres. Similarly in the Upton Award, which disposes of 803 acres, 720 acres went to the Lenthalls, and only one other person, Thomas Ansell, who received 41 acres, can be considered as a farmer.

It is, therefore, not difficult to understand why our enclosures took place early. Small farmers working their own land had almost disappeared. The new sources of prosperity had drawn back into the town the families of those who, in the sixteenth century, had first begun the creation of larger farms. They had been willing to be rid of their land, when Tanfield and the Lenthalls were putting together their estates, and had made way for the new race of tenant farmers.

Thus, as we leave the eighteenth century, our mental pictures, not only of Burford town, but of the country-side round it as well, have reached the last stage, and afford us already in all outward appearance the Burford of our own time.

The only topographical point in which change was yet to come was the direction of the main roads. It is strange that with all the amelioration of the coaching service and all the fierce competition in speed, so obvious an improvement as the avoiding of the descent into Burford, and the hill out again, should have been delayed so long as it was. A minor improvement took place early in the nineteenth century, when Mr. John Lenthall diverted the road beyond Sheep Street from its passage through the middle of the Priory woods, and gave the coaches a straight run to the hill by the quarries. This alteration, however, was due rather to his concern for the amenities of the Priory than to any intention to save the coaches a toilsome détour.

Not until 1812 do we hear of ' the new road ', which, by a re-making of the old track along the ridge, linked up the road between the turning down by White Hill and the turning up by Upton Quarries, so that the coaches could keep on the top of the hill. Naturally there was no little complaint in Burford. For while passengers would still come to the town to join the coaches, much casual trade would undoubtedly be lost. When a new inn was built at the cross-roads at the top of the town, the Bird-in-Hand—a somewhat gaunt house still surviving as two private houses—it may have seemed to portend a decline of the inns in the town ; especially when this was followed by the erection of another, the Ramping Cat, at the top of White Hill.

But a far more serious change was impending, which was to make anxiety about the new road of no account. Railroads were soon to divert the traffic of the country to wholly different lines of travel. For the principle of the new locomotion approached the problems of natural configuration in a way directly opposed to that dictated by the requirements of the coaches. Railways needed, not the dryness and firmness of the higher ground, but the most moderate gradients and the passage most nearly approximating to the level. The rise of the Cotswold could no longer be the best practical route to Gloucester and South Wales ; and on the other hand the valley of the Windrush lay just too far to the west to serve for the Worcester and Hereford route. Thus Burford found itself on none of the lines laid down by the Great Western Railway surveyors ; and, as the town had come to be very largely dependent upon chance traffic, not upon any well-developed industry, the blow must have been a heavy one.

But its effect was by no means immediate. Burford was still a market town, in a good agricultural district, and country folk were slow to avail themselves of the new locomotion in their business affairs. The evidence of the census figures throughout the nineteenth century is interesting. The figures are as follows :

	1801.	1811.	1821.	1831.	1841.	1851.
Burford	1,516	1,342	1,409	1,620	1,644	1,593
Upton and Signett	209	242	277	246	—	—

	1861.	1871.	1881.	1891.	1901.
Burford	1,434	1,403	1,312	1,346	1,146
Upton and Signett	245	248	259	—	177

The Worcester section of the Great Western Railway was opened in 1852. For ten years before that there was little change in the population. The ten years after reduced it by about 10 per cent.; and the next twenty years brought it 20 per cent. below the highest point, which it had reached in 1841.

Population is not, of course, the only test of the effect of new conditions upon the town. There must undoubtedly have been less money in the place, when the coaching traffic ceased. But a very rapid ruin was averted by the inordinate prosperity of agriculture during the first sixty or seventy years of the nineteenth century. There were enterprising and skilful farmers around Burford; Mr. Turner of Burford, Mr. Tuckwell of Signett, and Mr. Pinnal of Westhall are constantly cited by Arthur Young, in his *View of the Agriculture of Oxfordshire* (1809), for the value of their opinions on farming methods, and their experience of cultivation and cropping. The steadiness of the figures of population in Upton and Signett are in their way an indication of the circumstances that had come to the rescue of Burford. Farming was flourishing, and the town's trade as a market and shopping centre for the villages around was just enough to pull it through the shock of the withdrawal of the road traffic.

Yet the market was doomed. As a generation grew up accustomed to railways, and forced at the same time by the decline of agricultural prices to seek the larger markets with their more various openings for business, places like Burford could not hold their own against the wider range of Oxford. There are men still living who can remember the ' market ordinary ' room at the Bull, full on a Saturday of the farmers at their dinner. But in the late 'sixties of the the last century the numbers were beginning to grow smaller, and in the early 'seventies the market flickered out; it never came to a formal end, but about the year 1873 or 1874 it ceased from mere inanition.

One fair remains, a shadow of its former self; it is held on September 25, and is the old Holyrood fair, granted to the town by Henry VII. The fair of St. John the Baptist, which was a much older grant, was still represented in 1861 by a fair on July 5 for horses, sheep, and cows.

Saved as it had been for the time by agricultural prosperity Burford shared to the full in the effects of the great agricultural depression. After 1871 the population fell heavily, until by the end of the century both the town and the agricultural hamlets were left with no more than two-thirds of the population of 1841.

What was probably the last hope of a vigorous trade revival was offered by a project in the year 1864 for a branch line connecting the Midland Railway with the south-west of England, passing close to Burford on the south. But in the end a different route was chosen, and there is now no likelihood of any conjunction of through routes which would bring the railroad to the town.

Yet by a curious turn of the wheel of circumstance this final reaction upon the town of its natural situation has not been wholly disastrous. Modern refinements of taste, quickened by revolt against the dreariness of conditions in huge modern towns, have taught a keen appreciation of the country-side, keenest of all for the spots preserved by their remoteness from the activities that unheedingly spread ugliness elsewhere. Moreover, mechanical inventiveness, which a hundred years ago was all in the direction of draining life away from the roads to the railways, is now, by motor cars, restoring it to the roads.

The tale told by the census figures was for many years written also in empty houses declining into ruin. There are empty houses still, but there are many, like the Priory itself, which have taken on a new lease of life. A new resident element in the population, as in the seventeenth century, an influx of road travel, as in the eighteenth century, at least prevent this topographical study of Burford from ending on a note of irremediable decline.

There are towns in England, like Winchester, which have never been off the lines of human movement and intercourse since first such lines are traceable at all. There are others, like Stamford, which were always in older days upon great routes of travel, and were cast suddenly from their importance by the advent of the railways; and others, again, like

Swindon, which were as suddenly flung up into importance out of complete obscurity. Burford belongs to a class in some ways more interesting than any of these. Its relation to the routes of traffic has varied so much at different times that its topography is an unusually fascinating theme to pursue, and not the less fascinating because, in the face of modern valuations and modern appreciations, the final chapter is not yet written.

CHAPTER X

THE LEVELLERS AT BURFORD

THE following are the full titles of the contemporary pamphlets and periodicals of which use has been made in this chapter :

The Levellers (falsly so called) Vindicated, or the Case of the twelve Troops (which by Treachery in a Treaty) was lately surprised, and defeated at *Burford*, truly stated and offered to the Judgment of all unbyassed and wel-minded People, especially of the Army, their fellow Souldiers, under the conduct of the Lord *Fairfax*. By a faithful remnant, late of Col. *Scroops*, Commissary General *Iretons*, and Col. *Harrisons* Regiments, that hath not yet bowed their knee unto *Baal*, whose names (in the behalf of themselves, and by the appointment of the rest of their Friends) are hereunto subscribed.

A True Relation of the Proceedings in the Businesse of Burford with other Discourse of publike Concernment. By *Francis White*, Major to the Lord Generalls Regiment of Foot.

Englands Standard Advanced or A Declaration from M. Will. Thompson and the oppressed People of this nation, now under his conduct in Oxfordshire, dated at their Randezvous, May 6, 1649.

The Declaration of the Prince of Wales to the Commissioners of the King-dome of Scotland. . . . Also The Declaration and Speeches of Cornet *Thompson* and the rest of the Levellers, which were executed in *Burford* Churchyard in Oxfordshire on Fryday last, being the 18 of this instant May, 1649, touching the Parliament and Army And The Remonstrance and Speech of Lieut. Gen. Cromwell to the rest of the prisoners in the Church.

The Levellers Designe Discovered or the Anatomie of the late unhappie Mutinie Proved unto the Souldiery of the Army under the Command of his Excellency the Lord Fairfax ; for prevention of the like in others. Written by Henry Denne, an Actor in this Tragaedy.

Sea-Green & Blue See which Speaks True or Reason contending with Treason. In discussing the late unhappy difference in the Army, which now men dream is well composed. Wherein also is weighed, The Testi-mony of one lately risen from the dead Concerning the Levellers.

  [The above is a reply to Denne's pamphlet. Sea-green ribbon was the Levellers' badge.]

The Levellers Remonstrance sent in a Letter to His Excellency The Lord Gen. Cromwel concerning the Government of this Commonwealth, his wearing of the Crown of Honour, and preservation of the Lawes, Liberties, and Priviledges thereof.

Mercurius Britannicus, Number 4, from Tuesday May the 15 till Tuesday
    May 22 1649.
Mercurius Elencticus, Number 5.
Mercurius Pragmaticus, Pars 2, Numb. 5.
The Kingdoms Weekly Intelligencer, Number 312.
The Moderate, Number 45, From Tuesday May 15 to Tuesday May 22
    1649.
A Perfect Diurnall, Numbers 302, 303.
The Moderate Intelligencer, Number 217.
Antichrist unmasked in Two Treaties, The First, an Answer unto two
    Paedobaptists, . . . The Second, The man of Sinne discovered in Doctrine ;
    the root and foundation of Antichrist laid open. . . . By Henry Denne. . . .
A Den of Theeves Discovered Or certaine errours and false doctrines,
    delivered in a Sermon at a Visitation holden at Baldocke in the County
    of Hertford, Decemb. 9. 1641. By Henry Denne, Curate at Pyrton in
    Hertfordshire. And since Printed by his owne appointment Contradicted
    justly by many of the Auditors. And confuted by Thomas Attwood
    Rotherham Now Rector of St. John Zacharies, London, and sometimes
    Vicar of Ickleford in Hertfordshire, neare Hitchin.

The fact that Burford was the scene of the dramatic climax
of the mutiny among the Parliamentary troops in 1649 may
justify, in a history of Burford, a more particular examination
of that affair than histories of the period at large can give.
These treat, indeed, of the general aspects of the mutiny,
and its place in the political history of the time ; but they
cannot give space to the movements of troops on either side,
or to details which reveal how the sudden end was achieved
—points which in their ultimate association with Burford
become of great interest. Moreover an opportunity is thus
afforded of investigating the complaint, made afterwards by
some of the mutineers, that Fairfax and Cromwell had surprised them by deliberate treachery, and had in fact been
false to their own pledged word. Even if the investigation
throws no new light upon Cromwell, nothing that concerns
his character can be negligible.

The mutiny of 1649 was part of that extremist agitation
which, as we can now see, grew so inevitably out of principles
which the Parliamentary movement developed, yet was so
alien to the minds of the Parliamentary leaders. We are
familiar enough in our own day with democratic activities
to be well acquainted with the types of mind that they may

inflame—the irreconcilable doctrinaire, the unbending asserter of first principles against practical necessities, the man who can see no reason whatever for stopping short of the logical conclusion. These were the types that, after the final defeat of Charles I, had no patience with the Parliament's attempt to occupy the place he had left vacant, and could see in it only the substitution of one tyranny for another. By themselves they might have been, though troublesome, not very dangerous ; the danger came from the alliance between this kind of opposition to the Parliament and the Army's growing suspicion of the politicians. with their adherence to old constitutional forms. A third, and the most powerful, factor in the situation, was that Parliament for the most part represented the Presbyterian tendency towards a new religious intolerance, a new attempt to enforce conformity, against which Cromwell threw his whole weight. Those who believed the Parliament was merely substituting itself for Charles were reinforced by those who saw it also substituting itself for Laud ; and by Cromwell's attitude the Army's mistrust of the Parliament took a double edge.

As early as 1647 the first crisis had occurred, and the Army had asserted its authority in a way that must be referred to here, because it is constantly prominent in the events which culminated at Burford. The Parliament, envisaging its perils, and not unaware of the real seat of danger, had made an unwise attempt to disband a large part of the Army. The counter-stroke was a general rendezvous of the Army on Newmarket Heath, on June 5, 1647, followed within a few days by another at Thriplow Heath, near Royston,[1] at which the Army entered into an engagement to tolerate no disbanding or dividing until they saw the affairs of the country in a posture which they believed they had fought to secure. ' All wise men may see ', they said in one

---

[1] The reason for the two meetings of the Army does not readily appear, but it would seem from the accounts given by Whitelocke, in particular, that at the first the principal subject had been the disbanding, and that the second drew up more especially the political proposals. It is to be noted that the Thriplow Heath meeting is the one the mutineers usually mention, though they frequently mention both.

manifesto, 'that Parliament privileges as well as Royal prerogative may be perverted or abused to the destruction of those greater ends for whose protection and preservation they were intended, to wit, the rights and privileges of the people and the safety of the whole '.[1] The ideally democratic settlement of the country was set forth in these engagements; and a Council of the Army was appointed, on which two representatives of the rank and file of each regiment were to sit as equals with officers and the higher command. Fairfax and Cromwell had countenanced these proceedings; Ireton and Lambert were known to have lent their legal training to the drawing up of the published Declarations.[2]

There is no reason for supposing that Cromwell at any time regarded the political spirit in the Army as a weapon which he could use against the Parliament and drop at his convenience. He was probably under no illusions; yet he made three miscalculations. He did not realize the strength of the belief that the reign of pure democracy could arrive in a moment; he had no conception of the Council of the Army as a rival to Parliament in affairs of government; and he, in common with others, entirely missed the profound danger of the 'engagement' against disbanding *or dividing*. The fixed idea of countering the Parliament in that matter blinded every one concerned to the use that might be made of this engagement against the military commanders themselves, when detailing regiments for service. Within five months Cromwell was applying a drastic corrective to impatience, by the summary execution of a soldier in front of a disaffected regiment. That, and the renewed fighting of 1648, were effective for a time in keeping the Army in hand. But the logical democrats remained irreconcilably hostile; pamphlets poured forth in endless attack upon existing authority; Lilburne and three other leaders—Walwyn, Overton, and Prince—were clapped into the Tower, from which retreat they continued the most violent assaults upon

---

[1] Army Remonstrance of June 23, 1647; quoted by Firth, *Cromwell's Army*, p. 354.
[2] Whitelocke's *Memorials*, ii. 162.

the tyrant Cromwell. The name of 'Leveller' becomes almost as common in the varied periodical literature of those years as the name 'Anarchist' or 'Bolshevist' in our own day; and it is to be remarked that, like these later names, it was usually employed as a term of abuse and prejudice.[1] It was always repudiated by Lilburne and his followers, who strenuously denied that they had any intention of reducing all men to one level, or making any rough and ready redistribution of property. But a truly democratic government they never wearied of demanding; and there can be no question of the zeal with which they fomented discontent, wherever they found it. In the Army it was keen enough, the failure of the democratic Council of the Army, which had speedily declined into a committee of high officers only, being embittered by the standing grievance of pay in arrear, at a time when considerable grants of money were being made to military leaders.

In April 1649 a spark was set to the tinder by the decision for the campaign in Ireland, and the selection by lot of the regiments to proceed there on active service. The danger inherent in the Thriplow Heath engagement was now revealed. The leaders of disaffection could, and did, take the line that the preparations for the Irish campaign were a disguised attempt to break up centres of agitation in the Army—a 'dividing', such as they had undertaken not to tolerate. The inflammation came to a head simultaneously at Banbury and Salisbury. At the former town the disaffected men placed themselves under the leadership of one William Thompson, cornet of a regiment of horse, held a demonstration in force, and issued a declaration in the then common form against 'tyranny'. With this centre of trouble the troops

---

[1] There is a curious pamphlet called 'Terrible and bloudy Newes from the disloyall Army in the North', with a picture on the title-page of soldiers impaling babies on spears and swinging them up to dash out their brains. It proceeds to relate the terror of the inhabitants of Market Harborough when some Levellers arrived in the town on a market day; they ran hither and thither in fright. But the only facts to be related, when the point comes, are that the Levellers proclaimed that there was nothing to be afraid of, 'staid a while at the Crown, and so departed peaceably'. Evidently some methods of modern journalism are not new.

at Salisbury were already in communication. Thompson's manifesto states : ' We do own and avow the late proceedings in Colonel Scroops, Colonel Harrisons, and Major General Skippon's Regiments, declared in their Resolutions published in print ; As one man Resolving to live and dy with them, in their and our just and mutual defence.'[1] Less under the domination of a single leader, the movement at Salisbury was evidently in numbers the more formidable. Near that place were quartered two of the regiments of horse upon whom the lot had fallen for Ireland—Commissary General Ireton's and Colonel Scroops. The story may here use the words of some of those who were ultimately taken prisoner at Burford :

Our old solemn Engagement at Newmarket and Triplo Heaths, June 5, 1647, with the manifold Declarations, Promises, and Protestations of the Army, in pursuance thereof, were all utterly declined and most perfidiously broken, and the whole fabrick of the Commonwealth faln into the grossest and vilest Tyranny that ever English men groaned under . . . which, with the consideration of the particular, most insufferable abuses and dis-satisfactions put upon us, moved us to an *unanimous refusal to go* . . . till full satisfaction and security were given to us, as Soldiers and Commoners, by a Councel of our own free Election. . . . Whereupon we drew up a Paper of some Reasons, by way of Declaration, concerning our said refusal, to deliver to our Colonel ; unto which, we all chearfully subscribed, with many of our Officers (especially Cornet *Den*, who then seemingly was extream forward in assisting us to effect our desires) which being delivered a day or two after, immediately our Officers called a Rendezvous near unto Salisbury, where they declared, That the General intended not to force us, but that we might either go or stay ; and so certifying our intents to stay, we were all drawn into the Town again, and the Colonel, with the rest of the Officers, full of discontent, threatened us the Souldiers ; and because we were all, or most of one minde, he termed our Unity a Combination, or Mutiny ; yet himself, upon our request to know, told us, That he could not assure us, that he would go. Which forementioned Paper, with a Letter, we sent to Commissary General Iretons Regiment, who took it so well, That they were immediately upon their march towards our quarters, to joyn with us.[2]

---

[1] *England's Standard Advanced.*   [2] *The Levellers Vindicated.*

It may be remarked here that the permission to ' go or stay '
was not so simple as it sounds, since it meant in practice to go
or be disbanded, and struck upon another grievance ; for
it is asserted in this same pamphlet that men who took their
discharge, with months of pay in arrear, received nothing
but a few shillings for immediate needs and a certificate of
the amount of pay due, which certificates they were forced
by their poverty to sell at 3s. or 4s. in the £—the Parliament,
they allege, being actually so mean as to employ agents of
their own to buy back their own certificates at that price.

The officers took the obvious steps for stemming discontent
in the ranks, but without avail.

After this all politike means . . . were put in practice to work
us off from our Resolutions, as severing the Troops, and dealing
with them apart . . . All these devices working nothing upon
us (there being no satisfaction given to our just exceptions)
our Colonel fell to violent threats, and commanded us to put
our Horses in a Field two miles from our Quarters ; which
though at first we did, yet finding the bitterness of his spirit
to encrease, and that upon his information, That the General,
and Lieutenant General were preparing a force against us :
what could we do less, than put our selves into the best posture
we could to preserve our selves, which we immediately did
(and in this no man was more forward, and violently earnest,
than that perfidious Apostate, Cornet *Den*). . . . Hereupon our
Officers leaving us, we chose new ones, and disposed of our
Colours, and immediately drew up a Declaration . . . This
Declaration was publikely read at our Rendezvous in *Old
Sarum*, where four troops of Commissarie General *Iretons* met
us, and unanimously assented to by both Regiments ; whereupon our conjunction we advanced to Marlborough and so to
Wantage.[1]

The terms of the declaration we may see in a letter sent the
same day to Fairfax :

May it please your Excellency A Proposition was made unto
us for the service of Ireland, with a Declaration of your Excellencies pleasure, that it was lawfull for us to consent or deny,
for no man was to be forced ; although many of us were very
willing to put our lives in our hands for that service, yet were
we constrained to answer in the negative, in regard we did

[1] *The Levellers Vindicated.*

conceive it a breach of former ingagements, to suffer many of our fellow Souldiers, who could not go, to be disbanded without a competent pay in hand of their Arrears to carry them home, and inable them to follow their occupations : We perceive such a representation of the businesse hath been laid before your Excellency, rendring us so vile.in your eyes, that the next Newes we heard was of Forces marching towards us, which hath put us upon an unusuall yet a necessary way for our owne preservation, least we should be destroyed before we could be heard to speake, to relinquish our Officers, and fly for our present safety. And now we do earnestly beseech your Excellency patiently to heare us, and to take us under your protection ; all that we require is the performance of our ingagement at Triploe Heath, and we shall promise never to depart from your Excellencies command, in anything which shall not be contrary to the said ingagement, professing our selves very sorry, that we should have no better esteem in your Excellencies judgement.[1]

This was all very well, but to ' relinquish ' officers, ' dispose of ' colours, and leave quarters was mutiny. We may see now that Scroop and his officers had (as will happen in face of the disgrace of a mutiny) lost their tempers, and had not, perhaps, handled the situation with a calm discretion. But it may be doubted whether anything could have controlled the men then. Memories of the prompt execution at Ware in 1647 (and there had been another summary execution in London early in this same year of 1649) must have warned them that, however they formulated their grievances, Cromwell would not tolerate refusal of orders. By that time there was no course for them to take but the one they now attempted —to effect a junction with other forces of the disaffected. Banbury would clearly be their objective, for a brother of Cornet Thompson was among their number ; but believing that by taking Abingdon on the way they could pick up some troops of Harrison's regiment as well, they had directed their march first upon Wantage.

Their information that Fairfax and Cromwell were on the move was correct. News of the outbreak at Banbury had reached London on May 5 ; on May 7 it was known there

---

[1] White's *True Relation.*

that Scroop's regiment had refused duty, and on the next
day that Ireton's men were with them.[1] On May 11 these
two regiments left Salisbury, and on the evening of that day
the news reached Fairfax and Cromwell in camp at Andover ;
it may have been brought by Scroop himself, since he was
later given Fairfax's reply to the mutineers' letter, to carry
to them. The first step taken by the Generals was to dispatch
at once four officers, Major White, Captain Scotten, Captain
Peverell, and Captain Bayley with a communication to the
mutineers. Leaving Andover on the evening of the 11th,
they rode through the night to Marlborough, and finding
that the troops had already left that place they followed
them to Wantage. This was on Saturday, the 12th. Discussion was postponed till the next morning, when a meeting
was to be held at 10 o'clock at Stanford-in-the-Vale. The
four officers for some reason did not appear there (possibly,
if one may judge by some expressions in Major White's
account, because Scroop arrived just then), and had again
to follow the Levellers, who were on their way to Abingdon.
Near that place a halt was called, at which White read the
letter he had brought from Fairfax. With Scroop the men
would have no dealings ; they listened to what White had
to say—mainly an appeal to them, backed by Fairfax's
letter, to perceive the perils of disunion in the Army. But
the letter, they said afterwards, ' took but little effect upon
our Spirits ' ; they were set upon effecting the junction
they wished to make, and marched on till they met the
expected two troops of Harrison's men, to whom they read
their declaration.

The two Troops being very willing to be satisfied in the
lawfulnesse of the engagement, telling us they were marching
to *Thame*, and the next morning we should know their resolutions : But as we were marching back againe, before we were
half out of the field, we spied a party of horse, which it seemed
was the Apostate *Reynolds* with his mercenary damme crew
(such as in our hearing most desperately swore, That if the
Devil would come from hell and give them a groat a day more
than the State, they would fight for him against the Levellers

---

[1] Whitelock's *Memorials*, iii. 29.

or any others) well, upon this we drew out a Forlorne hope, and thereupon two troops of Colonel *Harrisons* marched with us towards them ; they retreated towards *New-bridge* and kept it by force against us, but we unwilling to shed blood, or to be the original occasion of a new war (though they have often branded us with it as if we wholly sought it) but our actions did then clearly manifest the contrary ; for we seeing Souldiers coming in a Hostile manner against us as aforesaid, did meet them, having forty or fifty of them at our mercy, and could have destroyed them, for we had them two miles from the foresaid bridg, but we did not then in the least offer them any violence, or diminish a hair of their heads, but let them go to their body againe, and withall marched to a Ford.[1]

It is necessary to modify this account in some respects by comparing it with Major White's. He says :

Reports came that the Bridge was made good against them by Colonell *Reynolds*, with 200 Horse and a party of Dragoons, and that my Lord Generall was coming to fall upon them in the Reer ; this news was strange to me and begat some heats amongst them, and put some upon resolution to Force the Bridge, and they tied up their cloaks and rode a Career with resolution to charge them, as far as I could perceive by their words and practice. I then made what hast I could to get before them, and to interpose between them to prevent hostility ; but by the way I met with Major *Abbot*, who asked my opinion, whether it were best for them to keep the Bridge, or let them passe ? I asked him whither he had command from my Lord soe to do, he answered he had ; then said I, you are bound so to do, or els you may be hanged if you do not : then coming to Colonell *Reynolds* at the Bridge foot, I there read the Paper which I had written, the which I thought so reasonable, as by that means to put a stop to any furious resolutions, the parties were perswaded to decline force, and marched a mile up the river, and forded over.[2]

By this time it was growing late in the evening of Sunday, May 13, and the mutineers began to think about quarters for the night. They left the decision to two of their officers, Lieutenant Ray and Cornet Denne, who decided to march them by Bampton to Burford, which was reached about nine o'clock at night. They disposed themselves about Burford and in two neighbouring villages, and appear to have settled

[1] *The Levellers Vindicated.* [2] White's *True Relation.*

PLATE XIV. ON THE SOUTH SIDE OF SHEEP STREET

DOUBLE-BAYED 16TH-CENTURY HOUSE IN CENTRE, LATE 17TH-CENTURY HOUSE TO LEFT

down without much apprehension.   They were horribly
surprised when, at midnight, troops poured into the town
from two sides, overwhelmed desultory attempts at resistance,
and finally imprisoned about three hundred and forty of
them in the church.   The remainder of the mutineers, who
had numbered in all some nine hundred, had escaped, but
the arms and horses of about eight hundred fell into the
hands of Fairfax.[1]   He and Cromwell had moved very
swiftly, having covered between forty and fifty miles in the
day, and they had actually been at Abingdon, having moved
from Andover by Theal, when the mutineers were crossing
just above Newbridge.[2]   The entry into Burford was made by
Colonel Reynolds with his horse, Colonel Okey with his
dragoons, and Major Shelborn with a Buckinghamshire
regiment of horse.   Fairfax himself brought up a party in
reserve, and Colonel Scroop had a command in the rear.[3]
Captain Fisher commanded the party that was sent round to
enter the town from the other side—the Sheep Street approach, no doubt, since the main advance of a force coming
up from Bampton would naturally be made along Witney
Street.

The mutineers afterwards made accusations of treacherous
dealings against Fairfax and Cromwell, asserting that they
had been lulled by Major White into a false security, had
been led to believe that time would be given them for
negotiation, and that there was no intention of using force
against them.

Being in treatic [says their own account] with the Commissioners, and having intelligence, that the General and
Lt. General were upon their march towards us, many of us
severall times, urged to Major *White*, and prest upon him,
that he came to betray us, to which he replyed, That the
Generall and Lieutenant Generall had engaged their Honours
not to engage against us in any Hostile manner till they had
received our Answer. . . . We gave the more credit to the
Major, who seemed extream forward and hastie to make the
Composure, pretending so far to approve of our standing for

[1] *Mercurius Britannicus*, no. 4.   [2] *The Moderate*, no. 45.
[3] *The Kingdom's Weekly Intelligencer*, no. 312.

the things contained in our engagement at Triplo-Heath, that himself with our consents drew up a Paper in Answer to the Generall for us ... During the time of treaty, while the Commissioners thus assured us *all security*, one of them, to wit, Captain *Scotten* privately slipt from us, and two others, to wit, Captain *Bayley* and *Peverill* left notes at every Town of our strength and condition, whilst Major *White* held us in hand, and told us, that if they fell upon us, he would stand between the bullets and us : So that when notice had been sufficiently given, and we with all the meanes that could be used, wrought into a secure condition at *Burford*, & after the setting of our Guard, which was commanded by Quarter-Master *More* who was thereupon appointed, by his Brother Traytor, Cornet *Den* (who himself) since his coming to London hath avowedly declared to Ma. W. W.[1] to this effect, that his beginning and continuing with the *Burford* Troops was out of premeditated and complotted designe, that so at last he might the easier bring on their destruction, holding all the time he was with them, correspondency with the Generalls creatures, which said Quarter-Master *More* after he had set the guard in this slight manner, and possest us with as much security as he could, and under the pretence of going to refresh himself and his horse, did most villanously and treacherously leave the guard without any Orders, and himself in person posted away to the Generals forces and brought them in upon us, marching in the head of them with his sword drawn against us ; And Quarter-Master *More* being afterward called Traitor by some of the Souldiers, Cap. *Gotherd* of *Scroops* Regiment made answer he was none, for that he did nothing but what he was sent to do ; so that most Treacherously, that same night the Generals forces came pouring on both sides of the Towne of *Burford*, where we had not beene above three houres, swearing Damme them and sink them, and violently fell upon us, and so by a fraudulent and Treacherous surprize defeated us, not expecting it during the Treatie, especially from them with whom we had joyned these seven yeares for the defence of Englands Liberties and Freedoms, and though divers of us had faire quarter promised us by Colonel *Okey*, Major *Barton* and the rest of the Officers there with them, as that not a hair of our heads should perish, yet did they suffer their souldiers to plunder us, strip us, and barbarously to use us, worse then Cavaliers.[2]

[1] Perhaps Lilburne's associate, Walwyn, whose Christian name was William.

[2] *The Levellers Vindicated.*

Rumours of treachery were also current in London circles unfriendly to Cromwell.

Oliver [says *Mercurius Pragmaticus*] having had a Taste of their Resolution given him in Hampshire about Alton (as Reynolds the Apostate had about Banbury) he gave them leisure to retreat out of Hampshire to joyn with their Friends in the County of Oxford, concluding his old engine, *money*, was like to bee more effectuall than force . . . Besides by the muttering and whispering of his men, he was not sure, whether they would engage unto *Bloud* against their *Fellow Souldiers*. And therefore having *Spies* and *Intelligencers* active among them, hee so ordered the matter, that their own *Scouts* betrayed them, and brought him on to surprise them.[1]

It was in answer to this accusation that Major White wrote his account of what had happened. Both accounts were published some months after the event—that of the mutineers being dated August 20, and Major White's September 17. Moreover it has to be remembered that, if the mutineers wrote in the bitterness of their failure, White wrote in his defence, and therefore the latter must be read with no less careful criticism than the former. On the whole it is not difficult to see the truth behind the two accounts. White is certainly frank in his statements, and he gives the text of various communications. He begins by saying definitely that when he received Fairfax's letter, he was given instructions to

use what meanes I thought expedient, according to my judgment and conscience, to produce a right understanding and procure a Union, to which Lieutenant General *Cromwell* added, that I should let them know, that although they sent Messengers to them, they would not follow with force at the heels ; which words my Lord Generall confirmed.

That is a perfectly clear assertion, and it conforms with White's account of his action at the moment of the surprise. He says :

About midnight, when the Papers were a drawing up by Cornet *Den* at my quarters, newes came in, that my Lord Generall and the Lieutenant Generall were at the Towns end with 2000 horse and dragoons, I then presently went forth in

---

[1] *Mercurius Pragmaticus*, Part II, no. 5.

my slippers, and made what hast I could towards my Lord, to beg of his Excellency to prevent bloodshed, but hearing the pistolls firing very thick, I ran as fast as I could, till I was stayed by a troop of horse, who threatened to pistoll me, but after information I passed them, and went forward, till I met with a single Trooper of the Northamptonshire horse, which would be satisfied with no account, but vowed if I stirred further he would pistoll me : I was forc'd to return back, and perswaded him to go with me to his Lieutenant, to be dismissed from being his prisoner, and then betook myself to my Quarters till the fury was over.

No man not genuinely surprised and distressed would have run such risks in the dark and the turmoil, when any one rushing out from the town would be taken for an escaping Leveller.

The accounts on both sides are quite consistent with an explanation that does not involve actual treachery. Fairfax's first letter, and the verbal message sent by White, were given on the very first news of the action taken by Scroop's and Ireton's regiments. At that stage, all that had happened, while serious enough, had not passed beyond the possibility of negotiation. The troops had left their quarters, but from the fact that White and the other three were sent to Marlborough it is clear that Fairfax hoped to stop them there. This is put beyond question by a letter written from the camp at Andover on the Saturday : ' They ', says the writer, referring to the disaffected regiments, ' lay last night at Marlbury, within 14 miles of us : the Gen. hath sent to them Major White, and Captain Scot, Captain Peverell, with a letter requiring their obedience, which if they refuse, he tells them what they are to expect, we much wonder we hear nothing of them again, for we have expected an Answer from them this 4 houres '. The information given here as to the tenor of Fairfax's letter is correct. ' If you shall returne to your obedience ', he wrote in the communication carried by Major White, ' these mischiefs are not yet gone so far, but that they may be healed by your submission and acknowledgement ; if you pretend to have done this unlawfull act for just ends, when did I ever refuse you, in referring

any just desire of the Armies to the Parliament? if you
refuse this tender to you, I must and I shall through God's
assistance, endeavour to reduce you by force to a just obedience.'[1] The key to the situation surely lies in the mutineers'
fixed idea of joining with other disaffected forces. That,
with a certain desperation which would be the natural result
of having burned their boats, prevented them from perceiving clearly that to pursue their immediate object completely changed the situation from Fairfax's point of view;
no sensible commander could have intended to be kept in
play while his opponents joined forces. This was distinctly
perceived by Fairfax's emissary officers. Major White says:

Then [i. e. after the halt for discussion near Abingdon] came
Captain *Modee* and Lievtenant *Pritchard* with a Declaration
from my Lord Generall, directed to me to communicate to
them; but the Regiment being marched to joyn with some
troops of Colonel *Harrisons*, it could not at present be com-
municated to the whole, but I read it to their Trustees and
Officers, and delivered it to them to communicate; at which
time they offered to dismisse us, unlesse we would grant, that
persons should go from them to my Lord Generals forces with
him, and that they might have liberty to speak to, and publish
Papers among them: this motion was like the former, of
desiring assurance my Lord should not fall upon them; things
without our power, and exalting their party to stand in competition with my Lord; this much incensed Captain *Scoten*,
and made him impatient to be gone, which I must needs say,
I was unwilling so to do, before I had gotten the bottom of
their desires and intentions, but Captain *Scoten* going away,
I desired him to present things to my Lord Generall with an
impartiall account, and how I had behaved myself among
them, and to let my Lord Generall know, I should prove my
selfe as faithful to him in that Businesse, as any Officer in the
Army, and that at what time he should send for me, I would
come to him, and however I would stay but a very little time
with them, but did intreat him to beseech my Lord Generall,
to call me away before any hostility was exercised.

There can be no doubt of the meaning of this passage;
White and his companions regarded their mission as over
when they saw the mutineers carrying out their plan, instead

[1] White's *True Relation.*

of remaining where they were for negotiations. Scoten actually went away; the message White sent back by him shows that he also thought he ought to go, but remained because he felt he could still be useful in continuing to try to bring the mutineers to terms. But he refused to give them any further assurances concerning Fairfax's intentions, or any further undertaking. We see a little more of his mind at a later stage; after the crossing of the river, on the road to Burford, he

desired that they would not neglect the use of their intended means of safety for my being with them, and did likewise expresse a great deal of confidence, that my Lord Generall would not fall upon them, and not without ground for it.[1]

In other words, he gave the mutineers fair warning that his continued presence did not mean that the original message from Fairfax and Cromwell was to be considered as applying in the existing circumstances. The confidence he expressed was not that the Generals were not in pursuit, but that they would not necessarily make an actual attack; he believed that the matter might pass without bloodshed. His surprise at the last moment was not because the Generals had followed, but because they had arrived so soon. Nor have we any reason to suppose that the Generals did mean to attack; on the contrary there is evidence of instructions to the troops making the entry into Burford that 'mercy should be tendered' to the mutineers, 'and in case they submitted, no hurt should be done to them';[2] there is also the mutineers' own assertion that Okey, Barton, and others offered quarter. But there was resistance. In part this was inevitable; men roused suddenly by the pouring in of troops would very likely be firing pistols before the offer of quarter could be made; and there would be confusion in the darkness. But there was at least one point of deliberate opposition; 'some refusing to surrender made good an inn out of which they made about sixteen shot; one of them was killed, and two or three of them wounded'. This seems to have been the work of an individual who did not belong to any of the revolted

[1] White's *True Relation*.   [2] *Perfect Diurnall*, no. 302.

regiments, or at this moment to the Army at all, but was among the leading extremists, Colonel Eyres, one of Henry Martin's associates. Throughout he showed an inclination to violence which the rest tried to avoid, and it was he who instigated the fighting which White just averted at Newbridge.

Colonell *Eyres* [says one account] is now brought a prisoner to *Oxford*, to be tried for his life ; Hee did in a high manner exasperate the Mutineers, and at *Newbridge* led the Forlorn Hope & would have charged Col. *Reynold* and Col. *Okey*, who made good the passe against him though they were but a handfull to their number ; he with divers others was in that house where that man was killed of our party, and shot divers of our souldiers before they would yield.[1]

The whole matter may perhaps be summed up in this way. We can feel a real sympathy for the mutineers, and that not only on the ground that they could hardly be expected to perceive clearly how their own action affected the validity of White's original message to them. They deserve sympathy also because at first they had not been very discreetly handled, but most of all (and this is an effectual criticism of Cromwell) because a night surprise of the kind that occurred could not possibly be a peaceful proceeding, whatever the Generals' intentions ; Cromwell should certainly have known that, if he wanted the affair to end without bloodshed, he should not have poured his men into Burford at midnight. He could have waited, with his much superior force, till the morning. But that is easy to see at this distance of time; and it has to be remembered that all the information which had reached the Generals had reported the mutineers as ' high and peremptory '. In any case, this is a criticism of a different nature from a charge of underhand dealing.

The captured troops were imprisoned in the church from that Sunday midnight till the following Thursday morning, and in that fact, more than in the ultimate executions, we may see Cromwell's handling of the disaffection. He could, as earlier events had shown, order executions on the instant,

---

[1] *Declaration and Speeches.*

when he chose to do so. He now waited three whole days and nights. He condemned the three hundred and forty to an interval of chill reflection and agonizing anxiety that must have been very effective for his purpose ; and the relic of those three days on the font in Burford Church—the words ' Antony Sedley prisner 1649 ' cut upon the lead lining—is perhaps grimmer than has been generally realized. Colonel Harrison, Colonel Okey, and Colonel Scroop appear to have been sent in to the prisoners with a general sentence of death ; this

so struck them, that when they had their monies sent them to buy provisions, they all refused to accept of it, saying they must take care to provide for the Soul, and not for the Body, and many of them wept bitterly.[1]

' The humble Petition of the sad and heavy hearted prisoners remaining in the Church of Burford ' is submissive enough in its acknowledgement of the offence and its unconditional prayer for mercy even on 'such detestable offenders'.[2] Fairfax and his Council of War were, in fact, already taking another decision ; on the Tuesday two marked men, Denne and Thompson (the latter, no doubt, from his relationship to the ringleader at Banbury) were separately condemned to death ; [3] but the rest appear to have been kept in suspense till the Thursday. Of Cromwell himself during this interval we have two glimpses. One is given by Major White, who relates how, when he went to see Fairfax and report himself, the General asked about the mutineers

and what they said of him, & whether I thought the business might have been composed ? to which I answered, that they generally spoke well of his Excellency, & that I thought the Business might have been taken up without that breach ; to these expressions the Lieutenant Generall discovered much dissatisfaction, and wondered I was not ashamed to inform my Lord things so ridiculous, as to talk of a composure.[4]

The other, a still more personal glimpse, is in a periodical, which, after stating that Lilburne and Thompson (the Banbury

---

[1] *Declaration and Speeches.*
[2] *Perfect Diurnall,* no. 302.
[3] *Declaration and Speeches.*
[4] White's *True Relation.*

Cornet of horse) were regarded as the authors of the discontent in the Army, proceeds :

For so it appears by the Examinations of several *Prisoners*, insomuch that righteous *Oliver* vow'd (in the presence of all the Officers) at *Burford*, and bound it with a solemn Thump on the Table, either *Lilburne* or himself should perish for it.[1]

Two others besides Denne and Thompson were in the end appointed to die, but we do not know how they were selected ; in some accounts both are spoken of as corporals, in others one is given no rank. Of the final scene there are several reports, agreeing, however, in details ; the following is the most vivid :

This day Coronet Thompson was brought into the Church-yard (the place of execution). Death was a great terror to him, as unto most. Some say he had hopes of a pardon, and therefore delivered something reflecting upon the legality of his engagement, and the just hand of God upon him ; But if he had they failed him. Corporal Perkins was the next, the place of death, and sight of his Executioners, was so far from altering his countenance or danting his spirit, That he seemed to smile upon both, and accompt it a great mercy, that he was to die for this quarrel ; and casting his eyes up to his Father and afterwards to his fellow-prisoners (who stood upon the Church-leads to see the execution) set his back against the wall, and bad the Executioners shoot ; and so died gallantly, as he had lived religiously. After him Master John Church was brought to the stake. He was as much supported by God, in this great agony, as the later ; for after he had pulled off his Dublet, he stretched out his Arms, and bad the Souldiers do their duties, looking them in the face, till they gave fire upon him, without the least kind of fear or terror.[2]

Another account adds some touches to the picture, expanding a little what Thompson said :

That it is just what did befall him, that God did not own the ways he went, that he had offended the Generall, and desired the prayers of the people, and told the souldiers that were appointed to shoot him, that when he held out his hand they should do their duties, and accordingly he was immediately after the sign given shot to death.

[1] *Mercurius Elencticus*, no. 5.   [2] *The Moderate*, no. 45.

This account mentions that Church, after pulling off his doublet, took his place 'a pretty distance from the wall', and confirms his lack of fear.[1]

Denne was reprieved at the last moment:

After these 3 Cornet Den was brought to the place of execution, he exprest himself with much penitancy, and said that he was more worthy to dy than live, with much remorse of conscience for being an occasion to lead others into this way of mutiny, and disobedience. But immediately before the act of Execution, The General sent him a pardon.[2]

The mutineers afterwards were convinced, as will already have been seen in various quotations, that Denne had been a traitor to them throughout; but it may be doubted whether this is based on more than the fact of his sudden reprieve, with the addition of their very natural dislike and contempt of the rather abject completeness with which he now went over to the other side. After the execution Cromwell had the mutineers back into the Church and there addressed them, 'and making', as the mutineers' own account says, 'his old manner of dissembling speeches, told us it was not they' (i. e. the officers who had offered quarter) 'that had saved our lives, but providence had so ordered it, and told us that he could not deny but that many of the things that we desired were good, and they intended to have many of them done, but we went in a mutinous way, and disobeyed the Generals Orders; but withal he told us that we should not be put off with dishonourable terms, because we should not become a reproach to the common Enemie.'[3] When Cromwell had had his say Denne was made to preach, and we are left in no doubt of what his fellows thought of him:

And to put an utter inconfidence and jealousie for ever amongst such upon all future engagements, they made that wretched *Judas Den*, to that end their pandor and slave . . . they enjoyne *Den* to preach Apostacy to us in the pulpit of *Burford* Church, to assert and plead the unlawfulnesse of our engagement, as much as before the lawfulnesse to vindicate, and justifie all those wicked and abhominable proceedings of the Generall,

---

[1] *Declaration and Speeches.* [2] *Ibid.*
[3] *The Levellers Vindicated.*

Lieutenant Generall and their Officers against us, howling and weeping like a Crocadile, and to make him a perfect Rogue and villain upon everlasting Record.[1]

His voice was made to reach beyond the walls of Burford Church, for he had also to publish a pamphlet against the mutiny—a pamphlet which apparently he had begun to write while a prisoner in the Church. It is much more likely that we are to see in these facts the reason for his reprieve, than to look for them in any treachery at an earlier stage. His treachery would have been of very little use to Fairfax, whose officers had, as the mutineers found out, left word at various points to guide him. Major White says nothing to reflect upon Denne; and it seems probable that, if he had had traitorous designs throughout, he would not have been in the town at the end, but would have slipped out with Quarter-Master More. We may be content with the explanation that Cromwell wished for a recantation from the Levellers' own side, as a useful weapon (they admit its effect in producing ' an utter inconfi- dence ' in such proceedings for the future), and perceived that Denne was the man to produce it. He had had some little reputation as a Puritan controversialist before the war ; tracts are extant by him against infant baptism, and also tracts by orthodox clergymen confuting certain ' schismatic ' sermons of his when curate of Pyrton in Hertfordshire.[2] Whatever explanation be given of his escape, he does not emerge as an heroic figure. Stories were told of his having ordered his winding sheet and coffin, on hearing of his condemnation, and this, accordingly as it was told by those who believed him to be a traitor or those who merely thought him a coward, appears as a disgusting hypocrisy or an ostentatious piece of abjectness.[3] Even the most friendly version of the reprieve says : ' But though he said this to save his life, yet the two last executed could not have said it, though they were sure thereby to gain their freedom.' We need not, however, conclude that Denne's change of opinion was wholly to save his skin ; two statements

[1] *The Levellers Vindicated.*
[2] See list of authorities at the head of this chapter.
[3] See, e.g., *Mercurius Elencticus*, no. 5, and *The Kingdom's Weekly Intelligencer*, no. 312.

seem to reveal him as the type of advanced theorist who becomes frightened by the pace at which any strong course, once it is developed, drives forward those who are committed to it. ' Cornet *Den* ', we read, ' did confesse that many of that party that were thus engaged with him, their hearts were so inraged, and full of bitternesse against the Parliament party, and all others that did not adhere unto them, that he did think in his conscience there would have bin greate cruelty used by these men, and that it was a blessed and happy hour they were surprized and prevented ' ; his own pamphlet takes much this line ,and draws its lessons from the differences he alleges between the ostensible objects of the mutineers and the temper which action roused in them. Denne recovered in the end some measure of respect ; he reappears in 1653 as a preacher held in esteem at Fenstanton, in Huntingdonshire, and later near Canterbury. But he remained no hero ; some of his people, Quakers and a few Baptists who joined the Quakers in their refusal to take oaths, were imprisoned : ' Mr. Henry Denne came forward, and addressed his brethren in prison, endeavouring to show them that to take an oath is a lawful act, sanctioned by the word of God.' Prison once more was giving him a respect for authority.

The mutiny ended at Burford. Those who had escaped had warrants issued against them, and the magistrates in all neighbouring counties were warned ; but we do not hear of any further trials or sentences. The remainder of the Burford prisoners were returned for a while to quarters near Devizes, to avoid disbanding them in poverty ; but it is plain from their account that many were shortly disbanded. Colonel Reynolds, who had been so useful throughout, was sent on to Banbury with a force to deal with Cornet Thompson ; Thompson's following was easily broken up, but he himself was determined not to be taken alive. He was pursued to a wood on the road to Wellingborough and there killed three men before a corporal, taking a musket charged with seven bullets, made an end of him, ' and there is an end of the Levellers' uproare '.

Our only local record is again to be found in the Registers, where, inserted on the top margin of a page (and the Vicar may well have been too agitated to make the entry at the time in the right place on the page) are the lines : ' three soldiers shot to death in Burford churchyard buried May 17.' Another entry : ' A soldier slaine at ye Crowne buried y 15 of May ' perhaps identifies for us the actual scene of the resistance organized by Colonel Eyres. He, we have seen, made good an inn ; the Crown was at the corner of Sheep Street and the High Street, in the centre of the town, a very likely place for resistance, and it is recorded that a man was killed there, and that a man was killed in that resistance ; that a man was killed at the Crown seems to identify the spot. The Church-wardens' Accounts enter payments ' to Daniell Muncke and others for cleansinge the Church when the Levellers were taken '. But this is all the record we have. We do not know where Fairfax and Cromwell stayed, but in a place where Speaker Lenthall had his house it may be taken for granted that that was the house they would occupy ; and it must have been there that Cromwell thumped on the table.

APPENDIX TO CHAPTER X

A few names of the prisoners have come down to us, besides those of the men who were executed and the name on the font. The copy of the petition from the Church, given in *The Moderate*, records these signatories: Hugh Hurst, Matthew Brown, John Roper, William Doegood, John Bishop, William Panck, William Orpin, John Cantloe, John Wilkinson, Thomas Atkins, and James Steel. Hugh Hurst was also one of the six signatories of the mutineers' own account of their proceedings, the others being John Wood, Humphry Marston, Robert Everard, William Hutchinson, and James Carpen.

A note is necessary as to the dates of the events. White's copy of the mutineers' first letter to Fairfax is dated May 13 ; this must certainly be a mistake for May 12, since Scroop arrived on the 13th with the answer, and Fairfax refers to the letter as ' of the 12 of this instant '. Again, two, at least, of the contemporary accounts state that the execution took place on Friday, May 18. But Cromwell was in Oxford (whither he went, with Fairfax, from Burford) on the night of Thursday, May 17. We may, therefore, rely upon the date of the burial as given in the Registers, and conclude that the execution took place on the Thursday morning.

Tradition points to the high wall enclosing the churchyard at the west end as the actual scene of the execution, and without regarding certain hollows in stones there as bullet-marks the tradition may well be accepted. We know that the rest of the mutineers were on the leads of the church (the account in the *Declaration and Speeches* says ' in the Church ', but there are two definite statements against this), and so large a number could only have found room on the leads of the nave and Lady Chapel. In that case this wall is much the most likely place to have been chosen for the execution; but it has to be remembered that the churchyard must at that time have been much more enclosed than at present; otherwise there would have been no need to take down a wall to carry straw into the church (see p. 206). There may therefore have been a suitable wall farther to the south, between the churchyard and what are now the Grammar School buildings.

CHAPTER XI

THE HISTORY OF BURFORD PRIORY

OF the origin of the small Hospital of St. John at Burford, which towards the end of its existence was sometimes called the Priory, no record has yet been found. The history of it, so far as documentary evidence is concerned, begins with an entry in the Close Roll of 1226, recording a gift of firewood to the Master and Brethren from the Royal Forest of Wychwood.

This date, however, taken in conjunction with certain other circumstances, opens the way to a reasonable conjecture, concerning the foundation of the hospital. From an early period the presentation to the mastership is found to be in the hands of the lord of the manor. Thus in 1268, in the course of a dispute concerning the lands of the hospital in Fifield, the Vicar of Burford states that John Giffard (who was then holding the manor) was ' the patron of the hospital '.[1] Again in 1327 Robert le Glasiere was presented to the mastership by the King ' by reason of the lands of Hugh le Despenser being in the King's hands '.[2] In 1389 the King presented one of his clerks, William Donne ; [3] and that presentation took place during the minority of Thomas le Despenser. Now the most probable cause of the patronage being vested in the lord of the manor would be the foundation of the hospital by a lord of the manor ; and it must moreover have been one who held the manor at some time previous to 1226. With that limitation, by far the most likely founder is to be discovered in William, Earl of Gloucester. He was a great benefactor to the Church and to religious foundations ; and there is good reason for connecting his possessions at Burford with his benefactions. He founded Keynsham Abbey ; and the rectory and advowson of Burford formed part of his original endowment of it. He may therefore be reasonably con-

---

[1] P. R. O. Assize Roll 702, 52 Hen. III.
[2] Part III, p. 573.   [3] Part III, p. 577.

jectured to have been also the benefactor to whom the Hospital of St. John owed its origin. The history of the manor after his death and before 1226 offers us no other probability as strong.

This is, however, but conjecture. All that can be definitely asserted of the beginnings of the hospital is that it was an independent foundation. It did not, as has sometimes been stated, belong to the Abbey of Keynsham. No evidence has ever been produced in support of that statement; and evidence against it is strong. There is, firstly, the fact that the Abbey did not present to the mastership; secondly, the fact that the stipend of the master is never entered on the Clerical Subsidies, as the Vicar of Burford's stipend was, among the benefices of Keynsham; thirdly, the fact that in Rentals, Surveys, and Particulars for Grants after the Dissolution of the Monasteries, the hospital appears quite independently and not as parcel of the possessions of Keynsham.

The hospital must have been small. At no time in its history did its revenue exceed £16 a year, which, when all allowance has been made for the different value of money, gives it but an insignificant place even in the class of pious foundations to which it belongs.

These were foundations essentially different from the great monastic and conventual houses; and by the very principle of their existence less likely to become powerful and wealthy. The monasteries, designed to maintain the service of God and the expression of worship and devotion, commanded the gifts of the faithful; and, being at the same time the only seats of learning and intellectual interest, were bound, in their communal life, to exert an enormous influence and attain a wide power. The hospitals, whose sole object was that relief of the poor and the sick which to the great monasteries was, so to speak, a matter of the crumbs from their table, had neither the conspicuousness of the monastic ideal nor the force of a large common life to assist them : their work, in times which had not embraced humanitarianism, was not greatly regarded for its own sake, and was on a small and rather perfunctory scale. ' Besides the poor and impotent ', says Tanner, ' there generally were in the Hospitals two or three Religious, one to be Master or Prior, and one or two to be Chaplains or Confessors.'

Of such was the Hospital of St. John at Burford, Augustinian in its rule, according to Dugdale's *Monasticon*, as the great majority of hospitals were. The reference to the master and brethren in the Close Roll of 1226, and a few other references to the brethren in similar entries during the next few years, together with the statement in 1327, regarding the appointment in that year to the mastership—that it was made on the representation of the brethren—must not be taken to indicate any larger community than Tanner thus describes.

This would, in any case, be obvious from the exiguous character of the revenues. Of the original endowment of the hospital we know as little as we do of its founding. Apparently its most prosperous period was from the middle of the thirteenth to the end of the fourteenth century, and from the group of references in the Close Rolls of 1226, 1231, 1232, 1233, and 1235, which all record gifts of firewood, we may perhaps conclude that at that time the hospital had very little landed property from which it could cut its own wood. After 1235 no more gifts of this kind are entered ; and it is to be remarked that within a very few years the hospital appears in possession of a fair amount of land. This may not be more than an accidental coincidence. In 1260–1 there is record of a gift of a messuage and a virgate of land in Fifield ;[1] and in 1279 the Prior is found in free tenancy in the same place of two holdings of 36 acres and 9 acres respectively, and also of ten virgates, of which he had five and a quarter in demesne.[2] In 1291 the hospital also possessed land at Rissington, which seems from later particulars to have been one virgate with certain meadow and pasture lands.[3] In 1320 Joan, widow of Richard de Cornwall, gave to the hospital five messuages, four crofts, two virgates of land, and 10s. of annual rent in Asthall and Asthally.[4]

Unfortunately we have no information as to the property

[1] Part III, p. 568.   [2] Part III, p. 569.
[3] Part III, p. 571.   [4] Part III, p. 587.

of the hospital in Burford at this time. The absence of any Burford return in the Hundred Rolls is chiefly responsible for this lack, but it is due also to the fact that, as an institution for the poor and the sick, the hospital was not assessed in the *Taxatio Ecclesiastica* of 1291. It is true we owe to that Subsidy the knowledge of the lands at Rissington, but a note appended to the entry explains this accidental circumstance.[1] No other reference to the hospital is to be found there. At the same time, we have clear proof that it did possess property in Burford in the entry of the Master of the Hospital on the Subsidy Lists of 1316 and 1326–7.[2] He would only be assessed on those lists for his temporal benefices; and he appears as paying in 1316 very little less, and in 1326–7 rather more, than Isabella de Clare, who held at this date that portion of the manor which lay in Upton. From this fact we can make certain deductions. At the time of the Dissolution the hospital's property in Burford and Upton was valued at £5 0s. 4d. In 1326–7, on an assessment of one-twentieth on land and movable goods, the Master paid 8s. Now even if we allow a considerable proportion of this for the tax on movables, it is obvious that at that time the hospital must already have been in possession of most of the land it held in Burford at the Dissolution.

This consisted of the hospital building with a close and a barn thereon; a tenement called Ivy House with one acre of land; another tenement in the town; three virgates of land in Burford Fields, and twenty-two acres of land in Upton Fields; a close, two gardens, and a little piece of land in Burford, and two closes in Upton. It may very well be that some small portions of this property were given by townspeople; but it has to be noted that the hospital seems to have appealed very little to Burford men as an object for considerable benefactions. Of all the mediaeval wills which we have, each of them containing large gifts to the Church and Gild, only one makes a gift to the hospital, and that is of 13s. 4d. in money, not a gift of property. Consequently it appears to be more probable that the greater part of such lands and tene-

---

[1] Part III, p. 571.   [2] Part III, pp. 594, 595.

ments as the hospital held in Burford were of its original endowment. That, however, like the identification of the founder, is but conjectural. All that can be said with certainty is that it must have acquired these lands and tenements by the early part of the fourteenth century.

If we take the rental of the Burford and Upton property at that time to have been about £4, and add to it 52s. 6d., the annual value in 1279 of the Fifield lands, and 32s. 1d., the annual value in 1320 of the lands at Asthall and Asthally, allowing 5s. also for the annual value of the virgate at Rissington, the total income of the hospital in the thirteenth century would amount to £9 9s. 7d. This might just suffice for the Master and the two or three brethren, but could hardly have supported a number of poor and sick people. Presumably they depended upon casual alms. The fact that a King's clerk was appointed Master in 1389, with the obvious implication that the office had at least some value, would make it clear that of so small an income none can have been expended upon the charitable work of the hospital.

At some time after the end of the thirteenth century more property was acquired, the most valuable item being the whole manor of Fifield, possibly given by that John de Fifield of whom the hospital held the land there entered in the Hundred Rolls.[1] The other lands were 28 acres of arable and some meadow at Widford, and a tenement with land at Little Barrington.[2]

In 1435–6 the Master of the hospital was joint tenant with Henry Spyser of the freestone quarry in Burford, at an annual rent of 5s.[3] This may possibly indicate that at that date new building was in progress at the hospital. Such remains of ancient building as have been found are of a style which would attribute them to the early fifteenth century ; and they may therefore be made to add their testimony to that of the quarry tenancy, and help to justify the belief that at that period a building was being erected which was probably the hospital as it stood at the time of the Dissolution.

Three fine pointed arches, now erected across the hall of the

[1] Part III, p. 569.   [2] Part III, p. 623.   [3] Part III, p. 609.

existing house, were found to have been incorporated in one of the walls of the mansion which Sir Lawrence Tanfield built on the hospital site. Another arch, in what is now a back passage, indicates that there was also an old wall running north and south along the western end of the building in which the three arches stood. The walls of a ruined wing at the back of the house show clearly ancient work, refaced with new stone, apparently in the seventeenth century.

It would be an impossible task to reconstruct, from such slight material, the hospital building. At any rate, the comparative poverty of the foundation forbids us to suppose that its buildings can have been extensive. The three arches first mentioned, appearing as they do to have belonged to a building lying east and west, may be remains of the chapel; and the wall running north and south might mark the site of the great Hall or refectory, carrying perhaps as an upper structure a solar for the Master's use, a dormitory for the two or three brethren, and an infirmary for the sick. If we imagine the ruined back wing to have contained kitchens, brew-house, store-houses, &c., we shall have provided all that seems to be required for a picture of the Burford Priory of the Middle Ages.

Around it was an area of enclosed land, consisting of meadows, pasture, orchards, and garden plots, the whole occupying very much the same space as the modern gardens and woods. The house called Ivy House was somewhere on this ground—possibly, if we may judge by indications so late as the map of 1797, at the upper corner of the grounds on the opposite side of Priory Lane from the Lamb Inn—and also a large barn, which, again judging by that map, may have stood at the far end of the grounds towards Upton.

It is probable that during the fifteenth century, when the increasing wealth of the townsfolk led to the establishment of more obits and commemorative Masses, the brethren of the hospital began to gain their living rather from emoluments as chantry priests than from the hospital revenues. We have, indeed, no definite evidence of this. The description 'capellanus' appended to the name of a priest, in the Clerical Subsidies, for instance, would be applied equally to a clerical

PLATE XV.   FIFTEENTH-CENTURY ARCHES IN BURFORD PRIORY

brother of the hospital, to a chantry priest, and to a man who was both one and the other. Even the Master of the hospital is, in the one Burford will which includes a bequest to him, described also as ' capellanus '. But though there is no direct evidence, there is, at any rate, a strong possibility. In a place of the moderate size of mediaeval Burford there would hardly be a sufficient number of obits to attract unattached priests from elsewhere ; and the insufficient revenues of the hospital would induce the brethren to be on the look-out for the money accruing from such obits as there were. In these circumstances one or two of the Clerical Subsidy lists of the fifteenth century become significant.[1] Those of 1420 and 1435–6 contain respectively three and two names of ' capellani ' ; that of 1448–9 contains the names of the Master of the hospital and four ' stipendarii in ecclesia '. The first of these Subsidies was levied on all ' capellani ' having benefices of seven marks and over ; the second on parish priests, stipendiaries and other priests receiving less than ten marks a year; and the third was a Subsidy on all ' capellani ', secular friars and other Religious serving parish churches, receiving stipends or annual payments or holding chantries not otherwise taxed. Now the second and third of these must certainly have included the brethren of the hospital and the chantry priests. Obviously, therefore, the numbers being so few, the two must have been the same ; there are not enough names to give us two or three brethren and a number of chantry priests as well.

Thus we can understand a little better the curious passing of the patronage of the hospital from the lord of the manor to the Corporation of Burford, which has already been noted in connexion with the Earl of Warwick's letter—undated, but written in some year between 1461 and 1471—to the Bailiffs and Burgesses, asking for leave to present to the mastership one of his chaplains.[2] If that loosening of the manorial control, which so remarkably increased the general importance of the Corporation, had allowed the nomination to the mastership to slip by default into the Corporation's hands, the assumption of a complete patronage would be much helped forward by

[1] Part III, pp. 594–6.   [2] Part III, p. 360.

dependence of the brethren upon obits founded by the towns-people. The combination of these two tendencies would rapidly make of the hospital something which it certainly had not been originally—namely, an appanage of the town.

This it became with singular completeness in the remaining fifty years of its existence. The last records we have of it as a religious foundation are a remarkable revelation of the extent to which the interference of the Corporation had grown. One of these documents, a petition from the dispossessed Abbot of Rewley to Thomas Cromwell, asking for support in his application to the Bailiffs and Burgesses of Burford for ' a grant of a service called the Priory in that town of £11 a year ' as a supplement to his pension, is, of course, much like the Earl of Warwick's letter.[1] But other documents show that, in the sixteenth century, leases of the hospital property were actually made by the Alderman, Steward, and Burgesses in conjunction with the Master, and were sealed with the Town seal as well as the Priory seal.[2] The dependence of the hospital upon the town could not have been more complete.

The hospital did not come under the operation of the first of the Acts by which the Dissolution of the Monasteries was carried into effect—the Act of 1536. It remained in existence, indeed, so late as September 1538, one of the joint leases by the Master and the Corporation bearing date in that month.[3] When the end came it was unheroic. The property was sur-rendered to the Royal Commissioners by the Master, who received a life pension of £3 6s. 8d. a year—about a quarter of the revenues.[4]

It appears from an Account of later date that the two bells which the hospital possessed became part of the depreda-tions of the notorious Dr. London.[5] The same Account

---

[1] Part III, p. 655.

[2] Incidentally it may be remarked that this condition of the hospital property is a final proof, if any more were needed, that the foundation never belonged to Keynsham Abbey. No monastic body would have permitted such intrusion upon the patronage of one of its possessions.

[3] Part III, p. 640.   [4] Part III, p. 612.

[5] Part III, p. 639.. I owe this reference to the kindness of Mr. Michael W. Hughes.

records that there was no lead on the building; the roofs would have been of stone slates, as would be natural in this district.

The last Master of the hospital, Thomas Cade, had held the mastership in conjunction with the vicarage. It is possible that this had happened before, since Thomas Mayowe, who was certainly Vicar in 1465, was Master of the hospital in 1448-9,[1] and may have continued his tenure after being presented to the vicarage. Cade was an old man at the time of the Dissolution, and had brought the hospital property into some confusion. In 1538 he granted a lease of the property as a whole to one John Barker, at an inclusive annual rent of £10. This farming of the hospital's revenue must have been a practice for some time before this, since there is no assessment of the hospital or the Master for temporal possessions on the Lay Subsidy lists of the town for 1524-5-6. But the lease to Barker was made apparently without regard to leases of separate portions of the property to other persons; and was actually followed in a few months by another lease of a separate portion. The tenants under these leases, which they had taken the precaution to have confirmed by the Court of Augmentations, obtained an injunction against Barker, upon his attempting to secure himself in 1541 by inducing the Court to grant him a new lease on the plea that he had been instrumental in securing the surrender of the hospital.[2] Barker contested the injunction, but, although the records of the Court of Augmentation do not state the result, it is clear from the tenant-rolls of the next stage in the history of the Priory that he lost his case.[3]

In 1543 the first step was taken towards converting the hospital into private property, though it was not yet sold outright. It was granted in that year to Edmund Harman, one of the King's barber-surgeons, for his life and his wife's; he paid for the grant £109 19s. 2d., ten years' purchase of the net revenues.[4] What Harman's first association with Burford had been we do not know; he had no family connexion

with it; or even with this part of England, his immediate
forbears being of Ipswich.[1] But he evidently had something
to do with Burford before he obtained the Priory ; for his
wife Agnes, mentioned in the grant, was a Sylvester of
Burford.[2]

Admitted to the freedom of the Barbers' Company in 1530,
Harman must have been born about 1509. By 1535 he was
one of the King's barbers ; and he also took rank as one of the
Grooms of the Privy Chamber.[3] He is mentioned once as
Keeper of the Wardrobe ; [4] and he obtained several of those
offices of profit, and small grants, which were then the normal
way of finding remuneration for the members of the King's
Household—stewardships of manors, minor appointments in
the Customs, and so on. His career was endangered in 1542,
when he was one of the persons of the Privy Chamber who
were informed upon as heretically inclined, and in association
with Anthony Pearson, the cleric whose preaching at Windsor
was made the chief occasion of the scenting out of Lutherans
there and about the Court.[5] But after the burning of Pearson
and two others with him, the persecutors lost the King's ear,
and some of them had to do penance as perjurers. Harman
and other servants of the Household had not fallen victims to
the informers, and he obtained the security of a pardon on all
heresy charges in 1543.[6]

After this crisis he prospered ; for, instead of gathering
miscellaneous small sources of profit, he begins to be seen
putting together a kind of modest estate. Within a few years
of obtaining for a term the dispossessed hospital at Burford
he acquired other property here. In 1545 he obtained a
grant of the rectory and advowson, with the chapelry of
Fulbrook, which he leased forthwith to Thomas Smyth ; [5]
and in the same year he bought from the Crown the various
mills in Burford and Upton, together with a meadow and
a piece of land.[6] In 1546 he sold his interest in some of the
hospital property—the lands at Asthall and Great Rissington

---

[1] Part III, p. 641.
[2] *Visitations of Oxfordshire* (Harl. Soc. Pub., vol. v), p. 157.
[3] Part III, p. 657. .   [4] Part III, p. 657.
[5] Part III, p. 643.   [6] Part III, p. 657.

—to Edmund Silvester, to whom he also sold one of the mills in Burford.[1] In or about 1547 he also took a lease from the Crown of the agricultural land of the manor of Burford.[2]

To what extent Harman ever lived in Burford or occupied the Priory is doubtful. He was, until the death of Henry VIII, discharging his office at Court ; he is entered in 1545 among members of the Royal Household having their diets at Court, and he was one of the witnesses to the King's will at Westminster in December 1546. He was still with the Court in 1547. Therefore he can only have been in Burford, at the most, occasionally, until 1547. After that, in so far as we have any indications, it is likely that he lived elsewhere. He had added in 1546 to the various grants he had obtained, one of the lordship and manor of Taynton, with the rectory and the advowson of the vicarage there. Now this was more likely to dictate his place of residence than a tenancy for life of the hospital at Burford, which cannot have afforded him any considerable house to live in, and carried with it no manorial position. Moreover, it is clear that he was living at Taynton in 1559, for in that year the entry of the marriage of one of his daughters appears in the Taynton registers. It is hardly likely that, if he had ever settled in Burford, or had (as has been sometimes said) built himself a house there, replacing the hospital building, he would so soon have moved away to a manor which was in his possession within a year or two after he obtained the hospital. It is more natural to conclude that he never took up his residence in Burford, or had much to do with the place, beyond receiving the rents of the properties he held there for his life, and the other properties he had bought. He caused to be placed in Burford Church in 1569 a monument which has the appearance of a sepulchral monument, especially in the tablets which represent, kneeling in tightly packed rows, his nine sons and seven daughters ; but the inscription gives no indication that he so intended it, merely recording that it was erected to commemorate the goodness of God to him throughout

---

[1] Part III, p. 657.   [2] Part III, p. 629.

his life, especially in the children with whom he and his wife had been blessed.

One of these children and a grandchild maintained for some time a connexion with Burford. His daughter Mary married William Johnson or Johnston of Leighton Buzzard ; [1] and he for a few years held the Burford manor lands jointly with Harman. In 1584 Mary and William Johnston and their son Harman Johnston obtained a grant of the Rectory of Burford and Chapel of Fulbrook (the original grant to Harman being about to expire) for three lives successively ; [2] and in 1596, as appears by two assessments in one of the fragments of the Record Book of the Borough Court, ' Mr. Harman Jhonson ' was living in Burford,[3] possibly occupying the Rectory house.

But meanwhile, Harman's death being followed within a few days by the death of his wife, the hospital, which was only granted for the term of their two lives, had, like the manor lands, reverted to the Crown. When next there is record of it, it is already in the hands of Sir Lawrence Tanfield, who had acquired it before he became lord of the manor and town of Burford. For in the deed of the sale of these lordships by the heirs of Sir John Fortescue to Tanfield, he is described as ' of the Pryorye nere Burford '.

Tanfield's association with Burford must have begun when he was quite a small child, if indeed he was not born here. His father, Robert Tanfield, was a younger son of a Northamptonshire family, which had acquired by purchase late in the fifteenth century the manor of Gayton, in that county ; [4] and he retained to the end of his life some connexion with Northamptonshire, for he is found presenting to the living of Harrowden Magna in January 1557. In that year or early in the following year he died, for the next presentation, in March 1558, is in the name of his widow, Wilgeford Tanfield.[5]

Robert Tanfield is usually described, in the accounts of

[1] *Visitations of Oxfordshire*, p. 3.
[2] Part III, p. 653.   [3] Part III, p. 543.
[4] Baker's *History of Northamptonshire* (1820, 1830), vol. ii, p. 275.
[5] Bridges's *History of Northamptonshire* (1791), vol. ii, p. 105.

his more famous son, as ' of Burford '. This appears to rest upon a single reference to him in the Herald's Visitation of ·Northamptonshire in 1564, wherein, under the family of Fermor of Easton Neston, it is recorded that a son of that family, Richard, married ' Dyonisia daughter of Robert Tanfield of Burford, Co. Oxon.' [1] No Tanfield pedigree appears in that Visitation. In the pedigree recorded by the Visitation of 1618–19 Robert's name is entered without any reference to Burford, though his son is duly described as of Burford.[2] Nor does the father's name appear anywhere in the Burford Records, nor on any of the extant Burford Subsidy lists of the time, nor among the tenants in the Edwardian Survey of the manor and town.

Still against the clear statement in the Visitation of 1564 negative considerations cannot easily prevail, and we must conclude that Robert Tanfield did live in Burford.[3] We may the more readily do so, since we know that he was not by any means a rich man, and must have lived here in unassuming conditions. There is just a glimpse of him in the curious *Life of Lady Falkland*, daughter of Sir Lawrence Tanfield, which opens, somewhat abruptly, thus :

She was born in the year of our Lord 1585 or 1586 in Oxfordshire, at the priory of Burford, her father's house. He was a lawyer, afterwards a judge and Lord Chief Baron; his name was Laurence Tanfield. His father was a younger brother, who, dying, left him a child, giving him all he had, which was not much ; but what it was, his mother parted among his sisters and herself, breeding him well ; and as soon as his age would permit, sent him to Lincoln's Inn to study law, where, as soon as he was capable of practice, she left him to•shift for himself. . . . He was called to the bar at eighteen years old.

[1] *The Visitations of Northamptonshire* (London, 1887), edited by W. C. Metcalfe, p. 20.

[2] *Visitations of Northamptonshire*, p. 140. Bridges (vol. ii, p. 263) reproduces the pedigree of the 1618–19 Visitation. Baker (vol. ii, p. 275) has incorporated, in his version of the pedigree, the statement found in the Visitation of 1564.

[3] As a young man he appears to have lived in London. His marriage licence, dated May 22, 1544, was obtained from the Faculty Office of the Archbishop of Canterbury in London, and he is described as of the diocese of Westminster (Harl. Soc. Publications, vol. xxiv [1886], p. 2).

These statements, which may certainly be taken as authoritative,[1] give us a view of Robert Tanfield's circumstances which may well account for his not appearing on any of our Records.

Lawrence Tanfield must have been a very small child when his father died, for he was not entered at the Inner Temple[2] till 1569. As he was called to the Bar at eighteen years old, he cannot have been much more than fifteen when he was entered, and must therefore have been about three years old at his father's death. The latter must presumably have lived some time at Burford, to be described in 1564 as ' of ' that place ; and hence it becomes quite likely that Lawrence was born there. This may perhaps have added to the bitterness of the feeling against him later on, when the townsfolk laid at his door the loss of their alleged privileges.[3] Where he had the education which his mother secured for him we do not know; the Burford Grammar School was not then in existence. But he must have been diligent ; and could very well be left ' to shift for himself '. His first case, the *Life of Lady Falkland* tells us, was against the Crown. A relation had given him his brief, not so much, we are frankly told, from belief in his powers as from the feeling that it would not matter much if an obscure lawyer lost the case. However, Tanfield won, and the Crown's counsel prophesied a great career for him.[4]

In 1584 he had advanced so far as to be sitting in Parliament for the Borough of New Woodstock ; and about this time he was already in possession of the Priory, since, as

---

[1] This *Life of Lady Falkland* is from a manuscript in the Archives of Lille. It was formerly in the possession of the English Benedictine nuns at Cambrai, the house at which her four daughters were received into Holy Religion. The manuscript, which was removed to Lille with the remains of the nuns' famous library after the troubles of 1793, appears to have been written by one of the daughters, and corrected in some details by a son—perhaps the youngest, Patrick Cary. The edition of the *Life* edited by ' R. S. ' (interpreted as Richard Simpson in the Catalogue of the Bodleian Library) was published in 1861.

[2] Foss, *Lives of the Judges*, vol. vi, p. 365. The reference to ' Lincoln's Inn ' in the *Life of Lady Falkland* is clearly a mistake, and the word ' Temple ' has been written in the margin of the manuscript.

[3] See Part I, p. 53.   [4] *Life of Lady Falkland*, p. 2.

we have seen, his daughter was born there in 1585 or 1586. That he had also other property in the town is shown by a document concerning some Grammar School property in 1599, containing reference to ' a barn of Laurence Tanfield Esq. ' on the north side of Witney Street.[1]

The words ' her father's house ', in the opening sentence of the *Life of Lady Falkland*, may imply that he had erected his fine mansion on the hospital site before 1585. Certainly there must have been a big house here when in 1603 King James I paid a visit to Tanfield, arriving on September 9 and staying till September 11.[2] Nothing could show better than this royal visit how successfully Tanfield had established himself and the Priory in the world. He was still plain Mr. Tanfield, Sergeant-at-Law since Easter of that year. Yet he had contrived to have Burford Priory included in the arrangements for King James's first great progress in his new kingdom, although there were many more notable family seats at which the King and Court might have stayed in this neighbourhood. Tanfield had good reason to commemorate the occasion by the erection of the large royal coat of arms still extant on the Priory wall.

Thus we come at last to that point in the history of the Priory which is common to the history of nearly all the religious foundations of England, the point at which they were converted, in varying degrees of size and importance, into the mansions of private estates. For some years, indeed, Burford Priory in its new conditions was much more of mansion than of estate. The old hospital brought to its lay owners none of those considerable territories which went with the majority of the monastic houses. Some parts even of the small property it had once possessed must have been disposed of before the Dissolution. The Asthall property, which at the time of Joan de Cornwall's grant in 1320 had

---

[1] Burford Records, S 28.

[2] *The Progresses of James I,* by John Nichols (London, 1828), vol. i, p. 257. The royal coat of arms, now on the south wall of the house, and formerly (though not, it would appear, originally) over the upper door into the Chapel, may have been put up to commemorate this visit. The arms are certainly of this period.

consisted of five messuages and various lands, valued altogether at 52s. 1d. a year, was only represented at the time of the Dissolution by a single messuage and some land, valued altogether at 33s. 4d., a greater decline than appears, since the value of money had decreased. Again, Harman had alienated what remained of the Asthall lands, and also the Rissington lands. Finally, the Fifield manor must also have become separated from the hospital property before Tanfield acquired it, since that manor never appears as part of his possessions. Thus the Priory estate, as such, can have been nothing more than the eight acres of grounds, a house or two upon these and in Burford, and a little arable in Burford and Upton Fields.

The Priory mansion, on the other hand, must have been a quite spacious and imposing edifice.[1] If we compare the deed of Lenthall's purchase from Tanfield's heir with that of Tanfield's own original purchase, we observe that the price recorded in the former is £7,000, and in the latter £1,900. Yet the only item in the former which is not in the latter is ' the capital messuage or mansion called the Priory House '. That must therefore account for the £5,000 of difference, a sum which, multiplied, as it has to be, by five or six to give its equivalent in modern money, can hardly represent anything less than the great house of the old prints.

But in due time Tanfield was able to correct this disproportion between his mansion and his estate at Burford. The death of Sir John Fortescue, who had bought the lordship of the manor and town from the Crown, gave him his chance. In 1617 he bought the lordship from Fortescue's heirs ; and by a later purchase extinguished separate leases of the Bury Barns house and farm land. With the lordship went several houses in the town which had passed into the hands of the Crown by confiscation, and had not been re-sold.

Thus was built up, in more senses than one, the Burford Priory which was to take its place among the family seats of

---

[1] The probable character of Tanfield's mansion, before it was altered and added to, is discussed at the end of this chapter.

Oxfordshire. Tanfield had put together, with a skill that approaches art, the requisite elements of a good country estate. In the hospital property he had the associations of an ancient tradition; and the Master had in the old days been described often enough as Prior to cause the hospital to be referred to occasionally as 'the Priory', so that even in the matter of the name of the estate Tanfield had secured an admirable measure of dignity. The purchase from Fortescue's heirs introduced both a position of authority and a respectable rent-roll. He also obtained for himself the additional position of patron of the living, by taking a lease of the Rectory; though this last he did not add to the estate by outright purchase.

How this opening of a new chapter in the history of the Priory involved also the opening of a new chapter, in a rather unfortunate sense, for the people of Burford has been told in the History of the Corporation. The result was that from the first the relations between Burford and the fine new estate were unpleasant. Such impressions of life in the Priory itself as it is possible to obtain are not pleasant either. Lady Tanfield was a daughter of Giles Symonds of Claye, Norfolk, and a niece of the famous Sir Harry Lee, of Ditchley, where a portrait of her, recognizably like her effigy on the Tanfield monument in Burford Church, is preserved. She was a woman as overbearing as her husband; and a note in the Church-wardens' Accounts, stating that her appropriation of space in the Church for the monument was without the leave of the Churchwardens, shows that she shared her husband's unpopularity in the town. Her daughter had no very happy childhood, being even reduced to bribing the servants in order to obtain candles for reading at night—a real hardship, for she was a studious child, and grew up a learned woman; and in later years, when Lady Falkland had forfeited her position and lost friends by joining the Roman Church, and was in real poverty, Lady Tanfield refused to receive her at the Priory, or to give her any assistance.

Tanfield himself did not live long after he had to the full asserted himself and his rights in the place. He died in

April 1625. His wife survived him in possession of the Priory for three years. On her death in 1628 it passed, not to the next generation, the daughter who had married the first Lord Falkland, but to the Tanfields' grandson, Lucius Cary, the second and more famous Falkland. This was by the direction of Tanfield's will. His daughter's marriage had not pleased him. She had allowed her dowry to be swallowed up in a constant vain effort to keep abreast of her husband's extravagant expenditure; and Tanfield was evidently determined that the remainder of his property should not go the same way.[1]

Lucius Cary was born at the Priory in 1610. His mother had been married to Lord Falkland in 1600, and their first two children had been daughters. Tanfield appears to have decided at once that the son now born should be his heir, for he kept the boy to live with him at the Priory.[2] At eighteen years old he succeeded to the Priory, and at the same time to the estates at Great Tew. Three years later, in 1631, he married Lettice Morison; and he seems, after his marriage, to have made Great Tew his principal residence. But he must still have continued to reside at the Priory occasionally, for his second son, Henry, was born here on November 6, 1634, and baptized on November 21. It is, therefore, possible that Burford Priory has some share in those gatherings of notable men which have given Falkland a place peculiarly his own among the intellects of his time. Great Tew is, in the main, the scene of the philosophic symposia to which Ben Jonson and Suckling, Cowley, Waller, Edward Hyde and Chillingworth brought their wit, their taste, and their learning. But the Priory may have had glimpses of them too.

Still, it is clear that it had not the first place in Falkland's affections; for when his circumstances compelled him to dispose of one of the estates, it was Burford Priory that he

[1] Tanfield was dead before Lady Falkland's conversion to Rome, so that event had nothing to do with her exclusion from the estates. It appears to have taken place in 1626.
[2] *Life of Lady Falkland*, p. 11.

gave up. He sold it in 1637 to William Lenthall, afterwards Speaker of the House of Commons.[1]

Coming of a family early settled in Herefordshire, one of whom by marriage acquired the manor of Lachford, and so founded at Haseley a branch of Oxfordshire Lenthalls, William Lenthall was born at Henley in 1591. The entry of the baptism records him as William Lenthall, son of John Lenthall; his father's name was William, and the name John was entered in error.[2] After being educated at Thame Grammar School and St. Alban Hall, Oxford, he took to the law, having an elder brother to succeed to the estates. He must have met with no little success, for when he purchased Burford Priory he was already owner by purchase of another estate, the manor of Besselsleigh. His connexion with Burford, however, began before he became owner of the Priory.[3] He must have been living here in 1626, for William, his second son, was baptized in Burford Church on January 8, 1626/7. In 1628, when the Royal Commission appointed a new body of Feoffees to hold the Charity Properties, one of the body was ' William Lenthall Esquire, of Burford '. In 1631 he acted as counsel for the town in the proceedings in the Court of Exchequer with regard to lands alleged to have been concealed from the Crown under the Act dissolving the Chantries.

In 1640, being by that time settled at the Priory, Lenthall was elected Member for Woodstock, the seat which Tanfield had once held, in that Parliament which was to change so violently the course of English history; and at the very outset of its career Lenthall was thrown into prominence by being elected Speaker of the House of Commons in flat

---

[1] Anthony Wood says that the date was ' about 1634 '; but the date in the deed of purchase is 25 November, 13 Charles I.

[2] See some letters written by Mr. F. Kyffin Lenthall in 1868 to the Rev. W. H. Turner, of Oxford, who edited the *Oxfordshire Visitations* for the Harleian Society. Mr. Lenthall provides good reason for holding that Speaker Lenthall was born at Henley. Bodl. MSS. Add. A. 289.

[3] His father, it may be noted, had owned property at Hailey, Witney, and Wilcote, at which last-named place he was buried. See the letters quoted in the previous note. Speaker Lenthall's purchase of Burford Priory thus grows out of previous associations with the district.

opposition to the known wish of the King for the appointment of Gardiner, Recorder of London. Speaker Lenthall has an uneasy place in history. His own death-bed protestation that he not only did not consent to the execution of Charles I, but actually did not know that the idea of it was seriously intended, his continuance in high place and offices of profit under the Commonwealth, his official welcoming of General Monk as the forerunner of the Restoration, and his immediate contribution of £3,000 to the Exchequer of the restored King—all these facts lend themselves but too easily to the view that he was at the best of indecisive character, at the worst, in Anthony Wood's slap-dash description, 'a knave'. The truth seems to be that he is a very good example of that curious and not uninteresting type, the instinctive House of Commons man. Such men are to be found at many periods since Lenthall's day, and not least in our own time. With a natural understanding and quick, almost unconscious, grasp of the subtleties of the relation between a nominal monarchy and an actually democratic governing principle, the House of Commons man is always constitutionally right; but very often politically ineffective, tactically unerring but strategically inconsistent. He is more aware of that subtle relation between forces, and the power which maintains the relation, than of the forces themselves.

In this light we can better understand Lenthall's career. It was real capacity, and not a more or less accidental choice, which had raised him to the Speakership, but capacity of precisely this narrow Parliamentary kind. We hear the very voice of it in his famous saying, which has become a maxim of the Speaker's Chair—his answer to Charles I when the King demanded to know if the five Members he meant to arrest were in the House: ' I have, Sir, neither eyes to see, nor tongue to speak, in this place but as the House is pleased to direct me, whose servant I am.' It is an almost incredibly perfect Parliamentary reply. At the same time it illuminates Lenthall's character, for on the one hand it is evidence of his singular fitness for the office he filled, and on the other hand it could only have been uttered by a man so penetrated

with the spirit of the House of Commons as to be in process
of surrendering any spirit of his own. It is significant that
Lenthall withstood in precisely the same official way the
determination of Cromwell to dissolve the Long Parliament ;
he would not leave the Chair without technical force being
used. He was not a mere time-server. He had sunk ·his
own individuality too much for even that kind of self-
expression to remain.

His acquisition of one office of profit after another—he
was Master of the Rolls, a Commissioner of the Great Seal,
and Chancellor of the Duchy of Lancaster, as well as Speaker—
is not to be judged by modern standards. Public opinion as
to all kinds of pluralities was looser than it is to-day. Nor
was he alone in virtually purchasing his pardon after the
Restoration. It is not difficult, once we have discovered the
mainspring of his character, to see him as guided at first
by the belief, natural to so good a House of Commons man,
that Parliament would be able to control the forces it had
aroused, yet acquiescing honestly enough in the Restoration
when he had found he had been mistaken.

After the Restoration he retired permanently to Burford
Priory. He must have lived here much throughout the
Commonwealth time, for he was on the Commission of the
Peace for the town appointed by the Commonwealth ; and
he had brought to the Priory, not to his other estate of
Besselsleigh, those famous pictures which he had purchased
from Charles I's collection at Windsor, including the Holbein
group of Sir Thomas More's family, the Van Dyck of Queen
Henrietta Maria, and two Correggios.

Yet it would be a mistake to think of Lenthall as con-
sciously retiring to Burford under a cloud. In 1660 he
presented himself as candidate for election to Parliament as
one of the burgesses for Oxford. General Monk supported
his candidature, and dispatched to Oxford ' one of his
captaines of horse, a gentleman of an estate (named Edmund
Warcuppe) nephew to the said W. Lenthall '.[1] This man we
can identify as a Burford resident ; he lived in the house

[1] Wood, *Life and Times* (Oxf. Hist. Soc.), vol. i, p. 311.

adjoining to the almshouse on the south side by Gildenford. John Lenthall, William's son, also busied himself on his father's behalf, giving dinners of beef and ale to the voters.[1] This candidature, unsuccessful though it was, could hardly have been undertaken at all, in Oxford of all places, if we are to imagine Lenthall as the discredited, double-faced person some of his critics have presented to us. It is, on the contrary, good support for the view that his apparent inconsistencies arose from a consistent faith in the House of Commons. That House failed in the great task it attempted after 1649; but this was no reason why Lenthall should cease to believe in it, or believe in his own fitness for membership of it, when it returned to its ancient position in the State.

He was not, however, to sit again in that Chamber which had seen so much of his life; and he settled down at the Priory. He had, since he first bought the place, made several alterations and enlarged the house. Unfortunately little that is good can be said for his work. Of its taste we have an instance in the clumsy ill-proportioned chimney-piece in the great drawing-room, as poor in execution as it is in design. Of its character as building we have an equally revealing instance in the flatness and poverty of the south wall of the south wing, and in the weak construction of the chapel, where a heavy vaulted ceiling was placed upon walls which had no foundations. This chapel was the work of his last years, perhaps after he had finally retired to the Priory. It is dated by a letter from the Bishop of Oxford to the Bishop of London, written on June 26, 1662,[2] asking for a copy of the 'uniform book of articles', and adding: 'If with the book of articles an uniform order of consecrating Churches and Chapels come along with it, it would add to the general satisfaction and please me much, who am called upon to consecrate a Chapel at Burford, a most elegant piece.' Much as the Chapel suffered in the long neglect of the Priory during the nineteenth century, enough remains to show that the most that can be said for it is that it was a good specimen of just what the taste of that age would call 'an elegant

---

[1] Wood, *Life and Times* (Oxf. Hist. Soc.), vol. i, p. 312.
[2] Bodl. MSS. Tanner, 48 (14).

piece '. It displays both the weakness and the floridness of design which vitiated Renaissance Gothic building of any but the first rank. The window tracery is uninteresting; and the fragments of the carved decoration of the interior show that it was feeble work, when it was not, as in the two statues flanking the doorway, grotesquely awkward.[1] Seen from a little distance in a merely picturesque relation to the main building, the Chapel, especially with the arcaded gallery leading to it, is certainly an effective addition to the general view of the Priory. But as a place of devotion the Chapel has no dignity or beauty ; and there is nothing in what survives of it to arouse regret for what decay has removed.

Speaker Lenthall can have had but brief pleasure in his chapel. He died on September 1, 1662, leaving a bequest of money to the town charities, and was succeeded in the Priory estate by his eldest son, John Lenthall, whom Anthony Wood describes in his bitterest style as ' the great Braggadochio and Lyar of the age he lived in ', and, more abruptly, as ' a beast '. He would certainly have exposed himself even more than his father to Wood's Royalist prejudices ; for he was a more out-and-out Parliamentarian. Elected Member for Gloucester in 1645, he received a Commonwealth ' baronetcy ' in 1658, and for a few months in 1660, before the Restoration, he was Governor of Windsor. The best of his reputation is due to Colonel Hutchinson, who in his account of the debate in the House of Commons in 1660, concerning the execution of Charles I, records that John Lenthall, refusing the quibbles of which some members availed themselves, spoke boldly and firmly of the policy and the course of events which had led to the condemnation of the King.[2]

In face of that evidence, Anthony Wood's characterization of the man can hardly satisfy us. John Lenthall evidently

[1] Gotch (*Architecture of the Renaissance in England*, Part I, p. 22) remarks on the ' combination of quasi-Gothic tracery with fully developed classical architrave and cornice ' in the windows of this chapel, which are, he says, ' genuine attempts to give to traceried windows a classic appearance, or at any rate an appearance other than Gothic.' Whatever the attempt, the effect is weak.

[2] *Hutchinson's Memoirs*, edited by the Rev. Julius Hutchinson, revised by C. H. Firth (1885), ii. 246.

had courage, and—perhaps because he had entered on the troublous times as a younger man—a more vigorous conviction of the rightness of the Parliamentary cause than his father held. Yet the fact remains that he weakened in it, and so far stultified himself as to receive knighthood from Charles II in 1677. He served as High Sheriff of Oxfordshire in 1672. Perhaps we may take it that Wood's view of him is an exaggerated representation of a phase of his life in which, having surrendered for the sake of safety and comfort the principles he had once maintained, he had lost respect.

The Burford Records show us very little of him, beyond his merely formal position in the town. Indeed, he may have been but little here ; and at one time during his tenure of the estate there was a possibility that Burford might have had a far more distinguished squire, the great Duke of Ormonde, who took a short tenancy of the Priory in 1672, and was living here from November in that year to February 1673. The Duchess of Ormonde writes under date November 16, 1672, to Captain Mathew, a business agent of the Duke's : ' We shall go within a few days to a place called Burford in Oxfordshire, where I may try whether we can live cheaper than at London ' ; [1] and again, under date December 21, 1672, from Burford : ' I am settled here for a while until my lord's going up into the Parliament, which will be the beginning of February next, at which time I purpose to go too ; whereby to avoid the excuse of keeping two houses. I was, I confess, desirous to try whether living in the country for a considerable part of the year would abate the charge we are at in London, and I find it will very considerably.' [2] That it was at the Priory at which the Duke and Duchess were staying is clear from a letter of some years later in which Colonel Edward Cooke, writing to the Duke about Charles II's visit in March 1680/1 to the Burford races, speaks of Lenthall as ' your Grace's quondam landlord '.[3] Evidently, from the phrases the Duchess uses, the

---

[1] *Ormonde Papers*, New Series (Hist. MSS. Com.), vol. iii, p. 451.
[2] *Ibid.*, p. 523.
[3] *Ibid.*, vol. vii, p. 618.

tenancy might have become more or less permanent ; but presumably the Ormondes did not much care for the place, or at any rate on trying Cornbury preferred that house, for in later years this economical *villegiatura* took place there.[1]

It appears that John Lenthall was not living at the Priory when the visit of Charles II took place. Colonel Cooke says that the King, as he came into Burford, ' was met by the reverend magistrates, welcomed with a hearty speech and a rich saddle, and so eat his dinner at your Grace's old quarters '. Anthony Wood says that the Burford Corporation ' accompanied him to Sir John Lenthall's house '.[2] But there is no mention of Lenthall himself ; and if he had been here at the time he would hardly have been absent or have left to others the conducting of the King to the Priory. He may already have been lying at Besselsleigh in his last illness, for he died at that place in November of this same year, 1681.[3]

His only son, William Lenthall, succeeding to the estates, made no attempt to carry on the baronetcy and title which John Lenthall had received under the Commonwealth. His tenure was a brief one, for he died in September 1686. But he seems to have lived at the Priory. He also comes under Anthony Wood's lash ; in recording young Lenthall's death, Wood ends his note : ' The grandfather, a knave ; the son, a beast ; the grandson, a fool.' Wood adds some scandal about young William Lenthall's wife. She had been Catherine Hamilton, and Wood records with uncompromising frankness

---

[1] In 1686, when, owing to the expectation that Lord Clarendon would be recalled from Ireland, the Duke of Ormonde foresaw that Cornbury might be no longer at his disposal, he again thought of taking Burford Priory. He writes from Cornbury, October 29, 1686 : ' I have been to see Sir Ralph Dutton's house at Sherborn, and was never more taken with the outside of a house, nor more deceived when I came in. Two parts of the three being either not finished or so fallen to decay, that there is not room to receive my family much less my friends . . . but that I may get as near as I can I am like to treat the new widow Lenthall for the house belonging to that family in Burford, where the want of rooms in the house will be supplied by very good ones in the town ' (*Ormonde Papers*, Hist. MSS. Com., vol. ii, p. 306). The ' new widow Lenthall ', however, had intentions of her own which did not leave her long a widow, and the Duke had to change his plans.

[2] Wood, *Life and Times* (Oxf. Hist. Soc.), vol. ii, p. 529.

[3] *Ibid.*, vol. ii, p. 559.

the reputation she bore before her marriage in the dissolute Court of that time, insinuating that it was not improved by her behaviour at Burford.[1] After Lenthall's death she married her cousin, the Earl of Abercorn; and a document bearing her signature after this marriage is among the Burford Records.[2]

The honours of the next royal visit to Burford fell to Lord and Lady Abercorn. On November 3, 1695, William III came to the town, receiving the customary Burford gift of a fine saddle, and spent the night at the Priory.[3]

The townspeople's attitude towards the Priory was not improving. In 1686 they took upon themselves to call Lady Abercorn, as lady of the manor, to account for remissness in the holding of the annual court at which the Bailiffs were appointed. The Burgesses seem to have had some intention of applying for a Mandamus. Lady Abercorn on her side retaliated by questioning the right of the Burgesses to present four persons at the Manorial Court for the selection of two of them to be Bailiffs; her case was that this custom had only arisen in days when the Steward of the Manor was not sufficiently acquainted with the town to make his own choice, and that she was not bound to pay any attention to the Burgesses' presentations. The matter collapsed without attaining to any importance; but it is significant as a sign of the continued ill-feeling.[4]

We need hardly be surprised, therefore, that there was plenty of malicious gossip when, on April 3, 1697, John Pryor, one of the trustees under William Lenthall's will for his two young sons, was found murdered in the Priory grounds. Tradition says that the body was discovered in a summer house in the upper part of the garden. As Lord Abercorn was accused of the murder, and as newspapers were beginning by that time to be spread abroad, there was plenty of excite-

---

[1] Wood, *Life and Times* (Oxf. Hist. Soc.), vol. iii, p. 195.
[2] Part III, p. 475.
[3] A letter of William III to an Alderman of Flushing, dated at Burford 17th November 1695, is preserved in the town museum of Flushing. See also Wood, *Life and Times*, vol. iii, p. 493.
[4] See Part III, pp. 389–90.

ment about the case. Both the newspapers and the diarists of the time were ready enough with accounts of how the murder had been committed, and with explanations of the reason for it. The theory most favoured was that Pryor, dutifully protecting the interests of the Lenthall boys, had refused to lend himself to schemes of Lord Abercorn's. The Earl was tried at the Oxford Assizes, the Duke of Norfolk and the Earl of Arran coming down to use their influence on his behalf; and he was acquitted.[1] No one was ever convicted of the murder.

The younger of William Lenthall's sons, who were both lads at this time, appears to have taken to the Bar as a profession, and to literature as an amusement. We have a glimpse of him in Hearne's *Diary*. Hearne notes under date December 3rd, 1705, that William Lenthall of Lincoln's Inn, gentleman, had had to insert an apology in the *London Gazette* for a libel on Mr. Manley and Mr. Walker in a poem which Lenthall had ' writ and published ', called ' A Trip to Leverpool '.[2]

The elder son, John, who succeeded to the estates, was to hold them for a very long time; he did not die till 1763. He figures considerably in Burford history, for he was the Lenthall whose concern for the disposition of the Speaker's bequest to the town charities, about which his two predecessors had not troubled themselves, led to the Royal Commission of 1738 and the Chancery suit of 1742, when the Corporation contested the Commission's authority. The fact that he was determined to inquire into the existing conditions of the bequest, and pursued his resolve so firmly, is enough to show that he was of a different calibre from his father and grandfather. A copy of the Commission's report, plentifully annotated by Lenthall himself, is preserved at the Tolsey; and the comments on it reveal the man. They are eloquent of clear-headedness in singling out and sticking to an essential point, not unworthy of a professional lawyer.

[1] Hearne says that the jury were drunk, as well as bribed, and that ' the Murther was clear '. *Hearne's Collections* (Oxf. Hist. Soc.), vol. ix, p. 221.

[2] *Hearne's Collections*, vol. i, p. 115.

The obvious contempt for the pettiness of the town's affairs is that of a man of the world ; and he is extremely impatient of anything he deems dishonourable. One has to remember that when he wrote these notes, the Corporation, discredited as they were by the report, had made up their minds to fight on a technical legal point, which could not clear their honour, but might save their self-importance ; the annotations are plainly intended for use in connexion with the Chancery suit. Therefore a certain amount of irritation may be excused in them. But even making that allowance, we cannot but see that Lenthall was rather intolerant and overbearing ; not at all the kind of man to be popular in the town.

So his long and steady tenure of the estate, while it no doubt restored the respectability of the Priory, somewhat tarnished by the Speaker's immediate successors, did not help on to any better footing the relations between the Priory and the townsfolk. . The Speaker, we may well imagine, had not been the kind of man to conciliate the resentment aroused by Tanfield's assertion of his rights and extinction of the town's privileges. Moreover, even if he had taken the trouble to be conciliatory, the town, in its flush of excitement with the races and the fine comings and goings of the Restoration, probably felt a new kind of resentment when it reflected that the Priory stood for the dull and now defeated Parliamentarians. Burford's opinion of John and William Lenthall would be, we may be sure, the summary one that Anthony Wood expresses. Following upon all this, the attack of the later John Lenthall upon the one public responsibility which remained to give the Corporation any importance banished finally any chance of more genial relations between the Priory and the town. To the end one cannot find that any Lenthall was affectionately, or even loyally, regarded by Burford people.

Of the mansion and grounds during John Lenthall's life we have one glimpse, and the account of them accords precisely with the character we have seen revealed in other ways. One John Borlase, a Gloucester engraver, who kept

up a voluminous correspondence with one of his patrons,
Lyttelton, at that time Dean of Exeter, and wrote to him
especially about possible subjects for engravings, made
a journey to Oxford in 1753 by way of Burford. After
a brief description of the Church Borlase says :

The Priory, now the house of Mr. Lenthall, seems to be a
mighty good old house in perfect repair—the Chapel adjoyning
has much Gothick ornament and some rich carvings over the
Door. The whole would make a good Print, if Justice be
done to it—but 'tis so neat that I can hardly think it prior to
ye Reformation ; and the Plantations round it are too close
and crowded for such a low situation.[1]

This last sentence shows that by the middle of the
eighteenth century the general aspect of the Priory must
have been almost exactly what it is now. The old fields and
pastures of the hospital had given place, in the century and
a half since Tanfield had made a country seat of it, to wooded
grounds covering the eight acres of the enclosure. The only
real difference from the conditions of the present day was
made by the course of the Cirencester road, which instead of
passing out from the town in a more or less straight line from
Sheep Street, turned down to the right towards the river,
cutting through the woods at an angle. The remark that
the Priory house was ' in perfect repair ' is exactly what we
should expect from what we have seen elsewhere of John
Lenthall. Precise, upright and rather exacting, he would be
just the man to hand over the estate in good order to his
successor. There are one or two documents among the
Miscellanea of the Burford Records which suggest that he
had the idea of improving the property by exchanging
detached and outlying portions for lands in other ownerships
adjoining to Priory lands, thus beginning that consolidation
of the estate which his successors were to have a better
opportunity of carrying out.

The first real step in this direction is the chief contribution
of the next owner of the estate to the history of the Priory.
John Lenthall died in 1763, and his son William succeeded

[1] Part III, p. 668.

him.   The fact that within ten years he carried through the
enclosure of the common arable land at Upton shows that
he was no unworthy successor to his father in management of
the estate.   For although he had practically no interests but
his own to consider—the Lenthall allotment at Upton being
720 acres out of 803 acres enclosed—yet his having decided,
at so early a date, to conform to the still new and contested
theories of agricultural betterment is proof of an intelligent
view of his opportunities as a landlord.   There were many
landowners of that time who were not to be convinced that
enclosure was an improvement, and maintained their estates
on the old strip system.   William Lenthall perceived the
advantage of compact distinct farms.

The other mark he has left upon the history of the Priory
was to prove less fortunate in its results.   He was unmarried,
and, perhaps for that reason, he was the first of the Lenthalls
to make an entailed settlement of the Priory, instead of
passing it on, as his predecessors had done, by simple testamentary disposition to the next heir.   He settled it to pass to
his brother and his brother's heirs.   The estate, which had
never been more than a pleasantly comfortable property,
not a really wealthy property, was within a very short time
to prove unequal to the strain of a settlement which made
mortgage the only means of meeting any large unusual
expenses.   Nor were the difficulties, when they came, lightened
by the fact that William Lenthall had charged the estate
with a considerable annual allowance to his sister Mary,[1] not
merely for her life, but subject to her own disposal at her death.

He died on October 22, 1781.   The brother, John Lenthall,
died soon after, in 1783.   His son, another John, was no
unworthy successor to the estates, in the matter of energetic
concern for improvements.   But he certainly allowed his
energy to outrun his discretion.   In so far as we can trace the
cause of the embarrassments under which the property began
to labour while he held it, the first of them was due to the very
natural sequel to his brother's enclosure of the Upton arable,

[1] The 'Molly Lenthall' of Mrs. Gast's letters in Archdeacon Hutton's
Burford Papers.

namely the enclosure of the Burford and Signett arable, which took place in 1795. Although other interests had to be consulted to a rather larger extent on this occasion, still there were only two persons seriously concerned in the matter, John Lenthall and the lay impropriator of the rectorial tithe. Between them these two received about 820 out of the 1,100 acres enclosed. This, while no doubt in one respect convenient, had the concurrent drawback of placing practically all the expense, whether of the making of the Award or the subsequent construction of walls, hedges, and the private roads, on only two men's shoulders. Now it is pretty clear that this came on top of a large amount of the expense of the Upton enclosure still outstanding. The road from Upton to Little Barrington which was being made as late as 1814, when the stone coffin was found, was one of the roads ordered to be made by the Award of 1773. The addition to these overdue burdens of fresh burdens in connexion with the Burford Award led to the beginning of a series of mortgages, placed upon the estate within the next twenty-five years.

At the same time it must be recognized that, as a mere estate improvement, the step was a good one. For, apart from the convenience and better cultivation of enclosed fields, Lenthall was able, by arrangements made at the time of the Award, and even in some measure guiding the decisions of the Award, to secure exchanges of the land allotted by the Commissioners, in such a manner as to gather the whole landed property of the Priory neatly around Bury Barns and the Priory itself, making the estate in the latter respect practically unbroken from the western side of Burford through Upton to the Barrington boundary. This satisfactory consolidation of the property might well seem worth the rather heavy expenses involved.

Equally an improvement, in a different way, was the diversion of the westward road out of Burford, whereby John Lenthall secured the privacy of the Priory woods and grounds. The improvement to the road itself was quite as great. The dip down to the river and up again, with the awkward slants in direction, was abolished, and a straight course provided more or less in a line with Sheep Street. But it may be doubted whether this, which was after all only an improvement in the amenities of the place, not in the practical working .of the estate, could also be considered worth the expenses involved. It was this costly scheme which, according to tradition, really brought the family into financial straits. The strain had, however, undoubtedly begun earlier, with the serious expenses of all the enclosing that had to be done in pursuance of the Awards of 1773 and 1795.

To the effects of this strain, and the narrowed prospects that were being forced upon him by various mortgages, we may safely attribute another manifestation of John Lenthall's energy, a lamentable one for the Priory. He reduced to its present dimensions the large mansion built by Tanfield and Speaker Lenthall. A detailed account of what he did is given later in this chapter. Possibly his reconstruction may have been partly suggested by the building having begun to fall out of repair. The alterations were begun in 1808;[1] and in the fifty years that had elapsed since John Borlase saw it in 1753, a time during which the estate had been held by men whose interest in the property had been so much taken up in other directions, the house may have fallen into a less happy condition. John Lenthall, confronted with the necessity of spending money on the structure, may well have decided, in view of the already crippled condition of the estate, to spend it in reducing the mansion to a size better adapted to the family's existing means, rather than in repairing a house which would always be a burden. That was, at any rate, the practical result of his work.

The last years of John Lenthall's life must have been very largely occupied with raising and readjusting the numerous mortgages which his activities had imposed on the property.[2] In addition to the cost of his improvements he had to find money to convert Mary Lenthall's charge upon the estate into an equivalent value in Consols; and also at intervals to

[1] The date is fixed by an advertisement in *Jackson's Oxford Journal*, April 30, 1808. I owe this reference to my wife.

[2] Abstracts of title to parts of the estate which were sold soon after his death contain interminable recitals of a quite confusing number of mortgages secured on the property.

maintain his son, William John, in the Guards; though it must in fairness be said that the young man made no excessive demands. The mortgages were consolidated ultimately into a single loan, and to meet the situation this loan had to be of no less a sum than £19,000.

Upon John Lenthall's death in November 1820 his son succeeded to a property encumbered even beyond that sum. He made little attempt to deal with conditions that must have been hopeless. One or two parts of the estate he soon sold. A considerable part of the Upton property was bought by the Kempster family; and the Bury Barns property was bought by the Faulkners, who had for some time been farming it as tenants. Part of the house property in the town was sold by public auction. Finally the Lenthall connexion with the Priory was severed outright in 1828, when the mansion and the remainder of the estate, with the lordship of the manor and town of Burford, were sold to Charles Greenaway, of Barrington Grove. He came of a family which had made a fortune in business in the city of Gloucester, and his father, Giles Greenaway, had bought Barrington Grove with the lordship of that manor a little before the end of the eighteenth century.

Under its new owner the Priory entered upon the dismal period of neglect and decay which finally reduced it to a ruin all but beyond hope of repair. The commonly accepted story was that, knowing his property would descend to a niece whom he disliked, Miss Youde, Mr. Greenaway deliberately allowed it to deteriorate. Another account was that the extravagance of this niece's father prevented any proper care being taken of the Priory.[1] Mr. Greenaway died on November 25, 1859; and the Priory estate was for some years in Chancery.

By the time it came into the hands of Mr. Hurst of Horsham Park, Sussex, a nephew of Mr. Greenaway's wife, in the year 1892 on the death of Miss Youde, the house was already ruinous. In that condition it long remained. During the latter part of the nineteenth century, with the increasing taste

---

[1] This was the reason given by the Rev. John Fisher, curate of Burford at the time of Mr. Charles Greenaway's death, in his *History of Burford*, published in 1861.

for touring about the country and observing picturesque places, Burford Priory became one of the favourite objects for expeditions from Oxford. The house and grounds were open to all comers, and were a favourite resort of Burford people. By a curious freak of destiny the place thus revived in its days of decay the fame which it had lost ; and just because it was open to any chance visitor it became far better known to the world at large than many finer houses of the county, such as Chastleton House or Shipton Court.

In course of time the Priory reached such an advanced state of ruin that nothing but sheer dissolution appeared to await it. However, Colonel La Terrière, buying it in 1908, set to work upon it, and in a very short space of time had made it again a human habitation. He introduced some structural alterations. The front door of the house as it stood led into a comparatively narrow hall, from which a dining-room opened on the right and a reception-room on the left. He took down the right-hand wall, thus throwing the dining-room into the hall and making the latter very spacious and pleasant. The left-hand wall of the hall was the one in which the three mediaeval arches were found ; these he removed, as they could not be displayed in that position, and re-erected them across his new hall, more or less on the line of the dining-room wall which he had taken down. By diminishing the size of the reception-room, and so enlarging an old parlour behind it, he was able to make a dining-room of the latter. The old kitchen was a very high room, some seventeen feet from floor to ceiling. By lowering this ceiling and other slight alterations, an extra bedroom was contrived, looking towards the river. The chapel, the roof of which had already been repaired to some extent by Mr. Hurst, Colonel La Terrière made sound and weatherproof, but did not attempt to restore internally.

In 1912 the Priory was bought by its present owner, Mr. Emslie John Horniman.

The difference between the Priory of to-day and the building engraved in Skelton's *Antiquities of Oxfordshire* calls for some explanation.

PLATE XVI. BURFORD PRIORY

The first mansion built upon the site of the mediaeval hospital was evidently a large **E**-shaped house, facing eastwards. To north and south were wings rising to a single gable, each of the same frontage-width as the present wings, but rather higher and much farther apart ; between the wings was a long central bay, and in the middle of it, set back from the line of the wings, was the existing porch, also higher than it is now. The windows of this façade would have been plain square-headed mullioned windows, in the same style as the two still surviving in the peak of the gables, though of course those on the lower levels would have been more ample in size. The two ornate bays now on this frontage were originally on the south frontage, facing the garden—a more natural position for windows of this open and elaborate kind.

That would appear to have been Tanfield's house, a simpler and more harmonious structure than that shown in Skelton's engraving. The house he drew was the result of later alterations. Who carried them out we cannot know for certain, but we may safely assume from the apparent date of the work, as well as from what we know of his successors, that it was Speaker Lenthall. First he removed the two bay windows from their original position, and re-erected them on the eastern faces of the two wings. The traces of this change are quite obvious, not only in the rather blank and patched-up appearance of the wall from which they were taken,[1] but in the facts that they are not bonded into the walls against which they stand, and that these walls have a distinct batter, while the bays are plumb upright. The most probable reason which has been advanced for this moving of the bays is that Speaker Lenthall wanted more wall-space in the south room for hanging the pictures he had acquired from Charles I's collection. This was certainly the room in which they hung, for the walls showed, within living memory, the marks of the places once covered by the pictures. Next he doubled the frontage-width of the north and south wings, and did not do it symmetrically. The south wing was extended on the side nearest the porch,

---

[1] There is stone from four different quarries in this wall as it stands— plain proof of patching.

and the north wing on the side nearest the river, with the result that the porch was no longer in the centre of the façade. Moreover, the bay windows, instead of being both on the outer half of the wings or both on the inner half, as symmetry would have ordained, stood on the outer half of the south wing and the inner half of the north wing. The proof of this later doubling of the width of the wings is that in the southern wing an outside chimney stack was discovered in what was then the middle wall of the wing, showing that the wings Tanfield built had later on been added to.

Thus we have at last, with the addition of Speaker Lenthall's chapel and arcaded gallery, the house which Skelton drew. It was also the house John Lenthall reduced in size about the year 1808 or 1809. Speaker Lenthall's building was all bad work. The one considerable piece of it which is left, the chapel, has actually no foundations. It is therefore likely that his additions to the north and south wings were in bad condition, for they were not incorporated in the reconstruction.[1] John Lenthall destroyed them, and also cut out completely the long bay of building between the wings. He was thus left with the two wings and the porch of the original Elizabethan house ; and proceeded to readjust them to make his new house. The south wing he was, of course, obliged to leave where it stood, partly because he could not move it without isolating the chapel, and partly because the long gallery with its elaborate plaster ceiling could never have been re-erected. So he brought the porch close up against this wing, and then brought Tanfield's north wing across to adjoin the porch on the other side. Besides thus telescoping the frontage to less than half its original length, John Lenthall also reduced the height of the gables and the porch. The whole roof, with the exception of the part above the kitchen, was lowered, and the topmost storey of the house practically destroyed.

From his own point of view John Lenthall, no doubt, did

---

[1] Knowledge of the character of Speaker Lenthall's work gives support incidentally to one of the reasons which have been offered for the rebuilding, for it becomes far more likely, in face of this knowledge, that the house had by that time fallen into a condition demanding some fundamental treatment.

the sensible thing. He had on his hands a large place which, though it must have contained, to judge by the gallery or great drawing-room, some fine and noble apartments, was so enfeebled by bad building that to maintain it would have involved heavy and continuous expense. He contrived out of it a house for himself which was comfortable, in an early nineteenth-century fashion, and yet presented, with the re-arranging of the façade, some reminiscence of its past. Still, the effect of such drastic rebuilding could not but be disastrous to the general character and dignity of the house. While the front retains some picturesqueness, there is no side or back view which has any consistent outline or appearance of con-sidered design. Every aspect save that of the façade produces a somewhat confused impression. Yet the house is not the less interesting for the marks it bears of the phases through which it has passed, once the signs of them have been made, so to speak, legible in its walls to-day.

MACES AND SEALS OF THE CORPORATION

PART III
CALENDAR OF THE RECORDS

SECTION I
THE CHARTERS OF BURFORD

THE originals of the earliest charters of Burford are not now in existence. Copies of them, however, are preserved on the Certificate made by the Burford Gild Merchant in response to the proclamation of Richard II, ordering all the Gilds to furnish returns to the Chancery setting forth their liberties and privileges, their rules and customs, and their possessions. The Burford Certificate is unfortunately damaged at the top, and the regnal year is missing from the date ; but as the first part of the date—xxviii die Ianuarii—is decipherable, and the proclamation was of the year 1388, the Certificate may be assumed to be of the year 1389.

It contains copies of eight documents, four emanating from lords of the manor and four from the Crown. They are not entered upon the Certificate in their true chronological order, but in two groups, the four from lords of the manor being placed before those from the Crown ; moreover, the first four, being undated, and the knowledge of the proper succession having doubtless been lost, appear in the order of their length and explicitness. Consequently rearrangement is necessary in order to present the chronological sequence of the documents.

The first charter is in its right place. It is the grant of liberties by Robert FitzHamon, which has already been discussed at some length.[1]

The second document on the Certificate is the charter of William Earl of Gloucester. But it refers to *two* previous grants—made by ' Robertus filius hamonis avus meus et Robertus Comes G. . . .'—and its place should therefore be third, if a document can be shown which should precede it. This is clearly the case with the fourth on the Certificate. That one opens with the words ' R regis filius Gloucestrie

---

[1] See Part I, pp. 5, 10..

consul ', the style commonly used by Robert, the natural son of Henry I, who took so great a part in Matilda's struggles against Stephen. He married Mabel, one of the daughters of Robert Fitz-Hamon, and obtained with her the Honour of Gloucester. But he never seems to have used the ordinary style of Comes Gloucestriae. His charters, as may be seen by several examples in the Cartulary of the Abbey of Gloucester,[1] open with a style identical with that employed in this Burford charter. Therefore that document must be placed second in chronological order, and is to be dated between 1107, the year of FitzHamon's death, and 1147, the year of Robert's death.

The charter of William Earl of Gloucester, Robert's son, may be placed third, since the two charters of Henry II are in the nature of confirmations of liberties granted by William. It may thus be dated between 1147 and 1155, the probable date of the first charter of Henry II. It is not difficult to see why the members of the Burford Gild who drew up the Certificate placed this document second. It recites in full and confirms the charter of FitzHamon, and the two might naturally be copied in succession. The recital is fortunate, since we are thus enabled to reconstruct those portions of FitzHamon's charter which have perished by the damaging of the Certificate.

The charters of Henry II, fifth and sixth on the Certificate, should stand fourth and fifth. Both can be dated with some accuracy. One was given at Northampton, and the witnesses are Reginald Earl of Cornwall, Humfrey de Bohun Dapifer, and Warin FitzGerold Chamberlain. Now Eyton gives no instance of Humfrey de Bohun signing as Dapifer after 1158, and none of Warin FitzGerold as Chamberlain later than that same year. But before that year he only records two visits of Henry II to Northampton, one in January 1155, and the other in July 1157. Consequently the Burford charter must belong to one of those two years, and as other charters tested by Reginald Earl of Cornwall and Warin FitzGerold as Chamberlain at Northampton are attributed by Eyton to the earlier year,[2] and as also Humfrey be Bohun signs as Dapifer in the same year,[3] there is sufficient ground for dating this Burford charter in 1155.

The case of the other charter is even more clear. The rather curious form of the dating clause, *apud Chinonem in excercitu regis*, is found in two charters quoted by Eyton, which he attributes to the year of

---

[1] *Historia et Cartularium Monasterii Sancti Petri Gloucestriae*, edited by W. H. Hart (Rolls Series, London, 1865), ii. 10, 48, 135.
[2] Eyton's *Itinerary of Henry II*, pp. 3, 27.   [3] *Ibid.*, p. 7.

the King's siege of Chinon in the war with his brother Geoffrey—1156.[1] It does not occur in the cases of any other charters given at Chinon in later years. Its occurrence here, therefore, would make the date of the second Burford charter of Henry II 1156.

This fact adds probability to the dating of the first charter in 1155 rather than 1157. In view of the chronological mistakes in the order observed on the Certificate there would, indeed, be no reason to speak of these charters in this way as first and second. It is, however, more significant that the Chancery of Edward III so arranged them in the Confirmation of that reign; and the coincidence of this arrangement with the apparent probabilities of dating is not quite negligible.

Next in point of time comes the charter of Richard de Clare, fourth on the Certificate, but properly to be placed sixth. His father, Gilbert de Clare, had succeeded to the Honour of Gloucester, *circa* 1217 in right of his mother Amice, one of the daughters of Earl William, after the death of Isabella, the daughter who had brought the Honour by marriage first to John, King of England, and after her divorce from him to Geoffrey de Mandeville. Richard de Clare, succeeding his father in 1230, held the manor of Burford till his death in 1262, and his charter is therefore to be dated between those years.

The last two documents entered on the Certificate are also the first two of the series of original charters preserved among the town Records—the Confirmations granted by Edward III and Richard II.

Of the reason why the series of extant originals opens with these two—of the circumstances that is to say, of the disappearance of the earlier charters—no account can be given. Dr. Plot makes a statement which would lead us to suppose that they must have been in existence in his day; he states that he saw a charter of Henry II granting liberties to the town of Burford. Against that must be placed the fact that, in the *Quo Warranto* case of 1620–1, no earlier charter than that of Edward III was produced on behalf of the Burgesses in defence of the privileges they had been exercising. It is hardly to be thought that, in a case in which the defence relied largely upon the plea of enjoyment of the privileges from time out of mind, the most ancient charters extant would not be produced. In other words, the course of that case leaves us no conclusion except that the earliest charters had already been lost. Plot, not concerned with extreme accuracy in such a matter, might in one sense say that he had seen

[1] Eyton, *op. cit.*, pp. 17, 18.

the charter of Henry II, after reading the transcription of it in the charter of Edward III.

Two originals of later dates have also been lost. The Confirmation obtained from Henry VI refers to a Confirmation by Henry V, but the latter is not in existence. As having some possible bearing upon this loss it may be remarked that among the charters is preserved a copy of Henry VI's Confirmation, with a note to the effect that this copy was sealed with the Common Seal of the town ' pro maiore securitate '. Unfortunately the copy is not dated ; but certain circumstances give a clue as to the time at which it was probably made. The Confirmation by Edward IV, issued in 1475, recites only the charter of Edward III, omitting all the intermediate reigns. Henry VII, in his turn, confirmed only the Confirmation of Edward IV. There would thus be a very good reason why the Burgesses should attach peculiar importance to the Confirmation by Henry VI, since it included all the reigns thus omitted. But they would not have been likely to go to the length of making a copy, unless they had had a warning given by the loss of one of their documents. Thus it may be offered as probable that the Confirmation by Henry V was lost at some time during the reigns of Edward IV and Henry VII. The Confirmation obtained from Henry VIII included both the Confirmation of Henry VII and also that of Henry VI, establishing the whole series up to that date ; so that the copy would have been less likely to have been made after Henry VIII's accession.

The other lost document of the series is the Confirmation by Queen Elizabeth. It is recited in that obtained from James I ; and the charges paid for it are entered in one of the Corporation Books.[1]

The instruments thus grouped under the general title of Charters of Burford are, technically speaking, of various characters, and hardly any of them can take rank as charters in the strictest sense. The earliest of them, in the absence of the originals, have to be classified by the form of their contents, without the guidance that might have been given by the shape of the parchments or the manner of attachment of the seals.

The first three, belonging to the rather obscure body of Anglo-Norman private diplomata, may perhaps be classified as charters. The Address in each case, though brief, is in general terms ; and the grant is conveyed in Concessive rather than Injunctive form. What remains of the Charter of FitzHamon is enough to show that it can be

---

[1] See *infra*, p. 411.

regarded as a good specimen of the diplomata of the time, free from unnecessary verbiage, and only introducing a clause subsidiary to the main grant, with the phrase ' Et adhuc concedo ', for the very definite and essential purpose of giving practical validity to the Gild Merchant grant.

The charter of Robert of Gloucester is, even for its period, a singularly curt confirmation of liberties. But it is on that account characteristic of so great a fighting man ; and it bears, in such details as the use of the present tense ' concedere ', instead of the past tense ' concessisse ', and the single witness, sound evidence of its genuineness.

The two charters of Henry II are quite distinct in character, and the differences appear to give us a reason for the procuring of two from that King. The first is not a true charter, but a writ. It has the particular Address to the Bishop of Lincoln and the officers of the County of Oxford, and its formula is purely Injunctive. The second, with a general, though rather abbreviated Address, contains an Injunctive clause concerning the rights and liberties at large of William Earl of Gloucester, and goes on to a Concessive clause concerning the free customs and the Gild Merchant of Burford in particular. It may therefore be classified as a Writ-Charter. The confined Address of the former document suggests that it was procured for a special purpose. Taking into account the fact that Burford, while in the County of Oxford and the Diocese of Lincoln, was part of the possessions of a great lord whose main possessions were in another county and diocese, and was attached to an Honour in another county and diocese, it is not difficult to see that trouble may have arisen between the authorities of the two counties and dioceses. The geographical situation of Burford may have led to some invasion of its feudal situation ; and the Writ of Henry II looks as if it were designed to correct some infringement of liberties.

From a constitutional point of view the second document of this reign, the Chinon Charter, is curious. It includes, in a confirmative writ to the lord of the manor, a direct grant of liberties from the Crown to men of the manor. At this period, when the niceties of diplomatic formula are still lacking in development, the phrases of a charter cannot be pressed too far ; but there is at least enough appearance of a direct Royal grant in this charter to show how it came about that the Burgesses imagined themselves to be above the level of the purely manorial boroughs at a later date.

The charter of Richard de Clare is an interesting specimen of the period when, with public diplomata becoming more formal and regular in outline, private diplomata, owing to their decreasing importance, were losing in formality, and becoming, in so far as they were still formal, perfunctory. The epistolary inversion of the formula of Address, the absence of any recital of the nature of the grants confirmed, the addition of ' et multis aliis ' to the list of witnesses, and the lack of any mention of a place in the dating clause, make it a poor specimen of a charter.

When, after a long interval, the Burgesses of Burford next bestirred themselves in the matter of their liberties, they found that the Royal Chancery had evolved a simple and comparatively inexpensive procedure for those who were not seeking new franchises—the system of Inspeximus by Letters Patent. As long as the borough lasted this system from henceforth sufficed for the Burford authorities, and with one exception the remainder of the ' Charters ' is composed of a series of these Letters Patent, which call for no comment. The exception is the grant to the town of a second annual fair by Henry VII. This, though in the form of Letters Patent, is a true charter, with an Expository clause and a complete Dispositive clause ; moreover, the Great Seal is procured not by payment of a fine in the Chancery, but by the process of a writ of Privy Seal.

In conclusion, the source, the sequence, and the character of the Burford Charters may be summarized as follows :

I. Gild Certif. 1	1088–1107	Robert Fitz-Hamon	Charter
II. Gild Certif. 4	1107–47	Robert of Gloucester	Charter
III. Gild Certif. 2	1147–64	Earl William	Charter
IV. Gild Certif. 5	1155	Henry II	Writ
V. Gild Certif. 6	1156	Henry II	Writ-Charter
VI. Gild Certif. 3	1230–62	Richard de Clare	Charter
VII. Burf. Rec. Bdle. AA	1350	Edward III	Letters Patent of Inspeximus
VIII. Ibid.	1379	Richard II	ditto
IX. Ibid.	1399	Henry IV	ditto
X. Ibid.	1437	Henry VI	ditto
XI. Ibid.	1475	Edward IV	Letters Patent of Inspeximus, but omitting all reigns since Edward III
XII. Ibid.	1486	Henry VII	ditto

XIII. *Ibid.*	1497	Henry VII	Charter of Fair
XIV. *Ibid.*	1510	Henry VIII	Letters Patent of Inspeximus, restoring those of Henry VI
XV. *Ibid.*	1547	Edward VI	ditto
XVI. *Ibid.*	1554	Mary	ditto
XVII. *Ibid.*	1605	James I	ditto

PUBLIC RECORD OFFICE. Chancery Miscellanea. Certificates of Gilds. Bundle 45 : Number 388 a & b.

Note.—The document is damaged at the beginning and at the end. The latter parts of the lines are missing throughout the first charter and the middle of the first two lines of the second charter. The middle of the last few lines of the certificate is also missing.

Certificatio Iohannis Wynrissh Thome Spicer Iohannis St . . .
. . . . facta xxviii die Ianuarii anno regni regis
nunc . . . .

Robertus Hamoni filius omnibus suis hominibus et amicis salutem
Volo . . . . de Oxenford videlicet istas ut
unusquisque domum suam et . . . . uxore
vel de quolibet alio absque ipsius domini requisicione heredem . .
. . . . Gilda mercatorum Et adhuc concedo ut quicunque ad mercatum . . . . lanam et corea
nisi homines istius ville . . . .

Willelmus comes Gloec dapifero suo et omnibus Baronibus suis
ffrancie et Anglie . . . . me concessisse
omnibus meis hominibus de Burford omnes illas consuetudines quas
Robertus filius hamonis avus meus et Robertus Comes G . . . unt
sicut carte illius testantur videlicet istas ut unusquisque domum et
terram et omnem pecuniam suam possit vendere et in vadimonio
ponere et de filio et filia vel uxore et de quolibet alio absque ipsius
domini requisicione heredem faciat et gildam et consuetudines quas
habent Burgenses de Oxenford in Gildam mercatorum et quicunque
ad mercatum venire volunt veniant et in ipso mercato habeant licenciam emendi quecunque volunt praeter lanam et corea nisi homines
ipsius ville Testibus Willelmo filio Iohannis Hamone filio Venfridi
constabulario Ruelano de Valomis Roberto de Almeri dapifero
Ricardo de Sancto Quintino fulco filio Guar Gilberto de Umframvilla
Rogero dapifero apud Oxenford

Omnibus Christi fidelibus hoc presens scriptum visuris vel audituris
Ricardus de Clara comes Gloucestrie et hertfordie salutem in domino
Noveritis nos concessisse et hac presenti carta nostra confirmasse
omnibus Burgensibus nostris de Burford eas libertates et liberas

consuetudines quas habent a predecessoribus nostris comitibus Gloucestrie quibus hucusque usi sunt In cuius rei testimonium huic scripto sigillum nostrum apponi fecimus hiis testibus domino Willelmo de Clare Waltero de Escoveny Willelmo de Sancta Elena tunc senescallo Gloucestrie Thoma de Bayuse Willelmo de la Mare Rogero de Wantone Willelmo de Langeleya Johanne Belew Willelmo de Cranleya Alano de Cranleya et multis aliis

R Regis filius Gloucestrie Consul omnibus suis amicis salutem sciatis me concedere meis burgensibus de Bureford omnes illas iustas consuetudines et lagas quas Robertus filius hamonis eis concessit Teste Roberto Soro

H Rex Anglie et Dux Normannie et Aquitanie et Comes Andegavie Episcopo Lincolniensi et iusticiario et vicecomiti et omnibus ballivis suis de Oxenfordscira salutem Mando vobis et firmiter precipio quod homines Willelmi comitis Gloecestrie de Boreford et de Mora sint ita bene et in pace et quieti de omnibus querelis et ita teneant omnes terras suas et omnia tenementa sua cum sac et soc et tol et theam et infanghenethef et cum omnibus aliis libertatibus et liberis consuetudinibus suis sicut melius et liberius tenuerunt tempore Regis H avi mei Teste Reginaldo comite cornubie et Umfredo de Bohun dapifero et Warenno filio Geroldi comite apud Norhampton

H Rex Anglie et Dux Normannie et Aquitanie et Comes Andegavie omnibus iusticiariis et vicecomitibus et ministris suis tocius Anglie salutem Precipio quod Willelmus comes Glouecestrie cognatus meus teneat omnes terras suas ita bene et in pace et libere et quiete et honorifice sicut comes Robertus pater eius eas tenuit tempore henrici Regis avi mei Et habeat in pace et integre et plenarie in omnibus locis et in omnibus rebus omnes illas libertatès et quietancias et liberas consuetudines quas habuerunt tempore comitis Roberti Et sciatis me concessisse liberis Burgensibus ville comitis Willelmi de Bureford omnes liberas consuetudines illas quas habere solebant tempore comitis Roberti et tempore willelmi comitis sicut carte illorum testantur et gildam et consuetudines quas habent liberi Burgenses de Oxenford in gilda mercatorum Quia volo ut ita sit Teste Ricardo de Humet constabulario et warenno filio Geroldi apud Chinonem in excercitu Regis

Edwardus dei gratia Rex Anglie et ffrancie et Dominus Hibernie omnibus ad quos presentes litere pervenerint salutem Inspeximus quandam cartam quam Dominus h quondam Rex Anglie progenitor noster fecit in hec verba h Rex Anglie—[etc]—apud Norhamptonam

Inspeximus etiam quandam aliam cartam quam idem progenitor noster fecit in hec verba h Rex Anglie—[etc]—excercitu Regis Nos autem libertates et consuetudines predictas ratas habentes et gratas eas pro nobis et heredibus nostris quantum in nobis est concedimus et confirmamus sicut carte predicte rationabiliter testantur In cuius rei testimonium has literas nostras fieri fecimus patentes Teste me ipso apud Westmonasterium tertio die Iulii anno regni nostri Anglie vicesimo quarto regni vero nostri ffrancie undecimo

Ricardus dei gratia Rex Anglie et ffrancie et dominus Hibernie [etc] Inspeximus literas patentes Domini E nuper Regis Anglie avi nostri in hec verba—[etc]—Nos autem literas predictas et omnia in eis contenta rata habentes et grata ea pro nobis et heredibus nostris quantum in nobis est acceptamus approbamus et ratificamus et ea prefatis hominibus et burgensibus de Bureford tenore presentium concedimus et confirmamus prout carte et litere predicte rationabiliter testantur et prout iidem homines et burgenses libertatibus et consuetudinibus predictis hactenus rationabiliter uti et gaudere consueverunt In cuius rei testimonium has literas nostras . . . . . .

. . . . . Teste me ipso apud Westmonasterium decimo die marcii anno regni nostri secundo

Qui quidem burgenses et homines predicti . . . . consuetudines et libertates prescriptas habuerunt et eis uti et gaudere consue . . . . seu catalla ad predictam gildam spectant

BURFORD RECORDS

Cheatle Collection, Bundle AA

1350. Letters Patent of Edward III.
(Transcribed on the Gild Certificate above.)
Portion of the Great Seal in green wax.
Fine paid for the grant, 20s.

1379. Letters Patent of Richard II.
(Transcribed on the Gild Certificate above.)
Good specimen, almost complete, of the Great Seal in green wax.
Fine paid, 2 marks.

1399. Letters Patent of Henry IV.
Reciting the Letters Patent of Richard II ; the liberties are confirmed to ' hominibus et Burgensibus de Bureford et heredibus et

successoribus suis . . . ' to be enjoyed ' prout iidem homines et Burgenses de Bureford et antecessores sui ' have enjoyed them. Dated at Westminster 8 October anno primo.

Seal lost.

Fine, not mentioned.[1]

1437. Letters Patent of Henry VI.

Reciting Letters Patent (not now extant) of Henry V, dated at Westminster 3 Henry V 1 February (1416), which recited the Letters Patent of Henry IV. Issued ' per ipsum Regem et consilium suum in parliamento '. 24 November, anno sexto decimo.

Good specimen, almost complete, of the Great Seal in green wax.

Fine, not mentioned.

A copy of Letters Patent of Henry VI, dated at Westminster 8 November 1 Henry VI (1422), reciting Letters Patent (date not copied) of Henry V. The copy makes Henry V, in reciting the Letters Patent of Henry IV, refer to him as ' avi mei '. This copy was sealed with the Common Seal of Burford ' pro maiore securitate ' ; this seal has been lost. The copy is not dated.

1475. Letters Patent of Edward IV.

Reciting the Letters Patent of Edward III with no reference to later grants. Dated at Westminster 8 November anno quinto decimo.

Portion of Great Seal in green wax.

Fine paid, 26s. 8d.

1486. Letters Patent of Henry VII.

Reciting the Letters Patent of Edward IV. Dated at Westminster 20 November anno secundo.

Small portion of Great Seal in green wax.

Fine, not mentioned.

1497. Letters Patent of Henry VII granting a fair to the town of Burford.

Henricus Dei gratia Rex Anglie et Francie et Dominus Hibernie Omnibus ad quos presentes litere pervenerint salutem Sciatis quod nos de gracia nostra speciali concessimus et licenciam dedimus pro nobis et heredibus nostris quantum in nobis est Dilectis ligeis nostris Ballivis Burgensibus et inhabitantibus ville nostre de Bourford in comitatu nostro Oxon quod ipsi et successores sui annuatim in perpetuum habeant et teneant ac habere et tenere possint infra villam nostram predictam unam feriam videlicet in festo Exaltacionis sancte

---

[1] The Fine Roll, 1 Henry IV, gives the fine: 33s. 4d.

Crucis et per tres dies immediate precedentes idem festum et per alios
tres dies immediate sequentes illud festum annuatim unam curiam
pedis pulverizati ibidem tenendam durante eadem feria unacum
omnibus exitibus proficuis et amerciamentis eidem ferie pertinentibus
sive provenientibus ác cum omnibus proficuis et emolimentis ad
eandem feriam pertinentibus sive spectantibus ullo modo· Ita tamen
quod feria illa non sit ad nocumentum vicinarum feriarum   Quare
volumus et per presentes concedimus pro nobis et heredibus nostris
quod predicti Ballivi Burgenses et inhabitantes Ville nostre predicte
et successores sui annuatim habeant et teneant ac habere et tenere
possint imperpetuum predictam feriam in diebus et festo predictis
cum dicta curia unacum omnibus exitibus proficuis et amerciamentis
de eisdem feria et curia provenientibus ac cum omnibus proficuis
et emolimentis ad eandem feriam pertinentibus sive spectantibus
ullo modo absque perturbacione impedimento molestacione seu
gravamine nostri heredum seu ministrorum nostrorum quorumcunque
Ita tamen quod feria illa predicta non sit ad nocumentum vicinarum
feriarum sicut predictum est   In cuius rei testimonium has litteras
nostras fieri fecimus patentes   Teste me ipso apud Westmonasterium
decimo nono die Ianuarii anno regni nostri duodecimo

> per breve de privato sigillo et de data
> predicta auctoritate parliamenti

Fragments of the Great Seal in white wax.

1510. Letters Patent of Henry VIII.
Reciting separately the Letters Patent of Henry VI as well as those
of Henry VII (thus including all the Royal grants).   Dated at West-
minster 12 March anno primo.
Portion of Great Seal in green wax.
Fine, not mentioned.

1547. Letters Patent of Edward VI.
Reciting the Letters Patent of Henry VIII.   Dated at Westminster
1 December anno primo.
The Great Seal, perfect, in brown wax.
Fine, not mentioned.

1554. Letters Patent of Queen Mary.
Reciting the Letters Patent of Edward VI.   Dated at Westminster
13 June anno primo.
The Great Seal, broken, in red leather cover.
Fine paid, £3.

1605. Letters Patent of James I.

Reciting Letters Patent of Queen Elizabeth (not now extant), dated at Westminster 10 November anno primo (1559), which recited the Letters Patent of Queen Mary. Dated at Westminster 14 June anno tertio.

The Great Seal, broken, in red leather cover.

Fine paid, £8.

Included in the same Bundle:

Two Commissions issued by the Keepers of the Liberty of England. 20 December, 1649. To William Lenthal, Speaker of the House of Commons and Master of the Rolls of the Court of Chancery, the Bailiffs of the Town of Burford, and the two ancientest Burgesses, and the Seneschal, appointing them Justices of the Peace. In Latin.

The Great Seal of the Commonwealth, almost perfect, in red wax.

26 May, 1659. To William Lenthal, John Lenthal, the Bailiffs, Seneschal, and two ancientest Burgesses, appointing them Justices of the Peace. In English.

Fragment of the Great Seal of the Commonwealth in red wax.

SECTION II

CALENDAR OF RECORDS PRESERVED IN THE TOWN

THE muniments of the ancient Corporation of the Bailiffs, Alderman, and Burgesses of Burford, which are still preserved in the town, are now in three ownerships. One portion, together with the maces and seals of the Corporation, is in the possession of Mrs. Cheatle, the late Mr. T. H. Cheatle having been the last surviving Burgess, and his father the last Alderman, of the Corporation. A second portion is in the possession of the Charity Trustees, who replaced the Corporation, and is kept at the Tolsey. The third portion, a small one, is in the possession of the Governors of the Grammar School, Mrs. Cheatle having handed over to them the foundation deeds of the School and a few of the leases of School property.

The main division of these muniments took place after the extinction of the Corporation in 1861. Before that event they were all kept in two ancient chests and a chest of drawers in one of the rooms above the Church porch. Thence they passed entire, when the Corporation had ceased to exist, into the possession of Mr. Cheatle.[1] By the Common Law, upon the extinction of a Corporation its property, in the absence of special provision to the contrary by the Act causing the extinction, becomes the property of the last surviving member. In the scheme of the Charity Commissioners, which abolished the Corporation, the provision concerning its property was worded thus : ' All lands, hereditaments, and other real estate and property whatsoever, heretofore vested in or held by the said Corporation, or by the Trustees or Feoffees of the above-mentioned Charities, or any of them, for the purposes thereof respectively, shall from and after the establishment of this scheme be vested in and held by the Official Trustee of Charity Lands and his successors in trust for the " Burford Charity Trustees ".' This clause contains no direction concerning the muniments. They

---

[1] I owe my information on this point to Mr. Charles East of Burford, who himself as a boy conveyed the whole of the documents from the room above the Church porch to Mr. Cheatle's house. One of the ancient chests and the chest of drawers are now in the Tolsey.

were quite unnecessary for the purposes of the Trusts, the nature and extent of the charitable property and the objects which it was to serve having been established by two Royal Commissions and reestablished by several Reports of the Charity Commissioners in the first half of the nineteenth century. Consequently the documents, following the course of the Common Law, became Mr. Cheatle's property.

A few years later, however, he made a division of them, handing over about half to the Charity Trustees in order to give them a share of the interest in these old records. Roughly speaking, the division appears to have been made on the principle of handing over to the Charity Trustees the greater bulk of the documents dealing with gifts to the Church and retaining those concerning property which had been more or less exclusively under the control of the Corporation. The numerous documents concerning the Royal Commission of 1738 and the Chancery proceedings of 1742 were divided into two parts, which in some cases duplicate and in other cases supplement each other.

The Burford Records were examined some years ago by the Rev. W. D. Macray, on behalf of the Historical Manuscripts Commission. But, as has already been remarked, only a very small portion of the Records can be regarded as true municipal records; and Mr. Macray, therefore, did not find it worth while to calendar many of them. The volume of the *Historical Manuscripts Commission, Various Collections*, no. 1, published in 1902, contains his account of the Records, with a calendar of the Charters, a transcript of the Roll of the Burgess Rules, and notes on a few of the more ancient grants of land and on later documents possessing a special interest, such as the one which bears the signature of the King-maker.

For the purposes of the Historical Manuscripts Commission it was not necessary to do more. But for the purposes of a history of the Corporation of Burford it was necessary to examine all the Records; and it was natural that the opportunity should be taken to make a complete calendar, and at the same time to reduce to order the mass of documents, which were in a state of confusion.

Classification of them was greatly assisted by the results of a previous classification. The Royal Commission which examined into the administration of the Charity properties in 1738 ordered, among other things, that the deeds and other documents then in the possession of the Corporation should be entered upon a schedule with a view to their better preservation. In the making of this schedule the documents were divided into several series, according to the Charities with which they were connected. Each series was given a distinguishing letter and the documents were numbered in chronological order. On the whole this classification was well done ; only in a few instances have documents been placed in a wrong series or out of their chronological order ; these instances are noted in the ensuing calendar.

The following is a summary of the Charities represented on the schedule of 1738, given in the order and with the series letter of the schedule :

(1) POOLE'S LANDS. Series letter P. Property bequeathed in 1500 by Thomas Poole, Citizen and Tailor of London, to the Burgesses, for the good continuance of the fraternity, the provision of a fund for paying the Chancery fees for confirmation of charters, &c. The earliest document is dated 1401. This series is a large one, owing to the fact that several documents not concerning these lands alone were included in it. Owing to the Trust being so specifically for Corporation purposes, and connected with the Charters, the Burgesses seem to have caused to be placed in this series all documents concerning in general their administration of the Charity lands, as, for instance, a copy of the Decrees of the Royal Commission of 1628, and the general Trust feoffments made in pursuance of the Decrees.

(2) SCHOOL LANDS. Series letter S. The Grammar School was founded in 1571. But many lands given to its maintenance at that date had previously been held for Church purposes. Consequently the documents go back to a much earlier period, the first of the series being dated 1374.

(3) CHURCH LANDS. Series letter CH. Property given or bequeathed for the maintenance of the fabric and services of the Church and the Gild Chapel. The earliest document is dated 1377.

(4) BRIDGE LANDS. Series letter B. A small property held in trust for the repair of the Bridge and the highways leading thereto. The earliest document is dated 1322. The property seems originally to have been given for the general religious purposes of the Gild, and no specific declaration of the use of the rents for the upkeep of the Bridge is made until 1560. There is, however, good reason for holding that the money had always been devoted to the Bridge. The date of the first document in this series is significant. It is the same date as that of the Letters Patent of Edward II, granting to the town for a limited period tolls on all merchandise passing over the Bridge to market, the grant being made because the Bridge was then in disrepair.

The occurrence of this date on the first document of the Bridge Lands series can hardly be a mere coincidence. It is more likely that the necessities of keeping up the Bridge, which had led to the issue of the Letters Patent, had also led to the gift of this property. The absence of any specific reference to the Bridge in early documents of the series is not surprising, since the repair of bridges was one of the customary objects of the early Gilds. But the Edwardian Act dissolving the Gilds and Chantries would make it advisable to declare for this Trust a use that did not come under the head of 'superstitious uses'. Hence the declaration in the Deed of 1560.

(5) ALMSHOUSE LANDS. Series letter A. Property of which the rents were devoted to the Almshouses founded by Henry Bishop in 1455. The document numbered 1 in this series has nothing to do with the Almshouses. It is a letter from the Earl of Warwick concerning the Priory or Hospital of St. John the Evangelist. It may have been included in this series by mistaken association with another document signed by the Earl, the true beginning of the series, giving his licence as Lord of the Manor to Henry Bishop to found the Almshouses. This is the document bearing one of the only two known signatures of the King-maker.

(6) FIFTEEN LANDS. Series letter T. A small property the rents of which were intended to accumulate to relieve the burden on the town when a tax of Tenths or Fifteenths was levied. The earliest document is dated 1382.

(7) COBB HALL. Series letter GS. A house given in 1590 by George Symonds (hence the initials of the series mark) with the intent that the rent should be used to supplement the weekly allowances to the poor in the Almshouse.

(8) LENTHALL AND HOLLOWAY CHARITIES. Series letter LH. A combination of two bequests of money for apprenticing poor children, the combined fund being invested in land at Standlake. The earliest document is dated 1677, but the investment of money was not made till 1726, though the Lenthall bequest had been in hand since 1662.

(9) MULLENDER'S LANE HOUSES. Series letter M. A similar investment of a monetary bequest by Lady Tanfield. The property purchased was in Mullender's Lane, now Swan Lane, Burford.

(10) CLEVELEY'S AND HEYLIN'S CHARITIES. Series letters CL and H. Similar investments made in the early eighteenth century.

(11) WILLS AND GIFTS. Series letter W. A collection of wills and extracts from wills, the earliest documents being the complete wills of

two Burford Burgesses, that of John Pynnock, dated 1473, and that
of Henry Bishop, dated 1478.

It is worthy of remark that the documents thus classified about
1738 have been preserved almost intact. Hardly any have been lost.

It was, of course, easy, in reducing to order the confused masses
of documents, to reconstitute the classification of the 1738 schedule
as far as it went ; and the bundles into which I have gathered the
documents concerning the Charity Lands follow that classification.
There remained, however, a large quantity of documents not entered
upon the schedule. The Charters of the Corporation come under this
head ; they have been collected together into a single bundle. The
bulk of the unscheduled documents were concerned with various
inquiries into the Charity administration of the Corporation, and
especially with the Royal Commission of 1738 and the Chancery
Suit of 1742 which arose out of the Commission's Decrees. All these
have been classified and sorted into bundles under the heading
' Commissions and Legal Proceedings '. A certain number of documents have had to be classified as ' Miscellanea '. Most of them have
some bearing on Corporation affairs, but a few have no traceable
relation to Burford at all. There is a small quantity of Apprenticeship Indentures of comparatively late date which were not worth
calendaring.

In classifying the documents I have lettered the labels of the bundles
to increase the ease of reference to the documents. A single letter
has been used for the Tolsey Collection, and a double letter for the
Cheatle Collection.

I. THE CHEATLE COLLECTION

Bundle

AA	Charters	1351–1659
BB	Fifteen Lands	1392–1732
CC	School Lands I	1375–1635
DD	School Lands II	1637–1736
EE	Poole's Lands I	1401–1659
FF	Poole's Lands II	1659–1729
GG	Almshouse	1456–1717
HH	Wills	1473–1672
II	Roll of the Burgess Rules	1605
KK	Cobb Hall	1590–1735
LL	Cleveley's, Heylin's, &c.	1691–1724
MM	Commissions and Legal Proceedings	16th and 17th centuries
NN	Commissions and Legal Proceedings	18th century
OO	Commissions and Legal Proceedings	18th century
PP	Miscellanea I	1472–1741
RR	Miscellanea II	18th and 19th centuries
SS	Miscellanea III (Warwick signature, &c.)	

THE FIFTEEN LANDS
Cheatle Collection, Bundle BB

T 1. Saturday next after the Feast of St. Lawrence, 16 Richard II (1392).

Conveyance by John Wenryche, ' Senior Gildae Borfordiae ', and Thomas Spycer, ' Senior dictae Gildae ', ' consensu fratrum nostrorum dictae Gildae ', to John Stowe. Two cottages lying together on the south side of ' Synt Jones Street ' between the messuage of John Wenryche on one side and the messuage of Robert Cotylere on the other side.

Witnesses: John Carswall, John Walkere of Bampton, Thomas Batyn, Robert Cotyler, William Nayler of Borford, John Abraham of Clanfield.

T 2. 7 February, 7 Henry VII (1492).

Conveyance by John Hyll of Burforde, to Richard Brame, Thomas Synde, John Hyll, and William Bowdelare, ' Camerarii de Burforde '. Two tenements situate together on the south side of ' Seynt Johnnes Street ' between the gate of John Neweman late of Richard Starr on the east side and the tenement of John Kenne late of Richard Mosyer on the west side ' habenda et tenenda predicta duo tenementa cum suis pertinentibus prefatis Ricardo Thome Iohanni et Willelmo et camerariis per dictam villam electis qui pro tempore fuerint existentibus in perpetuum sub forma sequente videlicet quod redditus illorum duorum tenementorum venient et persolvantur predictis camerariis ad proficuum villae quum taxaciones vel quintadecima domini regis advocantur seu ad omnia alia onera si petantur '.

Witnesses: William Flodyatt, Richard Brame, then bailiffs of the town of Burford, John Bysshope, Thomas Synd, John Lambard.

T 3. 1 December, 38 Henry VIII (1546).

Conveyance by Richard Hannes, Robert Johnson, Jhone Tomson, and John Fallor of Burford, yomen, to Simon Wisdom, William Hewis, alias Calcatt, Richard Hodges, Robert Bruton, Edmund Silvester, and Thomas Prickevannce, yomen. Two cottages lately held by gift and feoffment of William Hedges and Thomas Leper, in St. John's Street between the tenement belonging to Thomas (blank) chaplain of Charlbury on the west side and the way called the backside of the tenement where Walter Rose now lives on the east side. ' The contente of this present dede is that they above named feoffees shall take and receave the Rentes Revenewes and profettes that shalbe yerely comynge and growynge of the forsaide cotages over and above the Reparacions of the same cotages well and sufficiently to be made done and kepte And the same shall put in to one common Boxe to be had amonge them and there to be Reserved and kepte untyll suche tyme as any payment of the fyftenes shallbe levyed and gathered of the towne and Burroughe of Burforde aforsaid to the use and behoffe of our saide sovreyne lorde the kynge that now is his heirs and successours here after to come And that the saide Rentes Revenewis and profettes if any there be to be paide for the easemente of the poore people inhabitynge within the saide towne and Burroughe of Burfforde Or elles to be Imploide to any other honeste use By the discression of the said feoffees yf they shall deme the saide use to be for a common welthe to the said towne and Burroughe of Burfforde aforesaide.'

Witnesses : Robert Payne and Will. Hewes bailiffs of Burford, Walter Rose and Robert Starre constables, Robert Bruton sergeant, John Crouchman, Henry Perrott.

[For T 4 see below : the document was wrongly numbered in the making of the schedule.]

T 5. 3 May, 4 Elizabeth (1562).
Conveyance by William Hughes alias Calcott, Robert Brewton, Edmund Sylvester, Senior Burgesses of Burford, to Thomas Freers one of the bailiffs, Richard Chawreleye, Richard Dalby, Burgesses, William Partridge, and John Dallam yeomen. Two cottages (' illa duo cotagia nostra ') in St. John's Street between the tenement of Simon Wisdom on the west side and a way called the backside of a tenement in which Walter Rose, late of Burford, shoemaker, lately lived on the east, and abutting on the King's highway on the north, and the land of the foresaid Walter Rose on the south. Also a piece of ground lately in the tenure or occupation of Thomas Brayne alias Thomas George late of Burford, now deceased. Also two other arable lands lying in the south field of Upton belonging to the same piece of ground. All which the first-named parties recently had by gift and feoffment of Richard Hannes, Robert Jhonson, Thomas Tomson, and Thomas Fawler, lately Burgesses, now deceased, by charter bearing date 1 December 38 Henry VIII for the uses and intentions therein specified.

(After repeating these uses and intentions, with the additional detail that the ultimate use of the surplus money for the poor is to be by direction of 'the Alderman, Steward, and Burgesses or the more part of them, the deed enjoins that the ' pronotours ', or persons appointed by the feoffees to receive the rents, shall render yearly ' a wise and true account ' of the monies received and the amount spent in repairs ; and further that the feoffees or the longest-lived of them and his heirs shall enfeoff, upon requirement by the common assent of the said Alderman, Steward, and Burgesses and by the common assent of the more part of them, such person or persons as the Alderman, Steward, and Burgesses or the more part of the Burgesses shall appoint.

Witnesses : William Hughes, John Lord, John Smythar.

Witnesses to delivery of possession : William Grene one of the constables, John Craft, John Tyler, Henry Perrott, John Smythear the younger, Nicholas Smythe, and Thomas Arnolde.

T 6. 15 May, 4 Elizabeth (1562).

Counterpart of lease from the feoffees named in T 5, to Simon Wisdom, Alderman of the town of Burford. The two cottages with appurtenances situate in St. John's Street, lying as described in T 5, ' and the void piece of ground lyeth between a tenement of the late dissolved chantry in Burford on the east side and the said way leading to the said Walter Rose's tenement on the west side '. For 61 years at 12s. a year.

' And whereas also the said lands and tenements at the day of making of these indentures are utterly in Rewyn dikayed and fallen down as it is manifestly to be seen and perceived, and for that also the foresaid Simon Wisdom upon the consideration hereafter in these presents to be remembered hathe promised in the face of the most part of the inhabitants of the town and borough of Burford aforesaid to reedify make and buylde anew within four years next coming after the date hereof as well the aforesaid towe cottages or tenements well and sufficiently with timber sclatt stones and all other things to the same mete and expedient as also to build and set up one other new house or barne in the void piece of ground aforesaid well and sufficientlye made and buylded in forme aforesaid . . . ' this lease is granted by the feoffees with the consent of William Hughes alias Calcott, now Steward of the Fellowship of the Burgesses, Robert Brewton, John Lord alias Hughes, Edmund Sylvester the elder, John Smythar, John Hannes, John Heyter, Thomas Hynes, Hugh Colbrowe and Walter Mollyner, now Burgesses of the town, and with the consent of the most part of the inhabitants of the town.

Witnesses: William Hughes alias Calcott, John Hannes, Edmund Sylvester the elder, Burgesses, Bennett Fawler, Hugh Perrott, John Geast, Edmund Sylvester the younger, Robert Childe, John Taylor.

T4. 1 February, 29 Elizabeth (1587).

Conveyance by William Partridge, surviving feoffee, to John Lyme, one of the Bailiffs, Robert Sylvester, and Richard Dalby, Burgesses, Richard Merywether, William Webbe, and Edmund Sylvester, yeomen. Two cottages in St. John's Street on south side between a tenement of Simon Wisdom lately defunct on west and a way called the backside leading to the tenement in which the son of Walter Rose lived on east, and land of the said Walter Rose on south ; also one piece of ground on which a barn has lately been built. The intents specified as previously.

Witnesses : John Roffe, William Hewis, Thomas Penrise.

T7. 25 July, 22 James I (1624).

Conveyance by William Webbe the elder, surviving feoffee, to John Collier the elder, innholder, William Bartholomew the elder, mercer, Robert Jordan the elder, yeoman, John Hunt the elder, ironmonger, Thomas Silvester the elder, clothier, Burgesses, William Webbe the younger of Clifford's Inn, London, gentleman, eldest son of William Webbe the elder, William Huntt of New Colledge in the Universitie of Oxon, gentleman, eldest son of the said John Hunt, and John Jordan of London, grocer, eldest son of the said Robert Jordan. Two cottages with appurtenances in St. John's Street between a tenement of Symon Wisdome, lately of Phillipp Barrett on west, the gateway or passage belonging to the tenement sometime of Walter Rose lately of William Lambert on east ; also one cottage and stable in the same street heretofore in the tenure of John Lyme and now in occupation of John Hawkins, gentleman, and Thomas Russell ; and two acres of arable in the south field of Upton belonging to the said cottage and stable and occupied by Thomas Russell. The intents specified as previously.

Witnesses : William Lambert, Walter Veysey.

Note.—This deed seems to have been fully executed ; the witnesses are to the sealing and delivery of the deed and to the delivery of possession of the premises and to the formal attendance of the tenants. But the deed handing over the property to the trustees appointed by the Royal Commission seems to take no account of this document, and is executed again by William Webbe the elder as surviving feoffee.

T8. 23 February, 5 Charles I (1630).

Conveyance by William Webbe the elder of Burford, gentleman, to the trustees as in the Commission's decree. The Fifteen Lands as specified in the decree, ' the said William Webbe being the sole surviving feoffee '.

Witnesses : William Webbe, junior, Walter Hayter the elder, William Symons, Richard Norgrave.

Note.—The lands are described simply as charitable lands.

Note.—From this point the leases are all granted by the trustees appointed by the Royal Commission ; the names of the lessors are therefore not given.

T 9. 9 November, 17 Charles I, 1641.
Lease to Robert Perry the elder, slatter, and Margaret his wife. House on south side of St. John's Street between a tenement in the possession of the same on east and a tenement of John Hannes on west. For 21 years at 24s. a year.

Witnesses : Edward Watkins, Thomas Randolph.

T 10. 8 June, 6 William and Mary, 1694.
Lease to John Boulter, saddler. House on south side of St. John's Street between a tenement of William Jordan on east and a tenement of Christopher Kempster on west. For 21 years at 30s. a year.

Witnesses : Thomas James, Christopher Brooke, Richard Mathewes.

T 11. 8 June, 6 William and Mary, 1694.
Lease to William Jordan, broadweaver. House on south side of St. John's Street between the back gate of John Robins on east and tenement of John Boulter on west. For 21 years at 35s. a year.

Witnesses : Philip Sessions, Richard Mathewes.

T 12. 18 June, 3 George I, 1717.
Lease to William Jordan, broadweaver. The same house at the same rent.

Witnesses : John Boulter, Humphrey Gillett.

T 13. 24 May, 3 George I (1717).
Lease to John Boulter, carpenter. House on south side of St. John's Street between William Jordan on east and John Kempster on west. For 21 years at £1 10s. a year.

Witnesses : Benj. Woodroffe, Humphrey Gillett, Thomas Patrick.

T 14. 24 May, 3 George I (1717).
Counterpart of the preceding.

T 15. 25 March, 6 George I (1720).
Lease to John Andrues, weaver. House on south side of St. John's

Street between Widow Winfeild on east and Widow Jordan on west ; with 2 acres of arable land belonging to the same house. For 21 years at £3 10s. a year.

Witnesses : Wm. Applegarth, Humphrey Gillett.

T 16. 27 November, 6 George II, 1732.
Lease to Richard Parke, broadweaver. House late of John Boulter between Richard Coborne on east and John Kempster on west. For 21 years at 39s. a year.

Witnesses : Geo. Underwood, R. Griffiths.

THE SCHOOL LANDS
Cheatle Collection, Bundles CC and DD

S 1. Sunday after the Feast of the Assumption, 49 Edward III (1375).
Conveyance by Robert Whitteway of Boreford to Henry Taillor, draper, of Boreford. A half burgage with curtilage adjacent and all appurtenances in the High Street of Burford on the west side between a tenement of the said Robert on one side and a tenement of William Cotteswold on the other.

Witnesses : John Wynrish, John Crosson, Robert Coteler, William Nailler, John Kyngton, Thomas Spycer, William Cokerell, John Saleman, William Bernes, clerk.

S 2. Tuesday in the week of Pentecost and the last day of May, 7 Richard II (1384).
Conveyance by Geoffrey, Vicar of the parish church of Burford, to Thomas Causton, ' cognato meo '. Two messuages lying in the High Street on the west side Between the vicarage tenement on one side and the river called Wynrich on the other. The conveyance to take place after the death of Geoffrey.

Witnesses : John Crosson, John Wynrich, Robert Coteler, William Nailer, Thomas Spiser, William Ponter, John Sclatter, William Shulton, William Bernes, clerk.

S 3. Feast of St. John the Apostle in the week of the Nativity of the Lord, 10 Richard II (1386).
Conveyance by Thomas Causton of Burford, to John Cornewaill of the same. The two messuages as above.

Witnesses : The same.

S 4. Feast of St. Michael the Archangel, 6 Henry IV (1404).

Lease by Thomas Spicer, Senior of the Gild, Henry Coteler, Seneschal of the Gild, Thomas Wynryshh and Edmund Dyere, pronotours of the Gild of St. Mary, to John Spicer of Burford, with the assent of all the Burgesses of the town. A tenement with appurtenances in Witney Street on the north side between a tenement of William Coberley and a tenement of John Fawllere. For 60 years at 7s. a year. The tenant to have the boughs of trees within the close of the messuage, and to be allowed to cut down trees with the advice and consent of the Gild, as might be necessary to repair the house.

S 5. — May, 2 Henry VI (1424).

Conveyance by John Grene, Vicar of Fayreford, to John Leche of Burford. A messuage in Sheep Street on the north side between the tenement of Agnes Conyng on one side and the tenement of William Lynham on the other.

Witnesses : Thomas Spicer, William Coteler, Richard Lavyngton, John Ponter, Simon Mosyer.

S 6. 16 December, 8 Henry VI (1429).

Conveyance by Roger Coupe of Campden, to William Ingelby, Vicar of Burford, and Edmund Dyere of the same. One messuage with curtilage adjacent and all appurtenances on the east side of the High Street between the tenement of William Sterre on one side and the tenement of Robert Stowe on the other, 'which I recently had by gift and feoffment of Alice Ameryes of Burford'.

Witnesses : Thomas Spycer, William Coteler, Richard Lavyngton, John Ponter, Henry Blont.

S 7. 24 August, 6 Edward IV (1466).

Conveyance by John Egle of Oxford, 'gentilmon', to William Kempe of Borford and Isabella his wife. A messuage on east side of the High Street between a tenement of William Hylle on one side and a tenement of Nicolas Spaldying on the other.

Witnesses : John Pynnock, John Grove, Bailiffs, Thomas Brampton, William Hylle, Thomas Maiow.

S 8. 4 June, 16 Edward IV (1476).

Conveyance by William Freeman of Taynton, 'husbondman', to Walter Nymes, 'gentilman', and John Pynnok. A half burgage with appurtenances on west side of the High Street between the tenement of John Longe on the north and the tenement of William Wollyng on the south.

Witnesses : John Graunger, Robert Leveryche, John Banbury, William Flodeyate.

S 9. 12 July, 4 Henry VII (1489).

Conveyance by John Petur of Mynysterlevell and Marjory his wife, to Master Richard Chauncelere, Vicar of Burford, John Hyll, Thomas Jenyvere, William Smethyare, and George Moyese. Two tenements in Burford, one on east side of the High Street between the tenement of John Bishop on the south and the inn called the ' Bere ' lately of John Pynnocke on the north ; the other in Witney Street on the south side between the tenement once of Robert Coberley on the east and the tenement lately of John Mosyer on the west.

Witnesses : Thomas Bishop, John Boterell, Bailiffs, Robert Leveryche, William Flodyatte, Richard Brame.

Note.—Margery was the name of the granddaughter of John Pynnok the elder, by whose will (W 1) she was to have for her life the use of the house left by him ultimately to the Church.

S 10. 1 May, 17 Henry VII (1502).

Conveyance by Richard Chauncelere, clerk, Thomas Jenyver, and John Hill alias Prior, to Richard Brame, Thomas Boterell, Robert Osmond, Richard Harris, Robert Rile, and Peter Eynysdale. Two messuages in Burford, one near the inn called the ' Bere ', and the other in Witney Street near a messuage lately of Thomas Pole.

' The intent of this feoffment is that the said feoffees their heirs and assigns shall suffre the proctors of the chirche of Burford for the tyme beyng yerely for ever to take and receave all the issues and profettes of all the said ii messuages and on tyme in the yere for ever shall cause an obite to be kept in the said chirche that is to say in the xiithe day of Marche a dirige by note and on the morowe after a masse of Requiem by note to pray for the sowlle of John Pynnoke the eldyr and Ely his wiffe and all cristen sowllys and xs. of lawfull money yerely comyng of the Issues and Profettes of the said ii messuages shall distribute for the kepyng of the said obyte to prestys clerkes and pooremen And the residue of the said issues and profettes thereof to be disposed yerely to the use and behoffe of the said chirche as to them shalbe thought most profetable for the wele of the sowlls afore rehersed.'

Witnesses : Richard Bishope, William Flodeyate, Thomas Stanton. Endorsed in a later hand : ' Dalby's house and George Fawler's.'

S 11. A duplicate of the above conveyance.

Endorsed ' For Andrewe Wards House and a tenement in Witney

Street' and in a later hand ' Now the Bull and in the tenure of Edmond Serrell (the house in High Street) '.

S 12. 9 November, 23 Henry VII (1508).

Conveyance by John Tanner and Richard Brame, to Milo Gerard, John Bisshope, Thomas Pynnoke, William Fludeyatte, Thomas Stanton, and Richard Bagote. Lands and tenements 'which we had by gift and feoffment of Robert Leveryche, Henry Janyver, John Boterel, Thomas Sende alias Call, Henry Stodam, and William Janyvere'. ' The intent of this feoffment is this that the said feoffees theyr heyrs and assignys schal suffre the proctours of our ladye chapel in Burford aforesaid for the tyme beyng yerely to take and receve all the issues and profetes of all the landys or tenements and of theyr appurtenances for the exhibicion fyndyng and mayntenyng of a honeste preste in the said chapel dayly to singe there or to say be the quere aftyr the costom laudable and xs. iiij d. of lawful money yerely comyng of the issues and profetes of the said lands and tenements schal geve paye and delyvyr to the same said honeste preste to be chosen by the said feoffees for ever for his yerely servyce and the residue of all the Issues and profetes thereof to be disposed yerely to the use and behuffe of the said chapell and otherwise as to them schalbe thought most profetable.'

Witnesses : John Lauerance, William Bristo, Thomas Janyvere, John Billynge, John Prior, Robert Osemonde, Thomas Dylke.

Endorsed, 'A feoffment of our lady lands '.

S 13. 24 May, 7 Henry VIII (1515).

Conveyance by William Rose alias Smythe of Field in le Wychwode, to Robert Silvester of Burford. A close in Burford in Witney Street on the south between the King's highway on both sides, called Picked Close.

Witnesses : Peter Enysdale, Robert Riley, Bailiffs, Thomas Hoggs, Thomas Stodham, Robert Sharpe, Thomas Clerke.

S 14. 23 January, 1512.

Indenture of gift by Agnes Stodam, widow of Henry Stodam of Burford, to John Bysshope, Peter Aynsdale, Thomas Hedgys, and Robert Ryley, Burgesses. An annuity of 13s. 4d. out of the rent of a tenement of hers in High Street, occupied by Robert Silvester.

' Thententt off the graunte ys thatt they withyn named John Bysshoppe, Petrus Aynsdale, Thomas Hedgys and Robert Ryley and their heyrys and assignes yerely for ever shall kepe an obit Yn

the Chirche of Burford uppon monday nexte aftir Trinite Sonnday
for the saules off Wyllyam Stoddam and agnes his wyffe for the saules
off John Chestir and Isabell his wyffe for the saules of Henre Stoddam
and John hys son for the saules of John Morley and Jone his wyffe
and for the saule of agnes Stoddam the wyffe of Henry Stoddam and
for all crysten saules Wyth the summe off xiii*s*. iiii*d*. after the forme
folowyng thatt ys to say to prestys and clerks v*s*. and to the pore
pepull v*s*. and to the use of the chyrche off Burford ii*s*. and for the
labourers takyng yn thys behalfe every off the sayd J P T & R to
have and reteyn iiii*d*. for ever   And also I wyll that Thomas Stoddam
my son and his heyres and assigns to be oversears that thys my last
wyll be perfformed and keppyd for ever with the sayd summe of
xiii*s*. iiii*d*. goyng out off the sayd tenement.'

Witnesses : William Calaway, Curate of Burford, John Bysshope,
mercator, Peter Aynsdale, William Seyse, Thomas Hedges, and Robert
Ryley, Burgesses.

S 15. 18 ——, 29 Henry VIII (1538).

Conveyance by Peter Eynisdall of Burford, to John Johns, John
Lambert, Robert Eynesedale, Simon Wysdom, William Roberts alias
Fyscher, Robert Allflett. Two messuages in Burford, one near the
inn called the Bear, the other in Witney Street near a house lately
of Thomas Pole. The intents of the conveyance specified as in S 10.

S 16. Feast of the Annunciation, 30 Henry VIII, 1539.

Lease by Robert Payne, Thomas Fauler, Hewe Colborne, and John
Browne and Thomas Beynge, Churchwardens, with the whole assent
of the parishioners, to Richard Dawby of Burford, ' Bocher '. Messuage on east side of the High Street between the tenement of John
Cally and the Angel of William Pinnock on the north and the tenement
of Robert Browne on the south. For 41 years at 30*s*. a year, the tenant
to do the repairs.

S 17. 26 February, 4 Edward VI, 1550.

Conveyance by John Maynarde and Richard Venables ' armigeri ',
to Edmund Sylvester of Burford, gentleman. A tenement in Burford
called the Broadgates occupied by John Jones ; a tenement with
a little close now occupied by William Roberts alias Fisher ; a tenement
in Sheep Street occupied by Edmund Silvester ; a tenement occupied
by Marke Payne ; a close in Batts Lane occupied by Robert Browne ;
a meadow occupied by John Lambard ; a garden occupied by John
Hannes, Richard Wygpyt, and John Jons ; a tenement occupied

by Robert Browne; to be held of the King by reason of a certain Act concerning the dissolving of Chantries, Colleges, Gilds and Fraternities, passed at Westminster in the first year of his reign; to be held as John Maynarde and Richard Venables held the properties of the Royal manor of East Greenwich in Kent in free socage and not in capite, by Letters Patent bearing date at Westminster 21 December 3 Edward VI.

Attorneys for delivery of possession: Robert Bruton and Richard Hannes.

Witnesses: Richard Hedges and Robert Brewton, Bailiffs, John Hayter, Sergeant, Symon Wynchester and Rd. Hunt, Constables, William Hewes, Robert Ennisdale, John Hannes, Thomas Faller, Robert Jonson, Richard Dawby, Burgesses; John Jones, Phillipe Griffiths, Robert Allflett, Thomas Crouchman, Bedell; Henry Perrott, Town Clerk.

[S 18 will be found among the documents in the keeping of the Governors of the Grammar School.]

S 19. 1 May, 13 Elizabeth (1571).

Lease by William Partrige, John Lyme the elder, William Silvester, and Thomas Appar, churchmen of the parish church of Burford, Richard Dalby, Edmond Silvester, Bailiffs of the Borough of Burford, Symon Wisdom, Alderman of Burford, John Hannes, Steward of the Fellowship of the Burgesses of Burford, Thomas Fettyplace, William Mollyner, Richard Reynolles, William Symons, Bennett Fawler, Robert Chilld, John Williams, Robert Scarborough, William Phillips, Burgesses of Burford, Robert Starre, Thomas Butcher, William Stampe, John Hunt, John Wood, Robert Everest, Robert Silvester, Hugh Davis, Thomas Ward, Thomas Hooper, John Herne, with the assent and consent of the residue of the parishioners of Burford, to William Butcher of Burford. A messuage or tenement lying in the nether end of the High Street on the west side with a garden adjoining, between the vicarage of Burford on the north and a barne of Edmund Silvester on the south, late in the tenure of Philip Griffith, and now in the tenure of Thomas Butcher the younger. For 41 years at 13s. 4d. a year.

Endorsed: 'The colledge.'

The documents next in sequence are the Foundation Deeds of the Grammar School of Burford. S 20 and S 21 are (in duplicate) the deeds conveying certain properties from the Bailiffs and some of the co-feoffees of the parish lands to feoffees for the purposes of a free school ; S 22 is the deed by Simon Wisdom, conveying other properties, not to the same feoffees, and has attached to it the constitutions of the School written in Simon Wisdom's own hand.

These documents have been entrusted by Mrs. Cheatle to the keeping of the authorities of the School, and are therefore not calendared here.

S 23. 1 May, 13 Elizabeth, 1571.

Lease by the same lessors as in S 19, to John Wekens. House on North side of Witney Street with a Backside, garden, and a little piece of ground shooting down from the said garden to the river-side, between a barn of Alexander Hedges on east and a tenement called the Oxhouse occupied by Joan Silvester, widow, on west. For 41 years at 12s. a year.

S 24. 20 January, 29 Elizabeth (1587).

Conveyance by William Symons, tanner, Thomas Wysdome of Shipton-under-Wychwood, clothier, John Lyme of Burford, shoe-maker, William Partridge, smith, John Hunt, Raphe Wysdome, mercers, Symon Allflett, clerk, and Edmond Pittam of Stratton Audley, yeoman ; to Richard Chadwell, gentleman, Robert Silvester, Richard Dalbye, Symon Greene, Symon Symons, Symon Chadwell, gentleman, John Woode, John Roffe, John Hannes, Robert East, John Griffith, Symon Starre, William Webbe, Daniel Silvester, William Hewes, and Edmond Silvester the elder. Three tenements in one range adjoining to the common bridge, occupied by William Longe, Lawrence Holdinge, and John Scriven ; one tenement in High Street between a tenement of Symon Partridge on the south and a tenement belonging to the common bridge on the north, occupied by Thomas Prickevance ; two tenements in one range in Witney Street between Gildenford Lane on east and a tenement of Symon Allflett, clerk, on west, occupied by Thomas Cotton and Thomas Hiett ; one tenement on the hill in the High Street between a tenement of William Hewes on south and a tenement belonging to the parish church on north, occupied by Evans Floid. A lease of a house to Thomas Wysdom by Symon Wysdome excepted.

Witnesses : John Hanns, Richard Merywether, Richard Allflett, Thomas Penrise.

[S 25 in the keeping of the Governors of the Grammar School.]

S 26. 5 February, 36 Elizabeth (1594).

Indenture between Edmund Silvester of Burford, and Robert Maulthus of Reading. Marriage settlement upon the marriage of the said Edmund with Anne Hopkyns of Burford, widow. One messuage in Church Lane called Broadgates with garden and appurtenances, with 16 acres in the West and East fields of Burford and Signett and one acre in the common lot meadow called High Mead ; one tenement with garden and appurtenances on east side of the High Street occupied by Robert Hayter, between a tenement of Mr. Edmund Harman on south and a tenement of Richard (illegible) on north ; also a tenement with backside on east side of High Street occupied by John Scarborowe, shoemaker ; also the house called the Corner Tenement abutting upon Priory Lane on the south and upon the smith's forge on the east ; and two yard lands in the West and East fields of Burford and Signett.

Witnesses : Roger Webb, Humphry Finmore, William Finmore.

S 27. 3 April, 41 Elizabeth (1599).

Lease by Richard Merywether, yeoman, Alderman, and Symon Symons, Steward of the Fellowship, with the assent of Robert Serrell and William Sessions, Wardens or Proctors of the School, John Roffe and John Yate, Bailiffs, John Lyme alias Jenkins, William Webbe, and Toby Dallam, Senior Burgesses, to Richard Sowthe, curryer. House in Witney Street between Thomas Hiatt on east and Symon Allflett on west. Lease, for 21 years at 16s. a year, granted in consideration of a payment by the tenant of 6s. 8d. towards the repairing of the school.

Witnesses : John Roffe, John Yate, John Huntt, Andrew Ward, Raphe Wisdom, John Griffith, William Taylor, Edmond Serrell.

[S 28 in the keeping of the Governors of the Grammar School.]

S 29. 14 February, 41 Elizabeth (1599).

Lease by Richard Merywether, Alderman of the town, and Symon Symons the elder, Steward, to Symon Symons the younger, one of the sons of Symon Symons the elder. The three chambers over the Almshouse. Lease, for 90 years at 4d. a year, granted in consideration of a surrender of a term of 36 years unexpired of an existing lease granted to Symon Symons the elder. Common Seal of the Brotherhood to be affixed.

Witnesses : John Roffe, John Yate, William Webbe, John Huntt, Andrew Ward, Raphe Wisdom, John Griffith, Edmund Serrell.

[The above is an Almshouse document, placed in the wrong series.]

S 30. 14 February, 41 Elizabeth (1599).

Lease by John Lyme alias Jenkins, John Roffe, William Webbe,

John Huntt, John Griffith alias Phillippes, and Thomas Parsons, yeomen, Burgesses, to Nicholas Webbe, one of the sons of William Webbe. One acre and a swathe in High Mead late in the tenure of Thomas Hewis alias Calcott. For 31 years at 7s. a year.

Witnesses: John Collier, Thomas Hemyng.

S 31. 18 May, 1 James I, 1603.

Indenture between Edmund Silvester of Burford and Robert Maulthus of Reading, reciting an indenture of 18 January, 43 Elizabeth (1601), making a settlement upon Anne Hopkyns, 'his late wife', and his daughter Anne Silvester. Messuage called Broadgates, occupied by Thomas Silvester; house called the Corner Tenement abutting upon St. John's street; one close of an acre adjoining to Witney Street.

Witnesses: H. Heylyn, William Hunt, Richard Merywether, Robert Silvester.

[S 32 to S 39 in the hands of the School authorities.]

S 40. 2 August, 18 James I, 1620.

Lease by Symon Symons, tanner, Alderman of Burford, and William Webbe, yeoman, Steward, with the assent of John Hunt and David Hughes alias Floyde, yeomen, Wardens of the School, William Taylor and William Bartholomew the elder, Bailiffs, Thomas Parsons, John Templer, and John Collier, senior Burgesses, to Thomas Parsons the younger, chandler. House on east side of High Street between the tenement of Thomas Prickevance on north and the tenement of Symon Partridge on south. For 21 years at £3 10s. a year.

Witnesses: Richard Hanckes, Thomas Silvester, Leonard Mills, Walter Hayter senior.

S 41. 2 August, 18 James I, 1620.

Lease by the same lessors, with the assent of the same parties, to Paul Silvester. A house sometime occupied by Andrew Tayler, now by Paul Silvester; also the house next to it sometime occupied by Lawrence Holding, now by William Overbury; both being at the north end of the town between a tenement of Richard Tayler on south and a tenement sometime of William Wysdome, now of Paul Silvester. For 21 years at £4 a year.

Witnesses: as in S 40.

[S 42 in the hands of the School authorities.]

S 43, 44, 45. Three indentures fastened together, an Exemplification of a Recovery, and a Fine.

i. An indenture of 18 June, 41 Elizabeth, 1599, reciting Edmund Silvester's settlement in favour of his daughter. (The Corner Tenement is now described as abutting upon ' a little tenement of the Queen's Majesty ' in the place of the forge.)

ii. An indenture of 16 July, 3 Charles I, 1627, between Christopher Gale of Burford, gentleman, and Anne his wife, and Thomas Silvester of Burford, clothier, mutually agreeing to produce title deeds relating to lands and properties conveyed to each other.

iii. An indenture of 13 August, 21 James I, 1623, between Christopher Gale, late of the City of London, gentleman, and Anne his wife, daughter of the late Edmund Silvester, and John Chamberlayne of Reading, gentleman, and Christopher Hall of Thorburn in the county palatine of Durham, gentleman ; being a settlement of Broadgates and the two houses in High Street specified in S 26, and a close of arable or pasture in Witney Street.

iv. Exemplification of a Recovery between John Chamberlain and Christopher Hall plaintiffs and Christopher Gale and his wife defendants, 21 James I.

v. A fine of 43 Elizabeth between Robert Malthus and Edmund Sylvester, for £80 sterling.

The whole endorsed : ' A deed and fine of the house called Broadgates in the Church Lane belonging to the Free school of Burford.'

S 46. 23 February, 5 Charles I (1630).
Conveyance by John Collier of Burford, innholder, William Hunt of Farrington, mercer, William Bartholomew the elder of Burford, mercer, Richard Hancks of Burford, chandler, Robert Jordan of Burford, sadler, William Symons of Burford, tanner, William Webbe of Widford, gentleman, Symon Parsons of Burford, chandler, John Tayler of Burford, yeoman, and Edmond Serrell of Burford, haberdasher, to the trustees as in the Commission's decree. The School Lands as specified in the decree.

Witnesses : Richard Simeon, William Kempster, Thomas Prickevance, Thomas Ferryman, Thomas Martyn, Walter Hayter senior, Richard Hayter.

S 47. — September, 6 Charles I (1630).
Power of attorney by John Collier and the other parties making the conveyance S 46, to John Hunt of Burford, mercer. To hand over the School Lands to the trustees appointed by the Royal Commission.

Witnesses : Thomas Prickevance, Thomas Ferryman, Richard Symons, William Kempster.

S 48. 18 October, 6 Charles I (1630).

Lease to William Symons, tanner. The three chambers over the Great Almshouse, which Symon Symons had for 90 years at 4d. a year.

For 59 years, remainder of term, at the same rent, in consideration of costly repairs carried out on the said rooms. Also a half acre and a shurffe in High Mead, one acre arable in East field, and one acre in Upton field, being part of the School Lands. For 21 years at 20s. a year.

Witnesses : Thomas Richards, John Cole, Edmund Heminge, Symon Brookes, William Kempster, Daniel Berry.

[The above is again an Almshouse document, placed in the wrong series.]

S 49. 18 October, 6 Charles I (1630).

Lease to Richard Buckingham, labourer. House on north side of Witney Street between the tenement of John Abraham on west and lane turning down to Gildenford on east. For 21 years at 26s. 8d. a year.

S 50. 26 June, 1635.

Indenture of delivery and seizin of the house called Broadgates, the Pickes or Picked Close over against Patrick's Mill, and the garden now in possession of Christopher Gale, of Burford, gentleman—all which property is conveyed by Christopher Gale and Anne his wife to William Bartholomew and Richard Taylor, Bailiffs, Thomas Silvester, David Hughes, John Clarke, and John Taylor, Burgesses.

Witnesses : C. Glyn, Thomas Randolph, Thomas Bolton, John Bartholomew and Thomas Braggs, Constables.

S 51. 10 May, 12 Charles I (1636).

Indenture of sale by Simon Veysey of Chymney, Oxon., and Robert Veysey, his son and heir, to the trustees of the charitable lands. House on north side of Church Lane in the tenure of William Fayreford, bounded on the east by a tenement of Edmond Castle ; two houses in the occupation of Margaret Francklyn, widow, and George Peisley, a tenement of Thomas Silvester on north and a tenement of Richard Andrewes on south. The deed relates that these houses were bought for £52, part of a sum of 1,000 ducats (£260 sterling given as equivalent of this sum) left by Symon Reynolds, merchant, late deceased overseas, in his will bearing date at Roham in France 8 December 1626.

Witnesses : John Bartholomew, William Hayter, Edmond Heming, Thomas Tunckes, Thomas Hord, John Hobbes, William Collier.

Endorsed : The deed of three houses purchased for the free school in Burford vizt. the tenement on the south side of Thomas Silvester, One tenement on the south side of a tenement in the tenure of Roger Daniel and one other tenement in possession of Wm. Fairefield over against Broadgates now in possession of Alice Yate widow and Leonard Yate her sonne.

Belonging to this document is another, unnumbered, being a fine for £100 between the parties for these premises.

S 52. 25 March, 12 Charles I, 1637.

Lease to Nathaniel Noble of Burford, apothecary. House on north side of Witney Street between Richard Buckingham on east and Richard Sindrey on west. For 21 years at 26s. 8d. a year.

Witnesses : William Peislye, Thomas Randolph.

S 53. 18 October, 23 Charles I, 1647.

Lease to Paul Silvester the younger, tanner. Three houses near the bridge late occupied by Paul Silvester the elder ' together with all those erections or buildings lately had or made by the said Paul Silvester the elder '. For 21 years at £4 16s. a year.

Witnesses : William Hannes, Thomas Silvester, William Bartholomew, David Loyd alias Hughes, Paul Silvester, John Clark, William Sumner, Edmond Heminge, David Berry.

S 54. 27 November, 1649.

Lease to William Buckingham. House on north side of Witney Street between Phillip Collins on west and Guildenford Lane on east. For 21 years at 26s. 8d. a year.

S 55. 16 September, 1651.

Lease to Matthew Winfield, sieveyer. House on west side of High Street between Richard Thome on south and Edmund Vincent alias Greenhill on north, heretofore occupied by Walter Veysey, gentleman. For 21 years at £3 10s. a year.

Note.—The list of trustees is headed by ' William Lenthall, Speaker of the Parliament of the Commonwealth '.

S 56. 27 December, 1658.

Lease to Richard Smyth, blacksmith. House called the College, a court belonging to the Vicarage on north and a tenement belonging to Paul Silvester on south. For 21 years at £3 a year.

S 57. 18 February, 1658.

Lease to Mary Yate, widow. House called Broadgates on south side of Church Lane, adjoining to tenement of John Wells on west ; also the Picked Close belonging to Broadgates lying between the highways leading from Burford to Witney. For 21 years at £10 a year.

Witnesses : Rebekah Hughes, C. Yate, Symon Randolph.

S 58. 18 March, 1658.

Lease to Richard Veysey, innholder. Tenement in Witney Street heretofore occupied by Thomas Haynes, with a garden on north side of the street, now occupied by Andrew Smith, between Richard Sindrey on east and Henry Brisco on west. For 21 years at £2 13s. 4d. a year.

Witnesses : Lawrence Yate, John Jordan junior, Robert Jordan.

[S 59 is among the papers in the keeping of the School authorities.]

S 60. 29 December, 14 Charles II, 1662.

Lease to Roger Daniel, mason. House on east side of High Street between Margaret Haynes, widow, on north and Richard Andrewes on south. For 21 years at 34s. a year.

S 61. — — 25 Charles II, 1673.

Lease to William Buckingham. House on north side of Witney Street between Gildenford Lane on east and Phillip Collins on west. For 21 years at 26s. 8d. a year.

Witnesses : William Winchester, Symon Randolph.

S 62. 25 January, 29 Charles II (1678).

Lease to Richard Smith, blacksmith. House on west side of High Street called the College, between a court belonging to the Vicarage on north, and a house belonging to Paul Silvester on south. For 21 years at £3 a year.

Witnesses : Symon and Thomas Randolph.

S 63. 16 April, 30 Charles II, 1678.

Lease to Jacob Dix, fuller. House on north side of Witney Street between William Buckingham on east and Richard Hulls and others on west. For 21 years at £2 a year.

Witnesses : Symon and Thomas Randolph.

S 64. 25 March, 36 Charles II (1684).

Lease to Symon Partridge, clothier. House on north side of Sheep Street late occupied by David Berry between the garden of John Winsmore on east and the tenement of George Firbett on west. For 21 years at £1 15s. a year.

Witnesses : the same.

S 65. 8 July, 3 James II, 1687.

Lease to Andrew Lifollie, 'rooper'. House on north side of Witney Street between Robert Newman and others on east and Richard Wiett and others on west. For 21 years at £2 13s. 4d. a year.

Witnesses : Thomas and John Randolph.

[No document was numbered S 66 on the schedule. S 67 is in the keeping of the Governors of the Grammar School.]

S 68. 8 July, 3 James II, 1687.

Lease to Richard Winfield, 'siveyer'. House on west side of High Street between Margaret Greenhill on north and Edward Keble on south. For 21 years at £4 a year.

Witnesses : Alice Smith, Thomas Randolph.

S 69. 8 July, 3 James II, 1687.

Lease to Humphrey Greene, collarmaker. House on east side of High Street between William Dalby and others on north and John Mills on south. For 21 years at £1 10s. a year.

Witnesses : Thomas and John Randolph.

S 70. 28 May, 2 William and Mary, 1690.

Lease to Joanna Whiter, widow. House on north side of Church Lane late occupied by Anne Blackman deceased, between Thomas Daniel on east and the Almshouse on west. For 21 years at 13s. 4d. a year.

Witnesses : Richard Mathewes, Mary Ellis.

S 71. 26 April, 9 William III, 1697.

Lease to Jacob Dikes, fuller. Two tenements on north side of Witney Street between Charles Hague on west and a tenement occupied by Joseph Dikes, late by Mary Buckingham, on east, ' towards the lane turning down towards Guildenford '. For 21 years at £3 10s. a year.

Witnesses : Richard and Anne Mathewes.

S 72. 3 May, 11 William III, 1699.

Lease to Edward Townsend, maltster. House on west side of High Street between Thomas Newbury on north and Richard Winfield on south. For 21 years at £2 a year.

Witnesses : Anne Baylis, John Jordan.

S 73. 18 November, 2 Anne, 1703.

Lease to Drew Whiter, tailor, and Walwin Packer, carpenter. House called Broadgates, late occupied by Thomas Ashworth, gentleman, with the Picked Close on south side of the highway to Witney, adjoining a close called Kingshead close to the west. For 21 years at £10 a year.

Witnesses : John Jordan, Ambros Aston.

S 74. 28 February, 1704.

Lease to Jonathan Osman, mason. House on west side of High Street late occupied by Richard Winfield between Edmund Townsend on north and Edward Keeble on south. For 21 years at £4 10s. a year.

S 75. See Poole's Lands.

S 76. 2 March, 8 Anne, 1709.

Lease to Drew Whiter, tailor. House on north side of Church Lane between Thomas Daniel on east and the Almshouse on west. For 21 years at £1 a year.

Witnesses : Thomas Baxter, Humphrey Gillett.

S 77. 25 November, 13 Anne, 1713.

Lease to Thomas Green, collarmaker. House on east side of High Street between Walter Sessions on north and Thomas Boulter on south. For 21 years at 30s. a year.

Witnesses : Walter Sessions, Joseph Payton.

S 78. 28 April, 13 Anne, 1714.

Lease to Edmund Townsend, labourer. House on west side of High Street between Thomas Newberry on north and Jonathan Osmond on south. For 21 years at 40s. a year.

Witness : Sarah Bayley.

S 79. 29 September, 1715.

Lease to John Boyce, slatter. House on north side of Witney Street, late occupied by Andrew Lifoly, between Richard Wallington on west and Richard Palmer and George Sparrow on east. For 21 years at 40s. a year.

Witnesses : George Hart, William Castoll.

S 80. 26 March, 1716.

Lease to Richard Smith, blacksmith. House called the College, between the Vicarage on the north and Richard Monke junior on south. For 21 years at 50s. a year.

Witnesses : the same.

S 81. 26 September, 4 George I, 1717.

Lease to Paul Silvester, tanner. Three houses in his occupation with the new buildings erected by his father ; and 2 acres of meadow ground and a swath in High Mead. For 21 years at £8 4s. a year.

Witnesses : R. Griffiths, Edward Brown.

S 82. 3 March, 11 George I, 1725.

Lease to Joseph Dicks, fuller. Two tenements on north side of Witney Street now occupied by Henry Baylis and Widow Hague, between Widow Grimes on west and Widow Hague, formerly Mary Buckingham on east, towards a lane turning down toward Guilding ford. For 21 years at £4 a year.

Witnesses : Thomas Aston, Daniel Dicks.

S 83. 12 April, 13 George I, 1727.

Lease to Robert Osman, mason. House on west side of High Street late of Jonathan Osman, between Widow Townsend on north and John Keeble on south. For 21 years at £4 15s. a year.

Witnesses : Matthew Underwood, Humphrey Gillett.

S 84. 1 June, 4 George II, 1731.

Lease to Mary Townsend, spinster. House on west side of High Street between Martin Turner on north and Robert Osman on south. For 21 years at £2 a year.

Witnesses : George Underwood, Henry Walker.

[S 85 in the keeping of the School authorities.]

S 86. 2 December, 9 George II, 1735.

Lease to Thomas Boyce, slatter. House on north side of Witney Street between Joseph Midwinter on west and George Ward and others on east. For 21 years at £2 a year.

Witnesses : John Hall, William Jordan.

S 87. 18 January, 10 George II, 1737.

Lease to Malachi Gladwin, blacksmith. House on west side of High Street called the College, between the Vicarage on north and James Monk on south. For 21 years at £3 a year.

Witnesses : John Patten, William Jordan.

No number. 10 October, 1 George II, 1727.

Lease to John Fox, shoemaker. House late of Widow Cosins on east side of High Street, between Nicholas Willett on south and Honour Legg, widow, on north. For 21 years at £3 10s. a year.

Witnesses : Thomas Keeble, Humphrey Gillett.

POOLE'S LANDS

Cheatle Collection, Bundles EE and FF

P 1. Feast of Holy Trinity, 3 Henry IV (1402).

Conveyance by John Fawlour, Peter Webb, and Matilda formerly wife of John Cakebred, to Thomas Spycer of Burford. One messuage in Witney Street on south side between tenement formerly of William Purser East and tenement of William Brampton West . . . which we had by gift and legacy of John Cakebred.

Witnesses: Henry Coteler, John Stowe, Robert Cok, Thomas Wynryssh, John Cook.

P 2. 17 Jan., 5 Henry IV (1404).

Conveyance by William Brampton of Oxford, to Nicholas Chaloner, chaplain. Messuage in High Street on west side between tenement of Henry Cotiler on one side and tenement of the said William Brampton on the other . . . which messuage is twenty feet long and twenty-three feet deep.

Witnesses: Thomas Spycer, Henry Cotiler, Thomas Wynrysh, John Stowe, Robert Cok.

P 3. 22 Jan., 5 Henry V (1418).

Conveyance by Nicholas Chaloner, chaplain, to William Brampton and Margaret his wife. Messuage in High Street on west side between tenement of Henry Cotiler on one side and tenement of the said William Brampton on the other . . . which I lately had by feoffment of William Brampton.

Witnesses: Thomas Spycer, Henry Cotiler, John Stowe, Thomas Wynrysh, John Milton.

P 4. Sunday next before the Feast of St. Lucy Virgin, 7 Henry IV (1405).

Conveyance by John Cook and Christina his wife, to Thomas Alys and Matilda his wife. A certain shop in the High Street on west side between tenement of William Brampton on one side and tenement of the said Thomas on the other side . . . the shop being in length from the High Street to the lower part $17\frac{1}{2}$ feet, in breadth 7 feet, and in height 7 feet.

Witnesses: Thomas Spycer, Henry Cotiler, John Stowe, Thomas Wynrysh, John Iremonger, Robert Cok, John Milton.

Endorsed: Grant of Sadler's House.

[For P 5 and P 7 see the end of this series.]

P6. Fine, 6 Henry (IV).

Sale by William Brampton of Oxford, mercer, and Margaret his wife, to Thomas Alys of Burford and Matilda his wife. The sixth part of a messuage with appurtenances in Burford. Ten marks of silver.

P8. 7 Sept., 7 Henry V (1419).

Conveyance by John Blocklee of Abyndon, Berks, to Simon Mosyer of Burford. Two acres of arable land in the East Field of Burford of which one acre lies in Comefast furlong between the land formerly of Henry le Tayllour on one side and the land of John Longe of Seynet on the other side and the other lies in Coppdeslade furlong next the land formerly of Richard Mylton clerk on one side and the land formerly of John Dyte of Seynet on the other side.

Witnesses : Thomas Spycer, Henry Cotelere, William Cotelere, John Punter, Thomas Alys, Edmund Dyere, Richard Lanyngton.

· Endorsed : A feoffment of two acres of land in Burford Feilds. (Added in later hand) Called the Church lands.

P9. 3 July, 7 Henry VII (1492).

Indenture of sale by John Hill alias Priour of Burford, son of William Hill, wever, to Thomas Pole, Cittizen and Taillour of London. All that his close or piece of land and pasture called Culverhey with a Culverhouse as it is enclosed with wall and hedge lying in Ship Street between the tenement and ground belonging to the bretherede of the chapell of our lady there on the east part and the land of the Abbot and convent of Keynsham on the west part and the lands late of therle of Warwick on the south part and it abbuteth upon Ship Street on the north part.

Sold for £17. John Hill is indebted, according to the indenture, to Thomas Pole under the Statutes of the Staple for £30, which debt was to be void if John Hill carried out this sale.

P10. 14 Nov., 8 Henry VII (1492).

Indenture of sale by John Hille alias John Priour, to Thomas Pole, Citizen and Tailor of London. His whole Burgage or tenement, with a garden lying to, in Witney Street between a tenement lately of John Pynnok belonging to the parish church of St. John Baptist on west and another tenement of the same John Pynnok now belonging to the said church on the east and the street on the north and a curtilage belonging to John Bishop on the south. Also 18 acres of arable land belonging to the said burgage lying in sundry parcels in the fields of Burford . . . all which late belonged to Richard Mosyer.

For which Thomas Pole was to pay to and for John Hill £10 sterling—
£5 to Rauf Tilney citizen and alderman at the Feast of Pentecost next
coming, for which Thomas is to become surety to Rauf, and the other
£5 to John Hill at Pentecost. But if John Hill acquitted the £5 to Rauf
Tilney at Pentecost this deed was to be void.

(Attached to this indenture) :
Fine (two copies), 8 Henry VII.
Sale by John Hill and Margaret his wife, to Thomas Pole and
Petroniila his wife. A dovehouse, a garden, and three acres of pasture
with appurtenances in Burford on the Wold. £20 sterling.

P 11. 16 July, 9 Henry VII (1494).
Conveyance by John Hill alias John Pryour of Burford, to Thomas
Pole, citizen and tailor of London, Petronilla his wife, John Gardyner,
William Huntyngfeld (all of London), and Richard Brame of Burford,
yeoman. A cottage in Witney Street between a tenement lately of
Robert Stowe now of John Bysshop on east and north and a tenement
lately (? Annselrye) now of Thomas Maior on west and Witney
Street on south.

Witnesses : John Tanner, Bailiff of Burford, William Brame and
Robert James of Burford.
Endorsed : Polys lands. Andrew Yates house in Witney Street.

P 12. 8 Sept., 10 Henry VII (1494).
Release by John Hill alias Pryour, to Thomas Pole and others
(as in P 11) of the cottage in Witney Street (P 11).

P 13. 13 April, 10 Henry VII (1495).
Conveyance by John Hill alias John Prior of Burford, yeoman, to
Thomas Pole, citizen and tailor of London, Petronilla his wife, John
Percyvall knight, John Gardyner, citizen of London, Richard Braham,
Robert Leveryche, and Thomas Hubawde. A house in the High Street
formerly of Richard Mosyer bounded by the street on the east, a house
lately of William Brampton on west and north, and a tenement of
John Pynnok on the south.
Endorsed : A feoffment of sadler's house.

P 14. 3 June, 10 Henry VII (1495).
Release by John Kene of Kenkeham (county left blank), Thomas
Kene his son and heir, John Hille alias Pryor of Burford, yeoman, to
Thomas Pole and the rest (as in P. 13). The same house in High
Street ' with a shop cellars solars and all appurtenances '.
Endorsed : A release of Polys land. Sadler's house.

P 15. Extract from the registry of the Prerogative Court of Canterbury.

In the testament or last will of Thomas Poole, late citizen and tailor of London, deceased, bearing date the 4th day of April 1500.

Item as to the disposition of all my lands and tenements as well in Burford aforesaid as in Fulbroke I will that the said Petronilla my wife shall have the same for time of her life and after her decease I will the same lands and tenements in Burford shall be put in feoffment to such persons as shall then be of the most worshipful and honest parishioners Burgesses of the abovesaid Fraternity or Gyld in Burford to have and to hold to them their heirs and assigns for evermore to the use and intent that of the issues and profits of the same the poor people in the Almshouse shall have sixpence weekly to their refreshing to pray for my soul and my wife's soul and the residue to the maintenance of the priest of the said Fraternity and other such things as shall be to the good continuance of the same Fraternity.

P 16. 4 June, 19 Henry VII (1504).

Conveyance by John Gardyner and Thomas Preyers of London, to Thomas Stanton and Thomas Jenyver of Burford, burgesses. Two messuages and a close called the Colvirhey and a barn called the Woolhouse situate and lying in Burford aforesaid which formerly were the property of Thomas Pole citizen of London, ' and came to us John Gardyner and Thomas Preyers, executors of the will of the said Thomas Pole . . . '

(*In English*) Thintent of this feoffment is that the seid feoffees and their heyres schal yerely for evyr fulfyll a certen wylle declared yn the testament of the beforenamyd Thomas Pole concernyng the seid ii messuages close and wollehouse with theyr appurtenances the which be recityd and reported in a certen transumpt copye or exemplification of the seid wille in the custodye and kepyng of John Bisshope and William Fludeyate Burgesses of Burford aforesaid.

Endorsed : A feoffment of Poole's lands with the uses thereof sett downe in the deed in Englisshe. Also in a later hand—The first infeoffment of Poole's land by his overseers to Tho. Stanton and Tho. Jenyver.

P 17. 27 May, 5 Henry VIII (1513).

Conveyance by Thomas Stanton of Burford, burgess, to Peter Eynesdale, William Burrell, Thomas Hodges, Robert Rile, and John Harris. Two messuages, one close with dovecote, one cottage called the Woolhouse with twenty acres of arable land in the fields of Burford,

and one close in Fulbrok called Houndmylles with its appurtenances
. . . ' which messuages close with dovecot and cottage with twenty
acres and cottage with appurtenances in Fulbrook I lately held to
myself the aforesaid Thomas together with Thomas Jenyver now
defunct by gift and feoffment of John Gardyner gentleman and
Thomas Preyers of London goldsmith executors of the will of Thomas
Pole of London aforesaid Tailour '.

Witnesses : Robert Osmond, Thomas Pynnok, Robert Payne,
John Hille, Thomas Boterell, Robert Bagote.

Endorsed : ii messuages and i close the dowehouse the wollehouse
20 acres of land and i close in Fulbrooke. Also in later hand : The
2nd enfeoffment of Poole's land from Thomas Stanton to Peter
Senesdale, etc.

P 18. 27 October, 21 Henry VIII (1529).

Conveyance by Peter Eynesdale of Burford, Burgess and Alderman,
to Robert Jonson, Thomas Tomson, William Hughes alias Calcott,
and John Hayter, Burgesses. Two messuages, a close with a dovecote,
a cottage called the Woolhouse and twenty acres of arable land in
the fields of Burford.

Ad usus et intentiones in anglicis verbis subscriptos videlicet
That they the abovenamed feoffees shall permytt and suffer all and
every suche officer or officers being admitted nomynated and appointed
from tyme to tyme by the Alderman Steward and Burgesses of the
Bouroughe of Burford aforesaid perpetuallye to receave and take
all and singuler the yssues rentes revenues and profitts comynge
renewynge and growinge of all the forsaid lands tenementes and
hereditaments and their appurtenances at any suche daye and tyme
which are or hereafter shall be appointed lymyted and assigned for
the payments of the same or of any parte thereof quyetely without
contradiction or gaynesayinge of the said feoffees or of any of them
or their heires or of any other person or persons by their commandy-
ment or assent And that the said officer or officers and their successors
shall from tyme to tyme and at all tymes forever hereafter diligentlye
see that the said lands tenements and hereditaments aforesaid be well
and sufficientlye mayntayned and kepte in good reparacione And
whatsoever shall yerely remayne of the said rentes yssues revenewes
and proffitts of the said lands and tenements over and above the said
reparaciones shall yerely and forever be employd and bestowed by the
said officer or officers as followithe That is to say Everye Sundaye
in the yere they shall geve and distribute in almes to the twelve poore

people inhabitinge in the almes houses nowe beyng edifyed in Burford aforesaid sixe pense of lawfull moneye of England and what so ever shall yerely remayne of the said rentes Yssues revenewes and proffitts of the said lands and tenements over and above the said reparacions and almes as before is said shall yerely from yere to yere and tyme to tyme for evermore be reserved and kepte for ever towarde the payments and chargis which shall happen to growe and come at any tyme or tymes for the renewynge and confyrmacion of the charters gevyn and graunted for the liberties of this towne and Bouroughe of Burford aforesaid Or otherwise as theye the forsaid Alderman Steward and Burgesses for the tyme beinge and their successors or the more parte of them shall by their discressions thynke moste necessarye expedient and proffitable for the comon wealthe of the same towne.

(Clause providing for presentation of yearly accounts by the officers to the Alderman Steward and Burgesses.)

(Clause providing for new enfeoffment at demand of the same.)

Witnesses : John Sharpe, David Taylor, Bailiffs, Thomas Allflett, John Wykyns, Thomas Crouchman, Robert Eynesdale, William Roberts, John Jones, Burgesses.

P 19. 27 October, 22 Elizabeth (1580).

Conveyance by William Hughes alias Calcott, Burgess, to Simon Wisdom, Edmund Silvester the elder, John Hannes, Thomas Farrs, Richard Dalby, and Walter Molyner, Burgesses. One Messuage in High Street between the George on the north, the tenement of Robert Brewton chandler on the south and the highway on the east, occupied by Richard Chancelere yeoman. One messuage in Witney Street in the tenure of Simon Wisdom between land belonging to the parish church on the west and a tenement late of Richard Hodges on. the east and abutting on the highway on the north. One messuage in same street between a tenement of Benedict Fawler yeoman on the west and a barn lately of William Hodges baker on the east now deceased, occupied by John Wyckyns husbandman. Also a small barn called the Woolhouse in Witney Street, and a close called the Culverclose in Sheep Street, now in the tenure of Simon Wisdom. Twenty acres in the fields of Burford, Upton, and Signett occupied by Richard Chancelere, yeoman, ' which I had by feoffment from Peter Eynisdale by deed bearing date 27 October 21 Henry VIII '.

Ad usus et intentiones in Anglicis verbis subscriptos videlicet (as in P 18).

Witnesses : Richard Chancelere, John Smithyar, John Lloyd alias Hughes, Burgesses, John Geast, John Dallam, Edmund Silvester junior, Benedict Faller, William Grene, Griffith Jonnes, William Partridge, John Lyme, John Smithyar junior, Henry Perrott.

P 20. Michaelmas, 1580.

Lease by John Hannes the elder, Richard Dalbie and Walter Mollyner, feoffees of Poole's lands, Symon Wisdom, Alderman, John Hannes, Steward, Thomas Fettiplace, Richard Reynolds, Richard Chadwell, William Symons, Robert Silvester, William Partridge, John Lyme, Thomas Hewis, John Williams, Robert Scarborow, William Phillipps, and Benedict Fawler, with all the other burgesses, to Raphe Wisdom. The Culverhouse, with dovehouse and stable upon it, ' between a tenement late appertaining to the chauntree of our Ladie in Burford now dissolved on the East and the parsonage ground on the West and the common field there on the South and the highway on the North '. Also a tenement in Witney Street called Poole's house between a tenement of Richard Hodges on the east and the backside of the tenement of Richard Dalbie the younger on the west. Also one little barne over against this house between the backgate of William Stampe on the east and the tenement of John Wyckins on the west. All now in the occupation of Symon Wisdom. Fine of £10. Lease for 31 years at 30s. a year.

Witnesses : Symon Greene, Robert Stowe, Bartholomew Tanner, John Payton.

[P 21 is missing. As entered on the schedule it was the conveyance by Tipper and Dawe to Merywether and Dallam of the repurchased Charity Lands.]

P 22. 26 December, 41 Elizabeth (1598).

Conveyance by Richard Merywether, Alderman, and Toby Dallam, Burgess, to John Lyme alias Jenkins, John Roffe, William Webbe, John Huntt, John Gryffith alias Phillippes, and Thomas Parsons, yeomen, Burgesses.

In discharge of the trust and confidence reposed in them by their brethren the bailiffs and burgesses.

(i) Garden strip next to the river called Gyldenfforde occupied by William Hewes alias Calcott.

(ii) 18 acres in the arable fields occupied by William Taylor, chandler.

(iii) 2 acres of meadow in High Mead late occupied by William Partridge and William Hewes alias Calcott.

(iv) 1 acre of meadow in the common lott mead occupied by Alice Reynolds, widow.

(v) Messuage on east side of the High Street between the messuage of Robert Elston, gent., on the north and the messuage of Sir Anthony Cope on the south, occupied by Thomas Hemynge, barber surgeon.

(vi) Messuage with shop on east side of the High Street between the tenement of William Geast on the north and a tenement belonging to the Free School on the south, occupied by John Smart, smith, and Gryffin Lewes, cutler.

(vii) Messuage on west side of the High Street between the George Inn on the north and the tenement of the heirs of Agnes Brewton on the south, occupied by John Scarborough, shoemaker.

(viii) Messuage on west side of the High Street between the tenement of the heirs of Agnes Brewton on the north and the highway leading into Sheep Street on the south, occupied by Alice Reynolds, widow.

(ix) Messuage in Witney Street between a tenement of Sir Anthony Cope on the east and a tenement of Rychard Hodges on the west, occupied by George Fowler, 'cowper'.

(x) Messuage on the north side of Witney Street between a tenement and barn of Symon Partridge on the east and a tenement of the Queen's Majesty on the west, sometime occupied by John Wyckyns, now by Owen Thomas, clerk.

(xi) Barn on the north side of Witney Street between a tenement and barn of Symon Partridge on the west and the backgate of the tenement of William Geast on the east, occupied by George Fowler.

(xii) Messuage and garden on the east side of the High Street between a tenement of Richard Hodges on the north and a tenement of Edward Reynolds on the south, sometime occupied by Richard Dalby, now by Andrew Ward.

(xiii) Messuage on the north side of Sheep Street between a garden ground on the east and a tenement of Richard Chadwell, gent., on the west, sometime occupied by John West deceased, now by Robert Serrell.

(xiv) Little close of a third part of an acre on the south side of Witney Street, occupied by Alice Reynolds, widow.

(xv) The Culverclose with houses on the south side of Sheep Street between a tenement of the Queen's Majesty on the east and a pasture called the Leynes on the west, sometime occupied by Raphe Wisdom, now by Toby Dallam.

(xvi) Capital messuage with garden on Church Green between the

Almshouse on the north and a little close or garden strip and Gilden-ford Lane on the south, late occupied by William Symons, now by Symon Symons, tanner. The deed recites that all these properties were bought by Merywether and Dallam from William Typper and Robert Dawe of London by indenture dated 10 December 38 Elizabeth, enrolled in Chancery, Typper and Dawe having bought them of the Queen by Letters Patent dated 25 February 32 Elizabeth.

The intents of the present conveyance are specified as follows :

(A) The rents of numbers ii, iv, v, viii, xii, xiii, xiv are to be collected with the consent of the churchwardens and expended for the upkeep of the church and the bells.

(B) The rents of numbers iii and x are to be expended with the consent of the wardens of the school for the purposes of the school.

(C) The rent of number vi is to be expended on the repair of the bridge.

(D) The rents of numbers i and xvi are to be expended with the consent of the Alderman, Steward, and Burgesses for the poor people in the Almshouse.

(E) The rents of numbers vii, ix, xi, xv are to be expended with the consent of the Bailiffs, Alderman, Steward, and Burgesses for the payment of 6d. a week to the poor people in the Almshouse, according to the bequest of Thomas Poole, and as regards the remainder for the maintenance of the Fellowship of the Burgesses.

Witnesses : John Yate, Bailiff, Thomas Fowler and Thomas Silvester, Constables, Raphe Wisdom, William Taylor, John Collyer, Andrewe Ward, Edmond Serrell, William Sessions, Burgesses ; John Ward, Thomas Levett, William Huntt, Henry Hayter, Walter Hayter, Thomas Hardinge, William Wysdom, John Taylor, John Clarke, Thomas Hemynge ; Symon Symons, Steward.

Note.—The properties are not numbered in the original ; I have numbered them for convenience and clearness, and for purposes of comparison with later deeds concerning the transaction.

P 23. 14 February, 41 Elizabeth, 1599.

Conveyance by John Lyme alias Jenkyns, John Roffe, William Webbe, John Huntt, John Gryffyth alias Phillipps, and Thomas Parsons, yeomen, Burgesses, to Richard Meryweather, yeoman, Alderman of Burford. Messuage with appurtenances on west side of the High Street between the George on the north and a tenement belonging to the heirs of Agnes Brewton, widow, on the south ; and six acres of land in the corn fields alias Bury Barns. All which premises are described as having been bought by the six lessors from Richard Meryweather and Toby Dallam, 26 November 1597. The lease, for 90 years at 23s. 8d. a year, is specified as granted in consideration of a fine of £10 and a surrender of a term of 11 years unexpired of an existing lease granted by Meryweather to the widow of Simon Greene.

The common seal of the Fellowship or Brotherhood of the Corporation of the Burgesses of Burford affixed by Richard Meryweather, Alderman of the town, Symon Symons, Steward, John Roffe and John Yate, Bailiffs, John Lyme alias Jenkyns, William Webbe, Thoby Dallam, John Hunt, Andrewe Warde, Raphe Wysdome, John Gryffyth alias Phillippes, William Taylor, Thomas Parsons, Robert Serrell, Edmond Serrell, John Templer, John Collyer, William Sessions, Burgesses.

Witnesses : Symon Symons, John Templar, William Taylor, Thoby Dallam, Henry Perrott, Walter Hayeter, ' the wryter hereof '.

P 24. 14 February, 41 Elizabeth, 1599.

Lease by the same lessors, to Toby Dallam, clothier. The Culverclose and four tenements thereupon newly built, in the occupation of Thomas Sheppard, William Townesend, John Mare, and William Veysey ; between a tenement of the Queen's Majesty on the east and certain pastures called the Leynes on the west ; also a tenement in Witney Street occupied by George Fawler, between a tenement of Sir Anthony Cope, Knt., on the east and a tenement of Richard Hodges on the west ; also a barn in Witney Street over against this tenement between the back-gate of William Geast on the east and a tenement of Simon Partridge on the west. The same account of the purchase of the premises as in P 23. The lease, for 90 years at 32s. a year, is specified as granted in consideration of a fine of 40 marks and the surrender of a term of 15 years unexpired of a previous lease.

P 25. 14 February, 41 Elizabeth, 1599.

Lease by the same lessors, to William Taylor, chandler. 22 acres in the east and west fields of Burford, alias Bury Barns. The same account of purchase as in P 23 and 24. The lease, for 80 years at 11s. 4d. a year, is specified as granted in consideration of a fine of £5 and the surrender of a term of 13 years unexpired of a previous lease.

[No document numbered P 26 on the schedule.]

P 27. 20 March, 6 James I (1608).

Conveyance by William Webbe, yeoman, and Thomas Parsons, innholder, two of the elder Burgesses, to Robert Serrell, Thomas

Silvester, mercer, William Huntt, William Bartholomew, John Warde, Richard Hancks, and Robert Jordan, Burgesses.

Number in P 22.

(i) Arable lands containing by estimation 18 acres more or less, occupied by William Taylor, chandler ii

(ii) 1 acre of meadow in the common lott meadow . . iv

(iii) Little close containing a third part of an acre on the south side of Witney Street, occupied by Stephen Scott . . . xiv

(iv) Messuage on east side of the High Street between a tenement of Robert Elston, gent., on the north and the tenement of Robert Veysey on the south, occupied by Thomas Hemynge . v

(v) Messuage with appurtenances and shop on the east side of the High Street between the tenement of William Geast on the north and a tenement belonging to the free school on the south, occupied by Agnes Partridge, widow, and Peter Reynolds alias Hall vi

(vi) Messuage on west side of the High Street between the George Inn on the north and the tenement of the heirs of Agnes Brewton on the south, now occupied by John Collyer, lately newly erected by him, containing 32 feet from east to west and 22 feet from north to south, with 12 acres of arable land belonging to it vii

(vii) Messuage on west side of the High Street between the tenement of the heirs of Agnes Brewton on the north and the highway leading into Sheep Street on the south, occupied by William Taylor and Stephen Scott viii

(viii) Messuage in Witney Street between the tenement of Robert Veysey on the east and the tenement of Richard Hodges on the west, occupied by Gregory Patye ix

(ix) Barn on north side of Witney Street between a tenement and barn of Symon Partridge on the west and the backside and gate of the tenement of William Geast on the east, now occupied by Thomas Parsons xi

(x) Messuage, backside, and garden on east side of the High Street between the tenement of Richard Hodges on the north and the tenement of Edmond Serrell on the south, occupied by Andrew Ward xii

(xi) Messuage on north side of Sheep Street between a garden on the east and the tenement of Richard Chadwell, gent., on the west, occupied by Edward Taylerer xiii

(xii) The close called the Culverclose with all the houses on it on

the south side of Sheep Street between the tenement of Thomas
Bignell on the east and the pasture ground called the Leynes on
the west, sometime in tenure of Raphe Wisdom, now occupied by
Thomas Shepheard, Richard Busten, William Townsend, and
William Veysey xv

(xiii) Capital messuage with backside and garden and a piece
of ground heretofore called a garden strip, on Church Green
between the Almshouse on the north and gildenford lane on the
south, occupied by Symon Symons, tanner . . . xvi & i

The same recital of the purchase of these properties and the same
recital of charitable intents as in the deed, P. 22. Two clauses
are added : (A) that when only three of the present feoffees survive
they shall upon request made to them enfeoff the four elder Burgesses
inhabiting the town, the two Bailiffs, and the Steward, or such other
persons as shall be Burgesses ; (B) that all conveyances of these
properties are to be kept in the chamber over the Church porch, called
the Burgesses' Chamber.

The deed is endorsed to the effect that the tenants attended on a given
date and paid to Thomas Silvester one penny of silver each for and in
the name of his rent. It is also endorsed ' Affeoffment of the towne
lands among which Poole's lands are to the same uses with former
feoffment '.

Note.—It will be observed that numbers iii and x of the deed, P. 22,
do not appear in this deed. These two properties were conveyed to trustees
for purposes of a free school by the ' late co-feoffees of the parish lands
of Burford ' in 1571 (see S 20). But from the fact that they were obtained
by Typper and Dawe in 1590 from the Crown it may be inferred that the
title of the co-feoffees to these particular properties had been overruled.
They appear, therefore, in the deed of 1599 as if they had not been conveyed before ; but having been, by the purchase of Merywether and Dallam,
put upon a sound basis, they are then transferred to the school trustees,
and appear in the separate school conveyances (see S 36, which is dated
the same day as P 26).

P 28. 20 January, 3 Charles I (1628).

Conveyance by Robert Serrell, haberdasher, William Huntt late
of Burford, mercer, William Bartholomew the elder, mercer, Richard
Hancks, chandler, and Robert Jordan, yeoman, to Thomas Silvester,
William Bartholomew the younger, David Hewes alias Lloyd, Paul
Silvester, John Taylor, John Clarke, Richard Taylor, and Edmond
Serrell, Burgesses. All the town lands, as in P 27, with a few differ-
ences in the occupiers. The occupiers of number v (messuage with
shop on east side of High Street) were now Simon Hewes, shoemaker,

and Richard Dawson, sadler ; number x (messuage with backside
and garden on east side of High Street) had been occupied, after
Andrew Ward, by John Silvester, and was now occupied by John
Cooke ; number xii (the Culverclose) had Francis Turner in place of
William Townsend, and the holding of Thomas Bignell on the east
of it is described as a ' tenement, garden and croft '. The purchase
of the properties is recited as in the two preceding deeds.

Witnesses : William Webb junior, Richard Applegarth, Humphrey
Webbe.

[No document numbered P 29 on the schedule.]

P 30 & 31. VERDICT OF THE JURY and DECREES AND ORDERS OF
THE COURT under the Royal Commission of Charles I, dated 26 September, 4 Charles I, 1628.

The Commissioners were : Henry, Earl of Danby ; Sir John Walter,
Knt., Lord Chief Baron of the Court of Exchequer ; Sir Rowland
Lacy, Knt. ; Sir Giles Bray, Knt. ; John Fettiplace, Esq. ; John
Martyn, Esq. ; and Francys Gregory, Esq.

The jurors were : Anthony Bromsgrove of Kingham, Edmond
Weston of Cornewell, William Bridges of Churchill, Francis Collyns of
Sarsden, Richard Lissett of Bampton, Thomas Hinton of Alvescott,
John Fynnes of Kelmscott, Daniel Warwick of Kelmscott, Thomas
Fawler of Chipping Norton, John Higgins of Chipping Norton, William
Hodson of Witney, John Gunn of Witney, John Weekes of Witney,
and John Clarke of Witney.

The Commission was issued under the Act 43 Elizabeth, Concerning
the Misimployment of Lands heretofore given to Charitable Uses.

The jury found that the following were lands given in Burford for
charitable uses, and had hitherto been let at the rents mentioned :

POOLE'S LANDS :

i. House occupied by John Collyer on west side of the High
Street between the George Inn and a tenement occupied by George
Watkyns and Thomas Tonks, together with twelve acres of arable
land.

ii. The Talbott on south side of Witney Street occupied by Gregorye
Patye.

iii. Barn called the Woolhouse on north side of Witney Street over
against the Bull back-gate, occupied by Thomas Parsons.

iv. The Culverclose with four several houses occupied by Thomas
Smyth, Richard Bustyn, William Veysey, and Francis Turner.

v. 22 acres of arable land occupied by Robert Veysey, William Taylor, and William Fawkes.

Rents : number i . . . . 23s. 8d.
              numbers ii, iii, iv . . 32s.
              number v . . . . 11s. 4d.

GREAT ALMSHOUSE :

The Great Almshouse with a capital messuage on Church Green between Guildenford Lane and a tenement called Bavorks occupied by the heirs of John Templer, the capital messuage having been occupied by William Symons the elder and afterwards Symon Symons, and now occupied by Samuel Warcopp, gent.

Rent : 50s. 8d.

House or Inn called the Swan next the Bridge given by George Symons to the poor in the Great Almshouse, the new Almshouse, and otherwise, occupied by Richard Norgrave.

Rent : £6.

SCHOOL LANDS :

i. Three houses lying together near the Bridge occupied by Paul Silvester.

ii. House on east side of High Street between Symon Partridge on the south and Richard Dawson on the north, occupied by Thomas Parsons.

iii. Two houses lying together on north side of Witney Street next Guildenford Lane, occupied by Richard Buckingham and John Abraham.

iv. Two houses lying together on west side of the High Street on the hill between the lands of William Hewes alias Calcott and the lands of Richard Osbaston in the tenure of Jeremy Jellyman, occupied by John Dallam and George Greenhill alias Vincent.

v. Land in Bury Orchard, occupied by William Symons.

vi. A half-acre and a shurff in High Mead occupied by the same.

vii. One acre arable in East Field occupied by the same.

viii. The College, between the Vicarage on the north and the tenement of John Sympson on the south, occupied by Henry Sowdley, Joseph Boys and others.

ix. Two acres in High Mead occupied by Christopher Glyn, clerk, and William Bartholomew the younger.

x. House in Witney Street heretofore occupied by John Wyckyns, now by Robert Gray.

Rents : not specified.

CHURCH LANDS :

i. House or Inn called the Crown with a garden on west side of High Street, occupied by Suzan Scott.

ii. Little close at the furthest end of Witney Street between a tenement of Nicolas Franklyn on the west and a garden of William Taylor' on the east, occupied by the same.

iii. One acre in High Mead, occupied by the same.

iv. House on north side of Sheep Street between the garden of Suzan Scott on the east and the tenement of Anne Levett on the west, occupied by —— Steward.

v. House or Inn called the Bull on east side of High Street between the land of Edmond Serrell on the south and the Inn called the Angell on the north, occupied by John Cooke.

vi. House on east side of High Street between the tenement of Henry Hayter on the north and the tenement of Richard Hemynge on the south, occupied by Edmund Hemynge.

vii. A rent of 3s. 4d. out of an house next the Church, occupied by Mary Templar, widow.

Rents : numbers i, ii, iii .	.	.	.	25s.
number iv .	.	.	.	13s.
number v .	.	.	.	41s.
number vi .	.	.	.	21s.

BRIDGE LANDS :

Two houses on east side of High Street between a house of the Free School on the south and the tenement of John Taylor in the tenure of Thomas Bolton, glover, on the north, occupied by Symon Hewes and Richard Dawson.

Rents : not specified.

FIFTEEN LANDS :

i. Three houses in St. John's Street, occupied by Elizabeth Prickevance, widow, Robert Perry, and Thomas Russell.

ii. Two acres arable in Upton Field, occupied by Thomas Russell.

Rents : not specified.

CHARITABLE ANNUITIES :

The jury also found that the following annuities had been left for charitable purposes :

i. By Edmund Harman—£4 4s. a year out of the Port Mills.

ii. By John Lloyd alias Hewes, the elder—6s. 8d. to which John Lloyd the younger added 3s. 4d.

iii. By William Bruton—6s. 8d. out of his orchard at the end of Lavington Lane, now the land of Robert Veysey ; this payment was twenty years in arrear.

iv. Belonging to the Free School—A strip of ground called a garden strip, occupied by William Batson, gent., between his garden ground on the west and Gildenford Lane on the east ; the rent of 5s. a year was 50s. in arrear.

v. By Symon Wysdome—The new almshouse in Church Lane for four poor people.

vi. By Richard Hunt—15s. yearly out of the rent of a tenement at the furthest end of Witney Street, occupied by Nicholas Franklyn, of which 5s. was to be paid to the Church, 5s. to the poor, and 5s. to the schoolmaster.

vii. By Timothy Stampe—A gift of £40 to be lent out to four young tradesmen, who were to pay an interest of 12d. in the £ yearly, to be given to the poor.

viii. By George Tomson (1 James I)—A gift of £30 to be lent out for one year or not more than two years, the profits to be given to the poor.

ix. By William Edgeley—A gift of £10, the profits to be given to the poor.

x. By Alexander Ready, clerk (vicar of Sherborne)—A gift of £40, half to be lent in sums of £6 13s. 4d. to poor shopkeepers, one quarter to be lent to two poor maidens to help them in getting married, and one quarter to be lent to two decayed townsmen.

xi. By Edmund Silvester (1568)—£20 to be lent to young men for periods of five years.

xii. By Phillip Mullyner—A gift of £20 for the same purpose.

Upon this verdict the Commission decreed as follows :

New rents.

(A) That the rents of the various properties should in future be as hereunder :

POOLE'S LANDS :	£	s.	d.
i. Collyer's	4	0	0
ii. The Talbot	1	10	0
iii. The Woolhouse		5	0
iv. Smyth's house and close	1	10	0
v. Bustyn's		5	0
vi. Veysey's		5	0
vii. Turner's		5	0
viii. Arable lands	1	6	8
Total for Poole's Lands	9	6	8

ALMSHOUSE AND POOR :

	£	s.	d.
Capital messuage on Church Green . . .	4	0	4
Swan Inn	8	0	0

Out of the latter rent 8d. a week to be paid to the people in the Great Almshouse, and 16d. a week to the people in the new almshouse.

SCHOOL LANDS :

	£	s.	d.
i. Silvester's	4	16	0
ii. Parsons'	3	10	0
iii. Buckingham's and Abraham's . .	2	13	4
iv. Dallam's	2	10	0
v. Greenhill's	1	13	4
vi. Symons' land	1	10	0
vii. The College	2	0	0
viii. Two acres, High Mead . . .	1	0	0
ix. Gray's	2	0	0
Total for School Lands . . .	21	12	8

Out of this sum £5 was to be allotted to an usher and the remainder to the schoolmaster.

CHURCH LANDS :

	£	s.	d.
i. Susan Scott's	6	0	0
ii. Steward's	1	0	0
iii. The Bull	6	0	0
iv. Hemynge's	2	0	0
v. Annuity		3	4
Total for Church Lands . . .	15	3	4

Out of this sum £10 was allotted to the upkeep of the Church and the bells, and the residue to the poor, 16d. to be paid weekly to the people in the Great Almshouse and 8d. weekly to the people in the new almshouse.

BRIDGE LANDS :

	£	s.	d.
Hewes' and Dawson's	4	0	0

FIFTEEN LANDS :

	£	s.	d.
The three houses and the two acres to make a total of	3	10	0

(B) The Commission next decreed that there should be a new body of trustees, consisting of : Sir John Lacy, Knt., of Shipton-under-Whichwood, John Dutton, Esq., of Sherborne, Edward Fettiplace, Esq., of Swinbrook, William Lenthall, Esq., of Burford, Hercules

New body of trustees.

Osbaston, Esq., of Chadlington, Thomas Silvester, clothier, William Bartholomew the younger, mercer, David Lloyd alias Hewes, mercer, Paul Silvester, tanner, John Taylor, shoemaker, John Clarke, feltmaker, and Richard Taylor, tanner—all of Burford.

Enfeoffments were to be made in favour of this new body by :

Symon Chadwell, gent., heir to Symon Wisdome, surviving feoffee of Poole's Lands ;

Robert Walbridge, son and heir of John Walbridge, surviving feoffee of Church Lands ;

Richard Hannes, heir of Richard Hannes, his great-grandfather, surviving feoffee of the Great Almshouse and capital messuage adjoining ;

John Collyer, William Hunt, William Bartholomew the elder, Richard Hannes, Robert Jordan, Samuel Merywether, William Symons, William Webbe the younger, Symon Parsons, John Taylor, and Edmond Serrell, surviving feoffees of School Lands :

William Webbe the elder, surviving feoffee of the Fifteen Lands ;

Richard Allflett, son and heir of (blank), surviving feoffee of Bridge Lands.

The new trustees were to make a new enfeoffment when they come to be of the number of six or less, and were to choose for that purpose discreet persons of Burford and the parts adjoining.

Period of leases. In future leases were not to be for longer periods than twenty-one years ; but existing leases might be renewed for the remainder of their term, if it did not exceed thirty-one years.

An illegal sale. The Commission found that the capital messuage next to the Great Almshouse had been improperly dealt with. Mr. Samuel Warcopp had been allowed to buy for a considerable sum shortly before this date a very long lease, and on the strength of this lease William Symons had spent money on repairs. They were therefore to have special terms in the making of a new lease, if they surrendered the old lease without suit.

Fraudulent dealings. (C) The Commission next considered the case of the lands purchased by Merywether and Dallam from Typper and Dawe, who had obtained them by Letters Patent from the Crown. These lands comprised the whole of Poole's Lands, the Great Almshouse and house adjoining, the whole of the Church Lands, and two items of the School Lands (numbers ix and x in the above list).

The Commission stated that there was suspicion of 'fraud and cozen' in the obtaining of the Letters Patent ; they had been obtained on the representation that these lands had been concealed from the knowledge of the officers of the Crown at inquisitions into lands left for obits, lights in churches, etc., and ought to have been surrendered. The Commission found that there had been no such concealment, and that the Letters Patent to Typper and Dawe were therefore void.

Long leases had been obtained at small rents after the purchase depending on these Letters Patent ; these leases were also pronounced void. Yet since the lessees had spent money on repairs, they might, if they would surrender the old leases, have new ones from the trustees for the residue of their term, if it were not more than thirty-one years, or, if it were more, for the residue of the term at the new rents.

(D) The Commission made decrees for the rendering of accounts Accounts. yearly.

P 32. 23 February, 5 Charles I (1630).
Conveyance by Symon Chadwell ' being cozen and next heir of Symon Wisdome deceased ', surviving feoffee of the lands given by Thomas Poole, to the trustees as in the Commission's decrees.

[Describes the house on the south side of Witney Street as the Talbot, and the Woolhouse as ' over against the Bull back-gate ', and the 22 acres of arable as dispersed in the fields of Burford, Upton, and Signett.]

Witnesses : Richard Chadwell, Willm. Bartholomew, William Kempster.

P 33. 11 March, 6 Charles I (1630).
Writ of execution for carrying out the decrees of the Commission, addressed to John Collyer, Gregory Paty, Thomas Parsons, Thomas Smyth, Richard Bustyn, William Veysey, Francis Turner, Robert Veysey, William Tayler, William Fawke.

[*Note.*—Remains of a Great Seal attached to this document.]

Note.—From this point onwards the leases are all granted by the trustees appointed by the Royal Commission, and their due successors ; the names of the lessors are therefore dropped.

P 34. 23 September, 6 Charles I (1630).
Lease to Edmond Redman of London, gentleman. Part of Poole's Lands, viz. the Talbot, the Woolhouse, and the Culverclose with four houses. For 31 years at £4 a year.

P 35. 18 October, 6 Charles I (1630).
Lease to William Taylor of Burford, chandler. The 22 acres of arable land, of Poole's Lands. For 31 years at £1 6s. 8d. a year.

P 36 & 37. 28 March, 8 Charles I (1632).

Lease to Robert Veysey, of Chimney, Bampton, in consideration of a surrendered lease. House in the tenure of John Collyer, innkeeper, on west side of the High Street, lately added and adjoined to the George on the north side thereof, being in length on the street 23 feet and in depth 30 feet, containing six several chambers, a cellar, a parlour, a lodging-chamber over the same, and a cock-loft over that chamber, and two back rooms towards the kitchen, with 12 acres of arable land. For 31 years at £4 a year.

P 38. 30 September, 1657.

Conveyance by William Lenthall, Master of the Rolls, William Bartholomew, of Westalhill, gentleman, and Paul Silvester the elder, of Burford, tanner, surviving feoffees of the charitable lands, to Sir Anthony Cope, Knight and Baronett, Sir Edmund Bray of Great Barrington, Knight, John Lenthall, son and heir of William Lenthall, Esquire, Robert Jenkinson of Walcott in the parish of Charlbury, Esquire, Edward Hungerford of Black Bourton, Esquire, John Fettiplace the younger of Swinbrook, Esquire, John Hughes, mercer, David Hughes, clothier, John Knight, mercer, John Jordan, gentleman, Paul Silvester the younger, clothier, and Thomas Mathewes, innholder—all of Burford. The charitable lands set forth in the Commission's decree.

Witnesses : Robert Harleston, C. Glyn.

[*Note.*—This deed bears William Lenthall's signature.]

P 39. 4 November, 1659.

Lease to Margaret Haynes, widow. House now in her occupation on east side of High Street between Robert Cossen on north and Roger Daniel on south. For 21 years at 30s. a year.

P 40. 4 November, 1659. Lease to Thomas Smith. House on south side of Sheep Street between Thomas Newbery on west and John Newport on east ; and also the Culverclose containing by estimation two acres, between a close of Leonard Mills on east and a close called the Leynes on west now occupied by Thomas Taylor. For 21 years at £4 10s. a year.

P 41. 4 November, 1659.

Lease to Phillis Bignell of Burford and Alice Bignell her sister, spinsters. House on south side of Sheep Street now in occupation of Symon Hughes, between William Goram east and Robert Spurrett west, with garden plot and back-side. For 21 years at 30s. a year.

P 42. 4 November, 1659.

Lease to Thomas Newberie of Burford, yeoman. House on south side of Sheep Street between Thomas Smith on east and John Humphreys on west, with back-side and garden. For 21 years at 30s. a year.

P 43. 4 November, 1659.

Lease to William Goram of Burford, chapman. House on south side of Sheep Street between John Humphreys on east and Symon Hughes on west, with garden plot and back-side. For 21 years at 30s. a year.

P 44. 30 November, 12 Charles II (1660).

Lease to John Payton of Burford, clothier. The Talbot in Witney Street next adjoining the back-gate belonging to the Bull on west and the tenement of Richard Yate and others on east. For 21 years at £5 a year.

Witnesses: Edward Borham, John Lambert, Symon Randolph.

P 45. 26 December, 1659.

Lease to Thomas Parsons of Burford, chandler. A barn heretofore called the Woolhouse on north side of Witney Street next to the back-gate belonging to the three tenements of William Bartholomew, gentleman, Ralph Hicks, and Andrew Davis on east, and over against the back-gate of the Bull. For 21 years at 23s. 4d. a year.

Witnesses: Thomas Parsons the younger, John Sherrell, Symon Randolph.

P 46. 20 January, 1660.

Lease to Richard Veisey of Burford, innholder. House on west side of High Street adjoining to and occupied with the George, called the new building, the George on the north and the tenement of Margaret Watkins, widow, and John Collier on the south, with 2 acres of arable land. For 21 years at £6 6s. a year.

Witnesses: C. Glyn, J. Glyn, Robert Jordan.

P 47. 10 October, 1661.

Lease to Thomas Castle of Burford, innholder. 22 acres of arable land in Burford fields detailed in a schedule. For 21 years at £3 a year.

The Schedule:

½ acre in East Field shooting on Widford Hedge, ½ acre of parsonage land on north, and 1 acre late Richard Meryweather's on south.
½ acre at White Hill beneath the ridge way, ½ acre of parsonage land north, and 1 acre late of William Hall on south.

½ acre above the ridge way shooting north and south, ½ acre of parsonage land west, and ½ acre of Priory land east.

½ acre shooting on Sturt Quarre east and west, ½ acre of parsonage land north, and ½ acre late of Richard Meryweather south.

½ acre shooting upon Sturt Willow, ½ acre late of John Taylor east, and ½ acre of parsonage land west.

½ acre in same furlong, ½ acre Priory land east, and ½ acre parsonage land west.

½ acre in the Downs shooting north and south, ½ acre Priory land east, and ½ acre of Mr. Elston west.

½ acre shooting over Bampton way, 1 acre of John Hannes east, and ½ acre parsonage land west.

½ acre shooting into Bampton way, 2 acres of John Hannes land east, and ½ acre parsonage land west.

½ acre shooting upon William Combes headland, 1 acre of John Hame of Signett east, and ½ acre parsonage land west.

½ acre shooting upon the same, 1 acre of Richard Meryweather east, and ½ acre parsonage land west.

½ acre lying upon the ridge way east and west, ½ acre of Thomas Silvester south, and ½ acre parsonage land north.

½ acre beneath Bampton way lying north and south, 1 acre late of Mrs. Chadwell east, and ½ acre parsonage land west.

½ acre shooting over Bampton way, three ½ acres of the Bull land east, and 1 acre late of Richard Meryweather west.

½ acre shooting the same way, 1 acre of the Bull land east, and ½ acre parsonage land west.

½ acre shooting over Shilton path, ½ acre late of Thomas Hincks east, and 1 acre of Bull land west.

½ acre in the furlong at Shilton Bush, 1 acre of William Hunt east, and ½ acre parsonage land west.

½ acre in the furlong beneath Shilton Bush, 1 acre late of Robert Calcott east, and ½ acre parsonage land west.

½ acre shooting into Grove way, ½ acre parsonage land north, and 1 acre parsonage land south.

In West Field.

½ acre at the Conigree end shooting on W. Calcott's piece of Mr. Elston's land on east, and ½ acre late of John Taylor west.

Three ½ acres shooting into Deane Acre way, 1 acre late of Richard Meryweather north, and 1 acre of John Hannes south.

½ acre in Clay Furlong going north and south, 1 acre of John Hannes east, and ½ acre parsonage land west.

½ acre shooting into Deane Acre way, 2 acres of Thomas Silvester north, and ½ acre late of Richard Meryweather south.

½ acre shooting into Deane Acre, ½ acre parsonage land north, and land late of Richard Meryweather south.

½ acre shooting into Deane Acre way, 2 acres of Mr. Elston south, and ½ acre parsonage land north.

½ acre shooting in the same way, 1 acre Priory land north, and ½ acre late of Richard Meryweather south.

½ acre in Middle Furlong shooting into Signett path, ½ acre parsonage land north, and 1 acre late of Mrs. Chadwell south.

½ acre in the Oares shooting on the Downs, ½ acre parsonage land north, and 1 acre late of William Hall south.

½ acre shooting into Fulden Bottom in the Oares, ½ acre parsonage land east, and ½ acre late of Edmund Silvester west.

½ acre in the Oares, 1 acre late of Edmund Silvester belonging to Broadgates east, and ½ acre parsonage land west.

½ acre shooting upon Westwell Hedge, 2 acres late of Mrs. Chadwell east, and ½ acre parsonage land west.

½ acre shooting into Fulden Bottom, 1 acre late of Symon Partridge east, ½ acre parsonage land west.

½ acre shooting into Westwell way, ½ acre parsonage land north, and 1 acre late of Mrs. Chadwell south.

½ acre shooting into the same way, ½ acre late of Richard Meryweather north, and 1 acre late of Thomas Silvester south.

½ acre shooting upon Poole's Piece, ½ acre late of Samuel Gibbons east, and ½ acre parsonage land west.

½ acre shooting upon Edmund Silvester's headland, 2 acres late of Mrs. Chadwell east, and ½ acre parsonage land west.

½ acre shooting upon the same headland, 2 acres of the Bull land east, and ½ acre parsonage land west.

Witnesses: Richard Veysey, Edward Boarham, Robert Jordan.

P 48. 20 August, 13 Charles II (1661).

Lease to John Humphries of Burford, yeoman. House on south side of Sheep Street between Thomas Newbery on east and William Goram on west. For 21 years at 45s. a year.

Witnesses: Ambrose Berry, George Thorpe, Symon Randolph.

P 49. 3 September, 30 Charles II (1678).

Lease to John Payton the elder, clothier. The Talbot, between the Bull back-gate on west and the tenement of John Treenway on east. For 21 years at £5 a year.

Witnesses: John Payton, junior, Symon Randolph, Thomas Randolph.

P 50. 22 June, 35 Charles II (1683).

Conveyance by Sir Edward Hungerford and Sir Edmund Bray, surviving feoffees of the charitable lands, to Sir Edmund Fettiplace of Swinbrook, Thomas Horde of Cote, Esquire, Reginald Bray of Barrington, Esquire, William Lenthall of Burford, Esquire, Nathaniel Brookes of Burford, gentleman, David Hughes, mercer, Richard George, sadler, Paul Silvester, tanner, Thomas Castle, chandler, Richard Bartholomew, mercer, Thomas Silvester, tanner, and Francis Keeble, mercer—all of Burford. The charitable lands of Burford.

P 51. 29 September, 36 Charles II, 1684.

Lease to John Castle of Tewxbury, ' Physicion '. 22 acres in the common fields. For 21 years at £3 10s. a year.

Witnesses : John Payton, Hannah Castle.

P 52. 25 March, 36 Charles II, 1684.

Lease to Thomas Smith, yeoman. House on south side of Sheep Street between Thomas Newbery on west and Daniel Payton on east, with the Culverclose of two acres between the close of Daniel Payton on east and close called the Leynes occupied by William Taylor on west. For 21 years at £4 10s. a year.

Witnesses : Symon and Thomas Randolph.

P 53. 25 March, 36 Charles II, 1684.

Lease to John Humfryes, yeoman. House on south side of Sheep Street between Thomas Newbery on east and John Linsey on west. For 21 years at £2 15s. a year.

Witnesses : John Smith, Symon and Thomas Randolph.

P 54. 25 March, 36 Charles II (1684).

Counterpart of the same.

P 55. 25 March, 36 Charles II (1684).

Lease to John Linsey the elder, yeoman. House on south side of Sheep Street between John Humfryes on east and John Berry on west. For 21 years at £2 a year.

Witnesses : Symon and Thomas Randolph.

P 56. 26 August, 36 Charles II (1684).

Lease to Thomas Newbery the elder, yeoman. House on south side of Sheep Street between Thomas Smith on east and John Humphries on west. For 21 years at £1 10s. a year.

Witnesses : Symon and Thomas Randolph.

P 57. 8 July, 3 James II (1687).

Lease to Margaret Greenhill, widow. House on west side of High Street between Thomas Newberry on north and Richard Winfield on south. For 21 years at £2 a year.

Witnesses : Symon and Thomas Randolph.

P 58. 8 July, 3 James II (1687).

Lease to Richard Jordan of Witney, gentleman. The new building next the George, with 12 acres arable. For 21 years at £8 a year.

[Endorsed to the effect that, whereas only six rooms are mentioned in the lease, there are actually eight, the spence (?) chamber and a little square passage adjoining to it.]

P 59. 25 March, 8 William III, 1696.

Lease to Joseph Steele, sadletreemaker. House on south side of Sheep Street between Joseph Edmunds on west and Simon Partridge on east, with the Culverclose of two acres between the close of Simon Partridge on east and the Leynes occupied by William Taylor on west. For 21 years at £4 10s. a year.

Witnesses : Richard Osman, Richard Mathewes.

P 60. 8 July, 10 William III, 1698.

Lease to Richard Jordan of Witney, gentleman. The new building next the George, occupied by William Gossen, with 12 acres arable. For 21 years at £8 a year.

Witnesses : Ben Hawtyn, John Jordan.

P 61. 10 October, 10 William III, 1698.

Power of attorney by the trustees to Symon Partridge, clothier, and Richard Haddon, mercer, to recover the Sheep Street house and the Culverclose from Joseph Steele, saddletree maker, the rent being £13 10s. in arrear.

Witnesses : Mary Bartholomew, James Partridge, George Webb, John Jordan, junior.

[P 62 missing. It is entered on the schedule as an office copy of the Decrees of the Charity Commissioners at Witney in 1702. See Tolsey Collection, *infra*, p. 484.]

P 63. 21 September, 1 Anne, 1702.

Conveyance by Sir Edmund Fettiplace of Swinbrook, Thomas Horde of Coat, Esquire, David Hughes of Burford, gentleman, Richard Bartholomew the elder of Westhall hill, gentleman, and Richard George, late of Burford, saddler, to Edmund Bray of Barrington, Esquire, Philip Wenman of Caswell, Esquire, Charles Fettiplace of Swinbrook, Esquire, John Lenthall of Burford, Esquire, John Castle, gentleman, Richard Bartholomew the younger, gentleman, John Castle, chandler, William Forde, shoemaker, Dionysiùs Couzens, shoemaker, William Bowles, maltster, Paul Silvester, tanner, and Edward Sanders, mercer—all of Burford. The charitable lands of Burford.

Note.—Among the property of the Almshouses appears a house in Sheep Street described as the corner house on the west side of Lavington Lane. The house belonging to the School on the east side of the High Street was occupied by Denis Couzens. The Church Lands now consisted of the Crown inn and a close at the further end of Witney Street and an acre in High Mead, all occupied by John Castle ; a house on north side of Sheep Street occupied by George Sims next to the garden of the Crown ; the Bull, between land of John Jordan on south and the Angel on north ;

and a house on east side of High Street between Henry Hayter on north and a tenement of Mr. Jordan on south.

P 64. 26 August, 6 Anne, 1707.

Lease to Joseph Nunney, hatter. House on south side of Sheep Street between Robert Brown on east and John Bery on west, with garden plot. For 21 years at 40s. a year.

Witnesses : Richard Whitehall, Joseph Payton.

P 65. 26 August, 6 Anne, 1707.

Lease to Robert Browne, yeoman. House on south side of Sheep Street between Joseph Edmunds on east and Joseph Nunney on west. For 21 years at £2 15s. a year.

Witnesses : the same.

P 66. 26 August, 6 Anne, 1707.

Lease to Joseph Edmunds, yeoman. House on south side of Sheep Street between James Partridge on east and Robert Browne on west. For 21 years at £1 10s. a year.

Witnesses : the same.

P 67. 26 August, 6 Anne, 1707.

Lease to William Tash, innholder. The Talbot late occupied by John Payton, adjoining the back-gate of the Bull now occupied by William Tash on the east and the tenement of John Smith, Richard Berry, and Robert Patrick on west. For 21 years at £5 a year.

There is a memorandum to the effect that Tash had lately taken for the Bull the garden ground and back-side of the Talbot and one large stable of which the upper part adjoined a malt-house of Peter Rich.
This counterpart lease is not executed.

S 75. 21 April, 7 Anne, 1708.

Lease to John Berry the elder, slatter. House on south side of Sheep Street between Joseph Nunney on east and Robert Spurrett on west. For 21 years at 40s. a year.

Witnesses : Joseph Payton, John Randolph.

P 68. 6 April, 1713.

Lease to Richard Jordan of Witney. House called the new Building occupied with the George by Thomas Kennett, with 12 acres arable. For 21 years at £8 a year.

P 69. 20 February, 1 George I, 1715.

Lease to Richard Osmond, mason. House on south side of Sheep Street between Joseph Nunney on east and Robert Spurrett on west. For 21 years at £2 a year.

Witnesses : George Hart, William Castoll.   ·

P 70. 18 May, 5 George I, 1718.

Lease to Henry Tash, innholder, of the Bull. The Talbutt, between the back-gate of the Bull on west and the tenements of John Mills, Daniel Holiday, and Widow Wigins on west. For 21 years at £5 a year.

The previous inclusion of certain premises of the Talbot by the Bull recited as in P 67.

P 71. 16 October, 5 George I, 1718.

Lease to James Partridge, slatter. House on south side of Sheep Street between Joseph Edmunds on west and John Andrus on east, with the Culverclose of two acres between the close of John Andrus on east and the Leynes occupied by Robert Taylor on west. For 21 years at £4 10s. a year.

Witnesses : W. Applegarth, Humphrey Gillett.

No number. 16 October, 5 George I, 1718.

Lease of which P 71 is counterpart.

P 72. 13 December, 1 George II, 1727.

Conveyance by Philip Wenman of Caswell, John Lenthall of Burford, and William Bowles of Burford, to Sir John Dutton of Sherbourne, Sir George Fettiplace of Swinbrook, Reginald Morgan Bray of Great Barrington, William Lenthall, Charles Perrott, George Hart, brazier, Richard Whitehall, mercer, Matthew Underwood, mercer, Paul Silvester, tanner, John Green, chandler, and Daniel Dicks, maltster, being six of the present Burgesses—all of Burford. The charitable lands as before.

Note.—There were now five houses on the Culverclose.

P 73. 6 July, 3 George II, 1729.

Conveyance by William Bowles, to Robert Taylor, baker, Charles Perrott, George Hart, Richard Whitehall, Matthew Underwood, Paul Silvester, and John Green. The charitable lands as before.

Note.—This conveyance was apparently made owing to the former one never having been properly executed ; there is no endorsement of delivery of possession on P 72. It may be conjectured, in view of the near approach of another Royal Commission, that the state of the management of charitable affairs in Burford was such that the more important of the trustees named in P 72 refused to undertake the office.

[P 74 to 79 missing.]

Note.—The two documents which follow, though included on the Schedule in the Poole's Lands series, certainly do not belong to it. No part of Poole's Lands was in Church Lane. The situation of the property described here appears to correspond with the situation of

the Lesser Almshouse founded by Simon Wisdom, and the endorsement ' Domus Elimosinarius ' on one of them would support this
view. These appear to be the only documents among the Records
which have survived concerning that foundation. It is interesting
to observe that the semicircular shape of the close here mentioned
may perhaps be just traceable to-day in the slight curve of the line of
the Grammar School premises by the south-western corner of the
Churchyard.

P5. 12 October, 1 Henry V (1413).

Conveyance by William Brampton, to Thomas Alys of Burford.
A bakehouse in the eastern part of Burford in the upper lane leading
to the Church on the north side of the said lane, next the tenement
of Henry Spycer on one side, and it extends thence along the street
to the door which once was of John Sclatter, and in the lower part
the stable is built and abuts on a room of the said William Brampton
between the messuage of the said Henry and the tenement of the said
John Sclatter, and the close in the lower part extends in a semicircle
inclusively to the said door of John Sclatter from the said stable.

Witnesses : Thomas Spycer, Henry Coteler, Thomas Wynrysh,
John Punter, John Iremonger, William Coteler, John Baker.

Endorsed : ' Domus Elimosinarius '.

P7. 29 January, 8 Henry V (1421).

Conveyance by Henry Spycer and John Porter, clerks, to William
Brampton, of Oxford. The same property, ' which we had of the gift
and feoffment of Thomas Alys of Burford '.

Witnesses : Thomas Spycer, Henry Coteler, William Cotelere,
John Punter, Edmond Dyere, Robert Cok, Henry Gurney.

THE GREAT ALMSHOUSE

Cheatle Collection, Bundle GG

A 1. 5 August. (No year given, but it must be between 1455 and
1471.)

Copy of a letter from the Earl of Warwick to the Corporation.

Trusty and well beloved I greet you well and desire and pray you,
that at the instaunce of this my wrytynge you will graunt unto mee
the presentation of the next advowson of the Pryory of Burford that
thereunto I may promote a Chaplaine of myne whoe by God's grace
you shall fynde of suche good and priestly conversation rule and

governaunce, and so Demeane him amongest you, As you shall holde you pleased with God's mercy Whoe have you in Keepinge Wrytten at London the vth day of August

Richard Erle of Warwicke.

and captayne of Callais R. Warwyk

Endorsed : To my trusty and well beloved the Bailiffs and Burgesses of Burford And to every and eche of them.

Also : The Erle of Warwick's letter coppied out. The original itself included.

Note.—The original has been lost. The date of the letter can be approximately fixed by the fact that Warwick was Captain of Calais from 1455 to 1471. After the early part of 1456 he was abroad until 1459. Consequently this letter must be either of about the same date as A 4 (also dated from London), or after 1460.

A 2 and **A 3**. There are no documents with these numbers. The documents so entered originally on the Schedule were evidently noticed afterwards to be subsequent in date to A 4; they were renumbered A 5 and A 6 and the previous entry cancelled.

A 4. 26 February, 34 Henry VI (1456).

Ricardus Neville Comes Warrewici Dominus de Berguevenny Omnibus ad quos presentes litere nostre pervenerint salutem Sciatis nos concessisse et per presentes dilecto nostro Henrico Bushope de Burford in com Oxon heredibus executoribus et assignatis suis licenciam dedisse erigendi edificandi et sustentandi domum seu domos pro quadam elemosena ad pauperes sustentandos super duo crofta simul iacencia in le Cherchegrene in Burford predicto videlicet inter tenementum nuper Iohannis Bavok ex parte boriali et venellam vocatam Gildenfordlane ex parte australi et viam regiam ibidem ex parte occidentali et aquam sive rivulum vocatum Burfordwater ex parte orientali quorum quidem croftorum unum vocatur Fyssherscroft nuper in tenura Willelmi Cotiller et aliud croftum nuper fuit in tenura Willelmi Pynell et modo in tenura dicti Henrici Bushope Proviso semper quod nobis heredibus et assignatis nostris de annuis redditibus et serviciis pro eisdem clausis de iure debitis fideliter annuatim respondeant persolvent et perimpleant Et quod nos prefatum comitem et Annam uxorem nostram heredes et assignatos nostros eiusdem Elemosinarie sic edificande veros et licitos fundatores fieri facient et procurabunt In cuius rei testimonium has literas nostras fieri fecimus patentes Datum apud London vicesimo sexto die Februarii anno regni Regis Henrici sexti tricesimo quarto

R Warrewyk

Note.—This document bears a good specimen of the Earl's seal in red wax. As it also bears his signature—one of the only two specimens of the signature of the King-maker—and has therefore peculiar historical interest, it has not been placed in the bundle of Almshouse documents, but will be found in Bundle SS, Miscellanea III.

A 5. 23 February, 34 Henry VI.

Conveyance by Ralph Dominus de Suydeley, John Beauchamp Dominus de Beauchamp, John Norreys and John Nanfan armigeri, ' feoffati Domine Isabelle nuper Comitisse Warrwici ad instanciam nobilis Domini Ricardi Comitis Warrwici ', to Henry Bisshop of Burford. The two crofts as above, at a rent of 7s. 6d. a year.

Witnesses : Robert Harcourt knight, John Pynnok junior and Richard Lavyngton, Bailiffs, William Stodam, John Pynnok.

A 6. 8 October, 34 Henry VI.

Certificate that at the view of frankpledge held at Burford on the above date Henry Bishop came and took seisin of the two crofts as above to build thereon Almshouses for the poor, to pray for the souls of the Lord Richard and Anne his wife and all faithful souls.

Sealed by Robert Harcourt knight, seneschal of the Lord Richard in com. Oxon.

Note.—The dates of A 5 and A 6 are rather confusing ; A 5 makes the conveyance of the crofts take place three days before the Earl of Warwick's formal grant. October, 34 Henry VI, was October 1455.

A 7. Feast of St. Thomas the Apostle, 32 Henry VIII (1540).

Lease by Richard Manyngton, ' gentilman ', Alderman of Burford, and Richard Hans, Steward of the Borough Towne, Burgesses, to John Jones, one of the Burgesses. A tenement adjoining to the Almshouses on the south of them with a garden ground and a back-side ; also three chambers over the said Almshouses, with an entry going through the Almshouses and a garden ground appertaining to the said chambers. For 90 years at 34s. 8d. a year. Rent to be paid to the proctors of the Almshouses. (After the usual covenants) ' Over this the forseid John Jones do gyve graunte and permyt by these presents for hym and his assignes to and with the said Aldreman Stewarde and burgesses and to their successors Almanner suche Sylingis particions Ioynyng and Carvyng worke with portallis beyng in the hall and parler And also pales Yate and Suche other the whiche the said John nowe have Made or hereafter shall make upon the said Tenement and ground shall stonde and remayne in the said Tenement as Implements and stonders for evermore.'

Note.—This deed is a beautiful piece of writing and has a good specimen of the town seal attached to it.

A 8. Same date.

Counterpart of the above.

A 9. 30 October, 15 Elizabeth (1573).

Lease by Symon Wysdome, Alderman, and John Hannes, Steward, with the assent of the brethren, to William Symons, tanner. The plot or strip of ground part of the back-side of the Almshouses, 84 feet long by 22 feet wide, ' upon part whereof the said William hath erected and builded up a new tanhouse with other necessaries '. For 50 years at 4s. a year.

A 10. 5 December, 18 Elizabeth (1575).

Lease by the same lessors to Thomas Hewes alias Calcott, yeoman. The close or strip with the workhouse thereon builded commonly called the Tanhouse, between the tenement of William Symons north and Gyldenfoorde lane south. ' Excepting and always reserving unto the Alderman and Steward and Burgesses an annual rent of 2s. 8d. going out of the premises and to be paid by William Symons.' For 21 years at 8s. a year.

Witnesses : John Lyme, Robert Silvester, Bailiffs ; John Lloyde, Richard Chadwell, Thomas Feteplace, gentleman, Richard Reynolds, William Symons, Richard Dalby, Edmond Silvester, Benedicte Fawler, William Partridge, Walter Mollyner, John Wyllyams, Robert Scarboroughe, William Phillips ; John Smythar, bedle ; Bartholomew Cannan ' the wryter hereof and towne clerke '.

A 11. 14 February, 41 Elizabeth (1599).

Lease by John Lyme alias Jenkyns, John Roffe, William Webbe, John Huntt, John Gryffith alias Phillippes, and Thomas Parsons, yeoman, Burgesses, to Symon Symons, tanner, Steward of the Fellowship. Capital messuage with a garden strip late occupied by William Hewes alias Calcott lying near to the river called Gyldenford, all between the Almshouses on north and the highway and Gyldenford river on south. All which premises are described as bought by the lessors from Richard Merywether and Thoby Dallam, the title of sales being recited as in P 22. Lease, for 90 years at 50s. 8d. a year, granted in consideration of a fine of £30 and the surrender of a term of 36 years unexpired of an existing lease.

. Witnesses : John Yate, Bailiff, Thoby Dallam, Andrew Ward, William Taylor, Edmond Serrell, Raphe Wisdom, John Templer, John Collier, William Sessions, Walter Hayter, ' towne clerke and the wryter hereof '.

Endorsed: Md. that the third day of November 1606 Symon Symons within named did publishe unto the company then assembled that the ground lease contayninge the Lands within mencioned whereof this is a true counterpane assured unto his now wyffe for terme of her life ys remayninge in the custodye of John Saunders her brother in London to be safely kept according to true meaninge.

A 12. 23 February, 5 Charles I (1630).

Conveyance by Richard Hannes 'cosen and next heire of Richard Hannes his great grandfather surviving feoffee of Bishop's lands', to the trustees as in the Commission's decree. The Great Almshouse with the messuage and ground adjacent.

Witnesses: William Webbe junior, Walter Hayter the elder, Richard Alflat, William Kempster.

A 13. 17 October, 6 Charles I, 1630.

Lease to Samuel Warcuppe of Burford, gentleman. The capital messuage adjoining the Great Almshouse; also one 'lowe roome', one house called the Tannehouse, and one strip of ground adjoining. For 59 years at £3 a year for the capital messuage and 20s. a year for the low room and the tanhouse.

It is stated that this lease is granted because 'it appeared to the said Commissioners that the said Samuel Warcuppe for a great and full valuable consideration of one hundred and fower score pounds (and not being made acquainted that the premises were formerly given to any charitable use) purchased the said capitall messuage and other the premises then and nowe in his possession of and from William Symons of Burford, tanner, executor of Symon Symons deceased, and Robert Veysey the elder of Tainton, gentleman, who claimed the Residue of a Tenure of Ninetie yeares of and in the premises . . .' Reservation is made, until the point is settled at the Exchequer, of a possible yearly rent of 5s. to the Crown with arrears.

Witnesses: W. Batson, George Watkins, Thomas Richards, Christopher Gale.

A 14. 7 June, 1655.

Letter from William Lenthall, Speaker of the House of Commons, to the Bailiffs and Burgesses of Burford desiring them to grant him a lease of a parcel of ground in Berrie Orchard belonging to the town and formerly let by lease to Mr. Mathews.

A 15. 20 January, 27 Charles II, 1675.

Lease to Nathaniel Brookes of Burford, gentleman. Right of entry through the Almshouse to the house on north side of the Almshouse ; also of a parcel of ground in the back-side of the Almshouse fenced off and used for hay. For 21 years at a peppercorn rent. Granted in consideration of the surrender of a former lease and of the fact that the said Nathaniel Brookes had built a convenient house of office in the back-side of the Great Almshouse for the use of the poor people.

Witnesses : Symon and Thomas Randolph.

A 16. 29 September, 36 Charles II, 1684.

Lease to Thomas Gascoigne of Tainton, gentleman. The capital messuage adjoining to the Almshouse, now occupied by James Mady. For 21 years at £10 a year. The lease to determine if the lessee allowed two families to live on the premises.

Witnesses : Walwin Gascoigne, Elizabeth Gascoigne, Symon Randolph.

A 17. 30 August, 11 William III, 1699.

Lease to Anne Brooke, relict of Nathaniel Brooke. The same as in A 15, at a peppercorn rent, for keeping the building in repair.

Witnesses : Elizabeth Lambert, John Jordan.

A 18. 1 June, 3 George I, 1717.

Lease to James Gater, maltster. Part of the messuage on south side of the Almshouse, viz. two rooms below and three rooms above, all front rooms to the street on the south side of the said messuage ; also the barn, malthouse, dovehouse, little garden, and great back-side between the dovehouse and malthouse and that part of the orchard that is on the north side of the dovehouse straight from the north side of the dovehouse down to the river, where a mound is to be made and kept in repair by the trustees ; the tenant also to have access to the pump in the inner back-side of the Almshouse. For 21 years at £10 a year.

Witnesses : John Boulter, Humphrey Gillett.

WILLS

Cheatle Collection, Bundle HH

W 1. 29 November, 1473.

Will of John Pynnok.

(After bequests to altars, &c.) Item lego cuilibet filiolorum et filiolarum mearum duas oves matrices Item lego cuilibet famulorum et famularum mearum duas oves matrices Item lego Iohanni Graunger unam patellam eneam magnam Item lego Willelmo Spicer unam patellam eneam magnam Item lego Ricardo Barbero unum calefactorem Item lego margerie filie Iohannis Pynnok iunioris unam murram unam zonam stupatam viridis coloris unum capicium de scarlett Item lego Iohanni Gilmott unum plumale cum cervicali unum par lodicum unum par lintheorum duo cooptoria unam magnam cistam stantem in camera unam tabulam volventem stantem in parlario xii pecias de electro unam mappam duo manutergia unam murram unum craterem unam pelvim cum lavacro duas ollas eneas unam patellam eneam magnam unum cacabum cum pendentali unum verutum cum duobus popinagiis unum armorum vocatum pollax unam sellam cum freno unum gladium unam zonam stupatam sex cocliaria argentea unam ollam stanneam Item lego Matilde Nott unam maticiam unum par lintheorum unum par lodicum cum cooptorio unam armilausam vocatam Cloke unam togam de medley que quondam erat uxoris mee unam mappam duo manutergia unam ollam eneam unam patellam eneam unum calefactorem unum cacabum cum pendentali vi pecias de electro unam pelvim cum lavacro unam parvam tabulam volventem certa vasa lignea unum vocatum le vaate aliud vocatum cowle aliud vocatum paile et duos cados vocatos Barellis et omnes discos ligneos alia duo vasa vocata meelis unum verutum tripodem vocatam le brond yron unam ollam stanneam duo sacca unum urciolum eneum unam cistam stantem in camera que vocatur Hardyngs chamber unum ventilabrum et unum capicium que quondam erat uxoris mee.

[Bequest to John Pynnok, ' filio meo ', of a house in the High Street between a tenement of Henry Bishop on the south and one of John Pynnok junior on the north, and a house on the south side of Witney Street between a tenement formerly of Robert Coburley on the east and a tenement late of John Mosiar on the west, ten shillings to be paid yearly on testator's obit day to priests and poor people. The two houses to pass after the death of John Pynnok junior to his daughter Margery, and after her death to pass, the High Street house to the Vicar and proctors of the parish church, and the Witney Street house to the proctors of the Gild. John Pynnok to be residuary legatee and executor, and John Graunger supervisor.]

In cuius rei testimonium presentibus sigillum meum apposui et quia sigillum meum pluribus est incognitum presentem codicillum huic testamento indentato apponi procuravi Hiis testibus Thoma Maiowe Ricardo Barbero et aliis Datum die et anno supra notatis.

Note.—The codicil referred to is a certificate by John Sabyn, clerk, public notary of the diocese of Lincoln, that he was present at the making of the will, saw and heard the dispositions made, and himself drew up the will, and signed it with his usual signature and device. The device is a form of cross on a pedestal enclosing the words *Da Deo Cor Tuum* and *Serva Mandata.*

W 2. 29 October, 1478.

Will of Henry Bishop.

After various bequests for the maintenance of altars, lights, &c., he bequeaths two messuages in the High Street, two acres in the common fields, and a messuage called Gildenford gardeyne to his son John ; and to Margaret his wife and William his son the residue of all his goods and other lands and tenements in Burford that they may lay out £200 for the good of his soul.

Witnesses : Sir Thomas Pollard, by the grace of God bishop, and vicar of Burford, and Thomas Bisshope chaplain and bachelor of law.

W 3.

Extract from the will of Edmund Silvester the elder, late of Burford, clothier, giving £20 to be administered by the Alderman, Bailiffs, and Steward in loans to young tradesmen of the town on sufficient surety, for terms of five years, the sureties to be reconsidered every year. The recipients of the money to pay every Easter time 2*d.* to the Alderman, 2*d.* to each of the Bailiffs, and 4*d.* to the Steward, for their pains. If the money were ever retained in the hands of the Alderman, Bailiffs, and Steward unused for a period of three months, the testator's heir to have the right to recover the money for his own use. Note appended to the effect that at the Church Account held on 8 May 1575 by Richard Reynolds, Walter Mollyner, John Walburge, and Robert Brewtone, then churchwardens, the £20 was paid over by Edmund Silvester the younger to the Alderman, Bailiffs, and Steward, and by them lent out to the first recipients—Robert Evereste, ' glacier ', John Hiron, ' diar,', Symon Symons, tanner, and Richard Jurden, draper.

W 4. 17 March, 1576.

Gift by Edmund Harman, of £4 a year out of the rent of the Port Mills, to the poor, to be distributed on Monday before Easter and Monday before Christmas by the Constables.

W 5. 14 December, 22 Elizabeth (1579).

Bond of Robert Starre, in £4, to Symon Wisdom, clothier, Richard

Reynolles, woollen draper, and William Symons, tanner. The bond relates the bequest by Raphe Wyllett, clerk, parson of Kingham, of a cow for the relief of the poor of Burford. The cow had been delivered to Wisdom, Reynolds, and Symons, and by them hired out for 4s. a year. As the cow was ' very like to have perished through casuallty and ill keeping ', the three, in order to secure the testator's intentions, sold the cow to Starre for 30s., and added 3s. 4d. each to make up a sum of 40s. This sum was now lent to Starre for ten years, the interest, at the rate of 4s. a year, to be devoted to the relief of the poor.

Witnesses : John Hannes the elder, Raphe Wisdom, Miles Padelford, and Walter Hayter.

W 6. 29 December, 1580.

Copy of part of the will of William Bruton, leaving to Thomas Hewes the younger and his heirs ' the orchard which was my Brothers Roberts the which he bought of Bennett Fawler and my cosen Thomas to give yearly unto the poore uppon Good Friday 6s. 8d.'

Witnesses : John Huntt, Robert West alias Hallidayes.

W 7. 4 August, 1581.

Gift by John Floyde the elder, clothier, to Symon Wisdom, Alderman, and John Hannes, Steward, and their successors, of a yearly annuity of 6s. 8d. out of the rent of a house of his on west side of High Street between a tenement belonging to Brasenose College on south and the court hall commonly called the Towlsey on north. The annuity to be paid on Thursday before Easter and distributed on Good Friday.

Witnesses : John Lyme and John Williams, Bailiffs ; Richard Chadwell, Richard Reynolles, William Partridge, Richard Dalby, William Phillips, Benedict Fawler, John Griffiths.

W 8. 28 December, 2 James I, 1604.

Gift by George Thomson of Bampton to the poor of Burford, received by Andrew Ward and John Collier, Bailiffs of Burford, of £30 to be lent out £10 a year in sums of £2 10s. to beginners in trade, the interest to be distributed to the poor.

W 9. 24 January, 14 James I (1617).

Gift by William Edgley of London, gentleman, of £10, to be disposed of so that the profits might go to the poor.

W 10. 24 January, 1616.

Gift by Alexander Ready, Vicar of Sherborne (received from Richard Ready of Burford, yeoman, executor of the will, and Henry Heylin of Burford, Thomas Symons of Burford, and Alexander Ready, citizen and grocer of London, overseers of the will), of £40 to the town of Burford, half of the sum to be lent out in sums of £6 13s. 4d. to three poor shopkeepers, householders, &c., at interest of 4d. per 20s.; £10 of the sum to be lent to two maidens to help them to get married, the period of the loans to be for seven years; and the remaining £10 to be lent to two decayed tradesmen.

The interest, amounting at the rate mentioned to 13s. 4d. a year, to be disposed of thus: To the town clerk for drawing the bonds of the loans, 1s. 8d.; to the serjeant for warning the recipients to appear, 4d.; to the Registrar of the Bishop for supervising the administration of the bequest, 8d.; to eight of the Almshouse people, 1s. each on the Sunday before Christmas, 8s.; the residue of 2s. 8d. to the Alderman, Steward, Bailiffs, and chief minister to use as they appoint.

[W 11 and 12 missing. They were extracts from William Lenthall's will.]

W 13. 5 October, 1672.

Gift by John Harris of £200, 'out of the great love and respect which I bear unto the town of Burford where I was born'. Of this sum £100 to be lent out gratis to ten tradesmen, £10 apiece, repayable by 20s. a year, each of these tradesmen to pay 6d. to the Minister or Clerk who should read out the accounts of the charity in the Church on Tuesday in Whitsun week; the other £100 to be disposed of so that the profits should be employed in binding out apprentices.

· ROLL OF THE BURGESS RULES

Cheatle Collection, Bundle II

Note.—The Roll of the Burgess Rules has not been transcribed here, because it has been printed in full in the Reports of the Historical Manuscripts Commission, Various Collections, vol. i (1901).

COBB HALL

Cheatle Collection, Bundle KK

GS 1. 19 January, 1590.

Extract from the will of George Symons of Burford:

' Item I give and bequeath unto ye poore of Burford my now dwelling house in Burford called cobhall lying in the west part of the High Street with all edifices bacsides Courtyards gardens courts and easyaments and all other comodities and advantages whatsoever in as ample manner & forme as I the said George Symons have or doe or ought to have enioyed the same which house with the foresaid premisses are to be set yearely by Eight of ye poore people of Burford to be chosen by Voyces of ye said poore people out of their owne Company Wherof I will that fower of the eight shall at the time of their election vewe and survey the Reparacions of the said house for one yeare and to have authoritie to set the same house for one yeare and no more for the best and most advantage for all ye poore people of Burford And my will is the said yearly election of eight poore people should be done by them uppon St. Andrew's day Provided alwayes that all contracts promises compacts agreements bargaynes or graunts of theirs whatsoever contrary to ye true meaning of my will shalbe utterly void & of none effect.'

This will was proved 8 February, 1591.

GS 2. 16 October, 6 Charles I (1629).

Lease to Richard Norgrave. House or inn called the Swan lying near to the Bridge of Burford. For 21 years at £8 a year.

Endorsed in a later hand : ' Cobb Hall.'

GS 3. 1 May, 1650.

Assignment by Edmond Heming, barber surgeon, to Robert Collier of Tainton. Lease of the house or inn called the Swan next to the Bridge, formerly in the tenure of Richard Norgrave, with a signpost and sign of the Swan standing at the door thereof. Leased on 1 October, 23 Charles I (1648), to Edmond Heming, then in his occupation ; now let to Robert Collier for £31 a year and occupied by Richard Willett. Remainder of Heming's lease assigned to Collier, £8 a year to be paid to the trustees.

Witnesses : Edmond Heming junior, John Jordan.

GS 4. 14 January, 31 Charles II (1679).

Lease to William Savage of the City of London, grocer. House or inn called the Swan now occupied by Paul Silvester of Burford, clothier. For 21 years at £8 a year.

Witnesses : Robert Applegarth, Richard Mills, Richard Applegarth, Mary Applegarth.

GS 5. . . . 3 James II (1687).

Lease to William Rogers of Burford, clothier. Messuage or tenement called the Swan. For 21 years at £8 a year.

Witnesses : John Deacon, Thomas Randolph.

GS 6. 20 June, 13 William III (1701). ·
Lease to the same of the same premises, for same term and rent.

GS 7. 10 December, 3 George I (1717).
Lease to Daniel Flexson of Widford, clothier. The Swan. For 21 years at £8 a year.

Note.—The lessee signs his name Daniel Flexney, and the name appears so in an unnumbered counterpart.

GS 8. 1 March, 9 George II, 1735.
Lease to Joseph Flexney of Burford, clothier. The Swan. For 21 years at £8 a year.
Witnesses : Henry Tash, William Jordan.

GS 9. Same date.
Bond by Joseph Flexney, in £200. In consideration of a new lease replacing the unexpired three years of his late father's lease, at the same rent, the lessee undertakes to spend £100 in repairs ; otherwise his rent to be at £10 a year.
Witnesses : the same.

HEYLIN'S CHARITY, ETC.

Cheatle Collection, Bundle LL

H 1 and **H 2.** 26 and 27 May, 1691.
Indentures of a marriage settlement between Richard Abell of the one part and William Little, Edward Osborn, and Elizabeth Little, daughter of the said William Little, of the other part. A messuage or tenement with appurtenances in Clanfield and a yard lands and a quarter of a yard lands, and other premises, to be held upon trust to the uses mentioned, in consideration of the marriage intended between Richard Abell and Elizabeth Little.

H 3. 15 June, 1 Anne, 1702.
Indenture of sale by Richard Abell, citizen and haberdasher of London, Elizabeth his wife, and Thomas Abell his father, to the Trustees of charitable lands in Burford as in the decrees of the Royal Commission. Various arable and pasture lands in Clanfield, amounting to 17 acres and one farundell.

A Commission held at Witney in the year above mentioned having ordered that £200 given by Henry Heylin, late of Minster Lovell, Esquire, by his will dated 9 May, 1693, and also £20 given by Richard Sindrey, fellmonger, in 1660 for charitable purposes, should be employed in the purchase of lands, the rents thereof to be used for placing out two poor boys as apprentices.

H 4. 18 February, 6 Anne (1707).

Warrant addressed to John Sindrey and Henry Peacock. John Sindrey, of Bedford, merchant, is ordered to pay the sum of £20 bequeathed by his grandfather in 1660, which had not been paid either by his widow or by his son. Henry Peacock, executor of the will of Henry Heyling, gentleman, of Minster Lovell, is ordered to pay the sum of £200 given by that will. The money to be paid at Burford on 25 June next following.

Note.—The warrant is issued on the findings of the Royal Commission of 1702 at Witney. See Tolsey Collection, *infra*, pp. 485, 486.

CL 1. 1668.

Order by the Trustees of Charitable Uses to the Trustees of Cleaveley's Charity to distrain for the arrears of rent and when received to pay them according to the will.

CL 2. 27 October, 1693.

Conveyance by David Hughes, Thomas Parsons, and Richard Haynes, to John Bartholomew and others. Two several yearly rents of five pounds and three pounds given by the will of William Cleaveley to hold during the remainder of a term of six hundred years upon the trusts mentioned in the will.

CL 3. 26 September, 1724.

Conveyance by Paul Silvester the elder, to George Hart, Richard Whitehall, Paul Silvester the younger, Matthew Underwood, William Castle, and James Whiteing. The two yearly rents as above, to hold upon the trusts of the will.

CH 54. 16 July, 8 George II, 1734.

Lease to Nicholas Willett of Burford, apothecary. The Crown Inn with garden, on west side of High Street. Also a close at the further end of Witney Street between a close occupied by Henry Tash and a tenement occupied by Humphrey Nunny on west; also one acre of meadow in High Mead. This lease to include the end of a term granted to William Castle and assigned by his executors to Willett, six years yet to run. For 15 years from 25 March, 1749, at £14 a year.

Witnesses : R. Griffiths, William Jordan.

CH 56. 5 March, 9 George II, 1735.

Lease to Henry Tash, innholder. The Bull, between a tenement of

John Green on south and the Angel occupied by Edward Chavasse on north. For 21 years at £14 a year.

Witnesses : Joseph Flexney, William Jordan.

16 October, 5 George I, 1719.

A lease of which the counterpart is among the documents of Poole's Lands and duly scheduled : see P 71.

10 December, 3 George I, 1717.

A counterpart of a lease which will be found among the documents of Cobb Hall duly scheduled and numbered : see GS 7.

26 March, 1730.

Lease by the Trustees to Richard Clarke of Clanfield, butcher. Seven acres and a farundell of arable land. For 21 years at £9 a year. (Receipts enclosed.)

COMMISSIONS AND LEGAL PROCEEDINGS. I

Sixteenth and Seventeenth Centuries

Cheatle Collection, Bundle MM

5 July, 10 Elizabeth (1567).

Exemplification out of the Exchequer of a verdict concerning certain lands in Burford.

The lands in question were the following : one acre arable called Jesus Acre ; one acre of pasture in the occupation of the church-wardens, said to have been lately given for the maintenance of an anniversary in Burford Church ; one acre of meadow and a shurf in ' Heymeadow ' occupied by Thomas Calcott, given to maintaining a light in the chapel of St. Katherine ; a half-acre of meadow called Cakebred Land, occupied by Thomas Fryer, given for maintaining an anniversary ; a piece of ground called ' a platt of ground ' occupied by Simon Wysdome ; two acres arable in Upton occupied by the same, given to the maintenance of a light called the Torchlight ; a tenement occupied by Kenelm Chaunce ; a shop occupied by William Partridge, given to the maintenance of a priest to celebrate Mass in St. Thomas's Chapel ;

The Attorney General laid an information in the Court of Exchequer on 2 February, 9 Elizabeth (1567), to the effect that the lands mentioned had been given for the purposes named, that the jury at the inquisition held at Chipping Norton, 3 September, 7 Elizabeth (1564), had found that the lands were so given to the Church, and that they should therefore have been delivered into the hands of the Crown. The information laid proceeded to state that William Dalby and John Geste were trespassing in possession of the premises and converting them to their own use, and were so doing on 8 October, 8 Elizabeth (1565), and still continued to do so in contempt of the Queen and against her laws.

A writ was issued in pursuit of this information, ordering the attendance of Dalby and Geste at the Court of Exchequer, and they attended by their attorney allowed by the Court, John Marwood. They asked for time to reply to the information, and the case was adjourned. On its resumption at a later date Dalby and Geste protested that the information was vexatious, and denied in detail that the lands were ever given for the purposes alleged. They further protested that long before the inquisition at Chipping Norton, viz. on 20 June, 6 Elizabeth (1563), Simon Wysdome and Hugo Colman, Proctors of Burford Bridge, were seized of and in the premises specified, to apply the revenues thereof to the maintenance of the Bridge, and enfeoffed Dalby and Geste of the premises on the date mentioned.

The jury found on their oath that the premises were not given for the purposes alleged, and that Dalby and Geste had not been guilty of trespass.

The Court gave a verdict accordingly, with liberty to Dalby and Geste to enter on the premises.

17 June, 18 James I (1620).

Quo Warranto Proceedings in the Court of Exchequer concerning the franchises of Burford.

Per Trinitatis Recordum Anno Decimo Octavo Regis Jacobi.

Oxon
Memorandum quod Henricus Yelverton miles Attornatus Domini Regis Generalis qui pro eodem Rege in hac parte sequitur presens hic in curia decimo septimo die Iunii hoc termino in propria persona sua pro eodem Domino Rege dedit curiam hic Intelligi et Informari quod quidem Willelmus Taylor Willelmus Bartholomew Simo Simons Leonardus Mills Thomas Silvester et Iohannes Hunt et alii Inhabitantes Ville et Burgi de Burford in comitatu Oxon predicto per spaiam (*sic*) trium annorum iam ultimo elapsorum et amplius usi fuerunt et adhuc utuntur infra Villam et Burgum de Burford predictum in comitatu predicto absque aliquo warranto sive Regali concessione libertates privilegia et ffranchesias subsequentes viz : habere tenere et custodire unum mercatum ibidem infra Villam et Burgum predictum quolibet

die Sabbati qualibet septimana Ac eciam habere tenere et custodire
ibidem infra Villam et Burgum predictum quolibet anno duas ferias
annuatim viz : unam earundem feriarum in festo Sancti Iohannis
Baptiste et aliam earundem feriarum in die Exaltacionis Sancte
Crucis aliter vocate Holliroode day et in mercato et feriis illis habere
picagium stallagium et alias Iurisdictiones et privilegia ad mercatum
et ferias spectantia et pertinentia et pro eisdem picagio et stallagio
exigere levare et capere ad usus suos proprios diversas denariorum
summas de subditis dicti Domini Regis ad mercatum et ferias predictas venientibus et accedentibus ad bene cattalla mercimonia et
mercandisa sua in mercato et feriis illis vendenda seu vendicioni exponenda Ac eciam habere recipere et percipere ibidem in
mercato et feriis illis Tolnetum de omni genere frumenti et grani ad
mercatum et ferias predictas veniente et adducto ac Tolnetum pro
omnibus equis spadonibus bobus boviculis vaccis iuvencis ovibus
porcis et aliis averiis quibuscunque in mercato et feriis predictis
emptis et venditis Ac eciam habere et ad usus suos proprios convertere
et disponere omnia bona et cattalla felonorum bona et cattalla waviata
vocata waives bona et cattalla extrahura vocata straies infra Villam
et Burgum predictum contingentia et accidentia Necnon eligere
nominare et constituere de semetipsis fore Scenescallum Ville et
Burgi predicti necnon unum de semetipsis fore Deputatum Aldermannum eiusdem ville et Burgi ac ad libita sua propria quoscunque
officiarios infra Villam et Burgum predictum ab officiis suis amovere
ibidem necnon habere et tenere infra eandem Villam et Burgum unam
Curiam vocatam a Borrough Court de tribus septimanis in tres
septimanas ac omnia et singula proficua et emoleimenta infra curiam
predictam crescentia et contingentia ad usus suos proprios capere
convertere et disponere et in eadem curia tenere placita quaecunque
subter summam quadraginta solidorum ac insuper cogere et compellere
quascunque personas eis placuerint iurare et sacra praestare in curia
predicta in quibuscunque causis et materiis in eadem curia dependenti-
bus ad libita sua et easdem personas super sacramenta sua in omnes
(sic) causis et materiis illis examinare Ac eciam statuta ordinaciones
leges et articulos ad libita sua propria infra Villam et Burgum predictum facere ordinare et constituere et eos qui statutis ordinacionibus
legibus constitucionibus et articulis illis obedire negarent seu eadem
non observarent Imprisonare ac fines et amerciamenta super omnes
eis de causis taxare et imponere et ea ad usus suos propriis (sic) levare
et convertere Necnon sacris astringere tot et tales de Inhabitantibus

Ville et Burgi predicti quot et quales eis placuerint ad statuta ordinaciones leges constituciones et articulos predictos observandos et
custodiendos de quibus omnibus et singulis privilegiis libertatibus et
ffranchesiis supradictis iidem Willelmus Taylor Willelmus Bartholomew
Simo Simons Leonardus Mills Thomas Silvester et Iohannes Hunt et
alii Inhabitantes Ville et Burgi predicti per totum tempus supradictum
super dictum Dominum Regem usurpaverunt et adhuc usurpant in
dicti Domini Regis nunc contemptum et sue Regie prerogative grave
dampnum et preiudicium   Unde predictus Attornatus Domini Regis
pro eodem Domino Rege petit auditum in premissis et debitum legis
processum versus ipsos Willelmum Taylor Willelmum Bartholomew
Simonem Simons Leonardum Mills Thomam Silvester et Iohannem
Hunt et alii (*sic*) Inhabitantes Ville et Burgi predicti in hac parte
fieri ad Respondendum dicto Domino Regi quo warranto clamant
habere uti et gaudere libertatibus privilegiis et ffranchesiis supra
dictis   SUPER QUO concordatum est quod mandetur prefatis
Willelmo Taylor Willelmo Bartholomew Simoni Simons Leonardo
Mills Thome Silvester et Iohanni Hunt per breve Domini Regis nunc
de sub sigillo huius de essendi hic etc ad Respondendum in premissis
Et hoc sub pena Centum librorum quas etc. Si non etc Et predictis
eisdem Willelmo Willelmo Simon Leonardo Thome et Iohanni in
Forma predicta Ita etc ex die Sancte Trinitatis in tres septimanas
hoc termino Ad quem diem Predicti Willelmus Taylor Willelmus
Bartholomew Simo Symons Leonardus Mills Thome Silvester et
Iohannes Hunt venerunt hic per Willelmum Boucher Attornatum
suum ad hoc ex gracia Curia specialiter admissum Et habito auditu
Informacionis predicte iidem Willelmus Willelmus Simon Leonardus
Thomas et Iohannes protestandur (*sic*) quod Informacio predicta
minus sufficiens in lege existit ad quam ipsi necesse non habent nec
per legem Terre tenentur respondere per placita tamen iidem Willelmus
Willelmus Simo Leonardus Thomas et Iohannes dicunt quod dictus
Dominus Rex nunc ipsos Willelmum Willelmum Simonem Leonardum
Thomam et Iohannem occasione premissorum in informacione predicta
superius spectante impetere seu ottenare non debet quia dicunt
quod Villa et Burgus de Burford predictus est antiquus Burgus quod
quidem Inhabitantes eiusdem ville sive Burgi a tempore cuius contrarii
memoria hominum non existit fuerunt unum corpus Incorporatum
per nomen Ballivorum Aldermanni et Burgensium Ville suis (*sic*)
Burgi de Burford predicti Et quoad predictas libertates habendas
et ad usus eorundem Ballivorum Aldermanni et Burgensium pro

tempore existentium convertenda et disponenda omnia bona et cattalla
felonorum infra villam sive Burgum predictum contingentia et
accidentia iidem Willelmus Willelmus Simo Leonardus Thomas et
Iohannes Dicunt quod Dominus Edwardus quondam Rex Anglia
(*sic*) tercius per Litteras suas patentes magno sigillo suo Anglie
sigillatas Curieque hic ostensis gerentes datam eisdem die et anno
apud Burford predictum dedit et concessit eisdem Ballivis Aldermannis et Burgensibus ville sive Burgi predicti omnia et singula bona
et catalla felonorum infra villam sive Burgenses (*sic*) predictum
quovismodo contingentia sive accidentia habenda eisdem Ballivis
Aldermannis et Burgensibus et successoribus suis imperpetuum virtute
cuius iidem Ballivi Aldermannus et Burgenses fuerunt et adhuc
sunt de libertate illa seisiti ut de ffeodo et iure   Et quoad libertates et ffranchesie subsequentes in Informacione predicta spectant
superius iidem Willelmus Willelmus Simo Leonardus Thomas et
Iohannes dicunt quod predicta (*sic*) Ballivi Aldermannis (*sic*) et
Burgenses Ville sive Burgi predicti tempore existentes a toto tempore
supradicto cuius contrarii memoria hominum non existit habuerunt
tenuerunt et gavisi fuerunt et per totum idem tempus habere tenere
et uti consueverunt infra predictam villam sive Burgum de Burford
unum mercatum quolibet die Sabbati non existente festo die Natalis
Domini in qualibet septimana ac eciam infra villam et Burgum predictum quolibet anno duas ferias annuatim viz : unam earundem
feriarum in festo Sancti Iohannis Baptiste et aliam earum feriarum
in die Exaltacionis Sancte Crucis communiter vocato Hollyroode day
non existente dies Solis quolibet anno et in mercato et feriis illis per
totum idem tempus cuius contrarii memoria hominum non existit
habere picagium stallagium et alias Iurisdictiones et privilegia ad
mercatum et ferias spectantia et pertinentia   Ac eciam per totum
tempus supradictum cuius contrarii memoria hominum non existit
iidem Ballivi Aldermannus et Burgenses Ville sive Burgi predicti pro
tempore existentes habuerunt et receperunt et habere et recipere
consueverunt ad usus suos proprios de qualibet persona existente
forinsecto et minime libera persona Ville sive Burgi predicti pro
quolibet die quo talis persona exponit aliqua mercimonia in mercato
illo vendenda unum denarium pro exposicione Anglice showing
mercimoniorum suorum in mercato predicto et pro quolibet sacco
frumenti et grani locato Anglice pitched in Dicto mercato vendicioni
exponendo unum plenum discum Anglice one dish full continentem
unam pintam Anglice a pint huius grani   Ac eciam per totum tempus

supradictum cuius contrarii memoria hominum non existit habuerunt et habere consueverunt tolnetum pro omnibus equis spadonibus bobus boviculis vaccis iuvencis ovibus et porcis quibuscunque in mercato et feriis emptis et venditis Ac eciam iidem Ballivi Aldermannus et Burgenses ville Burgi (*sic*) predicti pro tempore existentes per totum predictum tempus cuius contrarii memoria hominum non existit similiter usi fuerunt et consueverunt habere et ad usus suos proprios converter et disponere omnia bona et catalla waiveata et bona et catalla extrahura infra villam et Burgum predictum contingentia et accidentia necnon per totum idem tempus cuius contrarii memoria hominum non existit usi fuerunt et consueverunt eligere nominare et constituere unum de semetipsis fore Senescallum Ville et Burgi predicti ac ad libita sua propria quoscunque officiarios infra villam et Burgum predictum ab officiis suis ibidem amovere necnon habere et tenere infra eandem Villam et Burgum unam Curiam vocatam a Burrough Court de tribus septimanis in tres septimanas ac omnia et singula proficua et emolumenta infra curiam predictam crescentia et contingentia per totum tempus supradictum ad usus suos proprios capere committere et disponere Et in eadem curia tenere placita quecunque subter summam quadraginta solidorum Ac eciam per totum idem tempus statuta ordinaciones Leges et articulos ad libita sua propria infra villam et Burgum predictum facere ordinare et constituere pro meliore Gubernacione ville et Burgi predicti modo non sunt contraria Legibus huius Regni Anglie et super omnes qui statutis ordinacionibus Legibus Constitucionibus et articulis illis obedire negarent seu eadem non observarent fines et amerciamenta eis de causis taxare et imponere et ea ad usus suos proprios levare et convertere Et iidem Willelmus Willelmus Simo Leonardus Thomas et Iohannes dicunt quod ipsi iidem Willelmus Willelmus Simo Leonardus Thomas et Iohannes sunt et per totum predictum spacium trium annorum in Informacione predicta specificatum fuerunt Burgenses Ville sive Burgi predicti Et eo warranto iidem Willelmus Willelmus Simo Leonardus Thomas et Iohannes predicti libertates privilegia et FFranchesie in Informacione predicta mencionata per tempus predictum in Informacione predicta superius specificatum usi fuerunt et adhuc utuntur prout eis bene licuit absque hoc quod iidem Willelmus Willelmus Simo Leonardus Thomas et Iohannes predicti libertates privilegia et ffranchesias predictas seu eorum aliquum super predictum Dominum Regem non usurpaverunt seu adhuc usurpant modo et forma prout per Informacionem predictam

pro dicto Domino Rege nunc superius supponitur Que omnia et
singula iidem Willelmus Willelmus Simo Leonardus Thomas et
Iohannes parati sunt verificare prout curia etc unde petunt Iudicium
et quod omnia et singula libertates privilegia et ffranchesie predicta
eisdem Ballivis Aldermanno et Burgensibus ville sive Burgi predicti
et successoribus suis imperpetuum deinceps allocentur et adiudicentur
Et quod ipsi quod illa ab hac Curia dimittentur etc ET predictus
Attornatus Domini Regis Generalis presens hic in Curia ad eundem
diem in propria persona sua quoad separales libertates privilegia et
ffranchesias subsequentes in Informacione predicta superius mencionatas et per predictos Willelmum Taylor Willelmum Bartholomew
Simonem Simonds Leonardum Mills Thomam Silvester et Iohannem
Hunt et alios Inhabitantes Ville et Burgi predicti usurpari allegatas
vizt : Eligere nominare et constituere unum de semetipsis fore
Deputatum Aldermannum eiusdem Ville et Burgi ac cogere et compellere quascunque personas eis placuerit Iurare et sacramentum
praestare in Curia in Informacione predicta mencionata in quibuscunque causis et materiis in eadem curia pendentibus ad libita sua Et
easdem personas super sacramenta sua in causis et materiis illis
examinare Ac omnes eos qui statutis ordinacionibus Legibus constitucionibus et articulis per ipsos Inhabitantes factis ordinatis et
constitutis obedire negarent seu eadem non observarent Imprisonare
necnon sacramentis astringere tot et tales de Inhabitantibus ville
et Burgi quot et quales eis placuerit ad statuta ordinaciones Leges
constituciones et articulos predictos observandos et custodiendos
Ex quo predicti Willelmus Willelmus Simo Leonardus Thomas et
Iohannes per placitum suum predictum non clamant habere uti seu
gaudere libertatibus privilegiis et ffranchesiis predictis ultimo mencionatis nec usum eorum vel eorum alicuius aliquo modo verificare
pretendunt nec aliquid dicunt pro manutenencione eorundem Idem
Attornatus Domini Regis pro eodem Domino Rege petit inde Iudicium
SUPER QUO visis premissis per Barones hic habitaque matura
Deliberacione inde inter eosdem CONSTITUTUM EST per eosdem
Barones quod predicte libertates privilegia et ffranchesie ultimo
mencionate per Inhabitantes predictos sic ut prefertur non clamate
in manu dicti Domini Regis capiantur seisiantur et de cetero omnino
extinguantur Ac quod prefati Willelmus Taylor Willelmus Bartholomew Simo Simons Leonardus Mills Thomas Silvester et Iohannes
Hunt et omnes alii Burgenses et Inhabitantes Ville et Burgi Predicti
et eorum successores ab omni usu et clameo utendi Habendi sive

Gaudendi libertates privilegia et ffranchesias predictas ultimo mencionatas et eorum cuiuslibet sive alicuius penitus excludantur et
eorum quilibet excludatur ET QUOAD predictam libertatem
habendam et ad usus predictorum Ballivorum Aldermanni et Burgensium pro tempore existentium convertenda et disponenda bona
et catalla felonorum infra Villam sive Burgum predictum contingentia
et accidentia in placito predicto superius specificatam Idem Attornatus
Domini Regis Generalis pro eodem Domino Rege petit auditum
Litterarum patentium predictarum in placito predicto placitatarum
Et predicti Willelmus Taylor Willelmus Bartholomew Simo Simonds
Leonardus Mills Thomas Silvester et Iohannes Hunt quia ad presens
non habent Litteras patentes predictas paratas hic in Curia petunt
ex gracia Curiae diem sibi dare ad proferendas easdem quod eis per
Curiam hic concessum est et super hoc et proviso quod Curia hic
vult advisare de placito predicto antequam ulterius etc datur dies
hic prefatis Willelmo Willelmo Simoni Leonardo Thome et Iohanni
secundum Statum quo nunc usque octavis Sancti Michaelis ad quem
diem iidem Willelmus Willelmus Simo Leonardus Thomas et Iohannes
venerunt hic ut prius Et Thomas Coventry miles Solicitator dicti
Domini Regis Generalis officium et locum Attornati ipsius Domini
Regis Generalis virtute Litterarum Dicti Domini Regis patentium
sub magno sigillo suo Anglie ei inde confectarum exercens qui pro
eodem Domino Rege nunc in hac parte sequitur presens hic in Curia
ad eundem diem in propria persona sua pro eodem Domino Rege
petit auditum Litterarum patentium predictarum in placito predicto
superius placitatarum ut predictus Attornatus Domini Regis prius
petebat Et ei leguntur in hec verba subscripta.

[*Note.*—Here follows a transcription of the charter of Edward III with
one or two small mistakes: the word *episcopo* between *Andegavie* and
Lincolnensi at the opening of the document is omitted ; *de Boreford et
de Mora* is transcribed *de Bereford de mora* ; and *Ricardo de Humet*, among
the witnesses, is transcribed *Ricardo de huius*.]

Quibus lectis et auditis quoad placitum predictum predictorum
Willelmi Taylor Willelmi Bartholomew Simonis Symons Leonardi
Mills Thome Silvester et Iohannis Hunt superius placitatum quoad
predictam libertatem habendam et ad usus predictorum Ballivorum
Aldermanni et Burgensium pro tempore existentium convertenda et
disponenda omnia bona et catalla felonum infra Villam et Burgum
predictum contingentia et accidentia Idem Solicitator Domini Regis
Generalis protestando non connoscendo aliquid in placito predicto
superius placitato fore verum pro Replicacionis pro eodem Domino

Rege dicit quod placitum predictum predictorum Willelmi Willelmi Simonis Leonardi Thome et Iohannis per ipsos modo et forma predictis superius placitatum ac materia in eodem contenta quoad predicta bona et catalla felonum minus sufficiens in lege existunt ad que ipse pro eodem Domino Rege necesse non habet nec per legem terre tenetur respondere unde obsufficiente eiusdem placiti idem Solicitator Domini Regis Generalis pro eodem Domino Rege petit inde Iudicium ac quod predicti Willelmus Taylor Willelmus Bartholomew Simo Symons Leonardus Mills Thomas Silvester et Iohannes Hunt et alii Inhabitantes ville et Burgi predicti de offenso et usurpacione in Informacione predicta versus eos allegatis quoad bona et catalla felonum convincantur etc Et ulterius quoad libertates privilegia et ffranchesias sequentes vizt. habere tenere et custodire unum mercatum ibidem infram (*sic*) villam et Burgum predictum quolibet die Sabbati in qualibet septimana Ac eciam habere tenere et custodire ibidem infra Villam et Burgum predictum quolibet anno duas ferias annuatim viz. unam earundem feriarum in festo Sancti Iohannis Baptiste et aliam earundem feriarum in die exaltacionis Sancte Crucis communiter vocato Hollyrood day et in mercato et feriis illis habere picagium stallagium et alias Iurisdictiones et privilegia ad Mercatum et ferias spectantes et pertinentes et pro eisdem picagio et stallagio exigere levare et capere ad visus (*sic*) suos proprios diversas denariorum summas de subditis dicti Domini Regis ad mercatum et ferias predictas venientibus et accedentibus ad bona catalla mercimonia et merchandisa sua in mercato et feriis illis vendenda seu vendicioni exponenda . . . etc. etc.

[*Note.*—The ensuing folio is a repetition, in the form of pleas on either side, of the Information and Answer given above, pp. 375–8.]

Et quoad predictam libertatem et privilegium habendi et disponendi bona et catalla felonum unde predicti Willelmus Willelmus Simo Leonardus Thomas et Iohannes superius placitando se posuerunt in mercia Curiae quia Curia vult advisare de Iudicio inde reddendo antequam ulterius etc dies datus est hic eisdem Willelmo Willelmo Simoni Leonardi Thome et Iohanni eodem statu quo nunc usque octavis Sancti Hillari Et quoad separales exitus predictos superius ad priam iunctos prescribitur vicecomiti Oxon predicti quod non omittatur etc Et veniri faciat hic in octavis Sancti Hillari predictis xii liberales et legales homines de Balliva sua de vicineto Ville et Burgi de Burford predicti in comitatu predicto Quorum quilibet etc per quos etc Et qui nec etc ad recognitionem noscendi in premissis Et idem dies similiter datus est hic prefatis Willelmo Willelmo

Simoni Leonardo Thome et Iohanni quoad exitus predictos et quoad
placitum predictorum Willelmi Willelmi Simonis Leonardi Thome et
Iohannis quoad residuas libertates privilegia et ffranchesias predictas
in placito predicto superius mencionatas et per ipsos per placitum
suum predictum modo et forma predictis clamatis quia Curia hic
vult ulterius advisare de placito. predicto quoad easdem libertates
privilegia et ffranchesias residuas etc antequam ulterius etc datus
est dies hic prefatis Willelmo Willelmo Simoni Leonardo Thome et
Iohanni eodem statu quo nunc similiter usque predictis octavis
Sancti Hillarii ad quem diem iidem Willelmus Taylor Willelmus
Bartholomew Simo Symons Leonardus Milles Thomas Silvester et
Iohannes Hunt venerunt hic ut prius Et quoad predictam libertatem
et privilegium habendi et ad usus predictorum Ballivorum Aldermanni et Burgensium Ville et Burgi predicti pro tempore existentium
convertendi et disponendi omnia bona et catalla infra villam et Burgum
predictum contingentia et accidentia visu placito predicto et litteris
patentibus predictis in eodem placito placitatis et ceteris premissis
per Barones hic habitaque matura deliberacione inde inter eosdem
Quia videtur eisdem Baronibus quod placitum predictum ac materia
in eodem contenta minus sufficiens in lege existunt ad manutenendum
clameum predictorum Willelmi Willelmi Simonis Leonardi Thome
et Iohannis habendi et ad usus predictorum Ballivorum Aldermanni
et Burgensium Ville et Burgi predicti convertendi et disponendi
bona et catalla felonum infra Villam et Burgum predictum contingentia et accidentia IDEO CONSTITUTUM EST per eosdem Barones
quod predicti Willelmus Taylor Willelmus Bartholomew Simo Symons
Leonardus Milles Thomas Silvester et Iohannes Hunt usurpacione
super dictum Dominum Regem libertatis et privilegii predicti habendi
et disponendi bona et catalla felonum infra villam et Burgum predictum
contingentia et accidentia modo et forma prout per informacionem
predictam versus eos superius supponitur convincantur Et quod
eadem libertas et privilegium ultime mencionatum in manu dicti
Domini Regis nunc capiantur et seisiantur Et quod Predicti Willelmus
Taylor Willelmus Bartholomew Simo Symons Leonardus Milles
Thomas Silvester et Iohannes Hunt et predicti Ballivi Aldermannus
et Burgenses ville et Burgi predicti pro tempore existentes et eos
(*sic*) alii Inhabitantes ville et Burgi predicti pro tempore existentes
de et in libertate privilegio et ffranchesia illis ultime mencionatis de
cetero nullatenus se intromittant nec eorum aliquis eorum se intromittat sed ab omni usu et clameo habendi sive disponendi bona aut

catalla felonum infra Villam et Burgum predictum contingentia
sive accidentia penitus excludantur et eorum quilibet excludatur
Quodque predicti Willelmus Taylor Willelmus Bartholomew Simo
Symons Leonardus Milles Thomas Silvester et Iohannes Hunt pro
usurpacione libertatis privilegii et ffranchesie predictorum ultime.
mencionatorum suo (sic) dictum Dominum Regem capiantur ubicunque etc ac faciendum finem cum dicto Domino Rege pro usurpacione
predicta etc   Et quoad separales exitus superius iunctos . . . etc.

[*Note.*—The following folio is occupied with the formal entry in the shape
of pleas of the Information and Answer concerning (i) the claim to waifs
and strays, (ii) the election of a Seneschal, (iii) the removal at pleasure
of officials, (iv) the holding of a Borough Court and the taking of its profits,
(v) the making of by-laws and the fining of offenders against them ; also
with the formalities of impanelling the jury and the appointment of Tuesday,
June 5th, following for the trial.]

Et Iurati dicunt super sacramentum suum quod predicti Ballivi
Aldermannus et Burgenses Ville sive Burgi de Burford predicti pro
tempore existentes a toto tempore cuius contrarii memoria hominum
non existit non habuerunt tenerunt et gavisi fuerunt nec per totum
idem tempus habere tenere et uti consueverunt infra predictam villam
sive Burgum de Burford predictum unum mercatum · quolibet die
Sabbati non existente in festo natalis Domino (sic) de qualibet septimana nec infra Villam et Burgum predictum quolibet anno duas ferias
annuatim . . . nec in mercato et feriis . . . habere picagium et stallagium
et alias Iurisdictiones . . .

Et Iurati predicti super sacramentum suum predictum ulterius
dicunt quod predicti Ballivi . . . non habuerunt et receperunt . . . unum
denarium pro exposicione . . .

Et ulterius Iurati predicti super sacramentum suum predictum
dicunt quod predicti Ballivi . . . non habuerunt nec habere consueverunt
tolnetum pro omnibus equis . . .

Et super hoc predictus Attornatus Domini Regis Generalis pro
eodem Domino Rege petit Iudicium set quia Curia vult advisare de
Iudicio suo de et super veredicto predicto reddendo antequam ulterius
etc datus est dies his prefatis Willelmo Willelmo Simoni Leonardo
Thome et Iohanni eodem statu quo nunc usque diem Sabbati 16 diem
predicti mensis Iunii . . . ad quem diem . . . viso veredicto predicto
et ceteris premissis per Barones hic habitaque matura deliberacione
inde inter eosdem CONSTITUTUM EST per eosdem Barones quod
omnia et singula libertates privilegia et ffranchesie illa in manu dicti
Domini Regis capiantur et seisiantur ac quod predicti Willelmus

Taylor Willelmus Bartholomew Simo Symons Leonardus Milles Thomas Silvester et Iohannes Hunt et predicti Ballivi Aldermannus et Burgenses ville et Burgi predicti pro tempore existentes de et in libertatibus privilegiis et ffranchesiis illis de cetero nullatenus se intromittant nec eorum aliquis se intromittat sed ab omni usu et clameo eorundem libertatum privilegiorum et ffranchesiarum et eorum cuiuslibet penitus excludantur et eorum quilibet excludatur Quodque predicti Willelmus Taylor Willelmus Bartholomew Simo Symons Leonardus Milles Thomas Silvester et Iohannes Hunt pro usurpacione libertatum privilegiorum et ffranchesiarum illorum super dictum Dominum Regem capiantur ubicunque etc ad faciendum finem cum dicto Domino Rege pro usurpacione predicta Et quoad residuas libertates privilegia et ffranchesias predictas in placito predictorum Willelmi Willelmi Simonis Leonardi Thome et Iohannis superius mencionato per placitum suum modo et forma predictis clamata viz. habere et tenere et ad usus predictorum Ballivorum Aldermanni et Burgensium pro tempore existentium convertere et disponere omnia bona et catalla waviata et bona et catalla extrahura infra Villam et Burgum predictum contingentia et accidentia et eligere nominare et constituere unum de semetipsis fore Senescallum ville et Burgi predicti ac ad libita sua propria quoscunque officiarios infra Villam et Burgum predictum ab officiis suis amovere necnon habere et tenere infra eandem villam et Burgum unam Curiam vocatam a Burrough Court de tribus septimanis in tres septimanas ac omnia et singula proficua et emolumenta infra curiam predictam crescentia et contingentia ad usus suos proprios capere convertere et disponere et in eadem curia tenere placita quecunque subter summam quadraginta solidorum ac statuta ordinaciones leges et articulos ad libita sua propria infra Villam et Burgum predictum facere ordinare et constituere pro meliore Gubernacione ville et Burgi predicti modo non sunt contraria legibus huius Regni Anglie et super omnes eos qui statutis ordinacionibus legibus constitucionibus et articulis illis obedire negarent seu eadem non observarent fines et amerciamenta eis de causis taxare et imponere et ea ad usus suos proprios levare et convertere predicti Willelmus Taylor Willelmus Bartholomew Simo Symonds Leonardus Milles Thomas Silvester et Iohannes Hunt nihil dicunt in Barram predicte replicacionis predicti Attornati Domini Regis Generalis per ipsum quoad predicta libertates privilegia et ffranchesias ulterius mencionata modo et forma predictis replicate IDEO CONSTITUTUM EST per eosdem Barones quod predicti Willelmus Taylor

Willelmus Bartholomew Simo Simonds Leonardus Milles Thomas
Silvester et Iohannes Hunt de usurpacione super dictum Dominum
Regem predictorum libertatum privilegiorum et ffranchesiarum ultime
mencionatorum modo et forma prout per Informacionem predictam
versus eos superius allegatur convincantur Et quod eadem libertates
privilegia et ffranchesie ultime mencionate in manu Dicti Domini
Regis nunc capiantur et seisiantur Ac quod predicti Willelmus Tayler
Willelmus Bartholomew Simo Simonds Leonardus Milles Thomas
Silvester et Iohannes Hunt et predicti Ballivi Aldermannus et Burgenses Ville et Burgi predicti pro tempore existentes de et in libertatibus privilegiis et ffranchesiis illis ultime mencionatis de cetero nullatenus se intromittant nec eorum aliquis se intromittat sed ab omni usu
et clameo eorundem et eorum cuiuslibet penitus excludantur et eorum
quilibet excludatur Quodque predicti Willelmus Taylor Willelmus
Bartholomew Simo Simons Leonardus Milles Thomas Silvester et
Iohannes Hunt pro usurpacione libertatum privilegiorum et ffranchesiarum predictorum ultime mencionatorum super dictum Dominum
Regem capiantur ubicunque etc ad faciendum finem cum Dicto·
Domino Rege pro usurpacione predicta etc.

20 February, 14 James I, 1617.

Orders made at Oxford by the Commissioners for Charitable Uses
for the County of Oxford, John Doyly, Esquire, Anthony Blincoe,
Chancellor of the Diocese, Rowland Searchfield, D.D., and John
Hawlie, D.C.L.

An inquiry had been held into a gift, bearing date 19 March, 5 James I,
1608, by Leonard Willmott of Clanfield, of various annuities out of
his farm and chief manor and lands at Clanfield to different parishes.
Burford appeared on the list for a gift of £4 a year for relief of poor
inhabitants living by their own labour and not relieved by the Poor
Law.

The inquiry was held in the presence of William Willmott ' who
pretendeth title unto the inheritance ', and had apparently not paid
the sums in question regularly. The Commissioners found that the
sums were to be paid after the death of Leonard Willmott, William
Willmott his brother, and Katharine wife of William Willmott.

Three documents annexed, viz.

i. Evidence of the death of Mr. Wilmott of Clanfield, ' Mr. Holmes,
vicar, sayeth that Mr. Wilmott died the 25th of June 1608 in June
next nine years '.

C C

ii. List of recipients of Willmott's charity in Burford on Good Friday 1617.

iii. ' It is ordered by the Comyssioners appointed for charitable uses whose names are hereunder subscribed That the Towns and Villages hereafter mencioned shall paye unto the bearer Bilson towards the chardges of the Comyssion the Jurye and drawing the decrees and for other chardges theis somes followinge . . . ' (Each place was adjudged to pay the amount of its annual receipt from the charity.)

The following is the list of recipients of the charity in Burford on Good Friday 1617 :

Margaret Daniell widow
Alexander Grynder
William Eve
Peter Lyfolly
Widow Kynborowe
Widow Hewes
Widow Renconde
Widow Greenaway
Thomas Horwood
Anne Evans
John Templer
William Jones
John Read
William Hedges
Widow Elmes
Anne Jenkins
Thomas Haynes
Edward Clarke
Margary Parre
Widow Wisdom
Jone Hiett
Mary Allen
Margery Hiett & daughter
William Wyninge
Widow Gladden
Andrew Hibbard
John Legge
Richard Sowthe
Widow Abram
William Horsman
Richard Levett
Edward Marshall's wife
Widow Poollen
Anne Jacobb
Henry Wylkins
Nicholas Franklen

William Phelpps
Thomas Hayward
Edmund Ryles
John Ludlowe
Thomas Jacobb
Richard Berry
Henry Hill
John Brande
William Haynes
John Baker
John Osmond
Thomas Bayly
Widow Collyns
John Massye
Thomas Prickevance
Anne Smart
Thomas Rowe
John Mare
Christopher Hayward
Thomas Daniell
Widow Leonard
Robert Harper
Thomas Cossom
John Cowper
Widow Clarke's children
John Ympe
Robert Parsons
George Swee
William Joyner
Richard Hiatt
Margett Jones
William Poole
Thomas Smyth
John Mason glover
Mary Warde
Olyver Monday

Edward Carter
Widow Wye's children
Susan Long
Robert Bedall
George Sudeley
Thomas Hughe
Thomas Lovering
Hugh Jones
Thomas Cockerell
Thomas Finche
Simon Walbye
Gryffin Hewes
William Hart
William Nealle
Richard Cowper
Richard Coock ruggemaker
Robert Perry
John Wheeler
Edmund Hynton
Thomas Russbee
John Burford
Thomas Sudeley
Widow Pattrick
Robert Somner
Thomas Graunger
Widow Waller
Edmund Apleton
John Greenaway
Tho. Tuncke's children
Richard Holding
Thomas Bolton
Robert Dallam
Edward Taylor's wife
William Jones Coock
John Greyven
Henry Hayter
William Fowler baker
Widow Cowlinge
Richard Smyth taylor
Humphrey Nunney
Elizabeth Winterley
Widow Gorram
Alice Joyner
Widow Nearle
John Berry
Thomas Ley
John Saunders
William Overbury

Henry Sudeley
Joseph Boyse
William Fairefall
Widow More
Widow Warde
Jone Jollyman
John Symson
Robert Hemynge
Walter Phillipps
Widow Lovett
Thomas Marshall
Wyllyam's children
William Hall
Richard Hewer
Edmund Revett
Widow Day
William Tull
Katharine Whiter
Thomas Pattrick
James Stransford
Jone Greene
Richard Taylor
Edith Holloway
Thomas Dixe
Thomas Elmes
Alex. Warde's wife
Widow Clark
Widow Reade
William Veysey son
John Colborne
Richard Buston
Thomas Bignell
George Halfepeny
John Wynterborne
Symon Smyth
William Foster
Richard Andrewes
Thomas Hewes
William Speeke
Peter Wyrer
Stephen Hincke's wife
George Peisley
William Potter
George Grenehill
Robert Prickyvans
John Wyllyams
John Cripps
Widow Wettmore

Mawrice Waters
Widow Duffen & daughter
Widow Hamlen
John Savage collarmaker
Richard Callire
Thomas Sheaphard
Morgan Powell

Anne Rosen
Elizabeth Launchebery
John Pattrick
John Coock
Mary Potter
Widow Harding
Walter Prickyvans

The sums given vary from 2*d*. to a shilling. The list is signed by William Webbe and William Huntt, Bailiffs; and by John Huntt, William Jurden, Thomas Joyner, and Simon Ward, Churchwardens.

26 November, 1631.

ORDER OF THE COURT OF EXCHEQUER.

Concerning the concealed lands. Recites the arrears as in the Constat (Tolsey Collection, Bundle K, no. 3) and records that Mr. Lenthall, being of counsel with the feoffees for the poor claimed that the lands were not concealed, but were heretofore given for the poor and were so administered as by the Decrees of the Royal Commission of 1628, and that the title to the lands was not claimed under the transaction with Typper and Dawe. It was ordered that, if the title were not so claimed, and if affidavit were made to that effect, the tenants and occupiers should be discharged of the arrears, the Crown auditor having laid his claim on the Typper and Dawe grant. William Bartholomew, one of the Burgesses, having made the necessary affidavit (Tolsey Collection, Bundle K, no. 2), the Court discharged the tenants and occupiers of the lands, and laid the arrears on Typper and Dawe their executors and assigns.

5 February, 1640.

Deposition by Leonard Yate in the Court of Exchequer with regard to charges in the Ministers' Accounts for £18 13*s*. 4*d*. for arrears of a rent of 13*s*. 4*d*. issuing out of a tenement in Burford in the tenure of Thomas Heminge, given for an obitt, and £9 upon the occupiers of another tenement called the Bull in the tenure of John Cooke, given for an obitt.

That £18 13*s*. 4*d*. had been paid to Sir Lawrence Tanfield and Dame Elizabeth Tanfield his wife for the period between Michaelmas 1611 and May 1627. The Court ordered that the Lord Falkland, as executor of the Tanfields, should be given a week to show cause why he should not pay this sum, the tenants and occupiers to pay the other sum in arrear.

Michaelmas Term, 20 Charles I (1644).

ORDER OF THE COURT OF EXCHEQUER.

The order demands payment of a sum of £18 13s. 4d. charged in the Ministers' Accounts for the county of Oxon, being arrears of the following rents due to the Crown :

A rent of 13s. 4d. a year from a tenement late in the tenure of Thomas Hemminge heretofore given for the maintenance of an obit, now in arrear for 18 years ended Michaelmas 14 Charles I (1638) and charged upon Robert Serrill, Thomas Silvester, William Hunt, William Bartholomew, John Ward, and Robert Jordan ;

A rent of 10s. a year upon the tenants and occupiers of a tenement called the Bull, now in the tenure of John Cooke, also given to maintain an obit, now in arrear for the same period as the foregoing.

The parties named pleaded at the Court that they, in trust for the Church of Burford, by the Statute of Charitable Uses, had paid the greatest part of these rents to Sir Lawrence Tanfeild, late lord of the manor, and after his death to Dame Elizabeth Tanfeild his executrix, now deceased, and after her death to Lucius Lord Viscount Falkland, her executor and owner of the manor ; and that they held the remaining portion of the arrears in their hands and were ready to pay the same.

The present order gives them time to look up their acquittances and notes of the transactions.

Lent Assizes, 1651.

Presentation by the Jurors to the Keepers of the Liberty of England concerning the ruinous condition of that part of Burford Bridge lying in the parish of Fulbrook, and asserting the duty of the parish of Fulbrook to repair that portion.

1686.

AFFIDAVIT by William Rogers of Burford, clothier,

That the ancient custom for the appointment of Bailiffs of Burford was for four persons to be nominated by the former Bailiffs and the Burgesses and presented to the Steward at the Court Leet within a month from Michaelmas in each year for the appointment of two out of the four to be Bailiffs for the ensuing twelve months :

that no Court Leet was held within a month from the Michaelmas last past :

that at a Court Leet held on November 2 four persons, viz. John Price, Thomas Silvester, John Haynes, and John Castle, were presented to the Steward, John Jordan, but that he appointed only one of them, John Haynes, and appointed to act with him John Payton :

that there were certain stocks of money and trust funds administered by the Bailiffs and therefore it was essential that they should be elected in the ancient manner.

AN OPINION of Counsel, Judge Levinz, on a case concerning the above, submitted by the Countess of Abercorn. A Mandamus had been taken out. The contention of the Lady of the Manor was that the presentation of four persons by the Bailiffs and Burgesses was only a survival from days when the Steward was a ' stranger ' and ignorant of suitable persons to appoint, and did not remain good when the Steward was acquainted with the town.

18 February, 6 Anne (1708).

WARRANT addressed to John Sindrey and Henry Peacock.

John Sindrey, of Bedford, merchant, is ordered to pay the sum of £20 bequeathed by his grandfather in 1660, which had not been paid either by his widow or by his son.

Henry Peacock, executor of the will of Henry Heyling, gentleman, of Minster Lovell, is ordered to pay the sum of £200 given by that will.

The money to be paid at Burford on 25 June next.

Note.—This warrant gives the names of the Commissioners who held the inquiry at Witney in 1702. They were Sir Robert Jenkinson, Sir Edmund Warcupp, Manwaryng Hamond, D.D., Henry Cole, Daniel Warwick, Matthew Prior, Thomas Abell, and Nicholas Marshall.

COMMISSIONS AND LEGAL PROCEEDINGS. II AND III

EIGHTEENTH CENTURY

Cheatle Collection, Bundles NN and OO

1. 7 June, 1 George II, 1728.

Indenture of Agreement between Richard Whitehall and James Partridge, Bailiffs, Charles Perrott, Alderman, George Hart, Chamberlain, William Bowles, Robert Taylor, Matthew Underwood, Paul Silvester, John Green, and Daniel Dicks, Burgesses, of the one part, and Richard Griffiths of the other part.

The Agreement sets forth that the Lords of the Manor had by pretence of a judgement in the Court of Exchequer seized upon the profits of the markets. A judgement had been obtained against the Bailiffs and Burgesses in their private capacity. No Execution of the judgement was ever taken, and the Burgesses' franchises had not been seized into the hands of the Crown. But the Lord of the Manor had used the judgement to intimidate the Bailiffs and Burgesses, in order to possess himself of the franchises.

The Bailiffs had been advised to sue out a writ of error to reverse the judgement. The rents of Poole's Lands were held on such terms as to admit of their being used for such purposes (the protection of the town's franchises), but they only produced clear £25 a year.

The present Agreement therefore is to the effect that Richard Griffiths is to receive this £25 a year in trust, and also, if necessary, a sum of £10 a' piece from the other parties to the Agreement, and an attempt is to be made to mortgage Poole's Lands for raising the moneys needed to proceed at once.

Witnesses : William Perrott, George Hart junior.

2. Two pieces of paper containing notes as to the ancient franchises of Burford, dated 1727, and evidently connected with the project outlined in the above Agreement.

3. THE ROYAL COMMISSION OF 1738

Not dated.

Verdict and Decrees of the Royal Commission of 1738.

i. William Lenthall's will. This had bestowed a sum of £50 to be added to £150 given to the town in his lifetime, the money to be lent out to poor tradesmen. He died in 1662.

The Commission found that the will was not proved till 1695. £100 of the whole sum had been put out on the security of land at Standlake and interest of £5 a year had been paid. The other £100 remained in the hands of the Bailiffs and Burgesses and no part of the money had ever been lent to poor tradesmen.

ii. Lady Tanfield's bequest of a house in Sheep Street of the yearly value of £4 for keeping the Tanfield tomb and aisle clean and in repair, 20s. of the money to be paid to a supervisor to see that this was properly done. Also a gift of £40 to bind poor lads apprentice at £10 each, the sum to be returned by the master at the end of the apprenticeship. Lady Tanfield died in 1628.

The Commission found that only £2 2s. 6d. had ever been spent on the care of the tomb, which was then in such disrepair that it would cost £36 9s. 2d. to put it in proper condition. The rent of the house had nevertheless been received by the Bailiffs all the time. None of the sum of £40 had ever been used to bind apprentices.

iii. Richard Hayter's charity, 1666 ; a sum of 8s. a year out of a house called Riches College on west side of the High Street, then occupied by John Robins, and a sum of 4s. a year out of a house adjoining then occupied by Thomas Miles ; the former sum to be given to 8 of the almspeople and the latter sum to 4 poor widows.

The Commission found that this charity had been regularly administered.

Also a sum of 6s. 8d., interest on a sum of 20 nobles (£6 13s. 4d.), the capital to be lent out and the interest paid to a Minister for a sermon on New Year's Day.

The Commission found that this also had been regularly carried out as regards the interest although no one had ever applied for the loan of the principal.

iv. John Harris's will (see W 13, p. 369).

The Commission found that the £100 to be lent to tradesmen had been administered properly except that the churchwardens had not been associated with the management of it. The second £100 for binding apprentices had been lent out, £50 to Alexander Ready and £50 to Richard Winsmore on his note of hand alone, and he dying insolvent the sum had been lost. One of the Burgesses to whom the note of hand was made out was a churchwarden, and should, the Commission held, have been more careful. The Corporation had themselves kept up the interest of £5 a year on the lost sum.

v. Alexander Ready's gift, 1616 (see W 10, p. 368).

The Commission found that a sum of £13 6s. 8d. had been lent to John Price, when Bailiff, and had been lost by his failure. The Minister had received no part of the 8s. bestowed on him by the will, and the charity had been administered at the Town Hall instead of at the Church as directed by the will.

vi. Cobb Hall.

The Commission had no comment to make, except that the premises were worth more than the existing rent of £13 a year. They put on record that Joseph Flexney had spent upon repairs more than was actually necessary.

vii. Gift of James Frotham, 1663, of a sum of 40s. a year from lands in Langford and Grafton, to be given to a maid-servant of six years' service, or failing that to be used to put out a boy or girl of Burford to service.

The Commission found that there was no complaint to be made, except that six years previously one of the Bailiffs, in bestowing the money, insisted that the recipient, a servant named Eliza Horne, should spend at his shop 20s. on things she did not want.

viii. Gift of Walwin Hopton of £50 to be lent to tradesmen in sums of £10.

The Commission found that the charity had been administered, but the accounts had not been read out in Church as they should have been.

ix. The School.

The Commission found that since 1717, when Richard Griffiths became schoolmaster, no usher had been appointed, the ' petties ' (junior boys) had not been taught their A B C ; no scholars had been registered. Griffiths had received all the rents, including that part which should have gone to the payment of an usher. The schoolmaster had not been elected annually, as Simon Wisdom's constitutions ordered.

x. Poole's Lands and Church Lands.

The Commission seemed chiefly occupied to prove that the 22 acres of arable land belonged to the Church, and maintained that this was proved by the Corporation and Church books from 1600 to 1689, and by a terrier of Church Lands deposited with the Bishop of Oxford about 1635 by the churchwardens ; also by the book drawn up by Symon Symons in 1600.

xi. Gift by Henry Heylin of £200.

The Commission found this duly administered.

xii. The Commission found that £30 of the gift of £40 by Lady Tanfield had been laid out in the purchase of a house in Mollynder's Lane, and the rent had been used for binding apprentices, but not according to the will.

xiii. Robert Veysey's gift of £20, the interest to be given to 12 poor widows.

In 1705 the Bailiffs' books display £10 laid out in church repairs at interest, but no such payment appears in the churchwardens' books. Three or four widows, the Commission found, had received some money in sums of 2s. 6d. at a time. There had been no other payments between 1704 and 1727. Between 1727 and 1736 the whole interest had been disposed of according to the will, except that the churchwardens had not been consulted.

xiv. Gift by Thomas Collyer, 25 October, 16 Charles II (1664), of £2 12s., the interest to be laid out by the Bailiffs in bread for distribution to the poor.

The Commission found that this had been administered, but the overseers of the will had not been properly consulted.

xv. Gift by Robert Gilkes of Burford of £10, to be lent out.

The Commission had no complaint to make.

xvi. Willmott's charity (see p. 385).

The Commission found that this had been administered, but not strictly, and no account had been delivered.

xvii. Edmund Harman's charity (see W 4, p. 367).

The Commission had no complaint to make.

xviii. Gift by John Castle, 1720, of 10s. a year out of a close in Bampton for a yearly sermon on Good Friday.

The Commission had no complaint to make.

xix. Gift by John Lloyd of 6s. 8d. (see W 7, p. 368).

The Commission had no comment to make except that an additional sum of 3s. 4d. promised by the son of John Lloyd had never been paid.

xx. Gift by Ambrose Aston, 1722, of a messuage producing £3 a year, to be used for apprenticing poor boys.

The Commission found that this had been done up to 1724. Then a year had been missed. From 1724 to 1738 the rents had been received by John Jordan, and £25 had been paid out ; the remainder he held ready to apprentice a boy when required.

xxi. Castle's Charity, 1726, of four houses in Gildenford Lane lying together, called Castle's Yard, to house four poor widows, and two messuages in Witney Street, and his garden, and two other houses in Gildenford Lane for maintenance of the widows.

The Commission found that this had been properly administered.

xxii. Gift by John Palmer of Bampton of £50, the interest to be given to the poor.

The Commission found that the money had been laid out in buying four houses in Mullender's Lane and the interest had been properly used.

xxiii. All Sorts of Money. Under this head came the following gifts : Timothy Stampe, £40 ; George Thomson, £30 (£20 of which had been lost) ; Alexander Ready, £40 ; William Edgeley, £10 ; Philip Mariner, £20 ; Edmund Silvester, £20 ; Attwell, 30s. ; Ralph

Willett's cow sold for 30s., made up to 40s. by Simon Wisdom, Reynolds, and Simon Symons. The total was given as £173 10s.

The Commission found that £29 16s. 8d. had been lost by being lent to John Price, who was one of the Corporation at the time. By the inquiry of 1702 the whole sum under the head of All Sorts of Money was ordered to be lent out in sums of £10 at a time, to be paid back by 20s. a year without interest. £125 was now out on 22 bonds.

xxiv. Gift by Elizabeth Meady of 17 acres to the overseers of her will; apparently invalidated by her failing to mention the heirs of these overseers.

xxv. Gift by John Hillary of £200, the interest to be laid out in bread for the poor.

The Commission found that £100 had been laid out in the purchase of land at Standlake and the interest properly used except in 1737, when George Hunt received the interest and had not accounted for it.

xxvi. Cleveley's Charity.

The Commission found this duly administered.

xxvii. The Almshouse and capital messuage adjoining.

The Commission found that the Corporation had spent between 1702 and 1738 a sum of £61 odd more than they had received. It did not appear to the Commissioners that the Corporation had any right to appoint widows to the Almshouses or to spend money on repairs.

Various minor points were also dealt with. The Church authorities complained that the Corporation had let a house belonging to the Church to William Bowles, one of their number; he had done no repairs, and after he left the house the Corporation put in an unskilful carpenter, so that it ultimately cost the Church £52 1s. 11d. to put the house in good condition.

A complaint was made that the Bailiffs had taken the rents of the houses of the Bridge instead of the trustees. Mr. Underwood was said to have received money for repairs to the bridge, but had not repaired it. By decree of the Commission of 1702 the Corporation should have received £2 10s. a year out of the Bridge Lands for repayment of a sum of £60 spent by them on the bridge. It did not appear to the Commission that they ever received this sum.

There was also an accusation of fresh entries having been made in the Corporation books after complaints had been made by Mr. Lenthall of the administration of the Lenthall charity.

THE JUDGEMENT OF THE COMMISSION was as follows :

Lenthall's Charity : The Bailiffs and Burgesses were ordered to refund the £100 spent in buying land, with £5 interest, and to produce within a twelvemonth the other sum of £100. They were also ordered to pay £135 damages, partly to Mr. Lenthall for their misuse of the money, and partly for the expenses of the Commission.

Lady Tanfield's Bequest : The Bailiffs and Burgesses were ordered to pay the sum of £38 9s. 2d. required for the repair of the Tanfield Chapel, and to pay £10 damages towards the costs. In future the sum of £40 was to be administered by the Minister, the churchwardens, and the Bailiffs.

John Harris's Bequest : The Bailiffs and Burgesses were to recover the £50 lent to Alexander Ready, to refund the £50 lost by Winsmore, and to pay £10 damages towards the costs.

Alexander Ready's Bequest : The Bailiffs and Burgesses were to produce the full sum of £40, refunding the sum of £13 6s. 8d. lost by John Price, and in future the Minister was to be summoned to share in the distribution.

Cobb Hall : Flexney's present lease was to be void and cancelled, a new lease being offered to him at a higher rent. The Bailiffs and Burgesses were to pay £20 damages towards the costs.

Frotham's Bequest : Matthew Underwood, the individual who had taken the 20s. from the servant girl, was to pay 40s. damages towards the costs.

The School : The rents, which in 1688 had been fixed at £21 12s. 8d., were now found to be £52 10s. An usher was ordered to be appointed at £13 a year out of these rents. Richard Griffiths was to pay £30 damages towards the costs. There being now no Alderman or Steward, the School wardens were to be supervised by the trustees, the Minister, the Bailiffs, the churchwardens, and the overseers of the poor, and these officers were to elect the schoolmaster.

Poole's Lands : The rents, after allowing for the payment of £2 12s. a year to the poor, were found to amount to £25 18s. Half of this sum was to be paid in future to the Vicar, the Vicarage, exclusive of Fulbrook, being of the value of only £6 a year. The Bailiffs and Burgesses were to pay £20 damages towards the costs.

All Sorts of Money : The Bailiffs and Burgesses were to refund the lost sum of £29 16s. 8d., and to pay £15 11s. 7½d. due to the Church. In general for the future these moneys were to be administered by the Bailiffs and the churchwardens, and not as hitherto by the Bailiffs alone or by the Bailiffs and Burgesses.

Bowles's House : The Bailiffs and Burgesses were to refund to the Church the sum of £52 1s. 11d. spent in repairs and to pay £10 damages towards the costs.

Bridge Lands : It was adjudged that the sum due to the Corporation had been paid though not entered on the Corporation books.* The Bailiffs were to pay £2 8s. 7d. due on the Bridge Account.

The Almshouse : In future the widows were to be appointed by the trustees.

The petitioners and defendants were to share the cost of entertaining the jury and paying the clerk, John Martin (the defendants, the Bailiffs and Burgesses, said they would refuse to bear a share of this cost).

Since the Bailiffs and Burgesses, by taking to themselves the sole management of the charities, had rendered this inquiry necessary, and since they had done everything in their power to delay it, they were adjudged to pay £163 damages over and above those already specified.

The following new trustees were appointed by the Commission : Sir Thomas Read of Shipton, Sir George Fettiplace, Sir John Dutton, William Lenthall, Esquire, Robert Stevens of Kelmscott, William Wanly the younger of Ayford, Francis Potter of Burford, clerk, Thomas Godfrey of Milton, gentleman, Henry Walker, maltster, Thomas Hunt, ironmonger, Robert Castle, mercer, Samuel Patrick junior, clothier, Thomas Clare, innholder, William Lawrence, maltster, James Faulkner, yeoman, and Richard Willett, joiner—all of Burford.

It was ordered that in future, when leases of town lands were within twelve months of determining, notice of the same was to be given in church.

The document is signed :

Harcourt	Tho. Martin	Tho. Snell
John Cope	Sam. Adams	Jno. Goodenough
H. Pye	John Coxwell	Jam. Chaunler
Henry Beeston		

4. Another copy of part of the same inquiry, but containing the Decrees alone without the recital of the charities.

5. A bundle of correspondence concerning the Royal Commission of 1738, especially concerning the attitude it would be wise for the

Corporation to take and the degree to which they should recognize the authority of the Commission. The Corporation were evidently in the dark as to the manner in which Mr. Lenthall was proceeding and the charges that would be alleged against them as a ground for the issue of the Commission.

6. A bundle of portions of Bailiffs' Accounts for various years between 1698 and 1734, possibly produced before the Royal Commission of 1738.

7. A copy of counsel's opinion, dated 1732, with regard to Cleaveley's Charity, a difficulty having arisen in connexion with the new appointment of new Trustees.

8. 9 May, 16 George II (1743).

Copy of the judgement in the Court of Chancery in the case Bailiffs and Burgesses of Burford exceptants *v.* Lenthall and others respondents.

The judgement will be found in full among the documents of the Tolsey Collection (*infra*, p. 486).

9 and **10.** Two small quarto volumes (damaged by damp) containing copies of the judgement, exactly similar to the volumes in the Tolsey Collection (see p. 486).

11. Copy of the petition of the Corporation to the Court of Chancery concerning the Royal Commission of 1738, and also some fragments of the depositions of witnesses in the suit of 1742–3.

12. A bundle of bills of the costs of the Corporation in the suit of 1742–3.

13. 29 November, 16 George II (1742).

Writ to Mr. Ingles, solicitor to the Corporation, ordering him to produce his books, &c., before the Master in Chancery to have his costs taxed, and also for examination as to payments on account alleged to have been made by the exceptants in the suit of 1742–3.

14. A portion (folios 1 to 30) of the pleadings in the suit of 1742–3.

Folios 1 to 4: Lenthall's bequest. Exceptants' case was that there was no evidence of deliberate misapplication of the money. Respondents' case was that there was such evidence, the copy of the will had been lost or concealed by the exceptants, and accounts not properly kept.

Folios 4 to 8: Tanfield Bequest. Exceptants' case was that the money had been properly applied. Respondents' case that the money had been received, but no work had been done on the tomb or aisle

The exceptants replied that they only had the management of the trust because the Trustees appointed by the donor had neglected their trust.

Folios 20 and 21 (*sic*) : Harris's Charity. Exceptants' case was that the Commission had no power to condemn them in costs, and that the loans improperly made were not so made by the whole Corporation. Respondents' case was that this could not be maintained, and they alleged that the books of accounts had been altered by the exceptants to bolster up their plea.

Folios 13 to 19 : Cobb Hall. Exceptants' case was that they had let the premises to the best of their ability, and that the Commission had no power to condemn them in costs. A considerable mass of depositions as to the letting of the premises and the repairs done on them.

Folio 22 : Fretham's Charity. Underwood pleaded that the Commission had no power to order him to refund the 40s.

Folios 22 to 30 : The Grammar School. Exceptants' case was that the Commission had no power to alter the constitutions of the School. Griffiths pleaded that he was not summoned by the Commission which therefore could not order him to pay damages. Respondents' case was that the constitutions had already· been altered by the Commission of 1628 and could therefore be altered again. As for Griffiths he ' did privately withdraw himself from Burford and conceal himself in London until after the Return or Close of the said Commission ', and the damages against him were reasonable.

Note.—The above document is not exactly the missing portion of the pleadings in the Tolsey Collection, *infra*, p. 509. The handwriting is different, and in this copy the pleadings with regard to the School run to folio 30 whereas in the Tolsey copy they end on folio 28. Probably one is a portion of the copy on the Respondents' side and the other a portion of that on the Exceptants' side. However, practically one is a complement of the other, and we have the pleadings almost complete.

With this copy in the Cheatle Collection is one folio (22) of the other copy—part of the pleadings with regard to the School.

15. A few fragmentary documents connected with the lawsuit, including a copy of depositions by Richard Griffiths's son and his sister-in-law concerning his mental weakness and his departure to Oxford to the care of a physician.

16. A copy of Counsel's opinion dated 20 September 1790, concerning the responsibility for repairing the Bridge.

MISCELLANEA. I

1397 TO 1741

Cheatle Collection, Bundle PP

1. Michaelmas Term, 21 Richard II (1397).

Copy of a fine between William Rosen of Fifhide plaintiff and John Cardygan and Alice his wife deforciants, for three messuages with appurtenances in Boreford. For 20 marks of silver.

2. 23 August, 12 Edward IV (1472).

Conveyance by John Mosier of Burford, to John Pynnock junior, John Granger, and William Hill. All his lands, tenements, meadows, and pastures, with all appurtenances, which he had in the town and fields of Burford and Kenkeham by bequest of his father John Mosier.

Witnesses: Henry Byschop, John Banbury, John Grove, Henry Stodham, John Boterell.

3. 1566.

Certificate of grant of the Common Seal at the Herald's Visitation.

The Seal was presented for confirmation by John Hannes and Rycharde Charley, Bailiffs, Symond Wysedom, Alderman, Edmunde Sylvester, Steward, Robert Bruweton, John FFlude, John Smythe the elder, Thomas Freere, Thomas Fetyplace, Rycharde Dalbye, and Walter Mollyner, Burgesses and late Bailiffs, and Henry Parrott, Town Clerk.

The certificate is signed by Will: Hervy, Clarencieux King of Arms.

Note.—The arms of the town are tricked at the head of 'the certificate; the lion is represented gardant to the dexter.

4. 14 January, 23 Elizabeth (1581).

Lease by Simon Wisdom, Alderman of the Borough of Burford, John Hannes, Steward of the Fellowship and Corporation, by and with the consent of John Lyme and John Williams, Bailiffs, and with the assent and agreement of all their brethren the Burgesses, to Richard Dalby of Upton in the parish of Burford and one of the Brotherhood of the borough. A shop lying and adjoining to the Tolsey of Burford, next unto Sheep Street, now in the tenure of Thomas Parsons. For 21 years at 5s. a year.

Witnesses: John Lyme, John Williams, Bailiffs; Thomas Phettyplace, Walter Mollynder, William Symondes, William Partridge, Thomas Hewis.

Endorsed: ' A lease of part of the Towlsey.'

5. 25 September, 18 James I (1620).

Letter from the Mayor and Commonalty of the City of Oxford to the Bailiffs, Alderman, and Burgesses of Burford.

Wee have receyved from you an instrument in writinge under your Common Seale purportinge your request to bee certified under our Common Seale touchinge our havinge and enjoyinge of waiefes, estraies, felons goods, pickadge, stallage and tallage For that amongst things it is by Diverse charters expressly graunted unto the Burgesses of Burford as yee relate that they and the Citizens of Oxon shalbee of one and the selfe-same lawe libertie and custome And further that the saied Burgesses of Burford shall in case of Doubte or question send unto the Cittie of Oxon to bee certified therein Now therefore for your satisfaccon on that behalfe and accordinge to our laudable custome of receyvinge certificates from London whereunto wee are in like manner referred and of advertisinge other places referred to us These are to lett you knowe that wee have and enjoy by auntient charters within our saied Cittie and the liberties thereof as part of that wee hould by fee farme and for which wee pay the same both waiefes estraies fellons goods pickadge stallage and diverse tolles.

6. 12 Charles I, 1637.

Two copies of a fine by William Bartholomew and Thomas Silvester for the purchase from Simon Veysey and Anne his wife and Robert Veysey and Anne his wife of three messuages and gardens in Burford. For £100.

Cf. S 51, Bundle CC.

7. 19 June, 14 Charles I (1638).

Lease by John Wheeler of Woolhope, com. Hereford, and Elizabeth his wife and Robert Lane of Ewis Harold in the same county and Elizabeth his wife, to Roger Bosworth of Woolhope, gentleman. A house and croft called Yeoman's Croft in Woolhope.

8. 27 May, 5 James I (1607).

Indenture of sale by John Hannes of Burford, yeoman, and Richard Hannes his son and heir, to Richard Merywether, yeoman, Alderman of the town. For £280.

Capital messuage or tenement on east side of the High Street over against the high cross there, known by the name of the Bull, now in occupation of John Silvester, innholder, abutting upon the High Street to the west, the tenement of Edmond Silvester the elder now occupied by Robert Jurdan, garden and back-sides of the tenements occupied by Edmond Serrell and Andrew Ward, and various tenements in Witney Street and Witney Street itself to the north; the back lane commonly called Batts Lane to the east; and the tenement and back-side of William Bartholomew, sometime part of the lands of Symon Wisdom, deceased, to the south.

Also a small close containing by estimation three acres commonly called the Long Bushy Close near the east end of the common lot meadow called High Mead, adjoining to the south side of the same mead, occupied by John Silvester.

Also an acre in the common lot mead occupied by John Silvester.

Also 63 acres in the common fields of Burford and Signett occupied by John Silvester. Excepting two butts of arable land containing by estimation two acres near to the High Mead gate in the East Field of Burford, adjoining to the spring or water running out of the bankside into the highway on the west and the lands of Richard Hodges to the east.

Also one acre of arable in the West Field in the fern furlong adjoining to the acre belonging to the Bull on the west and copyhold land late of John Gyvons deceased on the east.

Also an acre of arable in West Field shooting to the way from Burford to Signett, commonly called Dyne Acre way on the west side of the way and lying to the copyhold lands of John Hannes to the north and the land of Sir Lawrence Tanfield to the south; which two acres belong to John Hannes' now dwelling house and are sold in lieu of the two butts of land previously reserved.

Also an inclosed piece of pasture ground or Leynes about one acre stretching to the highway leading toward Upton and lying to the arable field there towards the west and ley ground or lands of Richard Merywether to the east, which piece of Leynes was sold by John Hannes and his father to Simon Wisdome deceased and was lately sold by one Hughe Maye, gentleman, to Richard Merywether. Also all the goods and chattels expressed in the schedule.

The Schedule:

Imprimis in the soler one table bord with a joyned bench to the same borde

Item in the same soler one other bench with a backe of wenscott to the same adjoyning one barre of Iron in the chymney and glasse in the windowes

Item one oriall in the soler chamber with glasse in the windowes

Item in the halle one benche a backe of wenscott at the upper borde
a barre of Iron in the chimney with glasse in the windowes

Item in the chambers the glasse in the windowes

Item in the kitchin the dresser bord with shylves and an Iron barre
in the chymney

Item all the goods and ymplements of houshold of the said John
Hannes and Richard Hannes his son remayning in or about the
messuage or tenement called the Bull

Witnesses : H. Heylyn, Ambrose Davis, Edw. Heylyn, Anthony
Rowles, Thomas Hardinge.

9. 25 February, 1651.

Deed of Exchange between Anne Atkinson of Chadlington, widow,
wife of Richard Osbaldeston late of Burford deceased ; Robert
Taylor, baker, and Anne his wife ; William Windowe of Gloucester,
gentleman, and Grace his wife ; John Smyth of Chadlington, carpenter,
and Frances his wife—three of the daughters and co-heirs of Richard
Osbaldeston, of the one part, and Edward Smyth of Chadlington tailor,
and Judith his wife, one other daughter and co-heir, of the other part.

By this deed the latter parties gave up all claim to a house on east
side of the High Street in Burford, occupied by John Jordan, and
a close of pasture occupied by John Woodward ; and the former in
return gave up all claim to a house in Witney Street between a tenement of Symon Hayter on east and a tenement and back-gate of John
Taylor on west.

10. 15 January 1655, 26 October 1659, and 1 November 1659.

Conveyances of property at Alvescott, consisting of the great close
called Great Ruxell, of 100 acres ; a ground called the Barn Ruxell ;
and a house ('new built' in the 1659 deeds) on one of the three closes
into which the Great Ruxell was divided ; all being part of the demesne
lands of the manor of Alvescott.

The Property was conveyed in 1655 to John Bicknell of Holwell,
yeoman, by Charles Trinder the elder of Holwell, John Trinder,
gentleman, his son and heir, Charles Trinder, and Richard Sackeville
of Bybury, Esquire. In 1659 it was conveyed by Charles Trinder of
Holwell, gentleman, one of the sons of Charles Trinder the elder,
deceased, John Bicknell of Yanworth, yeoman, and Charles Cooke of
Holwell, yeoman, to Nathaniel Brookes of Holwell.

11. 14 December, 22 Charles II, 1670.

Certificate by Sir Robert Long, Bart., Edward Fauconberge, and

John Lowe, gentlemen, officers under the Lords Commissioners of the Treasury and the Chamberlains of the Treasury.

One measure of brass containing one. bushel sized and seased by His Majesty's measure and standard kept in the Receipt of the Exchequer, by Thomas Taylor, citizen and founder of London, for and on behalf of the Bailiffs and Burgesses of Burford.

The seal of the office of Receipt of the Exchequer attached.

12. 1706.

Settlement by John Jordan senior on the marriage of his son John Jordan with Mary Coo of Sutton under Brailes, Gloucestershire, of the following property :

House now in occupation of John Jordan senior on east side of High Street between a house in the occupation of Richard Haynes on north and a house occupied by Mary Fox, widow, on south, with a carriage-way leading from the back-gate into Witney Street ;

House occupied by Daniel Dumbleton on east side of High Street between a house called the Bull, occupied by William Tash, on north and a tenement of Ann Harding, widow, on south ;

House occupied by Robert Smith on west side of High Street between a house of Amos Saintsbury occupied by Richard Freeman on north and a tenement called the Mermaid occupied by Joseph Overbury on south ;

House occupied by Joseph Payton on north side of Witney Street between Richard Wallington on east and John Randolph. on west ;

House on north side of Sheep Street occupied by William Partridge, between three barns on east and the house of Edward . . . (illegible) on west ;

These three barns and the ground on which a fourth stood, with an orchard and back-side adjoining ;

Two closes commonly called the Barley Closes on east side of Burford, and a close called the Lanes on west side of Burford, extending from the arable fields there on the south to the highway from Burford to Upton on the north ;

One and a half acres of meadow in the Common lot meadow ;

One acre of meadow in Upton near the river shooting upon Little Barrington fields ;

One parcel of arable land near Whitehill, now enclosed, of about 7 acres ;

All arable lands in the fields of Burford, of about 140 acres ;

Other lands in East field amounting to 21½ acres, and in West field 8½ half-yard-lands ;

Two closes in a lane on the east of Burford, one next the Barley Closes on east and one next Bear Close on west ; ·

One hamme or ground next the Water Crooke near to High Meadow towards the east and the high . . . (illegible) towards the west ;

All which are accounted four half-yard-lands, lately called Highlords Land.

13. 23 December, 8 Anne, 1709.
Deeds of Sale by Thomas Parsons of Burford, innholder, son and heir of Thomas Parsons, late of Burford, chandler, to John Jordan the younger, gentleman.   Close of pasture called the Bear Close, of two acres, in Batts Lane. For £65.

Included with this—formal lease of this close for a year at 5s.

Witnesses : Ralph Syndrey, John Coburn senior, John Coburn junior.

Also a fine, dated morrow of the Trinity, 10 Anne, between Richard Hall and John Baston and Susanna his wife, for a house, a garden, and orchard, ten acres of land and a pasture in Bampton and Aston. For £60 sterling.

The whole endorsed : ' My purchase deeds of the Beare Close I Purchased from Parsons in Burford.'

14. 12 William III (1700).
Exemplification of a Recovery of a house in New Woodstock, the proceedings being between William Batt and John Moulden.

15. 2 March, 11 Anne, 1713.
Deed of Exchange between John Lenthall, Esquire, and Paul Silvester, tanner.

The former gave up an end of a half-acre of arable lying in Battledge Field late of John Jordan, land of Mr. Silvester's on both sides ; and one acre in the same field between land of John Jordan on the east and land of Dr. Castle on the west.

The latter gave up one acre and two half-acre ends on the lower side of Battledge Field, land late of Peter Rich and now of John Lenthall on both sides.

Witnesses : John Jordan junior, Robert Collins, Ralph Wall.

16. 19 December, 15 George II, 1741.
Lease by Thomas, Lord Bishop of Oxford, to Elizabeth Pryor of Burford, widow of John Pryor, and administratrix of the will of

Matthew Pryor of Ducklington. The Rectory and Parish Church of Burford, the chapel of Fulbrook, the advowson of the Church, and the Vicarage, worth by estimation £80 a year. For the lives of William Collier of the parish of St. Mary Magdalen, Bermondsey, tallow chandler, son of Robert Collier, late of Witney, clothier; and John Pryor of Shipton-under-Wychwood, gentleman, son of Elizabeth Pryor; and Elizabeth Clarke Pryor, daughter of the said John Pryor the elder; and the life of the longest-lived of them; subject to trusts in the will of John Pryor and the will of Matthew Pryor. For an annual rent of £20.

The Bishop's attorneys for delivery of possession were Paul Silvester and William Jordan, schoolmaster.

Witnesses : Francis Potter, William Jordan.

Endorsed : ' Lives William Collier, John Pryor son of the lessee, and Elizabeth Clarke Pryor daughter of the said John who died 1772. After this the lives were

Mr. Nichols	i
then Mr. Jones	ii
then Mr. Caswell and Mr. Hayward	iii
then Mrs. H. Deane	iv.'

MISCELLANEA. II

Eighteenth and Nineteenth Centuries

Cheatle Collection, Bundle RR

1. 12 October, 1734.

Lease by George Hart and others, to William Taylor of Burford, gardener. A house and garden ground on the north side of Witney Street between the tenement of James Taynton on the east and that of William Hayeley on the west. For 21 years at £5 a year.

2. 19 October, 27 George II, 1753.

Lease by Paul Silvester and John Green, Bailiffs, Daniel Dicks, William Chapman, John Collier, and William Upton, Burgesses, to the same. The same property, for 9 years at the same rent.

Endorsed : ' William Taylor agrees at his death or at the expiration of the lease to leave the fruit trees (except gooseberries and currants) for the sole use of the Bailiffs and Burgesses.'

3. 1 June, 1793.

Lease by the Bailiffs and Burgesses of Burford, to Joseph Strafford of Burford, carpenter. Three houses in Mullender's Lane. For 21 years at £2 10s. a year.

Note.—This lease evidently belongs to the set in the Tolsey, Bundle F, see p. 462.

4 and **5**. 27 August, 1801.

Two copies of a lease of land in Ducklington Fields.

6. 6 May, 1807.

Lease by the Hon. and Rev. Francis Knollis and other Trustees, to John Tuckwell of Burford, gentleman. Charity Land situated on the Faringdon Road.

Note.—See Burford Enclosure Award, p. 694.

7. 10 June, 1815. A trust declaration concerning invested stocks of money held for the town. (Damaged by damp.)

8. A packet of correspondence concerning the claim of Robert Wisdom of Shipton-under-Wychwood to be the heir of Simon Wisdom, and, as such, Visitor of Burford Grammar School. The claim failed.

9. A packet of Bailiffs' Accounts for various years from 1754 to 1791.

10. A list, undated, of the Charity properties of the Corporation. It is identical with the list in the conveyance to new Trustees, Tolsey, Bundle M.

11. A packet of papers recording the appointment of Bailiffs, 1787–1801.

12. A packet of papers containing minutes of the Corporation concerning the Charity Lands, and minutes of Easter Vestry meetings, 1789–1805.

13 and **14**. Printed copies of the Enclosure Acts for Burford (1794) and Upton (1773).

15. Printed copy, undated, of Rules for the widows in the Almshouse.

16. A packet of apprenticeship indentures, 19th century, made by the Trustees of charitable moneys left for that purpose.

[The following are paper copies of documents of which the contents are recorded elsewhere in this Calendar.]

17. Copy of the Letters Patent of Edward III, probably made for the purposes of the Quo Warranto proceedings of 1620.

18. Copy of the will of Alexander Ready : see Cheatle Collection, Bundle HH, W 10, p. 368.

19. Copy of the will of Simon Reynolds : see Cheatle Collection, Bundle DD, S 51.

20. Copy of the will of Richard Hayter : see Cheatle Collection, Bundle NN, p. 392.

21. Copy and two translations of the Survey of Burford manor and town : see Public Record Extracts, p. 624.

22. Copy of the Upton Enclosure Award : see p. 701.

23. Copy in manuscript of what appears to be a draft clause intended for insertion in the Burford Enclosure Act, enabling the Vicar of Burford, the Rev. Francis Knollis, to borrow money for the purpose of enclosing lands allotted to him on the security of the lands so allotted.

MISCELLANEA. III

Cheatle Collection, Bundle SS

Parchment on small roller

This is a Roll of High Meade for Burry Barnes Signet and Burford, for them that shall Draw the Lotts hereunder written the Thirtieth Day of June Annoq: Domini 1729.

1. Imprimis the Serjeant and Reeve have the first Lay Acre Between them in the first Hide And then the nexte Acre in the first Hide is belonging to William Castell sen.

2. Item there be four Hides and in every Hide Tenn Acres, Whereof there be two Layne Acres in every Hide, so there remains eight Acres to be drawn for by Lott

3. Item These are the names of the Lotts as followeth First one of the Double Cross, The second of the single Cross, The third of the Three Pitts, The fourth of the Two Pitts, The fifth of Pitt and Dock, The sixth of Pitt and Dockseed, The seventh of Pitt and Stone, The eighth of Pitt and Thorne, and so these Lotts are to serve all the Meade

4. Item John Kempster may choose for Mrs Pryor's Land belonging to the parsonage, whether He will take the Lott of Double Cross, or single Cross, for four Acres, That is one in every Hide besides two Hales or ffarthendales att the upper end of the Meade

5. Item in the next Lott Martin Turner may Choose for Mrs Pryor's Land whether he will take the Lotts of Two Pitts or Three Pitts Throughout the Meade that is one Acre in every Hide

6. Item John Pearse have an Acre in every Hide off Pitt and Dock without Drawing for

7. Item Mrs Pryor have one Layne Acre in the second Hide, which Layne Acre is to be divided between Martin Turner and

John Kempster   The other Layne Acre in the second Hide belongeth to John Pearse

8. In the third Hide there are two Layne Acres the first belongeth to the School Land And the other belongeth to Edward Castle

9. Item in the fourth Hide are two other Layne Acres The first is belonging to the Town Land now in the possession of William Castle Chand : The second belongeth to John Pearse

10. Item Martin Turner hath an Acre of Pitt and Stone in the first Hide belonging to Mrs Pryors Land without Drawing for The other Three Acres of Pitt and Stone are to be Drawn for by John Pearse Clou de Chavasse and Martin Turner for Mrs Pryors Land

11. Item John Pearse hath one Acre of Pitt and Dockseed in the first Hide without Drawing for The other three Acres of Pitt and Dockseed are to be drawn for by Martin Turner for Mrs Pryors Land, John Pearse, and Martin Turner for Mrs Pryors Land

12. Item one Acre of Pitt and Thorne in the first Hide is between Martin Turner for Mrs Pryors Land and William Castle for Mr Veseys Land without Drawing for The other Three Acres of Pitt and Thorne are to be drawn for by Martin Turner for Mrs Pryors Land, John Pearse, and Martin Turner for Mrs Pryors Land

13. Item one Acre of Two Pitts or Three Pitts after Martin Turner have chosen for Mrs Pryors Land is Edward Castle's without Drawing for in the first Hide   The other three Acres of Two Pitts and Three Pitts after Martin Turner have chosen to be Drawn for by Martin Turner for Mrs Pryors Land Paul Sylvester for the School Land called St Katherine's and Edward Castle

14. Item For the Lotts of Double Cross or Single Cross after the parson have chosen there is one Acre belonging to John Pearse in the first Hide of Double Cross or Single Cross without Drawing for The other Three Acres of Double Cross or Single Cross William Castle for Mr Veseys Land Daniel Dicks for the Town Land and Henry Tash for Mr Aston's Land One of these Three to be divided between William Castell sen and Daniel Dicks for the Town Land Memorandum The Serjeant and Reeves Acre was at the Upper End of the Meade this present year 1729

John Pearse has without Drawing
  Pitt and Dockseed in the first Hide
  Pitt and Dock throughout the Mead
  The second Layne Acre in the second Hide
  The second Layne Acre in the fourth Hide.

Parchment on small roller

Burford, 1693. ‘A rent roll of the lands and tenements belonging to the Free School of Burford.

Note.—The names of tenants are as in the contemporary documents transcribed among the School leases.

In this bundle have been placed also the Almshouse document bearing the Warwick signature, A 4 ; and the Memorandum Book numbered 1 below ; these two documents being most frequently wanted for exhibition, it seemed better to put them apart.

MEMORANDUM AND ACCOUNT BOOKS

Cheatle Collection

1. Thin folio volume, bound in vellum, marked ‘ ffor matterys concernyng the Towne off Burfforde ’.

[*Note.*—This volume is a mixed record of accounts and memoranda. It appears to have been started and kept by Simon Wisdom, who was proctor of Poole's Lands as well as Alderman during a great part of the time covered by the volume. The accounts, therefore, consist for the most part of the receipts and disbursements (principally chief rent and wages for the serjeant and town clerk) of those lands. The following extracts give the items of interest among the entries apart from those accounts.]

fol. 1. Thys boke made and Begon at the Fest of Sent Mychaell the arkangell in the yere of our lord god a mvliii and in the Reyne of our Sovereyn lord Kyng phylyppe and quene mary Kyng and quene of england fraunce naples and Jerusalem and in the first and second for the Remembrance of acowmptes and thyngs belongyng to the Bretherhedde and Burgesses of the towne of Burfford they Beyng burgesses ther as folowythe by ther namys

Rychard Monyngton Alderman of the same Burgesses
Symon Wysdom Steward of the same felowship
Robert Jonson
Wylliam Hewys alias Calkott
Robert Ennysdale
Thomas Fawler
Robert Bruton
Edmunde Sylvester
John Hewys alias Floyd
Thomas Prykevans
John Smythear
John Hannys

Robert browne
Rychard Dawby
Wyllyam Colyns
John Hayter

fol. 1 rev. A memorandum as to the custody of the keys : the small keys of ' the deske wherein remaynethe our charter ' kept by the Steward ; the keys of the chest kept by W. Hewys and T. Fawler ; the keys of 'the dore where those thynges remayne' kept by Edmund Sylvester.

fol. 2. Names of Burgesses in 1559, Simon Wisdom being then Alderman.

The charges of the confirmacyon of our charter at the comyng of quene mary anº 1553.

payd for the fyne taxed by my Lord chancellor iii *li*.

pd for the Schynne floryschyng x *R*.

pd for the wrytyng and InRollement xvi*s*. viii*d*.

payd for the examynacon thereof iii *R*.

payd for the grett Seale xx *R*. iiii*d*.

payd for wex and lace iii *R*. iiii*d*.

payd to Mr Smythe for hys paynes iii*s*. iiii*d*.

   sma vii *li*. vii *R*. viii*d*.

fol. 2 rev. 1559. wherof payd in anº 1559 for the rennynge and conffirmacyon of our charter in anº primo Elizabethe viii *li*. ix*s*.

fol. 3 rev. 1561. a carpett cloth for the Tollysend vi*s*. viii*d*. and canvas to line the same and the doynge thereof   ii*s*.

To the mynstrelles viii*d*.

[*Note*.—A frequent entry is for ' our dener ' ; also there are frequent payments for ' dedes of infeoffment '—for conveyance of Poole's and other charity lands ; ' wyne and sugar ' is bought for the Judges at the Assizes, and also constantly for the visits of Sir Edward Unton, who had married Anne Countess of Warwick and so become lord of the manor.]

payd mr plowden at London for perusyng ower charter x*s*.

Resevyd more of xiii of the new bretherne xiii *li*.

fol. 7. payd to mr dyke for the last nisi prius over that he resevyd of mr Fryers vii*s*. ii*d*.

pd at oxffor to the clerk of the Syse for brekyng the last nisi prius xi*s*. viii*d*.

payd more to mr Fryers at London in money for ower law matters iiii *li*.

Note.—These Nisi Prius and other ' law matters ' would be the proceedings in connexion with the Charity Lands alleged to have been ' concealed ' ; cf. Bundle MM, no. 1, p. 373.

fol. 8. an⁰ 1569. yt ys agreyd by the consent of all the bretherne that Rychard Dawby schall pay for hys fyne for Reffusyng the baylyffe weke thys last yere *xs.* apon the condicon that he schalle not Reffuse the same the next yere or otherwyse to pay the whole sum wyche ys xl*s.*

fol. 9 rev. an⁰ 1570. as also that bartylmewe canon ys admytted to be towne clarke and to have the acostomed fee of the baylis xiii*s.* iiii*d.* a yere with the proffyttes of the courtes as ys now apoynted.

fol. 10 rev. wherof I have payd to Edmunde Sylvester towarde the byldyng of the schole howse x *li.*

fol. 11 rev. A payment of 10*s.* to the Herald for the Town seal.

more payd to Symon Allflett smythe the xii daye of Februarie for too casements for the scholehowse wyndowes at ii*s.* a peece iiii*s.*

m⁴ at the accompte made the daye above written there Remayneth to me Symon Wysdom that I have layed owte of my purse in Redye money for the schole howse and other wayes as it aperethe by the generall accompte thereof made the some of iiii *li.* xiii*s.* ii*d.*

fol. 12. 1575. Item more paid to Mr Bayliff Tanner for charges at wittney aboute the Almeshouse and poole's lands vi*s.* vi*d.*

Receyvd more of mr henry Barnarde of Greate Risington by the handes of Richarde Reynolds of Burforde towards the Buyldynge of the freschole x*s.*

fol. 12 rev. payde to Symon Wisdome by John Hanns at the laste churche accompte in parte of paymente of the some of the some (*sic*) of iiii *li.* xiii*s.* ii*d.* due to him at the last acompte xx*s.*

pd to Edmund Silvester for money layde oute for ye free schole xx*s.*

pd more unto him in parte of payment of ye some of xxviii*s.* layde oute at London for suinge owte the copye of our charter x*s.*

fol. 13. 1576. A further payment of 20*s.* to Simon Wisdom for money laid out on the school house.

fol. 14 rev. 1579. A payment of 22*d.* for repairing the pillars and stairs of the Tolsey.

Remember at the same Accompte there was receavid of Richard Chadwell and Richard Dalbie being Bailieffs this last yere for the fee of their ofice which was paid to Richard Reynolds for the matters in lawe xl*s.*

fol. 18. 1583. paid to Robert Silvester for obtayninge of counsell at Abington for the Towne matter x*s.*

yt is agreed with the whole consentes of the felowshipe at this accompte that the Bailiffes that nowe ys and the Bailiffes wch shalbee here after eny yere shall paye alwayse uppon the countye daye the some of vs. of lawfull money of Englande towards the Reparinge of the Stockes Pillary and couckinge stowle and otheres.

fol. 20 rev. 1585. paied to Symon Symons for ye reparacons of the Tolsend and other things xxxiiis. viiid. more towards the building of ye pillory viiis. ixd.

fol. 22. 1586. paied to mr Alderman mr Chadwell and Richard Dalby for the makinge of the pillory and for a payer of stocks in the same iiii li. xs. vd.

fol. 22 rev. 1587. Richard Chadwell entered as Alderman.

fol. 23. 1587. payed to William Symons and John Lyme for repayringe of the stocks vs. vid.

Recd of John Tailor, John Roffe, John Woode, Raphe Wysdome, Rychard Merywether, and Symon Starre elected Burgesses xxs. a peece the some vi li.

Note.—From this folio onwards the entries are nearly all memoranda. It looks as if when the book was started the early part was intended for accounts and the later for other entries ; but the distinction has not been entirely kept. However, this accounts for the fact that the later part is full of entries of dates as early as, or earlier than, those in the first part.

fol. 23 rev. anº 1568. The othe for the Stewarde of the Burgesses of the boroughe of Burforde made by Symon Wisdome Alderman mynystered to John Hannes Senior beinge elected steward the xith day of Marche in anno 1568 as followithe

ye shall take upon youe the office to be the steward of the Corporacon of the Burgesses of this towne of burforde the articles of your othe and charge are these

Firste ye shall to the best of your power wytte and discretion mayntayne and kepe and see to be mayntayned and kepte to the best of your power all suche frauncheses Lyberties and customes wch are graunted to this Corporacyon and conffirmed by our Soveraigne ladye the quenes maiestie that nowe is as allso by her noble progenytors kinges of this Realme

Seconderly ye shall assiste the Baylyffs of this towne in the execucon of their office to see Justice mynystered yf any of them do Require youe upon lawfull admonyssyon or warninge havinge nott Lawfull cause to the contrarye

Thirdly ye shall be allweyes assistaunte with the Alderman to see that all suche ordynaunces constitucyons and articles wch are made or shall be made by the assent and consent of the whole Corporatyon of the Burgesses or the more parte of them for the unyte and concorde of the same Fellowshyppe as also for the common welthe of the same towne to be allwayes observed and kepte and not to be infringed or broken by any of the saide Burgesses As also yf any of the saide Burgesses doe infringe or breake any of the said orders artycles or constytucons as is aforesaid that then youe as much as may come to your knowledge to bringe the same defawts in wrightinge at the day of accompte once or twise in the yere whereby Reformacion or punyshmente may be hadd by Amercyments penaltyes or otherweys accordinge to the constitucions and orders prescribed under our seales

fol. 24. Fourthley ye shall allweys be assystaunte with the said Alderman at such tyme or tymes as shall be Requysyte to see that all suche Deedes evidences charters Infeaments wyllis cownterpanes of Leaces artycles constytucions and orders in wrightinge and all other escrypttes or menuments appertayninge to our Corporacion or to any parte therof be orderly kepte so that they be nott Imbesellyd or taken awaye to any prevat use and to see once in the yere a trew accompte of all suche things as do appertayne or belonge to the said corporacyon.

Thus and all other things appertayninge to the office of the steward of this corporacyon beinge of ould antyquytye and custome ye shall well and trewly do and observe to the moste of your wytte power and dischressyon as god shall helpe youe and the holly contents of this booke

fol. 25. 1555. A list of the Bailiffs, starting from 24 Henry VII (1508), commences on this folio.

fol. 30 rev. Thes be the effecte of the words conteyned in owr charter of Burfford the furste yere of quene Elysabethe perused by lerned men as folowythe 1 Soke ys sewte of men in your courte affter the costome of the reame 2 Sacke that ys plee and amends of tresspace to be hadde of men in yowr courte ther kepte 3 And Sake ys seyd also for forfeture 4 Tolle ys that ye and the men of yowr homake schall be quytt of all maner tolle in all merkattes of thynges to be bowght and solde 5 Theme ys that ye schall have the hole generacon of the villayns with ther sewtes and chattellis where so ever they be fownde in England 6 Excepte yff any bondman have dwellyd in any prevelaged towne by a yere and a day quyettlye so as he be fownde on of them in the communalte or gylde therin he ys delyvered of hys vyllanage 7 Infangtheffe ys that theffes takene within yowr lordeschyppe or fee of thefftes commytted within yowr lordshippe schall be jugged   8 Outfangthef ys that theffte of your land or fee taken withowt yowr land or fee with haste (*Note*—This last word has been altered to ' thefte ') schall be recovered agayne and ther jugged.

fol. 31   (In the list of Bailiffs) 1561. Symon Wysdom beyng then Alderman Thomas ffryeres baylis for that yere.

(*Note in margin*) Thys presydent hadde never byn sene beffore that any affter beyng elected Alderlman (*sic*) to have the offyc any more of the baylyffe.

fol. 32. 1565 (Election of Burgesses). The same day above wrytten ther whas apoynted to be elected Edmunde Sylvester the yonger and John Gest and for that they dyd mysselyke one mr Fylyppes then elected in to the same Felowshyppe at the very day and howre of the eleccyon they wolde nott consent excepte the seyd Mr Phylyppes and one other schulde be dysmyssed and so apon ther obstynace they departed no thyng to ther commendacyon (*erased* and muche lesse to ther honeste).

fol. 32 rev. 1566. The Thewysday then next folowyng beyng the 9th day of October Sir Edward Unton whas chosen knyght for the parlement of Oxffordeschere with suche a voyce of the countie the lyke hathe not byn sene.

Remember the 9the day of August in an⁰ 1570 yong Edmunde Sylvester the sonne of Edmunde Sylvester decessed whas elected burges of Burfford by Symon Wysdom Alderman and John Hans Steward with the assent and consent of the burgesses ther and for and in consideracon of hys towardnes was placed in Senyoryte next to John Lymme then beyng one of the baylyffes of the towne.

fol. 33 rev. 1574. The Thewsday being the iii day of August the queens maiestye came from Langeley throughe the towne of Burfforde where shee was resevyd at the bridge by the Baylyffes then beinge Rycharde Reynoldes and Rychard Chadwell and Symon Wysdome Aldermane with all the Burgesses of the same towne presentinge her grace with a purse of gowlde and xxᵗⁱ Aungells in the same purse Offycers feys gyven at the charges of the whole towne as followethe

To the Clarke of the Markett xxvis. iiiid.

To the Sergeaunte of the Armes xiiis. iiiid.

To the quenes footmen xxs.

To the Trumpetors xiiis. iiiid.

To the Yeoman of the bottells vis. viiid.

God save the Quene.

fol. 34. 1577. A troblehus yere and grett charges with Mr Dutton.

fol. 37. A copy (unfinished) of Queen Mary's Letters Patent confirming the Charters.

fol. 38. The eleccyon of the cunstabullis of Burfford from tyme and accordyng to the olde auncient costome out of mans memory That ys to say the Alderman and Steward to commaund their bretherne the Burgesses to assemble together in ther counsell howse and ther with the hole assent to electe and apoynte within the towne iiii honest Inhabiters whyche eleccyon to be putte to the Steward at the Lawe day and the seyd Steward to apoynte ii of the same iiii to the offyce of the cunstabullis for the yere followyng

The eleccyon for the wardes men

Ther be within the towne iiii wards and for every warde a wardsman wyche wardesmen schalle at every lawe day bryng in wrytyng to the Stewarde all suche deffawtys as hathe byn commyttyd within hys warde that yere past as also schalle nomynate and apoynte one within hys sayd warde most meete to succede hym in hys offyce

1560.

The same yere was the pownde for the pygges made at the west ende of Scheppe Streete at the charges of the towne.

fol. 41. 1574. The yere above written the Syse and galedelyverye holden and kepte at Burfford beginninge the xiiii daye of Jullye and soe contynewed tyll the xviiith daye of the same monethe and there condempned to dye vii men and one woman that is to saye

> John Sturdye
> Robte Franckelyn } executed
> John Kyrbye

John Peppure beinge on the Lader and the Halter abowte his necke was commaunded downe and Repried till a further tyme.

And iiii other were executed whose names I know nott.

fol. 44. an° 1562. The yerely fynes of the Inhabytants of Scheppe strete to be payd yerely to the baylyffs off burford for ever taxed and Rated by Symon Wysdom and thomas Fryeres baylyffs in the yere of our lorde god 1562 and so to contynewe for ever and not to be Raysed as yt ys agreyd by and with the hole consent of all the burgesses that tyme beyng

To be payd alweys at mychelmas as folowythe for ther scheppe pennes

John Geste tenand to the crowne by the yere	xii*d.*
Item the tenement late in the tenure of mr phylyppes	iiii*d.*
Item wm dawbe for medeltons tenement	iiii*d.*

Wm wylcocks for mr Sylvesters tenement   vi*d*.
Wm Smythear for phylippe barretts tenement   iiii*d*.
Wm Smythe for mr brayes tenement   vi*d*.
John Wyllyams for colyns tenement   xii*d*.
Roger tunges   vi*d*.
wm grene   iiii*d*.
Agnes Jaxson   iiii*d*.
Symon Wysdom for the colver close walle   .iiii*d*.
Thomas Honyburn for mr hans tenement   iiii*d*.
Rychard tayler for peter payns tenement   iiii*d*.
Thomas Jenkyns for scheppe pennes afore hys dore and Symon
     Wysdoms barnes walle   vi*d*.
Thomas Devys for lamberts tenement   iiii*d*.
Alexander newbery for iii of fawlers tenements   iiii*d*..
Rychard yonge for another of fawlers tenements   iiii*d*.
hew worsalle for hys scheppe pennes   iiii*d*.
         S^ma viii*s*.

fol. 44 rev. Money resevyd by Symon Wysdom Alderman for
ordynary fees of our boke of Recorde begon añ 1557.

xii*d*.   Item resevyd of Walter Rose jun for the Recorde of hys
         tenement   •   xii*d*.
xii*d*.   Resevyd of John Hyett of mylton for the Recorde of hys
         dede of iii Tenements at the brygge   xii*d*.
xii*d*.   Resevyd of Symon Hyett for the Recorde of hys dede   xii*d*.
xii*d*.   Resevyd of Rycharde Sewell of mylton for the Recorde of
         hys dede made by John Hyett his father in lawe   xii*d*.
xii*d*.   Resevyd of Thomas Rycardes for the Recordyng off hys
         dede   xii*d*.
xx*d*.   Resevyd of thomas Fetyplace of Langford for the
         Recordyng off hys dede for hys tenement bowght of
         John Jenyvere   .   xx*d*.
12*d*.   Resevyd of phylyppe barett of mylton for Recordyng of
         hys ii tenements in owr boke of Record   xii*d*.

2. Quarto Book, bound vellum, containing accounts of the Bailiffs
from 1602 to 1658. Prefixed to the volume is a list dated 1600 of the
lands purchased from Typper and Dawe by Symon Greene, Richard
Merywether, and Toby Dallam, 'whoe were putt in trust for the
purchase thereof Amountinge to the some of fower score pounds'.
There is a gap in the accounts from 1618 to 1625, covering the period
of the Quo Warranto proceedings.

fol. 16. 1630. At this account Thomas Silvester William Bartholomew and Richard Tailor doe acknowledge themselves satisffied for
charges laid out concerning the decree.

[According to an entry on fol. 15 rev. it would appear that there had
been a subscription among the Burgesses amounting to £8 15s., perhaps
for this purpose.]

3. Folio book, bound vellum, marked ' A Booke for Schoole Accounts'. The accounts run from 1644 to 1735. After the beginning
of the eighteenth century no disbursements are entered ; the whole
of the rents seem to have been paid to the schoolmaster Griffiths.

4. Small duodecimo volume, bound in black, with brass clasps
containing the names of Bailiffs and of those returned from Burford to
serve on Grand Juries, 1664 to 1720. Also some notes of the names
of recipients of the Tanfield and Vesey Charities.

5. Folio book, bound vellum, containing assessments for the poor,
1658 to 1676. The names are arranged as follows : i. The Bailiffs
and Burgesses ; ii. Mr. Lenthall and one or two other residents ;
iii. East Ward ; iv. Church Ward ; v. West Ward ; vi. St. John's
Ward.

6. A narrow folio volume, bound vellum, containing Charity Accounts, 1656 to 1737.

7. Folio volume, bound vellum, containing Charity Accounts,
1698 to 1737.

8. A small book, bound in brown paper, containing a summary of
the charitable gifts, undated, but apparently about 1700.

9. One sheet of a Church tax, 1738.

10. Folio volume, bound vellum, containing Charity Accounts,
1739 to 1753.

11. A few leaves of an account book, folio, containing Bailiffs'
accounts for 1743-4 ; several entries record payments to Ingles,
Ashfield, &c., solicitors engaged in the Chancery suit of 1742.

12. Two small quarto volumes containing partial copies of the
judgement in the suit of 1742.

13. Folio, unbound, containing Charity Accounts, 1765 to 1776.

14. Folio volume, bound brown paper, containing Charity Accounts,
1776 to 1784.

15. Folio, unbound, containing Charity Accounts for 1790, John
Lenthall treasurer.

16. A copy bound in marbled paper boards of the Charity Commissioners' Report of 1822.

17. A small book, bound in marbled paper boards, containing names of recipients of the Tradesmen's Fund money, 1828 to 1857.

18. A quarto book, bound marbled paper boards, containing records of the Church Rate, 1831 to 1836.

19. Folio book, bound marbled paper boards, with records of the Poor Rate for 1838.

20. A small book, bound marbled paper boards, marked 'Widows' Book', 1840.

21. Small book, unbound, containing Charity Accounts, 1840 to 1847.

22. Some loose leaves of a ledger with accounts from 1841 to 1859.

II. THE TOLSEY COLLECTION

Bundle

A	Church Lands I	. . . . . .	1378–1544
B	Church Lands II	. . . . .	1567–1731
C	Bridge Lands I	. . . . .	1312–1601
D	Bridge Lands II	. . . . .	1629–1723
E	Two Burgage Rent Rolls	. . . .	1652 and 1685
F	Mullender's Lane Property	. . .	1649–1692
G	Lenthall and Holloway Charities	. .	1677–1732
H	Miscellanea I		
I	Miscellanea II		
K	Commissions and Legal Proceedings	. .	17th century
L	Commissions and Legal Proceedings	. .	18th century
M	Appointments of New Trustees	. . .	1745–1856
N	Nineteenth Century Documents I		
O	Nineteenth Century Documents II		

THE CHURCH LANDS

Tolsey, Bundles A and B

CH 1. 23 May, 1 Richard II (1378).

Conveyance by William Coteswolde of Boreford, to John Dyre of the same, cerveser. One acre and a half-acre of arable in the Eastfield of Burford ; the one acre lies 'desuper heygate in Monstyforlong' near the land of Blessed Mary on one side and the land once of Henry le Spicer on the other side ; the half-acre lies in the same furlong near

. the land of John Cakebred on one side and the land of John Knyte on.the other side.

Witnesses : John Wynrich, John Crosson, Robert Coteler, William Nailer, Thomas Spicer, John Sclatter, William Kokerell, John Alott (?), William Bernes, clerk.

CH 2. Sunday before the Feast of St. Peter in Cathedra, 8 Richard II (1385).

Conveyance by John Cakebred, Burgess of Boreford, to John Dyer of the same, corveser.   Two acres of common land in the Eastfield of Burford in Henacres furlong near the land of Blessed Mary on one side and the land late of Simon Haym on the other side.

Witnesses : John Crosson, Robert Coteler, Thomas Spicer, William Ponter, William Nailer, John Stowe, William Shulton, William Bernes, clerk.

CH 3.   Sunday after the Feast of St. Michael the Archangel, 17 Richard II (1393).

Conveyance by William Purser of Borfford, to Henry Coteler of the same.   A tenement in Burford in ' Wyteney stret ', between the tenement of Roger Hall on one side and the tenement of John Salamon on the other side.

Witnesses : Thomas Spyser, John Adynet (?), John. Hayer, William Taylur, John Lye, Thomas Catelyn.

CH 4.   Tuesday before the Feast of St. John Baptist, 1396.

In Dei nomine Amen   Die Martis proxima ante festum Sti. Iohannis Baptiste Anno Domini mill^{mo} ccc^{mo} Nonogesimo vi^{to}   Ego Iohannes Cakebred de Borefford Burgensis sanus mente et eger corpore condo testamentum meum in hunc modum   In primis lego animam meam domino deo et beate marie corpus que meum cemiterio ecclesie Sti. Iohannis Baptiste de Borefford   Item Lincoln xii*d*. Item domino vicario pro decimis meis oblitis vi*s*. vii*d*.   Item Thome Cussone capellano ii*s*.   Item Thome Benet capellano xii*d*.   Item Nicholao Chaloner capellano xii*d*.   Item duobus clericis xii*d*.   Item Galfrido Bemstere fratri minori iix^{ta}d.   Item Iohanni Lussulle ratri augustineo iix^{ta}d.   Item cuilibet ordini fratrum oxon. iix^{ta}d. Item alicui bono libro habendo et emendo in ecclesiam nostram x*s*. Item campanili nostro emendando x*s*.   Item pauperibus distribuendos die mee sepulture vi*s*. viii*d*. et ii dosen de russeto   Item Petro Webbe ix*s*.   Item Iohanni· Shulton clerico xviii*d*.   Item dedi et concessi Iohanni Faulor et Petro Webbe de Borefford et Matilde uxori mee

unum messuagium cum curtilagio in Wytteneystrete iuxta messuagium
Willelmi Purser ex parte orientali et messuagium Willelmi Brampton
ex parte occidentali habendum et tenendum predictum messuagium
cum curtilagio et omnibus aliis pertinenciis suis prefatis Iohanni
Petro et Matilde heredibus ac assignatis suis in perpetuum De
capitalibus Dominis feodi illius pro serviciis inde debitis et con-
suetis Dedi et dionisie Ynge de Borefford duas acras terre arabilis
quorum una iacet in campo orientali de Borefford iuxta terram dame
le Spenser Altera acra iacet in campo occidentali in vytulworth et
extendit se super Foreram Iohannis Knyte habendas et tenendas predictas duas acras prefate Dionisie heredibus ac assignatis suis in
perpetuum De capitalibus dominis feodi illius pro serviciis inde
debitis etc Item dedi et concessi Matilde uxori mee (*inserted above
the line* et petro Webbe) unam dimidiam acram prati in communi
prato sicut per sortem acciderit habenda et tenenda dicta dimidia
acra prati prefate Matilde (*inserted above the line* et petro) heredibus
ac assignatis in perpetuum De capitalibus dominis feodi illius pro
serviciis inde debitis etc Residuum vero omnium bonorum meorum
do et lego Matilde uxori mee Et ad istud testamentum bene et
fideliter exequendum constituo Matildam uxorem meam capitalem
executorem et Petrum Webbe capitalem supervisorem ut ipsi disponant
pro salute anime mee secundum quod eis melius videbitur expedire
Datum die et anno supradictis.

Endorsed as proved before the officer of the Archdeacon of Oxford,
1 September in the same year.

CH 5. 21 May, 1 Henry VI (1423). (Paper copy of a feoffment,
endorsed ' a coppie of ye crowne '.)

Conveyance by William More of Henley-on-Thames, to Thomas
Spycer of Burford and Christiana his wife. A burgage called Novum
Hospitium Angulare, with a close adjacent, and 18 acres of arable
land and two half-acres of meadow :

' quod quidem burgagium situatum est in Burford predicto ex parte
occidentali inter tenementum Henrici Cotelere et vicum nuncupatum
Sheepestreete ex altera parte et extendit se ab alta strata iuxta vicum
predictum usque ad tenementum Iohannis Ferrs ex parte occidentali :

' Predicte vero due dimidie acre prati iacent in communi prato
ibidem sicut in sorte Abbatis et sorte de Whitemeyes acciderit.'

All which premises the said William More had of Alicia, executrix
of Thomas Attorne.

To be held by Thomas Spycer and Cristiana his wife for the term of their lives and the longer lived of them ; after their death the whole to remain to Johanna, daughter of the said Thomas and Cristiana ; after her death to William, son of Thomas and Cristiana : and they are to maintain the premises in good repair ' sine vasto faciendo ' ; after the death of Johanna and William the premises to remain to Thomas, son of Thomas and Cristiana. If Thomas dies without heirs the property to pass to the heirs of William ; and if William dies without heirs then to the heirs of Johanna ; and if she dies without heirs then to the proctors of the Church of Burford and their successors.

' Tamen volo super omnia quod omnes predicti Thomas Spycer et Cristiana uxor eius Iohanna Willelmus et Thomas filii eorum et heredes eorum inveniant et renovent bis in anno annuatim et in perpetuum quoddam lumen quod est coram altare predicti Thome Spycer in ecclesia parochiali de Borford et quod predicti procuratores et successores sui onerentur ad predictum lumen in forma predicta sustinendum et innovandum sub pena censurarum ecclesiasticarum.'

After the death of all the heirs the rents of the property to be divided into three portions for three objects ' post lumen in forma predicta reparatum ' :

(i) to the sustentation of the parish church ;

(ii) to the chapel of Blessed Mary in the churchyard, belonging to the Burgesses ; [1]

(iii) to the relief of the poor.

Witnesses : William Brampton, William Coteler, John Spyser, John Punter, Edward Dyer, Richard Lavyngton, Henry Blont, Simon Hosier, John Iremonger.

CH 6. Feast of St. Edmund, Abbot, 14 Henry VI (1435).

Conveyance by Thomas Feyster of Northelecche, to Thomas Send, clericus, of Borford. One messuage ' in villa de Borford inter tenementum Abbatis de Keynsam ex parte una et vicariam ex parte altera '.

Witnesses : William Bramton, William Coteler, Richard Colis, Richard Lavyngton, John Ponter.

Endorsed : ' . . . of the tenement in which now Henry Walker dwellyth.'

CH 7. 20 August, 14 Henry VI (1436).

Conveyance by Edward Dyer of Borford, to Robert Bond, clericus, and Thomas Barber, ' custodibus ecclesie de Borford ' and their

---

[1] ' capelle beate marie in eodem cimeterio que est burgi.'

successors. A garden in the town 'ex parte boriali venelle que ducit ad ecclesiam de Borford inter gardinum Iohannis Russel tanner ex parte occidentali ex una parte et terram vocatam cherchegrene ex parte orientali ex altera parte et abuttat se.super gardinum quondam Thome Spicer ex parte boriali '.

Witnesses: William Coteler, Richard Lavynton, 'tunc ballivis ville ', John Ponter, John Mosier, Simon Hosier, Henry Blont, John Pynnock.

CH 8. 17 Henry VI (1438).

Conveyance by Henry Spycer, capellanus de Borford, to Robert Bond, clericus, and Thomas Barbor, 'custodibus ecclesie parochialis de Borford ' and their successors. One acre of arable land 'ad opus ecclesie in perpetuum ', lying in the Westfield upon Bunslade and extending into Denacre between the land of Thomas Hawker of Seynat on the south, and the land of William Spycer, son and heir of Thomas Spycer, on the north.

Witnesses: William Coteler, Richard Lavynton, Bailiffs, John Mosyer, John Punter, John Pynnok.

CH 9. 10 November, 23 Henry VII (1507).[1]

Conveyance by Richard Chaunceler, John Hill alias Prior, and Thomas Jenyvere, to John Bisshope, Richard Bisshope, Thomas Pynnoke, Robert Rile, Richard Harris, and Peter Eynysdale. ' Unum hospicium vocatum le Crowne' with appurtenances, in the High Street of Burford; which the first-named parties had by gift and feoffment of Thomas Smyth, clericus, Richard Brame, and others now defunct.

'Thentent of this feoffament is this That the beforenamyd feoffees theyr heyrs and assignys schall suffre the procuratours of the chirch of Burford for the tyme beyng yerely for ever to take and receve all the Issues and profettes of the seid Inne callyd the Crowne and of all thereto belongyng provided allwey that the seid procuratours and their successours schal kepe performe observe and fulfyll the laste wylle and testament of oon Thomas Spycer late Burgess of Burford aforeseid yerely for evyr as by the laste wylle and testament remaynyng of the same Thomas Spycer in the custodye and kepyng of Richard Brame Richard Harris Perys Eynysdale and John Hedgis nowe beyng procuratours more playnly hit aperith and shewith.'

---

[1] This document has been misplaced in the series, owing to the contraction ' septī ' in the regnal date being misread as ' sexti '.

Witnesses: John Tanner, Robert Osmonde, Nicholas Butler, Nicholas Clerck, William Burrell.

CH 10. Monday after the Feast of the Ascension of the Lord, 24 Henry VI (1446).

Conveyance by William Symonds of Boreford, to Thomas Sende and Robert Bond, clerici. One messuage in the High Street of Burford on the west side ' inter messuagia Abbatis de Keynsham ex utraque parte '.

Witnesses: William Coteler, Richard Lavynton, Bailiffs, John Pynnoke senior, John Mosyer senior, Henry Byschoppe.

CH 11. 26 February, 35 Henry VI (1457).

Conveyance by Walter Mareys and Robert Bond, clerici, of Borford, and Henry Hull of Swell, in Com. Glocestr., to Richard Sterre of Burford and Johanna his wife, for the term of their lives and the longer lived of them and the heirs of their bodies lawfully begotten. Lands and tenements which the first-named parties had by gift and feoffment of the said Richard and which were of the gift and legacy of William Sterre, father of the said Richard. If there are no heirs the property to follow the testamentary disposition of William Sterre.

Witnesses: Henry Bishope, John Pynnok junior, Richard Leveryche William Spiciour.

Endorsed: ' feoffment deeds for ye house next ye Vicaridge.'

CH 12. Penultimate day of October, 37 Henry VI (1458).

Release and quit-claim by John Lawyngton and Thomas Brampton of Borford, to Johanna Osbaston, late wife of Hamlet Osbaston of Hatherope. Lands and tenements, rents and reversions, meadows, pastures, and all appurtenances in Burford which recently belonged to John Dorset and once to Clement, son and heir of John Pryde, and are situated between the tenement of John Longe on the north and the tenement of William Wollynge on the south.

Witnesses: Robert Harecowrte, knight, Richard Harecowrte, armiger, Henry Byschop, John Pynnock junior, Bailiffs, William Stodam, John Pynnock senior.

CH 13. 15 October, 37 Henry VI (1458).

Conveyance by the same, to the same. The same premises.

Witnesses: The same, with the addition of John Granger.

CH 14. Feast of the Purification of the Blessed Virgin Mary, 39 Henry VI (1461).

Conveyance by Johanna Hamelet, widow of John Hamelet of Hathrope, 'in pura viduetate et legitima potestate', to William Freman of Teynton and Alice his wife. Half a burgage with appurtenances in the High Street of Burford on the west side, between the tenement of John Longe on the north and the tenement of William Wollyng on the south, which the first-named party had of Richard Lavyngton of Burford.

Witnesses : John Pynnock junior, Robert Coberle, Bailiffs, Thomas Brampton, Henry Byschop, Richard Leveryche.

CH 15. Feast of St. Leonard, Abbot, 4 Edward IV (1464).

Conveyance and release and quit-claim (fastened together by the seal-tags) by Thomas Mayowe, capellanus, John Pynnok senior, and John Pynnok junior, of Burford 'supra le Wold', to Robert Bond and Thomas Smyth, capellani. A burgage called Novum Hospicium Angulare, with a close and eighteen acres of arable land and two half-acres of meadow ; the burgage situate in Burford ' ex parte orientali (*sic*) inter tenementum Iohannis Pynnok iunioris et vicum nuncupatum schepe street et extendit se ad tenementum Iohannis Ferror ' ; the two half-acres of meadow as they shall fall ' in sorte Abbatis et sorte de Whitemays '. Which premises the first-named parties had by gift and feoffment of John Tylynger ' consanguinei et heredis Willelmi Spicer ut sibi de iure hereditario descendebat sicut per cartam inde confectam cuius datum est vicesimo primo die mensis martii anno regni regis Henrici sexti post conquestum Anglie primo plenius apparet '.

Witnesses : John Granger, John Lavyngton, Bailiffs, William Spicer, John Dauby, John Mosier.

CH 16. 6 January, 4 Edward IV (1465).

Conveyance by Robert Bond and Thomas Smyth, capellani, to Thomas Mayowe ' tunc vicario ecclesie parochialis de Burford ', John Pynnok senior, John Pynnok junior, Henry Bysshope, John Granger, John Lavyngton, John Grove, John Banbury, William Spycer, William Punter, Robert Mundy, and John Eyrys. The premises as described in CH 15.

Witnesses : Robert Harecourt, knight, ' tunc senescallo de Burford ', Richard Harecourt, William Bekyngham, armiger, John Mosyer, Richard Sterr, John Bele, John Orwell.

CH 17. Release and quit-claim by the same, to the same. The premises as described in CH 15.

Witnesses : Robert Harecourt, knight, Richard Harecourt, William Bekyngham, armiger, John Granger, John Lavyngton 'prioratus', Bailiffs, John Mosyer.

CH 18. 11 October, 12 Edward IV (1472).

Conveyance by Thomas Mayowe, clericus, vicar of the parish church of Burford 'supra le Wode ', to John Twynyho ' de Circetr. Recordatori ville Bristoll ', John Mores, Geoffrey Hewys, John Wellys. ' Omnes terras et tenementa mea Redditus servicia prata pascua et pasturas cum omnibus suis pertinenciis que habeo in villis et campis de Burford predicto Upton Teynton et Fulbroke.'

Witnesses : John Pynnok junior, John Granger, 'tunc ballivis ville et burgi de Burford ', William Flodyatte, sergeant, Henry Bysshopp, John Banbury, John Boterell, William Spycer.

CH 19. 22 July, 2 Richard III (1484).

Release and quit-claim by Richard Harecourt, knight, to William Bray and Elena his wife, daughter and heir of Robert Solas, formerly of Shipton Solas in com. Gloucest. A tenement in Burford on the west side of the High Street, ' inter vicariam eiusdem ville ex parte boriali et tenementum abbatis de Keynesham ex parte australi', which the first-named party had with William Garnon by gift and feoffment of Thomas Sende, formerly vicar of Burford.

No witnesses.

CH 20. Another copy on paper of the will of William More, identical with CH 5, except that the phrase ' que est burgi ' is omitted in the reference to the chapel of Blessed Mary.

CH 21. 6 August, 2 Henry VII (1487).

Conveyance by William Spicer and William Punter of Burford, to Thomas Smyth, capellanus, and Richard Brame of Burford. A burgage called Novum Hospicium Angulare, with a close adjacent, eighteen acres of arable, and two half-acres of meadow ; which the first-named parties had by gift and feoffment of Robert Bond, capellanus, and the aforesaid Thomas.

Witnesses : Robert Leverich, William Flodyatte, John Bisshopp, Thomas Send, John Bottrell.

CH 22. 6 October, 3 Henry VII (1487).

Conveyance by Thomas Smyth, capellanus, and Richard Brame of Burford, to Robert Leverich, William Flodeyate, John Bishopp, Thomas Send, John Bottrell, William Spicer, Thomas Umfray,

William Punter, John Legger, John Lambert of Upton, William Kempe, and William Smythiar of Burford. The same premises, described as in CH 15, except that 'ex parte orientali' is corrected to 'ex parte occidentali'.

Witnesses: William Nores, knight, William Harecourt, armiger, Henry Stodham, John Hille, William Smythe.

CH 23. 5 August, 7 Henry VII (1492).

Conveyance by Walter Tyckeford and Elena his wife, late the wife of Henry Howchyn of Burford, to Thomas Dodd, William Bryce, Robert Mayowe, William Lambarde, 'custodibus ecclesie parochialis de Burford', and their successors. A messuage with appurtenances in the High Street of Burford between a tenement of the Abbot of Keynsham on one side and the Vicarage on the other; and one acre of meadow lying in the meadow of Taynton 'iuxta Westbreve'.

Witnesses: William Fludyate, Richard Brame, Bailiffs, Thomas Eward, John Byschopp.

CH 24. 18 January, 29 Henry VIII (1538).

Conveyance by Peter Eynesdall to Richard Monington, armiger, John Scharp, Robert Payn, Thomas Faller, Robert Brown, and John Jurdan. 'Unum hospicium vocatum le Crown cum suis pertinenciis' lying in the High Street of Burford; which the first-named party had by gift and feoffment of Richard Chaunselar, John Prior alias Hyll, and Thomas Janiver, now deceased.

'Thintent of this feoffament ys this thatt the fornamid feoffees theyr heyres and assignes schall suffer the procurators off the chirche off Burford for the tyme being yerly for ever to take and receyv all thyssues and profects off the sayd Inne callyd the Crown and off all therunto belongyng provided allwey thatt the sayd procurators and ther successours schall kepe perform observe and fulfyll the last wyll and testament off the same Thomas Spicer remayninge in the hands and custodye off Richard Brame Richard Harris the sayd Peter Eynesdall and John Hedgs than being chyrche procurators more playnly ytt apperythe and shewythe.'

CH 25. 20 August, 36 Henry VIII (1544).

Lease by Robert Payne, Thomas Faller, Hewe Colborne, and John Browne, churchwardens of the parish church of St. John Baptist, 'with the holle ascent and condiscent of all the parishioners of the same towne', to Thomas West of the same town, 'sclatter'. A house on the north side of Sheep Street with a garden ground attached.

Lease for 41 years at 6s. 8d. a year. ' And the seid Thomás doth bynde hymsellffe by these presents to make or cause to be made the seid tenemente and eny parcell thereof sufficiently to be repayred and Teynauntable within the space of ii yeres next ensuynge the date hereof at his propere costis and expencis ', and thereafter to keep the same in repair.

CH 27. 5 July, 10 Elizabeth (1568).

Exemplification out of the Exchequer.

Information had been laid by the Attorney-General Gilbert Gerrard concerning : Sixteen acres of arable land in Burford now or lately in the occupation of Thomas Offlytt ; a tenement now or lately in the occupation of Philip Glover, lately given by Thomas Hynde for an anniversary ; a piece of a tenement with appurtenances now or lately in the occupation of John Impe ; a piece of meadow in Bury Orchard now or lately in the occupation of Thomas Fryer ; and four messuages in Burford and a barn now or lately in the occupation of the churchwardens ; all of which were alleged to have been given for the purpose of maintaining anniversaries within five years before 1 Edward VI ; and that William Harryson and John Hunt, church-wardens, were trespassing thereupon in contempt of the rights of the Crown under the Statute of 1 Edward VI, as appears by the inquisition taken at Chipping Norton, 3 September, 7 Elizabeth.

The Churchwardens replied in the Court of Exchequer by their attorney, John Marwood, that the premises were not given as alleged, and that the rents were not being used for any such purpose.

Inquisition taken at Oxford, Tuesday, 18 February, 10 Elizabeth, before Sir Edward Saunders, Chief Baron of the Exchequer, and Thomas Carus, Justice of the Common Pleas.

The jury found that the premises were not given to maintaining anniversaries within five years before 4 November, 1 Edward VI, and that the churchwardens therefore were not trespassing, and were acquitted.

CH 28. 20 August, 19 Elizabeth (1577).

Lease by Thomas Hewys, Robert Silvester, John Wedde, and Symon Greene, churchwardens, with the assent of the parishioners, to Richard Dalbye the younger of Burford, butcher. A messuage on the east side of the High Street of Burford between a tenement or inn called ' the signe of the Angell ' on the north and a tenement of Robert Silvester on the south. Lease for 41 years at 40s. a year.

Witnesses : Symon Wysdom, William Symons, Thomas Fetiplace, Robert Bruton (?), Thomas Sylvester, Thomas Plome, John Wodde, John . . . (*illegible*), Bartholomew . . . (*illegible*), the writer hereof.

Endorsed : ' Lease of the Bull to Dalby.'

CH 29. 29 June, 32 Elizabeth (1590).

Lease by John Tailor, Symon Starre, Toby Dallam, and Henry Reddy, churchwardens, with the assent of the parishioners, to Symon Allflett of Burford, clerk. Eleven acres and one ' farendelle ' of arable land called the Churchlands, as set out in a terrier annexed to these presents (*Note.*—Terrier missing). Lease for 21 years at 3s. a year.

' For and in Consideracon that the said Symon Allflett hath usually on the week daies for the space of twenty years past said and readde morning prayer in the parish church of Burford aforesaid.'

Witnesses : John Roffe, John Huntt, Benedic Fawller, Raphe Wisdom, Thomas Mynchon.

Note.—Besides the assent of the parishioners, the assent is also recorded of Richard Dalby and Richard Meryweather, Bailiffs, Richard Chadwell, Alderman, and William Symons, Steward, of Burford.

CH 30. 29 June, 32 Elizabeth (1590).

Lease by the same churchwardens, with the same assents, to Richard Tailor of Burford, chandeler. Ten acres and three ' farendells ' of arable land called the Churchlands, late in the tenure of Robert Scarborough, shoemaker. Lease for 21 years at 5s. a year.

Witnesses : Richard Dalby, Richard Merywether, John Roffe, John Huntte, Raphe Wisdom, Thomas Mynchon.

CH 31. 14 February, 41 Elizabeth (1599).

Lease by John Lyme alias Jenkyns, John Roffe, William Webbe, John Huntt, John Gryffith alias Phillippes, and Thomas Parsons of Burford, yeomen, Burgesses of Burford, to Andrew Warde of Burford, yeoman, one other of the Burgesses. A tenement on the east side of the High Street, between a tenement of Rychard Hodges called the Aungell on the north and a tenement of Edward Reynolds now occupied by Edmond Serrell on the south. Lease for 80 years at 41s. a year.

Witnesses : John Yate, Bailiff, Symon Symons, Steward of the Fellowship, Walter Hayter.

This lease was granted in consideration of the payment of a fine of £20 and the surrender of a term of 20 years or thereabouts of a lease of the said premises which Andrew Warde had acquired by marriage with Margaret, late the wife of Richard Dalby, deceased. In the course of the lease it is recited that the premises were purchased by the lessors of Merywether and Dallam in the previous December, they having purchased of Typper and Dawe, 38 Elizabeth, and they of the Crown, 32 Elizabeth. For the more effectual performance of the indenture the common seal of the Fellowship or Brotherhood of the Burgesses of Burford is affixed.

CH 32. 14 February, 41 Elizabeth (1599).

Lease, by the same Burgesses, to Robert Serrell, one other of the Burgesses, haberdasher. A messuage late in the occupation of John Weast, slater, in Sheep Street between a garden ground belonging to a corner messuage heretofore called the Crown on the east and a tenement of Richard Chadwell, gentleman, on the west. Lease for 80 years at 13s. a year. In consideration of a fine of £3.

The same account of the purchase of the premises as in CH 31. The common seal of the Fellowship attached as in CH 31.

CH 33. 14 February, 41 Elizabeth (1599).

Lease, by the same Burgesses (counterpart), to Thomas Hemynge of Burford, ' Barber Chirirgion '. Messuage on the east side of the High Street between a tenement occupied by Frauncis Perks on the south and a tenement of Henry Hayter on the north. Lease for 80 years at 21s. a year. In consideration of a fine of £5 and the surrender of a term of 36 years of a lease of the same premises.

The same account of the purchase of the premises as in CH 31, and the same attachment of the common seal.

Witnesses: John Yate, Richard Merywether, Symon Symons, Raphe Wisdom, John Templer, Edmond Serrell, Walter Sessions, Walter Hayter, ' the wryter hereof '.

Endorsed with an assignment of the lease after the death of Thomas Hemynge to Edmund his son, Elizabeth Alexander, spinster, and their issue: dated 10 April 1627. Witnesses: Thomas Coller, Thomas Rous, Walter Hayter senior.

CH 34. 14 February, 41 Elizabeth (1599).

Lease, by the same Burgesses, to Rychard Meryweather of Burford, yeoman, Alderman of Burford. Two parts of all that capital messuage with the appurtenances called the Crown now or late in the occupation of Alice Reynolds, widow, lying between a tenement of the co-heirs of Agnes Brewton on the north and the highway leading into Sheep

Street on the south ; also all shops, cellars, sollars, courts, &c., recently by agreement between Richard Meryweather, Alice Reynolds, and the lessors marked out as belonging to the two parts of the Crown now leased ; also a little close containing the third part of an acre lying in or near to Witney Street ; and one acre of meadow in High Mead. Lease for 90 years at 26s. a year.

The same account of the purchase of the premises as in CH 31, and the same attachment of the common seal.

Witnesses : As in CH 33, with the exception of Richard Mery-weather.

CH 35. 10 June, 41 Elizabeth (1599).

Indenture of agreement between the same Burgesses and Alice Reynoldes of Burford, widow. Sets forth that Typper and Dawe had bought and resold (as stated in CH 31, &c.) two parts of the premises called the Crown ; and that John Maynard and Richard Venables, esquires, had bought and resold to Richard Hodges of Burford, natural father of Alice Reynoldes, a third part of the premises. There had been 'suytes and controversyes' about the several holdings. It was therefore agreed, in order to stay these suits, that the premises should be divided as follows :

The two parts belonging to the Burgesses were to consist of : ' All the hall next to the High Street, the Inward parlour next to the Kytchin, also the Kytchin next to the same parlour, all the entre and comyng forth of the courte into the streete, the chamber over the said hall, the chamber next over the entrye, the chamber over the said parlour called the apple chamber, also the cellar or kaverne under the said hall, the lyttle stable called the Wolhouse next to the high raunge of howsinge, the stable next to the same lyttle stable, also the heyloftes over the said stables, the tymber howse nexte Bruton's house, also the haytallett or strawe lofte over the same howse, also all the waste of the inward courte and entrye aforesaid, and also the Wolhouse and pyggestyes, barne, backsyde, and garden ; one lyttle close beinge at Wytney streete's ende, one acre of meadow grounde beinge in the lott meade alias the highe meade in the paryshe of Burford aforesaid.'

Alice Reynoldes for her part of the premises was to have : ' Alle the shoppe nexte unto the highe streete, the warehowse next adioyning to the same shoppe, the lyttle enclosed roome adioyninge to the same warehowse and used for a buttrey in the inwarde entrye there, the chamber over the said shoppe called the Matte chamber, the chamber

next adioyninge to the same matte chamber being parcell thereof
and devyded with a partycon of waynescotte, the chamber next
adioyninge to the said partycon chamber, one other chamber to the
sajd last wryted chamber adioyninge, one other chamber adioyninge
and being over the yeldinge howse, one other chamber next thereunto
adioyninge and being over the inwarde courte gatehowse, one other
chamber in the gallerye called the corne lofte, one other lower roome
next the inward entrye dore called the mylhowse, and all the inward
courte gatehowse with all the roomes on both sydes thereof both over
and under tendynge and abowndynge soe farre as the highest raunge
of howsinge over and beyond the said inward gatehowse towarde
Shepestreete. And also three score and eighte foote in lengthe of the
sayde inward courte of the same syde thereof nexte to the said roomes
and inward gatehowse aforesaid which bredthe takethe begynnynge
by measure from the Inwarde entry dore next the said Mylhowse
and endynge at the furthest parte of the hyghe rawnge of howsinge
towards Shepe streete aforesaid And also sixe foote in bredethe of
the same inwarde courte of the same syde thereof nexte to the same
roomes and inward gatehowse aforesaide which bredthe taketh
begynnynge by measure from the said inward entrye dore next the
Mylhowse aforesayd and endynge at the Hether parte of the inwarde
gatehowse aforesaid tendynge towards the highe streete dore And
also twelve foote and a halfe in bredthe of the same inwarde courte
to begynne from the said hether parte of the inward gatehowse aforesaid dyrectlie over againste and towarde Bruton's tenemente And
also fowerteene foote in bredethe of the same inwarde courte to begynne
from the furthest syde of the sayd inward gatehowse nexte the back-
side towardes the sheepe streete and dyrectly over against and towarde
Bruton's tenemente aforesaide and in lengthe over against and towarde
Bruton's tenemente twentye foote to begynne from warde the kytchin
in Hughe Owen's tenure towards the backside of the holle tenement.'

Witnesses : Toby Dallam, Andrew Ward, Edmond Serrell, Robarte
Jackson, George Hodges.

CH 36. 26 September, 43 Elizabeth (1601).

Lease by Richard Merryweather, yeoman, to Hughe Owen of
Burford, yeoman. Two parts of the Crown late in the tenure of Alice
Reynolds, widow, deceased, between a tenement of the co-heirs of
Agnes Bruton on the north and the other third part of the said messuage
now in the occupation of Robert Jackson on the south'; also the little

close and the acre in High Mead. Lease for 91 years at £6 a year. In consideration of a fine not specified.

Witnesses : John Griffith, Thomas Harding, Walter Hayter junior.

CH 37. 23 February, 5 Charles I, 1630.

Conveyance by Robert Walbridge of Chipping Norton, chirurgien, to Sir John Lacy and the other feoffees named by the Royal Commission of 1628. (By order of the Commission, Robert Walbridge being son and heir of John Walbridge, surviving feoffee of the Church Lands.) A messuage being an Inn called the Crown with a garden belonging to it on the west side of the High Street ; a little close at the furthest end of Witney Street between a garden in the tenure of William Tayler on the east and a tenement of Nicholas Francklyn on the west ; one acre of meadow in High Mead ;—these three properties now in the tenure of Suzan Scott, widow ; a messuage now or late in the tenure of Anthony Steward on the north side of Sheep Street between the garden of Suzan Scott on the east and a tenement of Anne Levett on the west ; a messuage being an Inn called the Bull now or late in the tenure of John Cooke on the east side of the High Street between the land of Edmond Serrell on the south and an Inn called the Angell on the north ; a messuage on the east side of the High Street in the occupation of Edmund Hemynge between a tenement of Henry Hayter on the north and a tenement of Richard Heminge on the south ; and 3s. 4d. rent issuing out of a tenement next the church in the occupation of Mary Templar, widow.

Witnesses : William Webbe junior, Walter Hayter, clerck, Richard Alflet, William Kempster.

Endorsed : ' Noe land conveyd but what belonged to ye church.'

CH 38. 25 September, 6 Charles I (1630).

Lease by the Trustees to John Woodward of Burford, gentleman. The Crown and garden ' together with ground heretofore purchased of one Hedges lying at the furthest end of Witney Street '. Lease for 31 years at £6 a year. In consideration of the surrender of a previous lease.

Witnesses : William Tayler, Edmund Heming, David Berry, John Cole.

CH 39. 18 October, 6 Charles I (1630).

Lease by the Trustees to John Silvester of Burford, yeoman. The Bull, in the tenure of John Cooke. Lease for 31 years at £6 a year.

In consideration of the surrender of John Silvester's interest under the previous lease to Andrew Ward (see CH 31).

Witnesses : Richard Barnard, William Silvester, Leonard Yate.

CH 40. 18 October, 6 Charles I (1630).

Lease by the Trustees to David Berrye of Burford, mercer. A messuage on the north side of Sheep Street between the garden of Suzan Scott, widow, on the east and a tenement of Anne Levett on the west. Lease for 31 years at 20s. a year. It is noted that the premises had previously been granted under the common seal to Robert Serrell for 80 years (see CH 32).

Witnesses : Thomas Richards, Edmund Heming, William Symons, William Kempster, William Tayler.

CH 41. 13 October, 1658.

Lease by the Trustees to Edmund Heminge the younger of Burford, chirurgien. The Bull now in his tenure, between the land of John Jordan on the south and an Inn called the Angell on the north. Lease for 21 years from 18 October, 1661, at £14 a year.

Witnesses : Leonard Mills, Thomas Hughes, John Widdowes, John Payton, John Sindrey, Paul Silvester, Thomas Castle, Symon Randolph.

Note.—It is specified in the lease that the tenant binds himself to pay, over and above the rent, the sum of four shillings for chief rent issuing out of the premises to the Lord of the Manor.

CH 42. 18 March, 1658.

Lease by the Trustees to Lawrence Yeate of Burford, ' maulter '. A tenement on the east side of the High Street late in the occupation of Edmund Heming between a tenement in the occupation of Richard Hayter on the north and a tenement of Thomas Hughes on the south. Lease for 21 years at £6 6s. 8d. a year.

Witnesses : Richard Veyšey, John Jordan junior, Robert Jordan.

CH 43. 17 June, 1659.

Lease by the Trustees to David Berry of Burford, yeoman. A tenement on the north side of Sheep Street between a garden ground late of Susane Scott, widow, now in the occupation of John Syndrey, mercer, on the east and a tenement in the occupation of Richard Levett on the west. Lease for 21 years at 35s. a year.

Witnesses : David Hughes junior, Samuell Minty, Symon Randolph.

CH 44. (No date), 25 Charles II (1673).

Lease by the Trustees to Humfry Nunney of Burford, broadweaver.

A cottage now in his occupation on the south side of the highway from Burford to Witney between a tenement of Samuel Ferriman on the east and a tenement known by the name of the Kingshead on the west. Lease for 21 years at 24s. a year.

Witnesses : Symon Randolph, Thomas Randolph.

CH 45. 25 February, 30 Charles II, 1678.
Lease by the Trustees to Elinor Heming of Burford, widow. The Bull, described as in CH 41. Lease for 21 years at £14 a year.
Witnesses : Symon Randolph, Thomas Randolph.

CH 46. 25 March, 36 Charles II (1684).
Lease by the Trustees to William Bowles of Burford, collermaker. A tenement with garden on the east side of the High Street, late in the tenure of Lawrence Kemble, between a tenement in the occupation of Henry Hayter on the north and à tenement occupied by Jacob Marsh on the south. Lease for 21 years at £6 6s. 8d. a year.
Witnesses : William Holland, Symon Randolph.

CH 47. 26 April, 9 William III, 1697.
Counterpart lease by the Trustees to Robert Aston of Burford, innholder. The Bull, described as in CH 41. Lease for 21 years at £14 a year.
Witnesses : Richard Smith, Richard Mathewes, George Hawes.

CH 48. 18 November, 2 Anne, 1703.
Lease by the Trustees to Henry Hayter, in trust for William Bowles. The tenement described in CH 46, except that the tenement to the south is now described as of Mr. Richard Jordan. Lease for 21 years at £6 6s. 8d. a year.
Witnesses : John Jordan, Ceaser Harris.

CH 49. 26 August, 6 Anne, 1707.
Lease by the Trustees to George Hart of Burford, brazier, in trust for John Castle, now in occupation of the premises, The Crown Inn, on the west side of the High Street, with a garden ; one little close at the further end of Witney Street, between a close in the occupation of Tristram Wilton on the east and a tenement in the occupation of Humphry Nunny and John Nunny on the west ; and one acre of meadow in High Mead. Lease for 21 years at £14 a year.
Witnesses : Richard Whitehall, Joseph Payton.

CH 50. 29 September, 3 George I, 1716.
Lease by the Trustees to Humphry Nunny and John Nunny of

Burford, broadweavers. A tenement now in their occupation at the end of Witney Street between a tenement of Tristram Wilton on the east and a messuage formerly known as the King's Head on the west. Lease for 21 years at 36s. a year.

Witnesses : George Hart, William Castell.

CH 51. 20 May, 5 George I, 1719.

Lease by the Trustees to William Castle of Burford, chandler. The Crown Inn and other properties described as in CH 49. Lease for 21 years at £14 a year.

Witnesses : R. Griffiths, Phil. Birt.

CH 52. 29 May, 5 George I, 1719.

Lease by the Trustees to Henry Tash of Burford, innholder. The Bull, described as in CH 41. Lease for 21 years at £14 a year.

Witnesses : R. Griffiths, Phil. Birt.

CH 53. 29 December, 4 George II, 1730.

Lease by the Trustees to John Tomlin of Burford, woolcomber. A tenement on the east side of the High Street, late in the occupation of William Bowles, between a tenement of Benjamin Faulkner on the north and a tenement of John Jordan on the south. Lease for 21 years at £8 10s. a year.

Witnesses : John Hall, Henry Walker.

THE BRIDGE LANDS

1312 to 1607

Tolsey, Bundles C and D

B 1. Paper copy, dated 1650, of an extract from the Patent Roll of 1322.

Ex Rotulo patencium de anno Regni Regis Edwardi secundi decimo sexto ps2 m1.

Rex probis hominibus ville de Bureford Salutem Sciatis quod ad requisicionem dilecti et fideli (*sic*) nostri Hugonis le Despenser Iunioris et ad auxilium reparationis et sustentacionis pontis ville predicte concessimus vobis quod a die confeccionis presencium usque ad finem trium annorum proxime sequentium plenarie completorum capiatis de rebus venalibus ultra pontem predictum transeuntibus consuetudines subscriptas videlicet de qualibet summa bladi venali unum

obolum de quolibet equo et equa bove et vacca venali unum obolum
de quolibet corio equi et eque bovis et vacce frisco salito aut taniato
venali unum quadrantem de qualibet carecta ferente carnes salitas
vel friscas venales tres obolos de quinque baconibus venalibus unum
obolum de quolibet salmone frisco vel salito venali unum quadrantem
de qualibet centena mulewellorum congrorum et fricarum anguillarum
salitarum venali unum denarium de decem ovibus capris vel porcis
venalibus unum denarium de decem velleribus venalibus unum
denarium de qualibet centena pellium omnimodi lanutarum caprarum
cervorum bissarum damorum et damarum venali unum obolum de
qualibet centena pellium agnorum capricolarum leporum cuniclorum
vulpium catorum et squirrellorum unum obolum de quolibet sumagio
pannorum venalium unum obolum de quolibet panno integro venali
unum obolum de qualibet centena linee tele Carenacii pannorum
hibernie Galewyth et Woostede venali unum denarium de quolibet
panno de serico cum auro de samite diaspre et baudekyn venali
unum obolum de quolibet panno de serico sine auro et chiefe de seuro
dallo afforciato venali unum quadrantem de qualibet lampreda
venali unum obolum de quolibet dolio vini et Cudrus venali tres
obolos de quolibet sumagio cudrus venalis unum obolum de quolibet
sumagio mellis venali unum denarium de quolibet dolio mellis venali
duos denarios de quolibet sacto lane venali duos denarios de quolibet
trussello pannorum ducto per carectam venali duos denarios de
quolibet sumagio panni vel aliarum rerum diversarum et munetarum
transeuncium ultra pontem predictum venali unum obolum de qualibet
carectata ferri venalis unum denarium de qualibet carectata plumbi
venalis duos denarios de qualibet carectata tanni venalis unum
denarium de quolibet quarterio wayde venali duos denarios de duobus
miliaribus ceparum venali unum quadrantem de octo shavis alei
venalis unum quadrantem de quolibet miliari allecis venalis unum
obolum de quolibet sumagio piscis marini venali unum obolum de
qualibet centena ordi venali unum obolum de quolibet quarterio salis
venali unum quadrantem de qualibet pisa casei et butiri venali unum
obolum de qualibet carectata busce vel carbonum venali unum obolum
de quolibet miliari fagottorum venali unum denarium de quolibet
miliari turbarum venali unum denarium de averio de pondere scilicet
centena venali unum denarium de qualibet pisa cepi et uncti venali
unum denarium de qualibet centena de alinū cepose argayl et verte-
grece venali unum obolum de duobus miliaribus ceparum venalibus
unum quadrantem de quolibet miliari clavorum ad cumulum domus

venali unum quadrantem de duobus miliaribus omnimodorum clavorum exceptis clavis ad carectas et ad cumulum domus venalibus unum quadrantem de qualibet centena ferrorum ad equos et cliccorum ad carectas venali unum obolum de quolibet quarterio tanni venali unum quadrantem de quolibet quarterio farine fabarum et pisarum venali unum quadrantem de qualibet mola venali unum obolum de quolibet trussello cuiuscunque mercimonii transeunte ultra pontem illum et excedente valorem duorum solidorum venali unum quadrantem de qualibet centena stagni eris et cupri venali duos denarios de qualibet centena gaddorum aceri venali unum obolum de qualibet centena piscis de Aberden venali unum denarium de qualibet centena de stokfissh venali unum obolum de decem potys canoebi venalibus unum quadrantem de decem lagenis olei venalibus unum obolum de decem pnis venalibus unum obolum de quolibet calderio et plumbo ad braciandum venali unum obolum de qualibet alia mercandisa hic non specificata et excedente valorem quinque solidorum unum quadrantem Et ideo vobis mandamus quod predictas consuetudines usque ad finem dictorum trium annorum capiatis et denarios inde provenientes in reparationem et sustentacionem pontis illius et non in usus alios poni faciatis completo autem termino dictorum trium annorum dicte consuetudines penitus cessent et deleantur In cuius etc. per predictos tres annos durantes Teste Rege apud Eboracum quarto die Iulii per ipsum Regem

Convenit cum Recordo
Gulielmus Ryley

2do Iulii
1650

B 2. 26 March, 6 Edward IV (1466).

Release and quit-claim by Richard Harecourt, knight, to Nicholas Spaldyng of Borford. One tenement with the appurtenances in Burford 'in alta strata ex parte orientali in le cokerew inter tenementum Iohannis Egle ex parte australi et tenementum Henrici Byschop ex parte boriali '.

Witnesses : John Pynnock junior, John Grove ' tunc ballivis de Borford ', Henry Byschop, John Banbery, John Granger.

B 3. 3 August, 21 Edward IV (1481).

Conveyance by Thomas Herte of Gloucester, to William Kempe of Borford, ' corveser '. Tenement in the High Street of Burford on the east side, between the tenement of William Bisschopp on the north and the tenement of the aforesaid William Kempe on the south, ' quod quidem tenementum cum suis pertinenciis nuper habui ex dono et feoffamento Nicolai Spaldynge et Isabelle uxoris sue '.

Witnesses : John Pynnock, Robert Leveriche ' tunc ballivis burgi de Borford predicti ', William Bisschopp, John Boterell, John Granger.

B 4. 8 September, 21 Edward IV (1481).

Power of attorney by Thomas Herte, Burgess of Gloucester, to William Marshall of Gloucester, tanner, to take seisin of his tenement ' infra villam de Burford in Com. Oxon. in alto vico ibidem ex parte orientali de le Coke rewe inter tenementum Willelmi Byshope ex parte boriali et tenementum Willelmi Kympe corveser ex parte australi ' ; and to give seisin to William Kympe.

No witnesses.

Endorsed : ' The gift of Spalding and his wife ' ; and in another hand ' a feoffment of the Bridge lands '.

B 5. 23 October, 8 Henry VIII (1516).

Conveyance by Johanna Kempe of Burford, to John Chadwell of the same: Two tenements with appurtenances ' in parte orientali alte strate de Burford predicti videlicet inter tenementum Ricardi Byschup ex parte boriali et tenementum Iohannis Huggyns ex parte australi '.

Witnesses : Robert Osmund, Robert Payne, then bailiffs of Burford, John Bischup, Thomas Staunton, John Lane.

B 6. 11 March, 9 Henry VIII (1518).

Conveyance by Thomas Pynnok of Burford, gentleman, to Richard Hannys, Thomas Clerck, William Hedgis, (Robert Silvester erased), John Scharpe, and Robert Wigpitt. Two cottages lying together in the Cokerewe in the High Street of Burford, ' que nuper fuerunt Willelmi Kempe et que nuper habui simul cum Edmundo Harrison clerico per dimissionem testamenti ac ultime voluntatis predicti Willelmi Kempe prout mos in Burford predicto est et de tempore memoria cuius hominum non existit fuit '.

(In English) ' Thentent of this feoffament is this that the before-namyd Richard Thomas William John and Richard and their heyrs for evyr schall suffer the proctours of Seynt Thomas Chapell in the chirch of Burford aforeseid yerely to receve the issues Rents and pro-fettes growyng and goyng oute of the seid ii messuages to the use and behoffe of the servyce of god in the seid chapell and to the sustentation and mayntenance of the same chapell in Reparations.'

Witnesses : Peter Eynesdale, bailiff of the town of Burford, John Bisshope, Robert Rile, Nicholas Clerck, John ffrancklin.

Note.—Seal in good preservation—a shield of arms bearing two bars, in chief a lion passant guardant.

B 7. 12 March, 9 Henry VIII (1518).

Release and quit-claim by Johanna Kempe ' filia et heres Willelmi Kempe de Burford ', to the parties as in B 6. The same premises.

Witnesses : Thomas Pynnok, Peter Eynesdale, bailiffs, Robert Osemonde, William Smythe, John Chadewelle.

B 8. 13 March, 9 Henry VIII (1518).

Release and quit-claim by William Sabyn of Burford, to the same parties. The same premises.

Witnesses : Peter Eynesdale, John Bisshope, Robert Rile, Nicholas Butler, John Lane.

B 9. 12 October, 2 Elizabeth (1560).

Conveyance by John Hannes, one of the Burgesses, to Richard Chawrleye, Richard Dalbye, Burgesses, John Geaste, John Dallam, Edmund Sylvester junior, Benedict Fawler, of Burford, yeomen. Two messuages in the High Street between the tenement of Robert Eynesdale, late of Burford, woollen draper, on the north, and the tenement of Simon Wisdom, mercer, on the south ; now in the tenure of William Partridge, smith ; and also one acre of meadow in the common meadow of Burford called le highe meade, now in the tenure of Simon Wisdom ; and one acre of arable in the Eastfield of Burford now in the tenure of Simon Wisdom ; and another acre of meadow in High Mead now in the tenure of William Hughes alias Calcott, yeoman ; and a half-acre of meadow in the same called ' Cakebredd's ' now in the tenure of Thomas Fears, yeoman ; all which premises the conveyer had ' by gift and feoffment of Richard Hannes my father, defunct, Thomas Clerck, William Hodgis, John Sharpe, and Robert Wygpitt, all now defunct ', ' ad usus et intenciones in anglicis verbis subscriptas videlicet That theye thabove named feoffees and their heires shall permytt and suffer all and eny suche proctours or pronotours beinge admitted nominated and appoynted from tyme to tyme by the Alderman Steward and Burgesses of the Boroughe of Burford aforesaid speciallye to receave perceave collect gather and take all and singular those yssues rentes revenewes and profitts comynge renewinge

and growinge of all thabove saide lands and tenementes and their
appurtenances at eny suche daye and tyme whiche are or hereafter
shall be appoynted lymyted and assigned for the payments of the
same or of any parte thereof Quyetlye without contradiction or gayne
sayinge of the saide feoffees or their heires or of any other person or
persons by their comandyment or assente And that the saide proctours
or pronotours and their successours shall from tyme to tyme and at
all tymes for ever hereafter Diligentlye see that the saide lands and
tenements be well and sufficientlye mayntayned and kepte in good
reparation And whatsoever shall yerely remayne of the said Rentes
Yssues Revenewes and profitts of the said lands and tenements Over
and above the Reparations aforesaid Shall yerely and for ever be
employed and bestowed in and upon the Repayringe maynteyninge
and kepynge of the Common Bridge apperteyninge to the towne
and Boroughe of Burford aforesaid and for the amendinge of the
common highe wayes next adioyninge to the same towne Or otherwise
as theye the forsaid Alderman Steward and Burgesses for the tyme
beinge and their successours or the more parte of them shall by their
discression thinke moste necessarie expedient and profitable for the
common welthe of the same towne.'

Clause that the proctors are to render account upon reasonable
warning ' before the said Alderman Steward and their Bretherne the
Burgesses and other the parishioners of Burford at their yerely and
common accompte holden and made for the churche of the same
towne ': clause also providing for the making of a new feoffment by
the present feoffees or the longest lived of them upon requirement
' as well by thassente and agrements of the Alderman and Steward
of the saide towne and Bouroughe of Burford aforesaid as by the
common assente of the more number the Burgesses and parishioners
of the same bouroughe ', to such persons ' as theye the said Alderman
Steward and the more parte of the saide Burgesses for the tyme beinge
shall name and appoyncte '.

Witnesses: Simon Wisdom, William Hughes, Thomas Freers,
William Grene, John Taylor, Henry Perrott.

B 10. 6 May, 13 Elizabeth, 1571.

Conveyance by Richard Dalby and Edmond Silvester ' Balivi
Liberatis (sic) Ville de Burford ', Benedict Fawler, one of the Burgesses, and John Gest, mercer, to Thomas Freers, William Symons,
John Lymme senior, and Robert Chillde, ' quatuor burgienses Boragii
de Burfforde ', John Hunt of Burford, mercer, John Wood of Burford,

draper, John Flude junior, and Thomas Mollyner, of Burford, broad-weavers, and Simon Starre of Burford, baker. Two tenements in the High Street of Burford between a tenement of William Stampe, yeoman, on the north, and a tenement of Simon Wisdom, Alderman of the town, on the south ; now in the occupation of William Partridge, smith. The intents set out in English as before, except that ' the more part of the parishioners ' are joined in the appointing of new feoffees.

Witnesses (to livery and seisin): Symond Wisdome, Alderman, John Hannes, Steward of the Fellowship, Richard Reynolls, Edmond Sylvester, Robert Scarbrough, John Williams, William fyllyps, Richard Hedges, George Hedges.

Note.—No lands mentioned in this deed.

B 11. 1 February, 29 Elizabeth (1587).

Conveyance by John Geaste and Benedict Fawler of Burford, yeomen, to Richard Chadwell, gentleman, and Simon Grene, Burgesses, John Hiron, John Gryffiths, Robert East, and Richard Allflatt, of Burford, yeomen. Two messuages lying together in the High Street between a tenement late of Robert Eynesdale, defunct, on the north, and a tenement late of Simon Wysdome, defunct, on the south ; now in the separate tenures of William Partridge and Thomas Beare ; also one acre of Meadow in High Mead, late in the tenure of Simon Wysdome ; and a half-acre of meadow in the same, called Cakebredd, late in the tenure of Thomas Fryers, defunct. The intents in English as before, except that the parishioners are not included in the appointing of new feoffees.

Witnesses (to livery and seisin): John Roffe, William Hewes, Thomas (illegible).

B 12. 14 February, 41 Elizabeth (1599).

Lease by John Lyme alias Jenkins, John Roffe, William Webbe, John Huntt, John Gryffith alias Phillipps, Thomas Parsons, of Burford, yeomen, Burgesses, to John Smarte of Burford, smith. In consideration of the surrender of a term of 13 years of the messuage wherein he now dwells, and a fine of £4. A messuage and shop thereunto adjoining on the east side of the High Street between a tenement now occupied by Gryffith Lewes, belonging to the free school of Burford, on the south, and a tenement occupied by Thomas Fowler on the north. Which premises the lessors had by sale from Merywether and Dallam. 26 December, 40 Elizabeth ; and they by sale from Typper and Dawe,

10 December, 38 Elizabeth ; and they by sale from the Crown, 28 February, 32 Elizabeth. Lease for 39 years at 28s. 4d. a year. Covenants : (i) That Smart shall provide for Ann Partridge, widow, ' all things necessary to and for her dyett and Mayntenance as shalbe meete and agreeable to her aged estate and calling ' during all the period of the lease, if she shall live so long ; [1] (ii) That Smart will not use the premises as an alehouse or victualling house without the consent of the lessors.

Witnesses : John Yatte, Bailiff, Raphe Wisdom, Thomas Heminge, John Templer, Edmund Serrell, Walter Hayter (the ' wryter hereof ').

B 13. 7 December, 44 Elizabeth (1602).

Lease by John Lyme alias Jenkins, John Roffe, William Webbe, John Huntt, John Gryffith alias Phillippes, and Thomas Parsons, of Burford, yeomen, to John Yate of Burford, clothier, and William Taylor of Burford, chandler. For a fine not specified. A messuage in the tenure of Agnes Partridge, widow, and a shop adjoining, on the east side of the High Street between a tenement belonging to the free school on the south and a tenement of William Geaste on the north. Purchase of the premises recited as in B 12. Lease for 31 years at 28s. 4d. a year.

Witnesses : Symon Symons, John Collyer, Raphe Wisdom, Walter Hayter, Thomas Hardynge.

B 14. 23 February, 5 Charles I (1629).

Conveyance by Richard Alflett of Teynton, tailor, to Sir John Lacy and the rest of the trustees named by the Royal Commission. (By order of the court, Richard Alflett being son and heir of Richard Alflett, deceased, surviving feoffee of the lands commonly called the Bridge Lands.) Two messuages on the east side of the High Street between a tenement belonging to the free school on the south and the land of John Taylor, occupied by Thomas Dolton, glover, on the north ; now or late in the several occupations of Symon Hewes and Richard Dawson.

Witnesses : William Webbe junior, Walter Hayter the elder, Simon Ward, William Kempster.

B 15. 18 October, 6 Charles I (1630).

Lease by the Trustees to Richard Dawson of Burford, saddler. Messuage on east side of High Street adjoining to a house in the

---

[1] This would appear to be ' Ouldemother Partridge ', who was buried in 1615 (see Parish Registers).

tenure of Simon Hewes on the south. Lease for 21 years at 50s. a year.

Witnesses : William Symons, Symon Pearkes, Daniel Berry, William Taylor.

B 16. 26 December, 24 Charles I (1648).
Lease by the Trustees to the same. The same house, but described as adjoining to another house late in the tenure of one Symon Hughes on the *north*. Lease for 21 years at 50s. a year.
Witnesses : Rebecca Silvester, Tho. Randolph.

B 17. 29 September, 1649.
Lease by the Trustees to John Clerke of Burford, feltmaker. A tenement on east side of High Street, between a tenement occupied by Richard Dawson on the south and a tenement occupied by Elizabeth Davis, widow, on the north. Lease for 21 years at 30s. a year.
Witnesses : William Kempster, Tho. Randolph.

B 18. 8 July, 3 James II, 1687.
Lease by the Trustees to Samuel Wiett of Burford, butcher. Messuage on east side of High Street between a tenement occupied by Henry Overbury on the north and a tenement occupied by Denis Cossens on the south. Lease for 21 years at 50s. a year.
Witnesses : Thos. Randolph, John Randolph.

B 19. 8 June, 6 William and Mary, 1694.
Lease by the Trustees to Henry Overbury of Burford, glover. Messuage on east side of High Street between a tenement occupied by Richard Day on the north and a tenement occupied by Samuel Wyatt on the south. Lease for 21 years at 35s. a year.
Witnesses : Tho. James, Chas. Brooke, Richard Mathewes.

B 20. 2 September, 6 Anne, 1707.
Lease by the Trustees to Samuel Wyett of Burford, butcher. Messuage described as in B 18. Lease for 21 years at 50s. a year.
Witnesses : Ann Wyat, Joseph Payton.

B 21. 4 November, 9 Anne, 1710.
Counterpart lease by the Trustees to John Robinson of Burford, butcher. Messuage on east side of High Street between a tenement occupied by Widow Overbury on the north and a tenement occupied by Dennis Cousens on the south. Lease for 21 years at 50s. a year.
Witnesses : (To signature of Charles Fettiplace) Thomas Warren, Edward Fisher ; (To signature of Richard Bartholomew) Tho. Patrick,

John Faulkner ; (To signature of John Lenthall) Edward Moulder, Robert Gilkes.

B 22. 25 March, 7 George I, 1721.

Lease by the Trustees to James Legg of Burford, broadweaver. Messuage on east side of High Street, between a tenement occupied by William Eve on the north and a tenement occupied by Denis Cosens on the south. Lease for 21 years at 50s. a year.

Witnesses : John Stone, Humphrey Gillett.

B 23. 21 November, 10 George I, 1723.

Lease by the Trustees to James Legg of Burford, broadweaver. Tenement now in his occupation ; also a tenement now occupied by William Eve, between a tenement occupied by Denis Cosens on the south and a tenement occupied by Richard Day on the north. Lease for 21 years at £4 5s. 0d. a year.

Witnesses : Henry King, Humphrey Gillett.

TWO BURGAGE RENT ROLLS

1652 and 1685

Tolsey, Bundle E

1652

Burgus de Burford

A rent roll of the Chiefe Rents payable within the said Burrough

John Bartholmew his Land, sometyme the Land of Symon Wisdome the elder deceased

The Mansion house wherein John Hughes now dwelleth, on the east side of Burford, and Late the Land of Hugh May Esq   vis.

Mr John Highlords Land

Two closes and certaine Errable Lands and Meadowes Late the land of Symon Wisdome and now in the occupacion of Thomas Baggs   iiiis. viiid.

Item other Errable Lands in the ffields sometymes Pynnocks Land and now in the tenure of Thomas Baggs   vs.

Item a tenement on the eastside of the highstreete in Burford now in the tenure of Richard Bartholmew   vis. vid.

George Hide his land, late the land of Edward Heylin gent

A messuage or tenement on the eastside of Burford, and now in the possession of him the said ~~George Hide~~ Jo. Jurden Jo. Panter and others .... xii*d*.

John Jorden gent his land

A tenement on the Westside of the highstreete of Burford now in the tenure of Robert Jorden shoemaker .... xii*d*.

Item a tenement on the Northside of Witney streete, late the land of Thomas ffrancis and now in the tenure of Robert Newman .... viii*d*.

(*Interlined with above*—Item a Tenement on the east side of the high street in ye tenure of Samuel Wiatt It a Tenement neare Guildenford sometimes John Hanns his lands)

Nathaniel Noble his Land

A Tenement adioyninge to the dwellinge house of Richard Snowsell and now in the tenure of him the said ~~Nathaniel Noble~~ in the tenure of ~~John Warren~~ .... xii*d*.

Thomas Jorden his Land Late the Land of Robert Veysey

Two Tenements lyinge together on the Eastside of the high streete now in the severall tenures of Richard Snowsell and Beniamin Sessions .... xvi*d*.

Item a Tenement in Sheepestreete, sometyme Robert Silvesters Land and now in the tenure of Thomas Kemster iiii*d*.

Item a Tenement in the Priory Lane, in the tenure of John May .... iiii*d*.

Item an other tenement in the same Lane now alsoe in the tenure of the said ~~John Butler~~ Ri. Wheeler John Nunny ~~Jo. Cooke~~ .... iiii*d*.

Item an other Tenement in the same Lane in the tenure of John Cooke .... iiii*d*.

It a Tenement on the westside of the highstreete now in the tenure of William Rodes, late the land of Edmond Silvester vi*d*.

It a messuage on the westside of the high streete called the George now in the tenure of Richard Veysey, sometyme Richard Hodges Land .... iii*s*. iiii*d*.

Item a tenement adioyninge to the George now in the tenure of John Knight .... xvi*d*.

It a Tenement on the Eastside of Burford now in the tenure of ~~Robert Yate~~ Thomas Hughes .... xii*d*.

Item a Tenement on the Southside of Witney streete now in the tenure of the Widdow Haynes .... vi*d*.

Item an other Tenement on the same side now in the tenure of Richard Yate siveyer   vi*d*.

Item a Tenement on the westside of the highstreete now in the tenure of Richard Wakefeild   iiii*d*.

Item a Tenement on the westside of the highstreete now in the tenure of Robert Aston   vi*d*.

Item a Tenement in the Churchlane (*interlined* this is scoole land) now in the tenure of Judith Wie, Late the Land of Thomas Wiggpitt   iiii*d*.

Item a Tenement in the highstreete now in the tenure of Widow Watts, Late Parretts Land   vi*d*.

Item a Tenement on the Hill, now in the tenure of William Baylies late Parretts Land| vi*d*.

Item a Tenement in Sheepestreete in the tenure of Richard Levett   vi*d*.

John Scriven his land
A Tenement on the Westside of the high streete, and now in the tenure of him the said John Scriven   vi*d*.

Thomas Joyners Land late the land of ffrancis Hampson gent
A Tenement on the Westside of the high streete now in the tenure of Thomas Sansbury formerly the land of Anne ffisher widdow   ix*d*.

~~Thetfords Land~~ Mrs Rebecca Martins Land
A Tenement in the tenure of Henry Hayter late the Land of Anne ffisher   vi*d*.

Thomas Baggs his Land
A Tenement on the Eastside of the high streete now in the tenure of ~~John Canninge~~ ffrancis Craford   xii*d*.

Item a Tenement on the Eastside of the Hill now in the tenure of Henry Huggins late the Land of Joseph George   vi*d*.

Robert Taylors Land
A Tenement on the southside of Sheepestreete in the tenure of the said Robert Taylor   xxii*d*.

Item a Tenement on the Westside of the Hill, called the starre, and now in the tenure of Stephen Yate   vi*d*.

Item a Tenement on the Westside of the Hill, in the tenure of Richard Winfeild   vi*d*.

Lissence his Land, late the Land of one Ravenscroft
A Tenement on the southside of Witney streete, formerly called the Whitehart and now in the tenure of ~~Richard Lifollie~~ Wallin Hopton, with certaine arrable Lands in the ffeilds, late in the occupacion of John Huntt mercer   xi*s*. i*d*.

The ffifteene Lands
Three tenements in Saint Johns streete in the severall
tenures of the widdow Pottinger Elizabeth Prickavance
and Willm Hedges, graunted by Symon Wisdome senr by
lease to the towne of Burford towards the ffifteenes xviii*d*.

~~Slatters Land late the Land of John Clarke~~ Henry
Huggins his land
A Tenement on the eastside of the hill in the tenure of
Richard Mills baker vi*d*.

~~Thomas Silvester tayler his Land~~ now Mr William
Webb his land
A Tenement on the Eastside of the high streete in the
tenure of John Widdows ~~Richard Tustian~~ xii*d*.

The Almesland called Pooles Land
The Proctors of the same Land given by Poole to the
Almespeople of Burford vi*s*. v*d*.

Item of the Proctors for the Lands given by Henry
Bishopp to the Almespeople of Burford viii*s*.

The Churchland
Item of the Proctors thereof for the Lands appertaininge
to the parish Church of Burford xii*s*. vi*d*.

The Bridge Land
Item of the Proctors of the Lands, and an acre of meadow,
and an acre of arrable with two tenements thereunto
belonginge in the severall tenures of Richard Dawson and
Henry Overbury iii*s*. xi*d*.

Mr William Elstons land
Item for a Tenement on the Eastside of Burford now in
the tenure of William Haynes and one other Tenement
adioyninge to the same in the tenure of Richard Hayter,
and an other tenement in the tenure of John Lifollie, with
certaine arrable Lands in the feilds xvi*s*.

Mr Davis his Land late the Land of Mr Templer
The Tenement next the Churchyard, sometyme Pinnocks
Land now in the tenure of ~~Mrs Saunders~~ John Haynes and
Robert Smith ii*s*.

Item three Tenements in the Churchlane now in the
severall tenures of Oliver Munday, Daniel Muncke etc xii*d*.

Item a Tenement on the Eastside of the highstreete in
the tenure of ~~William Coules~~ Abraham Harding now the
land of Robert Collier xiii*d*.

It a Tenement on the same side in the tenure of Richard
Haynes xviii*d*.

Item a Tenement on the southside of Witney streete now in the tenure of ~~Miles Bancks~~ Alice Smith widdow   xii*d*.

Item a Tenement in the Priory Lane at the end of Sheepestreete in the tenure of ~~John Kempster~~ Thomas Boulton and a Barne to the same tenemente belonginge   viii*d*.

William Bartholmew, Ralph Hix and Andrew Davis theire land

Three tenements on the eastside of the highstreete adioyninge one to the other in the severall tenures of them the said William Ralph and Andrew   iiii*s*.

Michael Barretts Land now Symon Randolphs Land

A Tenement on the Southside of Sheepestreete in the tenure of the said Symon Randolph   xii*d*.

Thomas Chadwells Land

A Tenement on the Eastside of the high streete in the tenure of Elizabeth Hayter John ffletcher   iiii*d*.

Edward Beachams Land

Two Tenements on the Northside of Sheepe streete in the tenures of him the said Edward Beacham and Richard Taylor   xii*d*.

John Huntt his Land

A Tenement on the Eastside of the high streete and now in the tenure of him the said ~~John Hunt~~ William Hunt   xii*d*.

Leonard Mills his Land late the Land of Richard Huntt

A Tenement on the Southside of Sheepestreete now in the tenure of him the said Leonard Mills   ix*s*.

Brasenose Colledge Land

A Tenement lyinge on the Westside of the highstreete, now in the tenure of Miles Denton   vi*d*.

Item a tenement on the Eastside of Burford towards the Bridge now in the tenure of Thomas Huntt with certaine Lands thereunto belonging   ii*s*. vi*d*.

The Schoole Land

Two tenements lyinge together on the Northside of Witneystreete now in the tenures of William Buckingham and Phillipp collins   xii*d*.

Item an other Tenement on the Eastside of the highstreete now in the tenure of John Lambert   xviii*d*.

Item an other Tenement on the westside of the hill now in the tenure of Matthew Winfeild   xii*d*.

Item three Tenements neare the Bridge in the severall tenures of Paule Silvester, Richard Smyth etc   xii*d*.

Item a Tenement in the Churchlane called Broadgates in
the tenure of Leonard Yate   xii*d.*
(*Inserted*—A Tenement in the tenure of Widdow Blackman
and Thomas Daniel iiii*d.*)

Jellimans and ffords Land
A Tenement on the Northside of Sheepestreete now in the
severall tenures of Richard Wiett and John ffarmer, late
the Land of Henry Chadwell   vi*d.*

Henry Chadwell his Land
A Tenement on the Northside of Sheepestreete in the
tenure of Henry ffrancklin   vi*d.*
A Tenement on the Southside of Sheepestreete late in the
tenure of John Jorden butcher   vi*d.*

~~Edward Serrell his Land~~ Mr. Jo. Jurden his Land
A Tenement on the Eastside of the high streete and now
in the tenure of ~~John Sindrey~~ Bartholomew Avenell and
Samuel Wiatt   xii*d.*

Edmond Gregory his Land, late the Land of Willm
   Hewes
The Mansion house late in the tenure of Thomas Jorden
with arrable Land late Jennyvers Land (*interlined*—now
in the tenure of John Butler and others) lyinge on the
westside of the highstreete   viii*s.* viii*d.*
Item a Barne and three Tenements lyinge on the Westside
of the hill whereof one of them is in the tenure of William
Kinge   xii*d.*
Item two Tenements on the eastside of the highstreete
now in the tenure of Symon Belcher and David Davis   ii*s.* iiii*d.*
Item a little Tenement adioyninge to the Mansion house
in the tenure of John Boulton   iii*d.*
Item a Tenement on the Westside of the Highstreete and
certaine Arrable Land thereunto belonginge, in the
tenures of Edward Neale, ~~Symon Haynes~~ etc Thomas
Miles and others   vii*s.*

Thomas Silvester Clothier his Land
Item his now dwellinge house on the Eastside of the hill   iii*s.* vi*d.*
Item certaine Errable Lands sometyme ffords Land, now
in the tenure of ~~the said Thomas Silvester~~ Robert Gossen
and others   x*d.*
Item a Tenement on the southside of Sheepestreete in the
tenure of Thomas Willett   xii*d.*
Item a Tenement on the Eastside of the hill, and now in
the tenure of Paule Silvester   xviii*d.*

Item a Tenement on the Eastside of the highstreete, att the lower end of the streete Lately in the tenure of Thomas Sowdley Robert Andrewes   vi*d*.

Item a Tenement on the southside of Witney streete in Burford heretofore called by the ~~name of the~~ name of the Kingshead and lately in the tenure of Thomas Smyth (*added later*) now Matthias Blowin and others   vi*d*.

Item a parcell of Land sometyme Tainters Land devided into three partes between Thomas Silvester William Haynes and Robert Berry   .   vi*s*.

Item a Tenement on the Westside of the highstreete now in the tenure of ~~Edward Pebworth~~ Thomas Curtis   vi*d*.

Item a Tenement on the Eastside of the highstreete and now in the tenurè of Henry Williams   xii*d*.

Item a Tenement on the Eastside of the highstreete, in the tenure of Thomas Jorden   .   vi*d*.

Item a Tenement on the Eastside of the Hill in the tenure of Richard Evetts, with a Close in Witney streete and certaine Lands in the ffeilds   xvi*d*.

  Note.—The following items of T. Silvester's lands have marginal notes against them : Against the 3rd, 4th, and 5th items is written ' Mr. Winsmore ' ; against the 6th ' Js Silvester ' ; and below the 7th ' Ed Thorneton iis. Mr Castle iis. Widdow Brown iis. ' ; against the 8th ' Jo Minchin Paul S.' ; against the 9th ' Tho Silvester ' ; against the 10th ' Winsmore '.

    Thomas Parsons his Land
A Tenement on the Eastside of the highstreete called the Angell and now in his occupacion   iii*s*.
Item for a Close called the Beere close   vi*d*.

    Ambrose Berry his Land
A Tenement on the southside of Sheepestreete and now in the tenure of him the said Ambrose Berry   xii*d*.

    John Eve his Land
A Tenement on the Westside of the highstreete and now in the tenure of him the said John Eve   xii*d*.

    John Hanns his Land
The Mansion house, wherein hee now dwelleth on the Eastside of the highstreete   ix*s*.

    William Turners Land sometyme John Combes his Land
A Tenement on the Westside of the hill wherein hee now dwelleth   xii*d*.

    Richard Hayter his Land late the Land of William Lambert
A Tenement on the Westside of the high streete, in the

severall tenures of Thomas Miles, John Robins and
Thomas Waker xiii*d*.

Willm Hicks his Land, late the land of Willm Combes
A Tenement on the Eastside of the high streete, and now
in the tenure of him the said William Hicks xii*d*.

Thomas Hall of Bampton his Land
A Tenement on the Northside of Sheepestreete in the
tenure of John Maior xii*d*.

John Hughes his Land
A Tenement on the Westside of the high streete above
the Crosse sometyme Rylyes Land viii*d*.

Atkinsons Land, late the Land of Richard Osbaldeston
A Tenement on the Eastside of the hightowne in the
tenure of John Jordan gent xii*d*.
Item a little Tenement next the Common Gate in Witneystreete in the tenure of the Widdow Sessions iiii*d*.

John Dutton Esq his Land
A Tenement on the Eastside of the high streete now in
the tenure of Edward Allen xii*d*.

Symon Partridge his Land
A Tenement on the Eastside of the high streete with
certaine Errable Lands iiii*s*. ix*d*.

Richard Sindry the elder his Land
His now dwellinge house, att the further end of Witney
streete vi*d*.
Item a Tenement in Witney streete in the tenures of
Symon Wickins etc (*interlined* Edmund Dyer) vi*d*.
Item a Tenement on the Westside of the highstreete in
the tenure of William Hayter xii*d*.

Symmes Land sometyme Roffes Land
A Tenement on the Northside of Witney streete in the
severall tenures of ~~Robert~~ Strafford ~~Matthew Seaborne etc~~
John Payton and Thomas Kempster Richard Eve jun xviii*d*.
Item an other Tenement on the southside of Witney
streete called the blackboy in the severall tenures of John
Hardinge Daniel Dix and others xvi*d*.
  Note in margin against last item ' Mr Castle rem ii*s*. before '.

~~Richard Stanfeilds~~ Land Robert Jorden of ffulbrook
his Land late the land of Willm Wisdome
A Tenement on the Eastside of the high streete in the
tenure of John Colinge iii*d*.

Item an other Tenement thereunto adioyninge and belonginge, in the Churchlane, in the tenure of John May Jo Smith and Ri Panter Harry Panter   iii*d*.

Godfreyes Land Mr Masklins Land
A Tenement on the Westside of the hill in the severall tenures of ~~William ffoster~~ John King Simon Legg etc   vii*d*. ob

John Clarke his Land now Thomas Lugg his Land
His dwellinge house on the westside of the highstreete in Burford (*interlined*—' now in the tenure of Jo Cave ')   vi*d*.

Andrew Lifollie his Land
A Tenement on the Westside of the high streete in the tenure of the said Andrew Lifollie   vi*d*.

The Land late the Lord ffalklands Land
A tenement lyinge att the Lower end of the towne on the westside thereof called the Swan now in the tenure of Richard Willett and now Towne Land   iii*s*. iiii*d*.

Two tenements in Saint Johns streete in the severall tenures of ~~Henry Bocke, clerke~~ William Cowles and the Widdow Pope   xii*d*.

A tenement on the Northside of Sheepestreete in the tenure of Thomas Baggs   xii*d*.

Item a tenement on the Westside of the highstreete ad- ioyninge to the Pumpe in the tenure of Stephen Smyth   xv*d*.

Thomas Martins Land
One yard Lands now or Late in the tenure of the said Thomas Martin sometyme Bishopps Land   vi*d*.

~~Richard Piggott of Oxford his Land~~ now Mr. John Jurdens Land
A Tenement and an Orchard neare Guildenford now in the tenure of ~~Richard Gladden~~ Edmund Pebworth and others sometymes John Hanns his Land   xii*d*.

~~Andrew Davis his Land~~ now Paule Silvesters land
A Tenement on the Eastside of the high streete below the middle forge in the tenure of ~~Thomas Alkin~~ Thomas ffowler   vi*d*.

Waterfalls Land and other late the Land of Richard Tayler tanner
Three tenements on the Northside of Witney streete now in the severall tenures of ~~Richard Yate William Hobbs and~~ Thomas Waterfall Jo Alson Ed Wiatt   vi*d*.

(*In margin*—' Mr Castle ii*d*. Waterfall ii*d*. Widdow Ghossen ii*d*.')

Two cottages at the west end of Sheepestreete in the severall tenures of Robert Spurrett and Robert ffrancis Harper   iiii*d*.

An index follows in the original.

Note.—This roll is endorsed in a later hand ' Burgage Rents 1685'.

1685

Burgus de Burford

A Rent Roll of the Cheif ... payable ... the said Borrough

	£	s.	d.

John Bartholomew his land sometymes the land of Symon Wisedome the elder deceased

The Mansion house wherein ffrancis Keble now dwelleth on the east side of the high streete heretofore the Land of Hugh May Esq — 00 06 00

Mr Highlords Land

Two closes and certaine arrable lands and meadowes heretofore the land of Symon Wisedome and now in the occupacon of Henry Godfrey gent — 00 04 08

Allsoe other arrable Lands in the ffeilds sometymes Pynnocks Land and now in the tenure of the said Henry Godfrey — 00 05 00

A Tenement on the east side of the high streete of Burford now in the tenure of Richard Bartholomew — 00 06 06

Daniel Mosse his Land

A messuage on the east side of the high streete and now in the possession of the said Daniell Mosse — 00 01 00

John Jordan gent his Land

A tenement on the West side of the High streete now in the tenure of Robert Osbaldeston, Leonard Bennett and Robert Smith — 00 01 00

A Tenement on the Northside of Witney streete late the Land of Thomas ffrancis and now in the tenure of John Midwinter and others — 00 00 08

A Tenement on the East side of the high streete now in the tenure of the Widdow Harding — 00 01 00

A Tenement on the East side of the High Street and now in the possession of the said John Jordan — 00 01 00

A Tenement next to the Comongate on the Northside of Witney Streete now in the tenure of Robert Ghossen — 00 00 ·04

A Tenement and orchard nere Guildenford now in the tenure of Joseph Newbury and John Evetts — 00 01 00

	£	s.	d.
Marke Noble gent his Land			
A Tenement on the East side of the High streete now in the possession of Thomas Minchin	oo	oi	oo
Richard Jordan gent his Land late the Land of Robert Veysey			
Two Tenements lyeing together on the eastside of the Highstreete now in the severall tenures of George Hart and Henry Phelpes	oo	oi	o4
A Tenement in Sheepestreete called the Worldsend being the Corner house and now in the tenure of Richard Wickins	oo	oo	o4
A Tenement in the Priory Lane in the tenure of Robert Spurrett jun	oo	oo	o4
Another Tenement in the same Lane now in the tenure of Richard Eve etc	oo	oo	o4
Another Tenement in the same Lane now in the tenure of John Haynes	oo	oo	o4
A Tenement on the westside of the High streete in the tenure of Thomas Randolph	oo	oo	o6
A messuage or Tenement in the Highstreete called the George and now in the possession of Robert Aston	oo	o3	o4
A Tenement adioyning to the George now in the tenure of Richard Sheppard and John Bennett	oo	oi	o4
A Tenement on the Eastside of the High streete in the possession of Jacob Marsh and the Widdow Hughes	oo	oi	oo
A Tenement on the Southside of Witney streete in the tenure of Edward Neale	oo	oo	o6
Another Tenement on the same side in the tenure of John Bradshaw etc	oo	oo	o6
A Tenement on the West side of the high streete in the tenure of ffrancis Wakefeild etc	oo	oo	o4
A Tenement on the West side of the high streete in the tenure of Joseph Overbury	oo	oo	o6
A Tenement on the West side ot the high streete in the tenure of Thomas Williams	oo	oo	o6
A Tenement on the Hill in the tenure of Edward Wills	oo	oo	o6
A Tenement in Sheep streete in the tenure of George ffickett and John Kendall	oo	oo	o6
A Tenement on the West side of the high streete in the tenure of James Brag and John Phipps	oo	oo	o6
Mr Robert Pleydalls Land			
A Tenement on the West side of the high streete and now in the occupacon of James Mady	oo	oo	o6

	£	s.	d.
The Widdow Sansbury her Land			
A Tenement on the west side of the High streete and now in the possession of the said Widdow Sansbury and Joshua Brookes	oo	oo	o9
A Tenement on the Westside of the High streete in the occupacion of Henry Lambert Noah Newport and Alexander Luckett	oo	oo	o6
Widdow Baggs her Land			
A Tenement on the East side of the High Streete And now in the tenure of the said Widdow Baggs	oo	o1	oo
A Tenement on the East side of the hill now in the possession of John Legg	oo	oo	o6
Robert Taylor his Land			
A Tenement on the South side of Sheep streete in the tenure of the said Robert Taylor	oo	o1	10
A Tenement on the West side of the hill called the Starr in the possession of Robert Taylor the younger	oo	oo	o6
A Tenement on the West side of the hill in the severall tenures of Thomas Overbury John Wicks etc	oo	oo	o6
Becks Land			
A Tenement on the South side of Witney streete in the tenure of Mr John Loder with certaine arrable Lands in the ffeilds heretofore in the occupacion of John Hunt	oo	11	o1
The ffifteene Lands			
Three Tenements in St Johns streete in the severall tenures of the Widdow Hedges Edward Dyer and the Widdow Yate graunted by Symon Wisedome sen by Lease to the Towne of Burford towards the ffifteenes	oo	o1	o6
Widdow Huggins Land			
A Tenement on the East side of the hill in the severall tenures of the Widdow Huggins and John Buckingham	oo	oo	o6
William Widdowes his Land			
A Tenement on the Eastside of the High streete in the tenure of the said William Widdowes	oo	o1	oo
The Almesland called Pooles Land			
The Proctors of the same Land given by Poole to the Almespeople of Burford	oo	o6	o8
Item of the Proctors for the Lands given by Henry Bishopp to the Almespeople of Burford	oo	o8	oo
The Church Land			
Item of the Proctors thereof for the Lands apperteyneing to the Parish Church of Burford	oo	12	o6

	£	s.	d.

The Bridge Land
Item of the Proctors of the Lands and an acre of
meadow and an acre of Arrable with Two Tenements
thereunto belonging in the severall tenures of Samuell
Wyett and Henry Overbury   00 03 11

William Lenthall Esq his land late the Land of
Mr William Elstone
Item for a Tenement on the East side of Burford now
in the tenure of Richard George, and Another Tenement
adioyneing to the same in the tenure of Henry Hayter
and an other Tenement in the tenure of Thomas ffletcher
with certaine arrable Lands in the ffeilds   00 16 00

Mrs Saunders Land late the Land of Edward Davis
The Tenement next the Churchyard sometymes Pinnocks Land now in the tenure of Nathaniell Brooks
gent   00 02 00

Item Three tenements in the Church Lane now in the
severall tenures of John Jordan daniell Moncke and
others   00 01 00

Mr Robert Glyn his Land late the land of the said
Edward Davis
A Tenement on the East side of the High Streete in the
tenure of Richard Haynes   00 01 06

Item a new built tenement on the South side of Witney
Streete and now in the possession of the said Robert
Glyn   00 01 00

Item a Tenement in the Priory Lane at the end of
Sheepstreete now in the tenure of Thomas Jordan and
a Barne to the same Tenement belonging   00 00 08

Timothy Collier his Land
A Tenement on the East side of the High Streete now
in the severall tenures of Walter Whiter, William
Holford and John Jessett   00 01 01

Richard Bartholomews Land
Two Tenements on the East side of the High streete
in the severall tenures of John Mathewes and John
Minchin Baker   00 03 00

Two Tenements on the east side of the High streete
in the severall tenures of John Colborne and Richard
Norgrove   00 02 04

Symon Randolphs Land
A Tenement on the South side of Sheepe streete in the
tenure of the said Symon Randolph   00 01 00

	£	s.	d.

John ffletchers Land
A Tenement on the East side of the High Streete in
the tenure of the said John ffletcher — 00 00 04

Edward Strongs Land
Two Tenements on the north side of Sheep streete in
the tenures of George Webb and George ffickett — 00 01 00

William Hunts Land
A Tenement on the east side of the High Streete in the
possession of the said William Hunt Edward Keble etc — 00 01 00

Robert Astons Land
A Tenement on the Southside of Sheepstreete now or
late in the possession of Leonard Mills — 00 09 00

Brasenose Colledge Land
A Tenement on the westside of the High Streete now
in the tenure of William Hill — 00 00 06

A Tenement on the East side of the High Streete
towards the Bridge now in the tenure of Mercy Hunt
widdow with certayne Lands thereunto belonging — 00 02 06

The Schoole Land
Two Tenements lyeing together on the north side of
Witney Street now in the tenures of William Bucking-
ham and Jacob Dix — 00 01 00

An other Tenement on the east side of the High Streete
now in the tenure of Dennis Cousens — 00 01 06

An other Tenement on the West side of the Hill now
in the tenure of Richard Winfeild — 00 01 00

Three Tenements nere the Bridge in the severall
tenures of Paul Silvester and Richard Smith — 00 01 00

A Tenement in the Church Lane called Broadgates in
the tenure of John White — 00 01 00

A Tenement in the said Church Lane in the tenure of
The Widdow Blackman and Thomas Daniell — 00 00 04

ffords Land
A Tenement on the North side of Sheepe streete in the
tenure of Thomas Merry and Thomas Dix — 00 00 06

Margery Whiteings Land
A Tenement on the North side of Sheepe Streete in
the tenure of Edmund Wyett — 00 00 06

A Tenement in Sheepe Streete on the South side thereof
heretofore in the tenure of John Jordan Butcher — 00 00 06

Griffith Gregory his Land
The Mansion house late in the tenure of William

	£	s.	d.
Venfeild with Arrable Lands heretofore Jennyvers Land lyeing on the West side of the High streete and now in the tenure of John Carpenter	oo	o8	o8
A Little Tenement adioyneing to the said Mansion house in the tenure of Edward Scriven	oo	oo	o3
A Tenement on the West side of the- high Streete and certayne Arrable Lands thereunto belonging now or late in the tenures of John Legg Thomas Powell etc	oo	o7	oo

William King his Land

	£	s.	d.
A messuage on the west side of the High Streete and now in the tenure of the said William King	oo	oi	oo

Thomas Silvester his Land

	£	s.	d.
A messuage on the East side of the High Streete in the severall tenures of William Price and William Dalby	oo	o3	o6
Item certayne Arrable Lands sometymes ffords Land and now in the tenure of the said William Dalby and John Castle	oo	oo	io
A Tenement on the East side of the High Streete in the tenure of John Minchin	oo	oi	oo

John Winsmore his Land

	£	s.	d.
A Tenement on the South side of Sheepe Streete in the tenure of John Smith	oo	oi	oo
A Tenement on the East side of the High Streete upon the hill in the tenure of Mrs Jordan and William Goram	oo	oi	o6
A Tenement on the East side of the High Streete at the lower end of the Streete in the tenure of John Lambert	.oo	oo	o6
A Tenement on the East side of the High Streete in the tenure of Richard Mills	oo	oo	o6 .
A Tenement on the East side of the High Streete in the tenure of John Richins William Painter etc	oo	oi	o4

Paul Silvesters Land

	£	s.	d.
A Tenement on the west side of the High Streete in the tenure of Thomas Curtis	oo	oo	o6
A parcell of Lands sometymes Tainters Land devided into three partes betweene Anne Haynes Thomas Silvester and Robert Berry	oo	o2	oo
A Tenement on the South side of Witney Streete called the Kings head	oo	oo	o6

Thomas Parsons his Land

	£	s.	d.
A Tenement on the East side of the High Streete called the Angell and now in the tenure of the said Thomas Parsons	oo	o3	oo

	£	s.	d.
ffor a Close called the Beare Close	oo	oo	o6
A Tenement on the West side of the High Streete in the tenure of William Holland and John Vokins	oo	o1	oo
A Tenement on the North side of Witney Streete in the tenure of Richard Berry and others	oo	oo	o6

Ambrose Berry his Land
A Tenement on the South side of Sheepe Streete and now in the tenure of the said Ambrose Berry	oo	o1	oo

John Eve his Land
A Tenement on the West side of the High Streete and now in the tenure of the said John Eve	oo	o1	oo

Hanns Land
The Mansion house on the East side of the High Streete called the Greyhound and now in the severall tenures of Hercules Hastings Robert West Richard Davis etc	oo	o9	oo

William Turners Land
A Tenement on the west side of the High Streete wherein he now dwelleth	oo	o1	oo

Henry Hayters Land
A Tenement on the West side of the High Streete in the severall tenures of John Robins Charles Yate and Alexander Luckett	oo	o1	o1

Richard Hicks Land
A Tenement on the East side of the High Streete in the tenure of the said Richard Hicks	oo	o1	oo
A Tenement on the East side of the High streete in the tenure of Robert ffaxon	oo	o1	oo

Thomas Halls Land
A Tenement on the North side of Sheepe Streete in the tenure of Moses fford	oo	o1	oo

David Hughes his Land
A Tenement on the West side of the High Streete above the Crosse in the tenure of the said David Hughes	oo	oo	o8

Symon Partridges Land
A Tenement on the east side of the High Streete with certaine Arrable Lands	oo	o4	o9

Richard Syndryes Land
A Tenement at the further end of Witney Streete in the tenure of James Partridge and Joane Mills widdow	oo	oo	o6

	£	s.	d.

Giles Mills and Sarah Mills theire Land
A Tenement on the North side of Witney Streete in
the tenure of John Paynton and Thomas Kempster — 00 01 06

Thomas Castle his Land
A Tenement on the South side of Witney Streete called
the Black boy in the tenure of the said Thomas
Castle etc — 00 01 04

Certaine Tenements in Guildenford Lane with other
Lands which the said Thomas Castle lately purchased of
George Hyde — 00 02 00

A Tenement on the North side of Witney Streete in
the tenure of Richard Stryve — 00 00 02

John Jordan of ffulbrooke his Land
A Tenement on the east side of the High Streete in
the tenure of Richard Panter — 00 00 03

An other Tenement thereunto adioyneing and belonging
in the tenure of John Smith — 00 00 03

Henry Godfreyes Land
A Tenement on the West side of the hill called the
Sun in the tenure of John King — 00 00 07$\frac{1}{2}$

William Pagett his Land
A Tenement on the West side of the High Streete in
the tenure of the said William Pagett — 00 00 06

The Land heretofore the Lord ffalklands Land
A Tenement lyeing at the lower end of the Towne on
the west side thereof heretofore called the Swan and
now in the tenure of William Rogers — 00 03 04

Two Tenements in St Johns Streete, in the tenure of
Christopher Kempster and Anne Mathewes — 00 01 00

A Tenement on the North side of Sheepe Streete in
the tenure of Henry Godfrey gent — 00 01 00

A Tenement on the West side of the high Streete
adjoyneing to the Pumpe in the tenure of Timothy
Collier and Richard Burbree — 00 01 03

Mr Compeires Land late the Land of Thomas Martin
One yardlands in the tenure of John Crosse — 00 02 00

Thomas Waterfalls Land
A Tenement on the Northside of Witney Streete in
the tenure of the said Thomas Waterfall — 00 00 02

	£	s.	d.

James Hicks his Land
A Tenement on the North side of Witney Streete in the tenure of Elianer Ghossen widdow — 00 00 02

Two Cottages at the west end of Sheepe Streete in the severall tenures of Robert Spurrett and ffrancis Harper — 00 00 04

in all vis.   Thomas Tredwells Land
A parcell of Land sometymes Tainters Land devided into three partes betweene Anne Haynes Thomas Silvester and Thomas Castle — 00 02 00

Sir Ralph Dutton Barronett his Land
A Tenement on the east side of the high Streete in the tenure of John Perry — 00 01 00

Thomas Sindryes Land
A Tenement on the North side of Witney Streete in the tenure of William Palmer and Others — 00 00 06

10 19 9½

MULLENDER'S LANE

Tolsey, Bundle F

M 1. 8 April, 1649.

Assignment of Lease of ' an Oxhouse contayning by estimacion foure spaces or baies beinge lately builte in the backside belonging to the Capital messuage now in the Possession of John Hannes in Burford one end of the saide foure spaces or bayes abutting North into Mullenders Lane All the old Orcharde and Garden next adioyninge to the said foure spaces or baies on the east side thereof and now is bounded and seperated from the upper new Garden there from a Quine on the wall on the east side thereof to the Upper side of the Appletree next the garden gate where formerly the Mound was usuallie placed And one stripe or Plott of Grounde twelve foote square from the southend of the said foure spaces or Baies out of the backside there for the buildinge or erectinge of one baye of housinge more '.

The original lease granted by John Hannes of Burford, junior, gentleman, and George Hastings of Dalford in the county of Worcester, gentleman, dated 31 October 24 Charles I, 1648, to William Sessions for 99 years. Now assigned by Margaret Sessions, relict of William Sessions, to William George of Idson, Berks., son-in-law of William

Sessions, coverlett weaver. For a fine of £5 and a yearly rent to John Hannes of a couple of pullets.

Witnesses : C. Glyn, John Hughes, Tho: Randolph. .

M 2. 19 April, 1654.

Assignment of Lease by William George of Burford, coverlid weaver, to John Shorter of Witney, dyer. The same premises. For a fine of £30 and the same consideration to John Hannes.

Witnesses : G. Shorter, Fra: Horborne.

M 3. 28 March, 1673.

Lease for a year by Richard Hannes of Burford, gentleman, Mary Hanns his Mother, and Jane Hanns, spinster, his sister, to Edmond Wyett of Burford, tayler. The same premises, now containing five bays ; now in the occupation of Thomas Sessions, ' and were parcell or reputed parcell of the capital messuage or tenement situate lying and being in the Highstreet of Burford called the Grayhound in the tenure or occupation of the said Richard Hanns '. Lease for a year at 5s.

Witnesses : Henry Godfrey, Edward B . . . (*illegible*), Andrew Smyth, John Godfrey.

M 4. 5 August, 26 Charles II, 1674.

Indenture of Apprenticeship. Thomas Sessions, son of Benjamin Sessions of Burford, shoemaker, to Benjamin Sessions his father. With the consent of Gabriel Tooker of Chipping Farringdon, Berks., Gentleman, Anne Beck of Radcott, Oxon., widow, executors of Henry Beck of Eaton Hastings, clerk, and Paul Silvester the elder and Thomas Silvester, Bailiffs of the Liberty of the Borough of Burford.

M 5. 12 November, 29 Charles II (1677).

Assignment of Lease on Mortgage by Edmund Wiett of Burford, tayler, to Thomas Parsons of Burford, chandler. The premises as in M 3. Mortgage for £40.

Witnesses : Samuel Wiett, Symon Randolph, Thomas Randolph.

M 6. 25 March, 32 Charles II, 1680.

Lease for a year by Edmund Wyatt of Burford, tayler, to Richard Bartholomew, mercer, and John Price, clothier, Bailiffs of Burford, Thomas Mathewes, innholder, Thomas Hughes, bookseller, Paul Silvester the younger, tanner, Thomas Castle, chandler, Francis Keeble, mercer, Thomas Silvester, tanner, John Collier, sadler, Richard

George, sadler, and John Peyton junior, clothier, Burgesses of Burford. The same premises. Lease for a year at 5s.

Witnesses : John Minchin, Stephen Swayte, Samuel Wyett, John Jordan.

M 7. 26 March, 32 Charles II, 1680.

Indenture of Sale, by the same to the same. The same premises. For £80.

Witnesses : The same.

M 8. 26 March, 1680.

Receipt (on paper) by Edmund Wyett. For £40 2s. 6d., in full discharge of a sum of £80.

M 9. 26 March, 32 Charles II, 1680.

Bond, by the same, to the purchasers as in M 6. In the sum of £160. To observe the covenants expressed, concerning the guaranteeing of the purchasers in the matter of the mortgages.

M 10. 27 March, 32 Charles II, 1680.

Indenture, tripartite, between Thomas Parsons of Burford, chandler, and Edmund Wyatt of Burford, taylor, of the first part ; Richard Bartholomew and the purchasers as in M 6 of the second part ; John Winsemore of Burford, mercer, Robert Aston of Burford, innholder, Stephen Mathewes of Burford, cordwayner, and William Taylor of Burford, baker, also Burgesses, of the third part. Recites that whereas Edmund Wyatt had not paid the mortgage money due to Thomas Parsons of £42 8s., now in consideration of £40 paid to Edmund Wyett he with the consent of Thomas Parsons leases the premises to the parties mentioned above of the third part, the parties of the second part to receive the rents.

Witnesses : As in M 6.

M 11. 29 March, 32 Charles II, 1680.

Indenture of Trust between Richard Bartholomew and the purchasers as in M 6, and John Winsemore and the rest as in M 10. Recites that whereas the Bailiffs and Burgesses of Burford have been entrusted with the management and disposal of charitable funds, the moneys paid for the purchase of the before-mentioned premises were not the private moneys of the purchasers but were as to £30 derived from the bequest of Dame Elizabeth Tanfield for the apprenticing of poor boys, and as to the rest from the bequest of Mr John Palmer late of Bampton, gentleman ; and the moneys are declared to be upon trust, with clauses providing for the removal of trustees who may cease to reside in the town, and for the enfeoffment of new trustees when less than six remain.

M 12. 29 March, 32 Charles II, 1680.

Lease by the trustees with Winsemore and the rest of the lessees as in M 10, to Edmund Wyatt of Burford, tayler. The same premises, now described as a cottage in Mullenders Lane between a new erected cottage occupied by Benjamin Sessions on the east and the backgate of the Greyhound on the west. Lease for 7 years at £3 a year.

Witnesses : John Minchin, Stephen Swayte, Samuel Wyatt, John Jordan.

M 13. 23 May, 4 William and Mary, 1692.

Lease by Paul Silvester, John Collier, Richard George, and John Payton, to John Greenway of Burford, joyner. A messuage or tenement with garden, parcel of lands purchased by the Bailiffs and Burgesses of Burford and situate in the east end of Mullenders Lane next to a tenement of Joane Sessions, widow, on the west. Lease for 21 years at 45s. a year.

Witnesses : Thomas Minchin, Richard Mathewes.

LENTHALL AND HOLLOWAY CHARITIES

Tolsey, Bundle G

LH 1. 26 December, 1677.

Copy of Will of Lawrence Poole of Stanlake, Oxon., bequeathing to his wife, Anne Poole, his messuage in Stanlake with two closes adjoining, and after her decease to his two daughters, Elizabeth and Anne, and to their heirs in equal portions.

Witnesses : Edward Bartlett junior, Richard Griffin, Ruth Bennett, Richard Pratt.

Note.—The will was proved 28 March, 1682.

LH 2. 17 January, 13 George I, 1727.

Lease for a year by John Edwards of Hardwick in the parish of Ducklington, yeoman, to George Hart, brasier, Richard Whitehall, mercer, Matthew Underwood, mercer, and Paul Silvester, tanner,

of Burford. A close of Pasture in the liberty of Standlake containing
two acres, a little close of Thomas Aldworth's on the south-west and
one of Anderson Neasey's on the north-east, one end shooting upon
Standlake street and the other end abutting on the Church field.
    Witnesses : John Rushley, Thomas Leake.

LH 3. Easter Term, 13 George I (1727).
    Fine. Thomas Dolley, George Hart, Richard Whitehall, Matthew
Underwood, Paul Silvester junior, and Richard Aldworth, plaintiffs ;
John Jordan senior, gentleman, and Mary his wife, John Edwards
and Anne his wife, Absolom Harris and Jane his wife, defendants.
Two messuages, two cottages, two gardens, two orchards, and six
acres of land with appurtenances in Witney, Hardwick, and Ramsden.
Fine of £60.

LH 4. 18 January, 13 George I, 1727.
    Indenture of Sale, quinquepartite, between John Edwards of Hard-
wick, yeoman, of the first part ; Elizabeth Crell of the parish of
St. Anthony in the city of London, widow, and John Holloway, M.A.,
Fellow of Magdalen College, Oxford, of the second part ; Thomas
Smalbone and John Kempster, mason, churchwardens of Burford,
of the third part ; Edward Carter, yeoman, and John Bartlett, wheel-
wright, churchwardens of Bampton, of the fourth part ; George
Hart, Richard Whitehall, Matthew Underwood, and Paul Silvester
of the fifth part. Recites certain provisions of the will of John
Holloway, late of the parish of Cripplegate, Middlesex, deceased,
dated 10 February, 1723, whereby he left to Elizabeth Crell and John
Holloway his nephew the sum of £200 to be laid out by them in lands
or hereditaments upon trust, the rents thereof to go as to one moiety
to the churchwardens of Burford for buying as many twopenny loaves
as could be purchased for the money to be distributed to the poor
weekly upon Sunday ; and as to the other moiety to the churchwardens
of Bampton for a like trust. The present indenture is of the sale by
John Edwards to George Hart and the others of the fifth part of
the close of ground as in LH 2, upon trust to permit the churchwardens
of Burford for the time being to receive the rents.
    Witnesses : John Rushley, Thomas Leake, John Green, Thomas
Partridge senior, William Monk, Christopher Kempster, Benjamin
Haynes.

    [Enclosed with this document is a copy of part of the will of John
Holloway, as recited in the deed.]

LH 5. 18 January, 13 George I, 1727.

Bond by John Edwards, in the sum of £200, to observe the covenants in the indenture of sale.

[Folded with this document is a bill of share of costs for the documents of sale, &c., amounting to £2 18s. 10½d. receipted by Thos. Leake.]

LH 6. 24 May, 1727.

Counterpart Lease by George Hart and the others as in LH 4, to William Robinson of Stanlake, yeoman. The close of pasture as in LH 2. Lease for four years at £4 5s. a year.

Witnesses : William Spurritt, Geo. Hart junior.

LH 7. 16 November, 6 George II, 1732.

Indenture of Sale by John Edwards of Hardwick, yeoman, eldest son and heir of William Edwards and Anne his wife, deceased, and also nephew and next heir of Elizabeth Alder since also deceased, which said Elizabeth and Anne were daughters and co-heirs of Lawrence Poole, late of Standlake, and Elizabeth wife of John Edwards, to George Hart, Richard Whitehall, Matthew Underwood, and Paul Silvester. A close in Standlake containing half an acre, a close formerly purchased by the said feoffees on the east, and a highway or lane on the west, shooting up on Church field on the north, and on a garden lately purchased by one Thomas Collett on the south. For £25, ' part of £50 being charity money given by the last will and testament of one William Lenthal Esquire, deceased, the residue whereof being not received or else it hath been lost many years since '.

Witnesses : Nicholas Wrenford, Thomas Leake.

[Enclosed with this document is a lease for a year by John Edwards.]

LH 8. Hilary Term, 6 George II (1733).

Fine. George Hart, Thomas Collett, and Richard Brereton, armiger, plaintiffs ; John Edwards and Elizabeth his wife, and John Hawtyn, defendants. Three messuages, three gardens, two acres of land, two acres of pasture, and common of pasture in Standlake and Witney. Fine of £100.

MISCELLANEA. I

Tolsey, Bundle H

MERYDEN

14 January, 4 & 5 Philip and Mary (1558).

Conveyance by Edmund Swiffete of Wardley, com. Wigorn., yoman,

and Margery his wife, one of the daughters and co-heirs of Thomas
Mason late of Kenerseley, deceased, to William Stone of the parish
of Meryden, com. Warr., yoman. A close called Abraham Orcharde
with appurtenances in Alsepath, com. Warr., between a wood called
Hillwod on the west and a croft called Whichefylde on the east and
abutting on a coppice called okengrove on the south and extending
upon a pasture called brodheythe to the north. Sale for £6 13s. 4d.

Witnesses : none.

1 May, 12 James I (1614).

Conveyance by Thomas Stone of Woolstone in the county of
Warwick, husbandman, to Geoffrey Tasker of Great Packington in
the same county, yeoman. A croft called the little croft or Chauntrie
croft lying between the land of Clement Craddock called Dyve
Ryddynge on the west and a grove or parcel of ground of Widow Kent
on the east and the King's highway leading from Meryden to Fillongley
on the north and another close of Widow Kent on the south. Sale
for £11.

Witnesses : Tho. Holbeche, Thomas Whadcot, Henry Fynt, George
Shakspere, John Corbison.

4 November, 16 James I (1618).

Deed of Settlement by Thomas Greene of Fillongley in the county
of Warwick, yeoman, to George Pyender of Shustocke in the same
county and Arthur Myller late of Newhit . . . (?) in the same county,
yeomen. A cottage or tenement and a croft or close or meadow
to the same belonging ; and three other crofts or closes adjoining to
the cottage, lying in Old Fillongley, now in the tenure or occupation
of Francis Holbech, gentleman, and John Harris. In consideration
of a marriage to be solemnised between the said Thomas Greene and
Anne Chesshire daughter of Edmund Chesshire of Fillongley, wheel-
wright, and in consideration of the sum of £50 paid to Thomas Greene
by Edmund Chesshire.

Witnesses : John Dugdale, Edmund Cheshire, Richard Dynes.
Witnesses to livery and seisin : Edward Beck, Richard Harris,
William Harris.

24 March, 16 Charles II (1664).

Indenture of Sale by Thomas Greene the elder of Packwood in
the county of Warwick and Thomas Greene the younger of the same,
to Ann Shackspeare of Meriden in the same county, widow. The
remainder of a lease of 99 years of a cottage in Old Fillongley and

certain lands called Cotters Lands containing 25 acres belonging to
the cottage, all which the first-named held of Adrian Shackspere,
late of Meriden, by indenture dated 1 December, 7 Charles I, 1631,
at a rent of £6. Sale for £13 10s.

Witnesses : Martin Whadcock, Tho. Parsons, Tho. Whadcock.

Endorsed with a memorandum that Ann Shakespere assigns the
premises and all her title in them for the residue of the term specified
to Thomas Shakespere gentleman, her son.

Witnesses : Martin Whadcock, Benjamin Cockersall, Adrian
Shakespere (by mark), Tho. Whadcock.

JORDAN

19 July, 1658.

Conveyance in Settlement by Edmund Smith of Chadlington,
tayler, Judith his wife, and Thomas Smith of Chadlington, husbandman, son and heir of the said Edmund and Judith, to Walter Smith
of Burford, shoemaker, another of the sons of the said Edmund and
Judith. A messuage or tenement in Burford in Witney Street between
a tenement occupied by Symon Hayter and others on the east and the
backgate of John John (*sic*) gentleman on the west. In consideration
of the fact that Thomas Smith is to have after the death of his parents
certain lands and a tenement in Chadlington and a fifth part of several
messuages and yardlands left to Judith and her four sisters by Richard
Osbaldeston their father, and also in consideration of a payment of
£4 to be made ' at a day to come ' by the said Walter Smith to his
brother Richard Smith.

Witnesses : John Jordan, Robert Jordan.

24 March, 16 Charles II (1664).

Indenture of Sale by Judith Smith of Chadlington, widow of Edmund
Smith late of Chadlington, tailor, and Walter Smith of Chadlington,
shoemaker, one of the sons of the said Edmund Smith, to John Jordan
of Burford, gentleman. A messuage with appurtenances in Witney
Street between a tenement in the occupation of Symon Hayter and
others on the east and the backgate in the occupation of John Jordan
on the west, which messuage was in the occupation of Margaret
Sessions, widow. Sale for £37.

Witnesses : G. Shorter (?), Richard Greeneway, Robert Jordan.

5 June, 1 William and Mary, 1689.

Indenture of Sale by Richard Mace of Netherwestcott, Glos.,

yeoman, to John Jordan of Burford, gentleman. A messuage or tenement in Netherwestcott and one yardland with the appurtenances (lands and closes specified). Sale for £470.

Witnesses: Jo. Grayhurst sen., R. Jephson Holland, Jo. Ralegh, John Brookes, John Grayhurst jun.

6 July, 10 Anne, 1711.

Indenture in Bankruptcy (incomplete), between Daniel Warwicke Esq., John Jordan jun., and Charles Parrott, gentleman, of the one part, and John Townesend of Witney, chandler, of the other part. Relating to the bankruptcy of John Minchin of Burford, mercer, the three first-named parties being among the commissioners under the commission of bankruptcy.

5 September, 4 George I, 1717.

Lease for a year by Edward Hungerford of Black Bourton, Esq., son and heir of Sir Edward Hungerford, Knight of the Bath, deceased, and nephew and heir of Anthony Hungerford late of Black Bourton, Esq., deceased, to John Trevanion of Carhayes, Northumberland, Esq., and John Jordan of Burford, Esq. The manor or lordship of Black Borton alias Black Bourton, together with the capital messuage or mansion house in Black Bourton and with all rents, services, profits, courts, franchises, etc. For 5s.

Witnesses: James Partridge jun., Ralph Wall, John Jenner.

17 March, 4 George I, 1718.

Indenture of Sale by John Dyer of Kencott, to John Jordan junior, of Burford, Esquire. A strip of ground ' on parte whereof one Bay of the west end of the said John Dyers Barne belonging to his dwelling house in Kencott was formerly erected ', 112 feet in length and 23 feet in breadth, now bounded from the rest of John Dyer's close by a new stone wall and pales. Sale for £15 10s. 6d.

Witnesses: Anthony Clarke, George Ward, John Jenner.

HARDING

5 June, 7 William III, 1695.

Lease for a year by John Warwick of Curbridge, Witney, yeoman, Thomas Silvester of Curbridge, clothier, Ralph Trimbull of Witney, clerk, to John Harding of Burford, mercer. A messuage or tenement on the east side of the High Street now in the occupation of John Minchin, between a tenement of John Whiteing on the north and a tenement occupied by John Winsmore on the south; and 24 acres of arable land in the occupation of John Minchin in the common fields of Burford, Upton, and Signett, being one moiety of one yardland of 48 acres heretofore belonging to a capital messuage late of Thomas Silvester and now of John Warwick, on the east side of the High Street now in the occupation of William Price and Robert Strafford.

Witnesses: David Hughes, Charles Morlden, John Jordan.

6 June, 7 William III, 1695.

Indenture of Sale by the same to the same. The same premises. For £220.

Witnesses: The same, with the addition of John Peppin.

8 June, 7 William III, 1695.

Deed of Settlement by John Harding of Burford, mercer, to Thomas Harris of Lineham in the parish of Shipton-under-Wychwood, yeoman, George White of Little Barrington, yeoman, and Samuel Wheeler of Burford, clothier. The premises as above. In consideration of the love and affection of the said John Harding for his wife Anne, daughter of the said Thomas Harris, and for provision for her children, and in consideration of the sum of £220 advanced by Thomas Harris for the purchase of the premises.

Witnesses: Timothy Collier, Robert Osbaldeston, John Jordan.

Schedule annexed containing a terrier of the arable lands as follows:

In the East Feild
In the furlong lyeing on thest side of the pathway to Broadwell Grove neere the stile of the Inclosure

½ One halfe Acre thereof shooteing east and west on thest side of the footpath an half Acre of Mr Highlords land lyeing on the north side and an Acre of Mr Pryors on the south side thereof

¼ A ffarendell thereof on the south side of the said pathway in the same furlong lyeing to the land of the said Mr Pryor on the south

1 One acre thereof att thest end of the ffarrundell Mr Hughes land on the south Mr Jordans on the north side thereof

3 In the furlong Shooteing over Shilton pathway three single Acres two Acres whereof have the land of John Jordan lyeing between them and the third hath the land of Thomas Silvesters on thest and an Acre of Mr Pryors on the west thereof

½ One other half Acre thereof Shooteing upon Syenettway an Acre of Mr Pryors on the north and an half Acre of Mr Gregoryes on the south side thereof

½ A long half Acre thereof shooteing north and south upon Shilton way Mr Pryors half Acre on the west and Mr Highlords half Acre on thest

½ A shorte half Acre thereof shooteing north and south upon the same way Mr Highlords land east Mr Pryors land west thereof

½ One halfe Acre thereof in the next furlong above betweene an Acre of Mr Pryors on thest and Thomas Yates land on the west

¼ A ffarrundell shooteing north and south on the west side of Shilton way betweene an halfe Acre of Mr Highlords land lyeing on the west and three halfe Acres of Mr Pryors on thest thereof

1 One Acre at Sturte shooteing on Shilton way lyeing betweene an Acre of Mr Jordans land on the west and an Acre of Thomas Silvesters on thest side thereof

1 One Acre in the furlong at thest end of the Leaze Wall betweene the land of Mr Pryor on the south and a plott of Mr Winsmores land on the north thereof

½ One halfe Acre more in the same furlong lyeing betweene the land of Thomas Yates on the south and Mr Castle on the north thereof

1 One Acre more thereof lyeing at or neere the great Bush on the north side of Glouster way betweene the land of Mr Winsmores on thest and of Thomas Silvesters on the west

½ Halfe an Acre thereof lyeing on thest side of the Highway goeing by White Hill under the hedge of Mr Highlords Inclosuer betweene two halfe Acres of Mr Castles land lyeing on each side thereof

½ One halfe more thereof lyeing in the furlong on the west side of the same way between the land of Thomas Yates lyeing on both sides thereof

½ And one halfe Acre thereof

In the West Feild

2 Two Acres thereof in the furlong on the westside of the way to Synett two single acres of Mr Pryors lyeing betweene them

2 Two other Acres thereof lyeing together in the same furlong betweene an Acre of the said Mr Pryors on the south and an Acre of the said Thomas Yates on the north side thereof

1 One other Acre thereof being a fore shooter lyeing in Westwell Bottome on the south side of the Roade way therein A three half Acre peece of Mr Pryors land lyeing on the north side thereof

1 One Acre shooteing north and south upon the upper end of Westwell hedge betweene an Acre of Thomas Yates on thest and Mr Pryor on the west side thereof

1 One Acre in the Oares on the west side of the roade way there betweene an Acre of Mr Winsmores land on thest and an Acre of Mr Pryors land on the west sides thereof

1 One Acre more thereof in the furlong neerest Upton feild shooteing upon Thomas Yates headland betweene an Acre of the said Thomas Yates lyeing on thest side and an Acre of the said Mr Pryor on the west side thereof

½ One halfe Acre thereof lyeing in the furlong next below betweene Paul Silvesters peece on the west and an halfe Acre of Mr Highlords land on thest thereof

½ One other halfe Acre thereof lyeing in Hull Bush furlong betweene
an Acre of John Winsmores on the west and an Acre of Thomas
Yates on thest thereof

½ One other halfe Acre thereof lyeing next farme furlong betweene
an halfe Acre of Mr Pryors on thest And an Acre of Robert Aston
on the west

½ One other halfe Acre thereof lyeing at the Greene banck on thest
side of Westwell way betweene an half Acre of Mr Highlords land
on the north and an Acre of Mr Pryors on the south sides thereof

½ One halfe Acre more thereof lyeing in the Oares neere Westwell
hedge betweene three halfe acres of Mr Pryors land on thest and
an Acre of his land on the west sides thereof

1 One other Acre thereof lyeing in the midle furlong on thest side
of Westwell way betweene two Acres of Mr Highlords land on the
north and an Acre of Mr Pryors on the south

½ And one halfe Acre more in the same feild

Note.—Another copy of the same Deed of Settlement with the schedule
is in the same bundle.

7 June, 7 William III, 1695.
Lease for a year by John Harding, to George White and Samuel
Wheeler. The same premises, with schedule of lands.
Witnesses : The same.

1 August, 7 William III, 1695.
Indenture, tripartite, between John Southby of Caswell, Berks.,
Esq., and Mary his wife, of the first part ; John Warwick of Curbridge,
Thomas Silvester of Curbridge, Ralph Trumbull of Witney and Hester
his wife, of the second part ; Samuel Wheeler of Burford and John
Harding of Burford, of the third part. Declaring the purposes of a fine
to be levied concerning : (i) A messuage and two corn mills and two
fulling mills in Burford or the hamlets of Burford, meadow ground of
five acres belonging to the messuage and lying to the north of it and
adjoining to the mills, a ham lying near the meadow ground, and all
the closes adjoining the south of the tenement and mills—all which
are sold by the first-named parties to Samuel Wheeler ; (ii) the
premises purchased by John Harding as above.
Witnesses : John Jordan, John Peppin.
Enclosed in the above document : The fine referred to, Michaelmas
Term, 7 William III, for a sum of £120.

12 January, 1698. (*Date endorsed.*)
Mr. Hardings Title to a messuage with thappurts in Witney Streete
in Burford in the county of Oxon and to 5 acres thereto belonging

lying in the comon ffeilds of Burford and Signett and to a close of ground or pasture called the Wildernes and to a close of a meadow or pasture containing 2 Acres near the east end of Witney Streete, all which premises are now in the possession of Tristram Wilton or his assigns.

Sets out the following transactions :

11 May, 36 Elizabeth. The premises with the exception of the two-acre close sold by Walter Jones and Hellen his wife to Richard Meryweather for £120

12 August, 40 Elizabeth. Sold by Meryweather to Sir Anthony Cope

28 July, 2 James I. Sold by Cope tb Meryweather

23 May, 5 James I. The two-acre close sold by Thomas Silvester to Meryweather

17 January, 1619. The premises except the messuage conveyed by Meryweather to Thomas Church on mortgage for £205

11 September, 1620. Conveyed by Meryweather, Thomas Wiett, and Church to John Highlord and Susanne his wife

30 & 31 May, 1656. Premises brought into the marriage settlement of John Highlord son and heir of Zac. Highlord, on his marriage with Elizabeth Style

22 & 23 April, 1697. Premises sold by John Highlord of Micham, Surrey, Esquire, only brother and heir of Tho. Highlord Esq., deceased, who was eldest son and heir of John Highlord Esq., deceased, who was eldest son and heir of Zac. Highlord, who was eldest son and heir of John Highlord, sometime citizen and Alderman of London, to Sir John Cotton and John Stone the younger of London, merchant

11 & 12 January, 1698. Premises sold by Cotton and Stone to John Harding.

MISCELLANEA. II

Tolsey, Bundle I

RICH

12 January, 10 William III, 1698.

Certified Copy of an Indenture of Sale by Sir John Cotton of Landwade, Cambridgeshire, and John Stone the younger of London, merchant, to Peter Rich of Upton in the parish of Burford, papermaker. A Capital messuage sometime in the occupation of Richard Merryweather and now or late in the possession of John Winemore (*sic*—the name is later given as Winsmore ; endorsed in margin ' now of Timothy Abraham ') in the High Street of Burford on the east side of the street over against the High Cross, heretofore used for an Inn

and known by the name or sign of the Bull; also a close of pasture
ground containing three acres called the Long Bushy Close at or
near the east end of the High Mead; one acre of lot meadow in the
same High Mead; sixty-three acres in the arable lands of Burford
and Signett, except two acres, parcel of the said sixty-three acres,
called the Two Butts; one acre of arable land in the West Field in
the furlong called the Ferne Furlong; one acre of arable land in the
West Field shooting into the highway from Burford to Signett commonly called Dyneacre way, on the west side of the way. Sale for £545.
Clauses inserted guaranteeing the absolute title of Cotton and Stone.

2 May, 2 Anne, 1703.

Lease by Peter Rich of Upton, to Henry Hayter of Burford, ironmonger, and Katherine his wife. Part of a messuage or tenement on
the west side of the High Street, 'From the Quyne of the wall att
the Crosse house Doore streigh downe to the Quyne of the
wall of the entry Doore next the streete', between a tenement of
Thomas Curtis on the north and the other part of the said messuage
or tenement now in the occupation of Charles Yate and John Coeburne
on the south. At a peppercorn rent. As security for the payment
to Henry Hayter of a certain annual sum of £16 for a period of 200
years and of a certain capital sum in the event of the decease of Henry
Hayter or his wife during the ensuing five or ten years, money due
upon the sale by Henry Hayter and his wife to Peter Rich of the
premises above mentioned.

Witnesses: John Jordan, John Jordan junior, Joseph Payton.

29 September, 6 Anne, 1707.

Lease by Katharine, Countess of Abercorne, to Peter Rich of
Upton. A messuage or tenement in Upton late in the possession
of John Mutlow, deceased, now in the occupation of Joseph Thorneton,
with four yardlands of arable, meadow and pasture in the common
fields of Upton, and common of pasture. Lease for 21 years at £30
a year. Rich covenants not to sell any pease straw, barley straw, or
dung, but to use it on the land; and also to keep one hundred sheep
on the premises.

Witnesses: Ellen Winterborne, Wm. Lindsey, William Tomley.

Note.—Signature of Lady Abercorne.

— 8 Anne, 1709.

Lease by Peter Rich of Upton, papermaker, to John Lenthall of

Burford, Esquire. A moiety of the fulling mills and paper mills at Burford and Upton. Lease for a year at 5s.

Not executed.

— 8 Anne, 1709.

Lease by Peter Rich, to John Lenthall and Francis Broderick of Langford, Esquire. The Long Bushy Close ; one acre of lot Meadow ; 63 acres of arable except the Two Butts ; one acre of arable in Ferne Furlong and one acre upon Dyneacre way. Lease for 99 years at a peppercorn rent.

Not executed.

— 8 Anne, 1709.

Indenture of Sale by the same to the same. The meadow and arable lands as above.

Not executed.

— 8 Anne, 1709.

Indenture of Agreement between John Lenthall and Francis Broderick and Peter Rich. There being a possibility on the one side that a son of Peter Rich and Abigail his wife might have a claim on the meadow and arable lands above mentioned, Peter Rich makes a lease of a moiety of the fulling and paper mills as security that in the event of such a son being born the lands shall be properly conveyed by him to John Lenthall ; and on the other side since John Lenthall has the reversion at the death of Lady Abercorne of the fulling and paper mills and has undertaken to convey them to Peter Rich, he conveys to Peter Rich as security the meadow and arable lands as above.

Not executed.

23 March, 11 Anne, 1711.

Lease by Peter Rich to John Lenthall and John Frederick of Bampton, Esquire. The meadow and arable lands as above. For 99 years at a peppercorn rent.

Witnesses : John Jordan junior, J. Eykyn, Joseph Payton.

29 April, 1714. (*Date endorsed.*)

Endorsed : ' Peter Rich's mortgadge to Margarett Lay pro £40 Dat 29th Aprill 1714.'

A document mutilated (about one-third cut out) concerning premises apparently in the High Street of Burford late in the occupation of John Turner deceased . . . a tenement in the possession of John Jessett on the north side thereof together with three other tenements lately erected . . . Robinson, Thomas Spurryer, and . . . Coburne, and eight acres of arable land . . . except one cottage lately erected in the backside belonging to the . . . Rich lately sold to one John Deane and is now in the said John Deane's possession.

On back: Peter Rich's receipt for £40 witnessed by John Jordan junior and Ralph Wall.

The main document not executed.

12 July, 1 George II, 1727.

Counterpart Lease by John Aston of Suffolk Lane in the parish of St. Mary Abchurch, London, merchant, to Peter Rich of Upton, papermaker. A messuage or tenement with seven yardlands and common for 280 sheep, fourteen 'cow beasts' and seven 'horse beasts', commonly called Martin's Messuage or Tenement. For 21 years at £55 a year. Clause that John Aston shall be at liberty to open up a quarry at the upper end of the piece of arable adjoining the messuage. Also a clause that Peter Rich may plough up two of the closes belonging to the messuage, but not the enclosed lands called Newbrook Lands unless the tenant farmers and landlords agree to plough up their shares of those lands ; and Peter Rich will in that case sow 'two bushell of good sweet clean and merchantable saintfoyne seed to one bushell of corne for every acre of the said closes which shall be plowed up '.

Witnesses : John Jordan, George Mayer.

29 September, 13 George II, 1739.

Deed of Partnership between Joseph Flexney of Burford, clothier, and William Summerfield of Burford, distiller, of the one part, and Peter Rich of Upton, papermaker, of the other part. The paper mills to be worked in partnership ; Flexney and Summerfield are to provide capital ; Rich is to work in the mills as a journeyman, and to instruct the workmen, and also to instruct Flexney and Summerfield in the marketing of the paper ; Rich is to receive weekly wages, 1s. a week to be deducted as interest due upon a bond of £50 by Rich to Robert Raikes of the City of Gloucester, printer ; Rich is not to drink ale or strong drink with any of the workmen at the mills or elsewhere on pain of a fine of 5s. to be deducted from his wages ; nor is he to draw bills upon Flexney and Summerfield for more than is really due to him on pain of forfeiting twice the amount of the bill ; Rich is to enter all the manufacture of paper in a book and to write on every ream the quality of the paper ; Flexney and Summerfield are to receive all moneys and make all payments.

Witnesses : John Ingles, Benjamin Crossley.

23 May, 1746.

Copy of the will of Ann Abrahams, wife of Timothy Abrahams of Burford, mercer. Testator bequeaths certain houses in the High Street and Witney Street and 24 acres of land in the common fields belonging to a house in the High Street formerly a capital messuage of one ——— Silvester, in trust for various people including her niece Sarah Rich and her nephew Peter Rich. Testator mentions a mortgage on Peter Rich's estate for £400 and also a bond of Peter Rich for £180.

[There is another copy of the same will.]

Note.—Most of the Rich Papers have the name 'Padbury' written on the outside in pencil.

CHARITIES

A piece of paper in an eighteenth-century hand containing a copy of part of Thomas Poole's Will:

I Bequeath to the Brotherhood of Burgesses of the Fraternity of our Lady in the Church of Burford to be delivered to them after the decease of my wife my Bason of silver with a Boare's Head enamelled with black in the bottom, an Ewer of silver with a standing foot, to remain to them and their successors for ever. . . . (The gift of houses follows as in P 15 (Cheatle Collection).)

On the reverse of the piece of paper are various notes of payments:

Pd out of Pool's Land 52 shill a year to the poor £10 to the two Bayliffs That is whats for the feast & 50 shillings a piece for defraying other charges.

The Money that pays the Almespeople is as follows

	£	s.	d.
Out of Jonath: Harris's house	10	0	0
Out of Mr Rogers's house	5	4	
Out of the Church Rents	5	4	
Out of Pools Land	2	12	
	23		

21 December, 1725.

Note of Hand by William Webb to Wm. Bowles, Paul Silvester, and George Hart for £4. Agreement appended to receive payment in four instalments on dates named.

Endorsed: Harris's money.

14 May, 1803.

Two receipts by Pye Chavasse for £15 each, money received from Kenn. Esq. on a/c of the Corporation of Burford.

UNCLASSIFIED

23 March, 20 Charles II (1668).

Indenture of Mortgage by William Ford of Little Farringdon, Berks., yeoman, to John Francklin of Little Barrington, Glos., tayler. A messuage with backside and garden in Burford on the north side of Sheep Street between a barn in the occupation of Thomas Baggs on the east and a tenement occupied by Alice Taylor, widow, on the west. Mortgage for £45 ; and lease for 99 years at a rent of a penny.

Witnesses : Thomas Smyth, William Johnsons, Thomas Ford senior, Symon Randolph.

Also a counterpart of the same.

6 August, 31 Charles II, 1679.

Counterpart Lease by William, Earl of Craven, to William Washington of Ascott Dawley, Oxon. A messuage or tenement, a close, and half a yardland now in the tenure of the said William Washington by copy of Court Roll. Lease for 99 years, if Joan his daughter, wife of Francis Twinham, or Washington Twinham his grandson, shall happen so long to live, at 6s. 8d. a year.

21 December, 9 George I, 1722.

Lease for a year by Jonathan Harris late of Widford, Glos., now of Charlebury, Oxon., miller, to John Harris of Asthall, Oxon., miller. Four acres of arable land in Asthall and Astallingly belonging to a messuage occupied by Henry Midwinter.

Witnesses : Wm. Rolls, Ri: Wall.

The Presentation of John Eykyn. (*No date.*)

We whose names are hereunto subscrib'd Churchwardens of Burford in ye county of Oxon, doe present Mr John Eykyn Vicar of Burford afors'd for several Notorious Crimes & Scandals by him ye sd Mr Eykyn committed as followeth.

Imp^r. We present ye sd Mr John Eykyn for his Haunting Inns or Ale Houses continuing ther at unseasonable hours, immoderate drinking, Quarrelling, fighting, Gaming, using Chambering and wantonness, immodest Speech and behaviour there and elsewhere beneath ye dignity and gravity of a minister and wholly derogatory to ye Sacred Function.

Item. We P'sent ye sd Mr Eykyn for a common Drunkard, being

credibly inform'd yt he has been us'd to drink to yt excess as to have been seen reeling and often falling and sometime to ye degree of shamefull and loathsome spuing.

Item. For his Reveling, singing, Roaring, using Ribaldry of discourse even in private Houses as well as publick when he has had opportunity as at publick meetings, Christenings, weddings, discovering his vitious Inclinations, and Actions to ye great offence of all sober people.

Item. For his Blaspheming ye Dreadfull Name of Allmighty God, by his customary, rash, and profane cursing and swearing, And whilst he woud seem a minister of ye Gospell in a prodigious manner having been heard to damn his own wife.

Item. For having committed uncleanness, fornication and sinns of ye like nature and as by his own confession having lived long in ye guilt thereof, having not repented of ye same as he ought.

Item. For suffering and committing great Irregularity and Disorders in his own house by using ill hours, laying out at all hours of ye night, demeaning himself unseemly towards his wife making Games at her causing her shamefully to expose herself, not admitting her to his bed in his mad fits, treating her outragiously, causing her by threatening & terrifying of her to fly at middnight for her shelter and safety to some of her neighbours, at other times to take Sanctuary at a Neighbouring ministers for a considerable time, under his own roof giving his wife occasion of Jealouse and by ffewds and ffrequent Quarrells disturbing ye Neighbourhood.

Item. For keeping about him as his only serv^t a cheerwoman of evill fame, for incontinency and not putting her away when admonisht of it and suspected himself by some of his neare neighbours of too great familiarity with her untill a foul disease broke out upon her and she accused ye sd Mr Eykyn of having given it her.

Item. For omitting catechising of youth at his parish church since he came to Burford as required by ye cannon for refusing to visit ye sick when desird for delaying Christian buryal when in pursuit of his pleasures, for being absent often and in appearance upon frivolous occasions & having not order'd one in his room to read prayers but disapointing ye people.

Item. For not residing in his vicaridge house, as usual alwaies with his predecessors, but living at a Barbers in a meane manner and on several accounts not reputable for a minister.

Item. We p'sent ye said Mr Eykyn not only for his want of ye sober conversation requir'd in ministers but also for his promoting, encouraging, and propagating vice in several instances as will be made evident by his actually seducing and exciting others to filthiness and Lewdness to ye great danger of ye like corruption of manners, ye decay of piety, ye Dishonour of God and Scandal of Religion.

John Castle	
Richd Whitehall	Church Wardens
George Hart	

Note.—John Eykyn was Vicar of Burford from 1701 to 1734. This presentation is not dated; but it is clear from the Register of Officers, preserved with the Parish Registers, that the date is 1704. In that year John Castle was the Rector's churchwarden, and Richard Whitehall and George Hart the wardens 'pro villa'. In no other year are these three found as churchwardens together.

29 September, 9 Anne, 1710.

Counterpart Lease by Ward Smith of the City of London, silk thrower, to Edward Holmes of Fulbrook, clothier, and Phillis his wife. Part of 'an Auntiant Messuage or Tenement heretofore in the occupacion of John Bartholomew deceased, and late in the occupacion of Thomas Greene conteining two low Roomes and a buttery on the ground and the two Chambers over the said two Roomes and that bay of the old Barne that adjoyneth to the said roomes and the part of a garden ground and yard now bounded and fensed out of the residue of the premisses'.and the use of the brewhouse and of the pump and well, and 'way and passage from the said premisses into and from the churchway on the west side thereof'. For 59 years at 2s. 6d. a year. In performance of promises made by the lessor when purchasing the property of the lessee in Fulbrook.

Witnesses: John Jordan, Ralph Syndry.

COMMISSIONS AND LEGAL PROCEEDINGS. I

SEVENTEENTH CENTURY

Tolsey, Bundle K

1. A copy on paper of the decrees of the Royal Commission of 1628 (see P 31, Cheatle Collection); with a draft feoffment, apparently as a specimen, for transferring the charity properties from the old feoffees to the new body of trustees.

2. Michaelmas Term, 7 Charles I (1631).

Oxon. Memorandum quod Willelmus Bartholmewe de Burford in Com Oxon generosus venit Coram Barones huius Scaccarii xxiii° die Novembris hoc termino in propria persona sua et sacramentum suum prostitit corporale in his Anglicanis verbis sequentibus viz. That whereas there are diverse Inhabitants in Burford in the Countie of Oxon who did heretofore hould certaine messuages lands and tenements in Burford aforesaid under severall meane convciances made from Tipper and Dawes who were patentees thereof under the late queene Elizabeth uppon pretence that the same lands were concealed from the Crowne and whereas uppon examination of the said title by vertue or a Commission for charitable uses itt was found and declared thatt the said letteres patents were obtained uppon fraud and thatt the same were not concealed lands but were heretofore given to charitable and pious uses as by the said decree made uppon that commission to which this deponent refereth himself appeareth Now this deponent maketh oath that the seid all feoffees of the said lands trusted for the good of the poore of the towne of Burford doe not claime from by or under the said letteres patents and that this deponent being one of the Burgesses of the said Burrough and well acquainted with the affaires of the same Towne and being one of the feoffees by vertue of the said decree doth and soe doe all the rest of the feoffees disclaime to hold any interest from by or under the said letteres patents made unto the said Tipper and Dawes as aforesaid.

3. Constat of Concealed Lands.

Com. Oxon. In Compoto Henrici Lee armigeri Receptoris generalis revencionum domini Regis Comitatus predicti anno sexto domini nostri nunc regis Caroli inter alia continetur ut sequitur

Terre nuper Concelate

Tenentes et occupatores unius pecie terre vocate a gardenstripe in tenura Willelmi Symonds et xviii acrarum terre in Burford predicto modo in Tenura Willelmi Tayler que premisse nuper fuerunt in tenura Edwardi Bond Ricardi Rulfe et Simonis Alflatt per annum vi*s*. viii*d*. ac ii acrarum prati iacentium in prato vocato the high meade in Burford predicto nuper in tenura Willelmi Partridge et Willelmi Calcott et modo   Glynn et   Webbe per annum xii*d*. ac i acre prati iacentis in le common lott meade vocato le high meede in Burford predicto nuper Alicie Reynolds viii*d*. ac tenementum cum gardino in le highstreete nuper dicti (*sic*) Alicie xii*d*. que   Scott generosus modo tenet ac unum tenementum cum uno Shopp adiacente cum pertinenciis nuper Willelmi Partridge et modo   Dawson xx*d*. unum aliud tenementum nuper Walteri Robinson et modo Collar xx*d*. unum tenementum nuper in tenura Georgii Fowler et modo Gregorii Paty xii*d*. unum tenementum in vico vocato Sheepe-streete ibidem nuper in tenura Iohannis West et modo Anthonii Steward per annum xii*d*. unius parvi clausi continentis tertiam partem unius acre in Whitney streete nuper Alicie Reynolds vidue et modo   Scott generosi per annum iiii*d*. unius clausi vocati Culverclose continentis per estimacionem dimidiam acram in Sheepe-streete nuper Radulphi Wisdome et modo   Turner ii*d*. unum tenementum cum gardino in tenura vidue Silvester in le Churchgreene ibidem modo in tenura   Templer vidue per annum xii*d*. ac aliud tenementum gardinum et le Backside in le Churchgreene predicto nuper in tenura Willelmi Symonds per annum ii*s*. in toto ad xix*s*. ii*d*. per annum insolutos per xxviii^to annos sunt ad festum sancti michaelis archangeli anno regni domini nostri Regis Caroli sexto ultra c*s*. solutos receptori anno quarto dicti domini Regis et remanent adhuc insoluti

*l*xxi xvi*s*. viii*d*.

The said rentes were reserved upon letteres patents graunted to William Tipper and Robert Dawe theire heires and Assignes for ever bearinge date the xxvthe daye of Febr in the xxxiith yeare of the reigne of our late Sovereigne lady Queene eliz by vertue of wch graunte the said rents were putt in chardge

xxviii Iunii   ex p Edm
1631   Sawyer Audit

Note.—The blanks in the Christian names of tenants are as in the original.

4. 15 August, 10 William III (1698).
Writ of the Court of Chancery, addressed to Sir George Rivers Bart., Dorothy his wife, William Wallis, and William Smith. Concerning a gift by Thomas Collyer, late of Shoe Lane, London, brewer, by his will, of 52*s*. a year to the poor of St. Andrew's, Holborn, and a like sum to the poor of Burford, to be laid out at 1*s*. a week on 12 penny loaves to be given every Sunday to 12 poor children. .The gift was charged on a certain brewhouse bequeathed to Thomas Collyer junior, in or near Shoe Lane. The money was duly paid until

the time of the Fire of London, when the brewhouse was burned down. A Commission for Charitable Uses sitting at the Guildhall, London, 9 April, 1674, found that the new brewhouse standing on the site of the old one was chargeable with the annuity. Thereupon writs were taken out against Sir William Beversham, then holding under Collyer, and possession was taken. Beversham sued out an ejectment, but the debt was held due and the money was thereafter paid. Nine years before the date of the present writ Sir George Rivers and Dorothy his wife came into possession, and paid the annuity until about three years before this date.

The present writ, following upon legal proceedings, orders payment of a sum of £7 16s. adjudged by one of the Masters in Chancery to be due on arrears and £13 1s. costs.

COMMISSIONS AND LEGAL PROCEEDINGS. II

EIGHTEENTH CENTURY

Tolsey, Bundle L

1. Copy of the Decrees of the Commission of 1702.

The Commission sat at the house of Daniel Slaymaker at Witney.

The Commissioners were : Sir Robert Jenkinson Bart., Sir Edmund Warcupp Knt., Mainwaring Hamond D.D., Harry Cote Esq., Daniel Warwick Esq., Matthew Prior, Thomas Abell, and Nicholas Marshall, gentlemen.

The jurors were : Robert Harris, Jarvis Ashworth, John Humphreys, John White, William Gay, Francis Clements, William Young, John Saunders senior, William Allen, Thomas Martin, John Spier, John Camden, Richard Tuckey, John Nabbs, and Jethro Bunce.

The Commission first recited the Charity Properties as in the Commission's Decree of 1628 and confirmed the Trusts.

The Commission next recites certain gifts made since 1628 :

i. Dame Elizabeth Tanfield gave a house in Sheep Street being the corner house on the west side of Lavington Lane, for keeping up the tomb and aisle in the Church ; 20s. a year to be paid to ' a sufficient housekeeper of Burford ' to see that this was done ; and the surplus, if any, to six poor widows of good reputation on Christmas Day.

Also a sum of £40 for apprenticing poor boys.

ii. Robert Veisey gave a sum of £20, the interest to be distributed by the Bailiffs and Churchwardens of Burford to twelve poor widows on Christmas Day.

iii. (*Blank*) Atwell gave a sum of 30s. for the use and benefit of the town of Burford.

iv. William Cleavely gave a sum of £24 to be lent to four men for six years at £6 a piece. Also a sum of £20—uses unspecified.

v. John Palmer late of Weald in the parish of Bampton gave a sum of £50, the interest to be given to the poor of Burford.

vi. John Hawkins of Burford gave a sum of £20 for placing out apprentices.

vii. James Fretheram of Kencott gave a sum of 40s. a year out of his house and lands in Langford and Grafton to be given by the Minister and Bailiffs of Burford to a maidservant of six years' good service in one place; or failing that, towards the placing of a poor boy or girl as the Minister, Bailiffs, and Churchwardens should appoint.

viii. Richard Hayter of Burford gave a sum of 8s. a year out of one of his houses for eight almspeople; also 4s. a year out of another house for four poor widows; also 20 nobles to be lent at interest to any one in need, at the discretion of the Bailiffs and Churchwardens, the interest to be not more than 6s. 8d. a year which was to be paid for a sermon to be preached on New Year's Day.

ix. Richard Sindrey of Burford gave a sum of £20 to be lent to poor men in sums of £5, each to pay 3s. a year interest and this 12s. to be given to twelve poor people. The Commission finds that Sindrey left sufficient estate to pay this gift, his son John also left enough, and his grandson John, now of the town of Bedford, had confessed the debt and promised to pay.

x. Thomas Collier gave a sum of 52s. a year out of his brewhouse in London, to provide 12 penny loaves weekly for twelve poor children. The Commission finds that his brewhouse is still chargeable.

xi. Ralph Willett's gift of a cow, the proceeds of the sale of which, made up to 40s., had been put out to interest.

xii. The Right Hon. William Lenthall gave a sum of £100 during his lifetime to apprentice poor children; also a sum of £3 a year, 52s. to provide 10 penny loaves each Sunday for ten poor children and one 2d. loaf for the almspeople, and the remaining 8s. to the Minister of the parish. He also gave a sum of £50 by his will, the interest to be used for apprenticing children.

xiii. John Harris gave a sum of £200 to the Bailiffs and Church-wardens to lend out in sums of £10, repayable at £1 a year.

xiv. Walwin Hopton of Burford left a sum of £50, a debt due to him from Thomas Yate of Signett, to the Bailiffs and four Senior Burgesses, to be lent out to five tradesmen.

xv. Henry Hyling of Minster Lovell left a sum of £200 to Burford. The will was proved by Henry Peacock, and the Commission finds that sufficient estate was left to pay the sum.

The Commission records that the £50 given by John Palmer and £30 of Lady Tanfield's money and other moneys ' of the Company Stock ' belonging to the Bailiffs and Burgesses had been laid out upon the purchase of four tenements in Mullender's Lane.

The Commission finds that Stamp's, Thompson's, Ready's, Edgely's, Silvester's, and Marriner's money ' do several times ly in the hands of the persons above mentioned to have the disposing thereof ', and several of the sums after they are lent out have been likely to be lost and are often got in from the persons they are lent to ' by arrests and other great charges '. The Commission finds that it would be best for the recipients to have each the sum of £10 upon security for 10 years repaying 20s. a year without interest.

The Commission finds that the Bailiffs and Burgesses had laid out £16 on repairs of Burford Bridge, more than the Bridge Lands had brought in, and had paid £20 for expenses in recovering the gift of Collier ; and had laid out upon repairs of the Almshouse £40 more than they had received. Altogether they were £76 out of pocket. They were willing to accept £60, and requested that £2 10s. a year may be settled upon them for four years out of the Bridge Lands and £10 a year for five years out of the Church Lands.

The Commission finally records that there were then only five feoffees of Charity Lands—Sir Edmund Fettiplace and Thomas Horde, Esq., who were very ancient gentlemen, Richard Bartholomew, David Hughes, and one Richard George, who had absented himself from the town and had gone into another town or county.

2. A small quarto volume bound in marbled paper, lettered E on the front cover, containing in manuscript a summary of the decrees of the Commission of 1739, with the exceptions taken by the Bailiffs and Burgesses under each head in their appeal against the decrees, and the judgements of the Lord Chancellor thereon. The following is a complete transcript of the volume.

Lenthalls Charity.

Willm. Lenthall Esqr. by will gave £200 to the Poor of Burford And directed it to be lent to Poor Tradesmen that served their apprenticeships in that Town free from Interest as the Heir and the Bailiffs of the said Town should think fit so that no one Person should have more than £10 and security to be given for repayment thereof at 7 years end.

The Bailiffs and Burgesses of Burford received only £125 of the said £200 of which £100 was put out at Interest on a mortgage of lands at Standlake and £25 in another purchase the Bailiffs and Burgesses not knowing what were the directions of the Donors will had laid out the produce or Interest in Apprenticeing poor children.

The Commissioners of Charitable uses in 1738 Charge the said Bailiffs and Burgesses with the receipt of the other £75 and £135 for the Interest thereof together with £5 received for the Interest of the £100 placed on the said mortgage.

The Commissioners decree the £100 to be called in and paid within twelve months. And that the said Bailiffs and Burgesses do by sale of the purchased premises or otherwise Raise the said £25—That said £100 together with £5 the Interest in the hands of the said Bailiffs and Burgesses. The said £25 and the £75 amounting in the whole to £205 should for the future be preserved as a fund and applied as the Heir at Law of the said Donor Wm. Lenthall and Bailiffs of said Town shall think fit according to the directions of the said will.

The Bailiffs and Burgesses Excepted against that part of the Decree which Charged them with the payment of £75 and £135 upon arguing of which Exceptions the Lord Chancellor ordered them to be allowed and the Commissioners Decree to be reversed as to that part thereof.

So that the £100 is to be called in—the land sold upon which the £25 was laid out and that £25 together with the £100 and £5 the Interest of the £100 in the hands of the Bailiffs and Burgesses making together £130 to be a fund and applied in lending the same to Poor Tradesmen that served their apprenticeships in the Town of Burford free from Interest as the Heir of the Donor and the Bailiffs of the said Town shall think fit so that no one Person shall have more than £10 and Security be given for Repayment thereof at the end of seven years.

Tanfields Charity.

Dame Elizabeth Tanfield by Will dated 23rd May 1729 devised to Willm. Lenthall and others trustees and their Heirs a messuage in

Sheep Street Burford then in the possession of one Berry upon trust that they and the survivors of them should from time to time as need should require dispose of the profits thereof yearly for the repairing maintaining and Cleaning a monument in the said will mentioned and of the Isle wherein it stands—and also allow unto one sufficient Housekeeper of the same Town to be elected by the feoffees or the greater part of them 20s. yearly for his pains to see that the said Tomb be repaired and once in every year at the least and oftener if need require be made clean and the Isle be continually repaired. And the overplus of the Profits that shall arise in such years as there shall need no repairs or when it shall amount to more than needful to bestow thereon the same to be paid to the Hands of the Minister and Bailiffs of the said Town for the time being to be by them distributed on Christmas day in the Church immediately after Divine Service to six poor Widows of the same Parish who shall be reputed to be of Godly and religious conversation.

The Commissioners of Charitable uses Charge the Bailiffs and Burgesses with having received the Rent of the said House but had not regularly appointed any Person to take care of the cleaning and repairing the said Tomb and Isle but had suffered the same to run greatly out of repair so that to Perfect and Restore the said Isle and Tomb it would cost £38 9s. 2d.

Thereupon the Commissioners decree that the said Bailiffs and Burgesses shall pay the said £38.9s. 2d. to John Lenthall the Heir of the surviving Feoffee or Trustee and that it shall be applied by him for repairing the said Isle and Tomb And that the rents and profits of the same house for the future be received by the said Heir of the surviving Feoffee and after an allowance of 20s. a year to a substantial Housekeeper for the looking after the said Tomb that the residue shall be by him paid over to the minister and Bailiffs and shall be by them applied according to the said will.

The Bailiffs and Burgesses excepted against that part of the Commissioners Decree upon arguing thereof the Lord Chancellor ordered that so much of the said Decree whereby the said £38 9s. 2d. is directed to be paid to the said John Lenthall to be applied by him in Repairing the Tomb and Isle and whereby the £10 is directed to be paid towards the expenses etc should be Reversed.

And that the said Mr. Lenthall should appoint one workman and the said Bailiffs and Burgesses appoint another workman and that two such workmen should inspect and survey the said Tomb and Isle and make an Estimate of what it will cost to put the same into proper and sufficient repair and that if such two workmen cannot agree therein that then they do name an Umpire and that such repairs be made according to the Estimate that shall be made by the said two workmen or the Umpire and that the expence of such repairs be paid out of the rent of the said House then in arrear to grow due until the same shall be satisfied—and with these variations ordered that the residue of that part of the said Decree excepted unto be affirmed.

Harris's Charity.

John Harris by his will in 1672 gave to the Town of Burford £200 to be paid into the hands of the Bailiffs and Churchwardens of the Town of Burford upon trust that they and their Successors should lend out gratis to Ten such Tradesmen within the said Town as the Bailiffs of the said Town and the three eldest male persons above 14 years of age which should be of the name and family of the Silvesters in Burford or the major part of them should appoint by £10 a piece upon good Security to be approved of by them to be given by every such Tradesman to the said Bailiffs and Churchwardens for repairing the Ten pounds the yearly sum of 20s. for the space of 10 years then next ensuing into the hands of the Bailiffs and Churchwardens of the said Town. And that when £10 should be repaid into their hands the same to be let out to some other Tradesman in the manner before mentioned. And so to continue from time to time to be lent and repaid to the end of the world. And directs that if any of the said money should at any time remain in the hands of the said Bailiffs and Churchwardens the same should be paid into the hands of the succeeding Bailiffs and Churchwardens. And directs that if there should not be 3 such Persons of the name of the Silvesters living within the said Town at the time of such choice then the number of the said Persons should be made up out of the 3 senior Burgesses Inhabiting within the said Town. And directs that they should for ever Employ the profits of the other £100 in binding some poor Boy Born and living in Burford apprentice to some Trade yearly for ever The said Boy yearly to be elected as the said Tradesmen are to be elected. And directs that if any such Tradesman should die or in the Judgement of the majority of them be likely to become Insolvent That then the said electors should call in the money which should then become due from such Tradesman and that an account in writing how the said Charity is disposed of should be kept by the said electors and should be yearly in Whitsun week be publickly read in the parish church of Burford by the minister or Clerk there—And directs that every Tradesman who should receive any of the said £10 should pay thereout 6d. to be paid to the minister or Clerk who should so read the Account as aforesaid.

The Corporation received the £200 whereof £100 had been lent to Tradesmen pursuant to the Directions of the will—of the other £100 £50 was in Mr. Readys hands upon a promissory note and the other £50 had been lent to John Windsmore who became Insolvent.

The Commissioners decreed that the securities for £100 part of the £200 directed to be lent to Tradesmen should for the future be made to the Bailiffs and Churchwardens for the time being and that the same should be by them lent out according to said will—That the £50 in Mr. Readys hand should be called in and paid to the said Bailiffs and Churchwardens of Burford for the time being £50 Residue of said £100 lent by said Corporation to Said Winsmore and lost and that the Interests and profits of said last mentioned sum of £100 should be for ever applied by said Bailiffs and Churchwardens in apprenticeing poor Boys according to said Donors will That the minister of Burford for the time being should on Tuesday in Whitsunweek yearly read in the said Parish Church an account how the said Charities have been applied the preceeding year and that the minister should be paid for his trouble 6d. out of each £10.

Upon arguing an Exception to this part of the decree a variation was ordered that in the direction that the Bailiffs and Burgesses should be accountable to the Churchwardens of the Town of Burford the Bailiffs should be added to the Churchwardens.

Cobb Hall.

George Symons by his will in 1590 gave to the Poor of Burford his House with the Appurtenances there called Cobb Hall. In 1735 a Lease was granted to Joseph Flexney of Cobb Hall at the yearly Rent of £8 he repairing the same etc.

The Commissioners decree that the said Lease should be void and that it should be delivered up to the Feoffees therein after named to be cancelled—and Possession also to them and that said Feoffees should grant a new Lease to said Flexney if he should think fit for 21 years at £13 a year under the covenants in his said Lease That the rents and profits should be disposed of according to the Donors will.

The Bailiffs and Burgesses excepted against that part of the decree for setting aside the said Lease and upon arguing thereof

The Lord Chancellor allowed the exception and ordered that part of the Decree which was contained in such exception to be Reversed.

Frethems Charity.

James Frethem by his will in 1663 gave to the Town of Burford 40s. a year for ever to be paid out of his Lands in Langford and Grafton into the Hands of the Minister and Bailiffs of Burford which 40s. should be given yearly to a maid servant dwelling in a service six years not as an apprentice but an hired servant being of the age of 21 years And in that year wherein there should not be such a maid servant to receive it then he willed that the said 40s. should be bestowed towards the placing out to service a poor Child born within the said Town of Burford to be disposed of at the directions of the minister Bailiffs and Churchwardens or the major part of them with the good liking of the parents of such child (if any be).

Pools Charity.

Thos. Pool by his will in 1500 wills that his wife Parnell should have all his Lands and Tenements in Burford and Fulbrook for her life and after her death that the same Lands and Tenements in Burford should be put in Feoffment to such persons as should be of the most worshipful and honest Parishioners Burgesses of the abovesaid Fraternity to hold to them their Heirs and assigns for evermore to the Use and Intent that of the Issues and profits of the same The poor People of the Alms house should have every week 6d. to their refreshing and the residue of the same Issues and profits to be applied yearly to the maintenance of the Priest of the said Fraternity and of such other things as should be to the good Continuance of the same Fraternity for evermore.

By an Inquisition taken at Burford 1628 It was found that a Tenement with the Appurtenances lying on the west side of the High street and 12 acres of arable Land thereto belonging A Tenement called the Talbot on the south side of Witney Street A Barn called the Woolhouse on the north side of Witney street A parcel of ground and close on the south side of Sheep street whereupon had been built 4 Several Tenements and also 22 acres of arable Land in the Fields of Burford Upton and Signett were given by Thos. Pool to the Intent to pay weekly with the Revenues thereof for ever to the poor People of the Alms house of Burford 6d. and that the residue of the Revenues of the same Lands (if any) should be employed to the maintenance of the Fraternity of the Town of Burford.

By a decree made under the Inquisition it was decreed that out of the Rents of the Houses and Lands called Pools Lands by reason of the Improvement of the rents thereof the same being then to be let at £9 6s. 8d. yearly and the several Lessees to be charged with the repairs of the same there should be paid weekly for ever to the Poor people in the Great Alms house 12d. to be equally divided amongst them and that the residue of the Rents of the same Lands should be Employed according to the declarations of the will of the said Thos. Pool.

Simon Chadwell who was Heir of Simon Wisdom the surviving feoffee of Pools Lands by Indenture dated 23rd February 1629 did grant and enfeoffee to Sir John Lacy Jno. Dutton and ten others. A messuage or Tenement on the west side of the said High street and 12 acres of arable land in the Fields of Burford thereunto belonging. A messuage called the Talbot on the south side of Witney street—a Barn called the Wool house—a parcel of Ground and a close thereunto adjoining called the Culver close or culverhay whereon had been heretofore erected 4 messuages together with the same messuages—and 22 acres of arable land in the Fields of Burford Upton and Signett which premisses were commonly called Pools Lands to hold to Sir John Lacy and others the said Feoffees their Heirs and assigns for ever to the charitable uses in the Decree of 1628 particularly mentioned.

The Commissioners decreed that the rents and profits of the said 22 acres should for the future return to the use of the Parish Church of Burford aforesaid and should be received by the Churchwardens for the time being and should be by them applied for and towards the Reparation of the same Church and that the Churchwardens should yearly account for the same rents to the Parish Church at a publick vestry on Easter Tuesday decreed the said 1s. per week to be paid to the poor people in the alms house according to said Decree in 1628 And decreed that the Vicar of the parish Church of Burford for the time being (Being the only Person that can be esteemed to stand in the place of the Priest of the said Fraternity) should receive out of the said issues and profits which amount in the whole after an allowance of £2 12s. 0d. a year to the Poor of the said Almshouse to £25 18s. 0d. a year one moiety of the said Lands towards the maintenance of the said Vicar and decreed the other moiety of the said Issues and profits to the good continuance of the corporation of Burford for evermore—acording to the will of the donor And that the same Lands should be conveyed to Feoffees in Trust for the Use therein before mentioned.

The Bailiffs and Burgesses Excepted against the said Decree as to the 22 acres which the Commissioners had decreed to the Church and the applications thereof for the repairs of the said Church and likewise as to the dispositions of a moiety of the profits of the said Land or any part thereof for the augmentation of the Vicarage of Burford.

On arguing of which 2 Exceptions the Chancellor held them to be severally good and sufficient and ordered that the same should stand and be allowed and that such parts of the said Decree as were contained in these Exceptions should be reversed.

Fifteenths.

Three houses in St. Johns street and 2 acres of Land in Upton Field were heretofore given to the Intent that the rents thereof should be applied to repair the premisses and the residue to be kept by the Feoffees till any payment of Fifteenths or 10ths should be granted by Parliament and afterwards to be disposed of for the relief and Ease of the poor Inhabitants of Burford. The Bailiffs and Burgesses received the rents and applied them to charitable uses.

The Commissioners decreed that for the future the Bailiffs and Churchwardens to be chosen by the said Town of Burford and the Overseers of poor there shall receive the rents and profits of the said premisses and the surplus shall be by them disposed yearly on Christmas Eve amongst such of the poor Inhabitants of Burford as they shall think fit untill such time as Tenths and Fifteenths shall be Imposed again by Parliament.

The Bailiffs and Burgesses Excepted to that part of the Decree that directs that the Bailiffs and Churchwardens to be chosen and Overseers of the poor there shall receive and dispose of the rents and profits of the said premisses for by the Inquisition in 1628 it was found that the said premisses were given first to repair the same out of the profits And the residue of the said profits (if any) to be kept till any payment of Tenths or Fifteenths be granted by Act of Parliament and then the residue to be for the relief and easement of the poor Inhabitants of Burford or otherwise as the Alderman Steward and Burgesses of the same Town by their direction shall think fit for the common wealth of the Town which said premisses were by a Decree made under the recited Inquisition Decreed to be disposed accordingly and by another Inquisition and Decree therein in 1702 the jury found the same and Decreed the rents of the said premisses to be received by the Alderman Steward and Burgesses therein mentioned. And that the Commissioners had no reason or authority to vary the said former decree.

Upon the arguing of which Exception the Chancellor ordered that so much thereof as relates to the joining the churchwardens and overseers of the Poor in the Authority for distributing and disposing of the charity mentioned in the exception with the Bailiffs and Burgesses of the Town of Burford be allowed. And the rest of the said Exceptions be overruled and that so much of the said Decree as directs that the churchwardens and Overseers of the Poor should be joined with the Bailiffs and Burgesses of the said Town in giving the Authority for the distributing or disposing of the said Charity to be Reversed.

Heylins Charity.

Henry Heylin gave £200 for apprenticeing poor children. This was laid out in the purchase of lands in Clanfield and the Rents received by the Bailiffs and Burgesses and by them applied accordingly.

The Commissioners decreed that the Rents of the said Lands should for the future be received and applied by the Bailiffs Burgesses and Churchwardens to be elected by the Town of Burford and not by the Bailiffs and Burgesses only as had heretofore been for the apprenticeing poor children according to the decree in 1702 and that the same Charity lands should be conveyed to the Feoffees therein after mentioned by the (*blank*)

To which the said Bailiffs and Burgesses Excepted as to so much and such part thereof as directed that the Rents of the said Lands should be applied by the Bailiffs Burgesses and Churchwardens to be Elected by the Town of Burford—And likewise to that part thereof which directed the said Lands to be conveyed to the Feoffees therein named to be appointed by the (*blank*)

for that by the said Decree in 1702 the Commissioners ordered that when the said sum of £200 should be laid out in the purchase of lands that the rents and profits thereof should be received and applied by the Bailiffs Burgesses and Churchwardens of the Town of Burford or the major part of them.

Upon arguing upon this Exception the Chancellor held it to be good and sufficient and ordered it to stand and be allowed and that so much of the said Decree as this Exception related to be reversed.

Decree in 1702 says in placing out two poor Boys apprentices being
the children of such poor people of the said Town of Burford and do
usually frequent the Church of Burford and hear divine Service or
otherwise as the said Bailiffs Burgesses and Churchwardens for the
time being or the major part of them shall think fit.

Dr. Castles Charity.

John Castle Physician by his will dated 1706 gave to the Bailiffs
and 4 Senior Burgesses of Burford and to their Successors and assigns
for ever 4 messuages or Tenements lying all together in Guildenford
lane Called Castles yard with the appurtenances upon Trust that they
and their Successors should for ever from time to time place 4 Elderly
Widows of Burford who should be of honest sober life and conversation
as (they should approve of) in the said 4 Tenements to be held in such
manner as the same were then held by the then tenants and his will
was that such 4 poor Widows should enjoy the said Tenements for
their lives And he gave other houses and lands in Burford upon trust
that the said Bailiffs and 4 Senior Burgesses should dispose of the
clear rents after deduction for taxes and repairs towards the maintenance of such 4 poor Widows as aforesaid.

The Commissioners decreed that the said Bailiffs and 4 Senior
Burgesses shall yearly on Easterday give an account at the publick
vestry to the principal Inhabitants of the Town of Burford how and
to whom they have disposed thereof in order to prevent any misapplica-
tions for the future.

The Bailiffs and Burgesses Excepted to that part of the Decree for that
the Commissioners had no power nor had any just reason to impose such
Terms as to the account in a manner not warranted by the Donors Will.

Upon arguing of which Exception the Chancellor held the same to
be good and sufficient and ordered the same to stand and be allowed
and that such part of the said Decree to which the said Exception
relates to be reversed—And that the Bailiffs and 4 Senior Burgesses
to whom the Charity is given do annually make up a distinct account
of the said charity and from time to time deliver the same to the
Chamberlain for the time being—And such accounts to be kept in
the Chamberlains office.

Vesseys Charity.

Robt. Vesseys gave £20 the Interest therof to be disposed of by the
Bailiffs and Churchwardens of Burford on Christmas day to 12 poor
Widows of the Town of Burford.

The Commissioners decreed that the Interest of the said £20 should for the future be distributed by the Bailiffs and Churchwardens to be Elected by the Town of Burford for the time being according to the directions of the said will.

To which the Bailiffs and Burgesses Excepted for that they had no power to vary the directions of the said will.

Upon arguing whereof the Chancellor held the same to be good and sufficient and ordered to stand and be allowed and that the Decree so far as it related to such Exception should be reversed.

All Sorts of Money.

Timothy Stamp gave £40 Geo. Thompson £30 whereof £20 was lost with other Charities in the whole £173 10s. were thrown together into one fund called all sorts of money—By an Entry in the Corporation book in 1709 it appears that £29 16s. 8d. in the Hands of John Price was lost.

	£	s.
Timothy Stamp	40	0
Geo. Thompson	10	0
— Hawkins	20	0
— Atwell	1	10
Cow Money	2	0
Lady Tanfield pt	10	0
Alexr. Ready	40	0
Wm. Edgley	10	0
Edmd. Silvester	20	0
Philip Mariner	20	0
	£173	10

By Inquisition in 1702 it was found that these sums did several times lye in the hands of the persons mentioned to have the disposal thereof—And several Sums were lent out according to the respective wills of the Donors were likely to be lost—And that it would be for the advantage of the persons that were to have any moneys by any of the Gifts that they should have the Sum of £10 each lent by the Bailiffs of Burford for time being upon security for the Space of 10 years and the Persons who should borrow the same should pay only 20s. per annum without Interest for the said 10 years unto the Bailiffs of Burford for the time being.

And by a Decree under that Inquisition it was ordered that the same moneys should be lent to such persons upon such security and payable in such manner as last before mentioned.

	£	s.	d.
Bonds	125	0	0
Cash	18	13	4
	143	13	4
Lost	29	16	8
	£173	10	0

The Commissioners decree the Bailiffs and Burgesses to pay and make good the £29 16s. 8d. that was lent to John Price and was lost And that the £125 then standing out on said Bonds and the money in the hands of the corporation should for the future be applied according to the Donors will.

The Bailiffs and Burgesses Excepted to that part of the said Decree which orders them to pay and make good the £29 16s. 8d. Lent to Price and lost—and against that part that orders the said £125 then standing out on Bonds and the money in the hands of the said corporation shall for the future be applied according to the Donors will forasmuch as it appears by the said Inquisition that the said charities have been already settled by former Commissioners under a Commission of Charitable Uses in the year 1702 And to that part of the said Decree which charges them with having in their hands £18 13s. 4d. of the said Charity money whereas £13 13s. 4d. was only in their hands at the time of making the said Decree—

Upon arguing of which three several Exceptions the Chancellor held them to be good and sufficient and ordered them to stand and be allowed and that so much of the said Decree as the said Exceptions relate to be Reversed.

Church.

	£	s.	d.
The Bull in possession of Henry Tash at per annum	14	0	0
formerly the Crown an acre of meadow ground in High Mead a little close in Witney in possession of Nicholas Willett at per annum	1	15	0
A House in Sheep street Moses ford	1	15	0
A House late Willm. Bowles (void)			
An acre of arable land in Upton Field John Lenthalls	1	6	0
A yearly rent given by one Roffe		6	8
The 3d part of an house given by — Hunt	1	16	0
A yearly rent by Mr. Loder		3	4

For the reparation of the Church.

Bridge.

By Inquisition in 1628 it appears that 2 Tenements with the appurtenances on the East side of the High street of Burford were given to repair the said Tenements and the residue to repair the Common Bridge of Burford and amend the Highways adjoining to the said Town as the Alderman Steward and Burgesses of said Town of Burford and their Successors should think most Expedient for the common wealth of the said Town which premises were then applied accordingly —And by a Decree thereunder It was ordered that said 2 Houses should for ever then after remain and the rents thereof employed for repairing the common Bridge of Burford and amending the Highways adjoining to the said Town and the Feoffees of the same to receive and Keep the same untill occasion require to disburse the same in repairing the said Bridge.

By Inquisition in 1702 It was found that the same 2 Tenements were given to the same Uses as before mentioned relating to the same and were so Decreed.

A Strip of land in possession of Mr. Silvester formerly was given to repair said Bridge and way.

The Commissioners ordered and Decreed that £12 8s. 7d. appearing to be the Ballance due from the said Bailiffs and Burgesses to the said Bridge on an account in the year 1738 exclusive should be paid by the Bailiffs and Burgesses to the Feoffees therein after named for the use of the said Bridge and way and repairing of the same and that the rents of the said Bridge and Lands should be applied by the said Feoffees for repairing of said premisses and the surplus for repairing of said Bridge and Bridgeway aforesaid.

The Bailiffs and Burgesses (amongst other things) Except to the latter part of the said Decree but the Chancellor held the same to be sufficient.

Holloways Charity.

John Holloway by his will in 1723 gave £200 to be invested in Lands of Inheritance in Trust that one moiety of the profits thereof should be received by the Churchwardens of Burford and their Successors to be expended in purchasing as many 2d. loaves as the same would purchase to be distributed every Sunday after divine Service amongst the Poor people of Burford for ever and that the number of the said Loaves should every Sunday as near as might be, be equal.

18th Jany. 1726. By Indenture of that date £100 part of the £200 was laid out in the purchase of lands at Standlax Com. Oxon which were conveyed to Jno. Hart Richard Whitehall and others for the uses of the will so far as relates to the Town of Burford.

The Commissioners decreed that the rents and profits of the said Lands so purchased as aforesaid should for the future be received by the Churchwardens to be Elected by the said Town of Burford and be by them applied according to the Directions of the Donors will.

The Bailiffs and Burgesses Excepted against that part of the said Decree as directs the rents of the said Lands to be received by the Churchwardens to be Elected for the Town of Burford only.

Upon the arguing whereof the Lord Chancellor held the said Exception to be good and suficient and ordered it to stand and be allowed and that so much of the said Decree to which it related should be reversed.

Cheveleys Charity.

William Cheveley by his will gave £24 to be delivered to Trustees therein named In trust to be lent by them their successors or assigns to 4 poor Tradesmen within the said Town by equal portions for six years and then to 4 other poor Tradesmen for other six years and so in like manner for ever And that such poor Tradesmen should put in good security By Bond with sureties to the said Trustees their successors and assigns—to be allowed of by them for repayment at the end of every year—and in consideration thereof the said Tradesmen so holding the said money causing a sermon to be preached once every year at their own charges—within the Parish Church of Burford in the afternoon of the Sabbath next after the Burial day of the said Willm. Cheveley yearly for ever and that they should pay 4*d*. a piece yearly to the said Trustees their successors and assigns And gave £20 to the said Trustees and their Successors to be and remain among them for ever Whereof two of them to have it one year and Two another according to the succession for ever.

The Commissioners decreed that the said Charities given by the said Cheveley shall be received and applied by Sir Thos. Read and other the Feoffees therein after mentioned and placed out on Bonds in every respect according to the directions of the said will.

To which Geo. Hart Paul Silvester and Matt. Underwood Excepted as it orders that said charities to be received and applied by Sr. Thos. Read and others for they were the legal Trustees to receive and apply the said Charities pursuant to the directions of the will of the said Mr. Cheveley and no sufficient reason appeared in the said Decree for directing the Exceptions of the said Trust.

Upon arguing of which Exceptions the Chancellor held the same to be good and sufficient and ordered that it should stand and be allowed and that so much of the said Decree which the said Exception relates to be Reversed.

Alms House.

By an Inquisition in 1628 and another in 1702 It was found that one Tenement now called the great Alms house being houses and rooms both above and below together with one capital messuage with the appurtenances and also one lower room—One house called the Tan house and one strip of Ground thereto adjoining and belonging all situate in Burford on the Church green were long since given to the Use of the poor People of the Alms house of Burford aforesaid And were all given by Henry Bishop to the Intent to Employ the revenues thereof for ever to the Use of the Poor dwelling in the said Alms house.

By a decree made on the Inquisition in 1628 It was ordered that the lower rooms of the said Great Alms house with the appurtenances should for ever remain and be employed to and for the habitation and Lodging of 8 Poor people as the same had theretofore been used— and that the rents and revenues of the said upper rooms Capital Messuage Tanhouse strip of Ground and premisses then lett at £4 a year the Lessee to be charged with the repairs should for ever then after be employed and paid to and for the Benefit of the said poor People in the said great Alms House of Burford.

The Bailiffs and Burgesses received the Rents and revenues belonging to the said Alms house being £22 16s. od. a year from 1702 exclusive to 1738 exclusive amounting to £110 and have paid said poor People of the said Alms house and laid out on account thereof according to the Corporation books £171 19s. 10d. the Ballance being £61 19s. 10d. paid out of the corporation revenues.

The Commissioners Decreed that for the Future the rents and revenues of the said alms house shall be received and applied by the feoffees to be appointed for the charities Enquired into by the said Inquisition under that Commission who should also have the sole right and power of nominating and appointing the widows who from time to time shall be placed in the said Alms house.

The Bailiffs and Burgesses Excepted against so much and such part of the said Decree as orders the rents and revenues of the said Alms house to be received and applied by the Feoffees or Trustees in the said Decree mentioned—And also to so much and such part of the said Decree as directs the said Feoffees or Trustees to have the right of nominating and placing the said widows in the said Alms house.

Upon arguing of which Exception the Chancellor held the same to be good and sufficient and ordered that the same should stand and be allowed and that so much of the said Decree to which the said exception relates should be Reversed.

The Commissioners decreed that the charges and expences of entertaining the Jury and Bailiffs who attended on the Jury should be jointly defrayed by the Petitioners and Defendants during all the time of the Enquiry—and that Mr. John Martin appointed by the said Corporation to take down the minutes of the Inquisition of the said Jury under the Commission should be paid for his attendance and Trouble jointly by the Petitioners and Defendants.

The Bailiffs and Burgesses Excepted to so much and such part of the said Decree as orders them (Defendants aforesaid) to pay a moiety of the charges of entertaining the Jury and Bailiff and also to a moiety to the said Martin for his attendance for that the said Commissioners had not such power nor were the Bailiffs and Burgesses the only Defendants in the prosecution of the said Commission and proceedings thereon.

The Chancellor held this Exception to be good and sufficient and ordered it to stand and be allowed and that so much of the said Decree as the said Exception relates to should be reversed.

The Commissioners ordered and decreed that the Bailiffs Churchwardens Overseers and Constables of Burford aforesaid should for the future keep a Book wherein from time when and as often as anything should be done or transacted under or concerning any or either of the before mentioned Charities should be entered a full and exact Acct. thereof under proper and distinct heads and that such Entrys should be yearly on Easter Monday publickly read in the Town Hall of Burford aforesaid.

To this the Bailiffs and Burgesses Excepted and their Exception was held sufficient.

The Commissioners (after reciting that the Bailiffs and Burgesses had been remiss) Did order adjudge and Decree that the surviving Feoffee of the said several Charities or their Heirs should with all convenient speed by proper Deeds of Conveyance convey and assure the said Lands Hereditaments and premises to David Lea and Nicholas Willett and their heirs who should forthwith reconvey the same unto Sr. Thos. Read and others therein named their Heirs and assigns To for and upon the Uses Trusts powers Intents and purposes therein before particularly mentioned and Expressed of and concerning the same respectively.

The Bailiffs and Burgesses Excepted thereto.

Upon the arguing whereof It was ordered that the same should be overruled as to the appointment of the Feoffees and that the continuance and future nomination of the said Feoffees should be according to the Decree of 1629.

The Commissioners Decreed that the Bailiffs and Burgesses should make and deliver a Schedule of all Deeds wills minutes and records whatsoever belonging to the said charities to the Feoffees within 6 months also notice of the enrollment of the Decree—And that the said Deeds and writings should be kept in such places as the new Feoffees should direct and appoint.

The Bailiffs and Burgesses did Except against that part of the Decree for that the making of such Schedule would be a matter of great labour and expence upon them who denyèd. That they had not been guilty of any of the frauds misapplication or misemployments in the said Inquisition found or in the said Decree adjudged.

Upon the arguing of this Exception it was ordered that it be added to the said Decree that the Expences of making the Schedule be defrayed out of the Rents and profits of the respective Charity Estates and that the Schedules be respectively delivered within 12 months from that time.

Hoptons Charity.

William Hopton by his will gave to the Town of Burford £50 to be paid to the Bailiffs and 4 Senior Burgesses of Burford who should lend forth the same to 5 poor Tradesmen living in Burford by £10 a piece taking good Security by Bond of the penalty of £20 with 2 sureties for the payment thereof by 20s. a year for 10 years from the date of the said Bond—And when the sum of £10 should be received by the same Bailiffs and Senior Burgesses the same should be lent forth again to one other Tradesman he giving such Security as aforesaid—And directs that the same £50 should for ever remain to the Uses aforesaid and be lent forth in manner aforesaid And directs that any to whom the said money should be lent or any of the sureties for the same should die or become insolvent that then some other person should be procured to be bound for the remainder of the said Sum instead of the person so dying or becoming insolvent And that the same Bailiffs and Burgesses should in or about Easter yearly for ever cause to be made a note in writing by their officer and therein set forth in whose hands the said several sums of money were and who were their sureties for the same and procure the same to be openly read in the Church of Burford upon the Sunday after Easter day after Evening prayer yearly for ever by the Minister or Curate there and that the several Persons that should have the said Ten pounds lent them as aforesaid should severally pay yearly so long as they should hold the said money or any part thereof (*blank*) a piece for the officer for writing the said note and the like sum to the said minister or curate for reading the same.

Commissioners Decree that the £50 given by Hopton to be lent to poor Tradesmen shall be received by the Bailiffs and 4 Senior Burgesses of Burford and by them applyed according to the will of the Donor—And that notes of the disposition of the same charity shall for the future be read in the said Parish Church of Burford and the money paid for reading the same according to the direction of the same will.

Collyers Charity.

Thomas Collyer by his will dated 25th October 16th Car. 2nd gave to the Bailiffs of the Borough of Burford and the overseers of the Poor there £52 yearly for ever to be by them laid out by £12 (*sic*) every week in 12 loaves and by them bestowed on 12 Poor Children on every Sabbath day at their discretion.

Commissioners decree this to be received and applied by the Bailiffs and overseers of the said Poor according to the Donors Will.

Gilkes Charity.

Robt. Gilkes by his will gave £10 to the Vicar and Churchwardens of the Parish of Burford for the time being and their successors to be by them laid out at Interest and the Interest thereof Expended in Bread and to be distributed among the poor families of the said borough.

Commissioners decree this £10 to be laid out at Int. by the vicar and churchwardens and the Int. expended in Bread and distributed according to the Donors will.

Brutons Charity.

Willm. Bruton by his will Dated 1580 gave 6s. 8d. a year for ever Issuing out of an Orchard called Brutons Orchard (now in the possession of Benjn. Jordan) to be paid to the Poor on Good Friday yearly.

The Commissioners decree this to be received by the Churchwardens and Overseers of the poor of Burford and by them disposed to the poor of Burford according to the Donors will on Good Friday yearly.

Willmots Charity.

Leonard Willmott Dated 25th Feby. 14th James the 1st Gave £4 per annum to be disposed of to such of the poor Inhabitants as did not receive Alms by the Churchwardens who on Easter day are to give an Acct. to four the chief Inhabitants how and to whom they have disposed of it and the same Acct. from time to time to certify to the Justices of the peace of that division at their next assembly or meeting for the account of the Poor according to the form of statute in that case provided.

Commissioners decree this to be received and disposed of by the Churchwardens of the same Town according to the Will of the Donor and that they shall give an Acct. yearly on Easter Monday to four of the chief Inhabitants of the said Town how and to whom they have disposed of the same and shall certify the said Acct. to the Justices of the peace of that Division according to the Directions of the said will.

Harmans Charity.

Edmd. Harman Esqr. by his will gave £4 4s. od. to be yearly Issued out of Port Mills in Burford £4 thereof yearly to be distributed by the constable of Burford to the Poor of Burford at 2 several days in the year by equal portions for their pains in receiving and distributing the said £4 to and amongst the said poor.

Commissioners decree that the said £4 4s. od. shall be received by the said Constables and be by them disposed of to the said poor half yearly on St. Thomas Day and Good Friday by equal portions And that the said constables shall give an acct. in writing to the chief Inhabitants in Burford at the next publick vestry after the disposal thereof how and to whom they have disposed of the same And shall make a list of such poor Persons (Before the disposal thereof) to whom they intend to give the same which List shall be produced and shewn at the next general vestry.

John Castle.

John Castle by his will Dated 4th Novr. 1720 Gave to the minister of the Parish Church of Burford for the time being 10s. a year for ever to preach a Sermon in the parish Church of Burford in the morning on Good Friday yearly and Charged his little Close in Weald in the Parish of Bampton in the said county of Oxford called Marlbrook Close with the payment thereof for ever.

Decree that the 10s. shall be every year duly paid to the said Minister for preaching such Sermon.

John Loyd als Hughes.

Jno. Loyd als Hughes the elder by Deed dated 4th August 3 Elizabeth Granted to Simon Wisdom Alderman Jno. Holmes Steward and

the Burgesses of Burford and their Successors 6s. 8d. yearly for ever
Issuing out of his Tenement in Burford to be paid on Shew Thursday
being the Thursday next before Easter to be distributed by them
for ever on Good Friday to the most needy poor of Burford with a
Clause of distress. And that John Loyd the younger did add 3s. 4d.
to be yearly for ever paid and distributed as the 6s. 8d. is or ought to
be paid That David Loyd als Hughes Son and Heir Apparent of the
said John the Younger did in person ratify and confirm both the said
grants to be for ever had taken and employed as aforesaid.

Commissioners Decree both said 6s. 8d. and 3s. 4d. to be paid to
and received by the Bailiffs and Churchwardens and Overseers and shall
be by them applied according to the directions of the said Deed—And
in Case the said 3s. 4d. shall not be paid that then the Bailiffs Churchwardens and Overseers shall use all legal means for the recovery of
the same yearly sum.

Astons Charity.

Ambrose Aston by his will Gave to John Jordan Junr. Thos. Warren
and others and to the Heirs of the survivor for ever a messuage in
Burford in Trust to pay £3 a year for ever out of the profits thereof
towards the placing out a poor Boy of Burford yearly to some Trade.

The same was received and duly applied from 1713 to 1724 exclusive
But it did not appear by whom the £3 for 1724 was received or applied
or whether it was received or applied at all from 1724 exclusive to
Michs. 1738 Inclusive the £30 a year has been received by Mr. Jno.
Jordan the Heir of the surviving Trustee who has applied £25 part
thereof according to the said Donors will—And he is ready to apply
the remr. as soon as a poor boy of Burford shall be ready to be put
apprentice.

Commissioners decree the said Mr. Jordan to pay and apply the same
accordingly and that he and his Heirs shall for the future receive and
dispose of the said charity according to the will of the said Donor—
And ordered and decreed that the said Trustees or their Heirs shall
make good and pay the £3 for the year unaccounted for and apply
the same according to the directions of the said will.

Palmers Charity.

John Palmer gave by his will £50 to the Town of Burford the Benefit
thereof to be and remain for the Use of the poor for ever which has
been laid out with other charity money in the Purchase of 4 Houses
in Mullenders lane in Burford which are conveyed to the Bailiffs

and Burgesses of the same Town and 50s. part of the rents of the said
Houses have been received by the said Bailiffs and Burgesses and by
them constantly paid to the constable or constables of the said Town
for the time being who have constantly applied the same according
to the Intent of the Donor.

Commissioners Order and decree that the said Bailiffs and Burgesses
shall for the future receive and pay the said 50s. a year to the constables
and that the said constables shall apply the same according to the
directions of the said will and give an Acct. to the principal Inhabitants
of Burford at the publick vestry on Easter Tuesday how and to whom
they have disposed of the same.

Meadys Charity.

Elizabeth Meady gave to the Bailiffs and 4 Senior Burgesses of
Burford 17 acres of arable meadow and pasture Ground in Ducklington
in the county of Oxford with their appurtenances in Trust.

And appointed Mr John Green and Mr William Lawrence overseers
of the said charity.

Note. Here is no mention of their Heirs.

The Commissioners make no decree touching this Charity.

Hayters Charity.

Richard Hayter by his will dated 11th June 1666 gave 8s. a year
for ever to be paid out of the house wherein John Robins then dwelt
to the 8 poor Alms people that should be living in the Alms houses
next to the Church of Burford on the 21st of December yearly—And
gave 4s. yearly to be paid out of the rents of an house wherein Thos
Miles then lately dwelt to be paid to 4 poor widows of Burford aforesaid
of honest life and conversation for ever on the 1st of January yearly.
And gave £6 13s. 4d. to be sett out at Interest on good security by
the direction of the two Bailiffs and Churchwardens of the same Town
or any three of them for the time being unto such Inhabitants that
should have occasion for it—And directs that the Interest arising
thereby should be only 6s. 8d. and that the same should be to the use
of the Minister of the said Town for preaching a Sermon every New
Years day yearly for ever.

The £6 13s. 4d. has been paid to and kept in the hands of the Corporation of Burford and the 6s. 8d. the Interest duly paid to the
Minister for preaching a Sermon yearly on new years day no Inhabitant
having applied for the money.

The 8s. a year payable out of Riches College has been by the Landlord or Owner paid and applied according to the direction of the said will and payable out of Jno. Wilkins Tenement adjoining to the former house has been paid to the Bailiffs and by them constantly paid to 4 poor widows according to the will.

Commissioners order and decree the 8s. a year shall be paid for ever to the 8 Alms people in the Alms house next the Church and the 4s. given to 4 poor widows there shall be for ever paid to them according to the directions of the said will That the £6 13s. 4d. shall be placed out and the Interest thereof applied by the Bailiffs and Churchwardens to be Elected by the Town of Burford or any three of them for the future according to the directions of the same will and not by the Bailiffs only.

Vesseys. This is under the directions of the Bailiffs and Churchwardens.

All Sorts of Money seems wholly under the Directions of the Bailiffs and Burgesses of Burford and the Commissioners have not made any Decree as to the persons who are to place out the money on Bonds and receive the money when paid in again.

Bridge.

Holloway. This is under the directions of the Churchwardens.

Cheveley. This is in the surviving Trustee who should make a new assignment thereof pursuant to the Donors directions. The feoffees appointed by the Commissioners have nothing to do in the direction or application.

Almshouse. The Bailiffs and Burgesses are the sole persons concerned in this charity.

Hoptons. The Bailiffs and 4 Senior Burgesses are the sole Persons concerned in this charity.

Collyer. The Bailiffs and Overseers of the poor to dispose of this charity.

Gilkes. The Vicar and Churchwardens only concerned in this charity.

Bruton. The Churchwardens and Overseers of the poor to dispose of this charity.

Willmott. The Churchwardens to Distribute this Charity.

Harman. The constables to distribute this charity.

John Castle. This given to the minister of Burford.

John Loyd. Bailiffs Churchwardens and Overseers of the Parish to
als Hughes.   receive and pay this charity.

Aston. Mr John Jordan to pay and apply this charity.

Palmer. The Bailiffs and Burgesses to receive and pay this 50s. a year to the constables who are to apply the same according to the Donors will and give an acct. thereof.

Meady. Bailiffs and 4 Senior Burgesses solely concerned in this charity.

Hayter. Bailiffs and Churchwardens or any three of them to place out the £6 13s. 4d. and apply the Interest thereof as the will directs and not the Bailiffs only.

3. A thin folio volume, bound in grey paper, containing another copy, in identical terms, of the decrees of the Commission of 1738 with the exceptions taken by the Bailiffs and Burgesses and the judgements of the Lord Chancellor thereon.

The only point of difference between this and the quarto volume transcribed above is that the index summary, which concludes the quarto volume, is placed at the beginning of the thin folio, and includes some charities not mentioned in the index of the quarto volume. They are as follows :

Lenthals Charity. This Remains to be Applyed by the Heir of the Donor and the Bailiffs of Burford.

Tanfields. The Bailiffs and Burgesses must Appoint Workmen to View and Estimate the Repairs of the Tomb and Isle and when the Tomb and Isle Repaired and a person appointed to look after the same and his sallery and the Repairs paid for the Residue of the Rents of the House given for such Repairs of the Tomb is to be paid over to the Minister and Bailiffs of Burford and by them Applyed according to the will.

Harris. The Bailiffs and Burgesses are to be accountable for and pay to the Bailiffs and Churchwardens of Burford the £50 lent to Winsmore and Lost.

This is under the directions of the Bailiffs and Burgesses of Burford.

Cobb Hall. The Rent thereof is given to the poor of Burford.

Frethems. This 40s. to a maid servant is at the disposal of the Minister and Bailiffs of Burford.

Pools. This Remains in the power of the Bailiffs and Burgesses of Burford.

Fifteenths. This Charity is at the disposal of the Bailiffs of the Town of Burford.

Heylin. This seems to be wholly under the direction of the Bailiffs and Burgesses and Churchwardens as to the putting out Boys Apprentices.

Dr. Castle. This is under the Directions of the Bailiffs and four Senior Burgesses.

4. A thin folio volume, bound in vellum, containing a third copy of the decrees of the Commission of 1738, with notes in the margins obviously written from the point of view of John Lenthall and those who acted with him in attacking the management of the charities. Indeed some of the notes are actually in John Lenthall's handwriting. The general tenor of the notes is that the Bailiffs and Burgesses had usurped the sole management of trusts over which they had no right to be supreme ; that they had misapplied money, and in one or two cases were open to a suspicion of actual embezzlement ; that they had lost certain sums by carelessness and disregard of the donors' directions; that they had let trust property fall into ruin; and that in general they only disposed of the charity money to those who would be subservient to them, and would spend money at their shops.

5. A portion—folios 28–65—of a MS. copy of the pleadings in the lawsuit following the Commission, The Bailiffs and Burgesses of Burford Exceptants *v.* John Lenthall, Esq. and others Respondents.

Folio 28 (the end of the pleadings with regard to the Grammar School) contains a summary of the depositions of some witnesses as to the neglected state of the School and the mental condition of Mr Richard Griffiths.

Folio 29—The Fifteen Lands. The respondents' answer to the exceptants' case was that the rents of the houses being ultimately for the benefit of the town at large, the churchwardens and overseers were quite properly joined by the decree to the Bailiffs and Burgesses in administering the property; that there had not been for some time any Alderman or Steward, and the Bailiffs and Burgesses had no sole right in the property; and that the decree of 1628 appointed the feoffees to receive the rents.

Folio 30—Heylin's Charity. This folio is interesting as revealing the feelings at the back of the dispute. The exceptants' case with regard to the joining of ' the churchwardens to be elected by the town of Burford ' in the administration was that, there being four churchwardens—one appointed by the Rector, one by the Vicar, and two by the town—the two appointed by the town were ' always under the influence of the Lord of the Manor John Lenthall Esq and for this reason the exceptants apprehend the other two are excluded by the Commission's decree '.

Folios 31 & 32—Castle Charity. The respondents remark that they cannot conceive why the Bailiffs and Burgesses should object to giving an account, if they intend to administer the property justly.

Folio 32—Veysey Charity. Another interesting point about the churchwardens is made. The Bailiffs and Burgesses claimed the right to elect one of the two town churchwardens. The respondents' answer was that of the four the one chosen by the Rector was appointed for a ' Tything outside the said Borough ' which had separate officers and made separate rates, the one chosen by the Vicar was the normal Vicar's warden, and the remaining two were chosen by the inhabitants at large and no one by the Bailiffs and Burgesses alone. It appears from the summary of depositions on this point (Evidence of Henry

Walker, Fol. 33) that the outward tything was Upton and Signett. The exceptants do not seem to have pursued their point, but fell back again on the suspicion of the town wardens as being under the influence of Mr Lenthall.

Folios 33 to 35—All Sorts of Money. The respondents had no serious answer to make to the case of the exceptants' plea that the Corporation lands had been by a former decree made liable for recouping losses.

Folios 36 to 44—The Church Lands. The pleadings, mostly concerned with the damage done to Bowls's house, consist of directly contradictory evidence as to the responsibility for payments made or not made in the past.

Folios 44 to 48—The Bridge Lands. Similar counter-pleas and evidence with regard to payments alleged to have been made and the sum claimed by the Corporation as excess of expenditure over receipts. The two parties were in direct opposition as to the validity of entries in the Corporation books and the respondents alleged deliberate falsification of the books. There was dispute as to the due receipt of rents in the past, and some uncertainty as to the tenants of Bridge Land houses.

Folios 48 to 50—Holloway's Charity. The same points raised as on Folio 32 with regard to the appointment of the town churchwardens to receive the rents. The respondents raised the new point that the town churchwardens were the proper persons to appoint since the warden for the outward tything was in no way concerned with town affairs.

In this charity Hart pleaded that there was not sufficient evidence to charge him with the repayment of £5 which had been lost. He could have shown receipts for £4 and 20s. had been applied to ' another charity '.

Folios 50 & 51—Counter-pleas on the point that the Commission had no authority to over-ride a donor's appointment of Trustees and to order the payment of rents to the general body of Trustees.

Folios 52 to 54—The Almshouse. The same pleas by the exceptants against the power of the Commission to place the receipt of rents and the appointment of poor widows to the Almshouse in the hands of the general body of Trustees. The respondents declined to accept the Corporation books as sufficient evidence of the right of the Bailiffs and Burgesses to assume control of this charity ; and pleaded that the Bailiffs and Burgesses had ' misbehaved themselves ' in the matter of admissions to the Almshouse.

Folios 55 to 57. Pleadings with regard to the payment of the Commission's charges. The respondents' case was that there had been an agreement between the two parties to share the costs.

Folios 57 & 58. The infliction of £163 damages on the Bailiffs and Burgesses. Exceptants denied that they had obstructed the enquiry and contested the power of the Commission to order the payment of damages. The respondents affirmed that there had been deliberate refusal or neglect to produce deeds and documents needed for the purposes of the enquiry.

Folios 59 & 60. Order for the keeping of a book recording transactions in connexion with charity property and for the annual reading of accounts on Easter Monday at the Town Hall. The pleadings on this point are important in view of a dispute that arose as late as 1899 with regard to the ownership of the Tolsey. The exceptants say ' that ye sd Town Hall is the freehold of the exceptants and not within ye authority or jurisdiction of ye sd Comm^{rs} to order or direct anything to be done therein '. Respondents ' insist that the same was built by and at ye expence of ye Inhabitants of ye sd Borough & other contributors thereto and Intended and designd for ye Publick good and convenience of ye sd Town and that ye sd exceptants have no ffrehold or Interest therein and that there is no just foundation for their exception in relacion thereto '. The depositions for the exceptants relate to the ordering by the Bailiffs of repairs to the Tolsey and to payment for work done being made by the Bailiffs or some other of the Burgesses. Respondents only produced one witness who said that he did not know at whose expense the Tolsey was built.

Folios 60 to 62. Order appointing new Trustees. The exceptants relied on the appointment of Trustees made after the Commission of 1702. The respondents objected to the validity of that appointment as not having been made either by Mr Lenthall and Wm Bowls as surviving feoffees nor by the Bailiffs and Burgesses ' in their corporate capacity '. There was again dispute as to the power of the Commission to make orders over-ruling previous appointments.

Folios 62 & 63. Order as to the making of a schedule of the deeds and documents concerning charity property. The exceptants pleaded the expense of such a schedule. The respondents urge that the order should be enforced to prevent papers in future being ' secreted and concealed '.

On Folio 63 is the following : ' Note all ye feoffees of ye Charity Lands given to ye Town of Burford that are now living are ye Respondents

John Lenthal Esq., Paul Silvester, Matthew Underwood, John Green, Daniel Dicks Burgesses of ye sd Town of Burford '.

Folios 64 & 65. The beginning of the pleadings as to Pool's Lands. The document gets no further than the recital of the decree, and ends in the middle of a sentence.

6. Various bills of costs in the proceedings made out by Mr Ingles, solicitor, to Silvester, Underwood, Green and others, and the Bailiffs and Burgesses. 1738 to 1742.

7. A letter to Thomas Wainewright, solicitor, signed by J. Castle, Thos. Tash, and John Tash, authorizing him to pay money due for rent and arrears of rent.

8. A list of names of Trustees.

9. A copy of pleadings on the hearing as to costs of the action in Chancery, 9 May, 1743. The exceptants, besides a plea that the attack on the management of the charities had been vexatious and only designed to transfer the power over them into other channels, pleaded also that the enquiry had gone on so unreasonably long that their undertaking to pay a share of the costs could not be enforced upon them.

10. An Indenture Tripartite, dated 21 December, 25 George II, 1751, settling the incidence of the costs among those who had taken the action leading to the appointment of the Commission.

The indenture is between : William Upstone of Burford, maltster, of the first part ; John Lenthal of Burford Esquire, Samuel Patrick of Burford, clothier, and Thomas Clare of Burford, innholder, of the second part ; Robert Castell of Burford, glover, executor of the late William Castell, Edward Chavasse of Burford, innholder, John Andrews of Burford, clothier, Elizabeth Faulkner of Burford, widow, and John Faulkner of Burford, yeoman, executrix and executor of the late John Faulkner, William Griffin of Blackbourton, yeoman, executor of the late James Griffin, and Simon Badger of Burford, mason, of the third part.

The indenture sets out that whereas on or about 29 May, 1737, at a full vestry then held for the parish of Burford in the parish church there, ' it was agreed by general consent that a Commission of Charitable Uses should be sued out and that the churchwardens and overseers should be empowered to sue out the Commission ' ; and whereas Thomas Clare, Samuel Patrick, and the late John Faulkner, then churchwardens, and James Griffin and William Upstone, then overseers, did by writing on 17 June 1737 authorise Alexander Ready of Filkins, gentleman, to procure a Commission and engaged to pay his fees ; and whereas John Lenthall, Clare, Patrick, Upstone, Andrews, Castell, Chavasse, William Lenthall, Francis Potter, then Vicar of Burford, Thomas Hunt of Burford, brazier, Edward Deane of Burford, weaver, Henry Walker, John Faulkner, James Griffin, William Castell, and John Patrick—the nine last-named all since deceased— petitioned the Lord Chancellor for a Commission ; and whereas the Commission sat and made decrees, to which the Bailiffs and Burgesses made exceptions, and a case was heard by the Lord Chancellor, who gave judgement in May 1743 ; and whereas Alexander Ready sent in a bill for £719 13s. to William Upstone, and subsequently took out a writ against him for the money ; and whereas Upstone in Hilary Term 1749 entered a suit firstly against Alexander Ready asking for the taxation of his bill of costs, and secondly against Lenthall and all the rest of the parties named above asking that they be ordered to pay their shares of the costs ; and whereas the parties had agreed to come to terms ; the present indenture witnesses that in consideration of the payment to John Lenthall of the sum of £210 in the following shares :

	£	s.	d.
Robert Castell (as executor)	9	14	1
Upstone	26	19	5
Chavasse	23	5	5
Andrews	33	5	5
Castell (for himself)	26	19	5
E. and J. Faulkner	23	5	5
Griffin	33	5	5
Badger	33	5	5

Lenthall, Patrick, and Clare undertake to pay to Alexander Ready all his claims upon Upstone, Castell and the rest ; and Lenthall also acquits Upstone and the rest of all his claim upon them in connexion with a sum of £273 18s. paid to the Bailiffs and Burgesses on account of costs.

Witnesses : D. Lea, James Chavasse.

Enclosed with this indenture are various documents bearing on the agreement—a copy of Lenthall's receipt for the £210, the original authority to Ready signed by Patrick and the others, Ready's full acquittance, dated 20 December, 1751, for his charges and his written consent to the dismissal of the case brought against him by Upstone, a receipt by one Martin (who had acted as secretary to the Commission) for £20, etc., etc.

APPOINTMENTS OF NEW TRUSTEES

1745 to 1856

Tolsey, Bundle M

1. 25 January, 19 George II, 1746.

Conveyance by John Lenthal Esquire of Burford, as the only surviving feoffee of those named in the Trust Deed of 1702 (see Cheatle collection), to Sir Thomas Read of Shipton under Wychwood, Bart., William Lenthal of Burford Esquire, Robert Stevens of Kempscott Esquire, William Wanley the younger of Eyford, Glos., Esquire, Francis Potter of Burford Clerk, Thomas Godfrey of Hailey Esquire, Henry Walker of Burford maltster, Thomas Hunt of Burford ironmonger, Robert Castle of Burford glover, Samuel Patrick the younger of Burford clothier, Thomas Clare of Burford innholder, and John Falkner of Burford, yeoman.

Witnesses : Chas. Taylor, He. Edmonds.

2. 31 October, 17 George III, 1775 (*sic*).

Conveyance by William Lenthal of Burford Esquire, as sole surviving feoffee, to the Hon. and Rev. Francis Knollis of Burford Clerk, John Lenthal the elder of Burford Esquire, John Lenthal the younger of Burford Esquire, Charles Fettiplace of Swinbrook Esquire, George Davis of Ducklington Esquire, Henry Herries of Burford Clerk, William Chapman of Burford Esquire, William Chavasse surgeon, Thomas Kimber mealman, William Young brasier, and Thomas Clare innholder.

Witnesses : James Smart, James Benjamin Waters, James Baldwin.

3. 13 August, 16 George III, 1775.

Lease for a year, by the same to the same.

4. 30 October, 17 George III, 1776.

Lease for a year, by the same to the same.

5. 30 August, 1827.

Conveyance by the Rev. James Knollis of Penn in the county of Buckinghamshire Clerk, eldest and only son and heir at law of the Hon. and Rev. Francis Knollis, sole trustee and feoffee, to William John Lenthall of Burford Esquire, William Hervey of Bradwell Grove Esquire, Edward Francis Colston of Filkins Esquire, the Rev. William Birch of Burford Clerk, the Rev. Alexander Robert Charles Dallas of Burford

Clerk, the Rev. Charles Loder Stephens of Kencot Clerk, Robert Henry Pytt of Burford surgeon, Christopher Kempster Faulkner gentleman, John Large of Broughton gentleman, William Hine of Burford mercer and draper, Thomas Osman of Burford spirit merchant, and William Ward of Burford printer.

Note.—See the following bundle for documents bearing upon this transaction.

6. 20 October, 1838.
Appointment by Lenthall, Hervey, Colston, Birch, Dallas, Stephens, Pytt, Large, and Ward of the following as new Trustees to act with them, viz.: The Rev. Edward Philip Cooper, now Vicar of Burford, Thomas Cheatle of Burford surgeon, John Bartholomew Phillips of Burford gentleman, David Faulkner of Burford grocer, Thomas Edward Tanner of Burford draper, and Robert Durham of Burford baker.

7. 19 October, 1838.
Lease for a year, by the same to the same.

8. 1 March, 1851.
Appointment by Ward, Cheatle, Phillips, Faulkner, and Durham of new Trustees to act with them viz.: The Rev. James Gerald Joyce, now Vicar of Burford, William Pytt of Burford gentleman, William Robert Cooke of Burford surgeon, Charles John Tanner of Burford draper, Walter Stephens Ward gentleman, and Edward Ansell of Burford tanner.

Endorsed with the following further appointments on 9 February, 1856, viz.: Robert Dannatt Foster of Burford chemist, George Hambidge of Burford grocer, and William Gregory Westrope of Burford draper.

NINETEENTH-CENTURY DOCUMENTS. I

Tolsey, Bundle N

1. A packet of papers relating to the conveyance of the Burford Charity properties to new Trustees by the Rev. James Knollis in 1827.

A difficulty had arisen in this way. The Hon. and Rev. Francis Knollis had been left sole surviving feoffee of those appointed in 1776.[1] He had died intestate, and the Rev. James Knollis, as his heir at law,

[1] This conveyance—Bundle M, no. 2—is dated 1775 in error.

entered into responsibility for the Charity properties. His natural course would have been to appoint new Trustees, but it was discovered that the decrees of Royal Commissions regulating the Burford Charities made no provision for the appointment of new Trustees by the heir at law of a sole survivor.

Counsel's opinion was taken of Mr. T. C. Treslove, Lincoln's Inn. The case as submitted to him throws some significant sidelights upon the management of the charities at this time. One of the principal tenants of charity property was one Tuckwell, 'leading member of the Burford Corporation', who held the chief part of Pool's Land and some Church Land. He was at least seven years in arrear with his rents and was estimated to owe about £400. All the other charity tenants were also in arrear. Counsel is warned that one of the dangers is that, unless the disposition of the Trusts by Mr. James Knollis is flawless in law, the tenants, especially Tuckwell, will take advantage of any irregularity to escape payment of arrears. Mr Knollis confessed himself in ignorance as to who received the rents and when they were last paid (letter from him to Mr. Price, solicitor, Burford, 20 Sept. [1826]). The Hon. and Rev. Francis Knollis had, some twelve months before his death, taken steps to appoint new Trustees, and had made a list of twelve suggested feoffees, 'unconnected with the Corporation thereby meeting the views and wishes of the Commission'; a draft feoffment was made, but Mr. Knollis was growing increasingly feeble and never returned the draft.

Another important point submitted to counsel was about the collection of rents in arrear. His opinion was that these must be collected by the heir at law of the last surviving feoffee; the new feoffees could not claim them.

Ultimately it was decided that the best way to proceed would be by petition to the Master of the Rolls for authority to nominate new Trustees. This course had been rendered possible by a recent Act of Parliament (Sir Samuel Romilly's Act) for an easier way of redressing anything amiss with charity trusts. Previously the only way had been to lay an information with the Attorney General, which was a troublesome and expensive process (see letter from Mr. James Knollis to the Corporation 20 Sept. 1826).

A copy of the petition to the Master of the Rolls, signed by William John Lenthall, William Ward, and William Hine, requesting him to order one of the Masters in Chancery to consider a draft list of feoffees and authorize the transfer of the Charity properties to them, is in the packet. So also is a copy of the order made thereupon by a Master in Chancery giving the necessary authority.

On 21 April 1827 the Rev. James Knollis writes to Mr. Price giving him a list of the persons he nominates as feoffees. They are the persons named in the conveyance of 1827, Bundle M, no. 2. Mr. Knollis says he has been careful to choose ' three persons out of each of the four classes of society '. Evidently he means the upper class with the title of Esquire, the clergy, the ' gentlemen ', and those he calls ' respectable inhabitants '. It appears from some correspondence that an attempt had been made to persuade the Bishop of Oxford to accept nomination.

Tuckwell's final account is in the packet, dated 29 Nov. 1827. Presumably other arrears were paid on occasions when the Rev. James Knollis came to Burford to settle up the Trust business. There is much correspondence concerning these visits. There is also a good deal of correspondence with Tuckwell with regard to his rendering an account.

2 & 3. Two packets of papers concerning the survey of Charity properties in 1859 and the subsequent sale of certain portions in 1860 and 1862.

The survey was made in July 1859 by Mr. Francis Field of Oxford. The following is a summary of his report :

Almshouse Estate.

Dovecot House and large garden occupied by James Harris : in bad repair : sale recommended.

School room and two cottages in the tenure of the Vicar : not in good repair : sale recommended.

Common Poor Estate.

Cobb Hall and three cottages : a good deal out of repair : sale recommended.

Tanfield Estate.

House, stable, and garden in Sheep Street occupied by James S. Price : in excellent repair.

Church Estate.

The Bull Inn : parts out of repair and roof bad : sale recommended.

The Bell Inn, High Street : a dirty dilapidated place : sale recommended.

Chemist's shop in High Street: in indifferent repair: sale recommended.

Small house and inn in Sheep Street, occupied by Humphrey R. Porter: in good repair.

Fifteenths Estate.

Small house and garden in Priory Street: a newly built house.

Mullender's Lane.

First block—four small cottages, one sitting room and one bed room each: tolerable repair.

Second block—three similar cottages: also tolerable repair.

Poole's Estate.

Shop in High Street occupied by Griffin, watchmaker: poor house in bad repair: sale recommended.

Coach house and stable at bottom of Bull Yard, and a warehouse opposite on north side of Witney Street: in middling repair.

Public house in Sheep Street, the Fleece, with a cottage adjoining and another cottage: small cottages but in fair repair.

Cottage in Sheep Street occupied by Wm. Hill and a small close of pasture: in fair repair.

Castle Yard Estate.

Small cottage in Witney Street and two cottages in Guildenford: the first very dilapidated, the other two in very fair repair.

School Estate.

The Eight Bells public house: sale recommended. House occupied by Geo. Packer and Wm. Forest: in fair repair.

Wisdom's Almshouse.

A house of three rooms: very bad and unfit for habitation: sale recommended for site value.

Cottage occupied by Wm. Nunney adjoining: sale recommended.

Note.—The following were School property, though not so entered.

House and yard and currier's shop near the river: in fair repair.

House with timber yard occupied by Wm. East.

House occupied by Thos. Hall: fair repair.

House lately occupied by Thos. Wiggins: in very fair repair.

Two cottages occupied by Henry Pratley and Thos. Winfield: generally in a good state.

Cottage occupied by Benj. Charles.

Cottage occupied by E. Moss—both these cottages in fairly good repair.

Cottage occupied by James Hill: very dilapidated.

Small house occupied by E. Bastin : bad state.

Cottage occupied by H. Ball: fair repair.

Small house occupied by J. Faulkner : in middling repair.

Small House occupied by Widow Barnes : fair repair.

Cottage occupied by T. Beckley : not in good condition.

The following premises were put up for auction on 16 July, 1860 :

Lot 1. The Dovecot House etc.

Lot 2. The school room and two cottages.

Lot 3. Cobb Hall and three cottages.

Lot 4. The Tanfield House.

Lot 5. The Bull Inn.

Lot 6. The Bell Inn.

Lot 7. The chemist's shop in High Street.

Lot 1 was bought by James Wiggins for £210.

Lot 6 was bought by William Nunney for £200.

Lot 7 was bought by William Wheeler for £410.

The following were put up for auction at the Bull Inn on 6 June, 1862 :

Lot 1. Schoolroom and two·cottages.

Lot 2. Cobb Hall and three cottages.

Lot 3. The Bull Inn with the stable, warehouse, etc.

Lot 4. Mullender's Lane—four cottages.

Lot 5. Mullender's Lane—three cottages.

Lot 6. Shop (Griffin's) on Poole Estate.

Lot 7. The Fleece and two cottages.

Lot 8. Castle Yard cottage in Witney Street.

Lot 9. Wisdom Almshouse and cottage adjoining.

Lot 10. House with Currier's shop and next house.

Lot 11. Three cottages—Chowles, Hill & Moss.

Lot 12. House and yard (Wiggins).

Lot 13. Cottages—Bastin· and Ball.

Lot 14. Small house—Faulkner.

Lot 15. Small house—Widow Barnes.

Lot 16. Cottage—Beckley.

Lot 1 was bought by J. and C. Wiggins for £200.

Lot 8 was bought by Phoebe Tuckwell for £200.

Lot 9 was bought by G. Jennings for £65.

Lot 11 was bought by Miss Harriett Ansell for £180.

The following lots were subsequently disposed of by tender :

Lot 2 (purchaser not named) for £200.

Lot 12 to J. B. Walter for £180.

Lot 13 to T. Perrin for £160.

Lots 14 & 15 for £140 (purchaser not named).

4. A packet of leases of Charity properties, the first dated 2 February, 1828, and the last dated 24 April, 1861.

NINETEENTH-CENTURY DOCUMENTS. II

Tolsey, Bundle O

1. Various documents affecting the later history of the Charity Lands.

3 October, 1860.

Scheme of the Charity Commission on the dissolution of the Burford Corporation, vesting the Burford Charity properties in Trustees in trust for the Burford Charities. The only portions of the properties for which any particular arrangements were made were the Fifteenths Estate, the proceeds of which were ordered to be allotted to the National Schools ; Wisdom's Almshouse, which was ordered to be sold and the money allotted to the Great Almshouse ; and the Tradesmen's Fund, allotted to the Grammar School.

3 July, 1863.

Scheme of the Charity Commission under the Act 24 & 25 Victoria, amalgamating the funds of the Great Almshouse, the Tanfield Charity, the Widows' Fund (comprising Vesey's, Atwell's, and Willett's gifts), Meady's Charity, and certain holdings of stock into one fund for the benefit of the Great Almshouse.

5 April, 1869.

Exchange of a house forming part of the School Lands for another house near the School.

The School Lands house was on the north side of Witney Street, bounded on the north by the river Windrush, on the west by the cottage and garden of Letitia Smith, and on the east by cottages called Leather Alley. It was occupied by T. Beckley. The house for which it was exchanged belonged to J. Banbury and was in Lawrence Lane and bounded by the School playground on the south and east. Banbury received also a consideration of £20.

13 April, 1886.

Scheme by the Charity Commission consolidating the Great Almshouse, Castle's Almshouses, and Edmond Harman's Charity.

The Great Almshouse at this time possessed :

    i.   The buildings on Church Green.
    ii. A rood of land at Ducklington.
    iii. About 11 acres of land at Curbridge.
    iv. The Tanfield house in Sheep Street.
    v.   £3 a year from Poole's Lands.
    vi. £5 4s. a year from Church Lands.
    vii. £868 13s. 5d. Consols.
    viii. £221 15s. 1d. Consols.

Castle's Almshouses possessed :

    i.   The buildings in Guildenford.
    ii. A cottage in Guildenford.
    iii. £187 9s. 1d. Consols.

Harman's Charity of £4 4s. a year proceeded out of the Port Mills, then owned by Miss Youde.

12 May, 1891.

Order by the Charity Commission, since the County Council had taken over the Bridge as a County bridge, to transfer to the Council a sum of £87 9s. 8d. in 2¾ % Consols, belonging to the Bridge Estate.

—— 1893.

Draft of a scheme by the Charity Commission for the sale of the Fifteenths Estate, 18 perches of land and a cottage which had become ruinous in Priory Lane. The draft authorizes the sale of the property for £120.

2. A packet of papers relating to a dispute in 1899 as to the ownership of the Tolsey.

The Parish Council wished to obtain a lease of the building with a view to its preservation. The Charity Trustees claimed to be the owners, and had received a rent of 1s. a year from the Reading Room Committee as owners.

A case was submitted to counsel in which it was stated that the building ' had formerly always been used by the Lord of the Manor and the Corporation conjointly, by the Lord for holding his annual Court there, he claiming also a right to stallage underneath the building, and by the Corporation for an armoury for the Militia. The county magistrates prior to 1840 held their justices' meetings at the Tolsey with the permission of the Corporation '.

Counsel (Mr. Corrie Grant) held that probably the claim of the Lord of the Manor was barred by Statute, he having apparently made no claim since 1863. But whether no claim had been made was doubtful. This opinion is dated 11 Oct., 1899.

Subsequently, after the publication of the volume of the Historical Manuscripts Commission containing certain Burford documents, Mr. Corrie Grant's opinion was again asked, the new fact presented to him being that on p. 42 of that volume it appears in the course of the Rules of the Fellowship of Burgesses of Burford that the Corporation charged for stallage under the Tolsey in 1605. Mr. Corrie Grant was of the opinion that this reference did not help towards a solution of the main question ; to conclude from this that the Corporation were the owners of the building would be too large a deduction.

Included in this packet is a lease of the Tolsey by the Charity Trustees to the Parish Council.

FRAGMENT OF THE RECORD BOOK OF THE BURFORD BOROUGH COURT

1596 to 1597

Tolsey

Note.—The following fragment of the Record Book of the Borough Court was found by R. H. Gretton at the Tolsey in October 1915. Another fragment was found by the Rev. W. D. Macray among the Cheatle Papers, when he examined the Burford Records for the Historical MSS. Commission in 1899.

The handwriting is very crabbed. But the real difficulty in tran-

scription has been that the clerk knew very little Latin and had clearly
learned by rote certain formulas sufficient for the ordinary entries.
When he has to make other kinds of entries he uses words out of these
formulas without any regard for case of nouns or tense of verbs. At
times he gives up altogether and inserts phrases in English. All this
makes the transcription nonsense as Latin at several points. But the
meaning is clear enough.

The entries of pleas of debt repeat themselves so often that the
transcription has only been made in full for the first two folios. After
that it has been transcribed with the original abbreviations unaltered,
except where any unusual entry occurs.

The clerk's method was to enter in the left-hand margin the date
at which the action was entered, writing the word ' actio ' followed by
the date, and to enter under this date the various dates at which the
suit was heard. Most of the cases have at the head the words ' narr
de rec ' which I take to mean ' narratio debiti recepta '—' statement
of the debt received ' ; but occasionally the heading is ' non narr '—
which would mean that no statement had been filed. Two other
entries occur, on the right-hand side of the pages—' s fe pd ', which
appears to mean ' secta feodi predicti ' ; and ' attac p psons ', which
seems to be the clerk's way of saying that the parties attended in
person.

fol 13

Burford
in Com Oxon

William Webbe

Richard nuberi   Ballivi

Curia ibidem tenta 14° die mensis maii a° regni
domine nostre Elizabethe 38° coram
predictos Ballivos et William Symons aldrman Simonem Grene
stuard Iohannes Roffe et Radulphus
Wisdom Burgeses

Geast cler
ibidem
12° curia

1596

accon 15 maii

Willelmus fowler de Barington Glou querente
versus mychaell Burson in placito debiti quod
reddit ei   xs.

plegii pro querente Thomas Daniell et pro
defendente Iohannes Daniell Glover

4° Iunii   concordant ante hanc curiam

1596

accon 22 maii　　Edmundus Secole querente versus thomam howse
　　　　　　　　in placito debiti quod reddit ei
　　　　　　　　　　　pro defendente plegius Wm Webbe

1596

accon 29 maii　　Thomas Goddenoughe de bradwell querente ver-
　　　　　　　　sus Iohannem Dameye in placito debiti quod
　　　　　　　　reddit ei　　　　　　　　　　　　iii*s*. iii*id*.
　　　　　　　　　　concordant eodem die

1596

accon 14 Iune　　Edmundus hieron versus Edmundum Ryley gent
　　　　　　　　in placito debiti quod reddit ei　　　　x*d*.
　　　　　　　　　　plegius pro querente wm neale et pro defen-
　　　　　　　　　　dente Wm Walker
　　　　　　　　dies datur defendenti ad proximam responden-
　　　　　　　　dum.

25 Iune　　　　defendens confessus accionem in Curia ideo
　　　　　　　　iudicium datur per curiam solvetur debitum

26 Iulii　　　　et costagia apud proximam curiam debitum non
　　　　　　　　est solutum apud hanc curiam ideo plegius

6 augustii　　　est solvere eidem

fol 13 rev

1596　　　　　　　　　　　　　　narr de

accon 3º Iune　　Ricardus Walker de barrington magna querente
　　　　　　　　versus Iohannem Striver defendentem in placito
　　　　　　　　debiti quod reddit ei　　　　　　　vii*s*. iii*id*.

4º Iunii　　　　dies datur defendenti respondendum at proximam
　　　　　　　　aliter adward versus eum
　　　　　　　　　　concordant 6º Iunii

1596　　　　　　　　　　　　　　narr de

acco 4º Iunii　　Iohannes Ward querente versus Willelmum hall
　　　　　　　　in placito debiti quod reddit ei　　　　iii*s*.

14 maii　　　　dies datur per curiam pro defendente responden-
　　　　　　　　dum ad proximam curiam
　　　　　　　　Iudicium datur per curiam pro debito quia
　　　　　　　　defendens non apparet

25 Iune　　　　et pro costagiis de secta

20 Iulii　　　　　　concordant apud hanc curiam

1596
acco 3° Iunii   Ricardus meriwether querente versus Thomam
                 sowdley in placito debiti quod Reddit ei   viiis. xd.
4° Iunii   concordant ante curiam

1596
acco 3° Iunii   Ricardus meriwether querente versus Willelmum
                 Eve in placito debiti quod Reddit ei   viis. iiiid.

1596
acco 3 Iunii   Robertus Syrrell querente versus Ricardum
                 hodges in placito debiti quod reddit ei   xxiiis.
cur 4 Iune   continuatum est ad proximam curiam per p
cur 25 Iune   concordant apud hanc curiam 25 Iune

fol 15
                              te
1596   narr de in q Rec
accon 25 Iune   Ricardus swettnam de Burford miller querente
                 versus Danielle scheper in placito debiti
ı6 Iulii   quod reddit ei   xvs.
                     plegius pro defendente agnos hayt vidua
6 augustii   defendens essoigne per Edmundum Sutton

1596
acco 11 Iulii   Willelmus Barthelemew querente versus Ricardum
                 Walgrave alias Walldern in placito debiti quod
                 reddit ei   • xis. iiiid.
                     concordant eodem die et sic finis

1596
accon 14 Iulii   Iohannes shur(?) de Witney fuller querente versus
                 Ricardum Coocke de Strowd in com Gloc in
                 placito supra computaciones inter predictum
                 Iohannes et Ricardus ad valenc   xvs.
                     concordant eodem die et sic vacatum

1596   s fe pd
acco 14 Iulii   Willelmus Taylor querente versus Ricardum hancks
                 in placito debiti quod reddit ei   xvs. ixd. curia
16 Iulii   dat dies defendenti respondendum ad
6° augustii   proximam curiam
27° augustii   concordant

1596   s fe pd

accon 14 Iulii   Simon Grene querente versus Robertum Beddall
                    in placito debiti quod reddit ei   xxs.

16 Iulii   dies datur defendenti per curiam respondendum
                    apud proximam curiam

6° augustii   continuatum per assent querentis ad proximam
                    pro 1d. soluto per defendentem

27 augustii   defendens apparet in propria persona et

24 Sept   confessus accionem ideo iudicium versus eum
                    solvendum apud proximam aliter beware

fol 15 rev

Burford   William Webbe
Burg   Richard nuberi   Ballivi a° 1596
                    apud curiam ibidem tentam decimo· sexto die
                    Iulii a° Regine domine nostre Eliza-
                    beethe xxxviii° coram predictos   Geast cler
                    Ballivos Willm Symons alderman   15° cur
                    Simonem Grene stuard Jhon Lym Tobye Dallam
                    Burgesses
                            Wm Symons alderman
                            Symon Grene stuard

1596

accon 16 Iulii   Willelmus taylor istius ville Chandler querente
                    versus Iacobum hicks de cheppingnorton in   .

6° augustii   placito debiti quod reddit ei   xiis.
                    concordant eodem die

1596

accon 17 Iulii   michaele yong de ascot subter Whichewood
                    querente versus Willelmum peake de istius ville
                    baker in placito debiti quod reddit ei   iiis. iiiid.

6° augustii   plegius pro defendente Simon Dallam
                    concordant apud hanc curiam ante vocatur

1596   narr de rec   s fe pd

accon 29 Iulii   Thomas tuncks sadler querente versus Willelmum
                    haddon in placito debiti quod reddit ei iiis. iiiid.

6 augustii   Dies datur per curiam pro defendente apud
                    proximam curiam respondendum

27 august   concordant 27 august ante curiam

1596

acco 14 Iune	Edmundus hiron versus Edward Ryley in placito debiti quod reddit ei x*d*.
	plegius pro querente Wm neale et pro defendente Wm Walker
29 Iune	dies datur per curiam pro defendente respondendum apud proximam primam curiam
6° Iulii	defendens confessus accionem in curia 2° cur
6° augustii	ideo Iudicium datur per curiam solvere debitum et costagiis at proximam curiam ·
27 august	Wm Walker solvit debitum et costagia ad manum simonis Simons vz ii*s*. x*d*.

fol 16

1596

acco ultimo Iulii	Hewgone owen queritur vss Gryffin lewes in plit debit qd reddit ei iii*s*.	
6° augustii	concordant ante cur	feodem pro intrante non solutum

1596   narr de rec

acco ultimo Iulii	Thomas silvester q vss Edmd holiday in plit debit qd redit ei xix*s*.	
6° agustii	def non app ideo distreng vss eum˙sed nichill non inventus est apud hanc cur et non solvit Feod cúr	
27 agustii	Def app in ppria psona et cur dat diem defti respond apud px cur	
24 Sept	cont p q ad px cur	7 Janr cont
15 Octob*r*	cont p q usque px	cont 28 Jan
9 Novemb	cont p q usq px	18 feb
26 Nove*r*	cont p q usq px	11 mche
17 Dec*r*	cont p q p solut	1 aprill
		22 aprill

1596   narr de rec

acco 3 augustii	willmus Walker q vss Ihoem Iordan in plit debt reddit ei iii*s*. xi*d*.
	s fe pd
6 augustii	Cont est p q in px cur pro 2*d*. solut
29 agustii	essoygne per uxorem defendentis pro uno denario soluto usque px cur
24 Sept	concordant 24 Sept

1596   narr de rec   s fe pd
accon 3 augustii   Elizabeth Walclet vidua de Alington wroughton
                    in com Wiltes vidua q vss Ihoem Collyng de
                    Burford in placito detencionis pro divers parcelles
                    bonorum ut per narracionem suam apparet ad
                    somam   xviis.
                        pleg p q Ihoes Wallclet
                        concordant apud hanc cur

1596   narr de rec   s fe pd
acco 5 august   Simo star q vss thomam williams in plit debit
                    qd reddit ei   viis. iiid.
6 agustii   concordant ante cur

fol 16 rev.   1596

Burg de   William Webbe
Burford   .   Richard nuberi   Ballivi
                    apud curiam ibidem tentam 6° die augustii a°
                    regine domine nostre Elizabeeth dei gracia Anglie
                    francie et hibernie Reginae fidei
                    defensoris 38° coram pd Ballivos   Geast cler
                    Willm Simons aldermann Simo-   16e cur
                    nem Grene stuard Ihoes Lym Ihoes hannes Ihoes
                    Roffe et Radulphus Wisdom Burgesses

1596   narr de rec   s fe pd
acco 6 augustii   Agneta Hayter vid q vss Robertum Beddall in
                    plit debit qd reddit ei   vis. viiid.
6 augustii   Cont apd hanc cur p q p 2d. solut
27 Augustii   concordant 27 august ante cur
1596
accon 7 august   Ihoes Colborne istius ville q vss Ihoem Haslewood
                    in plit debit qd reddit ei   xviid.
                        concordant eodem die
acco 7 august   Edms Serrell q vss Robtum lifolie de plit debit
                    qd reddit ei pro duodecim boshells ordei ad valen
                        Concordant 8° agustii

1596   .   narr de rec   s fe pd
acco 7 august   Reginaldus gorram q vss Ihoem Iordan in plit
                    debit qd reddit ei   .   xxxixs. xd.
                        pleg p q Andrew ward

27° augustii	essoigne p uxorem def respond apd px
24 Sept	Concordant apd hanc cur et sic finalis
fol 17	

1596

acco 8 augustii	Georgius alltoste q vss Ihoem Chander alias Charm in plit debit qd reddit ei - xs.
	pleg p q Geor Serrell
	concordant eodem die et sic vac

1596   narr de rec   s fe pd

acco 10 August	Hughoe owen q vss ricardum lowman in plit debit qd reddit ei iiiis. iiiid.
27 Augustii	To hayt dies dat defti p cur respond pleg p def apd px cur
24 Sept	Iudic dat p cur p debit et costagiis

1596   s fe pd

acco 17 august	Willms Taylor q vss vid maior vid in plit debit qd reddit ei iiiis. viiid.
cur 27 augustii	concord 26 augustii uno die ante cur

1596   narr de rec   s fe pd

acco 20 august	Anna Chadwell vid q vss Ihoem taylor in plit debit qd reddit ea xxiis. viiid.
27 augustii	essoygne p Wm taylor respond ad px
24 Sept	Concordant ante cur

1596   narr de rec

acco 21 august	Samuell hurst q vss Edmd gorram in plit debit qd reddit ei xxxviiis. viid.
	pleg p q thoms arkell
27 augustii	Def apparet in ppria psona et petit dies respond apd px cur
24 Sept	Def non app ideo Iudic dat p q p debit et
15 Octob	p costagiis in secta concordant apd hanc cur et sic finalis

fol 17 rev

1596

Burg de	Willm Webbe	Ball
Burford	et Ric Nuberi	
	apud curiam Ibidem tentam xxvii° die augustii	
2304	M m	

a° regine domine nostre Elizabeethe
dei gracia 38° çoram pd Ball Willm   Geast
Simons allderman Simon Grene stuard   cleric
Simon Simons Richard Meriwether   17° cur
Toby Dallam Burgess

1596	narr de rec	s fe pd
acco 26 august	Willm Wisdom q vss Simonem fawler in plit	

1596	narr de rec	s fe p
acco 26 august	Oliverus lloyd alias hewes q vss Edmd Silvester Junior in plit debit qd reddit ei	xxiiii*s*. ii*d*.
27 augustii	Dies dat respond apd px p defti	
24 Sept	Concordant 24 Sept	

1596	narr de rec	s fe p
acco 25 august	Willm Wisdom q vss Simonem fawler in plit debit qd reddit ei	xviii*s*.
27 augustii	Cont p q ad px p soluc o	
24 Sept	Concordant ante cur	

1596	narr de rec	s fe pd
acco 26 august	Ihoes Ireland de barryngton parva q vss thomas baker in plit debit qd reddit ei	ii*s*. ii*d*.
27 Augustii	def non app ideo d est dist p un candebrum	
24 Sept	def non appar apd hanc cur	
15 Octob^r	def appar et confess acco ideo Iudic dat p debit et p costagiis	2*s*. 6*d*.
	baker tarde p toto feod	

1596	narr de rec	
acco 26 august	Edwds lloyd q vss thomam Baker in plit debit qd reddit ei	vi*s*. iiii*d*.
27 Augustii	def non app ideo d est deft est p un candelebrum	
24 Sept	def non appar apd hanc cur	
15 Octob^r	concordant ante cur et sic vac	

1596
fol 18

	narr de rec	s fe pd
acco 26 August	Robts veysye q vss anne tymson in plit debit qd reddit ei	xxiiii*s*.
27 augustii	essoignat p cur p denar	
24 Sept		

15 Octob^r	Cont p cur usq px cur p o
	narr de rec s fe pd
acco 26 August	Item eidem Robts vss pst anna in plit debit qd
	reddit ei xxiis. viiid.
27 augustii	essoigne p cur p denar
24 Sept	
15 Octob^r	Cont p cur usq px cur p o
	narr de s fe p
acco 26 august	Thomas arkell q vss Willm yeomans in plit debit
	qd reddit ei iis. viiid.
27 augustii	cont p q usq ad px cur p soluc o
24 Sept	cont usq px p soluc o
15 Octob^r	cont usq px p soluc o
5 Novemb^r	cont usq px cur p solut o
26 Novemb^r	cont usq px cur p solut o
17 Dec	cont usq px cur p solut o
7 Jan	cont usq px cur p solut o
28 Jan	cont usq px p soluc o
18 feb	cont usq px p o
11 mche	cont 11 mche o
	Cont 1 aprill o
	cont 22° aprill o

1596	s fe pd
acco ultimo	Willms Wisdom q vss margeria humfreyes als
augustii	maior vid qd redit ei xxviiis. xd.
	concordant 15 Sept

1596	narr de rec
acco 4 Sept	attac p psons
	Simon Dalbye q vss Ihoem tenman als tenpenny
	in plit detencionis p un ore (?) ad valenc xiiis. iiiid.
24 Sept	pleg p q hen davis et p def wm sessions
15 Octob^r	
5 Novemb^r	def app in ppria psona et petit copie narr respond
26 Novemb^r	apd px cur apd px
17 Dec	Def appar et ponit seipsum supra duos manus
7 Jan	approbatos quod non est culpabilis et sic dies
27 Jan	defendenti datur per curiam
28 feb	
11 mche	Def fecit legem per seipsum et duos manus
1° aprill	vz hen morris et thoma Davis ideo iudic vss
22° aprill	q pro costagiis 3s. 2d.

fol 18 rev

1596	fowler non solut sed 5 novemb
acco 18 Sept	Ihoes wood q vss Georgium fowler in plit debit qd reddit ei xxiii*s*.
24 Sept	Cont p q ad px p soluc *2d*. solut
15 Octob^r	Cont p q usq px cur p *2d*. solut
5 Novemb	Dies dat defti responda pd px cur deft confess
26 Novemb	acco ideo Iudic dat^r p q p debit et p costagiis

1596	narr de
acco 23 Sept	Simon star q vss andrew ward et margareta uxorem eius administratores bonorum Ricardi Dalbie defuncti in plit qd reddit ei xxxii*s*. Def petit dies respond apd px cur
24 Sept	Cont p q usq px cur p solut *2d*.
15 Octob^r	Dies dat defti usq px qd def approbat responden-
5 Novemb^r	dum suum quod querens outlegatus est vell non
26 Novemb^r	defendens demonstravit in curia brevis utlegati sub sigillo versus querentem ideo iudic dat pro defendente pro costagiis et accione vacato iiii*s*.

1596	narr de
acco 23 Sept	Thomas arkell q vss Walterum gryffyn in plit debit qd reddit ei xxxvi*s*.
24 Sept	Def appar in pson et confess accon ideo Iudic dat p cur p debit et costagiis ii*s*.
15 Octob^r	Concordant inter q et def qd def solvat wickle usq debit et costagiis solut v s et in def—t p uno solut tunc a levare p toto

1596	narr de
acco 23 Sept	Thomas Hathwaie q vss ihoem striver in plit debit qd reddit ei xx*s*. pleg p q Edmd Sutton essoigne per uxorem eius
24 Sept	Def appar et solvet debit et p costagiis 2*s*.
15 Octob^r	

	narr de
acco 23 Sept	Thomas hathewaie q vss agneta Tymson in plit debit qd reddit ei xxii*s*. pleg p q Edmd Sutton essoygne p cur respond apd px cur

24 Sept
15 Octob^r 15

Def confess accon et promissum dat querenti
recte secureti ante proximam curiam aliter levare
iudicium versus defendentem

5 Novemb^r

Concordant inter querentem et defendentem quod
defendens solvet every monthe   ii*s.*
et thomas parsons dat verbum suum pro predicta
solutione usque debitum solutum

fol 19

Burg de
Burford   1596

Simon Simons
Ric Meriwether   Ballivi

apud curiam ibidem tentam xxiiii° die mensis
Septembris coram predictos Ballivos Willm
Simons allderman Simonem Grene
stuard Ihoes Lym Ihoes hannes   Gest cler
Willm Webbe Burgesses   18° cur

narr de

Dalam non solut fe

acco 23 Sept

Thomas hathewaie q vss Simonem Dallam in
plit debit qd reddit ei   xviii*s.* vi*d.*
    pleg p q Edmd Sutton

24 Sept
15 Octob^r

essiyugne p Ihoem Geast apd hanc cur
Def appar apd hanc cur et confess accon ideo
iudic dat p q p debit et costagiis   2s.
Def solut debit et costagiis et sic finis

1596
acco 24 Sept in
cur

Willm Clarke q vss Reynoldus Gorram in plit
debit qd reddit ei   2s. 8*d.*
    pleg p def andrew ward
    concordant eodem die

1596
offycers sworne
at this courte

Memorandum at the court abovesaid were sworne
by m^r baylifs for cardners of the market for this
present yeare Robt Serrell and Walter gryffyn
and at the same time for aletasters Ihon Colling
and william neale

    Item 15 of octob was sworne by m^r baylifs
to be wardman for that yeare Ihon Saunders

1596
acco 2 octob[r] Rogerus Harrisson q vss Willm Woodward in
plit debit qd reddit ei   x*s.*
                pleg p q   et p def
                concordant eodem die et sic vac

fol 19 rev

1596   narr de
acco 9 octobr   Ricus Wheler de ydbury q vss Ihoem tappyn de
eadem in plit debit qd reddit ei   iii*s.* iiii*d.*
                pleg p q hew owen et p def thoms smythe
15 Octob   Concordant 15 octob[r] in cur et sic finalis

                                     dring non solut fe cur
1596   nec p 2° cur
acco 9 octob   Ihoes grenyng de cheppingfarrington in com
berks q vss Robtum dring de Shulton alias
Shillton in plit debit qd reddit ei   xxx*s.*
                deft   , q[q]
15 Octob   pleg p q Ric nubery et p deft Wm townsend
5 Novemb   Def non appar ideo cur dat dies penitorie respond
apd px° aliter levare vss def
26 Novemb   Def non appar ideo Iudic dat p q p debit et p
costagiis cur   ii*s.*

1596
acco 9 octob   Thomas hathewaye q vss edmd gorram in plit
debit qd reddit ei   xxii*s.*
15 octob   pleg p q   ·et p def
                Concordant apd stow et sic vac

1596
acco 9 octob[r] Thomas hathewaye q vss Georgium Cambrie in
plit debit qd reddit ei   ii*s.*
                pleg p q   et p def
                Concordant eodem die et sic vac

Note.—There is here a gap in the fragment, several folios being missing,
the middle portion of one of the binding sections of the book.

fol 30

The 8 of February 1596

Robert Beddall sheweth forthe to the bayliffs that one stephens a
stranger brought unto hym the 7th of this instant feb iiii q[trs] of mutton

at 7 a clock at nyght requesting him to sell the same for hym as he
would and pay for the same on fryday next when the said stephens
should make his returne to burford agayne

      the marke of

                             wm peake pleg p beddall

the said Beddall

The confession of mary Berry the wyfe of Jhon berry examyned
towchyng the matter abovesaid

Beyng examyned saythe that the said stephens beyng a butcher
did bryng into her howse certayne shepe and dressed them in a house
in her backsyde late in the occupation of the said Beddall / and saythe
she dothe know that the said stephens dyd kyll shepe in the said howse
iii tymes vz at one tyme beyng the fyrst tyme one sheppe / at the
second tyme ii shepe and at the third tyme beyng the sunday 7 of
Feb ii sheppe

Item that the said iiii q^{ts} of mutton were browght into the towlseie
before the bayliffs the day and yere abovesaid and prysed by andrew
ward thomas parsons and wm peake and wm clarke to be worth

                                        vis. viiid.

Item uppon searche made in the howse of the said Berry for suspycion
of stelyng of sheppe was found in a Barrell in the said Backhowse ii
good fells of two sheppe

Item the said Berry beyng examyned Dothe protest that she is
utterly gylteles of all the matter abovementioned

               Ihon neap pleg p berry

fol 30 rev

Burfford   Memorandum that a hewen cry sent from brodwell
by Ric mills cunstable 9th of Feb 1596 for then-
query of a white gelding with a red sadle uppon
him stowllen from brodwell aforesaid this present
nyght last past which came to the hands of the
bayliffs of Burford about 7 of the clocke in the
mornyng which was presently sent away to the
next tyothing

acco 20 Feb   attac p psons
1596   Iohes templer q vss thomam tuncks de plit debit
          qd reddit ei   xxxs.

11 mche   Cont p q usq px cur p solut   2–0

1° aprill	Cont p q usq px cur p solut	8–o
22° aprill	cont p q usq px cur p solut	2–o
	tarde p se p entran	
acco 22 Feb 1596	Willm more de aston husbandman q vss agnetam tymson vid istius ville de plit debit qd reddit ei	xx*s*.
11 mche	Cont est p q usq px cur	2–o
	cont p q usq px cur p solut	2–o
	concordabant inter seipsos 18 daye of mche 1596 et sic finis	

1596	narr de rec	s fe p
acco 16 Feb de p fe 8	Thomas Williams q vss Ric Cakebred de plit debit qd reddit ei	iiii*s*.
18 Feb 11° mche	Def confesseth ideo Iudic dat p debit et costagiis	18*d*.
1° aprill 22° aprill	concordabant et sic finis	

fol 31

1596	narr de rec	attach p psons
acco 16 feb	Fraunciscus peake q vss Daniell silvester in plit detencionis	
	debit qd reddit ei pro quinque boshells of wheate	xxxiii*s*. iiii*d*.
11 marche	concordabant et sic finis	

1596	narr de rec	s fe pd
acco 17 feb	Ihoes worthall alias crow q vss Georgium fowler de plit debit qd reddit ei	ii*s*. iiii*d*.
11 mche	cont p q usq px cur	
	cont p q usq px concordabant 2 4*d*. solut et f in cur	

1596		
acco 17 feb	Ihoes Iordan q vss Robtum Iordan de plit debit qd reddit ei	vi*s*. vi*d*.
	cont p q usq px cur p	2*d*.
11 mche	q non ideo acco vac 11° mche 1596	
1596	narr de rec	
acco 17 feb	Lodovic Iones cler q vss Ihoem Iordan de plit debit qd reddit ei	xxxii*s*. vi*d*.

11 mche	Def non app ideo distreng cpat p 16*d*. p embollina-tiones
1° aprill	Def confesseth accon ideo iudic dat p cur p debit
22° aprill	et p costagiis sect cur
	concordabant et sic finis
acco 17 feb 1596	Eidem Lodowic Iones cler vss Ihoem Iordan de plit debit qd reddit ei x*s*. i*d*.
22 mche 2 aprill 22 aprill	Def confessith acco ideo iudic dat p cur p debit et p costagiis sect de cur concordabant et sic finis

fol 31 rev

	1596	narr de	s fe pd
acco 17 feb	Thomas Williams q vss Ric Cakebred de plit debit qd reddit ei		xxx*s*.
18 feb 12 mche 1 aprill	Def confesseth accon ideo iudic dat vss eum p debit et p costagiis concordabant		xviii*d*.

	1596	non narr	attac p persons
acco 18 feb	Symon fildman de barryngton parva q vss Willm Broshe de Ensam et ursulam uxorem eius administ bonorum Wm hewes defunti in plit debit qd reddit ei		xxiiii*s*.
11 mche 1 aprill	pleg p q andrew ward et p def Thomas Sowdley q demonstravit in cur narrationem pro willmo per nominem thomas ideo vac		
concordabant p iudic Simon Simons et Ric meriwether	materia refert esse determinacione ad Simoni Simons et Ric[s] meriwether bayliffs in quinque libris eche to other ante px cur		

	1596	non narr	attac p psons
acco 18 feb	Symon fildman de barryngton parva q vss willm broshe de Ensam et ursulam uxorem eius administr bonorum Wm hewes defunti de plit debit qd reddit ei		xxxviii*s*. viii*d*.
11 mche	pleg p q andrew ward et p def thomas sowdley q demonstravit in cur narrationem p will° per nominem thomas ideo vac		

1 aprill

materie refertur ad iudicium et determinacionem
Simoni Simons et Ric meriwether bayliffs per
assensum q et def et obligati sunt in quinque libris
eche to other

Concordabant per iudic Simone Symons et
Ric meriwether Ball

1596   attac p psons
acco 19 feb

hen hollens q vss humfridum Cornsbye de plit
debit qd reddit ei   viiis. vid.
pleg p q Thomas smythe

11 mche

def solvit debit ad manum thome parsons ante
cur 11 mche

fol 32

Burford

Symon Symons   Ball
Ric merywether

apud curiam ibidem tentam 18º die feb 1596
coram ballivos predictos Wm Sy-
mons alderman Simonem Grene   Gest cler
stuard Ihoes Roffe andrew ward Wm   26 cur
taylor thomas Sessons Burgesses

Richd Goodman
Wm Hayter   cunstables
thos Williams
John Saunders   wardesmen

1596   narr de rec   attac p psons
acco 19 feb

Willms Broshe de Ensam q vss Symonem fildman
de Barrington parva millare in plit debit qd
reddit ei   xxvs.
pleg p q Symon Dallam et p def Andrew ward

12 mche
1 aprill
concordabant p
iudic Simon
Simons et Ric^s
merrywether Ball

def petit curiam narrationi respondendum apud
px cur aliter iudicium versus eum q et def stant
obligati to stand to thadward of the ii bayliffs
in v^ll eche to other for all matters depending
betwene them ante px cur

1596   narr de rec   attac p psons
acco 19 feb

Willmus Broshe de Ensam q vss Simonem fildman
de plit debit qd reddit ei   xxvs.

def petit curiam narr respond apd px cur aliter
iudic vss eum

12 mche   q et def stant obligati in 5^{ll} eche to other to abide

1 aprill   thadward of the ii bayliffs for all matters depending
betwene them ante px cur

      concordabant p iudic Simon Symons et Ric
meriwether

fol 32 rev

1596   narr de rec   attac p psons

acco 19 feb   Edward hongerford gen q vss Willm Edgeley
carriar in plit de computationis ad valent   xxxix*s.*
     pleg p q Raphe wisdom et p def Wm Bartle-
mew essoygne p Wm Bartlemew et dies dat
defti respond ad px cur

11 mche   Cont p cur respond apd px cur aliter Iudic vss eum

1 aprill   Def app p thomam Edgeley attornatum suum ideo
dies querenti def respond apd px cur aliter iudic
vss eum   et post hoc in eadem curia thomas
edgeley iurat quod   distring est bonorum q ad
vi^d sed sunt bonorum predicti thome

22 aprill   concordabant px cur eodem die in presentia
Wm Bartlemew

1596

acco 26 feb   Willmus (illegible owing to fading) de dodington
in com Gloc q vss peter peers de chippingnorton
cordwayner de plit debit qd reddit ei   vii*s.* viii*d.*
     pleg p q Edmd serrell
     concordabant eodem die

1596   narr de rec   s fe pd

acco 10 mche   Thomas prickevance q vss Robtum prickevance
de plit debit qd reddit ei   xxviii*s.*

11 mche   Dies dat defti p cur respond apd px cur aliter
1° aprill   iudic vss eum

22 aprill   Cont p q usq prx cur p solut   2–0

the ii of may 1597   Def non respond ideo iudic dat p cur p debit et
p costagiis solv ante px cur   2/6

Note.—Written in later in faded ink and overrunning the next entry.

     preysers of two bottles one barell one griddiron (?)

taken by Dystres of Robert Pryckevance and at vii*s*. viii*d*.

by Ihon Roffe Ihon hunt, Thomas (illegible) Thomas (illlegible).

1596
acco 10 mche   Thomas hayter q vss hewgone owen de plit detencionis
debit   qd reddit ei   xii*d*.

22 mche   Dies dat defti p cur respond apd px cur aliter iudic vss eum

1 aprill   Def dicit non est culpabilis et ponit seipsum supra duos manus approbatos apud

22 aprill   px cur   def fecit legem per ipsum et duos manus vz stephen wekmethe et nicolas temple ideo Iudic vss q p debit et p costagiis sect cur   iii*s*. ii*d*.
nondum solvitur

fol 33

26 feb a° 1596
memorandum the day and yere abovesaid there were comytted to m^r bayliffs by my lord cheffe barron at the assize then holden at Burford these persons folowyng subscribed

Katheryn wild
agnes Boothe   all of
Anne Wilkins   cheppingnorton
margery walker

at wch tyme
for saying of the said Bayliffs harmles Ihon myston and arthure wild of norton aforesaid dyd affirme and promysse and have hereunto Subscrybed thyr names accordingly as aforesaid

John miston
arthure
sign
willd

Burg de   Simon Simons   Ball
Burford   Richard meriwether
apud curiam ibidemt entam xi° die mensis martii

aº domini 1596 coram* predictos
Ballivos Wm Simons alderman Simo-
nem Grene stuard Ihoes Roffe Ihoes
Gryffyn Wm taylor thomas parsons Burgesses

Gest cler
27º cur

 Richd goodman
 Wm hayter cunstables
 Richd hawten
 thomas levet wardsmen

1596	narr de rec	attac p psons
acco 11 mche	Ihoes Roffe q vss Ric cobur de ffulbroke chandler	
	de plit debit qd reddit ei	iiiis.
	def essoygne p wm haddon usq px cur et tunc respond	
1 aprill	def app et dicit non est culpabilis et ponit seipsum supra duos manus approbatos apud px cur	
	materie ref ad iudic Symon Symons et Ric merywether ante px cur aliter . . . p lege	

Note.—The writing is so faded here as to be illegible.

1º die Iulii	Arbitrat . . . arbitrum . . . inter q et def ideo cont . . . usq ad px cur
27º die Iulii	continuat p q usq proxim cur
	Iudic conceditur versus deft de plit debit pfat cum costag curie iis. viiid. vis. viiid. solvend ante pxim cur

fol 33 rev

1596		attac p psons
acco 12th of mche	Ihoes makrethe de cheppingnorton in com draper q vss nicolaum Beard de plit debit qd reddit ei	xs.
1º aprill	cont p q usq px cur p	2–0
	cont p q usq px cur p	2–0
22 aprill	cont p q usq px p	2–0

1596		attac p psons
acco 14 mche	Edward gorrham de baryngton magna in Com berks q vss Robt chapman de plit debit qd reddit ei	xxxixs. xid.
	concordabant eodem die	

1596   •   attac p psons
acco 14 mche   Thomas parsons et Robt Serrell q vss Edwardum
1° aprill   Somner de plit   qd reddit eis   xxxiiis. iiiid.
22 aprill   Cont p cur usq px cur

1596   attac p psons
acco 14 mche   Thomas parsons et Robt Serrell q vss Edwardum
                  Somner de plit   qd reddit eis   xxxiiis. iiiid.
1 aprill   cont p cur usq px cur
22 aprill

1596   attac p psons
acco 14 mche   Thomas parsons et Robe Serrell q vss Edward
                  Somner de plit   qd reddit eis   xxxiiis. iiiid.
1 aprill   cont p cur usq px cur
22 aprill

1596   narr de rec   a fe pd
acco 14 mche   Iacobus morthew de eaton hastings in com berks
                  sheppard q vss Willm Iordan iunior de plit debit
                  qd reddit ei   xxxiiis.
                     pleg p Willm Webbe
1 aprill   def non appar ideo amerciatus est et distring
                  awarded vss eum
22 aprill   def non appar ideo amerc vss eum   vs.

1596   non narr   s fe pd
acco 19 m   Ricds Wilkins de Barington magna in com Gloc
                  weaver q vss Ihoem worthall alias crow de plit
                  detencionis pro una parcella ordini vocati a cone
                  or cocke of barley ad valent   xxs.
                     pleg p q henry sowtham
1 aprill   Cont est p q usq px cur p   .   2–0
22 aprill   concordabant inter seipsos

acco ultimo die   narr de rec   s fe pd
martii 1597   Ihoes ward q vss thomam smyth de plit debit
                  qd reddit ei   iis. viiid.
1 aprill   def confesseth acco ideo Iudic vss eum p debit et
                  p costagiis   iis.
22 aprill   def non appar et non solvet debit ideo amerciatus
                  est   xiid.

fol 34 rev

a taxacion 15 aprill 1596 towards the furnyshyng of sowdiars under the two lord generalls therle of Essex and 1d. admirall now at sea in her maiesties service for the some of 20s. ceassed by Wm Webbe Ric meriwether Symon Grene Ihon Roffe Burgesses henry sowtham Ihon hewes Ihon coliar Thomas hether Wm taylor Ihon hunt and Edmund Serrell as also for iiiis. iiiid. due to fryme (?) a sowdiar the same tyme into Ireland

Imprim Wm Webbe	vid.	Robt Cobar	iid.
Ric nuberi	vid.	Thos Cobar	iid.
Wm Symons	vid.	Thos Rossell	iid.
Symon Grene	vid.	Agnes hayter	vid.
Ihon Lym	vid.	Wm Wisdom	iiiid.
Symon Symons	vid.	Lawrence holding	iid.
Ihon Roffe	vid.	Thomas butcher	iid.
Ric merywether	vid.	Ihon Saunders	iiiid.
Ihon Hannes	vid.	Ihon Ward	iiiid.
Toby Dallam	iiiid.	Wm Daye	iid.
Raphe wisdom	viiid.	Samuell hurst	iiiid.
Mrs Chadwell	vid.	Wm Calkot	viiid.
Alice Reynolds	iiiid.	Ihon Gryffyn	vid.
Mary Reddy		Thomas hemyng	iiiid.
Ihon stryver	iid.	Ric harris	iid.
Gryffyn lewes	iid.	Francis perks	iid.
Andrew Yates	iid.	Thomas Kempe	iid.
Ric Levet	vid.	Ric Iordan	iid.
Wm Walker	iid.	Ihon Wood	iiiid.
Thomas luckyns	iid.	Watr hayter	iid.
Ric hodges	vid.	Wm taylor	iiiid.
mr harman jhonson	vid.	Wm hayter	iiiid.
George fowler	iid.	Thomas Daniell	iid.
Thomas Parsons	vid.	thomas fowler	iid.
andrew ward	vid.	Symon star	iid.
Edmond Serrell	iiiid.	Ric hanks	iid.
Widow maior	iid.	Thomas taylor	iid.
Ihon Scarbrow	iid.	Thomas axtell	iid.
Wm Sessions	vid.	Robt Iordan	iid.
Thomas hayter	iid.	Wm Bartlemew	iiiid.
Symon fawler	iid.	Ihon Walburge	iid.
Wm peake	iid.	Robt Moliner	iid.
Robt veyse	iiiid.	Ric hawten	iid.
Thos silvester	iiiid.	Innocent greneway	iid.
hew owen	iid.	wm eve	iid.
Ihon Iordan	iiiid.	henry lovering	iid.
Robt Serrell	iiiid.	Edward lloyd	iid.
Thos harding	iiiid.	Wm Combe	iiiid.

Petr lyfoly	ii*d*.	Symon taylor	ii*d*.
Wm Clarke	ii*d*.	Ric Cakebred	ii*d*.
Ihon hunt	iiii*d*.	Ihon hall	ii*d*.
henry sowtham	ii*d*.	Alexander grynder	ii*d*.
Ihon Templer	iiii*d*.	Thomas hayter	ii*d*.
Rich goodman	ii*d*.	Edmd silvester	iiii*d*.
Wm townsend	ii*d*.	henry hayter	ii*d*.
Ihon Hewes	ii*d*.	Wm Iordan	ii*d*.
Thos bygnell	ii*d*.	Jhon Coliar	ii*d*.
Symon Dalby	ii*d*.	Ric Carlton	ii*d*.

fol 36

1° die aprilis a° 1597

memorandum that the day and yere abovesaid Wm Veysye hathe yeven hys word that all his under (illegible) shall ffrom henceforth be of good behavior in the towne and that none of them shall goe a begging.

memorandum that allmatters depending in this cowrt betwene Wm Broshe of Ensam and Symon fildman of little Barryngton were by bothe theyr assents commytted at the cowrt here holden the first day of Aprill 1597 to Symon Symons and Richard merywether bayliffs to be determyned before the next cowrt here to be holden ffor performance whereof the said parties became bound eche to other in v^{li} apece to abyde by thadward of the said Bayliffs by geving of ii*d*. eche to other.

1597	non narr	attach p psons
acco 11 aprill	Willm Browne de cheppingfarrington in Com berks ostler q vss franciscum Bower de Stow in com Gloc de plit debit qd reddit ei	xx*s*.
22° Aprill	pleg p q Stephen Bateman Concordabant per dicentes stephen Bateman	

1597	non narr	attac p psons
acco 14 aprill	Ihoes Gryffin q vss Ihoem Wyet de plit qd reddit ei	ix*s*. xi*d*.
22° Aprill	Cont p q usqye px p	

fol 36 rev

A ceassment for the xvth rated by Wm Webbe Symon Grene Ihon Hannes and Ihon hunt the   day of   a° Domini 1596.

Imprim Wm Webbe	xii*d*.	Symon Grene	xii*d*.
Ric nubery	xii*d*	Ihon Lym	vi*d*.
Wm Symons	xii*d*.	Symon Symons	xii*d*.

Ihon Roffe	xiid.	Petr Lifolie	vid.
Ric meriwether	xiid.	Wm Clarke	vid.
Ihon Hannes	xiid.	Thos silvester	vid.
Toby Dallam	xiid.	Ihon Crow	iiiid.
Raphe Wisdom	ixd.	hew owen	iiiid.
Thomas Symons	ixd.	Ihon smart	iiiid.
Mrs Chadwell	xviiid.	Ihon iordan	vid.
Alice Reynolds	xiid.	Robt Serrell	ixd.
Mary Reddy	ixd.	Robt hemyng	iiiid.
!oane taylor	iiiid.	Tho harding	ixd.
Agnes hayter	xiid.	Robt coliar	iiiid.
Wm Wisdom	vid.	Tho Rossell	iiiid.
Lawrence holding	iiiid.	Edmd silvester	viiid.
Thos Harrisson	iiiid.	harry hayter	iiiid.
Thomas butcher	vid.	Edmd somner	iiiid.
Ihon Saunders	vid.	Thoms sowdley	iiiid.
Edwd Hieron	vid.	Thomas noke	iiiid.
Ihon ward	vid.	Samuell hurst	vid.
Ioane Ward	iiiid.	Wm Calkot	xviiid.
Thomas hincks	iiiid.	Ihon Colling	iiiid.
Wm Day	iiiid.	Ihon Gryffin	xiid.
Symon Dalby	iiiid.	Ihon Walclet	iiiid.
Ihon Muncke	iiiid.	Thomas hemyng	vid.
Ihon Striver	iiiid.	ffrancis perks	iiiid.
andrew yate	iiiid.	Ric harris	iiiid.
Ric levet	xiid.	Wm Haddon	vid.
thomas wyet	iiiid.	thomas Kempe	iiiid.
arthure Cotton	iiiid.	Ric iordan	iiiid.
Wm Walker	iiiid.	Ihon Wood	viiid.
Thomas luckins	vid.	Watr heyter	vid.
Ric hodges	xiid.	Wm taylor	vid.
mr harman Ihonson	xd.	Wm hayter	vid.
George fowler	vid.	Symon star	vid.
Thomas parsons	xiid.	Thomas fowler	vid.
Andrew ward	xiid.	Wm Smythiar	iiiid.
Edmd Serrell	vid.	Ric hancks	vid.
Wm Bartlemew	vid.	Gryffin lewes	iiiid.
Thomas axtell	vid.	Ihon hunt	xiid.
Ihon Walburge	vid.	Thomas waldron	iiiid.
Robt Moliner	iiiid.	harry sowtham	iiiid.
Ihon Coliar	vid.	Ihon Templer	vid.
Ric hawten	vid.	Ihon lloyd	vid.
Innocent Greneway	iiiid.	Rich goodman	vid.
Wm Eve	iiiid.	Thomas bignell	vid.
harry lovering	iiijd.	Symon Dalby	vid.
Edward lloyd	iiiid.	Symon Dallam	iiiid.
Simon lloyd	iiiid.	Symon taylor	iiiid.
Wm Combes	vid.	hew Davis	iiiid.

Thomas Williams	iiii*d*.	Thomas coliar	iiii*d*.
Ihon berry	iiii*d*.	Ihon Scarbrow	vi*d*.
Ric Cakebred	iiii*d*.	Wm Sessions	viii*d*.
Ihon hall	iiii*d*.	Symon fawler	iiii*d*.
Thomas marshall	iiii*d*.	Wm peake	iiii*d*.
widow prior	iiii*d*.	Wm Iordan	iiii*d*.
Thomas Imbry	iiii*d*.	Robt veysy	xii*d*.
Thomas hayter	vi*d*.	Wm jordan junior	iiii*d*.

VARIOUS BOOKS OF RECORD

TOLSEY

The following books are deposited at the Tolsey :

1. Fragment of the Book of the Borough Court, 1596–7. See transcription above.

2. A book of accounts roughly bound in vellum, containing entries for various years between 1735 and 1745. It appears from internal evidence to have belonged to Paul Silvester, who was Bailiff in 1734 and other years. The volume contains private accounts as well as some Bailiffs' Accounts. The latter show payments in connexion with the Royal Commission of 1738 to solicitors and others, receipts and payments in the Lenthall and Tanfield Charities, &c. The only entry of particular interest is as follows :

A Coppy of a Wrighting del to Jno. Lenthal Esq by the Corporation wch he was desired by them to be Read at a Vestry the 29 of May 1737 : wch he did not doe / Whereas divers aspersions are Industriously Cast on the Bayliffs of the Bourough of Burford relating to their disposeing of the Benefactions given to pious uses wch Representations in all Likelihood tends to create a Breach in our Neighbourhood & is Consequently destructive to the Commonwelth of the said town, Now we the Bayliffs and Burgesses of Burford aforesaid being conscious to ourselves that none of the Charitys have been by us either abused or Misemployed and being willing to prevent & set aside all faction and disturbance betwixt us & our Neighbours do hereby Consent & agree to all Such Measures as shall be properly proposed & taken and is thought most agreeable for the Ease & wellfare of the parish In order to wipe of the aforesaid aspersions and Satisfie every one Concerned, May the 29 : 1737.

3. A volume lettered A, bound in grey cardboard, containing accounts of the School, Poole's, the Church, the Almshouse, the Common Poor, the Bridge Estates. From July 3, 1747, to 1770.

4. A volume lettered B, similarly bound, containing the same accounts from June 16, 1747, to May 6, 1776.

5. A ledger lettered C, bound in vellum, containing the same accounts from December 16, 1776 to Michaelmas 1827.

6. A small quarto volume lettered D, entitled ' Feoffees entry book of Meetings ', containing memoranda of the meetings from December 9, 1776, to January 20, 1818.

7. A small quarto volume lettered E, bound in marbled paper, containing the account of the Chancery case. See transcription above.

8. A small quarto volume lettered F, bound in vellum, containing accounts of the Tanfield Charity from 1747 to 1786.

9. A ledger bound in red vellum, labelled 'Burford Charity Trustees', containing accounts from 1829 to 1856.

10. A ledger, bound in sheepskin, containing similar accounts from 1828 to December 1855.

11. A ledger, similarly bound, containing accounts from April 1856 to December 1867.

III. DOCUMENTS IN THE POSSESSION OF THE GOVERNORS OF BURFORD GRAMMAR SCHOOL

Burford Grammar School was founded in the year 1571. Simon Wisdom traditionally occupies the honoured position of the Founder ; but the documents which follow show that tradition in this instance requires some modification. The honour of the first movement in the founding of the school does not belong to him. His deed of gift is dated in October 1571 ; but in May of that year certain prominent Burford men had already set up an endowment for the purposes of a school.

Yet, since a school must have a Founder to revere, Simon Wisdom has no bad claim to the position, for more than one reason. Firstly, he gave to the school houses which were his private property, whereas the earlier deed is less a deed of gift, strictly speaking, than an allocation to new purposes of property long previously given to charitable uses. It is, in fact, a conveyance by certain co-feoffees of parish lands, to new feoffees, of lands and houses formerly given to the Church and the Gild. In the proceedings which followed the Edwardian Act dissolving the Gilds and Chantries much of the old charity property in Burford was confiscated. Some of it escaped for a time, only to be claimed later by the Crown. The claim failed, but the feoffees in possession of the property may well have felt that the best way to secure for the town any doubtful items was to allocate them to a new use much in favour with the Crown at that time—the provision of education for the young. That had been the more or less explicit intention of Edward VI's Commissioners in the scheduling of Gild and Chantry property, though private greed and the opportunity of profitable investment, by obtaining Crown grants of the confiscated lands, had vitiated the intention ; and the founding of schools, which had begun in his reign, had advanced rapidly under Elizabeth. It would, therefore, be very natural for these Burford feoffees to turn their minds in that direction when they felt their title to some of the charity lands to be insecure ; and in the wide and grasping inter-pretation then given to the term 'superstitious uses', it is obvious that property such as the Cakebred land, of which the original purpose —the endowment of an obit—was recorded in their muniments, or like 'Jesus acre', which betrayed its purpose in its name, might at any time be claimed for confiscation.

Nor is it only the different and more personal character of Simon Wisdom's gift which entitles him to rank as the Founder. Evidently the first movement had hung fire until he brought his energy to bear upon it, for although the conveyance of the charity property is dated in May 1571, the new feoffees did not actually enter into possession until February 1572. Moreover, the creation of an endowment was not the only necessity. The School could not come into existence until it had constitutions and a scheme of practical working drawn up for it ; and this Simon Wisdom did. Appended to his deed of gift are the Rules and Constitutions, written with his own hand. They are careful and thoughtfully devised, a little exacting, from the modern point of view, in the hours of teaching which they enjoin, and jejune, perhaps, in the subjects they propose for teaching. In one point they provoke a smile ; the clause concerning the daily recital of certain prayers ordains that one of these shall be the Collect beginning 'Almighty God, the fountain of all wisdom '—a singular way, to say the least, of commemorating the Founder's name.

Simon Wisdom does not in his own deed speak of himself as 'the Founder', but as 'one of the founders'. Still, it is fairly clear that his energy, and still more his love of organization and system, which is traceable, for instance, elsewhere in the form of oath which he drew up for the Steward of the Fellowship of Burgesses, were the main factors in the successful creation of the Grammar School ; and he may, therefore, be regarded as having done much more than just adding to the first endowment a sum which made the income sufficient, in the money of that time, for the engagement of a schoolmaster.

Endowment, however, was not all that had to be provided. A fund for the erection of buildings was also necessary. We gather from the constitutions that subscription was expected to provide this money ; provision is made for certain privileges, in connexion with the nomination of pupils and the official visiting of the school, to be enjoyed by those who should give sums of money. But it is also to be gathered, from the earliest leases of the lands and houses conveyed in 1571, that another method of raising the building fund was to grant leases at a comparatively small rent in consideration of cash payments.

Here, again, Simon Wisdom evidently helped the project forward. Entries in the Corporation Memorandum Book of this period recording sums repaid to him on account of the School, or due to him for repayment, show that he advanced ready money for paying the builders, and had it refunded to him as money came in from the other sources which have been mentioned.

Thus arose the building at the corner of Church Lane which survives to this day, plain and simple, but, in its comparatively humble way, of some dignity. The School, as originally founded, was for the youth of the town and parish, and was therefore what we should now call a day school. The master apparently lived in a house elsewhere in the town.[1] Thus the only building required was one that would provide class-rooms for the elder boys—the Grammar Scholars— and the younger boys, or ' petties ', as they were called, who were not beyond the stage of learning their alphabet ; hence the simple character and ground plan of the old school block.

Within a very short time Burford Grammar School had produced the first of its notable *alumni*, Peter Heylin and Marchmont Needham, both of whom attained some notoriety, if not distinction, among the partisan writers of the Civil War period. The Heylin name appears frequently in the preceding Records, and the Needham name is also to be found.

With the exception of these pupils the School may be said to have no history for the first century and a half of its existence. Its income was increased by the raising of rents which the Royal Commission

---

[1] Owen Thomas, for instance, one of the earliest masters, lived in Witney Street (see p. 340) and Richard Griffiths in Sheep Street.

of 1628 ordered in all branches of the Burford Charities. The two school 'wardens' were regularly appointed, as the Register of Parish Officers shows ; and the surviving early books of accounts are carefully kept.

Then, unfortunately, the School fell into that slough of mismanagement in which the whole of the charity administration in Burford had become involved early in the eighteenth century. The first sign of this is that soon after 1700 the school accounts, instead of containing entries of expenditure on various school purposes by the wardens, enter merely the payment of the whole proceeds of the school property to the master, Richard Griffiths. This would, of course, have been incorrect procedure, even if Griffiths had been an honest man, fit to be trusted with the entire responsibility. It becomes worse than incorrect when we find, from the proceedings of the Royal Commission of 1738, that he was idle, careless, and unfit for his post. The School was utterly neglected ; no usher had been appointed for years past to attend to the younger boys, and Griffiths himself made no pretence of teaching the elder ones. He was drawing the whole of the school income, and spending it himself. By the time the Commission was appointed, he was actually of unsound mind. He evidently had stood very well with the Burgesses, and they incorporated defence of him with their own defence in the Chancery suit that was the sequel to the Commission.

The School must have taken some time to recover from such neglect. But that it did so we may gather from the fact that before this century ended two more notable men had had their early education here. They were Sir William Beechey, the Royal Academician, who was born in Burford in 1753, and Charles Jenkinson, first Earl of Liverpool and Prime Minister. The Jenkinsons were seated at Walcote, and some of them served as Trustees of the Burford Charities, which may perhaps account for Charles Jenkinson being sent here to school.

But there was no real recovery. By the beginning of the nineteenth century the School had ceased to exist. An attempt to revive it was made in 1863, a meeting of the Charity Trustees with the Assistant Charity Commissioner was held, and the School was reopened. Five years later it was again in a very bad condition, and was the subject of an inquiry which resulted in the appointment of a competent Master, and since that date, with the present Constitution, drawn up by the Charity Commissioners in 1876, it has flourished, filling a very valuable place in the life of the country-side.

S 18. 1 May, 13 Elizabeth (1571).

Lease by William Partridge, John Lyme the elder, William Sylvester and Thomas Freer, churchwardens, Richard Dalby and Edmund Sylvester, Bailiffs of the Borough, Symon Wysdom, Alderman of Burford, John Hannes, Steward of the Fellowship of the Burgesses of Burford, Thomas Fetteplace, Walter Mollyner, Richard Reynolds, William Symons, Bennett Fawler, Robert Childe, John Wylliams, Robert Scarboroughe, and William Phillippes, Burgesses, Robert Starre, Thomas Butcher, William Butcher, John Huntt, John Warde, Robert Everest, Robert Sylvester, Hughe Davys, Thomas Hooper, Thomas Warde, and John Herne, parishioners, to Symon Wysdom, Alderman of Burford. A messuage or tenement with a close and garden adjoining on the west side of the High Street between a tenement of Symon Wysdom on the south and a tenement of John Floide alias Hewes on the north, now occupied by George Patrick ; one acre of meadow in High Mead occupied by Symon Wysdom ; one acre of arable in the East Field of Burford called Jhesu Acre occupied by Simon Wysdom. For 41 years at 20s. a year.

The lease contains a clause concerning the possibility that the premises may be put ' to any other more necessary or laudable use than before it hath been accustomed '.

S 20. 24 May, 13 Elizabeth (1571).

Indenture between Richard Dalby and Edmund Sylvester, Bailiffs, William Partridge, John Lymme the elder, and Bennett Fawler, three of the Burgesses, William Silvester, clotheman, and Thomas Freer, tailor, late co-feoffees of the parish lands of Burford, and Thomas Fettyplace, gentleman, Richard Reynollds, William Symonds, John Williams, and Robert Scarborough, five of the Burgesses, Robert Silvester, broadweaver, Thomas Silvester, John Hannes the younger, Richard Jordan, tailor, and Richard Hedges, son of Richard Hedges deceased. Setting forth that in consideration of the need for a school in Burford (expressed in terms almost identical with those of Simon Wisdom's foundation deed, transcribed in full below), the first-named parties purpose to enfeoff the second-named of lands and tenements to the annual value of £3 12s., namely : a barn now occupied by Thomas Lawrence ; the clerk's chamber ; tenement called Banks House on the north side of Church Lane ; a platt of mead in Bury Orchard and a half-acre in High Mead, occupied by Thomas Freers ; an acre of meadow in High Mead and an acre of arable in the East

Field now occupied by Symon Wysdom ; an acre in High Mead occupied by Thomas Hewis alias Calcott ; a tenement with appurtenances sometime occupied by Thomas Sambage now by Symon Wysdome ; a tenement once occupied by William Lawrence ; a tenement occupied by John Wyckins.

Endorsed : ' Lands enfeoffed by the Parishioners of Burford towards the erection of a free school in Burford.'

S 21. 24 May, 13 Elizabeth (1571).

Deed of Enfeoffment, by the same parties to the same parties. The premises named in the preceding document. Setting forth the intent of the feoffment, that the wardens of the school appointed or admitted by the Alderman, Steward and Bailiffs and others of the parish according to the constitutions of the school shall receive the rents and pay thereof the stipend of the schoolmaster.

Witnesses to livery and seisin (which did not take place till 1 February, 14 Elizabeth—1572) ; Thomas Hewis, one of the Bailiffs, Symond Wysdome, Alderman, John Floide, William Jordan, William Grene, John Floide junior, George Hedges.

S 22. 20 October, 13 Elizabeth (1571).

This Indenture made the Twentieth daye of October In the Threttenth yere of the Raigne of or Soveraigne Lady Elizabeth By the grace of god of England France and Ireland Quene Deffender of the ffaith Betwene Symon Wysedome of Burfford in the countie of Oxenford clothier on the one partie And John Hannes the elder Thomas ffryers Richard Reynolds Willm Symons Thomas Wisedome of Shipton under whichwood in the said countie clothier Richard Dawbye Edmonde Silvester John Lymm the elder Willm Partridge Thomas Hughes Thomas Silvester John Hunt Radulph Wisedome Symon Allflett Willm Silvester and Edmond Pittam on the other partie Wittenyssith that whereas the said Symon Wysedome heretofore have hadde consideracion and doth consider what greate nomber of yowth & yong children have been and yet are & in tyme to come maye be within the Towne of Burfforde aforesaid where many of their parents have benn not able to ffynde them at Schole whereby the more part of their yowth have Idely spent their tyme and hath not byn traded and brought uppe in no good order of Lernynge or knowlege wherby they myght the better apply their selffs to knowe their duty both towarde Almightie god their prynce and their parents as also to obtayne increase of vertue and Lernynge These considerations aforesaid consydered and for the advauncement of godes honour and glory and the good Seale that the said Symon Wisedome bearith to the comon wealth of the same Towne The said Symon Wysedome by the good mocyon of Almyghtie gode of his free will and mynde is contented to geve graunte & Infeaffe And by these presents do geve graunt and infeoffe to the said John Hannes the elder Thomas ffryers Richard Reynolds Willm Symons Thomas Wysedome Richard Dawlby Edmond Silvester John Lymm the elder Willm Partridge Thomas Hughes Thomas Silvester John Hunt Radulph Wisedome Symon Alflett Willm Silvester and Edmond Pyttam Certen lands and Tenements to the yerely value of ffyve pounds toward the ereccyon and maynetenaunce of a ffree Schole to be erected within the Towne of Burfforde aforesaid hereafter in these presents Indentures expressed and declared Hit is nowe covenanted condicended and agreed Betwene the said parties in manner and fforme ffolowinge That is to saye The said Symon wisedome for the consideracions aforesaid hath geven graunted and infeoffed and by these presents do geve graunt and infeoff to the foresaid John Hannes the elder (etc., names as before) . . . as feoffees in trust of and in all those his Three Tenements in one Raunge adyoynynge to the comon Bridge of Burfford aforesaid and now in the severall tenures and occupacyon of Willm Longe Richard Howldinge and John Sclatter or of their assignes by the yerely rent of Thyrtie Shillinges And also of and in one other Tenement with the appurtenances in the High Strete Lienge betwene the Tenement Late Allexander Hodges on the sowth parte and the Tenement belongynge to the comon Bridge of Burfford aforesaid on the northe parte And nowe in the tenure and occupacion of John Walbridge or of his assignes by the yerely Rent of Twentie six Shillings eight pence   And also of and in Twoo other Tenements with the appurtenances under one Raunge Sett lienge and beinge in a certen Streate there called Wytteney Streate in Burfford aforesaid boundinge uppon gildenforde Lane on the east parte And a Tenement of Thomas Alflett on the west parte and nowe in the severall tenures and occupacion of John Cotten and Roger Tunks or of their assignes by rent by yere Twentie shillings And also of and in one other Tenement with the appurtenances Sett Lienge and being on the hyll in the high Streate of Burfford aforesaid Betwene the Tenement of Thomas hughes on the sowth parte and a Tenement belonging to the parishe churche of Burfford aforesaid on the northe parte And now in the tenure and occupacion of Evan ffloyde or of his assignes of the rent by yere Twentie three shillings ffower pence And of and in all and Singuler howses edyfices buyldyngs Barnes Stables Orchards Gardens yardes Roomes and Esyaments proffitts and commodities whatsoever to the said severall Tenements or to everie or any of them belongyng remaynynge or apperteynynge the Chieffe Rents and Services therefore due and accustomed to the lord or lords of the ffee onely excepted And also one Indenture of Lease bering date the Twentie daye of August in the twelve[th] yere of the Raigne of o[r] Soveraigne Lady quene Elizabeth that nowe is made by the said Symon Wysdome unto the said Thomas Wisedome of Shipton under whichwoode in the countie of Oxenford aforesaid clothier and to his assignes of all the severall Tenements and other the premisses aforesaid ffor the terme of Twentie and one yeres Lykewise excepted and reserved To have and to hold the said severall Tenements and everie of them and all other the premisses aforesaid by what name or names soever thei be called with all and singuler their appurtenances and everie parte and parcell thereof Except before excepted Unto the said John Hannes (etc. as before) . . . to the onely use and intent as is aforesaid provided alweys and neverthelesse hit is covenanted graunted concluded condicended and ffully agreed betwene the said parties by these presents in maner and fforme ffolowinge That is to saye That if the said ffree Schole and Scholehouse and a house for the Scholemaister under one Raunge as it is appoynted be not errected within the said Towne of Burforde within the Space of three hole yeres next after the insealinge of this present dede of feoffement indented And also if the said yerely Rents to be taken of the said severall Tenements with the appurtenances or any of them be converted or bestowed to any other use intent or purpose Than is before in these presents declared That then these Indentures of feoffement and all and everie covenant grant clawse gyfte article and sentence therein conteyned to be utterly voide and of no effect in Lawe to all intents construccyons and purposes And that then and from thenceforth and everie daye after hit shall and may be Lawfull to and for the said Symon Wisedome his heires and assignes into all and Singuler the said Severall Tenements with their appurtenances and into everie parte and parcell thereof Holy to Reenter and the same to have againe holde possesse Reposede & enioye as in his or their ffirst and fformer estate or estates This indenture or eny thinge therein conteyned to the contrary in any wise notwithstandinge And hit is ffurther agreed Betwene the said parties by these presents That suche gode and Reasonable constitucions made by the advice of the said Symon Wisedome beinge one of the ffirste ffounders of the said Schole and by his Lerned councell ffor the goode order and ffor the contynuaunce of the same to be written in a Shedull and to be Annexed to this said dede of feoffement ffor this intent That if the said constytucions and articles and everie of them be not observed & kepte accordinge to the true intent and meaninge of the said constitucions and articles that then the Redresse and amendement of the same shalbe ordered Redressed and Reformed by the said Symon Wysedome and his heirs at all tymes hereafter To be ordered Redressed and Reformed accordinge to the said constitucyons and articles unto these presents Annexed   In witnes whereof to the one parte of this Indentures Remaynynge with the said feoffees the said Symon Wisedome have putt his hande and Seale And to the other parte Remaynynge with the said Symon Wisedome and his heirs the said ffeoffees ffor them and ffor their heires and Successors have putt their handes and Seales Geven the daye and yere above written.

THE intent of the above written ffeoffement is this That the said ffeoffees shall from tyme to tyme at alltymes hereafter quietly and peasably permytt & Suffer the wardens of the Schole whiche shalbe appointed or admytted by the Alderman and Steward of the ffelowshippe of the Burgeses of Burfford The twoo Bailiffs there ffor the tyme beinge and other of the parishe Accordinge to the constitucions and orders of the said Schole to take and receave all suche Rents proffitts and comodities yerely Renewynge cominge Rysinge and growynge owt of in or upon the said Lands and Tenements before inffeoffed Towards the Sellary or Stipend of a Scholemaister to teche a Schole there within the towne of Burfford aforesaid ffrom tyme to tyme without any Lett Denyall or interrupcion of the said ffeoffees or of any of them And the same Rents by them so Receaved to paie quarterly unto the said Scholemaister Accordinge as it is appointed by the constitucions & orders hereunto Annexed

By me Symon Wysdome
wrytten w^t myne owne hand.

THE CONSTITUCIONS And orders Indented and Made by Symond Wisdome Alderman of the Borowe of Burforde One of the ffirste ffounders of the free Schole in Burford aforesaid to be Erected as by his deede dated the Thirtenth yere of the Raigne of o^r Soveraigne Ladye quene Elizabeth within written et in Anno Domini 1571 Hereunto annexed apperith.

THE FIRST   INPRIMIS WHEARE I the said Symond Wisdome hath geaven and Enfeoffed to Certen Feoffeys in truste to the Nomb^r of Sixtene As by the Deede hit May appeare Certaine Landes and Tenementes To the yerelie value of fyve poundes towarde the Maynteynaunce of a free Schole in Burforde to be erected there PROVIDED ALWAIES that when hit shall fortune that Any of the said Feoffeys To deceasse So that there be nott paste the Nomb^r of eight at the Least then lyvinge The said Eight ffeoffeys then lyvinge shall within one Holle yere next after Make newe ffeoffeys to the nomber of Syxtene As ys aforesaid to the same use and entent as in the former Deede is declared SOE THAT THERE be never from tyme to tyme under the nomb^r of eight at the Leaste nott Above one hole yere AND THIS to continewe for ever.   And that the ollde enfeoffements to Remayne and be savely kepte from tyme to tyme for a president for ever.

THE SECOND   ITEM THERE SHALBE A Cheast made withe thre Lockes and thre keyes In the which Cheast there shalbe savely kepte from tyme to tyme all suche Money plate or Juells as also infeoffements deedes Evidences constitucions and orders Or whatsoever ys or shalbe geaven made or done By the ffownders and Benefactors of the same free Schole ffor the Goode order Maynteynaunce and continewance of the Same ffrom tyme to tyme as Oportunyte shall serve and Requyer Which thre keyes shall alwayes Remayne in such custody and kepinge as followith THE FIRST key with the Alderman and Steward of the fellowshippe of the Burgesses of Burford or with one of Them THE SECOND kaye with the two Baylyffes of the Towne of Burford aforesaid for the tyme Beyng THE THIRDE kaye with the two wardens of the free Schole for the yere appoynted soe that there shalbe nothinge taken owte of the same Chest nor nothing putt in But by the consent of the Syxe persons aforesaid And att eny chaunge of Alderman Steward Baylyffes or wardens They shalle deliver up their keyes to their successors with all writings Juells plate or money or Any other things That to the said free Schole dothe Belong or Appertaine WHICH BY Invitorye was delyvered unto Them AND BY THE SAME Invitorye to deliver the same ageyn WHICH Invitory to be indented The one parte thereof Remayning with the two wardens of the free Schole for the tyme beinge The other parte with the churchwardens of the Towne of Burford And every yere A newe Invitorye to be made atthe chaunge of the wardens By the over syght of the Alderman steward and the two Baylyffes And fowre of their auncient Brethren of the Burges AND THIS to continewe from tyme to tyme.

THE THIRD ITEM THERE SHALBE two Honest men of the Towne of Burford one Being a Burges the other a comyner to be wardens of the free Schole for one holle yere to be Elected and Chosen att the Church Account By the Alderman Steward and Burges And fower of the Beste and Auncient Comyners of the Towne beinge Elected and chosen By the Alderman Steward and two Baylyffes ffor the tyme beinge which wardens shall receave the free Schole Rents And see the Scholem^r payd quarterly AS ALSO take and receave all such profetts comyng and growing toward ye maintenance of the same free Schole By any constitucions and orders made for the same WHICH WARDENS shall yerely atthe day of the Church Account yeald up their account of their Charge And bring in their Bokes of Receytes and payments.

THE FOWRTH ITEM WHEN HIT shall fortune the Schole Maisters Rome to be voied to be electe and Chosen by thre voices That ys to saye the ffirst voyce shall be geaven By all suche as geave any Lands or tenementes for the Mayntenaunce of the said free Schole for ever they to have the first voice duringe their Lyves THE SECOND voyce to be geaven by the Alderman and Steward of the fellowshippe of the burgesses of Burford and their successors for ever THE THIRD voyce to be geaven by the Baylyffes of the Towne of Burford for the Tyme being And fower other of the auncient Burges of the same Towne for ever.

THE FIFTE ITEM THE SCHOLEM^r beinge Elected by the voices aforesaid the two wardens for the free Schole beinge for the tyme appointed with the Alderman and Steward of the same Towne shall compound and agree with the Scholem^r for the Nomber of Schollers that he shall teach Accordinge to his Stipend or wages As by their discretion shall seme good SOE THAT THE Nomb^r of gramarian Schollers Besyde the peties doe nott exceade above the Nomb^r of fortie AND ATTHE SAID tyme shall take order that the said Scholem^r shall by his discretion dayly and wekely appoynt from tyme to tyme One two or thre of his gramarian schollers of the said free Schole to enstructe and teach all such petye schollers nott able to learne accidence that shall come unto the said free scole being any of the inhabitaunce Sonnes of Burford aforesaid UNTYLL SUCH tyme there maybe some better or larger augmentacion or stipend gotten or atteyned to maynteyne or Recompence some other usher or mete Scholler to teach & enstruct the said petie schollers aforesaid AND YF HIT be thought by them that his Stipend appointed be not sufficient for his Lyvinge to lycence hym to take Certen Schollers by numb[r] to his own comoditie untyll such tyme that his Stipend maybe made sufficient to and for the Mayntenaunce of his Lyving PROVIDED ALWAIES that the Alderman Steward and wardens shall nott graunt any perpetuitie to any scholem[r] Butt from yere to yere uppon his diligence and good demener.

THE SYXT ITEM THAT SYMOND WISDOME being one of the firste fownders of the free Schole and his heires shall from tyme to tyme for ever Elect nominate and preferr into the same free Schole to Be taught freely ffower Schollers to be called Wisdoms schollers WHICH schollers attheir first entering into the free Schole TO PAYE TO THE WARDENS of the same for entering Their names in the free Schole Boke ffower pence apece AND SO FROM TYME TO TYME att every chaunge.

THE SEVENTH ITEM HIT SHALL nott be Lawfull to the Scholem[r] to take any Scholler into the free Schole there to be taught w[th]owt the consent or knowledge of the wardens WHICH WARDENS shall Register the names of Every Scholler in a booke AND TO TAKE for their entring Into the free Schole as ys appointed And to make a trewe account thereof once in the yere at the Church Account what Schollers hath been Receaved Into the free Schole AND WHAT THEY HAVE RECEYVED of them particulerly by name.

THE EIGHT ITEM THAT EVERYE Scholler that shalbe Receaved into the free Schole their parence Being dwelling in the Towne of Burford shall pay unto the wardens of the ffree Schole att the firste entring into the ffree Schole for every Scholler fower pence and to pence every quarter after AND EVERY Scholler that cometh owt of the Countrie to pay att his first entring into the ffree Schole twelve pence AND Syx pence every quarter for the tyme of their Contineweaunce EXCEPTE such as have ben Benefactors to the Edifieing and Buylding of the same ffree Schole howse They to pay for Their entring of every Scholler fower pence and fower pence every quarter during the said tyme ALL WHICH somes of Money to be collected and taken as ys aforesaid SHALBE EMPLOYD to the Reparacions of the ffree Scole howse and keping cleane of the same And towards the wages of such an usher as shalbe appoynted to teach the peties And otherwise as hit shall seme good to the Alderman Steward Baylyffes and wardens for the good Continuance of the same.

THE NYNTH ITEM THE SCHOLEM^r with his Schollers to be atthe Schole In the Summer tyme by Syxe of the clocke in the Mornynge AND IN THE WYNTER att seaven And there to continewe untill a Leaven And then to dynner And to be att schole ageyne By one of the Clocke And there to Learne untyll Syxe of the Clocke in Sommer and fower in The Wynter AND ATT their ffirst entringe into the Schole Every mornyng atthe howres Before appoynted to goe before their M^r or his depute two and two orderly from the Schole Howse to The Churche to the morning prayer yf any there be atthe said howres AND THERE TO SERVE god devoutlie in singinge or Sayinge of Salmes AS BY THEIR M^r they shalbe instructed AND YF HYTT be not morninge prayer atthe Churche Thatt Then the maister shall appoynt one of his scollers wekely by order att a deske in the Scholehowse To beginne to Singe or saye a salme or two by their maisters appoyntment And all the reste of the scollers to singe or saye with him And a Chappiter to be reed of the old testament or newe By The M^r or by one of his Schollers AND IN THEND thereof to singe a Salme to the praise of God And to reed thre Collects One to the laud and praise of god Another for the prince AND THE LASTE to be the Collect Begynnynge almightie god the fountaine of all wisdome and so furth etc AND THEN to their Bokes And att their departinge from Scholle att evenynge in Lyke manner to geave thankes to almightie god for the founders of the ffree Schole And to Singe a Salme By the appointment of their M and soe to departe

> by me Symon Wysdome
> wryttyn w^t myne awne hand.

THE TENTH ITEM THE ALDERMAN AND STEWARD of the fellowshippe of the Burges of Burford and their Successors from tyme to tyme shalbe Regarders and Hedmaisters of the Scole to over see the wardens that shalbe from tyme to tyme elected That they and every of them doe Justely truely and indifferently See all suche constitucions and orders Nowe made or hereafter to be made for the good order and contynuaunce of the Same schole to be well and truely observed and kepte withowt mede faver or affection of any manne AND YF THEY DOE THE CONTRARY Thatt Then the said Alderman and Steward withe the assystaunce of the two Baylyffes ffor the tyme beinge and fower of the auncient Burges of the same Towne To Reverse amend and reforme the same anythinge heretofore towchinge their office nott with Standinge.

THELEAVENTH ITEM THAT THE SAIED Alderman and steward with the two Baylyffes for the tyme beinge wth ye two wardens and ffower auncient Burges beinge Appoynted by the Alderman and Steward shalle fowre tymes In the yere THAT YS TO SAYE Every Quarter diligently to forsee that there be Alwayes one appoynted by Collection for his Stipend Or otherwise to teach and Enstructe the Petyes SOE THAT EVERYE man of the towne and parishe of Burford myndinge to sett his Childe to scole beinge men children havinge noe infirmite or sicknes Shalbe enstructe and taught in the same scole his abse Chathechissme his premer to wright & reed untyll he be able to be preferred to the grame^r schole payinge att his entring and Quarterly as appeareth in the Eighte Artycle above mencioned.

THE TWELFFE ITEM THAT THE SCOLEM^r ffor the tyme Beinge shall every Sondaye in the yere appoynt his Scollers to be atthe Scole howse or atthe Scolemaisters howse Atthe Second peale to Mattens or morninge prayer To wayte on their M^r to the church orderly Except some Reasonable cause to the contrary And there to serve god devoutly As by their M^r they shalbe enstructed And to Sett in such place in the Church as ffor them shalbe appoynted AND ALSO the saied Scolem^r shall fower tymes in the yere THAT YS TO SAYE att Christmas after Witsontyde & Alhollontyde att the Breakinge upp of their Scole for the tyme THE SAID M^r or one of his Scollers by him appoynted Shalle stand att a deske in the Scole Howse And there to exorte the Scollers to geave thankes To god And Resyte their names orderly of all the ffounders Benefactors And firste erectors of the Scole Which names to be wrytten in a Table which Table Always to Remayne in the scolehouse And there to singe or saye a Salme or prayer to the Laude and praise of god And soe departe the Scole

by me Symon Wysdome
Wrytten by & w^t my owne hand.

S 25. 13 December, 34 Elizabeth (1591).

Assignment of Lease by Andrew Yate, 'showmaker', to Owen Thomas of Teynton, clerk. Tenement on the north side of Witney Street with backside, garden and a little piece of land shooting down to the river between a barne of Alexander Hedges on the east and a tenement called the Oxhouse occupied by Joan Sylvester, widow, on the west. The document recites the lease of 1 May, 13 Elizabeth, to John Wekens (S 23: see p. 323) and sets forth that on Wekens's death the lease passed to his wife, from her to Symon Partridge, at his death to his wife, who then married Andrew Yate, who now assigns the remainder of the term of 41 years to Owyn Thomas for a consideration of £3 10s.

Witnesses : William Webbe, Jhon Scarbroughe.

S 26. 3 April, 41 Elizabeth (1599).

Lease by Richard Merywether, Alderman, and Symon Symons, Steward, with the consent of Robert Serrell and William Sessyons, yeomen, now wardens of the school, John Roffe and John Yate, Bailiffs, John Lyme alias Jenkins, William Webbe, and Toby Dallam, Senior Burgesses, to Thomas Bollton of Burford, glover. Messuage ' at the northe end of the towne ' between the tenement of Lawrence Holdinge on the north and the tenement of Thomas Butcher on the south. For 21 years at 26s. 8d. a year. Lease granted in consideration of a payment of 6s. 8d.

Witnesses : John Roffe, John Yate, Wylliam Webbe, John Huntt, Andrew Ward, Raphe Wisdom, John Griffith, William Taylor, Edmond Serrell.

S 28. 14 February, 41 Elizabeth (1599).

Lease by the same (excluding Merywether), to Richard Merywether. The tenement on the north side of Witney Street formerly leased to Wekens, now described as between a barn on the east occupied by Lawrence Tanfeild Esquire and the Oxhouse occupied by John Templer. For 90 Years at 13s. a year. Lease granted on surrender of an old lease having 14 years to run. The purchase of the premises by Merywether and Dallam from Typper and Dawe is recited.

Witnesses : John Yate, Bailiff, Symon Symons, Steward, John Templer, Tobye Dallam, Edmond Serrell, Walter Hayter, ' the wryter hereof '.

S 32. 14 October, 4 James I (1606).

Counterpart of Lease by Richard Merywether, yeoman, Alderman of the Town, Symon Symons, Steward of the Fellowship, Richard Merywether aforesaid and Toby Dallam, Bailiffs, William Webbe, Andrew Ward, John Yate, William Taylor and Thomas Parsons, four of the elder Burgesses, Andrew Ward aforesaid and William Huntt, wardens of the free school, to Richard Taylor, tanner. A little strip of ground being a water course or passage leading into the river there between a tenement in the tenure of William Wisdome belonging unto the free school on the east and the King's highway leading over Burford Bridge on the west. For 21 years at 20d. a year.

O O

S 33. 20 January, 4 James I (1607).

Lease by the same parties (with the exception of Symon Symons and Thomas Parsons), to Symon Symons, tanner, Steward of the Fellowship. A plot of meadow ground, ' being two croocks of ground marked and bounded out with three severall mearestones lying and being within the severall meadow ground nere unto the churchyard of Burford commonly called or known by the name of Burye Orchard and bounding upon the Ryver there over against a parcell of medow grounde of Samuell Cocks Esquire, now or late occupied by Edward Massye '; a half-acre of meadow called Cakebredd in the common lot mead called High Mead and usually allotted out with a half-acre belonging to the copiehold of John Hannes ; one acre of arable in the East Field called Jesus Acre shooting into Dean Acre way near unto Burybarnes ; one other acre of arable in the fields of Upton, now or late occupied by Andrew Warde. For 31 years at 20s. a year. Lease granted in consideration of the surrender of seven years term of an old lease and a payment of £10.

Witnesses : Thomas Parsons, Edmond Serrell, John Collyer, Walter Hayter junior, Thomas Hardinge.

S 34. Same date. Counterpart of the above lease.

Endorsed : ' This Lease shewes Burford a corporacion consisting of an Alderman, Bayliffes & Burgesses.'

S 35. 20 April, 5 James I (1607).

Lease by the same parties as in S 32, to Thomas Holdinge of Burford, yeoman. Messuage late occupied by John Floyd alias Evans upon the upper part of the hill on the west side of the high street between a tenement of Frauncis Perks on the north and a barn of William Hewes alias Calcott on the south, with garden and appurtenances. For 31 years at 50s. a year.

Witnesses : Thomas Parsons, Edmond Serrell, John Collyer, Walter Hayter junior.

S 36. 20 March, 6 James I (1609).

Counterpart of Conveyance by Symon Symons, tanner, Steward, Symon Chadwell, gentleman, William Webbe, yeoman, one of the elder Burgesses, John Hannes, William Hewes alias Calcott, and Symon Starre of Burford, yeoman, to John Collyer, Thomas Silvester, mercer, William Huntt, William Bartholomew, John Warde, Richard Hanks, and Robert Jurden, Burgesses, Samuel Merywether, William Symons, William Webbe the younger, Symon Parsons, John Taylor, and Edmond Serrell the younger, as Feoffees in Trust. Three messuages in one range adjoining to the common bridge, sometime occupied by William Longe, Lawrence Holdinge, and John Stryvens, now by William · Wysdome,, Lawrence Holdinge, and John Butt ; a tenement on the east side of the High Street between a tenement of Symon Partridge on the south and a tenement belonging to the common bridge on the north, now or late occupied by William Sessyons; two messuages in one range in Wyttney Street bounding upon Gyldenforde lane on the east and a tenement of Johanna Awflett, widow, on ·the west, occupied by Richard Sowthe and Thomas Hyett ; two messuages on the west side of the hill in the highe streete between a tenement of Wylliam Hewes on the south and a tenement of William Potter on the north, occupied by Thomas Hardinge and Frauncis Perks ; two acres of meadow ground in High Mead now or late occupied by Symon Symons and Nicolas Webbe ; a messuage on the north side of Wyttney Street between a tenement and barn of Symon Partridge on the east and a tenement of the King's Majesty on the west, sometime occupied by Owen Thomas, clerk, and now or late by Robert Grey ; a messuage on the west side of Burford near to the Vicarage sometime occupied by Thomas Butcher and now by Symon Horton ; a plot of Meadow being two croocks in Bury Orchard ; a half-acre of meadow called Cakebredd Half-acre ; an acre of arable called Jesus Acre ; an acre of arable in Upton. In trust for the purposes of the Free School.

Witnesses : John Templer, Edmond Serrell, Walter Hayter junior, Thomas Hardinge.

S 37. Same date. The conveyance of which the preceding is counterpart.

S 38. 13 April, 10 James I, 1612.
Assignment of Lease by Andrew Taylor of Taynton, to whom Thomas Bolton's lease of the house near the Bridge, now occupied by Thomas Sudeley, coverlet weaver, had been assigned, to Paul Silvester, tanner, for the remainder of the term.

Witness : Thomas Silvester.

S 39. 2 August, 18 James I, 1620.
Lease by Simon Symons, Alderman, and William Webbe, Steward, with the assent of John Huntt and David Hughes alias Floyd, yeomen, wardens of the school, William Taylor and William Barthollmew the elder, bailiffs, John Yate, Thomas Parsons, John Templer, and

John Collyer, yeomen, Senior Burgesses, to Richard Sowthe of Burford, curryer, and Katherine Abram, his daughter. Messuage on the north side of Witney Street between a tenement of Andrew Osborne alias Hibbarde on the east and a tenement of Thomas Hayter on the west, with backside, gardens, etc. For 21 years at 26s. 8d. a year.

Witnesses: Richard Hanks, Thomas Silvester, Leonard Mills, Walter Hayter junior.

S 42. Same date.

Lease by the same parties with the same assentors, to Andrew Osborne alias Hibbarde, roughe mason. The corner messuage or tenement where Andrew Osborne now dwells in Witney Street, between the tenement of Richard Sowthe on the west and the lane to Gildenford on the east. For 21 years at 26s. 3d. a year.

Witnesses: The same with the addition of Paul Silvester.

S 59. 26 December, 1659.

Lease by the Charity Trustees, to Thomas Huntt of Burford, tailor. Two acres and a swathe in High Mead. For 21 years at 24s. a year.

Witnesses: Thomas Parsons junior, Symon Randolph.

S 67. 21 March, 31 Charles II, 1679.

Lease to John White of Burford, tanner. Tenement called Broadgates, late occupied by Thomas Ashworth, gentleman, deceased, on the south side of Church Lane; and one little close or picked paddock belonging to the same, on the south side of Witney Street, a close called King's Head close to the west of it. For 21 years at £10 a year.

S 85. 1 December, 8 George II (1734).

Lease to William Strafford the younger of Burford, slatter and plasterer. Messuage with appurtenances on the east side of the High Street between a tenement late of William Hulls on the north and a tenement of William Midwinter on the south. For 21 years at 30s. a year.

Witnesses: William Holland, William Jordan.

Note.—The following document, though not one of the School series, is among those in the keeping of the Governors of the Grammar School.

CH 55. 28 December, 10 George II, 1736.

Lease to Humphrey Nunny and John Nunny, broadweavers. A house at the end of Witney Street on the south side, between a tenement of Edward Harman on the east and a house called the Meeting House and a yard thereto belonging on the west. For 21 years at 36s. a year.

Witnesses: George Underwood, William Jordan.

SECTION III

CALENDAR OF RECORDS PRESERVED ELSEWHERE

A. EXTRACTS FROM THE PUBLIC RECORD OFFICE

In the following Calendar of extracts from documents preserved at the Public Record Office, wherever the extract has been made from printed volumes of the Records the reference to the volume and page will be found at the end of the extract. In every case where no such reference is given the extract has been made from the original document.

The extracts are arranged in chronological order under the designations commonly used for the various classes of the Public Records, as follows :

(*a*) Exchequer and Chancery Rolls.
(*b*) Exchequer and Chancery Inquisitions.
(*c*) Lay and Clerical Subsidies.
(*d*) Ministers' Accounts.
(*e*) Early Chancery Proceedings.
(*f*) Rentals and Surveys.
(*g*) Records of the Augmentation Office.
(*h*) Letters and Papers, Henry VIII.
(*i*) Miscellaneous Documents.

(*a*) EXCHEQUER AND CHANCERY ROLLS

1176–7. Pipe Roll, 22 Henry II.
Oxinefordscira . . . De misericordia regis pro foresta . . . Clemens de Bureford debet v marcas pro eodem.

1177–8. Pipe Roll, 23 Henry II.
Oxinefordscira . . . De misericordia etc. . . . Clemens de Bureford debet v marcas pro eodem. In thesauro iii marcas et debet ii marcas.
Pipe Roll Society.

[Similar entries continue to appear in the Pipe Rolls for several years, the amercement being paid by instalments. As late as 1186–7 (32 Henry II) Clement of Burford still owed half a mark.]

1194–5. Rotuli Curiae Regis, Roll 3, 6 Richard I, m. 2.
Wiltescira, Placita et Assise. Baldewinus de Bureford ponit Robertum filium suum loco suo versus Thomam de Chereb‸c de placito terrae.—*Pipe Roll Society.*

119-. Pedes Finium, Richard I.

Inter Godehold que fuit uxor Ricardi filii Alani petentem et Thomam de Langele tenentem de tercia parte totius ville de Langele cum pertinenciis et de tercia parte unius hide terre cum pertinenciis in Hupton et de tercia parte quinque messuagiorum cum pertinenciis in Bureford . . . (*and other third parts*) . . . ut rationabilem dotem suam.

1200. Rotuli Curiae Regis, 1 John, m. 16.

dors. Oxon. Willelmus Clericus de Bureford qui tulerat breve de recto versus Willelmum de Upton et Paulinam uxorem suam de ii messuagiis et dimidio in Bureford unde ipse petiit rationabilem partem suam que eum contingit venit et relaxavit loquelam illam et dixit quod ipse tulit preceptum Regis Willelmo de Faleiser (Servienti Gloucestrie) de facienda inde inquisicionem.—*Rot. Cur. Reg., Rolls Soc.* (1835), vol. ii, p. 281.

1199. 'Fine Roll, 1 John, m. 2.

Honor Gloc. Willelmus Clericus et Ricardus filius Simonis dant Regi i marcam pro habenda inquisicione per legales homines de visnete de Bureford utrum particio que facta fuit inter ipsos et Willelmum de Hupton et Paulinam uxorem eius de ii messuagiis et dimidio cum pertinenciis in Bureford rationabiliter facta fuit aut non Cum assensu iusticiorum nostrorum Et si rationabiliter facta fuit teneat sin aliter patticio fiat rationabiliter.

1199-1200. Pipe Roll, 1 John.

Honor Gloecestr' . . . et de viii *li*. et *vs*. et x*d*. de redditu assise de Bureford de termino S Michaelis Et de vi *li*. de tallagio Et de xxv*s*. de feno vendito Et de xii*s*. et viii*d*. de perquisitis.

Oxinefordscira. . . . Taillagium factum per abbatem de Teokesberis et archidiaconum Staff' et Simonem de Pateshull et socios eorum. . . .

Villa de Bureford   vi marcas de taillagio.

1200-1. Pipe Roll, 2 John.

Oxenefordscira. . . . Amerciamenta facta per G. filium Petri et socios suos. . . .

Villata de Bureford debet vi marcas de Taillagio de quibus magister Suenus et Willelmus de Faleisia responserunt inde in compoto suo in anno preterito. Taillagium factum de sergiantiis et dominicis Regis. . . .

Idem vicecomes reddit compotum de vi marcis de Bureford de taillagio.

Honor Gloecestr'. Willelmus de Faleisia et magister swein reddunt compotum de xviii *li.* et x*s.* de firma de Bradested de dimidio anno antequam data erat Amalrico quondam comiti Ebroico . . . et de xvi *li.* et iii*d.* de firma de Bureford de eodem termino antequam daretur predicto Amalrico.

Pipe Roll, 4 John.

Oxenefordscira. . . . Taillagium factum de sergiantiis et dominicis Regis . . . vi marcas de taillagio de Bureford.

1205. Rotuli Chartarum, 6 John.

Confirmation to Bruern Abbey. . . . duo burgagia in Bureford ex dono Lowinilapis.

1205. Close Roll, 7 John, ps. unica, m. 3.

Mandatum est Willelmo de Lafaleis' quod statim visis litteris faciat habere Amalrico comiti Ebroico manerium de Bureford cum instauris et pertinenciis quia illud ei commisimus et quod domino Regi scire faciat quae instaura ibi fuerint T me ipso apud Lam xxx die Nov.

m. 7. Rex Willelmo de La Faleys' Precipimus tibi quod habere facias A comiti Ebroico omnia arreragia tam de Redditu quam taillagie de Bureford que retenta fuerunt quum manerium illud recepit et in summam nobis scire facias Teste me ipso apud Brehull xx die Dec.

1214. Close Roll, 16 John.

Petrus dei gratia episcopus Wintonensis vicecomiti Glouc' salutem Scias quod dominus Rex dedit dilecto et fideli suo Gaufrido de Mandevill Isabellam filiam Willelmi Comitis Glouc' in uxorem cum toto honore Gloec' qui fuit eiusdem Comitis in dominicis et redditibus . . . Excepto . . . etc. T me ipso apud Westm ix die Aug.

Idem mandatum est Vicecomiti Oxon de manerio de Bureford cum omnibus pertinenciis et de omnibus aliis sicut prius.

1215–16. Rotuli de Finibus, 17 John.

De (blank) que fuit uxor Gaufridi de Bureford viginti marcas pro habenda terra que fuit viri sui et pro se maritanda Mem quod pacavit x marcas ad custodiam castellani de Nobe.—*Rot. Fin. Records Comm.* (1835), p. 553.

1216. Close Roll, 18 John.

Mandatum est vicecomiti Oxon quod habere faciat Willelmo de Cantilupe iuniori plenariam saisinam de manerio de Bureford cum pertinenciis quod dominus Rex ei commisit quamdiu domino Regi placuit nisi dominus Rex alii illud contulit T ut supra (i. e. T Rege apud Albū Monasterium vii die Aug.).

1231. Close Roll, 15 Henry III, m. 12.

· De roboribus datis—Mandatum est Thome de Langele quod habere faciat priori Hospitalis Sancti Iohannis Bureford iii robora in foresta de Wichewood ad focum suum de dono regis Teste rege apud Otinton xxix die Maii.—*Cal. Close Rolls, 1227-31*, p. 510.

1232. Close Roll, 17 Henry III, m. 15.

De herieto perdonando—Rex perdonavit Edithe que fuit uxor Ricardi Caretter heriettam quod ab ea exigitur occasione mortis ipsius viri sui. Et mandatum est ballivo de Bureford quod eidem Edithe pacem inde habere permittat. Teste ut supra (i. e. Teste rege apud Theck' xxx die Decembris).—*Cal. Close Rolls, 1231-4*, p. 176.

1232. Close Roll, 17 Henry III, m. 10.

De roboribus datis. ' Mandatum est Thome de Langele quod in foresta de Wichewood faciat habere fratribus hospitalis de Bureford v robora ad focum suum de dono regis (Teste rege apud Otinton xviii die Maii).—*Ibid.*, p. 63.

[Similar gifts of wood are entered on the Rolls in 1233 (twice), and 1235.]

1233. Close Roll, 17 Henry III, m. 8.

De quadam equa data. Mandatum est P de Rivall' quod equam illam que inventa fuit in manu Hugonis de Cotingham et que iam remansit in manu regis eo quod nullus eam sequitur, faciat habere fratribus hospitalis Sancti Iohannis Baptiste de Bureford de dono regis (Teste rege apud Oxoniam xxx die Iunii).—*Ibid.*, p. 233.

1260-1. Pedes Finium, 45 Henry III. ·

Inter Agnetam la Vylane petentem et Robertum priorem hospitalis Sti Iohannis de Bureford quem Agneta de Tancy vocavit ad warantum de uno messuagio et una virgata terre cum pertinenciis in Fifhyde Et inde placitum fuit inter eos in eadem curia scilicet quod Predicta Agneta la Vylane remisit et quietum clamavit de se et heredibus suis predicto Priori et successoribus suis et fratribus et sororibus predicti Hospitalis totum ius, etc.

1261. Close Roll, 47 Henry III, m. 12.

Writ to the Keepers of the Honour of Gloucester to take the manors of Thornbury, Bureford and Fairford into the King's hands, and render account at the Exchequer.

On the dorse of this membrane a copy of the Inquisitio Post Mortem concerning the lands of Richard (de Clare), late Earl of Gloucester. See *infra*, p. 581.

1273. Patent Roll, 1 Edward I, m. 8.

Licence to Lambert le Fraunceis of Burford to export 20 sacks of wool.—*Cal. Pat. Rolls.*

1276. Hundred Rolls.

Extractum Inquisicionum factorum per preceptum domini Regis in comitatibus . . . etc. . . . de iuribus et libertatibus domini Regis subtractis et excessis viceComitum Coronatorum Escaetorum et aliorum Ballivorum domini Regis quorumcunque aliorum Ballivorum (*sic*) quoquomodo dominum Regem spectantibus . . . anno regni Regis E filii Regis H quarto.

Villata de Bureford

Iurati illius villate dicunt de feodis domini Regis et tenentibus eius qui ea modo tenent etc.

Dicunt quod Comes Glouc' tenet duas carucas terre apud Bureford de Rege in capite et burgum similiter tenuit de Rege. Et modo tenet Iohannes Giffard ex dono Comitis ad terminum vite sue sed nesciunt pro quo servicio predictus Comes tenet de Rege nec predictus Iohannes de Comite.

Qui eciam alii a Rege clamant habere returnum brevium et alias libertates etc.

Dicunt quod Iohannes Giffard habet assisas panis et cervisie sed nesciunt quo waranto.   *Rot. Hund.* (1818), i. 37.

Note.—In the more detailed Roll of 7 Edward I there is no mention of Burford under Com. Oxon.

1279. Hundred Rolls, 7 Edward I.

Hundredum de Bampton

Astallingeleye. Lib. Ten.   Prior Hospitalis de Burford tenet in eadem vi acras terre de feodo Ricardo Cornubie in puram et perpetuam elemosinam.

Fifhide. Lib^e Tenent. Dicunt quod Prior Hospitalis Sancti Iohannis de Bureford tenet de predicto Iohanne xxxvi acras terre in puram et perpetuam elemosinam. Dicunt etiam quod idem Prior tenet de predicto Iohanne[1] ix virgatas terre cum pertinenciis reddendo forins' qun curr' et hidag' et aliud forins' cum villat' per annum. Forins'. Dicunt quod Prior Hospitalis Sancti Iohannis de Bureford

---

[1] i. e. Iohannes de Fifhide.

tenet x virgatas terre et dimidiam de Iohanne de Fifhide ut patet supra De quibus tenet in dominico suo v virgatas terre et quartam partem unius virgate que valent liis. vi*d*. et quinque virgate et quarta pars virgate tenentur de eodem ut patet infra.

WOTTON HUNDR'.

Nerer Orton. De feod' Comitis Glou'. Ricardus Parson tenet ii virgatas terre de dono Iohanne de Bremesfeld. Idem Iohannes tenet de Comite Glou'nie de feodo de Bureford reddendo dicto Iohanni x*s*. annuos et sectam curie de iii septimanis in tres septimanas de Bureford pro omni servicio.

Rot. Hund. ii, pp. 694, 732, 842.

1285. Proceedings before Itinerant Justices, 13 Edward I.

Villata de Bureford venit per xii iuratos De pannis dicunt quod Henricus de Blunham vendit pannos contra assisam Ideo in misericordia De libertatibus dicunt quod Iohannes de Giffard tenet Manerium de Bureford de heredibus Gilberti de Clare Comitis Glouc' ad terminum vite ipsius Iohannis et in eodem clamat habere furcas tumbellas assisas panis et cervisie pillory mercatum singulis septimanis per diem sabbatis et feriam in vigilia in die et in crastino sancti Iohannis Baptiste nesciunt quo warranto et quia predicte libertates spectant ad Comitem predictum Et habent hic diem in crastino purificacionis beate Marie.

circa 1291. Taxatio Ecclesiastica.

Taxacio ecclesiarum Pensionum et Porcionum personarum ecclesiasticarum.

Linc. Dioc. Decanatus de Wytteneye.

	£	s.	d.
Abbatis de Keynsham. Ecclesia de Bureford deducta porcio	30	0	0
Porcio Abbatis de Ibreya in eadem	4	0	0
Item porcio Prioris de Munster in eadem		13	4
Vicarius eiusdem	6	13	4
Beneficia Ecclesiastica ad x marcas et infra taxata quorum possessores aliunde non sunt beneficiati.			
Vicar' de Bureford	6	13	4
Taxatio bonorum temporalium reddituum et proventuum Religiosarum personarum			
Abbas de Keynsham habet in Bureford in redditu		3	0

Wygorn. Dioc.

    Taxacio bonorum temporalium Archidiaconatus Gloucestr'

      error Hospitalis Sancti Iohannis de Bureford

      Magister Hospitalis Sancti Iohannis de Bureford

      habet in Rysindon unam virgatam terre que valet

      decem solidos   summa 10.

        et est error quia pauperum et mendicantium.

            Tax. Eccles. (ed. of 1802), pp. 32, 41, 44, 238.

1297. Close Roll, 25 Edward I.

Orders to sheriffs to restore to certain prelates and clergy their lands and tenements together with goods and chattels taken by the sheriffs under the King's orders concerning all lay fees. Among the clergy so reinstated in Oxfordshire were : Adam, Vicar of the church of Burford, Robert the Chaplain, warden of St. John's House, Burford.—*Cal. Var. Chanc. Rolls* (1912), p. 58.

1300. Charter Roll, 28 Edward I, m. 1.

Inspeximus and Confirmation of a charter of Henry I to the church of St. Mary at Tewkesbury, confirming gifts by Robert FitzHamon and others. . . . duas domos in Bureford de dono Radulfi Sacerdotis.— *Cal. Chart. Rolls,* vol. ii, p. 490.

1301. Close Roll, 29 Edward I, m. 10d.

May 4. John son of Richard le Sumenur of Bureford came before the King on the morrow of the Invention of the Holy Cross and sought to replevy his land in Bureford taken into the King's hand for his default before the bailiffs of Ralph de Monte Hermeri, earl of Gloucester and Hertford, and of Joan his wife in their court of Bureford against Ralph de Whitindon and Richard his brother. This is signified to the bailiffs.—*Cal. Close Rolls, 1296–1302,* p. 491.

1302. Forest Roll, 30 Edward I.

Inquisicio apud Cherlebury A° 30 Edwardi tertii de statu foreste de Wychewood in Com. Oxon. . . . Qui dicunt quod quidam venerunt . . . cum sex leporariis in campo de Shipton in balliva de Burford ad malefaciendum domino Regi.

1306. Close Roll, 34 Edward I, m. 10d.

William de Bureford, clerk, came before the King on Sunday after St. Botulph and sought to replevy to Walkelin le Espicer of Bureford the latter's land in Bureford which was taken into the King's hand for his default before the justices of the Bench against Agnes, daughter of Robert le Vykere of Bureford. This is signified to the justices.—*Cal. Close Rolls, 1302–7*, p. 450.

Testa de Nevill.

Com. Oxon. Hundredum de Bampton. . . . Bureford est in manu domini Regis et fuit dominium Comitis Glov'nie.—*Testa Nev.* (ed. of 1807), p. 103.

1314. Close Roll, 8 Edward II.

Delivery of lands to Matilda, late wife of Gilbert de Clare, assigned by the King as dower, including lands at Bureford, Netherorton and Heyford at Bridge, of the yearly value of £14 6s. 6d.—*Cal. Close Rolls, 1313–18*, pp. 131, 135.

1322. Fine Roll, 15 Edward II, ps. 1, m. 9.

Commitment during pleasure to Richard de Foxcote of various manors in the King's hand, including Shipton and Burford in Com. Oxon, late of Maurice de Berkele. (April 21.)—*Cal. Fine Rolls, 1319–27*, pp. 122–4.

1322. Patent Roll, 15 Edward II, ps. 2, m. 16.

William Aylmer appointed to keep and survey the stock of various manors, including Burford.

m. 7. Grant of the manor of Burford to Hugh le Despenser, late of Maurice de Berkeley, rebel. (May.)—*Cal. Pat. Rolls.*

1322. Charter Roll, 16 Edward II, m. 6.

Gift for good service rendered and to be rendered by Hugh le Despenser the younger to the said Hugh and Eleanor his wife of £20 of rent in Burefford, Co. Oxford, late of John Giffard, a rebel and enemy to the King, by whose forfeiture it has escheated to the King. (York, July 16.)—*Cal. Chart. Rolls, 1300–26*, p. 449.

1323. Charter Roll, 16 Edward II.

Grant to Hugh le Despenser the younger and his heirs of a yearly fair at their manor of Boreford, Co. Oxford, on the seven days before the feast of the Nativity of St. John, the feast, and eight days after. (York, July 3.)—*Ibid.*, p. 353.

1327. Patent Roll, 1 Edward III, ps. 1, m. 26.

Grant to Robert de Prestbury, King's yeoman, of all cattle, wool and hay late of the Despensers, rebels, and William Aylmere, their adherent, in the manors of Burford, Shipton and elsewhere in Oxon and Glouc.—*Cal. Pat. Rolls, 1327–30*, p. 22.

1327. Patent Roll, 1 Edward III.

Grant to John de Wysam of the manors of Fulbrook and Westhall with members in Burford, Upton and Swynbrok, of the value of £48 18s. 2¾d.—*Cal. Pat. Rolls.*

1327. Patent Roll, 1 Edward III, ps. 3, m. 6.

Admission of Robert le Glasiere, chaplain, one of the brethren, to the custody of the Hospital of St. John, Bureford, void by the death of John de Sutton ; the presentation of Robert to the office being made by the brethren to the King by reason of the lands of Hugh le Despenser and Eleanor his wife being in the King's hand.—*Cal. Patent Rolls, 1327-30,* p. 195.

1327. Close Roll, 1 Edward III.

Order to the sheriff of Oxford and Berks to deliver to Isabella de Clare the manors of Shipton and Burford, except the borough of Burford, the King having learnt by inquisition that Gilbert de Clare granted the premises to his sister Isabella and she so seized of them married Maurice de Berkeley. Maurice de Berkeley's lands were forfeit, but not the lands of Isabella, which included the manor of Burford except the borough, worth £10 yearly in all issues.—*Cal. Close Rolls, 1327-30.*

1328. Close Roll, 2 Edward III.

Order to the keeper of the manor of Bureford to deliver the premises to Eleanor, late wife of Hugh le Despenser, as the King did not consider it consonant with justice that her lands should be forfeited by the forfeiture of her late husband's lands.—*Cal. Close Rolls, 1327-30.*

1332. Patent Roll, 6 Edward III, ps. 2, m. 25d.

Commission of oyer and terminer to John Inge, Richard de Coleshull, William de Shareshull, and Robert de Aston on complaint by John Goudhyne that William de Horwod the younger, Thomas Corbot, William de Clynton, clerk, Richard de Berton, Giles de la Mote, Thomas de Bykenet of Witteneye, Nicholas Touwe of Burford, Nicholas Cayfestre of Cirecestre, John de la More of Witteneye, ' boucher ', John de Kyngeston of Abyndon, marchaunt, and Henry Blonham of Burford and others carried away his goods at Burford, co. Oxon.—*Cal. Pat. Rolls, 1330-4,* p. 350.

1341. Close Roll, 15 Edward III, ps. 3, m. 1.

To the assessors and collectors in co. Oxford of wools granted in the last Parliament : orders to sell up wool to satisfy various persons for wool taken from them, including . . . William, parson of Bureford for one stone of wool.—*Cal. Close Rolls, 1341–3*, p. 334.

1344. Patent Roll, 18 Edward III, ps. 1, m. 3.
Licence for the King's kinsman Hugh le Despenser to enfeoff Edward de Grymesby and William de Osbertson, clerks, of the manors of . . . Shypton and Burford . . . with intent to regrant the same to the said Hugh, his wife and their heirs.—*Cal. Pat. Rolls, 1343–5*, p. 268.

1344. Patent Roll, 18 Edward III, ps. 2, m. 8d.
Commission of oyer and terminer to John de Stonore, Thomas de Besyle, John de Alveton and Thomas de Langeley on complaint by Henry Dauwes of Burford that Roger de Thornham, vicar of the church of Burford, Richard de Bureford, chaplain, and others assaulted him at Burford so that his life was despaired of.—*Ibid.*, p. 424.

1349. Close Roll, 23 Edward III, ps. 1, m. 20 & m. 13.
Orders to the escheators of Oxford and other counties not to intermeddle further with the manors of . . . Shipton and Burford, and to deliver them to Elizabeth, late the wife of Hugh le Despenser, tenant in chief. Guy de Brian and John de Alveton had had them in charge while they were in the King's hand ; Inquisition now had shown that Hugh and Elizabeth at Hugh's death held the manors for themselves and their heirs.—*Cal. Close Rolls, 1349–54*, pp. 15, 17.

1350. Patent Roll, 24 Edward III, ps. 2, m. 23.
Entry of Letters Patent of Confirmation of the Burford Charters of Henry II. By fine of 20s. paid in the hanaper.—*Cal. Pat. Rolls, 1348–50*, p. 546.

1352. Patent Roll, 26 Edward III, ps. 3, m. 20.
Licence for Guy de Briane, 'chivaler', for the said Guy and Elizabeth his wife to grant to Richard de Hornyngton and Martin Moulissh, clerks, the manor of Rotherfeld and the hamlet of Ernerugge, co. Sussex, the manors of Shupton and Burford and the town of Burford, co. Oxon, and the manor of Stanford, co. Berks, and the advowson of the church of this manor, held in chief, as is said, to hold for the life of the said Elizabeth with the knights' fees, views of frank pledge, and all other appurtenances of the manors, town and hamlet.—*Cal. Pat. Rolls, 1350–4*, p. 351.

1352, Dec. 20. Patent Roll, 26 Edward III, ps. 3, m. 5.
Licence to the two clerks mentioned above to grant the manors, etc. as above to John de Briane and John Seys, clerks.—*Ibid.*, p. 379.

1353, Apr. 20. Patent Roll, 27 Edward III, ps. 1, m. 10.
Similar licence to Briane and Seys to grant to David Vaghan and
Simon Johan, clerks.—*Ibid.*, p. 430.

1354, Mch. 30. Patent Roll, 28 Edward III, ps. 1, m. 17.
Similar licence to Vaghan and Johan to grant to Walter de Briene
and Thomas de Bentham, clerk.—*Cal. Pat. Rolls, 1354–8*, p. 26.

1354, May 17. Patent Roll, 28 Edward III, ps. 1, m. 6.
Similar licence for Briene and Bentham to grant to Guy de Bryene,
chivaler, and Elizabeth his wife, to hold for the life of Elizabeth.—
Ibid., p. 47.

1355. Patent Roll, 29 Edward III, ps. 1, m. 28.
Pardon to John le Sclattere of Burford of the King's suit for the
death of Thomas le Vikory, as the King has learned by the record
of William de Shareshull and his fellows, justices appointed to deliver
the King's gaol of the castle of Oxford, that he killed him in self-
defence.—*Ibid.*, p. 172.

1355. Patent Roll, 29 Edward III, ps. 3, m. 8.
Licence to Thomas de Langele, chivaler, for him to enfeoff Geoffrey,
vicar of the church of Shipton under Wicchewode, and Walter, vicar
of the church of Boreford, of the manor of Langley, for them to re-grant
to him and his wife with remainders to their heirs.—*Ibid.*, p. 317.

1359. Close Roll, 33 Edward III, m. 19.
Order to the escheators to deliver to Edward, son of Edward le
Despenser, kinsman and heir of Hugh le Despenser, the manors of
Shipton and Burford, etc.—*Cal. Close Rolls, 1354–60*, p. 582.

1363. Close Roll, 36 Edward III, m. 39.
Reference to Walter, vicar of Burford, in connexion with Thomas
de Langeley's enfeoffment of the manor of Langley.—*Cal. Close Rolls,
1360–4*, p. 314.

1364. Patent Roll, 38 Edward III, ps. 2, m. 36d.
Commission of oyer and terminer, in the following circumstances :
Whereas at a Parliament held 36 Edward III, it had been complained
that Chaplains were dearer in salaries and stipends since the pestilence,
to the damage and depression of the people, and the Archbishop of
Canterbury and the Bishops and clergy, at the motion of the King
and other magnates had advised that parish Chaplains taking more
than 6 marks yearly, and chaplains not having cure of souls taking
more than 5 marks yearly, for stipends or salaries without dispensation

should incur suspension, John Bishop of Lincoln had sent commissioners to proceed against such chaplains ; and they, while in session at Leicester, had been violently assaulted and brought in fear of their lives by a number of people, including Walter de Burford, who had since bound themselves by oaths to maintain one another, and who lay in wait for the Bishop and his commissaries.—*Cal. Pat. Rolls, 1364-7*, p. 67.

1374. Patent Roll, 48 Edward III, ps. 1, m. 63.

Commission for the arrest of various persons including John Ravenser, ' bocher ', of Boreford, co. Oxon, and William Bakere of Burford for divers felonies, they being now vagabond in various parts of the realm.—*Cal. Pat. Rolls, 1370-4*, p. 489.

1377. Patent Roll, 51 Edward III, ps. unica, m. 26.

Mention of the fact that Elizabeth late the wife of Edward le Despenser, the King's kinsman, had the keeping of the manor of Burford, in the King's hand by reason of the minority of Edward's heir.—*Cal. Pat. Rolls, 1374-7*, p. 442.

1378. Patent Roll, 1 Richard II.

Commission to Robert Tresilian, John de Nowers, William Hervy, Robert de Charleton and Hugh Poure to enquire touching divers forestallings, regrating of wools and other merchandise, concealments, false weights and measures and withdrawals of presentments therefor before the late King's ministers at Bureford and other merchant towns adjacent to the marches of Codeswold.—*Cal. Pat. Rolls, 1377-81*, p. 250.

1379. Patent Roll, 2 Richard II.

List of loans to the King, including John Wynriche of Burford, £10.—*Ibid.*, p. 636.

1379. Patent Roll, 2 Richard II, ps. 2, m. 24.

Entry of Letters Patent of Confirmation of Burford Charters.

1380, Mch. 9. Close Roll, 3 Richard II, m. 11.

To Simon de Burle, constable of Wyndesore castle, or to his lieutenant there. Order to deliver William Hykeboy, neif of Thomas son and heir of Edward le Despenser of his manor of Burford, co. Oxon, who is imprisoned in that castle in custody of the constable, to Elizabeth who was wife of the said Edward or to Richard Earl of Arundell and Surrey and Guy de Brien knight in her name, or to any other whom she shall depute to receive him, as the said Earl and Guy have mainperned for her that she shall deliver him, if living, to the said Thomas, a minor in the King's wardship, when he shall come to the lawful age.—*Cal. Close Rolls, 1377–81*, p. 298.

1380, Mch. 8. Close Roll, 3 Richard II, m. 16d.

Richard Earl of Arundel and Surrey and Guy de Bryene knight to the King : Recognisance for £40 to be levied in Surrey. Memorandum of defeasance upon condition that when Thomas son and heir of Edward le Despenser shall come of age, Elizabeth who was wife of the said Edward shall deliver to him William Hykeboy of Upton his neif of his manor of Burford if then living. Cancelled by the King's command under the Privy Seal, which is upon the Chancery file of 7 Richard II, for that the said Earl delivered the said William to the King and he is imprisoned in the Flete at the King's will.—*Cal. Close Rolls, 1377–81*, p. 361.

1389. Patent Roll, 13 Richard II, ps. 2, m. 31.

Grant for life to the King's clerk William Doune of the wardenship of the Hospital of St. John, Boreford, notwithstanding any prior grant thereof by the King to any other person not yet executed.— *Cal. Pat. Rolls, 1388–92*, p. 156.

1390. Patent Roll, 13 Richard II, ps. 3, m. 2.

Pardon at the supplication of John Aubill, parson of Whalton, to Roger Horold, cordewaner, dwelling against the tavern called the ' cardinalishat ' by Billyngesgate, London, of suit of the King's peace and outlawry, if any, for that being appealed by William Palmere of Burford on the Wold, co. Oxford, 21 May, 12 Richard II, before Adam Carlill and Thomas Austin, sheriffs, and John Chauncye, coroner of London, as having with him and others between Midsummer and the Feasts of SS. Peter and Paul in the year 7 Richard II between Godestowe and Witteneye in that county, after the hour of nine, robbed a man unknown of a bay horse with a saddle and bridle, a pack of woollen cloth of divers colours value 100s., and 40s. in money, whereof the said William Palmere had as his share 40s. and the said Roger and others the goods, he was convicted ; the said approver, before Robert Cherlton, William Venour mayor of London, John Cassey and other justices appointed for delivering Newgate gaol having retracted the said charges.—*Ibid.*, p. 264.

1390. Patent Roll, 14 Richard II, ps. 1, m. 36.

Pardon to John Blaunchard for not appearing to answer John Milton of Boreford, chaplain, touching a debt of 40s.—*Ibid.*, p. 282.

1394. Patent Roll, 18 Richard II, ps. 1, m. 33.

Licences for those born in Ireland to remain for life in England, notwithstanding the proclamation requiring all those born there to return there : Walter Bryan of Boreford, for a fine of 6s. 8d.—*Cal. Pat. Rolls, 1391–6*, p. 457.

1395. Patent Roll, 19 Richard II, ps. 1, m. 26.

Pardon at the supplication of the King's aunt, the Duchess of Gloucester, to Cristina wife of John Cook of Boreford for, with others, murdering and robbing William Schulton of Boreford at Boreford at night on the Feast of St. Katherine, 17 Ric. II.—*Ibid.*, p. 604.

1396. Patent Roll, 20 Richard II, ps. 3, m. 20.

Pardon to John Hay of Burford for not appearing when sued with Maud his wife to answer Edmund Olyver touching a debt of 44s.—*Cal. Pat. Rolls, 1396–9*, p. 128.

1397. Patent Roll, 20 Richard II, 4s. 3, m. 10.

Licence for Geoffrey Walker alias Ludlow to accept the vicarage of the parish church of Burford in the diocese of Lincoln, void by the death of Henry de Norfolk, to which he has been provided by the Pope, notwithstanding the Statute of Provisors.—*Ibid.*, p. 142.

1399. Patent Roll, 1 Henry IV, ps. 1, m. 27.

Entry of Letters Patent of Confirmation of the Burford Charters : for a fine of 33s. 4d. paid in the hanapar.—*Cal. Pat. Rolls, 1399–1401*.

1400. Patent Roll, 1 Henry IV, ps. 5, m. 4.

Grant for life, in aid of her estate, to the King's kinswoman Constance, late the wife of Thomas late lord le Despenser, of the manors of Caversham, Burford, and Shipton, co. Oxford, and others.

Ibid., ps. 5, m. 4.

Similar grant of goods and chattels in various castles and manors, including Burford, to the value of £200.—*Ibid.*, pp. 204, 224.

1400. Patent Roll, 1 Henry IV, ps. 6, m. 4.

Inspeximus and confirmation to William Hamme Esquire of the county of Hereford of an indenture (French) dated at London 27 October, 1 Henry IV, witnessing that Thomas le Despenser Earl of Gloucester has retained him for life at a yearly fee of 10 marks from the manor of Burford, and if the Earl shall go to war out of the realm with the King or in his service the said William shall go with him, and if he is commanded to come to the Earl at any parts in England or Wales he shall come with a yeoman, a groom and three horses ... and shall bring with him any number of men required, unless he has a reasonable excuse.—*Cal. Pat. Rolls, 1399–1401*, p. 263.

1402. Patent Roll, 4 Henry IV, ps. 1, m. 27.
Ratification of estates as parsons of churches: Walter Eymer, vicar of the church of Boreford in the diocese of Lincoln.—*Cal. Pat. Rolls, 1401–5*, p. 156.

1403. Patent Roll, 4 Henry IV, ps. 1, m. 4d.
Commission to Richard Drax, serjeant at arms, to arrest various persons, including John Hostiller of Burford.—*Ibid.*, p. 200.

1405. Patent Roll, 6 Henry IV, ps. 2, m. 30.
Grant to the King's consort, Joan Queen of England, of the custody of the manors of Caversham, Burford, and Shipton, co. Oxon., with others (as in the grant to Constance late wife of Thomas le Despenser), during the minority of Richard, son and heir of Thomas.—*Cal. Pat. Rolls, 1405–8*, p. 4.

1406. Patent Roll, 7 Henry IV, ps. 1, m. 9.
Pardon to Walter Aymere, clerk, alias Walter Eymer, vicar of the church of Burford, for not appearing to answer Henry Colbache, clerk, and Robert Bridlyngton touching debts of 40 marks and £10 respectively.—*Ibid.*, p. 136.

1415. Patent Roll, 3 Henry V, ps. 2, m. 13.
Entry of Letters Patent of Confirmation of the Burford Charters; for a fine of 4 marks paid in the hanaper.—*Cal. Pat. Rolls, 1413–16*.

1422. Patent Roll, 10 Henry V, m. 12.
Pardon to Edmund Dyer of Burford, co. Oxon, dyer, for not appearing before the Justices of the Bench to answer Robert Yorke of Wanteynge and John Wodestok of Abendon mercer touching a debt of 112s.—*Cal. Pat. Rolls, 1416–22*, p. 434.

1431. Patent Roll, 9 Henry VI, ps. 1, m. 26. [t]
Pardon of outlawry to John Sely of Chepyngfaryngdon, co. Berks, yoman or citizen and fellmonger of London, for not appearing before the Justices of the Bench to answer William Townesende, executor of Henry Cotelere or Cotiller of Boreford or Burford and Richard Colas and Agnes his wife, executrix and late the wife of the said Henry Cotelere, touching a plea that he render £50.—*Cal. Pat. Rolls, 1429–36*, p. 93.

1436. Patent Roll, 14 Henry VI, ps. 1, m. 25.

Pardon of outlawry to John Hill of Bampton, co. Oxon, esquire or gentilman, or late of Burford in the Wold, gentilman, for not appearing before the Justices of the Bench touching a plea of debt and other matters.—*Ibid.*

1439. Patent Roll, 18 Henry VI.

Licence for Isabel Countess of Warwick to grant in fee by a fine to be levied in court to Ralph Boteller, John Beauchamp, William Mountfort, and William Thomas, knights, John Throkmorton, John Noreys, John Nanfan, and William Menston, the manors of Tewkesbury and . . . Burford, co. Oxon., and . . . held in chief, to the intent to fulfil thereof her last will to them to be declared.—*Cal. Pat. Rolls, 1436–41,* p. 359.

1446. Patent Roll, 24 Henry VI.

Grant to the King's Esquire for the body John Noreys that he be chief steward of all manors, lordships and lands pertaining to the lordship of the Spensers . . . except the stewardship of the honour of Gloucester in Bristol, to hold as they were held in the lifetime of Henry late Duke of Warwick, during the minority of the Duke's heir.—*Cal. Pat. Rolls, 1441–6,* p. 434.

1465. Patent Roll, 5 Edward IV.

Pardon to John Pynnok of Burford in le Wolde the younger, merchant alias mercer, of his outlawries for not appearing before the Justices of the Bench to answer the Prioress of Westwode touching a debt of 5 marks and to satisfy others of a debt of £20—he having surrendered to the Flete prison and satisfied the other debtors but not the Prioress.—*Cal. Pat. Rolls, 1461–7,* p. 470.

1477. Close Roll, 17 Edward IV.

Entry of the transfer of a house in Burford from William Brampton to Henry Bishop.

1478. Patent Roll, 18 Edward IV.

Grant to the King's servant John Harcourt, one of the gentleman ushers of the King's chamber, of the office of custody of the King's laund called Burfordlaund with the lodge of the same within the forest of Wychwode . . . with wages of 6*d.* daily, during the minority of Edward son of George late Duke of Clarence, from the issues of the lordship of Burford with all other profits.—*Cal. Pat. Rolls, 1476–85,* p. 103.

1479. Patent Roll, 19 Edward IV.

Grant to William Noreys, knight, during the minority of Edward, son and heir of Isabel late the wife of George Duke of Clarence, of . . . the stewardship of the manors of Boreford, Shipton and Spellesbury and the Hundred of Chadlyngton, and 13 marks yearly from the issues of the same lordships with all other profits.—*Ibid.*, p. 157.

1482. Patent Roll, 22 Edward IV.

Grant to William Hugford Esquire of an annuity of £5 from Michaelmas last during the minority of Edward Earl of Warwick, from the issues of the lordship of Burford.—*Ibid.*, p. 311.

1486. Patent Roll, 1 Henry VII.

Grant to William Huggeford, as above.—*Cal. Pat. Rolls, 1485–94*, p. 79.

1486. Patent Roll, 1 Henry VII.

Grant to Anthony Fetyplace Esquire, king's servant, of the office of launder of the laund of Burford in the forest of Whichwood.— *Ibid.*, p. 36.

1489. Patent Roll, 5 Henry VII.

Grant for life to Anne Countess of Warwick of the manors and lordships of Tewkesbury . . . Burford . . . etc.—*Ibid.*, p. 298.

1492. Patent Roll, 8 Henry VII.

Grant for life to Robert Harcourt Esquire of the office of . . . steward of the manors of Burford, Skypton and Spelesbury . . . which offices are in the King's hand by reason of the death of Anne Countess of Warwick . . . With such fees as Reynold Bray enjoyed for the said offices.—*Ibid.*, p. 405.

(b) EXCHEQUER AND CHANCERY INQUISITIONS

1261. Inquisitions Post Mortem, Henry III, File 27, No. 5, m. 41. 46 Henry III.

Extenta terrarum que fuerunt R quondam Com Glouc' . . . Bureford cum burgo et ceteris pertinenciis et libertatibus lxiii *libr.* xi*s.* i*d.* ob. q̄ā. Et inde redduntur annuatim per manus prepositi de Bureford de firma molendini ad partem de Merlawe 32*s.* ob. q̄ā. Et sic remanet ad partem de Tokesbur' lxi *libr.* xix*s.* i*d.*

(Later in roll of knights' fees) . . . G de Fanencourte dimidium feodum in Bureford.

1295. Inquisitions Post Mortem, Edward I, File 77, No. 3. 24. Edward I.

Inquisicio capta trecesimo die Decembris Anno regni regis Edwardi vicesimo quarto super articulos subscriptos videlicet quantum terre Gilbertus de Clare Com Gloucestr' et Hertford' tenuit de domino Rege in capite in Com Oxon. . . . etc.

[*Note.*—The jurors' names are very indistinct ; the name Robertum le Maiorem can be discerned and the name Robertum Dolbe.]

. . . Item dicunt quod tenuit hamelettum de Opton pertinentem ad manerium de Bureford de domino rege in capite pro servicio sexte partis feodi militis in quo sunt c acre terre arabilis pretium acre iii*d*. summa xxv *sol.* Item sunt ibidem x acre prati pretium acre vi*d*. summa v*s.* Item sunt ibidem viii custumarii quorum quilibet tenet unam virgatam terre operaturi a festo Sti Michaelis usque festum Sti Iohannis Baptiste qualibet septimana per tres dies cum uno shore et valet opus diei obolum summa operum DCCCCXII summa in denariis xxxviii*s.* si dies operum eorum in aliquo festo evenerit allocatur eis per annum   Item a festo Sti Iohannis Baptiste usque gulam augusti qualibet septimana per tres dies operatur pro operibus   Summa operum cxx summa in denariis x *sol.* Item a gula augusti usque ad festum Sti Michaelis qualibet septimana per tres dies ac valet opus diei . . . summa operum cIIII^xx XII opera summa in denariis xxii*s.* Item debent talliagium ad xiii *sol.* iiii*d*. placita et perquisita valent vi *sol.* viii*d*. summa hambleti de Opton vi *li.* ii *sol.*

1299. Inquisition Post Mortem, Edward I, File 91, No. 2.

Oxon. Bureford. Inqui. . . . facta ibidem die veneris proxima post festum Translacionis Sti Thome martyris anno Regni Regis Edwardi vicesimo septimo per . . . cramentum Thome de Lincoln Willelmi Whyteman Ricardi de Whytinton Willelmi de Hayles Willelmi le Mareschal de Bureford Henrici de Gerdun Iohannis Stodham de Bureford Thome Oseberne Iohannis Martyn Michaelis le ffeure de Bureford Iohannis le ffeure et Thome de Shipton Quantum videlicet terre Iohannes Gyffard de Brummefeld nuper defunctus tenuit de domino Rege in capite in dominico suo ut de feodo die quo obiit in Com Oxon   Et quantum de aliis   Et per quod servicium et quantum terre ille valeant per annum in omnibus exitibus et quis propinquior heres eius sit et cuius etatis.

Iurati dicunt per sacramentum suum quod predictus Iohannes nullas terras aut tenementa tenuit de domino Rege in capite in dominico

suo ut de feodo in Com predicto die quo obiit Set dicunt quod tenuit
villatam de Bureford et quoddam hamelettum cum pertinenciis quod
vocatur Seynat iuxta Bureford de Gilberto de Clare quondam Comite
Glouc' et Hertford' per homagium et servicium unius feodi militis
faciendo inde scutagium cum acciderit Quia dicunt quod predictus
comes dedit prefato Iohanni per cartam suam feoffamenti quicquid
habuit in predictis villa et.hameletto tenendum de eodem Comite
per servicium predictum sub hac forma videlicet quod si predictus
Iohannes heredem habuerit de corpore suo legitime procreatum tunc
ipse Iohannes et heredes sui de eodem legitime procreati haberent
et tenerent viginti libratas annui redditus in eisdem villa et hameletto
per servicium predictum imperpetuum Et si predictus Iohannes
obierit sine herede de ipso legitime procreato tunc predicte viginti
librate annui redditus simul cum toto residuo in eisdem villa et hameletto post decessum predicti Iohannis prefato Comiti et heredibus
suis integre reverterentur et remanerent inperpetuum Per quod
dicunt prefatus Iohannes tenuit predictas viginti libratas redditus
in eisdem villa et hameletto in dominico suo ut de feodo die quo
obiit Et totum residuum ultra predictas viginti libratas redditus
tenuit ad terminum vite sue tenendas per formam doni superius
expressi Et dicunt quod nichil tenuit de aliquo alio in comitatu
predicto.

Dicunt quod sunt ibidem cv libere tenentes qui reddunt per annum
xx *li*. xiii*s*. vi*d*. ad quatuor anni terminos videlicet ad festum Nativitatis Sti Iohannis Baptiste cii*s*. iiii*d*. ob. q̄ā. Et ad festum Sti Michaelis
cvi*s*. iii*d*. ob. q̄ā. Et ad festum Nativitatis Domini cii*s*. iiii*d*, ob. q̄ā.
Et ad festum Pasche cii*s*. iiii*d*. ob. q̄ā. Est ibidem quoddam mercatum
quod valet per annum simul cum feria stallagio et tolneto cervisie
ibidem xii *li*. Sunt ibidem xxx acre prati que valent per annum
iiii *li*. x*s*. per acram iii*s*. Est et apud Upton quoddam molendinum
aquaticum quod valet per annum lx*s*. Dicunt quod placita et perquisita curie ibidem et visus ibidem valent per annum xx*s*.

Summa de Bureford xli *li*. iii*s*. vi*d*.

Seynat. Dicunt etiam quod apud Seynat sunt xii villani virgatarii
quorum quilibet tenet unam virgatam terre in villenagium que
continet xx acras Et de eisdem villanis quilibet eorum pro se reddit
per annum pro redditu tallagio et pro omnimodis operibus de certo
xii*s*. vi*d*. ob. q̄ā. ad quatuor anni terminos videlicet ad festum Nativitatis Sti Iohannis Baptiste xv*d*. Et ad festum Sti Michaelis viii*s*.
ix*d*. ob. q̄ā. Et ad Natale domini xv*d*. Et ad festum Pasche xv*d*.

Sunt et ibidem iii dimidii virgatarii quorum quilibet tenet x acras
terre in villenagium Et quilibet eorum pro se reddit per annum de
certo pro redditu tallagio et omnimodis operibus suis vi*s*. iii*d*. q̄ā. ad
predictos terminos videlicet ad festum Nativitatis Sti Iohannis
Baptiste vii*d*. Et ad festum sti michaelis iiii*s*. iiii*d*. ob. q̄ā. Et ad
Natale Domini vii*d*. Et ad festum pasche vii*d*. ob. Et predicti villani
tam virgatarii quam dimidii virgatarii dant de certo ad terminum
de la Hokeday xxxi*d*. Dicunt etiam quod Iohannes filius predicti
Iohannis Gyffard est propinquior heres eius et est etatis xiii annorum
In cuius rei testimonium predicti Iurati huic inquisicioni sigilla sua
apposuerunt Datum ut supra

Summa de Seynat viii *li*. xii*s*. i*d*. ob. q̄ā.

Summa totalis de Bureford et Seynat xlix *li*. xiiii*s*. q̄ā. (*sic*).

Bureford. Inquisicio facta ibidem die mercurii proxima ante
festum Sti Iacobi apostoli anno Regni Regis Edwardi viçesimo septimo
per sacramentum Henrici de Grey Iohannis de Haddon Stephani de
Wyndsor Ricardi de Fretewell Iohannis Turfrey Roberti de ffernhull
Iohannis le Brun Iohannis le Cur Iohannis Pòmeray Roberti de
Westwell Thomae le Baroun et Willelmi Purnele Qualem videlicet
statum Iohannes Gyffard de Brymmefeld nuper defunctus habuit in
Maneriis de Bureford in Com. Oxon et Baggeworth in Com. Gloucestr'
. . . etc. etc.

[The form of John Giffard's tenure sworn to as above. The only differences in this separate Inquisition are that it is expressly mentioned that
from the lease of the town were exempted lands and tenements which
Geoffrey de Phanacurt held of Gilbert de Clare ; and that the jurors
responded to a certain inquiry that John Giffard had not done homage
for his holding to Joanna the widow of Gilbert nor to Ralph de Monthermer.]

1307. Inquisitions Post Mortem, Edward I, File 128, No. 4.

Oxon. Manerium de Bureford.

Extenta ibidem facta coram Escaetori domini Regis xiiii die Iuni
Anno regni regis Edwardi xxx quinto De terris et tenementis de quibus
Gilbertus de Clare quondam Comes Gloucestr' et Hertford' et Iohanna
uxor eius ex feoffamento domini Regis tenerunt Habenda ad totam
vitam eorum et heredibus de corporibus eorum exeuntibus et que
terre et tenementa ultra feoffamentum predictum heredibus predictis
iure hereditario descendent et que per escaetam vel alio modo et
qualiter et quo modo acciderunt et quantum terre idem Comes tenuit
de domino Rege in capite die quo obiit et quantum de aliis et . . . et
quantum terre ille valeant per annum in omnibus exitibus et quis

propinquior heres eorum sit et cuius etatis per sacramentum Willelmi Whiteman Laurencii le Clerke Willelmi de Faireford Nicho Richeman Iohannis le Hay Iohannis atte Stone Thome le Mestre Iohannis le Taillur Henrici Gerdon Ricardi de Bureford Radulfi de Hilworks et Clementis le Vatte.

Qui dicunt per sacramentum suum quod est iuxta villam de Bureford manerium de Bureford cum hameletto de Upton unde predicta Iohanna non fuit coniuncta quod quidem manerium et hamelettum de Upton Dominus Rad de Monte Hermeri tenet per commissionem domini Regis usque ad plenam etatem heredis predicti Et dicunt quod predicta tenementa tenentur de dono Regis in capite ut de Comitatu Gloucestr' set per quod servicium teneantur pro se ignorant Et dicunt quod est ibi quedam grangia que nichil valet ultra reprisas Et dicunt sunt ibi ix^{xx} acre terre arrabilis que valent per annum xxxii$s$. pretium acre ii$d$. Et xx acre prati que valent per annum xxx$s$. pretium acre xviii$d$. Summa dominicorum lxii$s$.

Et sunt in eodem hameletto de Upton predicto (*blank*) de redditu villanorum de quibus Thomas atte Vorde tenet i virgatam terre et reddit per annum ix$s$. ad quatuor terminos principales equaliter vel operabitur per annum et opera appunctantur ad predictos ix$s$. et si operabitur nichil dabit per annum extra tallagium Et Iohannes Simond Iohannes Tretons Iohannes atte Hurne Robertus Hikeman Rogerus Hikeman quilibet istorum faciet in operibus sicut predictus Thomas atte Vorde Et Iohannes le Sutherne tenet dimidiam virgatam terre et faciet in omnibus medietatem servicii predicti Thome atte Vorde pro omni servicio Et dicunt quod sunt ibi viii custumarii . . . quorum quilibet . . . reddet et faciet in omnibus sicut predictus Thomas atte Vorde. Summa reddituum et operum vi li. xx$s$. (*sic*) vi$d$.

Et omnes predicti custumarii dabunt ad festum Sti Martini de certo tallagio xxvi$s$. viii$d$. Et dabunt quolibet anno ad la Hokkeday de dominico visu iiii$s$. Et placita et perquisita curie valent per annum iiii$s$. Summa tallagii et visus perquisiti xxxiiii$s$. viii$d$.

Summa totalis extente predicte xi li. xvi$s$. ii$d$.

Villa de Bureford. Et predicti Iurati dicunt quod predictus Comes diu ante mortem suam feoffavit Iohannem Giffard de villa de Bureford cum hameletto de Seynat Habendum sibi ad totam suam (*sic*) et post mortem predicti Iohannis predicta ten. . . . den. . . . in manu domini Regis eo quod predicta Comitissa non fuit inde coniuncta Et dicunt quod predicta villa cum hameletto tenentur de Domino Rege in capite et de Com Glouc' Set per quod servicium pro se ignorant Et dicunt quod omnia supradicta tenementa heredi predicto iure hereditario descendebunt   Et dicunt quod sunt in eadem villa cum hameletto predicto xxx *libr*. vi*d*. de quodam redditu per annum   Et dicunt quod Tolloneum dicte ville valet per annum xi *libr*. xviii*s*.   Et est ibi unum molendinum ad predictam villam pertinens quod valet per annum lx*s*.   Et est ibi quoddam pratum quod valet per annum iiii *libr*. xvi*s*.   Et dicunt quod placita et perquisita curie valent per annum xx*s*. (v*s*. vi*d*. interlined above)   Et dicunt quod Gilbertus de Clare filius et heres predicti Gilberti de Clar Com est propinquior heres eius et est etatis xvii annorum.   In cuius rei testimonium huic excaete predicti Iurati sigilla sua apposuerunt . Datum ut supra.

[*Note*.—This Inquisition was made on a writ of Diem Clausit Extremum touching the death of Johanna, wife of Gilbert de Clare, daughter of Edward I.]

1314.   Inquisitions Post Mortem, Edward II, File 42.   (*Document damaged at the top*.)

Excaeta . . . reford . . . quarto die Septembris Anno Regni Regis Edwardi Octavo De terris et tenementis qu. . . . fuerunt Gilberti de Clare Com Gloucestr' et Hertfordis nuper defuncti quantum videlicet terre Idem Gilbertus tenuit in dominico suo de feodo de domino Rege in capite die quo obiit et quantum de aliis et per quod servicium et quantum terre de aliis et per quod servicium et quantum terre ille valeant per annum cum omnibus exitibus et quis propinquior heres eius sit et cuius etatis per sacramentum Thome de Lyncolne Willelmi le Mareschal Egidii de Wytinton Willelmi de Wegewolde Symonis le Spicer Ricardi Russel Radulfi Chastelton Edmondi de Dene Iohannis de Epewelle Symon de Tardiu Nich de Estcote et Roberti le Mason   Qui dicunt per sacramentum suum quod predictus Gilbertus fuit seisitus in dominico suo ut de feodo die quo obiit de dominio ville de Boreford quod quidem dominium tenetur de domino Rege in capite tanquam parcella honoris Gloucestr' per quod servicium pro se tenetur ignorant   Et sunt ibi xiii burgenses qui reddunt per annum xiiii*s*. vi*d*. ad iii terminos videlicet ad festum Nativitatis beati Iohannis Baptiste Beati Michaelis Beati Thome Apostoli et festum palmarum equis porcionibus   Et quoddam mercatum per annum per diem sabbatis cuius proficuum valet una cum tollonio Nundinarum ibidem die Nativitatis beati Iohannis Baptiste existentium valent per annum x *li*.   Et placita et perquisita curie eiusdem ville valent per annum lx*s*.   Et dicunt quod si Matillda que fuit uxor predicti Gilberti pregnans non existet quod Alianora uxor Hugonis le Despenser et Margareta que fuit uxor Petri de Gavàrston et Isabella que fuit uxor Iohannis de Burg sorores predicti Gilberti de Clare sunt propinquiores heredes eius et predicta Isabella tertia nata est etatis sexdecim annorum Item dicunt quod dictus Comes habuit die quo obiit xs. redditus per annum de Ricardo parson de Netherverton in Com. Oxon. Item habuit dictus Comes die quo obiit ii*s*. per annum de certo annuali visu apud Heyford ad Pontem in com. predicto

Summa extente de Boreford ad.redditus et forins' xiiiili. vis. vid.

[*Note*.—A number of writs and other documents are affixed to this Inquisition, the husbands of the three co-heiresses named having seized upon the estates on the ground that the time had passed within which the Countess might be pregnant. The matter went to the Chancery, who would not advise ' because of the strangeness of the case '.]

1320.* Inquisitions Ad Quod Damnum, File 145, No. 15.

Inquisicio capta coram Escaetori domini Regis citra Trentam apud Asthallyngeley die Lune in festo Translacionis Sci Thome Martyris anno regni regis Edwardi filii regis Edwardi quartodecimo incipiente secundum tenorem brevis huic inquisicioni consuti per sacramentum Roberti de Esthalle Iohannis Turfrey Iohannis de Camswelle Rogeri de Heuxheye Iohannis Bruyn Henrici de Fyffhede Iohannis de Lewe Roberti de Fernhulle Willelmi le Maryschal Galfridi Turfray Salamonis le Grete et Nich Whitemay iuratorum Qui dicunt per sacramentum suum quod non est ad dampnum nec preiudicium domini Regis nec aliorum si dominus Rex concedat Iohanne que fuit uxor Ricardi de Cornwaille quod ipsa quinque messuagia quatuor crofta duas virgatas terre et decem solidatos redditus cum pertinenciis in Asthalle et Asthallyngeley dare possit et assignare dilecto sibi in Christo Priori hospitalis sti Iohannis de Boreford Habenda et tenenda eidem priori et successoribus suis ad inveniendum quendam capellanum in ecclesia Sti Nicholai de Asthalle divina singulis diebus pro anima ipsius Iohanne et predicti Ricardi viri sui celebraturum inperpetuum Et dicunt quod predicta Iohanna tenet predicta messuagia crofta terras et redditus de Edmundi de Cornubia in capite ut de manerio de Astalle per fidelitatem et servicium unius denarii per annum pro omni servicio Et dicunt quod Abbatissa de Godestowe a tempore quo memoria non extat percepit et percipere consuevit annuatim de una virgata terre eiusdem tenementi quod quondam fuit Willelmi de Feor duodecim solidos Et dicunt quod predicta messuagia crofta et terre valent per annum cum omnibus exitibus quinquaginta et duos solidos et unum denarium iuxta verum valorem eorundem Et dicunt quod non sunt plures medii inter dominum Regem et predictam Iohannam . . . etc. etc . . .

[*Note*.—The licence in mortmain to alienate this property, Aug. 6, 1320, is entered on the Patent Roll 14 Edward II, ps. 1, m. 22.

In connexion with this grant see *The English Register of Godstow Nunnery*, edited by A. Clark (E.E.T.S., 1905), p. 212 : ' A covenant i-made by the abbas of Godstowe to the prior of Burford. The sentence of thys convencion is, that Margerye Dyne, abbesse of Godstowe and the covent of the same place graunted & yaf licence for hyr & hyr successours to the prior of the hospital of Seynt Iohn of Borforde and to the covent of the same place and to her successours for to appropour a yerde londe with the pertinens in Estallingleie the whyche Iohn of Cornewayle helde of the seyd abbas and covent so that the for-seyd prior and covent of the same place and her successours pay ther-of yerly to the fornamyd Abbas and covent xii shillings at iiii termys of the yer for all seculer exaccion and demand. I-yef at Godstowe the xii yere of Kynge Edward.' Cf. *infra*, p. 622.]

1327. Inquisitions Post Mortem, Edward III, File 5. (*Document in bad condition.*)

Inquisicio facta apud Bampton coram Thomam de Harpden escaetorem domini Regis in com. Wigorn. . . . Oxon Berks. . . . die februarii anno regni Regis Edwardi primo. . . .

Qui dicunt super sacramentum suum quod Iohannes Gyffard de Brym. . . . tenuit in dominico suo ut de feodo die quo obiit viginti libratas in villa de Burford in predicto Com Oxon . . . Et dicunt quod predictus redditus tenetur de heredibus comitis Gloucestrie pro servicio quarte partis feodi unius militis pro omni servicio Et requisiti etiam quis sit propinquior heres predicti Iohannis Gyffard dicunt quod penitus ignorant.

1337. Inquisitions Post Mortem, Edward III, File 51.

Inquisicio facta apud Bureford coram escaetorem domini Regis in Com Oxon xx° die Iulii anno regni Regis Edwardi tertii post conquestum undecimo Iuxta tenorem Brevis domini Regis huic Inquisicioni consuti per sacramentum Salamonis le Grete Rogeri Yathman Nicholai Whytemay Nicholai Sely Thome Whytemay Thome Note Ricardi Salaman Willelmi de Fayrford Ricardi Turfray Nicholai Cokerel Willelmi le Mareschal et Willelmi. . . . qui dicunt quod Elionora la Despenser quum diem suum clausit extremum fuit seisita in dominico suo ut de feodo die quo obiit de octodecim solidis uno denario uno obolo et uno quadrante Redditus assisi per annum de quibusdam libere tenentibus in Bureford in Comitatu predicto solvendis ad quatuor anni dies usuales per equales porciones Et dicunt est ibidem quoddam mercatum cuius tolnetum valet per annum 1*s.* Et sunt ibidem quedam Nundine ad festum Sti Iohannis Baptiste quarum tolnetum valet

xxvi*s*. viii*d*. Et est ibidem quidam visus franci plegii tenendus ad
le Hockeday qui valet iii*s*. iiii*d*. Et dicunt quod placita et perquisita
curie valent per annum xiii*s*. iiii*d*. Que tenentur de domino Rege
in capite ut de honore Glouc' Per quod servicium ignorant Et
dicunt quod Hugo le Despenser filius primogenitus ipsius Elianore
iun. . . . est propinquior heres eius et est etatis viginti none annorum
et amplius In cuius rei testimonium predicti iurati huic Inquisicioni
sigilla sua apposuerunt Datum die anno et loco supradictis.

1344. Inquisitions Ad Quod Damnum, File 269.

Inquisicio facta apud Boreford coram Iohanne de Alnetone escaetore
domini Regis in Com Oxon 'et Berks octavo die Aprilis anno Regni
regis Edwardi tertii post conquestum xviii iuxta tenorem brevis
domini Regis huic inquisicioni consuti per sacramentum Iohannis
de Hyntone Thome Blakeman Nicholai de Ascote Nicholai de Kyrtlen-
tone Reginaldi de Dene Thome ffrankelayn Iohannis Whitefeld
Willelmi Isaac Thome le Quareour Nicholai Whitemay Willelmi le
Lepere et. . . . Qui dicunt per sacramentum suum quod non est ad
dampnum seu preiudicium domini Regis nec aliorum si dominus
Rex concedat dilecto et fideli suo Hugoni le Despenser quod ipse de
manerio de Schipton et manerio de Burford cum pertinenciis in dicto
Com Oxon feoffare possit Edmundum de Grymesby Iohannem de
Hamslape et Willelmum de Oseberston clericos Habenda et tenenda
eisdem Edmundo Iohanni et Willelmo et heredibus suis de domino
Rege et heredibus suis per servicia inde debita et consueta in perpetuum
ita quod ipsi habita inde plena et pacifica seisina dare possint et
concedere predicta maneria cum pertinenciis prefato Hugoni et
Elizabethe uxori eius Habenda et tenenda eisdem Hugoni et Elizabethe et heredibus ipsius Hugonis de Domino Rege et heredibus suis
per servicia in perpetuum Et dicunt quod predictum manerium de
Schipton . . . etc. etc. . . . .

Item dicunt quod predictum manerium de Burford tenetur de
honore Gloucestr' per servicium unius feodi militis Et dicunt quod
capitale messuagium dicti manerii valet per annum ii*s*. Et dicunt
quod est ibidem unum molendinum aquaticum quod valet per
annum xiii*s*. iiii*d*. Et sunt ibidem due carucate terre in dominico
continentes cc viii acras quarum medietas seminari potest per
annum Et valet acra seminata iii*d*. cuius summa est xxvi*s*.
Et sunt ibidem xlv acre prati quarum xx acre valent per annum
xxx*s*. pretium acre xviii*d*. et xxv acre prati valent per annum xxv*s*.
pretium acre xii*d*. Et dicunt quod liberi et nativi tenentes ibidem

reddunt per annum xiiii *li*. x*s*. Et dicunt quod placita et perquisita. curie ibidem valent per annum x*s*. Et sic dicunt quod predictum manerium de Burford valet per annum in toto xix *li*. xvi*s*. iiii*d*.

The following entries concern the half knight's fee held in Burford by the family of de Fanencourt.

1386. 10 Richard II. Hugo Comes Stafford'. Burford—Unum feodum de honore de Gloucestr'.

1392. 16 Richard II. Thomas Comes Stafford'. Boreford—Medietas unius feodi.

1398. 22 Richard II. Willelmus frater et heres Thome Comitis Stafford'. Boreford—Dimidium feodi per heredes W. Fanacourt.

1402-3. 4 Henry IV. Edmundus Comes Stafford'. Burford —Medietas unius feodi.   •

1460-1. 38 & 39 Henry·VI. Humfridi Dux Buckinghamie. Boreford—Dimidium feodi per heredes Willelmi de Fanacourt.

Cat. Inquis. Post Mort. iii. 85, 152, 245, 288, iv. 155.

1460. Inquisitions Post Mortem, Henry VI, File 96, No. 3. 18 Henry VI.

Oxon. Inquisicio capta apud Oxon xxiii die mensis Maii anno regni Regis Henrici sexti post conquestum decimo octavo coram Petro ffetiplace escaetori domini Regis in comitatu predicto virtute brevis domini Regis eidem escaetori directe Et huic inquisicioni consute per sacramentum Willelmi Roseno Ricardi Purcell Thome Chevenhurst Iohannis Mery Roberti ffyffyde Willelmi Candy Thomas Chalkeleyn Iohannis Swyft Iohannis Radby Thome Cozener et Iohannis Tyllynger Qui dicunt super sacramentum suum quod Isabella nuper comitissa Warrwick in dicto brevi nominata nulla tenuit terras seu tenementa in dominico suo ut de feodo nec in servicio de domino Rege in capite nec de aliquo alio in comitatu predicto die quo obiit. Set dicunt quod quidam finis levavit in curia Domini Regis nunc a die sti Michaelis in quindecim dies anno regni eiusdem domini Regis nunc decimo octavo Inter Radulphum Boteler militem Iohannem Beauchamp militem Willelmum Mountfort militem[1] Willelmum Thomas militem Iohannem Throkmarton Iohannem Norys Iohannem Nanfan Willelmum Menston et Iohannem Say clericum querentes et dictam Isabellam in dicto brevi nominatam per nomen Isabelle que fuit uxor Ricardi nuper comitis Warrwick comitisse Warrwick deforciantem de manerio de Shipton . . . etc . . . Dicunt etiam predicti Iuratores

[1] This name interlined.

quod in curia domini Regis nunc videlicet a die sti martini in xv dies
anno regni eiusdem domini Regis nunc decimo octavo quidam alius
finis levavit inter Radulphum Boteller et alios in eodem fine nominatos
querentes et dictam Isabellam in dicto brevi nominatam per nomen
Isabelle que fuit uxor Ricardi nuper. comitis Warr comitisse Warr
deforciantem de manerios de Caversham et Burford cum pertinenciis
inter alia in eodem comitatu licencia regis inde prius habita per quem
finem eadem Isabella recognovit eadem maneria cum pertinenciis inter alia esse ius ipsius Radulphi et aliorum in eodem fine nominatorum
ut ea que idem Radulfus et alii in eodem fine nominati habuerunt
ex dono ipsius Isabelle prout in eodem fine dictis Iuratoribus ostenso
plenius potest apparere virtute cuius finis ipsi de eisdem maneriis
cum pertinenciis inter alia fuerunt seisiti in dominico suo ut de feodo
in vita ipsius Isabelle et tempore mortis eiusdem Isabelle Et de tali
statu adhuc inde seisiti existunt Et dicunt quod dicta Isabella obiit
in festo Sti Stephani ultimo preterito Et quod Henricus nunc comes
Warr est filius et heres propinquior ipsius Isabelle et fuit etatis
quindecim annorum xxii die martis ultimo preterito in cuius rei
. . . etc.

1466. Inquisitions Post Mortem, Henry VI, File **123**, No. **43**.
25 Henry VI.
Inquisicio capta apud Oxon in com Oxon xviii die Novembris
anno regni Regis Henrici sexti post conquestum vicesimo quinto coram
Waltero Wyghthyll escaetori dicti domini Regis in comitatu predicto
virtute cuiusdam brevis . . . etc. . . .

[Upon the death of Henry de Bello Campo, Duke of Warwick. Gives
the same account of the fine of 18 Henry VI as the preceding Inquisition,
and of the existing tenure of the manor of Burford.]

Et dicunt quod dicta maneria de Caversham et Burford non tenentur
de domino Rege set de quo vel de quibus tenentur Iuratores predicti
ignorant.

1486. Inquisitions Post Mortem, Exch. Series II, File **775**, No. **9**.
2 Henry VII.
Inquisition dated 26 September, 2 Henry VII, concerning the lands
of Thomas Farmer, including the manor of Chadlyngton Estende,
seven houses and land in Witney, a house and land in Coggs and in
Filkins, and one cottage with the appurtenances in Burford, the last
held of the Earl of Warwick at a service of one penny a year, and
valued at 6s. 8d. a year.

1486. Inquisitions Post Mortem, *Ibidem*, No. 16. 2 Henry VII.

Inquisition dated penultimate day of October, 2 Henry VII, concerning the lands of Richard Mosyer. The jurors found that he held no lands of the King *in capite*. Set dicunt predicti Iuratores quod Iohannes Pynnok Iohannes Graunger et Willelmus Hill alias dictus Willelmus Priour fuerunt seisiti in dominico suo ut de feodo de et in omnibus illis terris et tenementis cum suis pertinenciis iacentia in Burford et Kenkham in comitatu predicto que nuper fuerunt Iohannis Mosyer patris Ricardi Mosyer in dicto brevi nominati ad usum et commodum eiusdem Ricardi heredum et assignatorum suorum Qui quidem Ricardus Mosyer pro eo quod nullum habuit heredem ac pro eo quod Willelmus Hill alias dictus Willelmus Priour fuit proximus consanguineus eius diu ante obitum suum voluit et ordinavit quod idem Willelmus Hille post mortem suam heret omnia supradicta terras et tenementa cum suis pertinenciis . . . prout Willelmus Pole Robertus Coke et Iohannes Fyssher super captionem huius Inquisicionis examinati testificaverunt . . .

[The lands in Burford held of the Earl of Warwick and valued at 20*s.* a year.]

1495. Inquisitions Post Mortem, Chanc. Series II, vol. 10, No. 143. 10 Henry VII.

Inquisition held at Crowmarsh, 20 February, 10 Henry VII, concerning the lands of William Eyston, who had died the previous 23 December, leaving a son and heir Thomas Eyston. His lands included three messuages in Burford of the annual value of £3.

Et dicunt quod dicta tria messuagia cum pertinenciis tenentur de domino Rege ut de Ducatu suo de Glous' Set pro quo servicio iuratores predicti penitus ignorant.

1578. Inquisitions Post Mortem, Chanc. Series II, vol. 182, No. 43. 20 Elizabeth.

Inquisition at Chipping Norton 16 January, 20 Elizabeth, coram Herculi Raynsford et Thoma Penistone et Thoma Richards generosis per sacramentum Willemi Bond Iohannis Wythinge Iohannis Rawlinge Thome Wodward Iohannis Crippes Iohannis Sessions Iohannis ffiecher Henrici ffiecher Ricardi Busbye Iacobi foster Henrici Baker Willelmi Brooke Thome Norden Thome Carike Willelmi Huchines Simonis Turfrey et Roberti Haris . . .

Qui dicunt super sacramentum suum quod Edmundus Silvester

pater predicti Edmundi in dicta commissione nominati fuit seisitus in dominico suo ut de feodo de una virgata terre cum pertinenciis in Risington magna in com Glouc ac de et in uno messuagio uno curtilagio uno tofto et uno crofto et diversis aliis terris tenementis et hereditamentis in Esthall et Esthall langlye in comitatu Oxon nuper hospitali Sti Iohannis Evangeliste de Burford dudum spectantibus ac etiam de et in uno messuagio cum pertinenciis in Burford predicto in tenura cuiusdam Ricardi Dalam et de et in uno gardino ibidem in tenura Iohannis Haynes uno alio gardino ibidem in tenura Ricardi Wigpit uno clauso ibidem in tenura Roberti Hayter ac de et in uno messuagio vocato The Corner House in Burford predicto cum curtilagio et gardino adiacentibus nuper cantarie Beate marie virginis de Burford spectantibus necnon de et in uno tenemento in Burford predicto in alta strata ibidem et uno clauso in Burford predicto vocato Picked Close in Wittneye Street . . .

The jurors found that Edmund Silvester the younger succeeded as son and heir to the above properties, and was also himself seised ' de et in duabus virgatis terre arrabilis iacentibus in villa et campis de Burford et Signett in comitatu predicto et de et in duabus acris prati iacentibus in quodam prato de Burford predicto vocato High Meade et de et in uno clauso vocato Samon's Close '.

The jurors found that Edmund Silvester died 29 July, 19 Elizabeth (1577), having left to Thomas Silvester, his second son, the messuage occupied by Dalam and the close called Hayter's Close ; and to William Silvester, another son, Salmon's Close in St. John's Street. The rest of his property descended to Edmund Silvester, his son and heir.

The lands in Risington, Asthall, and Asthally held of the Queen *in capite*, by service of a twentieth part of a knight's fee, and valued at 40s. a year.

The house with a garden and close (valued at 13s. a year), the Corner House (valued at 20s. a year), the High Street tenement (valued at 13s. 8d. a year), and the Picked Close (valued at 2s. a year), all in Burford, held of the Queen as of the manor of East Greenwich.

The other lands and tenements in Burford valued at 25s. a year, ' et tenentur de domina Regina ut de Burgo suo de Burford in libero Burgagio '.

(c) LAY AND CLERICAL SUBSIDIES

1316. Lay Subsidies, Oxfordshire : 161, 8.

Boreford

De Isabella de Clar	xvis. vid.
De Thoma Corbet	xiiis. iiiid.
De magistro Hospitalis	xis. iid.
De Iohanne Mokes	iiiis. iid.
De Ricardo Sely	iiiis.
De Willelmo Fynely	vis. vid.
De Iohanne Fabro	iiiis. vid.
De Willelmo Bond	iis. iiiid.
De Iohanne de Sotham	vis. vid.
De Salamone le Grete	viiis. vid.
De Ricardo Pakedam	iis. iid.
De Michaele Fabro	xixd.
De Iohanne le Viker	iis. vid.
De Ricardo de Wintarton	xiiiid.
De Henrico Laszine	iiiis. vid.
De Ricardo de Churchill	xxd.
De Nicholao Richeman	iis. vid.
De Clemente le Vatter	ixs.
De Iohanne le Napper	xs.
De Nicholao Whitemay	iiiis. viid.
De Willelmo Faireford	iiiis. vid.
De Thoma Note	xviid.
De Willelmo Whitemay	xxiiid.
De Iohanne le Baker	xxd.
De Rogero Machmen	iiiis.
De Henrico Blondam	iis. vid.
De Ricardo Pistore	iis.
De Thoma de Lincoln	iiiis.
De Egidio de Whitinton	vs. iid.
De Ricardo Rossel	iiiis. viiid.
De Thoma Eaward	iiiis. viiid.
De Thoma Martyn	iiiis. viiid.
De Willelmo de . . .	iiis. vid.
De Matthew le Canone	vs. iiiid.
De Cristina . . .	iiiis. ixd.
De Iohanne le Star	vs. iiid.
De Galfrido Bitheweye	iiiis. iiiid.
De Willelmo le Long	vis.
De Iohanne ad Aulam	iiis. vid.
De Roberto Abraham	vs. vid.
De Thoma Hykeman	vis. viiid.
De Thoma Iones	iiiis. viiid.
De Hugone Crikel	iiiis. xd.

De Thoma Roberd	viis. iiii*d*.
De Willelmo atte Ford	iiiis. viii*d*.
De Thoma atte Ford	iis. viii*d*.
De Iohanne Symond	iis. viii*d*.
De Iohanne Tritones	iis. viii*d*.
De . . . . Selewynes	iis. viii*d*.
De Iohanne Alis	iiiis. ii*d*.
De Ricardo Herdman	vs.
De Ricardo Chont	iiiis. i*d*.
De Symone le Spicer	iiiis.
De Waltero de Whitinton	vs.
De Willelmo le marschal	xii*d*.
De Willelmo Wygewold	iis. vi*d*.
De Thoma Osebarn	viii*d*.

Summa xiii *li*. iiis. iii*d*.

1326-7. Lay Subsidies, Oxfordshire : 161, 9.

Subsidy of a Twentieth, 1 Edward III.

Villata de Boreford

De Isabella de Clare	vs. vii*d*.
De Thoma Corbet	iiis.
De Magistro Hospicarii	viiis.
De Reginaldo Pynchet	xis. ii*d*.
De Symone Haym	xs. ii*d*.
De Nicolao le Towe	viiis.
De Henrico Blonham	vis. viii*d*.
De Iohanne Gilkes	iiis. vi*d*.
De Iohanne Mokes	iis. vi*d*.
De Henrico Nespis	xix*d*.
De Nicholao Scotham	vis. viii*d*.
De Willelmo Ayneld	iis.
De Michaele Fabro	vi*d*.
De Galfrido de Schipton	vi*d*.
De Ricardo Torfrey	vi*d*.
De Willelmo de. Ergewold	iiis. vi*d*.
De Ricardo de Beardon	xviii*d*.
De Ricardo le Couper	iiis.
De Alicia Silewyne	vi*d*.
De Iohanne Giles	vi*d*.
De Waltero Aloto	xviii*d*.
De Ricardo Pakedam	vi*d*.
De Iohanne le Vikery	iis. vii*d*.
De Iohanne Phelip	vi*d*.
De Willelmo le Taillur	vi*d*.
De Ricardo de Cherchehull	xv*d*.
De Clemente le Vatter	iiiis. vi*d*.
De Iohanne Pynchard	vi*d*.

De Iohanne le Riche	vi*d*.
De Thoma Whitemay	xii*d*.
De Thoma de Lincoln	vi*d*.
De Iohanne le Smyth	ii*s*.
De Thoma Note	iii*s*.
De Alicia Hodes	v*s*. i*d*.
De Roberto de Hercote	xii*d*.
De Willelmo Magete	xii*d*.
De Willelmo de Wydforde	iii*s*. iiii*d*.
De Ricardo Pistore	xii*d*.
De Nicholao Kokerel	vi*d*.
De Willelmo de Westwelle	x*d*.
De Iohanne Stubian	ii*s*.
De Roberto le Taillur	vi*d*.
De Willelmo le Mareschal	iii*s*.
De Magistro Rogero	iii*s*. xi*d*.
De Ada le Towe	xviii*d*.
De Egidio de Whitynton	iiii*s*. vi*d*.
De Ricardo Rossel	ii*s*. vi*d*.
De Iohanne Saleman	xviii*d*.

Summa vi *li*. x*s*. iiii*d*.

Hamelettum de Seynatt

De Thoma Eaward	iii*s*. iiii*d*.
De Simone Rolf	iiii*s*. ix*d*.
De Iohanne Martyn	xxiii*d*.
De Willelmo Haddon	iiii*s*. xi*d*.
De Matilda Canones	iii*s*. iii*d*.
De Rogero Saundres	iii*s*. iii*d*.
De Iohanne le Ster	iii*s*. iiii*d*.
De Galfrido Eitheweye	iiii*s*. i*d*.
De Isaac le Nemige	iii*s*. vii*d*.
De Iohanne atte Halle	xvii*d*.
De Roberto Keite	v*s*. vi*d*.
De Iohanne Abraham	ii*s*. vii*d*.
De Waltero Killyng	xi*d*.
De Agneta de Eynesham	xiii*d*.

Summa xliiii*s*.

Hamelettum de Uptone

De Roberto Chont	iii*s*. viii*d*.
De Ricardo Herdman	iii*s*. ix*d*.
De Thoma Hobbes	iii*s*. xi*d*.
De Alicia Cholber	vi*d*.
De Roberto Selewyne	xix*d*.
De Roberto in le Hurne	xvi*d*.
De Iohanne le Tretone	v*s*.
De Iohanne Symondes	xii*d*.
De Willelmo Seynet	xxi*d*.

De Willelmo atte Forde	xxii*d*.
De Thoma Roberdes	v*s*. iii*d*.
De Iohanne Cassebel	ii*s*. iii*d*.
De Willelmo Iones	xvi*d*.
De Hugone Crikel	xii*d*.
De Thoma Iones	iii*s*. ii*d*.
De Thoma Hikeman	v*s*. i*d*.
De Nicholao . . .	iii*s*.
De Salamone le Grete	iii*s*.
De Willelmo de Fairford	iii*s*.
De Iohanne Bernard	iii*s*.

Summa liiii*s*. v*d*.

1316. Lay Subsidies, Oxfordshire : 161, 16.

Nonarum Inquisitiones. (*This file in very bad condition.*)

Ecclesia de Boreford Decanat' de Witeneye et hundred' de Bampton — Inquisicio capta apud Wyttneye die Iovis proximo post festum Annunciacionis beate marie virginis anno regni Regis Edwardi tertii a conquestu Anglie quintodecimo et regni sui francie secundo coram Alano Abbati de Eynesham et sociis suis collectoribus None garbarum vellerum et agnorum per com Oxon assignate per sacramentum Salamonis le Grete de Boreford Ricardi . . . legh de eadem Henrici Blonham Thome Note Ricardi Sely et Iohannis Wyggewold Qui dicunt per sacramentum suum quod ecclesia de Boreford extendit in lii *marc'* de qua taxacione nona garbarum . . . anno concessionis valuit ibidem xx *marc'* x*s*. Et nona vellerum valuit illo anno v*s*. iiii*d*. Et nona agnorum valuit illo anno ii *mrcs* et dimid' Summa garbarum vellerum et agnorum xxviii *mrcs* iii*s*. iiii*d*. Et . . . Rectoris ibidem valuit illo anno xx*s*. vi*d*. Et . . . valuit illo anno lxxiii*s*. iiii*d*. et redditus illo anno valuerunt lxix*s*. vi*d*. . . . oblacionis . . . minutis decimis valuerunt illo anno viii *li*. Summa abrenacionis extraordinarie causis supradictis xxiiii *mrcs* iii*s*. iiii*d*. Et sic remanent adhuc ad opus Domini Regis de nona garbarum vellerum et agnorum Domino Regi concessa xxviii*m*. iii*s*. iiii*d*. et nichil de catallariis.

1347. Lay Subsidies, Oxfordshire : 161, 20.

A Tenth and Fifteenth, 20 Edward III.

Hundredum de Bampton . . .

Boreford ix *li*. xvi*s*. ii*d*.

1383-4. Lay Subsidies, Oxfordshire : 161, 52.

Half of a Tenth and Fifteenth, 7 Richard II. The name of John Wynrysh of Burford among the Collectors of the Subsidy.

Hundr' de Bampton. . . .
Villate de Opton et Seynet xliis. viid.
Villata de Boreford iiii li. xviiis. id.

1385–6. Lay Subsidies, Oxfordshire : 161, 53.
A Tenth and Fifteenth, 9 Richard II.
Hundr' de Bampton. . . .
Villate de Upton et Seynatte iiii li. vs. iid.
Villata de Bureford (amount illegible).

1392. Lay Subsidies, Oxfordshire : 161, 54.
Half of a Tenth and Fifteenth, 16 Richard II. The name of Thomas
Spicer of Boreford among the Collectors of the Subsidy.
Vill' de Upton et Seynet xliis. viid.
Vill' de Boreford iiii li. xviiis. id.

1420. Clerical Subsidies, Oxfordshire : 36, 252. 7 Henry V.
Compotus collectorum de vis. viiid. de quibuscunque capellanis
etc in archid' Oxon . . . (holding benefices of the value of seven marks
and over).
Decanatus de Wyteney

De Domino David de . . . rford	vis. viiid.
De Iohanne Port capellano ibidem	vis. viiid.
De Roberto Clere alias fflyng capellano ibidem	vis. viiid.

1435–6. Clerical Subsidies, Oxfordshire : 37, 411.   14 Henry VI.
· Collection of a subsidy of 6s. 8d. from certain parish priests,
stipendiaries and other priests having chantries and other chaplains
in the archdeaconry of Oxford, receiving less than 10 marks a
year.

De Richardo Monmouth capellano de Boreford	r ix *marcas*
De Waltero Mares capellano de eadem	r viii *marcas*

1448–9. Clerical Subsidies, Oxfordshire : 38, 557. 27 Henry VI.
Compotus ffulconis Bermyngeham archidiaconi Oxon collectoris
cuiusdam subsidie vis. viiid.de singulis capellanis secularibus fratribus
et aliis religiosis ecclesiis parochialibus deservientibus seu stipendia et
annualia recipientibus sive ab aliis capellanis quibuscunque cantarias
non taxatas habentibus et infra archidiaconatum Oxon commoranti-
bus . . .
   Dec' de Wytteney. De Domino Thoma Mayhow magistro hospitalis
Sti Iohannis Baptiste de Borford   vis. viiid.

(On the dorse of the same membrane.)

De Domino Roberto Bonde stipendiario in ecclesia
de Borfford   vis. viiid.

De Domino Waltero Morys stipendiario in eadem ecclesia vis. viiid.

De Domino Roberto Shepard stipendiario in eadem   vis. viiid.

De Domino Iohanne Breknok stipendiario in eadem   vis. viiid.

1450–1. Clerical Subsidies, Oxfordshire: 38, 603. 29 Henry VI.
Spiritualia and temporalia of the Abbey of Keynsham.

Spiritualia in the Archdeaconry of Oxford : videlicet ecclesia de
Boreford in Decan' de Wittney que ad xlv *marcas* taxatur per annum
de qualibet librata 2s.

et de iiiid. de bonis temporalibus que quidem bona ad iiis. taxatur
in Boreford.

1524. Lay Subsidies, Oxfordshire: 161, 172. 15 Henry VIII.
Villat' de Burford for goods and londs subsidium.

De Petro Annesdale in goods	xl *li*.	xls.
Iohanne Sharppe in bonis	xx *li*.	xxs.
Iohanne Bysshoppe p bon	vi *li*.	iiis.
Roberto Payne p bon	xx *li*.	xxs.
Iohanne Pryour p bonis	vii *li*.	iiis. vid.
Nicholao Philippys de bonis	vii *li*.	iiis. vid.
Roberto Hannys de bon	xx *mks*.	vis. viiid.
Iohanne Osmonde in bon	xls.	xiid.
Iohanne Colyns de bon	xls.	xiid.
Iohanne Tryell in bonis	xls.	xiid.
Iohanne Wyllyngton in bon	xx *li*.	xxs.
Iohanne Crampton in bon	xls.	xiid.
Iohanne Wodowys in bon	xls.	xiid.
Thoma Ryle in bon	vi *li*.	iiis.
Iohanne Salthouse in bon	xls.	xiid.
Thoma Tesedale in bonis	xl *li*.	xls.
Iohanne Lambert in bon	xl *li*.	xls.
Willelmo Spycer in bon	vii *li*.	iiis. vid.
Willelmo Est in bon	viii *li*.	iiiis.
Roberto Ithell in bon	xls.	xiid.
Iohanne Smyth in bon	xxvis. viiid.	vid.
Thoma Lepar sen in bon	xls.	xiid.
Iacobo Grene in bon	x *li*.	vs.
Willelmo Colyns in bon	vii *li*.	iiis. vid.
Roberto Crouner in bon	xls.	xiid.
Thoma Thomson in bon	vii *li*.	iiis. vid.
Thome Straunge in bon	vii *li*.	iiis. vid.
Willelmo Harper in bonis	lxs.	xiiiid.
Iohanne Agar in bon	cs.	iis. vid.

Willelmo Fyssher in bon	xl*s*.	xii*d*.
Thoma Frethorne in bon	xl*s*.	xii*d*.
Roberto Forde in bon	vi *li*.	iii*s*.
Nicholao Tame in bonis	xl*s*.	xii*d*.
Thoma Croucheman in bon	xl*s*.	xii*d*.
Henrico Baker in bon	xl*s*.	xii*d*.
Roberto Whytepytt in bon	vii *li*.	iii*s*. vi*d*.
Thoma Kyng in bon	xl*s*.	xii*d*.
Iohanne Beller in bon	vii *li*.	iii*s*. vi*d*.
Iohanne Hyter in bonis	v *li*.	ii*s*. vi*d*.
Willelmo Nethall in bon	xl*s*.	xii*d*.
Thoma Grene in bon	xl*s*.	xii*d*.
Thoma Clere in bon	vi *li*.	iii*s*.
Willelmo Wincester in bon	xl*s*.	xii*d*.
Thoma Adams in bon	lx*s*.	xviii*d*.
Henrico Bocher in bon	xl*s*.	xii*d*.
Willelmo Dyll in bon	iiii *li*.	ii*s*.
Thoma Cok in . .	xl*s*.	xii*d*.
Iohanne . . .	xl*s*.	xii*d*.
(Five names illegible)		
Iohanne	xv *li*.	vii*s*. vi*d*.
Iohanne Ionys in bon	xl*s*.	xii*d*.
Roberto Iohnson in bon	vi *li*.	iii*s*.
Roberto Smyth in bon	lx*s*.	xviii*d*.
Thoma Lepar in bonis	lx*s*.	xviii*d*.
Thoma Fawler in bon	iiii *li*.	ii*s*.
David Tailor in bon	xx *marc*.	vi*s*: viii*d*.
Ricardo Edmonds in bon	lx*s*.	xviii*d*.
Willelmo Smyth in bon	x *li*.	v*s*.
Georgio Chadworth in bon	xl*s*.	xii*d*.
Georgio Lambert in bon	xl*s*.	xii*d*.
Iohanne Stokdale in bon	xl*s*.	xii*d*.
Iohanne Wellok in bon	v *li*.	ii*s*. vi*d*.
Willelmo Ienyver in bon	vi *li*.	iii*s*.
Christofero Stoddale in bon	lx*s*.	xviii*d*.
Edwardo Smyth in bon	vii *li*.	iii*s*. vi*d*.
Iohanne Colyns in bon	vi *li*.	iii*s*.
Roberto Eynesdale in bon	vi *li*.	iii*s*.
Roberto Towe in bon	lx*s*.	xviii*d*.
Thoma Crowe in bon	x *li*.	v*s*.
Roberto B . . . in bon	xl*s*.	xii*d*.
Roberto P	lx*s*.	xviii*d*.
Editha Far . . . vid in bon	x *li*.	v*s*.
Matilda Stanton vid in bon	iiii *li*.	ii*s*.
Agneta Laurens vid in bon	lx*s*.	xviii*d*.
Al	viii *li*.	iiii*s*.
Alicia	lx*s*.	xviii*d*.

(Eight names illegible ; one, perhaps John Busbye, rated at £100 and taxed £10 ; the rest all taxed 4d.)

Hugone Ionys pro stipendio	iiii*d.*
Willelmo . . . servo pro stipend	iiii*d.*
Roberto Andrewes servo pro stipend	iiii*d.*
Iohanne . . . p stipend	iiii*d.*
Thoma . . . . p stipend	iiii*d.*
Thoma Alf . . . . p stipend	iiii*d.*
Iohanne Gryffyn S Iohannis Apost p stipend	iiii*d.*
Iohanne Delk p stipend	iiii*d.*
Iohanne ffeld servo Rob Smyth p stipend	iiii*d.*
De Terris pertinentibus ecclesie de Burford	xviii*d.*
De terris pertinentibus capelle beate marie virginis de Burford	xviii*d.*
Thoma Inglond in bon	xl*s.* xii*d.*
Iohanne Grove p stipend	iiii*d.*

1525. Lay Subsidies, Oxfordshire : 161, 173. 15 Henry VIII.
The township of Burford.

De Iohanne Sharp	xx*s.*
Iohanne Bysshop	iii*s.*
Roberto Payn	xx*s.*
Iohanne Pryor	iii*s.* vi*d.*
Nicholao Phyppys	iii*s.* vi*d.*
Roberto Hannys	vi*s.* viii*d.*
Iohanne Osmonde	xii*d.*
Iohanne Colyns	xii*d.*
Iohanne Togill	xii*d.*
Iohanne Myllyngton	xx*d.*
Iohanne Brampton	xii*d.*
Iohanne Wodowys	xii*d.*
Thoma Ryley	iii*s.*
Iohanne Salthouse	xii*d.*
Thoma Teysdale	xxxvi*s.*
Iohanne Lambert	xxx*s.*
Willelmo Spycer	iii*s.* vi*d.*
Willelmo Est	iiii*d.*
Roberto Ithell	xii*d.*
Iohanne Smyth	vi*d.*
Thoma Lepar seniore	xii*d.*
Iacobo Grene	x*s.*
Willelmo Colyns	iii*s.* vi*d.*
Roberto Browne	xii*d.*
Thoma Tomson	iii*s.* vi*d.*
Thoma Straunge	iii*s.* vi*d.*
Willelmo Harper	xviii*d.*
Iohanne Agar	ii*s.* vi*d.*
Willelmo Fyssher	xii*d.*

Thoma Frethorn	xii*d*.
Roberto Forde	iii*s*.
Nicholao Tame	xii*d*.
Thoma Crowcheman	xii*d*.
Henrico Baker	xii*d*.
Roberto Whytpyt	iii*s*. vi*d*.
Thoma Kyng	xii*d*.
Iohanne Bellar	iii*s*. vi*d*.
Iohanne Haytar	ii*s*. vi*d*.
Willelmo Noveller	xii*d*.
Thoma Grene	xii*d*.
Thoma Clarke	iii*s*.
Willelmo Banaster	xii*d*.
Thoma Adame	xviii*d*.
Lawrencio Bocher	xii*d*.
Willelmo Dylke	ii*s*.
Thoma Beky	xii*d*.
Iohanne Clemson	xii*d*.
Ricardo Ithell	xii*d*.
Iohanne Hannys	vi*s*. viii*d*.
Christofero Perkins	xii*d*.
Thoma Sadler	xii*d*.
Thoma George	xii*d*.
Iohanne Yong	vii*s*. vi*d*.
Iohanne Ionys	xii*d*.
Roberto Iohnson	iii*s*.
Roberto Smyth	xviii*d*.
Thoma Lepar	xviii*d*.
Thoma Fowlar	ii*s*.
David Tayllor	vi*s*. viii*d*.
Ricardo Edmunds	xviii*d*.
Willelmo Smyth	v*s*.
Georgio Chadworth	xii*d*.
Iohanne Stokdale	xii*d*.
Iohanne Willok	ii*s*. vi*d*.
Willelmo Ienyver	iii*s*.
Christofero Stokdale	xviii*d*.
Edwardo Smyth	ii*s*. vi*d*.
Iohanne Colyns	iii*s*.
Roberto Eynysdale	iii*s*.
Roberto Lowe	xviii*d*.
Thoma Crow	v*s*.
Roberto Grantham	xii*d*.
Roberto Payn jun.	xviii*d*.
Editha Brame vidua	v*s*.
Mawd Staunton vid	ii*s*.
Agneta Laurens vid	xviii*d*.
Alicia Hoggs vid	vii*s*.

Alicia Cox vidua	xviii*d*.
Thoma Prat famulo Ricardo Payn	iiii*d*.
Ricardo (blank) famulo dicto Ricardo	iiii*d*.
Christofero Cabter famulo Iohanni Colyns	iiii*d*.
Rogero Smyth famulo Willelmo Hoggs	iiii*d*.
Thoma Waltermer famulo predicto Willelmo	iiii*d*.
Ricardo (blank) famulo dicto Willelmo	iiii*d*.
Hugone Ionys famulo Willelmo Smyth	iiii*d*.
Willelmo Couper famulo Christofero Stokdale	iiii*d*.
Roberto Andrewes famulo Iohanni Colyns	iiii*d*.
Iohanne Roo famulo dicto Iohanni	iiii*d*.
Thoma Pynnok famulo dicto Iohanni	iiii*d*.
Thoma Alflete famulo Iacobo Grene	iiii*d*.
Philippo Gryffyn famulo Iohanni Gwyllyam	vi*d*.
Iohanne Bell famulo Thome Adame	xii*d*.
Iohanne (illegible) famulo Roberto Smyth	iiii*d*.
Terris pertinentibus ad capellam beate marie de Burford	xviii*d*.
Thoma Inglonde	xii*d*.
Iohanne Grove famulo Willelmo Colyns	iiii*d*.
Terris pertinentibus ad ecclesiam de Burford	xviii*d*.
Summa xv *li*. vi*s*. iiii*d*.	

1526. Lay Subsidies, Oxfordshire: 161, 179. (*Document illegible in many places.*) 16 Henry VIII.

Hundred' de Bampton . . . . .

Fyrst the Borough of Burford

De Iohanne Busbyne pro cc *li*. in bonis	. . . .
Willelmo Hoggs p lxxx *li*. in bonis	. . . .
Iohanne Sharp p xx *li*. in bonis	. . . .
Iohanne Bishope p vi *li*. in bonis	iii*s*.
Iohanne Prior p vii *li*. in bonis	. . . .
Roberto Payne sen p xx *li*. in bonis	xx*s*.
. . . . p vi *li*.	. . . .
. . . Hannys p xiii *li*. vi*s*. viii*d*.	vi*s*. viii*d*.
Iohanne . . . . p xl*s*.	xii*d*.
Iohanne . . . ett p xl*s*. in bon	xii*d*.
Iohanne Mylyngton p . . . in bonis	xii*d*.
Iohanne Brampton p xl*s*. in bonis	xii*d*.
Iohanne Wedowes p xl*s*. in bonis	. . . .
Thoma Ryley x *libr*. in bonis	. . . .
Roberto S. . lt. . se p xl*s*. in bonis	xii*d*.
Thoma Teysdale p.	. . . .
Iohanne Lambard p xxx *li*. in . .	. . . .
Willelmo Spycer p vii *li*.	iii*s*. vi*d*.
Willelmo Est p octo *libr*. in bonis	iiii*s*.

Roberto Ythell p.xls. in bonis .... xii*d*.
Iohanne Smyth p terris viginti ...　　　.　.　✦　....
Thoma Bepar sen p xls. .... xii*d*.
Iacobo Grene p x *li*. in bonis ....
Willelmo Colens p vii *li*. in bonis .... vi*d*.
Roberto Browne p xls. in bonis .... xii*d*.
Thoma Tomson p vii *li*. in bonis　. .... iiis. vi*d*.
Iohanne Straunge p vii *li*. . . . . iiis. vi*d*.
Willelmo Harpare p iii *li*. in bonis .... xviii*d*.
Iohanne Agar p v *li*. in bonis .... iis. vi*d*.
Willelmo Fysher p . . . in bonis' .... xii*d*.
Thoma Frethorne . . . . in bonis .... xii*d*.
Roberto Foord . . . *li*. in bonis .... iiis.
Nicholao Ta . . . . xls. in bonis .... xii*d*.
Thoma Crocheman p xls. in bonis .... xii*d*.
Henrico Baker p xls. in bonis .... xii*d*.
Roberto Wygpyte p vii *li*. in bonis .... iiis. vi*d*.
Thoma Kyng p xls. in bonis .... xii*d*.
Petro Ensdale p xl *li*. in bonis .... xls.
Iohanne . . . . p·v *li*. in bonis .... iis. vi*d*.
Willelmo Newell p xls. in bonis .... xii*d*.
Thoma Grene p xls. in bonis ✦ .... xii*d*.
Editha Brame vidua p x *li*. in bonis ....
Willelmo Banaster p xls. in bonis .... xii*d*.
Thoma Adams p iii *li*. in bonis .... xviii*d*.
Laurenc . . . her p xls. in bonis .... xii*d*.
Willelmo D . . . . p iiii *li*. in bonis ....
. . . Hoggs vidua . . . viii *li*. . . . . iiiis.
. . . . xviii*d*.
Iohanne . . . . xii*d*.
Ricardo Ythell p xls. in bonis .... xii*d*.
Iohanne Harres p xiii *li*. vis. viii*d*. .... vis. viii*d*.
Christofero Parkyns p . . . .
Thoma Saddler p . . . .
Thoma George p . . . .
Iohanne Younge . . . .
Iohanne . . . .
Roberto . . . .
Roberto . . . . xviii*d*.
Thoma Lepar p iii *li*. in bonis .... xviii*d*.
Thoma Faller p iiii *li*. in bonis .... iiis.
David Taylor p xx *mrcs*. in bonis .... vis. viii*d*.
Ricardo Edmonds p iii *li*. in . . . . xviii*d*.
Willelmo Smyth . . *li*. . . . . vs.
Georgio Chadworth p xls. in bonis .... xii*d*.
Georgio Lambert p xls. in bonis .... xii*d*.
Iohanne Wellooke p v *li*. in bonis .... iis. vi*d*.
Iohanne Stocdale p xls. in bonis .... xii*d*.

... Ienyver p vi *li.* in bonis	iiis.
... ofero Stocdale p iii *li.* in bonis	xviiid.
Edwardo Smyth p vii *li.* in bonis	iiis. vid.
... e Colly ... vi *li.* in bonis	iiis.
Roberto Ensdale p vi *li.* in bonis	iiis.
Roberto Lowe p iii *li.* in bonis	xviiid.
Thoma Crowe p x *li.* in bonis	vs.
Roberto Grauntham p xls. bon	xiid.
.... Payne iun p iii *li.* bon	xviiid.
Th ... Alflete p xxs. stipend	iiiid.
Philippo Griffyn p xxs. stipend	iiiid.
Feoffatoribus terrarum spectantium ecclesie ibidem annue valoris iii *li.*	iiis.
feoffatoribus terrarum spectantium capelle beate marie virginis ibidem annue valoris iii *li.*	iiis.
Summa xxx *li.* xiiis. iid.	

Upton et Synet

De Willelmo Dy ... p xx *li.* bon	xxs.
Iohanne Lamberte p viii *li.* bonorum	iiiis.
Iohanne Wynchester p xls. bon	xiid.
Iohanne Patens p viii *li.* bon	iiiis.
Rogero Worthey p xls. bon	xiid.
Willelmo Patens p v *li.* bon ·	iis. vid.
Iohanne Mourhyne p iii *li.* bon	xviiid.
Iohanne Tame p xxs. stipend	iiiid.
Iohanne Hoggs p xxs. stipend	iiiid.
Thoma Grene p xxs. stipend	iiiid.
Summa xxxvs.	

[For extracts from the Clerical Subsidy of this year see p. 122, note 2.]

1527. Lay Subsidies, Oxfordshire : 161, 197. 18 Henry VIII..

To the Barons of the King's Eschequier.

This Indenture made the fourthe day of February in the xviiith yere of the reign of oure sovereign lord King Henry the eight witnesseth that we Symond Harecourt knyght Thomas Unpton esquyar and Rychard Waynman gentilman thre of the Commissioners of our said sovereign lord the King assigned to the hundred of Bamton in the countie of Oxenford to rate tax and assesse all and singular personne and persons temporall intrityng abyding and most resorting within the said hundred havyng goods and catalls to value of fyfty pounds and above chargeable to the iiiita payment of the last subsydie granted unto our said sovereign lord the King in the xiiith yere of his reign by tertue of his commission under his gret seall unto us and other in that behalf directed taxed rated and assessed all

and singular such personnes within the said hundred being of the
value abovesaid whoys names and surnames with their value and
the summes payhable and the name and surname of the high
collectour chargeable with the gedering leveyng and payng of the
seid summes to thuse of our seid sovereign lord the king at the receipte
of his Eschequier herafter particularly doth ensue   In witnesse
wherof we the seid commissioners to this Indenture have set our
sealls the day and yere aboveseyd

John Busby merchaunt in goods cc *li*. subsidie   x *li*.
William Hoggs in goods iiii^{xx} *li*. subs.   iiii *li*.
Richard Smyth in goods L *li*. subs   l*s*.

summa totalis xvi *li*. x*s*.

John Secole de Southlee high collectour
  p Symon Harecourt k
   Thoma Unton
   Rychard Waynman

1535. Lay Subsidies, Oxfordshire : 161, 209. 26 Henry VIII.
Half of a Fifteenth and Tenth.
Boreford. ix *li*. xviii*s*. vi*d*.

1538. Lay Subsidies, Oxfordshire : 161, 210. 30 Henry VIII.
The document is badly decayed, and the Burford entry has perished.
It is entered here because Symon Wysdome was the Collector for the
Hundreds of Bampton and Chadlyngton.

(d) MINISTERS' ACCOUNTS

1232-3. Min. Accts., Bundle 1117, no. 13. 16 to 18 Henry III.
Compotus Radulfi de Wileton per P de Rivall thesaurarium de
quibusdam escaetis a die s Matthaei anno xvi usque ad sextum diem
Iunii anno xvii^{mi}.

m. 2. Oxonia. Et de vii *li*. vii*s*. x*d*. et ob. de firma forinseca de
Bureford de hoc anno et termino s Michaelis anni precedentis . Et de
liii*s*. iiii*d*. de firma burgi molendini et fori Et de c & v*s*. de operationibus parvis ad firmam Et de vii *li*. vi*s*. et ii*d*. de placitis et perquisitis et feno et herbagio vendito Et de xl*s*. de taillagio Et de vii *li*.
vi*s*. et iii*d*. de frumento vendito Et de iiii *li*. viii*s*. de de (*sic*) xlii
quartariis et dimidio ordei et ii bussellis et uno quartario et ·dimidio
corallum de eodem vendito Et de xvi*s*. et vi*d*. de xi quartariis avene
vendite Et de xii *li*. xvii*s*. et vi*d*. de ii^{xx} bovum et de feno attracto
et de c et xxxv multonibus de instauro.

1235-9. Min. Accts., Bundle 1109, no. 6. 20 to 23 Henry III.

Expensa eiusdem a crucifixione domini anno xx usque ad purificacionem Beate marie anno xxi.

m. 2. Bureford. In ferro et acero ad carucas cum ferratura averiorum iiii*s*. viii*d*. in ii novis carucis emptis cum vii iugis ii harnesiis cum i curta empta ii axibus et xii clittis ferri et in uncto ad caretas iii *sol*. xi*d*. Et ferratura pro averiis viii*s*. vii*d*. Et in i sacco i besca i scala i capistro ii cordis ii clittis ad carectas iii seruris iii criblis emptis ii*s*. iii*d*. ob. Et in plantis porri et caulium et in sale ad potagium familiorum emptis xii*d*. ob. Et in quadam parte unius prati perfalcanda vi*d*. ob. Et falcatoribus pro multone suo de consuetudine xii*d*. Et pro bladis metendis pro iiii^xx et iiii^or messoribus x*s*. vi*d*. pro cuilibet in die iii*d*. ob. Et cuidam homini cum equo et careta sua per sex dies ad bladum cariandum iii*s*. Et in xxxiiii summis et xxxi quartariis de draggio et lx quartariis avene cariandis xi*s*. ii*d*. ob. pro carianda i summa frumenti ii*d*. et quartario de draggio iii quadrantes eodem quartario avene Et in eisdem xxxi quartariis draggii et lx quartariis avene ventilandis xii*d*. et in vi summis de predicto frumento vannandis viii*d*. Et in precariis xxxvi carucarum iii*s*. Et in stipendio ii carucatorum per annum x*s*. in stipendio i caretarii xv*d*. Et in stipendio cuiusdam messoris per annum vii*s*. Et in defectu redditus prepositi xv*d*.

[Expenses for the second and third years much the same. In the second year a sum of 5*s*. is entered as expenses of repairing a barn and ox-house.]

[*Note*.—These Accounts are entered as arising from escheats of the lands of Richard de Clare.]

1292-6. Min. Accts., Bundle 1109, no. 7. 20 to 24 Edward I.

Compotus Horreorum Honoris Glouecestr anno regni regis Ed xx . . .

Frumentum. Et de viii quartariis de exitu horrei de Bureford et De x quartariis de emptis . . . Et in semine apud Bureford xvii quartaria . . . Ordeum. Et de xv quartariis et dimidio de exitu horrei de Bureford et de xxvi quartariis de emptis. . . . Et in semine apud Bureford xv quartaria et vi busselli.

Dragium. Et de xiii quartariis et dimidio de exitu horrei de Bureford . . . Et in semine apud Bureford xiii quartaria et dimidium.

Avena. Et de liii quartariis de exitu horrei de Bureford Et de vi quartariis de empto . . . Et in semine apud Bureford liii quartaria . . .

Et apud Bureford in liberacione ii carucatorum i messoris per annum xv quartaria et vi bussellos scilicet ad x septimanas i quartarium.

[Accounts for the other years much the same.]

1435–6. Exchr. K. R. Min. Accts., 957, 10.

Boreford
Manerium.

Compotus Iohannis Williams praepositi ibidem a festo Sancti Michaelis archangeli anno regni regis Henrici sexti quartodecimo usque idem festum Sancti Michaelis anno predicti regis henrici quintodecimo videlicet per unum annum integrum. Arreragia. Idem computat receptum de x *li*. xv*s*. receptis de arreragiis ultimi compoti anni proximi precedentis.

Summa x *li*. xv*s*.

Redditus
Assisae.

Et de xv*li*. xiiii*s*. v*d*. ob. receptis de redditu assisae per annum cum firma nativorum ad quatuor anni terminos et patet parcellatum in compoto de anno regni regis Ricardi secundi nuper regis Angliae tertio.

Summa xv *li*. xiiii*s*. v*d*. ob.

Firma.

Et de xii *li*. vi*s*. viii*d*. receptis de firma omnium terrarum pratorum et pasturae dominicalium ibidem quae Thomas ultimus Dominus le Despenser defunctus tenuit in sua manu in cultura die quo obiit sicut dimissa Roberto Atkyns Isabelle uxori eius et Willelmo filio eiusdem Roberti tenenda eisdem ad terminum vitae eorum viventis ad quatuor anni terminos per annum per Indenturas inter consilium Domini et dictum firmarium inde factas quarum datum apud Burford die dominica in festo apostolorum Philippi et Iacobi anno regni regis Henrici quinti post conquestum septimo. Et de v*s*. receptis de Willelmo Pynnell pro firma x acrarum terrae dominicalis Domini ibidem sicut eidem dimissarum per rotulum curiae quartidecimi anni precedentis ad eosdem terminos per annum Et de ii*s*. receptis de firma quinque acrarum eiusdem terrae dominicalis nuper dimissarum Iohanni Pounter et nunc dimissarum Thome Dorne ad terminum vitae suae per rotulum curiae anni precedentis tamen debet esse iii*s*. Et de iii*s*. receptis de Iohanne Mason pro firma ix acrarum terrae dominicae sicut eidem concessarum per annum ad terminum vite sue per Rotulum curiae anni precedentis Et de ii*s*. receptis de Thoma Dorne pro firma iiii acrarum eiusdem terrae sicut eidem dimissarum per annum ad vite terminum Et de xvi*d*. receptis de Thoma Fifeld pro firma iiii acrarum terrae eiusdem nuper in tenura Roberti Cooke tamen . . . esse ii*s*. Et de ii*s*. receptis de Philippo Iames pro firma iiii acrarum eiusdem terrae sicut dimissarum hoc anno ad eosdem terminos Et de v*s*. receptis de firma unius quarreriae vocatae le Stertequarell de petris tegulis sicut dimissae Iohanni Eyre ad terminum xx annorum per rotulum curiae hoc anno Et de v*s*.

receptis de firma unius quarreriae vocatae Whiteladiesquarell liberarum
petrarum sicut dimissae Henrico Spyser et magistro hospitalis Sancti
Iohannis de Boreford tenendae eisdem ad terminum xx annorum
proxime sequentium et plenarie completorum per Rotulum curiae
anni precedentis hoc anno Et ii*s*. de firma unius quarreriae petrarum
tegularum vocatae le Wortquarrie sicut nuper dimissae Willelmo
Cutteler nichil hoc anno per defectum firmarii Et receptum de iiii*d*.
receptis de Iohanne Atkyns pro firma unius crofti quondam Edwardi
Dyere sicut dimissi eidem Iohanni hoc anno. Et de viii*d*. receptis
de firma unius crofti nuper Iohannis Fraunceys sicut dimissi eidem
Iohanni Fraunceys iuniori hoc anno.   Summa xiii *li*. xiii*s*.

Firma
molendini.
Et de iiii *li*. xiii*s*. iiii*d*. receptis de firma molendini aquatici
Domini ibidem vocati Upton mille sicut dimissi Willelmo
Gough hoc anno.   Summa iiii *li*. xiii*s*.*iiii*d*.

Exitus
manerii.
De vi*d*. de tak porcorum custum ad festum Sancti Martini
accidentem infra tempus compoti (nichil hoc anno *inserted
between the lines*) de porcis salitis neque corticibus nihil
hic quod nullum habendum accidit hoc anno.   Summa nulla.

Vendicio
pratorum
et
pasturae.
Nec de xlvi*s*. viii*d*. de herbagio quinque acrarum et
xxxii perticarum prati in Overham Nec de xiii*s*. iiii*d*.
de pastura yemali in Biriorchard Nec de xiii*s*. iiii*d*. de
una acra et una pertica prati in Wirmham Nec de iii*s*.
iiii*d*. de herbagio pasturae friscae in Fernehill tempore
estumali Nec de xx*d*. de pastura ibidem tempore yemali Nec de
vi*d*. de herbagio in le Serte Nec de x*s*. de herbagio de herbagio (*sic*)
pasturae in Powkputte Nec de xi*s*. de agistamento animalium
agistato cum animalibus Domini Nec de xxii*s*. de iiii acras dimidia et
xv perticis in Wilmore Nec de xxvi*s*. viii*d*. de herbagio vi acrarum
ii perticarum prati in Bateling nec de xii*d*. de secunda vestura
eiusdem prati nec de x*s*. de herbagio pasturae in Ordingham post
fenum abductum Nec de iiii*s*. de herbagio pasturae in prato de
Fernehulle vocato Westmede nichil hoc anno quia omnia prata et
pasturae predicta conceduntur prefato Atkyns Firmario omnium
terrarum Domini supremi.   Summa null.

Perquisita
curiae.
Et de vii*s*. v*d*. receptis de perquisitis ii curiarum ibidem
tentarum hoc anno prout patet per Rotulum earundem
Et de vi*s*. viii*d*. receptos de certo fine de ca ... ad terminum
de Hokday accidentem infra tempus compoti prout patet per dictum
rotulum curiae huius anni.   Summa xiiii*s*. i*d*.

Recepio · Et de iiii *li*. x*s*. vi*d*. ob. receptis de seipso Iohanne Wyllyams
forinseca. praeposito terrarum et tenementorum pratorum et
molendinorum ac redditum terrarum tenementorum quondam
Iohannis Salmons in Boreford unde Idem praepositus exoneratur in
pede compoti sui accidentis infra tempus compoti de Boreford Salmons
finale tallia seu Indentura per recognicionem ipsius praepositi.

Summa iiii *li*. x*s*. vi*d*.

Summa Totalis Recepti cum arreragiis i *li*. v*d*.

Allocationes
et defectus
redditus.
De quibus computat in allocatione redditus praepositi
causa officii sui per tempus compoti x*s*. Et computat
in allocatione redditus unius tofti et dimidiae virgatae
nuper Thomae Fyfide qui valebant per annum vi*s*.
viii*d*. et modo dimissi Willelmo Pinnell pro iiii*s*. ii*s*. viii*d*. Et in
allocatione redditus unius virgatae terrae quondam Henrici Williams
et unius aliae virgatae terrae vocatae Caskales quae valebant inter se
xx*s*. ac unius parvi crofti vocati Cornerscrofte qui valebat per annum
ii*d*. et modo dimittuntur eidem Willelmo Pinnell pro xiiii*s*. per annum
et sic in decasu redditus vi*s*. ii*d*. Et in allocatione redditus unius
virgatae terrae quondam Thomae Robert et unius aliae virgatae
terrae quondam eiusdem Roberti et unius aliae virgatae terrae quondam Leggere quae valebant per annum inter se xxx*s*. et modo dimittuntur Iohanni Crosson pro xxix*s*. per annum et sic in decasu redditus
xii*d*. Et in allocatione redditus ii virgatarum terrae quondam Willelmi
Colles et unius aliae virgatae terrae quondam pooles quae valebant
per annum inter se xxx*s*. et modo dimissae Willelmo Leyneham pro
xxvi*s*. iiii*d*. per annum et sic in decasu redditus iii*s*. viii*d*. Et in allocatione redditus ii virgatarum terrae quondam Willelmi Grene quae
valebant per annum xx*s*. et modo dimittuntur Iohanni Williams
pro xiii*s*. iiii*d*. per annum et sic in decasu redditus per annum vi*s*.
viii*d*. Et in allocatione redditus unius virgatae terrae vocatae par-
triches et unius aliae virgatae terrae vocatae Swaiers quae valebant
per annum inter se xx*s*. et modo dimissae eidem Iohanni Williams
pro xviii*s*. per annum et sic in decasu redditus hoc anno ii*s*. Et
in allocatione redditus unius messuagii et iii virgatarum terrae
quondam Iohannis rokke quae valebant per annum xxx*s*. modo
dimittuntur Thomae Patyn pro xxii*s*. per annum et sic in decasu
redditus iiii virgatarum terrae quae valebant per annum inter se
xl*s*. modo dimittuntur Thomae Haukes pro xxxviii*s*. et sic in decasu
redditus hoc anno unius virgatae quondam Willelmi Symmes et unius

aliae virgatae terrae quondam masons quae valebant per annum inter
se xx*s*. modo dimittuntur Thomae Lovel pro xviii*s*. per annum et
sic in decasu redditus hoc anno ii*s*. Et in allocatione redditus dimidiae
virgatae terrae vocatae Saunders et unius virgatae terrae vocatae
hilleplace et unius aliae virgatae terrae quondam Roberti Bonde
quae valebant per annum inter se xxv*s*. modo dimittuntur Willelmo
Rokke pro xxii*s*. sic in decasu redditus iii*s*. Et in allocatione redditus
dominicalis terrae et tenementorum in manu Domini existentium
ubi ignorat nec ubi pro dicto redditu distringere debet nescit x*s*.
tamen in compoto precedente xlii*s*. xi*d*.   lvii*s*. ii*d*.

Feodum   Et computat solutos Iohanni Goloffre armigero in plenum
senescalli. solucionem vi *li*. xiii*s*. iiii*d*. cuiusdam feodi sui concessi
ad terminum vite sue pro suo bono servicio in presente et in postea
impendendum percipienda singulis annis de exitibus huius manerii
et manerii de Schipton.   lvi*s*. viii*d*.

Expensa   Et in expensis senescalli curie ad eius adventus · hic
senescalli   existentes pro ii curiis tenendis   xi*s*. iiii*d*.
curie cum   Et in expensis ipsius prepositi computat   xviii*d*.
solucione
feodi.   Summa xii*s*. x*d*.

Annuetates. Et computat solutos Iohanni Nansen et Henrico Slak
             armigeris in plenam solucionem xiiii*s*. cuiusdam
annuetatis concessae Iohanni Fulleford magistro Theologiae ad terminum vitae suae percipiendae singulis annis de exitu huius manerii
per manus praepositi ibidem qui pro tempore fuerit terminis Annunciacionis beatae mariae et Sancti Michaelis equaliter per annum per
literas patentes Dominae comitissae dum sola fuit supra compotum
xii annorum precedentium . . .   Summa vi *li*. xiii*s*. iiii*d*.

Custus   Et computat in stipendio i tegularii per iii dies reparantis
domini   diversos defectus coopture domus dicti manerii ibidem
manerii.   hoc anno capientis per diem v*d*. xv*d*. Et in clavis vocatis
             latchenaills ad idem iiii*d*. Et in clavis vocatis bordenaills
pro reparacione orrei dicti manerii.   iiii*d*.
                                       Summa xx*d*.

Annuetas.   Et computat solutos Thome Berkeley armigero pro
             quadam annuetate ad terminum vite sue x *li*. per annum
per literas patentes domine comitisse.   Summa x *li*.

Liberacio denariorum.

Et computat liberatum Iohanni Hygeford Receptori denariorum . . . de onere Roberti Atkyns firmarii terrarum dominicalium ibidem de parte nonarum exituum officii sui huius anni   cxis. viiid.

Duo tallia remanent quarum prima tallia continet lxvis. viiid. et altera continet xlvs.

Et eidem Receptori per manus Iohannis Williams prepositi ibidem nunc computoris de parte nonarum exituum officii sui huius anni. xs.

Summa omnium allocacionum et liberacionum   xxix li. iiis. iiiid.
Et debentur   xx li. xviis. id.

(Other allowances—to William Gough, farmer of the lord's mills xxs. for repairs to the mill; to John Williams for help in building a new grange on his tenement   xxvis. viiid.
Et debentur   xviii li. xs. vd.)

1539. Min. Accts., Henry VIII, no. 3144.
(Possessions of Keynsham Abbey, account for 31 Henry VIII.)
An account of Thomas Bayllye, tenant at farm of the Rectory of Burford and Chapelry of Fulbrook, the annual rent being £10, of which £2 10s. was paid in pension to the late Abbot of Keynsham.

Min. Accts., Henry VIII, no. 2928.
An account of John Barker, tenant at farm and Collector of the rents of the possessions of the late Hospital of St. John in Burford. The property and tenants are entered as in the Rental Survey, *infra*, p. 621. The total rental is entered at £12 17s. 2d. Of this sum 33s. 4d. was paid in pension to Thomas Cade, late Master of the Hospital, half a year's payment of the pension granted to him by Letters Patent dated 20 November, 33 Henry VIII.

(e) EARLY CHANCERY PROCEEDINGS

circa 1386–7. E.C.P.: Bundle 74, no. 26.
Petition by John Dyer of Burford for a writ sub. poena against John Sclatter, John Stowe, and others of their company. Setting forth that John Sclatter ' le ioesdy apres la feste de Seinte Dionis lan du regne de le tresnoble seigneur Roy E que dieux assoille ayel a notre seigneur le Roy qui ore est xlviiime vient ove force et armes et encountre la pes al meson du dit suppliant en Boreford et diloques prist et amesna un cheval du dit suppliant pris de iiii *marcs*. Et auxi le viii^e joar de martz lan du dit Roy E xlixme le dit John Sclatter ove plusoeurs

autres ovesque lui de sa comyne vient ove force et armes et encountre
la pes al meson du dit suppliant et diloques prist et amesna iii ochides
de Reyne pris x*s*. Et auxi le dit John Sclatter le ioesdy al noet en
la semaigne du pasque lan viiime du regne notre seigneür le Roy
Richard avauntdit par force prist et amesna une Alice fille et servaunte
du dit suppliant ove ses biens et chateux et encountre sa volunte ele
atort detenoit pour un an et demy Et ensement les avauntditz John
Sclatter John Stowe et autres de loeur commune par diverses foitz
depuis ount venuz ove force et armes al dit meson et pris et emportez
certeins biens et chateux du dit suppliant cestassavoir chevals draps
hostelements et autres biens a la value de xx *li.* a damages du dit
suppliant de xl *li.* Et en outre ills luy ount amenassez de vie et de
membre parount il nose·par doute de mort aprocher son dit meson.'

circa 1410. E.C.P.: Bundle 69, no. 300.
Petition by John Hatter of Burford and Margery his wife for a writ
sub poena against Thomas Alys of Burford and John Irnemonger of
Burford. Setting forth that Alys and Irnemonger 'le Ioesday Devant
le feste de Nowell firent assaut a Burford en la dite margerie et mesme
la margerie illoques baterount naufrerount et malement treterount
par ensy que ele fuit despaire de sa vie et mesmes les John Hatter
et margerie ne purront avoir remedie en cest partie al commune ley
des ditz malefaisours pourtant que le viscount et subviscount de mesme
le comite sount favorables as ditz Thomas et John Irnemonger.'

[No Chancellor being named, this document, like the preceding one,
cannot be accurately dated ; but the names mentioned occur in Burford
Records of 1406, 1413, 1419, & 1422.]

1413–25 (probably). E.C.P.: Bundle 27, no. 485. (Chancellor,
The Bishop of Winchester.)
Petition by William Stodham of Burford for a writ sub poena against
Thomas Porthaleyn. Setting forth that ' your seid besecher bounde
hym by his byll and dede enseslled with his seall to deliver to Thomas
Porthaleyn xx *li.* sterling the which he dyd accordyng to his seid
word in reasonable and sufficient meane and forme as evidently shall
be provyd which notwithstandyng your seid besecher the seid bill
and dede enseallyd left of gret trust in the kepyng and hands of one
Philip Sewale now dede then servant of the seid Thomas to which
Philip the seid bill was only deliveryd after whos deces the seid bill
came to the possession of the seid Thomas and so hit resteth he ayenst
all right and conscience sore vexith and troublith your said besecher
for the repayment of the same xx *li.*'

The answer of Thomas Porthaleyn denied that the petitioner had ever paid any part of the £20.

[*Note.*—It appears from other petitions in the same bundle that Porthaleyn was Receiver to Cecile Duchess of Warwick.]

1452-3. E.C.P.: Bundle 22, no. 116.

Petition for a writ sub poena by Henry Philip against John Pynnok of Burford, concerning a debt of £80. Setting forth that Pynnok 'sotelly and disseynably contrarye to good conscience and to trouth to thentent to delaye your seid Suppliaunt of his seide dewete hathe yefe awey all his londes tenementes and godes for the whiche he is not sufficiaunt ne may not contente your seide suppliant of the seide somme as he myght before tyme '.

The answer of John Pynnok pleads that he is 'fallen and so much impoverished that he may not content him of the said sum '.

1456-9. E.C.P.: Bundle 26, no. 400.

Petition by William Kyng for a writ sub poena against Robert Shepherd alias Robert Natgrove of Burford, priest. Setting forth that Shepherd was one of the feoffees of John Colas, who had enfeoffed John Neweman, John Nelen of Northleach, and Shepherd of certain burgages and tenements in Northleach, to sell them for the good of his soul. The petitioner had bought three parts of the burgages, and complained that Shepherd refused to carry out the bargain.

1459-66. E.C.P.: Bundle 27. (Chancellor, The Bishop of Exeter.)

Petition by Roger Snyperell and Margery his wife for a writ sub poena against James Dodde otherwise called James Synde of Burford. Setting forth that the petitioners had enfeoffed Dodde of a messuage with appurtenances in Burford with intent that he should re-infeoff them when required, which he now refused to do, though duly requested.

1467-72. E.C.P.: Bundle 45, no. 239. (Chancellor, The Bishop of Bath.)

Petition by Thomas Brampton and Thomas Barbour for a writ sub poena against Thomas Send, Vicar of Burford. Setting forth that 'where William Brampton late of Burford in his life prayd and desired Thomas Send clerk vicar of the church of Burford aforesaide to write and make his testament after his last will and to sette and write in that testament the wyfe of the seid William Brampton and youre besechers executours of the same in the presence of divers

persons of Burford aforeseid the seid Thomas Send having the seid
testament so by hym written in his owne governance by a certain
tyme in the life of the seid William wrote in the same testament
Hymself to be one of the executours of the seid William and wold
afore the ordynari have taken the charge of the admynystracion of
his godes as his executour and openly in presence of people affermed
hymself to be one of the executours of his testament and whan that
the contrary yereof bi grete proves and witnesses was duely provyd
byfore the Ordynari the seid Thomas prayd your besechers to do what
yei couthe for the savacion of . . , in yis matter and yat sum thyng
myght be don and made bytwene thaym that hit myght appere to
the people yat he had sum interesse in the rule of the godis of the
seid testator in eschewyng of grete . . . and desired amonges othre
thynges your seid besechers to be bound unto hym in an obligacion
of a grete notable summe yat yey sholde duely execut all the last
will and ordynacion of the seid William promyssyng to thaym that
they by suche an obligacion shold never be vexed nor troubled but
whan that he had schewed hit openly to divers persones for the cause
and entente aforeseid hit schold . . . to thaym and your seid besechers
havyng trust and feyth in the wordes of the same Thomas Send were
bound to hym at his grete prayer and Instance in obligacion of the
summe of M *li.* . . . condicion aforeseid and notwithstandyng yey have
don . . . true devoir and diligence to the fulfillyng of the last will of
the seid William . . . the seid Thomas Send . . . yat yey by the rygour
of the lawe schal be compelled to pay the seid summe of M *li.*'

1475–80 or 1483–5. E.C.P.: Bundle 53, no. 88.
Petition by John Derehurst of Hardewyk, Com. Glouc., gentleman,
for a writ sub poena against William Byschopp of Burford, merchant.
Setting forth that the petitioner and Byschopp were severally seised of
certain lands and tenements in the town of Gloucester, to all which
divers charters belonged, which charters petitioner had sealed in a
box. He had 'bayled' the box to Byschopp, the latter promising to
'rebayle' the box with the charters to petitioner upon due request
made. Petitioner was now unable to recover the charters, and being
unable therefore to prove his title to the severalty of the lands and
tenements he could not convey them, which he wished to do.

1475–80 or 1483–5. E.C.P.: Bundle 57, no. 276. (Chancellor,
The Bishop of Lincoln.)
Petition by William Bisshop for a writ sub poena against Thomas

Fermor. Setting forth that one John Tanner in his life was seised of a messuage with appurtenances in Burford, 'which is a Bourough where londes and tenementes of tyme that no mynde is have and yet be dyvysible by testament'. He devised the messuage to his wife Johanna, and after her death to his son Walter and his heirs ; and if Walter died without heirs, then the vicar and churchwardens of Burford were to sell the house and dispose of the proceeds at their discretion ' for the wele of his soule and the soule of his wife '. Walter died without heirs, and the vicar and churchwardens sold the house to William Bisshop. But the charters and deeds and all other evidences came into the hands of Thomas Fermor, who refused to give them up.

The reply of Thomas Fermor sets forth that the aforesaid Walter, being duly seised of the messuage with another adjoining to it in Burford, sold the two messuages to him for twenty marks, and he denied that the vicar and churchwardens had made any such sale as alleged.

The further answer of William Bishop was that his allegations were true, and that Fermor knew perfectly well of the ultimate disposition of the property by John Tanner's will.

The further reply of Thomas Fermor is that his reply is good and sufficient, and that he knew nothing of any such disposition.

1486–93. E.C.P. : Bundle 92, no. 37. (Chancellor, The Archbishop of Canterbury.)

Petition by Thomas Everard and Elizabeth his wife, Thomas Pynnock and John Alane, executors of one John Pynnok, for a writ sub poena against John Longe. Setting forth that John Pynnock with one John Longe by the assent and agreement of Thomas Say of Abyndon, Thomas Fermer and John Buttrell bargained and sold unto Ralf Astereche of London and others ' an c̄ and iiii sakkes of Cotteswold wolle for the some of a mlxxxiii li. ixs. and ixd.' Of this sum it was agreed between the parties that John Pynnock should have to his own use £92, and Pynnock, for the trust he had in John Longe caused the buyers to be bound to Longe for the payment of the sum of £92 for the only use of Pynnock, payable at certain dates. Petitioners say that John Longe had paid none of it.

The reply of John Longe sets forth that Fermor, Say, Pynnock and Boterell, being severally possessed of the wools mentioned, thomas Fermor by their consent sold it to Rauf Astryche and the others for a certain sum to be paid severally to the parties after certain days, and for the payment were bound to Fermor and Longe ; that John

Pynnock's share was £80, which Longe had well and truly paid to Pynnock during the latter's lifetime. Also that Longe himself never ' medelyd with the sale of the seid wollys '.

In the same Bundle, no. 40.

Petition by Everard and his wife, Thomas Pynnock and John Aleyn ' chapelyn ', for a writ of Certiorari to the Sheriffs of London. Setting forth that John Long of London, ' Bruer ', when witnesses in the preceding case had been examined and the matter rested upon judgement, commenced an action of debt against the petitioners for £120 before the Sheriffs of London and by force of this suit had attached three horses belonging to the petitioners. The action was feigned ; and if the claim were true, it depended upon the judgement now pending. The action was vexatious, and was intended to make the petitioners drop their previous action.

1486–93 or 1504–15. E.C.P. : Bundle 128, no. 20. (Chancellor, The Archbishop of Canterbury.)

Petition by William Colton for a writ sub poena against Agnes Colton. Setting forth that petitioner had lent to Richard Colton of Burford, his brother, 40s. of ready money. Richard made Agnes his wife his executor, and since his decease petitioner had made repeated application for payment but had been unable to obtain it. He is without remedy at the Common Law ' for that an accion of dett uppon a prest or a nude contract is not mayntenable ayenst executours '.

1486–93 or 1504–15. E.C.P. : Bundle 144, no. 25. (Chancellor, The Archbishop of Canterbury.)

Petition by John Kene of Kenkham, com. Oxon, for a writ against John Pryour of Burford. Setting forth that one John Moisier of Burford ' was seasid of viii messuages with their appurtenances in Burford foresaid In his demenys as of fee and soo seasid thereof Infeoffed one John Pynnoke Rychard Granger and Willm Pryour to have to them and to ther heires to the use and behofe of the said John Moysier and of his heires by force whereof they were seasid of the said messuages with their appurtenances in their demenys as of fee '. John Moisier died and the property descended to his son and heir, John Moisier. John the younger died, and the property descended to Richard Moisier, his son and heir. Richard Moisier died without issue, and the right in the property descended to the petitioner as cousin and heir to John Moisier the elder, being son and heir to Agnes sister and heir to the said John Moisier. Then John Pynnoke and

William (*sic*) Granger died, and William Pryour, outliving them, became sole seised of the property. He died, and the property descended to John Pryour, his son and heir, who entered into possession. John Pryour, though frequently requested to do so, refused to make an estate in the property to the petitioner.

1493–1500. E.C.P.: Bundle 197, no. 84. (Chancellor, The Archbishop of Canterbury.)

Petition by Thomas Dorman of Burford, ' bocher ', for a writ sub poena against Thomas Janyver of Burford. Setting forth that certain ' evidences charters and munuments ' concerning a messuage, eight acres of arable land and two acres of meadow lying in Burford, whereof petitioner was seised in right of his inheritance, had come into the hands of Thomas Janyver, who refused to give them up. Petitioner had no remedy at Common Law, ' forasmoche as he knoweth not the nowmbre of the saide evidences charters and munyments nor wherein they be conteigned '.

1501–2. E.C.P.: Bundle 251, no. 14. (Chancellor, The Bishop of London, Archbishop elect of Canterbury.)

Petition by Margaret Stodham, widow, for a writ sub poena against Agnes Stodham. Setting forth a complaint of detention of deeds of a messuage in Burford.

1502–3. E.C.P.: Bundle 273, no. 50. (Chancellor, The Bishop of London, Archbishop elect of Canterbury.)

Petition by Hugh Warham for a writ sub poena against John Haster. Setting forth that ' one Robert Martyn of Depford in the countie of Kent Yeoman was seised of a tenement with a barne stable and a crofte to the seid tenement belonging conteyning one acre and iii Rodes of assise set and lying in the parisshe of Westgrenewich in the seid countie. And he being so seised therof bargayned and solde the seid tenement and other the premises to one John Pynnoke of Burford in the Olde in the countie of Oxenford for a certeyn summe of money betwene them aggreed Whiche money and every parte therof the seid Pynnoke truly contented and payed to the seid Robert Martyn Wheruppon the same Robert Enfeoffed one John Haster of Depford aforeseid, the seid John Pynnoke and Sir John Alane, priest, to thuse of the seid Pynnoke and his heirs for evir And the seid John Pynnoke had issue Thomas and dyed And after that died the seid Sir John Alane and the seid John Haster then survyved by Reason wherof the same John Haster was sole seised of the premisses.' He died,

and the premises descended to his son John. Thomas Pynnoke had
sold the premises to petitioner, but John Haster the younger refused
to make an estate of the premises to petitioner.

1504-15. E.C.P.: Bundle 278, no. 17. (Chancellor, The Archbishop of Canterbury.)

Petition by Richard Adams of Sodbury, com. Glouc., for a writ
sub poena against Richard Somerby of Tetbury and his wife. Setting
forth that petitioner and one Harry Adams had bought certain wools
of one Thomas Stanton of Burford for the sum of £68, for which
sum they were jointly bound. The wools had been equally divided.
Petitioner had paid £30 and Harry Adams became debtor for ' the
resydew that is to say xxx li.' Harry Adams died, having made a will
declaring himself thus indebted, and making Margery his wife his
executor. She married Richard Somerby, and the two had paid £5
in part payment of the debt. Now Thomas Stanton had commenced
an action of debt against Richard Adams, petitioner, for the residue
of the debt, which he contended Somerby and his wife ought to pay.

1504-15. E.C.P.: Bundle 291, no. 88. (*Document very imperfect.*)

Petition by William a Chambre and Margaret his wife for a writ
sub poena against William Crane. Setting forth a complaint of detention of deeds concerning a half burgage in Burford.

The reply of William Crane sets forth that petitioners had no right
to the premises, which were claimed by one Thomas Stodham, and he
requests that Stodham may be joined in the suit.

Another document apparently sets forth Stodham's case, claiming
the half burgage by inheritance from Agnes Pynnok, who had held
it as heir of William Symonds.

1504-15. E.C.P.: Bundle 361, no. 15.

Petition by Thomas Stodham for a writ sub poena against William
Crane. Setting forth a complaint of detention of deeds concerning
certain lands and tenements in Burford belonging to petitioner as
heir of his father Henry Stodham.

1504-15. E.C.P.: Bundle 300, no. 8.

Petition by Thomas Cokks of Burford, yeoman, for an injunction
against Robert Eggerley, attorney of Edmund Bury and John Salbrigge, and for a writ sub poena. Setting forth that petitioner had
taken ' a place and certen londys ' in Windrush in March, 24 Henry VII,
from one John Salbrigge, late servant to Richard Guison, deceased,
for six years at £4 for the first year and £5 a year afterwards. During

the first year Guison was taken and ' emprisoned ', and one Edmund Bury of Hampton Poyle became owner of the premises and put one John Fisher into them. Fisher bought such corn and chattels as the petitioner had there at the time. Petitioner paid £4 for the first year's rent, ' and so departed '. Fisher had since paid the rent. But now Bury had taken action against petitioner in the county of Gloucester and ' caused by hys grete labour a Jury to pass ayenste your seid oratour by their verdit in the sum of xiiii *li*. and over that by his like speciall labour hath caused an other Jury to passe with the seid John Salbrigge uppon an accion of dette for the seid ferme by their verdit in the sum of iiii *li*. xiii*s*. iiii*d*. and xl*s*. costs in the county of Oxon '. As yet no judgement had been given, ' but nevertheles the seid Edmund will make quyk and hasti labour for jugement.'

1504–15. E.C.P. : Bundle 327, no. 36.
Petition by Agnes Jenyver widow, of ' Burforth ', for a writ sub poena against John Priour and Robert Reley. Setting forth a complaint of detention of deeds concerning two messuages and other premises in Burford.

1504–15. E.C.P. : Bundle 360, no. 27.
Petition by Agnes Smythier, widow, cousin and heir of Agnes Cace of Burforde, for a writ sub poena against John Ingram otherwise called John Tanner. Setting forth a complaint of detention of deeds concerning two messuages with appurtenances in the town of Burford, Tanner by detaining the deeds having entered on the premises.

1515–18. E.C.P. : Bundle 415, no. 66. (Chancellor, Thomas lord cardinal, legate a latere.)
Petition by William Hele and Elen his wife for a writ sub poenà against Marion Wastell, widow. Setting forth a complaint of detention of deeds concerning a messuage and a garden with appurtenances in Burford.

1515–18. E.C.P. : Bundle 512, no. 1.
Petition by Thomas Grene, priest, and William Smyth, executors of the will of Agnes Sylvester, widow, of Burford, against John Sharpe and Thomas Tyesdale, or Teysdale. Setting forth that Agnes Sylvester left goods appraised at the sum of £50, and Thomas Teysdale and John Sharpe offered to buy them for £50. The goods were handed over, the money to be paid ' at the festes of Ester St. John the Baptist Michell messe and Christe masse '. Sharpe and Teysdale now refused to be bound by a bond to pay.

1515-18. E.C.P.: Bundle 546, no. 72.

Petition by John Mille of Southampton for a writ sub poena against Johanne, widow of Thomas Staunton of Burford, merchant. Setting forth that Staunton had ordered of petitioner on 11, December, 7 Henry VIII, by William Pokley, carrier, one thousand pounds weight of iron and one butt of roney (?), the total value being £6. Staunton received the goods and promised to pay. He made his will, being ' yn extreme siknes ', and died, and his widow, his executor, refused to pay.

(f) RENTALS AND SURVEYS

1539. Rentals and Surveys : Portfolio 18, no. 66. 30 Henry VIII.

Burford in Com. Oxon. valet in

Firma scitus dicti nuper hospitalis cum columbariis stabulis curtilagiis Gardinis cum uno clauso ibidem vocato le pryory close accum uno Tenemento vocato Iveyhouse continentibus inter se per estimacionem uni (sic) acram terre et valentes per annum   xxxiiis. iiiid.

Firma unius horrei scituati infra clausum dicti nuper hospitalis in tenura Iohannis Iones per Indenturam datam xviiito die Septembris anno regni Regis Henr' viiivi xxixno Habendum ad terminum xxx annorum Reddendum inde per annum   xiiis. iiiid.

Firma trium virgatarum terre arabilis iacentium et existentium in campis ibidem cum duabus acris prati iacentibus in quodam prato vocato highmed cum communi pasture pro omnibus catallis suis pascendis in campis de Burford predicto In tenura Iohannis Sharpe sic sibi dimissa per Indenturam datam xxvto die Septembris anno regni Regis Henr' viiivi xxxo habendum ad terminum xxi annorum Reddendum inde per annum   xxs.

Firma sive redditus unius tenementi ibidem dimissi Iohanni Hardgrave ad voluntatem reddendum inde per annum

     vis. viiid.

Firma i clausi cum duabus parvis pecie (sic) terre nuper Gardinis modo dimissa Thome Richards per Indenturam datam xxviiio die Septembris anno regni xxxmo Domini Regis nunc Henrici viiivi habendum ad terminum xxi annorum Reddendum inde per annum

     vis. viiid.

Firma unius pecie terre iacentis prope salmans close Dimisse Thome Faller Reddendum inde per annum   iiiid.

Summa iiii li. iiiid.

Upton in
eodem Com.
Oxon.
valet in

Firma i clausi cum pertinenciis iacentis ibidem dimissi
Roberto Ensdale Reddendum inde per annum

vi*s*. viii*d*.

Redditus sive firma unius clausi ibidem dimissi Roberto
Browne ad voluntatem Reddendum inde per annum

iii*s*. iiii*d*.

Firma xxii acrarum terre arabilis et duarum acrarum prati iacentium
in campis de Upton predicto predicto (*sic*) in tenura Iohannis Wynchester sicut sibi dimissa per Indenturam Datam xxviii° die Septembris
anno regni Regis Henrici viii^vi xxx° Habendum ad terminum xl
annorum Reddendum inde per annum . x*s*.

. Summa xx*s*.

Astall seu
Astale in
dicto Com. Oxon.
valet in

Firma messuagii curtilagii toftorum croftorum
pratorum terrarum arabilium pascuae et pasture
cum pertinenciis ibidem dimissorum Henr' Cockerell
per Indenturam Datam xiii^mo die Septembris anno
regni Regis Henr' viii^vi xxvii° Habendum ad ter-
minum quinque annorum Reddendum inde per annum   xxxiii*s*. iiii*d*.

Summa prout patet.

Terre et
possessiones
nuper hospitalis
sti Iohannis
Evangeliste de
Burford in Com.
Oxon. pertinentia
iacentia in
diversis comita-
tibus ut infra

manerium de
ffyfhede alias
dicta ffyfyld
in predicto
comitatu Oxon
valet in

Firma scitus et capitalis man-
sionis dicti manerii cum terris
dominicalibus pratis pascuis et
pasturis Dicto capitali mansioni
pertinentibus necnon unius crofti
seu clausi separaliter iacentis ad
finem orientem ville de ffyfhede
prope campum ibidem vocatum
henmed Ac eciam unius hide
terre cum omnibus et singulis

pertinenciis in ffyfhyde predicto Necnon serviciorum custumariorum
tenencium Dicti manerii viz in plowyng carteyng repyng and mowyng
ac unius quartarii terre ibidem quod Thomas Clerke tenet Exceptis
omnibus aliis terris custumariis et tenencium Redditibus serviciis
Dicto manerio pertinentibus Que omnis et singula (exceptis prout
excepta) Dimissa sunt Thome Clarke per Indenturam Datam primo
die Decembris anno regni Regis Henrici viii^vi xxxi^mo Habendum ad
terminum xxi annorum Reddendum inde per annum   xlvii*s*. x*d*.

Redditu unius cotagii cum una virgata terre Dimissi Iohanni
Humfrey per copiam curie Habendum sibi et Iohanne uxori eius ac
Elizabethe filie eorundem Reddendum inde per annum • viii*s*.

Redditu unius Tenementi cum cotagio et una virgata ibidem vocati Kymers Dimissi Roberto Secoll per copiam curie habendum ad terminum vite sue et Roberti filii sui Reddendum inde per annum

xs.

Redditu unius messuagii et unius virgate terre cum suis pertinenciis continentis xxx^ta acras terre arabilis nuper in tenura Iohannis Torfrey necnon unius alii messuagii et unius quartarii terre cum suis pertinenciis nuper in tenura Ricardi More modo Dimissi Thome Riche per copiam curie Habendum sibi et Edithe uxori eius ac Agneti (sic) filie dicte Edithe pro termino vite eorum ac eorum diutius successive viventis Reddendum inde per annum   xiis.

Redditu assiso unius messuagii et unius virgate terre que Willelmus Hale libere tenet reddendum inde per annum   xvid.

Redditu unius parcelle terre iacentis ibidem quam Willelmus percy tenet libere Reddendum inde per annum   vid.

Redditu unius domus sive tenementi ibidem quam Gardianus dicte ville tenet libere reddendum inde per annum   iiiid.

Summa iiii li.

Wydford in Com. Glouc' valet in	Firma unius tofti viginti et octo acrarum terre arabilis necnon unius pecie prati cum tribus acris et dimidia prati iacentium in Westmed de Wydford predicto in tenura Georgii Cotton Reddendum inde per annum xiis.

Summa prout patet

Rysyngton magna in Com. Glouc' valet in	Firma unius prati iacentis in parochia de Shereborne infra decennaria de Rysyngton magna in dicto comitatu Glouc' Dimissi Thome Bygge ad voluntatem Reddendum inde per annum vs.

Firma omnium illorum terrarum pratorum et pasturarum iacentium et existentium in villa et campis de Resington magna in dicto comitatu cum omnibus pertinenciis dimissorum Simoni Wysdome per Indenturam Datam in festo sti michaelis archangeli anno regni Regis Henrici viii^vi xxviii° Habendum ad terminum vite dicti Simonis Reddendum inde per annum   xxiis.

Summa xxviis.

Barington parva in Com. Glouc'. valet in	Firma unius tenementi cum certis terris ibidem dimissi Iohanni Willeshire ad voluntatem reddendum inde per annum iiiis. vid.

Summa prout patet

Summa totalis omnium et singularum
Revencionum predictarum xii li. xviis. iid.

Memor⁴ their ys a lease made to John Barker of all and singular the premisses
apperteyning to the said late hospitall under the seale of Thomas
Cade late mʳ of the sayd late hospitall for the terme of iiiixx yeres
yeldyng therfor yerely x *li.* and to bere and supporte all maner of
Reparacions as in the said lease beryng date the iiiith day of may in
the xxxth yere of our Sovereigne lorde King Henry the eight many-
festely shall appere

Exᵐ per me Gregorium Richardsone deput'
Willelmi Cavendissh audit' ibidem.

1552. Misc. Books, Land Revenue : vol. 189. 4 June, 6 Edward VI.

fol. 85a

Manerium de Berybarre et manerium de Burforde in comitatu Oxon parcella terrarum et possessionum predicti Iohannis nuper ducis Northumbr' modo in manu Domini Regis Racione excambii.	Supervisus ibidem factus per predictum Michaelem Camsewell Generalem supervisorem domini Regis in Comitatu Oxon quarto die Iunii Anno Regni Edwardi Sexti dei gratia Anglie ffrancie et Hibernie Regis fidei defensoris Ac in terra Ecclesie Anglicane et Hibernie supremi capitis sexto Ac per sacramentum diversorum tenenciuni manerii predicti.
Redditus liberorum tenencium in Upton et More ac in Netherworton parcellis manerii predicti.	Oliverus Hyde de Abendon in com Berk generosus tenet libere unum messuagium et quatuor virgatas terre cum suis pertinenciis iacentia et existentia in Upton Reddendum inde per annum iis. iiiid. et pro secta curie annuatim xiid. et alia servicia iiis. iiiid.

Thomas More armiger tenet manerium suum vocatum Le More
cum pertinenciis infra parochiam de More in dicto comitatu Oxon
libere Reddendum inde per annum viis. et sectam curie cum aliis
serviciis   viis.

Thomas parsons tenet libere unum messuagium cum suis pertinenciis iacentem et existentem in Netherworton Reddendum inde
per annum xis. et sectam curie cum aliis serviciis   xis.

Redditus iiis. iiiid. pro libero redditu exeunte extra manerium de
fulbroke in Com Oxon domino Cobham nuper pertinens Eo quod
dominus Rex habet dictum manerium in excambio de dicto domino
Cobham pro aliis terris sibi in compensacione datis Responsus est
inde eidem Domino Regi simulcum proficuis eiusdem manerii in Curia
Augmentacionum et Revencionum Corone Domini Regis   null.

Summa liberorum tenencium in Upton More et
Netherworton per annum xxis. iiiid.

Adhuc Manerium de Berybarre alias Burforde

8 5a
rev.

Redditus Custumariorum tenencium per copiam curie in Upton Seynatt et in villa et campis de Burforde parcella manerii predicti

Georgius Chedworth tenet per copiam curie datam vi{to} die Octobris Anno regni nuper Regis Henrici viii{vi} xvi{to} unum messuagium et tria virgatas terre cum pertinenciis iacentia et existentia in villa et campis de Upton unum clausum vocatum Notts Clause continentem i acram unum clausum adiacentem separale continens i acram ii acras prati in Veron Hill meade in Wyldermoremeade i acram In Southefeld lxxii acras terre arrabilis in Northefeld lxxi acras terre arrabilis cum pertinenciis Habendum et tenendum sibi et Elizabethe uxori eius Ac Iohanni filio eorundem pro termino vite eorum et alterius eorum diutius viventis successive Reddendum inde per annum xxvi*s*. servicia et herietum cum acciderint   xxvi*s*. viii*d*.

Willelmus Collens filius Iohannis Collens defuncti tenet per copiam curie datam secundo die Maii Anno regni nuper Regis Henrici viii{vi} xviii° factam predicto Iohanni Collens et Willelmo filio eius secundum consuetudinem manerii predicti Unum messuagium edificatum et iiii virgatas terre cum pertinenciis in Upton predicto Necnon scitum alii messuagii cum uno clauso adiacente continente ii acras et tribus virgatis terre ac cum uno clauso adiacente dicto messuagio continente ii acras In Vernell medowe vii acras prati In Wyldmore medowe iiii acras prati et iii acras prati ibidem Ac in Southefeld Clxviii acras terre arrabilis et in Northefeld Clxviii acras terre cum pertinenciis Habendum et tenendum predicto Iohanni et Willelmo filio suo pro termino vite eorum et alterius eorum diutius viventis secundum ii herieta consuetudinem manerii predicti Reddendum inde per annum lxvii*s*. viii*d*. et alia servicia Finem et herietum cum acciderint
                   lxvii*s*. viii*d*.

Thomas Symmes tenet per copiam curie datam die Iovis Septimane Pasche Anno Regni nuper Regis Henrici viii{vi} xxxvi{to} unum messuagium edificatum unum clausum adiacens continens unam acram unam virgatam terre in Upton predicto viz in Southefeld xxiiii acras arrabiles in Estefeld xxiiii acras arrabiles in Veronhill meade Dimidiam acram prati cum pertinenciis Habendum et tenendum sibi et Agnete uxori eius pro termino vite eorum et alterius eorum diutius viventis secundum consuetudinem manerii predicti Reddendum inde per annum vii*s*. et sectam curie proficua et herietum cum acciderint
                   vii*s*.

fol. 86   Adhuc Manerium de Berybarre alias Burforde

Ricardus Dawbye tenet per copiam curie datam xiiii^{to} die Maii anno regni nuper (*sic*) Regis Edwardi Sexti quarto unum messuagium et unum clausum adiacens ac iiii virgatas terre cum pertinenciis in Upton iiii acras prati inde iacentes in Vyrynshills meade iii acras in Wyldmore i prati et in Southefeld iiii^{xx} xvi acras terre arrabilis ac in Northefeld iiii^{xx} xvi acras terre arrabilis Habendum sibi et Margerie uxori sue et Ricardo filio eorundem pro termino vite eorum et alterium eorum diutius viventis secundum consuetudinem manerii predicti

finis viis.   Reddendum inde per annum xxxi*s*. et sectam curie proficua et herietum cum acciderint Reparaciones ad onus predicti Ricardi et assignatorum eius durante vita sua   xxxi*s*.

Ricardus Hobbes tenet per copiam curie datam xi^o die Octobris anno regni nuper Regis Henrici viii^{vi} xxx^o unum tenementum edificatum trees (*sic*) virgatas terre iii clausa adiacentia continentia iii acras unum clausum iuxta terram Iohannis Hannes continens i acram iii acras prati in Highmed iacente in Synett ac in Westefeld lxxii acras in Estefeld lxxii acras terre arrabilis cum pertinenciis Habendum sibi et Elizabethe uxori eius pro termino vite eorum et alterius eorum successive secundum consuetudinem manerii predicti Reddendum inde per annum xxii*s*. servicia et herietum cum acciderint   xxii*s*.

Henricus Patent tenet per copiam curie datam ultimo die mensis marcii anno regni nuper Regis Henrici viii^{vi} xxxiiii^o unum messuagium edificatum unum clausum adiacens continens i acram cum alio clauso separali super venellam que ducit ad le Holwell continente ii acras cum pertinenciis in Sygnett unde iacent in Westfelde xlviii acre in Estfelde xlviii acre et ii acre prati in Hyghmeade cum pertinenciis Habendum et tenendum sibi et Agnete uxori eius ad terminum vite eorum et successive secundum consuetudinem manerii predicti Reddendum inde per annum xviii*s*. et sectam curie ac finem et herietum cum acciderint   xviii*s*.

Ricardus Hannes tenet per copiam curie datam xxi die Octobris anno regni nuper Regis Henrici viii^{vi} xix^o unum clausum in villa de Burford vocatum Cellynges continens i acram et dimidiam virgatam terre in Sygnettfeld et dimidiam acram prati in Hyghmede Habendum sibi Alicie uxori eius et Iohanni filio eorundem secundum consuetudinem manerii predicti Reddendum inde per annum v*s*. vi*d*. et sectam curie et finem et herietum cum acciderint   v*s*. vi*d*.

fol. 86   Adhuc Manerium de Berrybarre alias Burforde
rev.

Iohannes Hannes tenet per copiam curie datam xxvii^o die Septem-

bris anno Regni nuper Regis Edwardi Sexti tertio unum messuagium
edificatum et iiii^{or} virgatas terre in Signett unum clausum adiacens
continens ii acras unum clausum iuxta tenementum Ricardi Hobbes
continens unam acram unum clausum iuxta terram Ricardi Patents
continens dimidiam acram iiii^{or} acras prati iacentes in prato vocato
Burford meade in Westfeld iiii^{xx} xvii acras arrabiles in Estfeld iiii^{xx}
xvii acras Habendum et tenendum sibi Alicie uxori sue et Iohanni
filio eorundem et alterius diutius viventis (*sic*) secundum consuetudinem manerii predicti Et predicti Iohannes Alicia et Iohannes
filius eorundem sustinent et manutenent reparaciones predicti messuagii durante termino predicto Reddendum inde per annum xxxviii*s*.
et sectam curie finem et herietum cum acciderint   xxxviii*s*.

Idem Iohannes Hannes tenet per copiam curie datam ix° die
Octobris anno regni nunc Regis Edwardi sexti secundo unum horreum
cum clauso adiacente continente unam acram scituatum et existens
ex parte australi ville de Burford et dimidiam virgatam in campis
vocatis Sygnett feld xii acras terre arrabilis et xii acras terre arrabilis
in campis orientalibus de Burford super viam secundum (blank) et
xii acras terre excedentes nuper in tenura Iacobi Grene et Petri
Grynfeld Habendum sibi Alicie uxori sue et Iohanni filio eorundem
pro termino vite eorum et alterius eorum diutius viventis secundum
consuetudinem manerii predicti Reddendum inde per annum xiii*s*.
vi*d*. et sectam curie ac herietum acciderit (*sic*)   xiii*s*. vi*d*.

Iohannes Turner tenet per copiam curie datam ix° die Aprilis anno
regni nunc Regis Edwardi vi^{ti} secundo unum messuagium unum
clausum adiacens continens iii acras unum clausum iuxta terram
Ricardi Hobbes continens i acram et trium (*sic*) virgatas terre et
dimidiam in Signet viz in Westfeld iiii^{xx} iiii acras terre in Estfeld
iiii^{xx} iiii acras arrabiles in Hyghmede iii acras et dimidiam prati cum
pertinenciis Habendum et tenendum sibi et Margarete uxori sue pro
termino vite eorum et alterius eorum diutius viventis secundum
consuetudinem manerii predicti Reddendum inde per annum xxix*s*. fin viii*s*.
et sectam curie finem et herietum cum acciderint   xxix*s*.

Adhuc Manerium de Berrybarre alias Burforde Edmundus Sylvester fol. 87
tenet per copiam curie datam penultimo die Aprilis anno Regni
nuper Regis Henrici viii^{vi} xxxviii° unum messuagium edificatum
iacens in vico vocato Wytneystret infra Burgum de Burford unum
clausum vocatum oxehouse close continens ii acras unum clausum
iuxta tenementum continens dimidiam acram Ac unam virgatam terre in Signet feld viz in Westfeld xxx acras terre arrabilis

in Estfeld xxx acras arrabiles cum pertinenciis nuper in tenura (blank)
Hogges Habendum sibi ac Willelmo filio suo pro termino vite eorum
et alterius eorum diutius viventis secundum consuetudinem manerii
predicti Reddendum inde per annum xxs. et sectam curie fines et
herietum cum acciderint   xxs.

Summa custumariorum tenencium in Upton Signet
& Burford per Annum xiiili. xviiis. iiiid.

Diverse terre et
quarrerie demisse
diversis tenencibus
domini Regis ad
voluntatem iacentes
in Upton Fulbroke et
Holwell ac in campis
ibidem parcella ma-
nerii predicti

Oliverus Hyde de Abendon generosus tenet
unum acram terre arrabilis iacentem occidentali parte messuagii predicti Oliveri in
Upton felde ad voluntatem Domini Regis
ibidem de Anno in Annum Reddendum inde
per annum   viiid.

Tenentes de Holwell qui habent viam
ducentem oves suos ad aquam apud Gelden-
forde ex gratia et licencia Domini Regis ad
voluntatem de Anno in Annum Reddendum inde per annum   iiis.

Edmundus Harman tenet unam parcellam prati iacentem in Milne-
ham in Taynton continentem i acram et unam parcellam prati in
Wyldmore continentem per estimacionem iiii acras Reddendum
per annum

[*Note.*—No sum of money is entered here. Instead is written in different
ink—'id quod pertinet predicto Edmundo Harman heredibus et assignatis
suis parcella firme de terris dominicalibus manerii predicti dimissis prefato
Edmundo per Indenturam sub Redditu xili. iiis. iiiid. ut postea '.]

fol. 87
rev.

Adhuc Manerium de Berybarre alias Burford pd.

Ricardus Hannes tenet unam acram terre arrabilis in campo vocato
Fulbrokefeld inter pontem Vocatum Burford Brige et Westellhill
ad voluntatem domini Regis Reddendum inde per annum viis. quod
dictus prepositus occupavit ad voluntatem Domini Regis Racione
officii sui   viis.

Georgius Lambert tenet unam Quarreriam vocatam Whichelate-
quarrye iacentem et existentem in campo de Burford nuper ad
xxs. per annum et modo arrentatam per Supervisorem Domini
Regis in dicto comitatu ad vis. viiid. per annum solvendum
ad festum Annunciacionis beate Marie virginis et Sti Michaelis
Archangeli per equales porciones prout per copiam curie ut dicitur
                                                             vis. iiiid.

(blank) tenet unam Quarreriam vocatam Strete quarry petrarum
et tegularum nuper in tenura Iohannis Evynger nuper ad viis. per

annum Aliam quarreriam vocatam le Slatte iacentem in Signett
sicut nuper dimissam Willelmo Slater   vii*s.* modo in decasu
Summa reddituum ad voluntatem per annum
xvii*s.* iiii*d.*

Redditus vocatus Tenentes de Upton solventur annuatim ad
Hedsylver in Upton festum pasche domino Regi pro certo Redditu
& Signet vocato hedsylver per annum   iiii*s.*

Tenentes de Signet solventur annuatim ad

festum pasche dicto domino Regi pro certo redditu vocato hedsylver
per annum   ii*s.* viii*d.*

Summa certi Redditus vocati hedsylver per
annum vi*s.* viii*d.*

Adhuc Manerium de Berrybarre alias Burforde pd.   fol. 88

Firma scitus Manerii Edmundus Harman armiger tenet per Inden-
vocati Berreybarre turam sub sigillo Curie Augmentacionum Re-
cum terris Domini- vencionum Corone Domini Regis datam (blank)
calibus ibidem die (blank) anno Regni Regis nunc Edwardi
 Sexti (blank) totum scitum manerii predicti
vocati Berreybarres cum omnibus Domibus eidem manerio sufficienter
spectantibus viz unum clausum vocatum the Conynggree continens
iii acras unum pratum vocatum Berrye orcharde continens viii acras
unum pratum vocatum Wornam separale continens iiii acras Unam
pasturam vocatam Batelenche separalem a festo purificacionis Beate
Marie virginis usque ad festum Sti Martini continentem quinque
acras Unum pratum vocatum Hyghemeade vii acras super unum
clausum separale vocatum Hammes continens Duas acras separale
a festo purificacionis Beate Marie usque ad festum Sti Petri
Sex virgatas terre arrabilis unam pasturam vocatam Sturke continentem xl acras separalem per annum a festo annunciacionis Beate
Marie virginis usque ad festum Sti Martini Unam pasturam et pratum
iacentia apud Upton vocata Veronhill continentia xxiiii acras separaliter et unam parcellam prati iacentes in Millham in Taynton continentem i acram et dimidiam acram unam parcellam prati in Wyldmore
continentem iii acras   xi*li.* iii*s.* iiii*d.*

Summa Totalis Manerii de Berrybarre alias fol. 88
Burfforde pdict. xxvii*li.* vii*s.* rev.

Limita et Banna Incipit a Cepe vocata Woodfordehedge et sic inde
dicti Manerii per viam usque ade le Sturke et sic inde per rivulum
 vocatum Shiltonbroke usque ad sepem vocatam
Westwellhedge et sic inde per quandam sepem vocatam Westwellhedge

usque campos vocatos Barryngtonfelds et sic inde per le hade usque ad le Veronhill et sic inde per Ripariam vocatam Wenderushe usque ad sepem vocatam Woodfordehedge ubi incipit continens vi millia

Ricardus Hannes tenens domini Regis electus est in officio prepositi manerii predicti hoc anno ad colligendum Redditus dicti Domini Regis et facere compotum inde ad usum Domini Regis predicti

Dictus Dominus Rex habet Communem ibidem vocatum Seynet Down continens per estimacionem C acras.

fol. 89

Burgus de Burford cum membris in com Oxon Parcella terrarum predicti Iohannis nuper Ducis Northumbr' modo in manu Domini Regis Racione perquisiti

Supervisus ibidem factus per Michaelem Camsewell Generalem Supervisorem Domini Regis in dicto comitatu Oxon sexto die Iunii Anno regni regis Edwardi Sexti Sexto per sacramentum Ricardi Hannes Roberti Iohnson Symonis Wysedome Willelmi Hewes Iohannis Lembert Thome ffawler Roberti Enisdall Iohannis lloyde Iohannis Hayter Thome Prykevance Thome Alflett Ricardi Rogers Roberti Bruton Ballivorum Domini Regis ibidem Willelmi Collens Alexaunderi Hegges Roberti Browne et Hugonis Colborne Tenencium Burgi predicti cum aliis   viz

Redditus liberorum tenencium in vico vocato Wyttneystret in villa et Burgo de Burford Ac diversarum terrarum iacentium in campis de Burford Upton & Signett

Ricardus Hogges tenet libere unum messuagium et Burgagium et dimidium cum gardino vocatum le signe of the George ibidem Habet primam vesturam inde et non ultra quinque acrarum et dimidie arrabilium iacentium in campis de Upton Unum clausum vocatum le Georgeclose continens unam acram Unum Burgagium et dimidium iuxta pontem cum gardino adiacente et dimidium Burgagium adiacens Dicto Burgagio et dimidio aliud Burgagium iuxta Burgagium Walteri Rose cum gardino Et aliud dimidium Burgagium iuxta Burgagium Willelmi Hewes cum gardino adiacente et aliud dimidium Burgagium cum gardino iuxta Burgagium ecclesie Iohannis Baptiste Aliud Burgagium cum gardino et unum clausum adiacens continens unam acram et dimidiam iacens in Wytneystreate et aliud dimidium Burgagium cum gardino iacens in Wytnestret iuxta Burgagium Alexaunderi Hogges Aliud Burgagium cum gardino accum duobus clausis vocatis Wyldernes continentibus iiii acras et Reddit per annum cum secta curie bis in anno   xvs. viiid.

Willelmus Hewes de Burforde tenet libere sex Burgagia cum gardino adiacente scituata in vico vocato Wytney Stret ibidem et trees (*sic*) clausos continentes quinque acras et dimidiam unum vocatum Hawllecrofte iacentèm prope Burybarres et alium iuxta altum vicum et tercium iacentem in Wytneystret ibidem iuxta le Walkemylle cum centum et decem acris terre arrabilis in separalibus campis de Burforde Upton et Signett cum una acra et dimidia prati iacentibus in Upton meade de quibus terris arrabilibus habet primam vesturam et non ultra Secta curie et Reddit per annum   xix*s*. iii*d*.

Adhuc Burgus de Burforde pd.

Robertus Smythe tenet libere unum Burgagium cum gardino adiacente scituatum in Wyttneystrete cum iiii^{or} acris terre arrabilis in campis de Burforde de quibus terris arrabilibus habet primam vesturam inde et non ultra Et Reddit inde per annum xviii*d*. et sectam curie   xviii*d*.

Alexandreus Hedges tenet libere unum et dimidium Burgagium scituatum in Alto Vico et Duo Burgagia et dimidium cum gardino adiacente scituata in Whytneystrete cum sexaginta acris terre arrabilis in campis de Burford Upton et Signett de quibus acris terre habet primam vesturam et Reddit inde per annum vi*s*. x*d*. et sectam curie   vi*s*. x*d*.

Thomas Allflett tenet libere Dimidium Burgagium cum gardino adiacente scituatum in vico vocato Wytney strett predicto cum pertinenciis Et Reddit per annum vi*d*. et sectam curie   vi*d*.

Willelmus Pynnock de Ensham in Com Oxon generosus tenet libere tria Burgagia cum gardinis adiacentibus scituata in alto vico et Duo Burgagia et dimidium cum gardino adiacente scituata in Wytney stret cum uno clauso adiacente iuxta Batts lane continente ii acras Et Reddit inde per annum   vi*s*.

Summa redditus liberorum tenencium in Wytney stret pdict per annum xlix*s*. ix*d*.

Redditus liberorum tenencium in Wytney stret et Shepstret ac Churchelane in villa de Burford ac diversarum terrarum in campis de Burford Upton & Signet

Ricardus Hannes tenet libere tria Burgagia cum gardino adiacente scituata in altero (*sic*) vico unum Burgagium cum gardino adiacente in vico vocato Wytneystret et duo Dimidia Burgagia cum gardino adiacente scituata vocato (*sic*) Shepstret et ii clausos continentes iiii acras quorum unus iacet apud Upton et alterus (*sic*) apud Whyttehill et dimidiam acram prati in prato de Upton predicto et ii acras prati et dimidiam in Hyghmeade cum sexaginta ac duabus acris terre arrabilis in campis de Burford Upton & Signett de quibus terris habet primam Vesturam et non ultra Et Reddit inde per annum xiiii*s*. et sectam curie fol. 90 Adhuc Burgus de Burforde pd.

Iohanna Iones tenet libere iiii°ʳ Burgagia cum gardino adiacente scituata in alto vico et duo Burgagia cum gardino adiacente in Wytnestrett et unum gardinum in eodem vico Dimidium Burgagium cum gardino adiacente scituatum in churche Lane et duos clausos continentes ii acras iacentes in Wytneystret unus clausus continens dimidiam acram iacentem in Hyghmeadeforde cum quadraginta duobus et dimidia acris terre arrabilis in campis de Burford Upton et Signett de quibus terris arrabilibus habet communam pro duodecim acris vocatis Howselands cum ceteris tenentibus manerii de Bury-barnes et dabit sectam curie eiusdem manerii pro eisdem terris vocatis Howselands Et de ceteris terris arrabilibus habet primam vesturam et non ultra et Reddit inde per annum   xixs. vid.

Ricardus Hoges tenet libere tria Burgagia et iiii°ʳ dimidia Burgagia cum gardinis adiacentibus scituata in alto vico et duo Dimidia Burgagia cum gardino adiacente scituata in vico vocato Wytney streete et unum Burgagium cum gardino adiacente scituatum Church Lane et tria clausa iacentia iuxta predictum vicum de Wytneystret continentia per estimacionem quinque acras cum quinque dimidia acris terre arrabilis iacentibus in campis de Upton de quibus terris arrabilibus habet primam vesturam et non ultra Et Reddit inde per annum xvs. viiid. et sectam curie   xvs. viiid.

Summa reddituum liberorum tenencium in Wytneystret Shepestret ac Chirchelane in dicta villa de Burford   xlivs. vid.

fol. 90 rev. Adhuc Burgus de Burford pdict.

Redditus liberorum tenencium in vicibus vocatis Shepestret & sanct Iohnes strete infra Burgum de Burford ac in campis de Upton Burford et Signet pdict.

Simon Wysdome de Burforde tenet libere octo Burgagia cum gardinis et pomariis adiacentibus scituata in alto vico et unum Burgagium et dimidium cum gardinis et pomariis adiacentibus scituata in Shepestret cum centum quadraginta et tree (sic) acris terre arrabilis in separalibus campis de Burford Upton & Signett et unam acram prati iacentem in le Hyghmeade de quibus terris arrabilibus habet primam vesturam et non ultra Et Reddit inde per annum xviis. ixd. et sectam curie   xviis. ixd.

Philippus Maryner de Cicestr' in com Glous' tenet libere unum Burgagium cum gardino et clauso adiacentibus in vico vocato Shepestret cum quinque acris et dimidia terre arrabilis iacentibus in campis de Burford de quibus terris habet primam vesturam inde et non ultra Et Reddit inde per annum xxii*d*. et sectam curie   xxii*d*.

Edwardus Ryley de Burford tenet libere unum Burgagium sine gardino adiacente scituatum in vico predicto Et Reddit inde per annum viii*d*. et sectam curie cum aliis serviciis etc   viii*d*.

Ricardus Busby de Islyngton in com Midd tenet libere unum Burgagium cum gardino adiacente scituatum in alto vico cum uno clauso iacente in Batts lane continente iiii^or acras cum xxvi acris terre arrabilis in campis de Burford et Signett accum uno prato iacente et existente in Upton meade de quibus terris acris (*sic*) arrabilibus et prato habet primam vesturam inde et non ultra Et Reddit inde per annum xiii*s*. vi*d*. et sectam curie cum aliis serviciis Debet et consuetudinem pro predicto Burgagio cum pertinenciis

xiii*s*. vi*d*.

Adhuc Burgus de Burforde pdict.   fol. 91

Petrus Payne tenet libere unum Burgagium cum gardino adiacente scituatum in vico vocato Shepestrete predicto cum pertinenciis Reddendum inde per annum xii*d*. et sectam curie   xii*d*.

Marcus Payne de Burforde tenet libere unum Burgagium et dimidium cum gardinis adiacentibus scituata in alto vico Accum xliiii^or acris terre arrabilis in campis de Burforde et Signett de quibus terris arrabilibus habet primam vesturam inde et non ultra Et Reddit inde per annum iiii*s*. iiii*d*. et sectam curie   iiii*s*. iiii*d*.

Magister et Socii Collegii de Brasenose in Civitate Oxon tenent libere unum Burgagium et dimidium cum gardinis adiacentibus scituata in alto vico cum sex acris terre arrabilis in campis de Burford de quibus acris terre arrabilis habent primam vesturam et non ultra Et Reddit inde per annum iiii*s*. et sectam curie   iiii*s*.

Iohannes Hannes tenet libere unum Burgagium et dimidium cum gardinis et uno clauso adiacentibus continente ii acras scituata in alto vico Accum sexaginta et una acris terre arrabilis in campis de Burford et Signett de quibus terris habet primam vesturam et non ultra Et Reddit inde per annum ix*s*. et sectam curie   ix*s*.

Iohannes Smythear de Burforde tenet libere unum Burgagium cum uno clauso adiacente scituatum in Shepstret predicto cum pertinenciis Et Reddit inde per annum xx*d*. et sectam curie   xx*d*.

Willelmus Bayley de Kevoller in Com Wiltes' tenet libere unum Burgagium et quarterium Burgagium cum gardino adiacente scituatum in alto vico de Burford Et Reddit inde per annum xv*d*. et sectam curie   xv*d*.

Adhuc Burgus de Burforde pdict.

Thomas Collyns de Southlye in Com Oxon tenet libere unum Burgagium cum gardino adiacente scituatum in Shepestrete predicto et uno clauso iacente in Wytneystret iuxta frontem vocatum fforest wall continente per estimacionem unam acram et dimidiam Accum uno prato iacente in le Hyghemeade et xx acris terre arrabilis iacentibus in campis de Burford Upton et Signett de quibus terris arrabilibus habet primam vesturam inde et non ultra Et Reddit inde per annum ixs. et sectam curie   ixs.

Iohannes Halle de Sherborne in Com Glous' tenet libere duo Burgagia et dimidium cum gardinis adiacentibus scituata in vico vocato le Shepestrete cum pertinenciis Et Reddit inde per annum xiid. et sectam curie   xiid.

Iohannes Gay de Civitate London tenet libere dimidium Burgagium cum gardino adiacente scituatum in alto vico de Burford cum pertinenciis Et Reddit inde per annum vid. et sectam curie   vid.

Willelmus Hulls de Risington parva in com Glous' tenet libere dimidium Burgagium sine gardino scituatum in alto vico predicto cum pertinenciis eidem spectantibus Et Reddit inde per annum vid. et sectam curie   vid.

Hugo Colbrow tenet libere unum Burgagium cum gardino eidem adiacente in alto vico predicto cum pertinenciis eidem spectantibus sine pertinenciis (sic) Et Reddit inde per annum xiid. et sectam curie
                                                                 xiid.

Thomas Chadwell de Baryngton parva in Com Glous' tenet libere dimidium Burgagium cum gardino adiacente scituatum in alto vico predicto Et Reddit inde per annum iiiid. et sectam curie
                                                                 iiiid.

Robertus Edmunds de Tetbury in Com Glous' tenet libere unum Burgagium et dimidium cum suis pertinenciis scituata iacentia et existentia in alto vico predicto Et Reddit inde per annum xviiid. et sectam curie   xviiid.

Adhuc Burgus de Burforde pdict.

Thomas Pyme de Islyngton in Com Middx generosus tenet libere unum Burgagium cum gardino et uno clauso adiacentibus in alto vico predicto cum tribus acris terre arrabilis iacentibus et existentibus in campis de Burforde et Upton de quibus acris terre arrabilis et (sic) habet primam vesturam inde et non ultra Et Reddit inde per annum xviiid. et sectam curie   xviiid.

Iohannes Pope de Astall in Com Oxon tenet libere dimidium Bur-

gagium cum gardinis adiacentibus scituatum in alto vico predicto
cum suis pertinenciis Et Reddit inde per annum vi*d*. et sectam curie
vi*d*.

Philippus Barrett de Mylton in Com Oxon tenet libere unum
Burgagium cum gardinis adiacentibus scituatum in vico vocato
Shepestret et dimidium Burgagium cum gardino adiacente scituatum
in vico vocato Seynt Iohns stret Et Reddit inde per annum xviii*d*.
et sectam curie   xviii*d*.

Thomas Fetiplace de Langford in Com Oxon tenet libere unum
Burgagium cum gardino adiacente scituatum in Shepestrete cum
iiii*or* acris terre et dimidia arrabilis iacentibus et existentibus in
campis de Burford de quibus terris arrabilibus habet primam vesturam
inde et non ultra Et Reddit inde per annum xix*d*. et sectam curie
xix*d*.

Iohannes Legge de Burford tenet libere ut in iure Margarete uxoris
eius Dimidium Burgagium cum gardino adiacente scituatum in alto
vico Et Reddit inde per annum vii*d*. obolum et sectam curie
vii*d*. ob.

Robertus Ensdale de Burford tenet libere Duo Burgagia et dimidium
cum gardinis et uno clauso adiacentibus scituata in alto vico Et Reddit
inde per annum iiii*s*. vi*d*. et sectam curie   iiii*s*. vi*d*.

Adhuc Burgus de Burford pdict.   **fol. 92**
rev.

Willelmus Collyns de Upton in Com Oxon tenet libere unum Burgagium et dimidium cum gardino adiacente scituatum in alto vico
et unam acram terre arrabilis iacentem in campis de Burforde de
quibus terris arrabilibus habet primam vesturam inde et non ultra
Et Reddit inde per annum xviii*d*. et sectam curie   xviii*d*.

Rosa Ryleye de Burford vidua tenet libere dimidium Burgagium
cum gardino adiacente scituatum in alto vico cum pertinenciis Et
Reddit inde per annum vi*d*. et sectam curie   vi*d*.

Thomas Dutton de Sherborne in Com Glous' tenet libere ut in iure
Marie uxoris sue Dimidium Burgagium cum gardino adiacente scituatum in vico vocato Shepestret Et Reddit inde per annum vi*d*. et
sectam curie   vi*d*.

Iohannes Lamberte de Upton in Com Oxon tenet libere dimidium
Burgagium cum gardino adiacente scituatum in Shepestret cum duabus
acris terre et dimidia in campis de Upton De quibus terris habet
primam vesturam inde et non ultra Et Reddit inde per annum vi*d*.
et sectam curie   vi*d*.

Georgius Lambert de Burford tenet libere unum Burgagium cum

gardino adiacente scituatum in Shepestret predicto Et Reddit inde per annum xii*d*. et sectam curie xii*d*.

Idem Georgius tenet libere dimidium Burgagium sine gardino pertinens Ecclesie de Cicestr' in Com Glous' scituatum in alto vico cum pertinenciis Et Reddit inde per annum iiii*d*. et sectam curie iiii*d*.

Walterus Rose tenet libere unum Burgagium cum gardino et parvo clauso adiacentibus sciatuatum in alto vico cum ix acris terre arrabilis in campis de Burford et Signet de quibus terris habet primam vesturam inde et non ultra Et Reddit inde per annum xiii*d*. et sectam curie

xiii*d*.

Adhuc Burgus de Burford pd.

Summa Reddituum liberorum tenencium in Shepstret & Senct Iohns Stret in villa de Burford per annum iiii*li*. iii*s*. vi*d*.

Redditus liberorum tenencium in vico vocato Seint Iohns Strete et Wytneystret Necnon certarum terrarum in campis de Burford Upton & Signett pd.

Thomas Faller tenet libere iiii^or Burgagia cum gardinis adiacentibus et unum pomarium scituata in alto vico et Duo Dimidia Burgagia cum gardinis adiacentibus scituata in vico vocato Saynte Iohns Stret et uno clauso vocato Salmans close iacente in eodem vico continente i acram et alio clauso iacente in Wytney stret continente i acram et duas virgatas terre arrabilis in campis de Burford Upton et Signett et quilibet (*sic*) virgata continet xxiiii acras terre arrabilis et duo acras prati iacentes in le highemede de quibus terris et prato habet communam cum ceteris tenentibus Manerii de Burybarnes et Debet sectam curie eiusdem Manerii Et Reddit inde per annum xvi*s*. et alia servicia xix*s*. (*sic*)

Iohannes Euston de Estehendred in Com Berk generosus tenet libere duo Burgagia et duo dimidia Burgagia cum gardinis adiacentibus scituata in alto vico cum quatuor virgatis terre arrabilis in campis de Burford Upton et Signet ac iiii^or acris prati in Hyghmeade et quilibet (*sic*) virgata continet xxiiii^or acras terre arrabilis et habet communam pro eisdem terris cum tenentibus Manerii de Burybarnes et debet sectam curie dicti Manerii de Burybarnes Et Reddit inde per annum xvi*s*. cum aliis serviciis xvi*s*.

Willelmus Sheperde de Chorlebury in Com Oxon tenet libere dimidium Burgagium et unum quarterium Burgagium cum gardino adiacente scituata insimul in vico vocato Seynt Iohns stret in villa de Burford Et Reddit inde per annum ix*d*. et sectam curie ix*d*.

Thomas (blank) de Chorleburye in dicto com tenet libere duo Burgagia et dimidium iacentia et scituata in Seynt Iohns stret predicto in villa predicta cum pertinenciis Et Reddit inde per annum xviii*d*. et sectam curie   xviii*d*.

Idem Thomas tenet libere Duo Burgagia et dimidium cum gardino adiacente scituata in eodem vico pertinentia (*sic*) Et Reddit inde per annum xii*d*. et sectam curie   xii*d*.

Rector de Burford tenet libere duo Burgagia et dimidium cum gardinis adiacentibus pertinentia eidem Rectori scituata in alto vico Et Reddit inde per annum xii*d*. et sectam curie   xii*d*.

Iohannes floyde alias Hewys de Burford tenet libere Duo Burgagia et dimidium cum gardino adiacente scituata in alto vico Et Reddit inde per annum xii*d*. et sectam curie   xii*d*.

Edmundus Sylvester tenet libere unum Burgagium et dimidium cum gardino adiacente scituatum in alto vico Accum uno clauso iacente in batts lane vocato Pykedclose continente dimidiam acram Et Reddit inde per annum xviii*d*. et sectam curie   xviii*d*.

            Summa Reddituum liberorum tenencium in vico
            vocato Seynt Iohns stret in villa de Burford per
                     Annum xxxviii*s*. ix*d*.

Adhuc Burgus de Burford pdict.   fol. 94

                     Ricardus Wygpytte tenet libere dimidium
Redditus liberorum   Burgagium sine gardino adiacente scituatum
tenencium in Churche   in Churche Lane cum pertinenciis Et
Lane in Villa Burford   Reddit inde per Annum iiii*d*. et sectam
                                curie iiii*d*.

Robertus Browne tenet libere unum Burgagium cum gardinis adiacentibus scituatum in Alto vico ibidem Et Reddit inde per annum xii*d*. et sectam curie   xii*d*.

Iohannes Yonge tenet libere Dimidium Burgagium cum gardino adiacente in alto vico de Burford Et Reddit inde per Annum vi*d*. et sectam curie   vi*d*.

Elizabeth Tomson vidua de Burford tenet libere unum Burgagium cum gardino adiacente scituatum in alto vico Et Reddit inde per Annum xii*d*. et sectam curie   xii*d*.

Iohannes Bredocke de Wantag in Com Berk tenet libere unum Burgagium cum gardino adiacente scituatum in alto vico Et Reddit inde per Annum xii*d*. et sectam curie   xii*d*.

            Summa Reddituum liberorum tenencium in villa
            de Burford in vico vocato Churche Lane per
                     Annum iii*s*. x*d*.

Quietus Redditus exeuns Canterie de Burford	Quodam annuali Redditu exeunte de terris et tenementis pertinentibus predicte Cantarie in villa de Burford per Annum xxs.

Summa prout patet.

Adhuc Burgus de Burford pdict.

Terre et tenementa concessa ad susten-tacionem pauperum de Burforde per Henricum Bysshope.

Tenentes sive gardiani ecclesie de Burford tenent quatuor Burgagia scituata simul in Churche Lane cum gardino et uno clauso adiacentibus continente i acram et Reddunt per annum viiis.   viiis.

Summa prout patet.

Terre et tenementa concessa ad susten-tacionem pauperum eiusdem ville per Thomam Pope (sic)

Predicti gardiani ecclesie de Burford predicto tenent unum Burgagium scituatum in alto vico et unum Burgagium et dimidium cum gardino adiacente scituatum in vico vocato Wytneystret Unum Burgagium cum uno clauso vocato Cowerclose continente iii acras iacente in vico vocato Shep-stret cum xii acris terre in campis de Burford et Signett de quibus terris habent primam vesturam inde et non ultra per Annum

vis. vd.

Summa prout patet.

Terre et tenementa pertinentia de Reparacionem ecclesie de Burford pdict

Predicti gardiani ecclesie predicte tenent iiiior Burgagia et dimidium cum gardino adiacente scituata in alto vico et duo Burgagia cum gardino adiacente scituata in Churche Lane et Dimidium Burgagium cum gardino adiacente scituatum in Shepestret cum xviii acris terre et dimidia iacentibus in campis de Burford et Signett cum una acra et dimidia prati in Bury orchard de quibus terris habent primam vesturam inde et non ultra Et Reddunt inde per annum

xiis. vid.

Summa prout patet.

Terre et tenementa pertinentia ad Reparacionem pontem (sic) iuxta Burford predicto

Supradicti tenentes tenent unum Burgagium et dimidium iacentia in vico vocato Seynt Iohnes stret et dimidium Burgagium scituatum in Churche Lane cum tribus acris terre iacentibus in campis de Burford et Upton cum duabus acris de ffarendell prati iacentibus in highmeade de quibus terris habent primam vesturam inde et non ultra Et Reddunt inde per Annum   iiis. xid.

Summa prout patet.

Adhuc Burgus de Burford pd.

Tolnetum mercatorum de Burford — Et denarii provenientes diversis tenentibus et aliis personis per Tolnetum Marcatorum in villa de Burford communibus annis x*s*.

xs.

SUMMA TOTALIS BURGI DE BURFORD PREDICTO xiiii*li*. v*s*. vi*d*.

circa 1556. Land Rev. Bundle 1392, File 10/1.

(John Carleton's Accompt of lead and bells for Berks, Bucks and Oxon.—Chantries, &c.)

Co. Oxon—the hospitall of Burforde — the Leade ther—none as apperyth by the certificate of Edmunde Harman gent and others hereupon seen and wth thaccomptaunte Remaynyng.

the bells—ij sold by Doctor London one of the Commyssioners by certificate of Edmond Harman esquier w^t the accomptaunte remaynyng.

[*Note*.—In another account (Land Rev. Bundle 1392, File 9/1) there is a reference to Thomas Barten, Surveyor of Hampton Court, with a note in the margin—' The wyff of Barten dwellyth beside Burforde '.]

(g) RECORDS OF THE AUGMENTATION OFFICE

1541. Decrees of the Court of Augmentations. Exch. K. R. Augm. Office : Misc. Bks., vol. 93.

fol. 167. Michaelmas Term, 22 October, 33 Henry VIII.

Richard Hannes produced a lease from Thomas Cade, Master of the Hospital of St. John the Evangelist at Burford, dated 22 September, 28 Henry VIII, granting him the Hospital's property at Asthall for a term of 21 years at a rental of 33*s*. 4*d*. a year. It is stipulated that the tenant is not to cut down ' oke asshe nor crabbetre but in sight of and by the assente of the said Thomas Cade clerke or his successors '.

The lease was recognized by the Court, and allocated to Richard Hannes.

fol. 168 rev. Same date.

Thomas Clarke similarly produced a lease of the manor of Fifield for a term of 41 years at a rental of £4 a year.

The preamble of the lease is as follows : ' This Indenture made the 27th daye of Marche in the eight and twentie yere of the reign of our soveraigne lord king Henry the eight betweene Master Thomas Cade master and prior of the hospytall of saynt John the Evangelist

founded within the town of Burford in the countie of Oxford and
Peter Annysdale Alderman and Richard Hannys steward of the
Burgesses of Burford aforesaid and all other of the saide Burgesses
very true and perpetuall patrons of the foresaide hospytall of the
one partie And Thomas Clerke of ffyffhyde otherwise called ffyfeld
in the countie foresaide yoman of the other partye wytnessyth that
the foresaide Thomas Cade prior at the speciall ynstance and requesté
and with the full and clere assente and consente of all the foresaide
Alderman Steward and Burgesses hath demysed ' . . . etc. . . . .

The sealing clause is as follows : ' The foresaide master and prior
of the hospytall . . . have put the comen and auncyent seale of his
said hospytall and for the full assente and clere consente of the said
Alderman Steward and Burgesses very true and perpetuall patrons
of the same hospytall for them and their successors they have caused
the comen and auncyent seale of their ffraternitye to the same to be
sett '.

Lease recognized and allocated.

fol. 172. Same date.

John Sharpe produced a lease of three yards of arable land and
two acres of meadow, dated 25 September, 30 Henry VIII, for a term
of 21 years at a rental of 20s. a year.

In the lease Thomas Cade is described as ' master or keper of the
hospytall ' ; and the lease is granted ' with the assente and consente
of Rychard Manyngton Gentilman and Aldermañ of the borough
town of Burford aforesaid Richard Hannys Steward and their brethren
Burgesses there patrons of the said hospytall '.

Lease recognized and allocated.

Proceedings of the Court of Augmentations. Exch. K. R. Augm.
Ct. Proc. : 13, 10.

John Barker against John Jones, Thomas Clark, Richard Hannes,
and John Sharp.

Barker complained that defendants were in possession of lands
of the late Hospital relying on leases from Cade which, he pleaded,
were void in law, whereas he himself held a lease of the whole property
of the late Hospital, including ' the mancyon howses of the said
hospitall and manor '. He pleaded that Cade had no right to make
leases without the consent of his brethren for a longer period than
that of his own life. He admitted that a lease which he himself held
from Cade of the whole property was equally void ; but he stated

that he had been instrumental in persuading Cade to hand over the Hospital to the Crown, and had therefore obtained a new lease from the Crown for a term of 21 years at a rent of £11 22d. by indenture under the seal of the Court of Augmentations dated 23 March, 32 Henry VIII. The defendants, however, had craftily obtained an injunction against him.

An answer by John Jones and Richard Hannes sets forth that Barker had done nothing to persuade Cade to surrender the Hospital, and that their leases were good in law.

Augm. Off. Misc. Bks. : vol. 402.

A Survey of the possessions of the late Hospital of St. John the Evangelist in Burford. The details are as recorded above (Rentals and Surveys, p. 621, *supra*) with the following exceptions :

Against the entries of the holdings of John Sharpe, Hardgrave, Richards, Faller, Ensdale, Browne, Wynchester, Cockerell, Clarke, Cotton, Bygge, and Willeshire is marked ' vacat '.

Several of the rentals are altered ; the Hospital site is entered at 43s.; Hardgrave's holding at 13s. 4d., Ensdale's at 15s., Browne's at 4s., and Fifield Manor at 53s. 4d. The total rental thus becomes £14 9s.

1544. Exch. L. T. R. Augm. Off.: Particulars for Grants. No. 541, 35 Henry VIII. Harman Grantee.

Firma domus et scitus dicti nuper hospitalis Sti Iohannis Evangeliste de Burford predicto in dicto com Oxon cum omnibus edificiis columbariis stabulis curtilagiis et pomariis gardinis terris et solo infra scitum septum ambitum circuitum et precinctum eiusdem nuper hospitalis existentia Ac unius clausi vocati le priorie close Ac unius tenementi vocati Ivey house iacentis et existentis in Burford predicto Necnon trium virgatarum terre arrabilis iacentium in campis de Burford predicto et duarum acrarum pratorum iacentium in quodam prato vocato hygh mede in Burford predicto et communam pasture pro omnibus animalibus et catallis Iohannis Tucker firmarii ibidem nuper in tenura Iohannis Sharpe ac unius tenementi ibidem nuper in tenura Iohannis Hardgrave ac unius clausi terre cum duabus parvis peciis terre cum pertinenciis nuper in tenura Thome Rychards in Burford predicto ac unius pecie terre cum pertinenciis iacentis prope Salmons close nuper in tenura Thome Faller in Burford predicto Necnon unius clausi terre et pasture cum pertinenciis in tenura Roberti Ensdell iacentis et existentis in Upton ac unius clausi terre cum pertinenciis nuper in tenura Roberti Browne iacentis et existentis in Upton predicto accum omnibus illis viginti duabus acris prati iacentibus et existentibus in campis de Upton nuper in tenura Iohannis Wynchester Necnon omnibus illis messuagiis curtilagiis toftis croftis pratis terris arrabilibus pasturis pascuis cum suis pertinenciis nuper in tenura Henry Cotler iacentibus et existentibus in Asthall ... etc ...

[And the manor of Fifield and the lands at Risington.]

Total annual value £12 3s. 10d.

M^d that ther is no more landes belonging to the hospitall of Burford then is before conteyned per Willm Cavendyssh audit'.

These parcells above specifyed with there appurtenances as I have lernyd ar ffrom eny of the Kyngs houses whereunto hys maiestie hathe eny accesse and repayer two myles and ffrom eny the Kynges parkes forests and chases two myles They ar no parcell of eny manor or other hereditament excedynge the clere yerely value of xli. There be no patronage advowsons ne chantries belongyng to the same I have not made eny partycular of the premysses to eny person but only thys and what fyne or Income wylbe gyven for the same I know not ne can not lerne Item the hospytall of Burford is graunted to Mr Harman thys berer for terme of hys lyfe and hys wyfe by the Kynges letteres pattents ex^d per Willm Cavendyssh audit'.

The clere yearly value of the hospytall of Seynt Johns in Burford with the londs to the same which the same Edmund and Agnes his wyff hathe for terme of their lyffes without fyne payenge for the same £12 3s. 10d. Inde pro decima 24s. 5d. Et remanent clare £10 19s. 5d. whiche to be purchased at x yeres is £109 14s. 2d.

Item certeyn parcells of the monastery of Bruerne ... etc ...

And so the hole sume the same Harman must paye is £180 18s.

1546. Exch.L.T.R.: Particulars for Grants. No. 542.37 HenryVIII. Harman Grantee.

Parcella terrarum et possessionum nuper monasterio sive prioratui de Keynshame in com Soms pertinentium.

Firma Rectorie de Burfford predicto cum una capella eidem annexata vocata Fullbroke Necnon cum omnibus terris tenementis pratis pascuis et pasturis Redditibus et suis decimis oblacionibus obvencionibus fructubus proficuis et commoditatibus quibuscunque eisdem Rectorie et capelle quoquomodo spectantibus seu pertinentibus sicut dimissa Thome Baylie executoribus et assignatis suis per Indenturam sigillo conventuali dicti nuper monasterii sigillatam datam sexto die maii anno regni regis Henrici octavi xxiii Videlicet a festo sti michaelis archangeli adtunc proximo futuro post diem datam Indenture usque finem termini nonaginta annorum extunc proxime sequentium et plenarie complendorum Reddendum inde ad festa Annunciacionis Beate Marie Virginis et sti Michaelis archangeli equaliter per annum   x*li*.

The said parsonage lyethe nere none of the Kynges maiesties houses parks forests or chases reserved for thaccesse or Repaire of his highnes   Also I have made the particulers herof to no other person nor I know any other desynes to by the same

ex^d per Ricardum Lambe deputat'

Mathie coltehirste audit' ibidem

Note the trees growyng about the scytuacion of the sayde parsonage and in the hedgs inclosing the glybe lands perteyning to the same wyll barely suffyce for staks for hedgeboote to repayre and meynteyne the sayd hedgs and fencs therfore not valuyd   ii*li*.

         ex^d per me David Clayton

Exch. L. T. R.: Particulars for Grants. No. 705. (*Not dated.*)

Entry of a lease of the Rectory of Burford and the Chapelry of Fulbrook granted by Edmund Harman and Agnes his wife to Thomas Smyth, generosus, for a term of 60 years from the year 1546, at a rental of £15, out of which 20s. is reserved as rent to the Crown.

[*Note.*—This document and the preceding one bear the signature of Edmund Harman.]

1547. Exch. L. T. R.: Augm. Off. Certificates of Chantries. No. 38. 1 Edward VI.

The certificat of Sir John Williams Knyght John Doyly and Edward Chamberleyn Esquyers commissioners appoynted by the Kyngs maiesties commyssion to them directed and berynge date the vi^th of Februarye in the fyrst yere of the reigne of our sovereigne lorde by the grace of God Edward the Syxt . . . etc . . .

The parissh and town of Burford   The guilde of our Lady in the howselyng people dxliiii.   said parishe Churche.

Certeyn lands and tenements gyven by divers persones to the fyndyng of a prest and to gyve to pore people of the towne yerely and to the mendynge of hyghways and comyn brydges of the same towne and the said prest to pray and synge for the founders and all Crysten soules for ever.

Thomas Plomtre Incombent there of thage of xl[ta] yeres a man well learned able to kepe a cure had for hys salary yerely vii*li*. and hathe non other lyvynge nor promocion but only this stipend.

The value of all the lands and tenements to the same belonging ys
yerely xvi*li*. x*s*. x*d*.
Repryses yerely xxxii*s*. ix*d*.
And so remayn clere (left blank).
Plate and Jewels weyng by estimation x ounces.
Ornaments valued at xx*s*. xx*s*. x *oz*.

Obits there Founded by divers persons whiche gave certeyn Annuall rentes going oute of theyre lands to have certeyn obitts theyre for ever.

Incombent none.
The said Annuall rents goinge oute of the said lands be of the yerely value of xxx*s*.
Ornaments plate & jewells to the same none.

Memor[d] that the saide towne of Burford ys a very greate markett towne Replenyshd with muche people And needfull to have a Scole there And the said lands was gyven to the mayntenance of hyghwayes and Brydges and to pore people And the Bretherne of the said Guylde at theyr costs and charge dyd Builde a chapell of our Lady annexed to the parishe church there of theyre devosion and dyd fynde a prest to mynyster ther and to teache chylderne frely and after that at divers tymes certeyn men of theyr devosione dyd gyve by will and feofment unto the said Guilde the lands and tenements aforesaid amountyng to the some of xvi*li*. x*s*. x*d*. to fynde a prest and to helpe pore people and to mend hyghwayes and the Comyn Brydges of the towne and so yt hath ben all wayes used so.

1547. Exch. L. T. R.: Augm. Off.: Particulars for Grants. No. 1618. 1 Edward VI.

Exchange of lands between the College of Fotheringhay and Edmund Harman.

The Rectory of Burford and Chapelry of Fulbrook, as above, as leased to Thomas Smyth. The rental is now given as £20 less the reserved rent to the Crown of 20*s*. a year. The date of Harman's Letters Patent for the grant to him is given as 6 May, 37 Henry VIII. (See *infra*, Letters and Papers, Henry VIII, p. 657.)

1548. ˙Exch. L. T. R. : Particulars for Grants. No. 1420. 2 Edward VI. John Bellowe Grantee.

Parcella terrarum pertinentium ecclesie parochiali de Burforde in dicto com Oxon ex donacione Willelmi Byshoppe.

Duae acre prati iacentes in Teynton ad ecclesiam de Burford ptin.	˙Redditus duarum acrarum prati in uno prato vocato lott meade in Teynton predicto modo in occupacione Ricardi Taylour ad voluntatem Reddendum inde per annum vi*s*. viii*d*.

Redditus resolutus predicto Edmundo Harman armigero exeuns de terris in Teynton predicto per annum   ii*s*..

Et valet clare ultra Reparaciones   iiii*s*. viii*d*.

There are not woods growyng upon the premysses suffycyent to ffens and enclose the same.

M^d that the forsaid Willm Bysshope dyd gyve the said lond in Teynton aforsaid to fynde a lampe Lyghte in the parishe churche of Burford.

1549. Exch. L. T. R. : Particulars for Grants. No. 2046. 3 Edward VI. Earl of Warwick Grantee.

An Exchange between the kings maiestie and the right honorable the Erle of Warr'.

Parcella terrarum et possessionum domini Regis vocatorum Warwikes lands in comitatu predicto.

Manerium de Burford in com pd.	Firma scitus manerii de Burforde dimissi Willelmo Ertons per literas domini Regis nuper Henrici vii^mi datas xviii^mo die ffebruarii anno regni sui xvii^mo ad terminum xxi annorum exceptis et

omnino reservatis domino regi et successoribus suis omnibus Boscis subboscis minerriis quarreriis ac aliis regali dignitati pertinentibus sive spectantibus omnibus reparacionibus eiusdem scitus ad onus domini Regis faciendis durante dicto termino et valet per annum

xi*li*. iii*s*. iiii*d*.

x & xii Decemb 1549

per Anth. Bochier auditorem.

Burford officium prepositi.	Redditus assisi diversorum tenencium domini regis ibidem solvendo ad terminos principales per annum xiiii*li*. vii*s*. ix*d*. ob.

Redditus sive firma xv acrarum terre Dominicalis in tenura Roberti lane v*s*. (*blank*) acrarum terre in tenura Margarete Dorne ad terminum vite ii*s*. iiii acrarum terre Dominicalis nuper in tenura Iohannis Barbor pro termino vite iiii*s*. iiii acrarum terre nuper in tenura Margarete Dorne ii*s*. cuiusdam campi continentis iiii acras terre nuper in tenura philippi Iames xii*d*. cuiusdam quarrerie domini regis vocate Whiteslate quarrey dimisse Willelmo Graunte ad terminum vite sue xiii*s*. iiii*d*. Unius crofti nuper in tenura Iohannis Frauncis per annum iiii*d*. firma unius crofti nuper in tenura Iohannis Frauncis per annum viii*d*. Firma cuiusdam quarrerie petrarum et tegularum vocate Strett quarry nuper in tenura Iohannis Evinger per annum vii*s*. Firma cuiusdam parcelle terre vocate ffefeld continentis iiii acras terre per annum xvi*d*. in toto xxxv*s*. viii*d*.

Redditus forinsecus viz de exitibus terre et centorum pasture molendini ac redditus diversorum tenencium quondam Iohannis Cale per annum' iiii*li*. x*s*. vi*d*. ob.

Nona reddituum ibidem per annum viii*s*. iiii*d*.

Inquisicio reddituum ibidem per annum vi*s*. viii*d*.

Perquisita Curie ibidem communibus annis will valew them if I be commanded.

xx*li*. ix*d*.

Allocationes reddituum terrarum in villa de Burford et Upton per annum xii*s*.

Expensa Computoris venientis ad compotum suum reddendum xx*d*.

Decasus redditus unius quarrerie vocate Whitslate quarry superius onerate ad xiii*s*. iiii*d*. per annum et in titulo nostro reddende ad vi*s*. viii*d*. eo quod remanet in manu domini regis.

Decasus ii quarreriarum quarum una vocatur Strete quarry et altera de novo invenitur per annum xi*s*. viii*d*.

Allocatio reddituum exeuntium de dicto manerio domino Cobham per annum iii*s*. iiii*d*.

Ricardi Hannes prepositi ibidem per annum xx*s*.

cxviii*s*. & vii*d*.

Et valet clare per annum li*s*. xi*d*.

ex^{d} xvii December 1549
Anth Bochier audit'

Burford Burgus Redditus assisi tenencium domini regis ibidem per annum xiiii*li*. ix*d*. ob.

Tolnetum cum stallagio nundinarum et marcatorum ibidem per annum viii*s*. x*d*.

Perquisita curie ibidem communibus annis I will value them if I be commanded.

xiiii*li*. ix*s*. vii*d*. ob.

Allocationes reddituum ibidem per annum   xx*s.*

Et valet clare per annum   xiii*li.* ix*s.* vii*d.* ob.

1549. Exch. L. T. R. : Particulars for Grants. No. 2025. 3 Edward VI. Venables Grantee.

Com. Oxon. Certe Terre et tenementa pertinentia ad Gildam sive fraternitatem Beate Marie in Burford in comitatu predicto ut sequitur

> parcella possessionum nuper
> gilde sive fraternitatis beate marie
> in Burforde in com predto

Redditus firme unius tenementi existentis in Burforde predicto vocati le brodeyates cum gardino adiacente modo in tenura Iohannis Iones ad voluntatem reddendum inde per annum   xxvi*s.* viii*d.*

Redditus firme duorum messuagiorum existentium in le highe strete et in vico vocato Seint Iohns Strete dimissorum Roberto Allflett per Indenturam datam xiiii die Ianuarii anno xxxi° h octavi pro termino triginta unius annorum reddendum inde per annum

                            xxii*s.*

Redditus firme unius tenementi cum gardino ibidem dimissi Willelmo Roberts alias Fyssher per Indenturam datam xiiii die Ianuarii anno xxxvii Regis pro termino triginta unius annorum reddendum inde per annum   xx*s.*

Redditus firme unius tenementi cum gardino et uno horreo in Wytney Strete dimissi Iohanni Wylkyns per Indenturam datam die et anno supradictis reddendum inde per annum   xxi*s.*

Redditus firme unius tenementi iacentis in vico predicto cum horreo et gardino dimissi Willelmo Hedges per Indenturam datam xiiii die Ianuarii anno xxxi h viii*vi* pro termino triginta unius annorum reddendum per annum   xi*s.*

Redditus firme unius horrei cum gardino adiacente dimissi Thome Tomson per Indenturam datam xii die Ianuarii anno xxxiiii h viii*vi* pro termino triginta annorum reddendum inde per annum

                            vii*s.*

Redditus firme tertie partis hospitii ibidem vocati le Crowne in tenura Simonis Wynchester ad voluntatem reddendum inde per annum   xii*s.* iiii*d.*

Redditus firme unius tenementi ibidem dimissi Ricardo Hodges per Indenturam (ut dicitur) reddendum inde per annum   x*s.*

Redditus firme unius tenementi ibidem dimissi Iohanni Browne per indenturam (ut dicitur) reddendum inde per annum   xiii*s.* iiii*d.*

Redditus firme unius clausi iacentis in venella vocata batts lane dimissi Iohanni Browne per Indenturam datam xiiii die Ianuarii anno xxxiiii h viii^vi pro termino viginti unius annorum reddendum inde per annum · x*s*.

Redditus firme unius gardini iuxta gildenfforde dimissi Ricardo Wynpytt per Indenturam datam in festo Sti Thome Apostoli anno xxxiii° h viii^vi pro termino septuaginta annorum reddendum inde per annum viii*d*.

Redditus firme unius gardini dimissi Ricardo Chawley per Indenturam (ut dicitur) reddendum inde per annum xii*d*.

Redditus firme unius gardini in tenura Iohannis Hans ad voluntatem reddendum inde per annum x*d*.

Redditus firme unius gardini in tenura Iohannis Ionys predicti ad voluntatem reddendum inde per annum viii*d*.

Redditus firme cuiusdam parcelle prati ibidem vocate le ladys hame dimisse Ricardo hans per Indenturam (ut dicitur) reddendum inde per annum x*s*.

Redditus firme unius tenementi iacentis in vico ibidem vocato Shepe Strete dimissi Edmundo Sylvester per Indenturam (ut dicitur) reddendum inde per annum xviii*s*.

Redditus firme unius tenementi in alto vico ibidem cum gardino dimissi Marco Payne per Indenturam pro termino annorum reddendum inde per annum · vii*s*. iiii*d*.

Redditus firme xi acrarum terre arrabilis in campis de Upton in tenura Iohannis Lambert ad voluntatem reddendum inde per annum ii*s*. viii*d*.

obit Willm Flodyate infra ecclesiam de Burford prdto in com predto. Redditus firme trium acrarum prati cum pertinenciis iacentis et existentis in quodam prato ibidem vocato le highe mede concessarum per Willelmum Flodyate predictum pro le obit eiusdem Willelmi per annum vi*s*. viii*d*.

M^d that there ys no other landes perteyning to the tenements above mencyoned other then suche as ys heryn declared other then orchards and gardenplots Summa totalis x*li*. xiiii*d*.

[*Note.*—As entered on this document the properties are placed in seven groups. The first comprising the first nine entries, the second comprising the Batts lane close alone, the third comprising the next four items, and the fourth comprising the Ladyham item alone, are marked 'in libero socagio'. The two next items make a fifth group, and the arable land at Upton and the obit each stand alone.

A calculation of the value at 23 years' purchase has been roughly made on the membrane.]

1564. Exch. L. T. R. : Augm. Off. : Particulars for Leases. Elizabeth : Oxon. Roll I, no. 47.

Com. Oxon. Parcella Terrarum et possessionum nuper Gilde sive fraternitatis Beate Marie in Burforde in dicto comitatu pertinentium.

Burford Villa. Firma unius tenementi cum uno clauso et gardino modo vel nuper in tenura Simonis Wysdome pro annuali redditu

vis. viiid.

Firma unius messuagii cum gardino modo vel nuper in tenura Roberti Smythear pro annuali redditu   xiii<i>s</i>. iiii<i>d</i>.

Firma unius domus vocati a wollehouse modo vel nuper in tenura Roberti bruton pro annuali redditu   xiii<i>s</i>. iiii<i>d</i>.

Firma unius horrei modo vel nuper in tenura sive occupacione Thome Plommer pro annuali redditu   vi<i>s</i>. viii<i>d</i>.

Firma unius tenementi cum gardino modo vel nuper in tenura Ricardi Hunte pro annuali redditu   xvi<i>s</i>.

Firma unius tenementi cum pertinenciis modo vel nuper in tenura sive occupacione Ioanne Iones vidue per annum   viii<i>s</i>.

Firma unius cotagii nuper in tenura Elizabethe Dodde pro annuali redditu   iii<i>s</i>.

Firma unius tenementi cum pertinenciis modo vel nuper in tenura sive occupacione Ricardi Crompe per annum   viii<i>s</i>.

Firma unius tenementi cum pertinenciis modo vel nuper in tenura sive occupacione Roberti Iohnson per annum   xii<i>s</i>.

Firma unius tenementi cum pertinenciis modo vel nuper Thome Waterman per annum   vi<i>s</i>. viii<i>d</i>.

Firma unius tenementi cum pertinenciis modo vel nuper in tenura Stephani Grene per annum   vi<i>s</i>. viii<i>d</i>.

Firma unius tenementi cum pertinenciis modo vel nuper in tenura Rogeri Tuncks per annum   viii<i>s</i>.

Firma unius tenementi cum pertinenciis modo vel nuper in tenura Thome percyvall per annum   vi<i>s</i>. viii<i>d</i>.

Firma unius tenementi cum pertinenciis modo vel nuper in tenura Thome Hoke pro annuali redditu   viii<i>s</i>.

Firma unius tenementi cum pertinenciis modo vel nuper in tenura Rogeri Baker per annum   ix<i>s</i>.

vili. xiis.

Decasu redditus unius tenementi nuper in tenura Ioanne Iones vidue et postea Thome pecock superius onerati ad viii<i>s</i>. per annum   Reprise
Eo quod modo totaliter in decasu existit   viii<i>s</i>.   ut in

Redditu Resoluto domino Manerii de Langley et Burford per annum

xxs.

xxviiis.

Remanet ultra per annum   ciiiis.

M^d the premisses be so farre and greatly in Decay that xxx*li*.
will not Repayre them as by an Inquysycyon taken the thyrde day
of September in the fourth yere of the Reigne of the Quene that nowe
is before James Longeworthe esquyre and John Smythe gent appereth
Notwithstandinge one Thomas Smythe and Thomas Devyes are
contented to take the same by lease for lx yeres without fyne byndinge
them selves to all Reparacyons and payenge the Quene cxii*s.* by yere
So that they may have great tymber yerely allowed duringe theyr
terme for the Repayringe thereof And also have a lease of the parsonage of Holywell of the yerely Rente of xl*s.* for xxx yeres without
fyne.

[Follows a valuation of the Rectory of Holwell, and a memorandum that
' there be but two or three farms whereof the farmer of the Rectory hath
tythe Although it is commonly called a Rectory yet in deed it is but the
tythe of Holywell within the parish of Bradwell '.]

22 Aug. 1564 Make out ii lesses of the premysses unto Thos Smythe
and Thos Devyes viz of the houses for lx yeres and of the parsonage for
xxi yeres and the sum to be without fyne for consideracyon they
shall retayne the sume of viii*s.* now divertyd and at theyr own charges
see the howses well repayred.   (Signed—Winchester.)

1564. Exch. L. T. R.: Augm. Off.: Enrolments of Leases. 6 Elizabeth, Roll 17.

Oxon. Regina omnibus ad quos . . . etc . . . Salutem.

Cum Redditus octo solidorum per annum de et pro quodam cotagio
in Burforde in comitatu nostro Oxon modo vel nuper in tenura sive
occupacione Iohanne Iones vidue parcella possessionum dicte nuper
guilde sive fraternitatis beate marie in Burforde predicto nobis aut
progenitoribus nostris per multum tempus Responsi non fuerunt
Cumque diversa messuagia et cotagia in Burford predicto in dicto
com Oxon parcella possessionum dicte nuper Guilde sive Fraternitatis
beate marie in Burford predicto in eodem comitatu adeo in ruina et
decasu existunt ut vix pro summa triginta librarum valeant reparari....

And whereas nevertheless Thomas Smyth and Thomas Devyse
wish to have a lease of the premises, a lease is therefore granted to
them for 60 years at a rental of £4 18s. 8d. a year of the following
premises, possessions of the late Gild :

Cottage`	—occupier	Simon Wisdome
Messuage—	,,	Robert Smyth
Barn —	,,	Thomas Plommer
Cottage —	,, .	Richard Hunt
,, —	,,	Johanna Jones
,, —	,,	Elizabeth Dodde
,, —	,,	Richard Crompe
,, —	,,	Robert Johnson
,, —	,,	Thomas Waterman
,, —	,,	Stephen Grene
,, —	,,	Roger Tuncks
,, —	,,	Thomas Percyvall
,, —	,,	Thomas Hocke
,, —	,,	Roger Baker.

Dated 22 October, 6 Elizabeth.

Same Roll, No. 13.

Cum una domus vocata a Wollehouse in Burforde in comitatu nostro Oxon nuper in tenura sive occupacione Roberti Bruton parcella possessionum nuper Guilde sive Fraternitatis beate marie in Burforde predicto annui valoris tresdecim solidorum et quatuor denariorum magnopere in ruina et decasu existit ut sine magno sumptu reparari non possit. . . .

(Similarly leased to Smyth and Devyse with a parcel of land, and with the Rectory of Holwell, now or late in the tenure of Simon Wisdome, part of the preceptory of Quenington, for a term of 21 years at a rental of 13s. 4d. for the Woolhouse and 40s. for the Rectory.)

Dated as the preceding.

1565. Same Roll, No. 24.

A lease of the Woolhouse and the Rectory of Holwell to Simon Wisdome for a term of 20 years, as lately leased to Thomas Smyth and Thomas Devise, the total rental now to be 53s. 4d. a year, and the lessee to pay a fine of two years' rent, 106s. 8d.

Lease signed W. Burghley.

1566. Exch. L. T. R.: Augm. Off.: Particulars for Leases. 8 Elizabeth : Oxford, Roll I, no. 3.

Com Oxon. Terre a Regine Maiestate concelate et iniuste detente in com predicto.

Parochia de Burford.

Redditus sexdecim acrarum terre arrabilis iacentium et existentium in Burford predicto modo vel nuper in tenura sive occupacione Thome Offlytt antehac per quosdam ignotos ad inveniendum et manutenendum unius anniversarii in ecclesia de Burford predicto date et appunctuate existens per annum . iiii*s*.

Redditus unius acre terre arrabilis vocate Iesus acre et unius acre pasture in alto prato de Burford iacentis et existentis in Burford predicto modo vel nuper in tenura sive occupacione Gardianorum ecclesie de Burford antehac per quosdam ignotos ad inveniendum et manutenendum unius anniversarii in ecclesia predicta data et appunctuata existentia per annum ii*s*.

Redditus unius acre prati et ashurve vocate a swath . . . modo vel nuper . . . Thome Calcote . . . ad inveniendum . . . cuiusdam Luminis in capella Ste Katherine in Burforde . . . xiiii*d*.

Redditus unius dimidie acre prati vocate Cakebred land . . . modo vel nuper . . . Thome Freer . . . unius Anniversarii . . . viii*d*.

Redditus unius tenementi . . . modo vel nuper . . . Philippi Glover antehac per Thomam Hynde clericum ad inveniendum . . . unius anniversarii . . . xiii*s*. iiii*d*.

Redditus medietatis unius tenementi viz the moiety of an house . . . modo vel nuper . . . Iohannis Impe . . . unius anniversarii . . . xii*d*.

Redditus unius pecie terre vocate a plott of grownde iacentis atque existentis in platea Sti Iohannis anglice St Iohns Strete ac duarum acrarum terre arrabilis iacentium et existentium in campis de Upton . . . nuper . . . Willelmi George et iam in tenura Simonis Wysdome . . . ad inveniendum . . . unius luminis vocati a torchelight in ecclesia de Burforde predicto . . . vi*s*. viii*d*.

Redditus unius pecie prati vocate a plott of medowe iacentis et existentis in Bury Orchard . . . nuper Thome Freer . . . unius anniversarii . . . v*s*.

Redditus unius tenementi . . . modo vel nuper . . . Kellam Chaunce . . . ad inveniendum . . . presbiteri ad celebrandum missam in capella Sti Thome in Burford predicto . . . xvi*s*. viii*d*.

Redditus unius shope viz a shopp . . . modo vel nuper . . . Willelmi Partridge . . . ad inveniendum . . . presbiteri ad celebrandum missam in Capella Sti Thome . . . vi*s*. viii*d*.

Redditus quatuor tenementorum cum pertinenciis et horreo . . . modo vel nuper . . . Gardianorum ecclesie de Burford . . . unius anniversarii . . . iiii*li*. vi*s*. viii*d*.

[Against this last item is noted : ' This parcell and thother parcell of xiii*s*. iiii*d*. aforsaid passed in the name of Henrie Farre and all the residue except iiii*s*. in Bampton passed in the name of Henrie Hawthorne '.]

19 June, 1566.   Make a lease of the premisses to the saide Henrie Hawthorne for terme of twenti one yeres.   (Signed—Winchester.)

1566. Exch. L. T. R. : Augm. Off. : Enrolments of Leases. 8 Elizabeth, Oxfordshire, Roll IV, no. 5.

A lease to Henry Hawthorne of the premises specified.

It appears in the preamble to the lease that the lessee was the informer upon whose allegations the lands had been confiscated. The preamble runs : ' Cum omnes terre tenementa et alia hereditamenta cum pertinenciis inferius in presentibus specificata diu antehac a nobis et progenitoribus nostris subtracta et concelata fuerunt usque in tertium diem Septembris ultimo preterito Quo modo ad sectam et ex industria sumptibus et oneribus dilecti nostri Henrici Hawthorne ad manus nostras traducta et inventa sunt . . .', etc.

Lease granted for 21 years at the rents given in the preceding. Dated 12 July, 8 Elizabeth.

1566. Same Roll, no. 7.

A lease to Henry Farre of Barrington, com. Berks. ' at the instance and request of Henry Hawthorne ', of the tenement mentioned above occupied by Philip Glover and of the four tenements occupied by the Churchwardens ; for 21 years at the rents specified above. Dated 12 July, 8 Elizabeth.

1584. Exch. L. T. R. : Augm. Off. : Particulars of Leases.

Com. Oxon.   Rectoria de Burforde et   Parcella possessionum nuper
          Capella de Fulbroke. ·   collegii de Foderinghaie.

Described and valued as above (p. 642), as let to Thomas Smyth under the seal of Edmund Harman.   .

Make a lease of the premisses to the said Mary, Harman, and William Johnston for terme of their lives successively yeldinge to the Q Ma[tie] the said yerly rent etc.   (Signed—W. Burghley.)

8 Nov. 1584, unto Mary Johnston wief of Willm Johnston, Harman Johnston their sonne, William Johnston of Greys Inne gent, for iii lyves successively.

(h) LETTERS AND PAPERS, HENRY VIII

1510, 8 June. For William Gower, groom of the Chamber. Grant during pleasure of a tenement or inn called the George in the town of Burford on the Wolde, Oxon., with the lands thereunto belonging, forfeited by William Brampton to Henry VII, and by that King granted in tail male to John Basket, his servant, who has died without heirs male (Pat. Roll, 2 Henry VIII, ps. 2, m. 16).—i. 162.

1521, April. To Thomas Wildyng, Yeoman of the Ewery. Lease of Burford Mills and Upton Mill in the lordship of Burford, and a fulling mill in Burford, part of the late Earl of Warwick's lands ; for 21 years at a rent of £12 13s. 4d. and £4 of increase (Pat. Roll, 12 Henry VIII, ps. 1, m. 23).—iii, pt. 1, 480.

1526, April. To William Gittyns. Lease of the site of the manor of Burford, parcel of Warwick's Lands, for 21 years at the annual rent of £11 and 3s. 4d. of newly approved rent.—iv, pt. 1, 955.

1526, 29 Dec. Letter from Dr. John London to Mr. Larke, concerning the progress of Cardinal Wolsey's College. ' This last summer stone come in from Burford, Toynton, Barendon and Hedyngton, sufficient to find many mo masons than yet be here until Midsummer . . .'—iv, pt. 2, 1219.

[References to the use of Burford stone in the building of Christ Church are also to be found in vol. iv, pt. 3, p. 2681—' batering of toles at Burford ' entered on a list of accounts.; and p. 3042—a payment for ' quarries at Burford ' and ' Leper's quarry at Taynton '.]

1529, 28 Sept. Sir Richard Cornewayl to Thomas Cromwell. Asks him to send a man to Richard Monyngton at Haryngton one mile from Burford on the Wold, to purchase out the writ for the knight's expense for the time of Parliament.—iv, pt. 3, p. 2659.

1534, 4 Feb. Petition to the Commons in Parliament by Thomas Phillip, citizen of London, who has been three years a prisoner in the Tower. The Bishop of London has . . . ' untruly surmised against him that he has been a preacher, a teacher, a schoolkeeper, now at Salisbury, then at Burford . . . and a reader of damnable lectures '. An accusation of heresy had been made against him, alleging that he possessed a New Testament in translation.—vii. 64.

1536, June. List of persons appointed to various offices. ' . . . Sir John Brudges and Thomas Brudges . . . the keeping of the manor and park of Langley, the stewardship of Mynster Lovel, Burford, Shipton, Spellesbury, Langley . . . the bailiwick of Chadlyngton and the keepership of Cornbury Park.—x. 358.

[Note.—Cf. the sepulchral tablet in the church of Charlbury, Oxon., to ' Iohanna nuper uxor Thome Bridges Armigeri, Senneschalli excellentissimi ac metuendissimi viri Henrici octavi, Dei gracia . . . etc . . . Hundredi sui de Chadlington . . . necnon maneriorum et villarum suarum de Burford et Minster Lovell . . . etc . . .']

1536. Accounts of Henry Norres, Esquire to the Body. ' Arrearages
. . . Stewardship of Burford Town, £8 12s. 4d.'—x. 364.

1537. Nicholas Austen, late Abbot of Rewley, to Thomas Cromwell.
Asks him to write in his favour to the bailiffs and burgesses of Burford
in the Wolde for a grant of a service called the ' Priory ' in that town
of £11 a year, the holder of which, one Mr. Cade, is very old and sickly.
The town favours him because of his kindness shown to them in the
past. His pension allows him to take any ecclesiastical dignity so
that it pass not his pension.—xii, pt. 2, p. 476.

1538, Feb. To John Johnes of Burford, Oxon. Lease of two
corn mills built under one roof called ' Burford mylles ', a corn mill
called Upton mill in the lordship of Burford, and a fulling mill in
Burford, part of the lands of the late Earl of Warwick, for 21 years
at £16 13s. 4d. rent and 4d. increase, on surrender by the said John
of a Patent, dated 3 May, 13 Henry VIII, granting a similar lease to
Thomas Wildyng, now deceased, his daughter and administrator
having sold her remaining interest to the said John.—xii, pt. 1, 139.

1538, 22 Feb. Sir Richard Ryche to Thomas Cromwell, reporting
a survey made by him and other officers of the lands of the late
monastery of Abingdon.

' . . . Besechyng you to sygnyfye to the Kyngs magestie that the
town ys sore decayed and lyke dayly more to decaye onles provysyon
there be made to sett the people on worke to drape clothe wherby
undowghtydly his grace shulde moche contente the people and
Inhabytaunts thereabought whiche assurydly ben a greatt nomber.
Sygnyfying to you also there ys a certen Clothemaker callyd Tucker
dwellyng in Burtheforde whiche hathe requyryd me to advertyse
the kyngs magestie yf his grace wyll leatt to hym too fullyng mylles
now decayed, the flottgates the ffysshyng and farme callyd the Rye for
suche Rents as they shalbe surveyed with a convenyent howse for his
occupacon Affyrmyng to me he wyll bestowe wykely duryng his lyff in
wages to clothe makers in the sayd Towne a c markes sterlyng whiche
shulde moche inryche the Towne And kepe the people from Idelnes. . . .'

4 March. Thomas Cade to Thomas Cromwell.

' Plecythe ytt your good lordshyp to be advertysed thatt I am In-
formyd by thys Berar thatt he hathe entryd communicacion wythe
Mast^r Rytche and oder Commyssionars to the kynges hyghnes and
hathe made sewt to them to take to ferm certeyn landes mylles pasturs
medows and waters wythe oder commodities belonginge to the same
late in use off the kynges monastery off abyngdon now in the possession

off the kynges sayd hyghnes and for hys further spede in the premisses
he Intendythe to make sewt to your lordshyp and hathe made me
Desyr to be peticioner and sewter to your s^d gode lordchyp for hym
and hathe gode trust thatt the rather att my pore contemplacioun
you wylbe the better lord to hym and be the rather content to here
hys resonabull sewtes and soo gode my lord I moste hartylye beseche
yow and soo beynge ye schalbe assured off my contynewell prayer
duringe my schort lyff and over thatt my lord ye schall have hym
redy att all tymes aswell in hys own person as also wythe xx tall men
att hys leadynge to serve the kynges hyghnes att yowre comaundement
/ my lord ye schall nott fayll to approve hym a very substanciall and
just man in hys dealings bothe in word and dede and he settythe in
occupacione dayly fyve c off the kynges subjetts of all sortys and yff
he myght have kardinge and spynnynge he wolde sett many moo in
worke than he dothe for thys I know for trewthe my lord thatt yff
ye be gode lord to hym he wyll sett the Inhabitants off the kyngs
Town off Abyngton yff they woll wyrk / on occupacion soo thatt they
schall gayn more in few yeres commynge than they have done in
xx^{ti} yeres past for thys I know my lord thatt wekely ned constreyneth
hym to send to abyngdon hys kart lodyn wythe woll to be kardyd
and spann or els many tymes hys workmen schuld lak work and
lykewyes he sendythe to Strodwater my lord I know the man soo
substanciall and just off hys word and dede thatt ytt gyvethe me
Boldnes to wryte in hys favour trustinge my lord thatt ye wyll be
the better lord to hym att thys my pore sewte and in soo beynge he
schall gyff yow xx^{ti}li. to by yow a sadell and hys servic wythe my
dayly prayer as knowys best the holy trynite who ever have yow my
lord in hys blessyd tuicion wythe longe contynewans in Joyous selyate
/ from Burford on the wold the iiii day off marche wythe rude hande
of yower daylye orator   Thomas Cade.

[*Note.*—The two preceding extracts have been copied in full from the
originals as bearing upon the population of Burford at this date.]

1538, 11 April. Certificate of Sir Simon Harecourt knight and
Will. Fermour of an examination taken at Burford, co. Oxon, on a bill
of complaint by Will Hedgys the younger of Burford against John
Jones one of the Bailiffs.

On Thursday before Midsummer Day last John Jones was charged
by Thomas Thomson, then also Bailiff, to arrest one Bayman, whom
Thomson undertook to prove a traitor. Jones attached him and put
him to ward, but next day let him go.

Answer of Jones that Thomson called him out of bed to arrest Bayman, who had attempted to prevent the door of the town gaol being shut ; and only next day charged him with treason for assaulting the King's officers. Thomas Weyman, justice of the peace, to whom they referred the matter, charged them to take Bayman home again and punish him as an unthrift.

Hedgys's witnesses were Robert Jacobb, Humphrey Pyper, Wm. Nicholas, Nicholas Riley, Edmund Sylvester, and Richard Darnell.

Thomson confirmed Jones's defence. Witnesses for him were Wm. Hedges the elder, John Sharpe, Robert Jonson, Thomas Richards, Robert Payn, and Wm. Hewys.—xii, pt. 1, 278.

1539, 23 Aug. In Thomas Cromwell's accounts : ' Roger the falconer, for his charges at Burford, 10s.'—xiv, pt. 2, 342.

1542, March. To Thomas Edgare. Lease of the site of the manor of Burford for 21 years from the expiration of a 21 years' lease to Will Gittons by Patent 18 Feb., 17 Henry VIII, at £11 3s. 4d. rent.—xvii. 101.

1542, April. To Anthony Berker, clerk. Presentation to the perpetual vicarage of Burforde super Wolde, Lincoln diocese, void by death.—xvii. 161.

1542, Oct. Entry from the Books of the Court of Augmentations of the grant to Edmund Harman and Agnes his wife of the possessions of the late Hospital of St. John in Burford.—xviii, pt. 1, 547.

1543, Nov. Grant in fee of the above for £198 6s. 0½d., bells, lead and advowsons excepted.—xviii, pt. 2.

1545, May. Grant in fee to Edmund Harman and Agnes his wife of the Rectory of Burford and Chapel of Fulbrooke, with the advowson of Burford Vicarage, formerly of Keynsham Priory, Somerset.—xx, pt. 1, 424.

1545, July. Grant in fee to Edmund Harman of two grain mills called Burford Mills, another grain mill called Upton Mill, and a fulling mill in Burford, with a meadow called Le Holme and land called Piggehill in Burford, all in tenure of John Jones. For £187 3s. 8d.—xx, pt. 1, 662.

1546, Feb. Licence to Edmund Harman and Agnes his wife to alienate to Edmund Sylvester certain lands of the late Hospital of St. John, viz. the lands at Asthall in tenure of Henry Coteler and the lands at Rysyngton Magna in tenure of Simon Wysdome.—xxi, pt. 1, 150.

(j) MISCELLANEOUS DOCUMENTS

1487. Ancient Deeds : A 11056. 13 December, 3 Henry VII.
Grant by Anne Countess of Warwick to Henry VII, of a great
number of castles, manors and lordships, including ' maneria et
dominica de Burford Shipton Spellisbury Chadlyngton hundredum
Langley cum pertinenciis in Com Oxon '. Endorsed as enrolled on
the dorse of the Close Roll 3 Henry VII.

1542. Exch. K.R. : Accounts, Bundle 60, no. 11.
The Musters for Bampton Hundrede, Anno xxxiiii° H. 8.

Burforde Burroughe with the Parryshe

Ablemen

John Sharpe	Nycholas Stane	
Robert Ennysdale	John Hardgrove	
Wyllyam Roberts	Robert Aulflett	
Henry Stringfellowe	Phillip Gryffith	
Nycholas Ryley	Willyam Kenner	
Thomas Taylor	Edmond Cordywell	
Nycholas Hyatt	Thomas Walbridge	
John A Wod	Thomas Haynes	
John Rogers	Henry Bacon	
Richard Hunte	fflower his fellowe	
John Roberts	Bytan Clawylde	ARCHERS
John Jurden	Henry Teynton	xlvii^ti
Alexsander Hodgis	Thomas Tucker	
John Smythiar	Rawfe Hyatt	
John Nychollys	John Myller	
Wyllyam Watt	Thomas Dunsden	
Willyam Barton	John Yate alias Huyet	
Thomas Dryng	John Dallam	
Edmund Sylvester	Willyam Nenwey	
John Lyones	George Stafforde	
Thomas Dyos	Thomas Butler alias Lawrence	
John Hans	Gyles Jones	
Thomas Colles	Thomas Spenser	
Willyam Hyatt		

John Jones	John Wylkens
Symond Wysdome	Thomas Aulflett
Robert Payne	John Fars
Willyam Hewys	Thomas West
Robert Browne	Jamys Myller
Robert Johnson	John Huys
Thomas Tomson	Richard Stanborne
Willyam Collens	John Adamson

Kenelme Chaunte
Crystofer Baker
Richarde Dawby
John Davys
Thomas Smyth
Robt Moppas
John Ympe
John Dodde
Hugh Colborne
Edwarde Ley
Willyam Harding
Willyam fflowre
Richard Elye

Roger Tuncke
Robt Bruton
Thomas Halyday
George Bell
Morres Lewis
Thomas George
John Browne
Willyam Grene
Willyam Lawrence
Willyam Kenner
Roger Togood
Alexsaunder Thomas

BYLMEN
xli[ti]

Le Armoure

The Borough Towne of Burford with Upton and Sygnett to finde
xxiiii[ti] men furnysshed vi Archers on Horsback xii Archers on foote
And vi Bylmen on ffoote.

Upton and Signett

Thomas Lamberte
Henry Patten   **ARCHERS iii**
Richard Nellys

[*Note.*—The Burford Muster roll is the largest of the Hundred. The
total is 88, and the Witney total is only 70 ; also Burford provided 47
archers and Witney only 27. The 'armoure' of Witney is 10 men against
24 from Burford.]

1546. Court Rolls : Portfolio 197, no. 15.

Court held at Burford on Tuesday next after the feast of St. Michael
the Archangel, 38 Henry VIII.

Richard Manyngton ⎱ Bailiffs.
Simon Wysdome   ⎰

Presentations : For being common bakers of bread and breaking
the assize : William Roberts and William Hodges, amerced 4*d.*
Thomas Tomson amerced 2*d.*, and Robert Starre 4*d.*

For being common bakers of bread and selling it in Burford for
excessive gain : Richard Ramsell of Stowe, John Fretherne and Thomas
Grye of Stowe—4*d.* each.

For selling fish there and making excessive gain : Simon
Wysdome, Richard Hedges, Edmund Sylvester and Robert Bruton—
6*d.* each.

And thereon the bailiffs aforesaid came and placed their offices in
the hands of the King, on which the Seneschal of the King elected

in their places Robert Payne and William Hewys to perform the duties for one year and they took the oath.

Robert Bruton was similarly elected Constable and took the oath.

1547. View of frank pledge, 6 April, 1 Edward VI.

Presentations : As common bakers : William Hodges, William Roberts, Robert Starre, 6d. each ; Thomas Tomson and Richard Dawby, 4d. each.

As common Brewers : Richard Chyld, William Collyns, John Wyddowes, and Richard Stayne, 1s. each.

As common alehouse keepers : Willm. Roberts, John Hewys, Alice Bocher, William Saunders, Robert Awflett, Thomas Awflett, Henry Stringfellow, Hugo Collyns, William Foster, Thomas Plomer, Kenelm Chaunce and Walter Mollyner, 2d. each.

As keepers of common hostels : Agnes Grene, widow, Thomas Barton, and Symon Wynchester, 4d. each.

As sellers of fish : Simon Wysdome, Richard Hodges, Edmund Sylvester and Robert Bruton, Wysdome 12d., Hodges 8d., and Sylvester and Bruton 4d. each.

As common Vintners : Richard Hannys and Agnes Grene, 6d. each.

1548. Court of the manor of Bury Barns, held 9 October, 2 Edward VI.

Upton Presentations : Oliver Hyde owes suit to the court.

Richard Dawby for ploughing contrary to ordination, 4d.

Signett Presentations : Thomas Moore gentleman owes suit to the court.

Simon Wysdome for ploughing on the ' merys ' to the damage of his neighbours, 4d.

William Hodges and William Patten, copyhold tenants, reported as having died.

1549. Burford Burgus, Extracts of the lawday there holden for our sovereign lord King Edward the sixth the third year of his reign.

Presentations : As keepers of common hostelries : Richard Teyne, Thomas George, 4d. each.

As common bakers : William Roberds and Robert Starre, 8d. each, Thomas Tomson, 2d. William Saunders, 4d. Thomas Gayes 6d. John Hill, Robert Smyth 2d. each.

As common Brewers : Richard Child, 2d. Will Collyns, 3d. Alys Bocher, widow, 2d. William Saunders, 4d. Richard Dalby, Thomas

Alflete, Walter Mollyner, 2d. each, Thomas George, 4d. Thomas Richards, 6d.

As common butchers : Richard Dalby, Symon Wynchester, 4d. each, John Jordan, 6d. Thomas Plomer, 4d. Edward Grene, 6d.

As common fishers : Symon Wysdome, Richard Hodges, Edmund Sylvester, 4d. each, Robert Brewton, 2d.

As common innholders : Richard Charley, 4d. Edward Maddok, amercement not entered.

As common vintners : John Hannys, Richard Charley, 6d. each.

1549. Augm. Off. : Deeds of Purchase and Exchange, G. 12. 3 Edward VI.

Grant of the town and manor of Burford by Edward VI to the Earl of Warwick, in exchange for other lands granted by Warwick to the King.

1597. Ancient Deeds, C. 7782. 1 August, 39 Elizabeth.

Release and quit claim by Lawrence Tanfeilde of ' the Pryorye neere Burford ', to Thomas Hewes alias Calcott, William Hewes alias Calcott, and Robert Hewes alias Calcott, of Burford,—all manner of actions as well real as personal trespasses escates rights titles interests claims debts duties suits quarrels judgements and demands whatsoever up to the last day of July last past.

(The deed bears Tanfield's signature.)

STAR CHAMBER PROCEEDINGS, Henry VIII, vol. vii, ff. 51–71 :—

Bill of Complaint of Rychard Hannes and John Lambart, bayliffs of the Towne of Burford in the countie of Oxon :—John Jones, collector of the xths and xvths within the Hundred of Bampton, directed his precept vnto the said bayliffs for the leuying and getheryng of the tax graunted by Parliament in the 32nd yere of the King's (Henry VIII) reign. Thereupon the said bayliffs caused all the Inhabitants wythin the towne of Burford to be assembled together in theyre common hall, and then and there, accordyng to theyre olde and auncyent vsage, caused a bill to be made and wryten of the names of all such persons inhabytynge within the said towne as were and shuld be contrybutory to the payment of the tax, with the somes of money that eury of them was then taxed att. In this bill Edmond Sylvester, oone of the inhabytants of the towne, was taxed and sessed at xxd., John Barker at iijs. iiijd., and Thomas Barton at iijs. iiijd., after the rate of oon peny of the shelyng of the rent of eury of theyre howses, like as all othyr were sessed. The bill was delivered to Symon Wynchester and Robert Alflete, constables of Burford, for the due collection of the money ; who repayred and cam vnto the seyd Edmond Sylvester, John Barker, and Thomas Barton dyvers and sundry tymes and requyred theym to make payment of the sayd somes of money sessed and taxed vpon them according as is aforeseyd ; but they, nothyng consyderyng theyre dutyes in that behalf, nor the olde and auncyent vsage and custome vsed and accustomyd within the towne, in most obstynat peruerse maner vtterly refused and denyed to paye the sayd somes. Moreover, they confederated themselves together with diuers others of the same towne, intendyng not only to wythholde and withstande the payment, but also to sett disordre and dyuysion amongst theyre cobrethren and the comyns of the towne, sayinge that they wolde make a comon wealth. Wherevppon certeyn of the auncyent men of the towne were sent vnto Sir John Bruggs, Knight, the King's Steward of the towne, desiring him to come vnto the towne for Reformacon and Redres of these abuses ; who coming, found the towne greatly owte of order and good Rule, and all mysordered persons suffered to go vnpunysshed. Certain of the seditious persons he therevppon comyted to warde ; notwithstanding which, there is still such great discorde and contencon stirred and moued amongst the Inhabytants, that the said Bayliffs dare not at this tyme ponysshe any offenders, or doo anythynge concernynge the good orderyng of the towne.

Defendant John Barker, in his Answer, says the complaint is made only of malyce and envy. He himself is none of the inhabytants of the towne, but is taxed with them of the owtwarde, that is, as he alleges, according to his goods and not according vnto the rents of theyre howses. Further, his howse, as a spirituall howse, ought not to be taxed. For the rest, he declares that whereas the tax was sessed at the rate of one penny in the shilling, the Bailiffs have levied it at the rate of twopence. Moreover, he denies that he hath at any tyme vsid himself in the sayd towne in any soche vnlawfull maner or fasshion as by the sayd bill is supposed. On the other hand, whereas there was a boke made and streted vnto the constables of the towne for the spedy collecon on the tax, when defendants desired to see this boke the bayliffs vtterly denied theyre request, saying how that they, nother none suche as they, shuld be made privie to know what the boke wold or dyd com vnto. Wherefore diuers of the inhabytants were privately and vnlawfully (as already alleged) chargyd vnto a further some then the some which they were (taxed) att.

A commission was appointed by the King to inquire into the alleged disturbances and abuses. It was composed of Sir Walter Stoner, knt., Sir John Bridges, knt., William Fermour and Thomas Bridges (Sir John's brother), and sat at Burford on the 20th of Sept., 33 Henry VIII, when the following witnesses were examined :—

William Hodges of Burford, baker, aged 60, 'borne within the towne of Burford, and hath kept his household there continually by the space of xl yeres ', who deposes that a hundred persons at least, being householders, were present in the Guild Hall when the taxation was made ; that the house called Ivy House, which defendant Barker now holdeth in Burford, hath been ever contributory to the common charges of the towne, such as the watch, and hath given the holy loff ; And furder he sayeth that he hath seen one John Clemson, somtyme dwelling within the house of the Hospital of Saint John in Burford, and there keping household, and having the Priour boarding in his howse, chosyn owte of the same howse to be constable of the towne of Burford.

Symon Wynchester, constable of Burford, bocher, aged 36 yeres.

Robert Johnson of the same town, showmaker, aged 50 yeres and above.

Thomas Richards of the same town, sadler, aged 66 yeres.

Robert Browne of the same towne, mercer, aged 50 yeres.

Jamys Grene of the same town, bocher, aged 46 yeres.

Robert Ennysdale of the same town, wullen draper, aged 46 yeres.

William Hewis of the same town, glover, aged 40 yeres.

William Roberts of the same town, baker, aged 40 yeres.

Who depose that the deposition of William Hodges is in everything true ; that the wief of Edmond Sylvester payed her husbonds porcyn to the constable, prayenge hym that he would speake nomore to her husbond for itt ; that there was nomore money gethered by the sessment than was truly accompted, but only the some of ijs. xd., which was gyven agayne to xij poor men ; that a true and perfect boke was made of the same, which boke was openly brought before Sir John Bridges and Thomas Bridges, Stewards of the towne ; that certain of the defendants, asserting the contrary, and resolved to have the matter newly examined and redressed, went with pen and inke and paper from howse to howse, to the number of twentie houses, requiryng eury man to take their parties, saying they wold make them as free as Bayliffs of the towne by Cristmasse Day, and that they should by and sell as freely as any Burgesse ; that after that the towne grewe into suche murmor and controuersye that there was like to ensue greate inconvenyence, insomuche that William Hiatt said vnto John Jones in the strete : Come forthe, and all thy men with thee, if they be fortie, for now wee are prouided for thee ; and the said Hiatt sayed vnto his owne wief, in the hyringe of one John Hannys of Burford, then constable : I trust ones to be Bayliff of the towne, and see some of the Burgesses hangyd, and to sitt vppon them my silf ; that Sir John Bridges and Thomas Bridges came to the towne and tooke vppon them the exaumynacon of the matter openly and thoroughly, and could fynde no falte in the officers nor Burgesses, on which occasion the said Sylvester, being askyd what was the cause of the grudge, aunsweryd that they could shewe none, forasmuche as the matter was before the Lord Chauncellor and the King's Counsaill, but said that that they did was for a comon wealthe ; and the forsaide Hiatt, then stondyng by, said Yea, and for the King's advauntage ; whervppon the said Sir John Bridges and Thomas Bridges wyllyd them to fynde suretie, which to doo they vtterly refusyd, and therevppon they were comyttyd to warde and letten owte agaynst the daye that they should appeare before the King's Counsaill.

The above were witnesses for the Burgesses and Bailiffs. Against the Burgesses and Bailiffs there were called the following :—

Henry Parratt of Burford, towne clerke, aged 32, who hath dwellyd within the towne but only fyve yeres.

Robert Alflet, smith, aged 40.

John Hayter, yeoman, aged 57, who sayth that he was in the Guild Hall in the mornyng, the daye of the assessment, when there weare no mo in the Hall but only the Bayliffs and oon John Jones, and ij mo with hym.

John Smythyer, husbondman, aged 50.

Thomas Ockford, wever, aged 26.

John Colyns, showmaker, aged 60, and Nicholas Stanes, laborer, aged 50, who sayeth that he was nother at the begynnyng nor at the end, and therefore what was doone for the taxacon he knoweth not.

Other witnesses, called on behalf of Edmond Sylvester, John Barker, and other defendants, were :—

John Barker of Burford, gent (one of the defendants).

Edmund Silvester, mercer.

Wllliam Hiatt, baker.

Thomas Barton, innkeeper.

Robert Wigpit, fletcher.

John Hewes, wever.

John Sands, servant to Thomas Abridges, Esq. and constable of Burford, who deposes that he had William Hiatt, and fyve others, to warde in the stokhowse for their misdemeanors.

The result of the inquiry is not disclosed by the documents.

B. EXTRACTS FROM MSS. AT THE BRITISH MUSEUM

B.M. Harl. 56, B. 3.

1372. 15 July, 46 Edward III.

Grant by William Sewale to William Kokerell of Boreford. ' Unum messuagium cum pertinenciis in Boreford scituatum inter messuagium predicti Willelmi Kokerell ex parte boriali et messuagium Iohannis Cakebred ex parte australi.' Of the chief lords, &c.

Witnesses : John Crosham, John Wenryssh, John Bruere, John Saleman, William Naylere.

B.M. Harl. 49, D. 36.

1380. Feast of St. George the Martyr, 3 Richard II.

Release and quit claim by Elizabeth, late the wife of John Deonye of Gloucester, ' in pura mea viduetate ', to Thomas Cawlyn, burgensis de Boreford. ' Omne ius in uno burgagio cum curtilagio adiacente et omnibus pertinenciis suis scituato in Wytteney stret de Boreford ex parte australi inter tenementum beate marie ex una parte et tene-mentum meum ex altera parte.'

Witnesses : John Wynrich, John Crosson, William Nailer, Robert Coteler, John Sclater, Roger Wynrich, Thomas Spicer, William Bernes, clerk.

B.M. Harl. 47, C. 47.

1404. 20 April, 5 Henry IV.

Indenture of lease between William Brampton of Oxford, mercer, and Margaret his wife, of the one part, and John Baker of Gloucester, draper, and Isabella his wife of the other part.

A tenement with garden adjacent ' in villa de Burford ' between the tenement of John ffauelour on the north and the tenement of Thomas Alys on the south.

Lease for seven years at a rent of ' quatuor libras argenti fidelis monete Anglie ' payable at the four usual terms of the year, the Feast of St. Michael, the Feast of St. Thomas the Apostle, the Annunciation of the B.V.M., and the Nativity of St. John the Baptist.

Clause providing that the lessors are to repair and maintain the house.

Clause providing that the lessees are not to sublet.

Clause providing for distress to be taken if the rent be fifteen days in arrear, and in the event of failure of the distress for right of re-entry and recovery of the house.

Witnesses : Henry Coteler, Thomas Spycer, Thomas Morcok, John Mason, John Stowe.

B.M. Add. Ch. 39958. 10.

1577. Exchequer Acquittance.

De Iohanne Moore Thoma Cooke et margareta Curteis Hertford Essex pro fine dimissionis in revercione certarum terrarum et alibi in Barkhamsted certarum terrarum mariscarum in No xxv^to 1577. Barking et scitus maneriorum de Estimanneo et Burford de eodem fine   xlii*li*. viii*s*. quadraginta duas
                                              libras octo solidos
                         Mich^is anno regni Regine Eliz' xix^mo

B.M. Add. Ch. 39971. 14.

1613. Exchequer Acquittance.

Oxon. 4 Nov. 1613.   De Reginaldo Edwards et Humfrido Repington pro redditu Rectorie de Burford et capelle de ffulbroke debito pro dicti anni fructu ad festum Sancti Michaelis Archangeli anno Regis Iacobi xi^o   x*li*. decem libr'

B.M. Add. Ch. 39971. 15.

1618. Exchequer Acquittance.

Oxon. 7 Nov. 1618.   De Lawrencio Tanfeild milite capitali Barone scaccarii pro redditu Rectorie de Burford et capelle de ffulbrooke debito pro dicti anni fructu ad festum Sancti Michaelis Archangeli anno Regis Iacobi xvi^to   x*li*. decem libras.

B.M. Add. Ch. 38960.

635. An Inventorie of the Goods and Chattels of Roberte Veysey

late of Chymney in the Countie of Oxon gentleman taken and appraysed the one and twentieth day of Iulie Anno dni 1635 . . .

[Follows an inventory of goods and chattels at Chimney, another of goods and chattels at Tainton, another of goods and chattels at Duckling-ton, and another of goods at Broadwell.]

1634. This part of the Inventorie followinge was taken the sixt day of October Anno dni 1634 at Burford by Christopher Glin Clerke and Tho. Randolph.

Item in the chamber over the hall one Chest one box and hamper

viis.

Item gloves, handkerchiefs, Points, a purse and three smale peeces of Lynnen Cloth and other lumber and a Cheste wherein these thinges lie

xxxvs.

[Follows a list of leases and mortgages in various places including these:]

A lease from Robert Collier of foure Yeard lands in Upton in Com Oxon for 86 yeares to come with promise that if 50^{li} p ann be paid for foure yeares with consideration then the lease to be voide dated 16th April Anno octavo Re Car valued att — cc<i>li.</i>

the mort-gager saith he hath paid this

A lease from Thomas ffrancis of a house in Burford for about 96 yeares to come valued att — c<i>li.</i>

A lease from William Hunt of a tenement in Burford for about 27 yeares to come with a provisoe that if thirtye pounds be paid then to be voide — xxx<i>li.</i>

[The total of the value of leases, mortgages, and debts by bond is entered at £7158 6s. 5d.; and the total value of ready money, household stuff, and cattle £324 11s. 6d.]

B.M. Stowe MSS. 752.

Letters from William Borlase to Lyttelton, Dean of Exeter.

1753. Fol. 155.

From Cirencester we came along the Foss, which, tho' call'd thus, is a Ridgeway and Roman, to Burford.

The Church at Burford has been built at several times : The Tower on which the Spire is erected, is near the middle of the building, and is of ye Saxon style : the Arches on which it stands are semicircular, low, and solid, and have a very ill effect on the inside of the Ch: being design'd doubtless for a much smaller building, than the Ch: is at present.—On the Outside of this Tower which is much more antient than the rest, there are three pannells or sham-windows, on the south side with a window of a very singular structure between them, and a window of a semicircular arch below them, all in ye Saxon style, which I therefore send you. All above this in the tower is more modern, but of no despicable gothick taste—On the outside coving of one of the windows in Saxon letters is this Inscr^n ORASE (for Orate) pro animabus Patris et Matris Iohannis Leggare per quem ista Finestra decoratur—This Ch: is not at all uniform, and divided into several Chancels and Isles—

The Priory, now the house of Mr. Lenthall, seems to be a mighty good old house, in perfect repair—the Chapel adjoyning has much Gothick ornament and some rich carvings over the Door. The whole would make a good Print, if Justice be done to it—but tis so neat than I can hardly think it prior to ye Reformation ; and the Plantations round it are too close and crowded for such a low situation.

[A little sketch follows of the Roundheaded windows on the south side of the Church tower, described ' Saxon Remains in the Tower of the Church at Burford June 30, 1753 '.]

C. EXTRACTS FROM THE MUNIMENTS OF BRASE-NOSE COLLEGE, OXFORD

BURFORD LEASES

circa 1250. Release and Quit-claim.

Sciant presentes et futuri quod ego Seyld uxor quondam Ricardi Beaufront de Bureford concessi et quietum clamavi pro me et heredibus meis in perpetuum Priori et canonicis de Nortun omne ius quod habui vel habere potui in illo dimidio Burgagio cum pertinenciis suis quod predictus Ricardus quondam vir meus et ego tenuit de prefatis canonicis in villa de Bureford Et in huius rei testimonium commune sigillum de Bureford rogatu meo huic scripto feci apponere Testibus Radulfo capellano Iohanne Annor Hugone Urri Martino fratre suo Radulfo camerario Henrico filio Nicholai Rogero le Nobble Ricardo pistore Aluredo le bonde Rogero Cockerel et curia burgencium de bureford.

1264. Indenture of Lease.

Anno dni mcclxiiii ad festum beati Gregorii Haec conventio facta inter Simonem priorem et canonicos prioratus de Caldenorton ex una parte et Walterum Adgar de Bureford ex altera parte videlicet quod dicti prior et canonici concesserunt et dederunt dicto Waltero unum dimidium burgagium cum domibus et curia edificatis cum curtilagio et pertinenciis suis in villa de Bureford ad terminum vite sue . . . que

Ricardus Beaufront quondam tenuit . . . Reddendum . . . sex solidos argenti. . . . Et non licebit dicto Waltero dicta edificia . . . alienare sine assersu et consensu dicti prioris . . .

Witnesses : Richard the Vicar, Henry Pride, Will Osebern, Robert de Bradeston, Will le Coluns, Ralph de Dicheley, Richard Wale, Ralph the cook, Walter the draper.

Same date. Counterpart of the above.

To the clauses providing against subletting, &c., is added the following clause : ' Et ad ista predicta fideliter observanda supponit se et omnia catalla sua mobilia et immobilia sub pena dimidie marce solvende dictis priori et canonicis et ballivis de bureford.'

Witnesses : The same.

1367. Tuesday next after the Feast of the Conversion of St. Paul, 41 Edward III.

Lease by the Prior and convent of Cold Norton to Robert le Cotelir ' seniori burgensi de Boreford '. A half burgage with appurtenances lying in the High Street of Burford in the western part between tenements of the said Robert le Cotelir on either side. For 60 years at 4s. a year.

Witnesses : Robert le Pope, Richard Saundres, John Wynrich, John Bruere, Thomas Stowe, John Crosson, Will atte Berne clerk.

1416. Sunday next after the Ascension, 4 Henry V.

Grant by Philip James of Borford to Robert Legg of the same. ' Dimidiam acram terre arabilis iacentem in campo de Borford super beldame furlong inter terram domini vocatam Mullelond ex una parte et terram Thome Spicer ex altera parte. . . .'

Witnesses : Thomas Spicer, Henry Coteler, William Coteler, John Spicer, John Punter.

1423. 26 June, 1 Henry VI.

Grant by Elizabeth Payne de Boreford in pura viduetate et legitima potestate to Richard Martyn and Johanna his wife. ' Dimidium Burgagium cum curtilagio adiacente cum omnibus pertinenciis suis iacentia in Boreford predicto in le Newelond inter tenementum beate Marie ex una parte et tenementum quondam Thome Wygewolde ex altera parte. . . .'

Witnesses : Thomas Spycer, Will Coteler, Richard Lavyngton, John Ponter, Simon Hosyer.

1429. Feast of St. Edmund the Archbishop, 8 Henry VI.

Lease from the Prior of Cold Norton to William Coteler, of

Boreforde, Burgess. Half Burgage on the west side of the High Street between tenements of the said William on either side.

1431. 7 April, 9 Henry VI.

Grant by Johanna late the wife of Richard Martyn of Boreford in pura viduetate to Roger Mylton and Johanna his wife. Half Burgage in le Newelond, described as above.

Witnesses : William Coteler, John Ponter, John Moysyer senior, Henry Bysshop, William Pynneller.

1435. 20 September, 14 Henry VI.

Grant by Roger Mylton and Johanna his wife to Robert Coburley of Boreford. The half Burgage as in the last.

Witnesses: William Coteler, Henry Bysshop, John Pynnok junior, William Pynneller, Richard Leverych.

1461. Feast of St. Mary Magdalen, 1 Edward IV.

Grant by Robert Coburley burgensis to Robert Mondy of Burford chawndeler. The half burgage 'in le newelond inter tenementa procuratorum beate Marie virginis ex partibus orientali et occidentali'.

Witnesses : John Pynnok junior, Henry Byschop, John Pynnok senior, Robert Cace, Richard Leverych.

1462. 14 April, 2 Edward IV.

Grant by Robert Coburley of Burford Shearman to Robert Mondy and Alice his wife. The half burgage as above and 4 acres of arable in the town and fields of Burford. ' Quod quidem Dimidium Burgagium cum curtilagio adiacente situatum est in Borford predicto ex parte orientali inter clausos procuratorum beate marie virginis in newlond ex utraque parte vocatum the berehowse quod nuper habui ex dono et feoffamento Rogeri Mylton et Iohanne uxoris sue Que quidem quatuor acre terre iacent in campis de Borford predicto quarum due acre iacent super le Worthe iuxta terram custodis Sti Iohannis hospitalis ex parte occidentali et alia acra iacet super Whitston furlong iuxta terram Iohannis Maddock de Seynat ex parte orientali et una dimidia acra terre iacet et abbuttat super viam que ducit versus Westwelle inter terram custodis hospitalis Sti Iohannis ibidem ex parte australi et terram quondam Thome Spicer ex parte boriali alia vero acra iacet super Beldamys forlong inter terram Domini vocatam Myllonde ex una parte et terram dicti Thome Spicer ex alia parte.'

Witnesses : Henry Byschop, John Pynnock senior, John Pynnock junior, John Stowe, John Maior.

1462. 14 April, 2 Edward IV.

Grant by Robert Coburley, hosyer, to Robert Mondi, chawndeler. Two half-acres of arable land, ' quarum una dimidia acra terre iacet in campo occidentali inter terram custodis hospitalis Sti Iohannis ibidem ex parte australi et terram quondam Thome Spicer ex parte boriali altera vero dimidia acra terre iacet in campo orientali super le Beldamysforlong inter terram Domini vocatam Millonde ex parte una et terram dicti Thome Spicer ex parte altera.'

Witnesses : Henry Bischop, John Pynnock senior, John Grove, John Mayor, Thomas Dyere.

1471. 11 May, 11 Edward IV.

Grant by John Wynchecombe of Borford chawndeler and Alice his wife to Richard Haddon. The half burgage and four acres of arable as above.

1488. Mortgage.

Be hytt knowyn to all men y^t I John Cubberly off ye towne off Burford in ye County off Oxenfordshere son and ayre off Robert Cubberly latte off Burford hath sold grantyd and promyssyd to Thomas Everard marchaunt off Burford ii cottagys and a crofte w^t ye pertynse ye whych I sold sum tyme to John Pynnoke ye younger as hytt a peryth in a dede wryttyn and selyd w^t my sele to ye foresayd John Pynnoke in ye ere of ye raigne off Kyng Edward ye fforeth sixteneth ere The whyche ii cotages and croft and ye pertynens when I ye forsayd John hath made a statte to ye forsaid Thomas Everard for ye forsayd ii cotages w^t a croft and ye pertynens att such day and tyme as ye forsayd Thomas Everard will desyre The whyche statte gevyn ye sympull obligacion bownd to y^s byll shall stond as voyd and yff hytt benott then to stond in hys grett strenkyth and power Wrytten in burford ye last day off september The er off ye reyne off Kyng hary ye viith after ye conquest ye iiiith in ye presens wrytyn and selyd off Rychard Hamdyn and John Hanne.

Bond attached (in Latin) for £30.

1488. 17 October, 4 Henry VII.

Grant by John Cobberley to Thomas Everard and Elizabeth his wife. Two cottages and a croft in Witney Street on the north side between a tenement of Thomas Umfry alias Maior on the west and a tenement of Richard Mosyer on the east, containing in length 30 feet and in width from the street to the close of Henry Bysshope on the north 20 feet ; the croft lying in a certain place called the

Newlond between a croft of John Pynnok on the east and a croft of the chantry of Blessed Mary on the west.

Witnesses : John Bysshope and John Botterell, then Bailiffs of Burford, Thomas Stawnton, John Hanne.

1493. 15 July, 8 Henry VII.

Grant by Robert Coke alias Moke of Chylliston to Thomas Everard and Elizabeth his wife. A messuage in Burford and seven acres of arable land. ' Quod quidem messuagium scituatum est in magna strata eiusdem ville ex parte orientali inter tenementum predicti Thome Everard ex parte australi et venellam que vocatur que (*sic*) Bordem-wetlane que se extendit versus ecclesiam ex parte Boriali.'

Witnesses : Thomas Dodde then Bailiff, John Laurans, William Glover, John Grene, William Bryce.

1514. 20 October, 6 Henry VIII.

Grant by Lambert Goughman of Burford, tailor, and Matilda his wife, lately wife of Thomas Parsons of Burford, smith, defunct, to John Fornby clerk, Rowlande Messynger clerk, and Henry Rathbone. A tenement in St. John's Street in Burford between a tenement of Thomas Kene on the east and a tenement of John Faller on the west.

Witnesses : Peter Aynesdale and Robert Reyley, then Bailiffs of Burford, Nicholas Butler, Nicholas Phippys.

1526. 2 August, 17 Henry VIII.

Grant by Katerine Evarard, late the wife of Thomas Evarard in pura viduetate, to Robert Syngulton, clerk, pro suo bono servicio michi. A tenement or messuage in Burford and sixteen acres of land with meadow and pasture, the messuage situate in the High Street between a tenement of William Este on the south and a way leading to the church on the north.

Witnesses : Ralph Bostoke, Johanna Turnor, William Bradshaw. Executed at Merston.

1526. 25 September, 17 Henry VIII.

Indenture of Sale by Robert Syngulton, clerk, to Matthew Smyth, John Hawardyn, and William Sutton, for 20 marks. The same property as in the last.

Peter Eynesdale and Richard Hannes appointed attorneys to give possession.

[*Note.*—The above is the Deed by which this property passed into possession of Brasenose College. From this point onwards the documents are leases granted by the College.]

1552. 22 November, 6 Edward VI.
Lease to Symon Wisdome of Burford, yeoman, of a half-burgage house with a garden platt. For 30 years at 6s. a year.

1559. 7 December, 2 Elizabeth.
Lease to Elyzabeth Sambiche of Burford, widow, and Andrew Sambyche, son to the said Elizabeth, of a messuage with seven acres of land in Burford field. For 21 years at 20s. a year.

1567. 5 December, 10 Elizabeth.
Lease to Willyam Wisdome of Burford, clothier, of the house leased to Simon Wisdom, for 30 years at 6s. a year, upon expiry of the term granted to Simon Wisdom or any forfeiture of the lease.

1600. 9 April, 1600.
Lease to John Templer, clothyer, of the house as leased to the Wisdoms.

1620. 8 November, 1620.
Lease to Symon Perkes, shoemaker, of the house as leased to Sambyche ; rent now 13s. 4d.

1636. Lease to the same with a heriot of 20s. added to the rental.

1651. Assignment of lease to Thomas Hunt, son in law to Symon Perkes.

1732. Lease to John Jordan of Burford, gentleman, of the house as leased to John Templer.

1743. Lease to Elizabeth Beesley of Burford, widow, of the house as leased to Hunt, described as next to the Three Goats Inn.

1753. Lease to William Jordan, schoolmaster, of the same, described as having a house of Robert Castle on the north and Elizabeth Clarke's messuage called the Three Goats' Heads on the south, and a house of William Taylor on the west.

1788. Lease of the same to John Kempster, perriwig maker.

D. DOCUMENTS PRESERVED IN THE BODLEIAN LIBRARY, OXFORD

Bodl. MSS. Arch. Oxon. b. 40 (Terriers).

Visus terrarum pertinentium Rectoriae et glebe ibidem xxiii^tio Anno mensis Iunii anno Regis Henrici septimi xvi^to per informationem Dni. 1501. Roberti Maihowe Gulielmi Patten Iohn Calaber Richardi Davis et aliorum fide dignorum   Est fylde

       Rectoria de Burford

Fyrste in a furlonge besydes Angecrosse at Halcrafte ende ii acres lyinge between the land of Jhon Howse on the west parte and the land called Kyllings land on the est parte

ıc. fur. abutting upon Bamptone waye. Item in a furlonge abuttinge upon Bampeton waye iiii acres lyinge together betwene the lande of Richarde Bisshope on the west and the lande of the lorde in the tenure of Wylliam Shepperd of Synett in the este.

Bampton waye fur. Item in a furlonge that goeth over Bampeton waye iii acres whereof di acre lyethe betwene the churche lands of Burforde on the est and the land called Heystonysland on the west and one lyethe betwene the land of Thomas Pole one bothe syde est and west and di unius acre abuttethe upon the northe ende of the same Acar towarde the northe and lyethe betwene the lande of William Patten of Synete on the west and the lands of the churche of Burford on the est and di an acre in the same furlonge lyinge betwene the land called Heystonisland on the west parte and the lande of Wylliam Shepperd on the est & di an acre abuttinge upon the north ende of the same di acre stretcheth unto Henfurlonge and lyethe betwixt the land of Thomas Pynnocke on the west and the lords land of Burford lyinge to his farme on the est.

Item besydes the said furlonge ther lyethe i acre & di whereof di acre abuttethe upon coppyd crosse towarde the southe and upon Henfurlonge towarde the northe & lyethe betwene the lande of Wyllyam Patten of Sinet on the west and the churche lande on the est, another acre abuttethe upon the sayd coppyde crosse towards the northe & lyethe betwene the lande of Robert Osmunde on the west and the land of Richard Byshop on the est.

Brodhedden furlonge. Item in a furlonge called brodehedden furlonge ii acres & di wherof lyethe di acre abuttinge upon Henfurlonge betwene the land of Thomas Pynnocke on the west and the land of the churche of Burford on the est & ii acres betwene the land of Sʳ Jhon Neweman one the west & the land of the pryor of Saint Jhon on the est.

Esterhen furlonge. Item in a furlong called Esterhenfurlonge one acre wᶜʰ lyeth betwene Moysers land south & the land of William Patten north.

Westerhen furlonge. Item in Westerhenfurlong di an acre wᶜʰ lyeth betwene the land of Wᵐ ffludyate north & yᵉ church land south.

Ridgwaye furlonge. Item in a furlonge besyds ridgway iii acres and di acre lying betwene the land of Jhon Lammer on the northe & the churche land on the southe Item i acre lyinge above the waye that ledethe from Burford to Whit hyll besyde the hedg called Shednills betwene the said hye waye north and Salmons slad southe Item another acre by the said (*sic*) lying betwene the said land called Salmons land south & the land of William Patten of Synet northe Item half an acre Besyde the Whit hyll betwene the land of Jhon marriner southe & the land of Jhon Lammer northe.

Item in moresty furlonge abuttinge upon Whit waye half an acre betwene the land of William Patten the younger southe and the pryor of St. John northe. *moresty furlonge.*

Item in Hiot half an acre betwene Salmons land on the northe & the churche land on the southe Item in the west syde of Whit waye di acre betwene the land of Jhon legger south and the land of William patten ye younger north. *Hiot.*

Item in Uphedfurlonge i acre betwene the land of Robert Jennens on the est & the land of William ffludyate west Item di acre lying betwene the church land on the est (*sic*). *uphed furlonge.*

Item in Brodhedden furlonge iiii acres wherof one acre lyethe betwene the land of Jhon Byllinge on the est & the land of Wm Patten on the west Item ii acres lyinge betwene the land of William Shepperd west & the heystons land est Item i acre lyeth betwene the land of Jhon fan west & the land of Richard Davy est Item one acre betwene Heystons land on the west & the land of William ffludyate est. *Brodhed-den furlonge.*

Item in Offley furlong i acre inter terram nescitam. *Offley furlonge.*

Item in Sawnfyfe ffurlonge i acre betwene the land of William Shepperd north and southe. *Sawnfyf furlonge.*

Item in Hedsondye furlonge i di acre called the head-half acre betwene the churche lande on the southe. *Hedson-dye furlon*

Item juxta Stertwell halfe one acre betwene Heystonisland on the west & the land called the Stert on the est Item in a furlonge abutting upon brodhedden furlong on the south di an acre betwene the Churche land est and heystonysland west Item in the same furlong di an acre that is to say di an acre betwene the church land est & St. Jhon west Item in the sayde furlong i acre betwene the land of Wm Patten est. *Stertwell.*

Item in Bampton waye furlonge at copyslade di an acre betwixt the land of the churche est & Jhon Marriner west Item one acre betwene the land of Thomas Pynnocke Northe & Jhon Byshops land southe Item in the southe syde of Bampton waye i acre betwene the land of Jhon Byllinge est & the land of Edmund Tame west *Cope-slade.*

Item in the same furlonge di an acre betwene the churche land est & the land of Wm Pattyn west   Item ibidem halfe an acre besyd Shilton way betwene the land of the churche est & the land of William ffludyate west.

Bellam Furlonge.   Item in a furlonge abuttinge upon Bellam Furlonge i acre betwene Heistonsland west and Salmons land est.

Item di an acre betwene the land of Richard Davy west and the churche land est   Item in the nether end of Bellam furlonge i acre betwene the land of William Patten est and Salmons land west.

Whitston furlong.   Item in Whitstone furlong ii acres of Hedlands betwene Heystonys land est.

Comfast furlong.   Item in comfast furlong one acre betwene ye land of Jhon newman north & ye land of Wm Patten south.

Salmons pathe.   Item i acre goinge over Salmons pathe betwene the land of Richard Davy northe & Salmons land south   Item a fferdelland abutting upon Salmons path   Item one ley and a half betwene the churche land north and Richard Davy southe.

Downe ffurlonge.   Item in Downe furlonge i acre betwene the land of Wm Patten west & Jhon márriner est   Item one acre abuttinge upon the Downe acre way betwene the land of Thomas Pynnock south & the land of the pryorye of Saint Jhon north   Item one acre goynge over Salmons pathe betwene Jhon Marriner southe   Item one acre in Deane acre betwene the land of William Patten south and the land of Janyver northe.

Summa acrarum in le est

ffyld   xlvii

et di. ffer.

1576

Est West ffylde

Juxta Ship-strete.   ffyrst in est fylde at the townsende of Burford besyde Shepestret crosse ii acres wher one lyeth betwene the colverhey est & the land called Heystones west and one other acre lyeth in the west syde of the same Heystonys next to the waye.

Item in the same furlonge lyethe ii acres betwene the land of thomas Pynnocke southe & the land of Richarde Davy northe   Item in the same ffurlonge besyde Ridgway at longe crosse i acre betwene the sayd Ridgwaye northe & the land of Richard Davy southe   Item in the same ffurlong i acre lyinge betwene the land of Richarde Davy north

& the lande of Thomas Jeniver southe   Item in the same furlong i acre
lyinge betwene the land of Jhon Byllinge northe & the land of Thomas
Pynnocke southe   Item in the same furlong one acar lying betwene
the land of John Bottrell northe & a pece of heyland no man knowethe
whose it is southe.

Item in Cheyney ffurlonge lyethe ii acres hedland & the land called Cheyneye
Heystonyse land on the northe parte. furlonge.

Item in Cley ffurlonge lyeth i acre betwene the land of Thomas Cley
Pynnocke west and the land of Anyse Dod est. furlong.

Item in Deane acre furlong lyeth ii acres wherof i acre lyeth betwene Deane
the land of Jhon Byllynge northe and the land of William Patten acre waye
southe & the other acre lyethe betwene the land of Wylliam Patten ffurlong.
north & the land of Jhon Bylling south.

Item in Cleyt ffurlong lyeth di an acre betwene ye land of the church Cleyt
est & ye land of William Patten Junioris west. ffurlong.

Item in a furlonge of the est syde of Westwell waye lyeth ii acres Westwell
wherof one acre lyethe betwene the land of Wᵐ fludyeate northe & way est
the land of Richard Davy southe the other acre lyethe betwene the ffurlong.
land of Thomas Pynnocke northe & ye land of Heystonyst southe.

Item in long furlonge on the est syde of Westwell waye di an acre Longe
betwene the land of Robert Jennens northe & the land of the churche furlong.
of Burford southe   Item another half acre lyethe betwene the land
of Jhon ffarmer northe & the land of thomas Pynnocke southe.

Item in a furlonge abuttinge upon Deane acre waye lyeth i acre A ffur-
betwene ye land of Moysers southe and Heystonise land northe   Item long
in the same furlonge lyethe halfe an acre betwene the land of Jhon abutting
Davy northe & the land of the churche of Burford southe   Item in super
the same ffurlonge di an acre lying betwene the land of Robert Jennes acre
(sic) & the churche land southe. waye.

Item in the myddle furlonge lyethe one acre betwene the land of Myddle
William Patten northe and Heystonyseland southe. furlong.

Item in northe furlong abutting fuldenslade lyeth one acre betwene Northe
the land of Wᵐ Patten est and the land of Jhon Howse west   Item furlong
in the same ffurlong di an acre lyinge betwene the land of the churche abutting
of Burford est & Jhon Bottrell weste   Item in the est part of Westwell super ful-
waye lyeth one acre betwene the land of the pryor of St. Jhon in Bur- denslade.
forde northe & the land of Richard Davy southe.

Item in ffuldenslad lyethe i acre of Hedlande by the land of Sʳ Jhon
Neweman on the northe syde   Item in the ffurlong abutting upon

ffulden-slad. the same hedacre lyeth one acre betwene the land of Wylliam fludyeat est & the land of Wm Patten Junior west Item in the same furlong lyeth di an acre betwene the church land est & the land of William Patten west.

the worthye. Item upon the worthye lyeth one acre of hedlande besyd the church land of Burford on ye south part.

Item in the same furlong lyeth i acre abuttinge upon the tyle quarry betwene Heystones land northe & the land of Wm Patten ye younger southe Item in ye same furlong i acre abutting upon the same tyle quarry & lyethe betwene the land of thomas Pynnock northe & the land of Wm Patten junior south Item upon the worthye lyeth di an acre of hedland besyde ye churchland on ye est syde Item Ibidem half an acre lying betwene the land of est (*sic*) and Southeweks land west Item one acre of pyckedland lyinge betwene the land of Wm Semer and the land of William Shepperd southe.

owld hull. Item upon the owld hull lyeth i acre betwene the land of Jhon Lane northe & the land called Salmons southe Item in the same owld hull in a furlong abutting upon ffuldene lyeth one acre betwene the land of Jhon Bylling est & ye land of Thomas Janiver west.

Goryse furlong. Item in a furlonge called the Gowrys lyeth one acre betwene the land of Jhon Byshope south and the land of William Patten northe.

ffuldeane hill. Item in a furlonge upon ffuldenschull lyeth i acre betwene the land of the pryor of St. Jhon west and the land of Jhon Howsse est Item in a furlong abuttinge upon westwell waye lyeth i acre betwene the land of Thomas Janyver southe and Heystons land northe.

a furlong juxta hyllslade. Item in a ffurlong besyde hyllslade lyethe i acre betwene the land of William ffludyeate est and the land of Richard Davye west Item in the same ffurlong lyeth half an acre betwene the churche land est and the land of Jhon Byllinge west.

mydle furlong. Item in mydle furlong lyeth ii acres upon the hull betwene the land of Jhon Botrell west and the land of Richard Davy est.

short furlorg. Item in a short furlonge abutting upon the hull towards the southe lyethe i acre betwene the land of William Patten est & the land of Sr Jhon Neweman west.

Bright-hyll furlong. Item in a furlong abuttinge upon Bright hyll towards the northe lyeth one acre betwene the land of Jhon Lane est & the pryor of St Jhon west Item i acre abuttinge upon the same towards the southe betwene the churche land & the land of Jhon Chadwells west.

Item in a ffurlong by ridgwaye lyethe one acre betwene the lande **Ridg-waye.**
of Heystonyse on the northe & the sayd Ridgwaye on the southe.

Item in ferny ffurlong lyethe i acre betwene the land of Thomas **ferny furlong.**
Pynnock on every syde Item in the same furlonge di an acre lyinge
betwene the land of Edmunde Tame west & the churchland est.

Item in a ffurlong abuttinge upon Whyteslade lyethe di an acre **Whit-slade furlong.**
betwene the churchland south & the land of Wm Patten north Item
in the same furlong lyethe di an acre besyde the land of the churche
southe.

Item in elerstubfurlonge lyethe ii acres betwene the land of Wm **Elerstube furlong.**
Patten west & the land of Richarde Davy este Item in the same
furlong lyeth di an acre betwene the land of Wyllyam Patten west
& the churche land est Item in the same furlong di an acre betwene
the land of thomas est (*sic*) & the land called o^r ladys lande west
Item in the same ffurlong di an acre betwene the land of the pryor of
St Jhon west & the land of Thomas Everarde est

Summa acrarum arabilium

lii in est west ffylde

finis.

This recorde was caused to be renued & written agayne by Mr Edmund Harman Esquir the vth day of maye 1576 in the xviii^th yere
of the raigne of o^r most gracious Soveraigne Ladye Elyzabethe by
the grace of God Quene of England ffraunce & Ireland defender of
the ffaythe.

On the dorse of the same parchment.

Burforde

A Rentall renovated and renewed w^t the oversyght of the lands
pertaynynge to the parsonage in the morowe after the nativytie of
Saint Jhon Baptist in the xvi^th yeare of the raigne of King Henry
the vii^th & in anno domini 1501.

In primis the feoffurs of the lands pertayninge to the
churche of Burforde for one tenement in Burford wch is
called the crowne the quit rent bye the yere   ii*s.*

Item one tenement of late in the tenure of Sr Jhon
Neweman for one messuage in Burford in St Jhons strete
de quit   xii*d.*

Item of the land of o^r blessed virgin Mary in Burford for
ii tenements in the hye streat by the yere of quit rent   v*s.*

Item ye tenements of one of the mylls of Burford   xii*s*.

Item one tenement in the hye stret of Burford late S^r
Jhon Shene after Sir Thomas may pryst quit rent by the
yere   xii*d*.

Item Jhon Bylling for i tenement in Burford late Robert
Leverege the rent therof by the year   xviii*d*.

Item Jhon Taylor for i tenement & i garden in the hye
strete tennaunt at wyll by ye yere   xi*s*. iiii*d*.

Item Richarde Haynes for i cottage & a garden beinge
tennaunt at wyll yerly   xi*s*. iiii*d*.

Item Thomas Stamford for a cottage & a garden tennaunt at will yerly   v*s*.

Item Jhon Calaber for a cottage & a garden tennaunt at
wyll yerly   iiii*s*.

Item Wm Baker for a garden next the parsonage garden
yerly for ye same   xvi*d*.

xxxiii*s*.

Summa totalis reddituum liii*s*. vi*d*.

Bodl. MSS. Arch. Oxon. b. 81

Burgus de   A true Terrier of the Messuages houses and lands given
Burford.   to the parish Church of Burford   vi*d*.

The tenements

Imprimis one messuage standing in the streate there
called the Bull now in the tenure of John Cooke rent per
annum   vi*li*.

Item one other messuage in the same streate called the
Crowne now in the tenure or occupacion of John Woodward
rent yerely   vi*li*.

Item one Messuage in Sheepstreate in the tenure of David
Berry yerely rent   xx*s*.

Item one Messuage in the highstreate there in the tenure
of Edmund Heming rent per annum   xl*s*.

Summa   xv*li*.

The lands

Item Twenty two Acres of errable Lands lying in the
feilds of Burford & Signett now in the tenure of William
Tailor of Burford chaundeller Rent per annum   xxvi*s*. viii*d*.

Some totall   xvi*li*. vi*s*. viii*d*.

Wherof doth belong to the poore in Burford as by
a decree in his Ma^ts highe cort of Chauncery plainlie
appereth   vil*i*. vis. viiii*d*.

The rcsidue belongeth to the aforesaid Church of the
parish of Burford being   x*li*.

William Barthollmew ⎞
thomas precavance   ⎬ Church
Will Veysey   ⎰ wardens
Richard Sessions   ⎠

[*Note*.—This document has on the dorse the certificate of its production
in the Chancery case of 1742 between the Burgesses of Burford and John
Lenthall and Others.]

E. BURFORD AND UPTON ENCLOSURE AWARDS

The Enclosure Awards for Burford (1795) and Upton (1773) are
preserved at the Office of the Clerk of the Peace at Oxford. The
following transcripts have been made from the original documents,
and are in full, with a few obvious abbreviations of detail. The
Award maps, which should be preserved with the Awards, are in both
cases missing. But when the exchanges of enclosures provided for
in the Burford Award took place a small map was prepared for the
purpose, which must have been copied from the Award Map. This
small map exists, and is preserved at the Tolsey, having been presented by the late Mr. Jonathan Banbury. It is dated 1823.

BURFORD ENCLOSURE AWARD

INDEX

BURFORD ENCLOSURE AWARD

The Award is dated 28 February, 35 George III, 1795. The Commissioners appointed by the Act, 34 George III, for enclosing the common fields, common meadows, common pastures, and other commonable lands of Burford, were John Chamberlain of Cropredy;

the Rev. John Horseman of Souldern ; and John Davis of Bloxham.
With them were·joined, as participating in the award, Edward, Bishop
of Oxford ; John Lenthal, of Burford Priory ; the Rev. Robert
Clarke Caswall, as Lessee of the Bishop of the Impropriate Rectory of
Burford ; the Hon. and Rev. Francis Knollis, Vicar of Burford ;
the Rev. Robert Clarke Caswall, as proprietor of certain freehold
lands ; Mary Legg, of Burford, widow ; Richard Weller, of New
Woodstock, ' slatter and plaisterer ' ; Edward Ansell, of Burford,
tanner ; John Kenne, of Alvescot, attorney and agent of John Williams
Willaume, Esquire, Trustee of the estates of Robert Fettiplace for the
benefit of his creditors ; Thomas Hunt, of Burford, surgeon, for and on
behalf of his father, James Hunt ; the Rev. Francis Knollis, John
Lenthal, Charles Fettiplace, late of Swinbrook and now of Taynton,
Thomas Kimber, of Burford, mealman, and William Young, of Burford,
brazier, as acting feoffees or trustees of the land called the Church
Land, the School Land, and the Fifteens ; and the Rev. Francis
Knollis as surviving Trustee of the land for the poor of Upton.

The Award begins by establishing the following roads :

1. One public carriage road and drift way of breadth of sixty feet
being the present turnpike road from Burford to Witney.

2. One other public carriage road and drift way of the like breadth
of 60 feet leading from and out of the top of a certain street in Burford
aforesaid called the High Street and extending eastward by certain
old inclosures in Burford aforesaid known by the name of the Garden
Ground and the Upper Leasow to a certain furlong known by the name
of the Furlong crossing Alvescot way from thence extending in a
southward direction over the said furlong Bush and Pie furlong
Butt furlong Radcot furlong and Barley park piece to the west corner
of a certain common called Sturt Down common from thence over
the said common by the side of certain old enclosures known by the
name of Sturt Farm Grounds into the new inclosures of Shilton in
the county of Berks being the intended track of the Turnpike Road
leading from Burford aforesaid to Faringdon in the county of Berks.

3. One other public Carriage Road and Drift Way of the like
breadth of sixty feet leading from and out of the top of the said High
Street in Burford aforesaid and extending southward to the Turnpike
Gate at Signet in the said county of Oxford being part of the present
Turnpike Road from Burford aforesaid to Lechlade in the County
of Gloucester.

4. One other public Carriage Road and Drift Way of the breadth

of forty feet branching out of the said first described Road at or near the West corner of a certain Piece of Ground known by the Name of Hell Acre, and extending Eastward to Widford Lane in the said county of Oxford being part of the present Road from Burford aforesaid to Widford aforesaid.

5. One other public Carriage Road and Drift Way of the like breadth of forty feet branching out of the second described road at the Upper Leasow and extending Eastward of the said Upper Leasow along the present track called the Bird in Hand Road to High Park Grounds to join the first described Road being the present turnpike Road from Burford aforesaid to Witney aforesaid.

6. One other public Carriage Road and Drift Way of the like breadth of forty feet branching of (*sic*) the second described Road at Radcot Road furlong and extending south westward over the same furlong and Barley Park Piece to a certain gate leading into Sturt Farm being part of the road from Burford aforesaid to Shilton aforesaid.

7. One other public Carriage Road and Drift Way of the like breadth of forty feet leading from the West End of a certain lane in Burford called the Bird in Hand Lane at the North West corner of certain old Inclosures called eighteen Acres Piece and extending Westward by Kempster's Corner into the Hamlet of Upton being part of the present road from Burford aforesaid by the Bird in Hand Inn towards Cirencester in the said County of Gloucester.

8. One other public Carriage Way and Drift Way of the like breadth of forty feet leading out of a certain Lane in Burford aforesaid known by the Name of Tanner's Lane and extending southward by the two trees to join the last described road at the South West corner of a certain old Inclosure known by the Name of thirty Acres Piece.

9. One other public Carriage Way and Drift Way of the like breadth of forty feet branching out of the seventh described Road at or near the North East corner of a certain furlong called Fern Furlong and extending in a South western direction over the same furlong the Furlong south of Fern Furlong Hull Bush Furlong the Furlong south of Hull Bush Furlong the Pikes and Short Furlong to the Gate in the parish of Westwell in the said County of Oxford being part of the Road from Burford aforesaid to Westwell aforesaid.

10. One public Bridle and Drift Road of the Breadth of twenty feet leading out of a certain road in Upton aforesaid at the south west corner of a garden known by the Name of Phipps's Garden and

extending southwards over Apple Pye Corner to a Gate leading into Westwell Grounds.

11. One public Bridle Road and private Carriage Way of the breadth of twenty feet leading out of Hollwell Grounds and extending westward over the Furlong between the old Pits and Westwell Hedge into Westwell Grounds for the Use of the Inhabitants of Westwell Burford and Signet aforesaid and of Hollwell in the said County of Oxford.

12. One other public Bridle Road and private Carriage Way of the like breadth of twenty feet leading out of the second described road at or near the East Corner of Park Piece and extending eastward over Sturt Down Common into the parish of Swinbrook aforesaid for the use of the inhabitants of Westwell Hollwell Burford and Signet aforesaid.

13. Also one other public Bridge Road and Private Carriage Way of the like breadth of twenty feet leading out of Shilton new Inclosure and extending Northward to High Park ground for the use of all persons resorting to and returning from the Mill at Widford aforesaid.

The Award proceeds :

And we the said Commissioners do hereby order and direct that the Grass and Herbage of all and every the Public Bridle roads and Private Carriage and Drift ways shall be and remain to and for the use of the several persons over whose allotments the said Roads are hereinbefore respectively directed to go . . . and that the grass and herbage of all and every the public Carriage and Drift Ways shall be and remain to and for the use of the several persons whose allotments adjoin thereto.

Clause appointing John Lenthal Surveyor of all the public Carriage and Drift Ways and directing him to cause the said Ways to be properly found and put in good and sufficient repair and afterwards to certify the clerk of the peace of Quarter Sessions—Yearly salary of £10.

The following Foot Ways are next established :

1. One public Foot Way of the breadth of four feet leading out of the first described road called the Witney Road and extending Eastward through and over the first allotment herein awarded to the said Mary Legg the third allotment herein awarded to the said Robert Clarke Caswall in lieu of his freehold Lands the fifth allotment herein awarded to the said Lord Bishop of Oxford and Robert Clarke Caswall his Lessee in Lieu of rectorial Tithes the first allotment herein awarded

to Benjamin Cutler Finch Matthew Finch and Mary Eleanor Tebbut wife of John Tebbut the third allotment herein awarded to the said Mary Legg into Widford Inclosures being part of the present Foot Way from Burford aforesaid to Widford aforesaid.

2. One other public Foot Way of the like breadth of four feet leading out of the said third described road opposite Bury Barns Homestall and extending through and over the second allotment herein awarded to the said Robert Clarke Caswall in lieu of his freehold lands to a certain stile leading into Sturt Farm being part of the present Foot Way from Burford aforesaid to Shilton aforesaid.

3. One other public Foot Way of the like breadth of four feet leading out of the said second described road opposite a lane in Burford aforesaid called the back lane and extending through and over the said second allotment herein awarded to the said Robert Clarke Caswall in lieu of his freehold Lands through and over the said fourth allotment herein awarded to the said Lord Bishop of Oxford and Robert Clarke Caswall his Lessee in Lieu of rectorial Tithes through and over the said second allotment herein awarded to the said John Lenthal to a certain stile leading into Signet Inclosures being part of the present Foot Way from Burford aforesaid to Signet aforesaid.

4. One other public Foot Way of the like breadth of four feet leading out of the said seventh public Road herein described at or near the North West Corner of eighteen acres piece and extending through and over the said third allotment herein awarded to the said Lord Bishop of Oxford and Robert Clarke Caswall his Lessee in Lieu of rectorial Tithes to join the said ninth public road herein described at the Pikes being part of the present Foot Way from Burford aforesaid to Westwell aforesaid.

The Award proceeds :

The said Commissioners ... have by virtue of the powers and authorities etc. .... set out and appointed for stone gravel pits or quarries for the materials for making the public roads the following seven plots parts of the land directed by the Act to be inclosed.

a. r. p.
2. o.   (1) One plot or piece of land or ground situate on Whitehill containing two Roods as the same is now admeasured staked and set out Bounded on the north by the first described Road called the Witney Road on the south by the fifth described Road called the Bird in Hand Road and on the West by the fifth allotment herein awarded to the said Mary Legg.

2. 1.   (2) One other plot or piece of land or Ground situate on Whitehill

aforesaid containing two roods and one perch as the same is now admeasured staked and set out Bounded on part of the north by the said fifth described road called the Bird in Hand Road on the remaining part of the north by the said first described Road called the Witney Road and on the South by a certain old inclosure in Burford aforesaid known by the name of High Park Ground.

(3) One other plot or piece of Land or Ground situate on Sturt Down Common containing two Roods as the same is now admeasured staked and set out Bounded on part of the north by the second allotment herein awarded to the said Francis Knollis in lieu of vicarial Tithes on the remaining part of the north and the South East by the third allotment herein awarded to the said John Lenthal and on the south west by the second described road called the Faringdon road.   2. 0.

(4) One other plot or piece of land or ground situate near the Leasow Wall containing three Roods as the same is now admeasured staked and set out Bounded on the north by the said fifth described road called the Bird in Hand Road on the south east by the allotment herein awarded to Margaret Faulkner and on the south west by the second described road called the Faringdon Road.   3. 0.

(5) One other plot or piece of land or Ground situate in Windsmoor Hedge Quarter containing two Roods as the same is now admeasured staked and set out Bounded on the North and East by the second allotment herein awarded to the said Robert Clarke Caswall in lieu of Freehold Lands on the south by the fourth allotment herein awarded to the said Lord Bishop of Oxford and Robert Clarke Caswall his Lessee in lieu of Rectorial Tithes and on the West by the third public Road herein described called the Lechlade Road.   2. 0.

(6) One other plot or piece of Land or Ground situate in Abigal's Bush Quarter containing three roods as the same is now admeasured staked and set out Bounded on the north by the seventh public Road herein described on the south East and South West by the third allotment herein awarded to the said Lord Bishop of Oxford and Robert Clarke Caswall his Lessee in lieu of rectorial Tithes and on the north West by the ninth public Road herein described called the Westwell Road.   3. 0.

(7) One other Plot or Piece of Land or Ground situate in Abigal's Bush Quarter containing one Rood as the same is now admeasured staked and set out Bounded on the West and North by the second allotment herein awarded to the said Lord Bishop of Oxford and Robert Clarke Caswall his Lessee in Lieu of rectorial Tithes and on the South   1. 0.

by the said ninth public road herein described called the Westwell Road.

ALLOTMENT in lieu of Glebe Lands and right of Common to Edward Lord Bishop of Oxford and Robert Clarke Caswall as his lessee.

Glebe
a. r. p.
92. 3. 25.

Ground in Abigal's Bush Quarter containing 92 acres 3 roods and 25 perches Bounded on the north by road 7 on S.E. by road 9 on S.W. by the second allotment to the Bishop and Caswall in lieu of rectorial Tithes and on several parts of North West and North by old inclosures in the Hamlet of Upton, and every part thereof next to the tenth allotment to John Lenthal for the purpose of being exchanged.

ALLOTMENT to Bishop of Oxford and Caswall and to Francis Knollis in lieu of Rectorial and Vicarial Tithes of tithable parts of Common fields.

Tithes
a. r. p.
471. 1. 10.

Nine plots part of common lands containing 471a. 1r. 10p.

(i) Situate in the Garden Ground in Upton 7a. 3r. 12p. Bounded on N. by fourth allotment to Lenthal for exchange on several parts of S.E. and S. by the second allotment to Bishop of Oxford and Caswall and on West by road from Upton to Westwell.

(ii) Situate in Hull Bush Quarter 52a. 2r. 39p. Bounded on N.E. by Glebe Lands allotment on several parts of S.E. and S. by 9th road and 7th stone allotment on S. and W. by the old inclosures of Westwell on several parts of N. and N.W. by the 1st allotment for rectorial Tithes on other parts of W. and on S. by 4th allotment to Lenthal for exchange and on rest of west by other inclosures in Upton.

(iii) Ground in Abigal's Bush Quarter 252a. 2r. 33p. Bounded N. by road 7 on several parts of E. S. and N. by old inclosures in Burford called the Eighteen acres on E. by Lechlade Turnpike Road on S.E. by Signet Green on several parts of S. and W. and E. by old inclosures in Upton on S. and S.W. by the 1st allotment to Caswall for freehold Lands on N.W. by road 9 and on N. and N.W. by 6th allotment for stone.

(iv) Ground in Sturt Quarter 41a. 2r. 31p. Bounded on part of N. by 5th allotment for stone, on rest of N. and on E. by 2nd allotment to Caswall for freehold lands on part of south by 2nd allotment to Lenthal on remaining part of S. by allotment to Trustees for poor of Burford and Signet and on W. by Lechlade Turnpike Road.

(v) Ground in High Meadow 4a. 3r. 36p. (exclusive of footway passing over same as hereby directed) Bounded on N. N.E. and N.W.

by Windrush on E. by 1st allotment to B. C. Finch, M. Finch, and Eleanor Tebbut on part of S. by an old inclosure in Burford called Bob's Ham on rest of S. by Witney Turnpike Road and on W. by 3rd allotment to Caswall for freehold lands.

(iv) Ground in Sturt Common set out with intent to exchange with John Lenthal 11a. or. 9p. Bounded N.W. and N.E. by 3rd allotment to John Lenthal on S.E. by Shilton new Inclosures on S.W. by 7th allotment to Mary Legg for exchange.

Boundary fences to 2nd allotment 3rd allotment 4th allotment and 5th allotment to be made with quick set hedges or stone walls by the commoners except the Bishop, Caswall, and Knollis and kept up for 7 years—after that by the Bishop, Caswall, and owners for the time being.

TITHES (VICARIAL).

To Francis Knollis and his successors.

(i) Ground in Sturt Quarter 10a. 1r. 35p. Bounded on N.W. by Faringdon Turnpike on S. by old inclosures in Signet called Sturt Grounds.

(ii) Ground in White Hill Quarter 84a. 2r. 23p. Bounded on N. by 5th public road on E. and N. by 6th allotment to Mary Legg on several parts of S.E., S.W. and part of S. by 3rd allotment to John Lenthal on rest of S. by 3rd allotment for stone on S.W. by 2nd public road called the Faringdon Turnpike Road and on N.W. by 2nd allotment to Finches and Tebbut.

(iii) Ground in High Meadow 5a. or. 32p. exclusive of footway over same Bounded on N. and N.W. by Windrush on E. by second allotment to Mary Legg on several parts of S. and E. by an old inclosure in Burford called Long Close on rest of S. by 4th public road and on N. and W. by 6th allotment to Finches and Tebbut.

Similar provision as to fencing.

JOHN LENTHAL AS LORD OF THE MANORS OF BURFORD AND BURY BARNS.

Ground in Sturt Down Common 1a. 1r. Bounded on N.E. by 7th allotment to Mary Legg for exchange on S.E., S.W., and N.W. by 3rd allotment to Lenthal—this allotment as compensation for lord of manor's right and interests in waste lands.

Division of residue of open and common fields common meadows common pastures and other commonable lands among their several owners and proprietors and other people interested therein.

JOHN LENTHAL, in lieu of rights and in lieu of his two meadows called Chavasse's Ham and Stevens's Ham. 11 plots of ground.

(i) Ground in Batledge Quarter 7a. 2r. 28p. Bounded on N.W. and N.E. by 4th allotment to Caswall for freehold lands for exchange on S.E. by 8th public road on S. by seventh public road.

(ii) Ground in Windsmoor Hedge Quarter 17a. or. 13p. exclusive of footway Bounded on S. by 4th allotment to Bishop of Oxford and Caswall for rectorial tithes on E. by second allotment to Caswall for freehold lands on S. by ancient inclosures in Signet on part of W. by 6th allotment to Lenthal for exchange and on rest of W. by allotment to trustees for the poor of Burford and Signet.

(iii) Ground in Sturt Down Common 68a. 3r. 1p. exclusive of 2 Bridle roads Bounded on several parts of N.W., N. and N.E. by 2nd allotment to Knollis for vicarial Tithes on rest of N. and part of E. by ancient inclosures in Burford called High Park Grounds on E. by open and common fields of Swinbrook on part of S.W. and S.E. by 6th allotment for rectorial tithes for exchange on other parts of S.E. and N.E. by 7th allotment to Mary Legg for exchange on part of S.E., N.E. and N.W. by allotment to Lenthal for manorial rights on rest of S.E. by new inclosures of Shilton on rest of S.W. by 2nd public road on rest of N.W. and on S. by.3rd allotment for stone.

(iv) Ground of Edward Ansell in Upton 6a. or. 21p. with a piece of land of Edward Ansell being an old inclosure called Ansell's Ham 2r. 16p.—in lieu of a meadow of John Lenthal in Fulbrook called Bridge Meadow of 2a. or. 1p., allotted for purpose of passing in exchange to Bishop of Oxford and Caswall Bounded on part of N. and N.W. by old inclosures in Upton on rest of N. and on S.E. by 2nd allotment for rectorial Tithes on S. by 1st allotment for rectorial Tithes and on W. by other old inclosures in Upton.

(v) Ground in Further White Hill Quarter for exchange with Mary Legg 12a. 2r. 28p. Bounded on N. by allotment to James Hunt for exchange on parts of E., on S. and on N.E. by old inclosures in Widford on S. and W. by 4th allotment to Mary Legg.

(vi) Ground in Sturt Quarter for exchange with Trustees for poor of Upton 2a. 2r. op. Bounded on N. by allotment to trustees for poor of Burford and Signet on E. by 2nd allotment to Lenthal on S. by an old inclosure in Signet on W. by Common Green of Signet.

(vii) Ground in Windsmoor Hedge Quarter for exchange with feoffees of Fifteens land 1a. or. 24p. Bounded on N.E. by 2nd public road on S. by 8th allotment to Lenthal for exchange on W. and N.

by allotment to feoffees for benefit of Bailiffs and Burgesses of Burford aforesaid.

(viii) Ground in Windsmoor Hedge Quarter for exchange with feoffees of Church lands 0a. 1r. 31p. Bounded on N.E. by 2nd public road on S. by 3rd allotment to Finches and Tebbut on W. by allotment to feoffees for benefit of Bailiffs and Burgesses on N. by 7th allotment to Lenthal for exchange.

(ix) Ground in Whore's Quarter for exchange with Caswall 90a. 2r. 9p. Bounded N. by 1st allotment to Caswall for freehold lands on several parts of E., S., S.E., N.E. and S.W. by ancient inclosures in Signet and on several parts of S.W., S.E., S. and N.W. by old inclosures in Westwell.

(x) Ground in Abigal's Bush Quarter for exchange with Bishop of Oxford and Caswall for Glebe 1a. 0r. 7p. Bounded on N., E., S., and W. by allotment for Glebe.

(xi) Ground in Stevens's Ham for exchange with James Hunt 1a. 0r. 0p. Bounded on N., part of N.W. and part of S.E. by Windrush on rest of S.E. by allotment to Richard Weller on part of S.W. and on E. by old inclosure in Signet called Hunt's Close on S. by Witney Turnpike Road and on N.W. by 1st allotment to Richard Weller.

ALLOTMENT TO EDWARD ANSELL. In lieu of 4th allotment to Lenthal.
Bridge meadow of John Lenthal 2a. 0r. 1p.

ALLOTMENT TO ROBERT CLARKE CASWALL *in lieu of his freehold rights. Four plots.*

(i) Ground in Whore's Quarter 40a. 0r. 32p. Bounded on part of N.W. by 9th public road called Westwell Road on N.E. and N. by 3rd allotment for rectorial tithes on E. by an old inclosure in Signet called the tenacres on S. by 9th allotment to Lenthal for exchange and on S.W. by an old inclosure in Westwell.

(ii) Ground in Sturt Quarter 119a. 2r. 30p. exclusive of footways Bounded on part of N.E. by 2nd public road called Faringdon Turnpike Road on S.E. by allotment to Thomas Minchin for lands purchased of Matthias Padbury on part of E. by allotment to Ann Rich, widow, on remaining part of E. by allotment to feoffees for benefit of Bailiffs and Burgesses on other part of N.E. and N. by 3rd allotment to Finches and Tebbut on rest of N.E. by Faringdon Turnpike Road on S.E. by 6th public road on several parts of S.W., E. and W. by Sturt Grounds on part of W. by 2nd allotment to Lenthal on rest of W. and other part of S. by 4th allotment for rectorial tithes on part of N.W. and remaining part of S. by 5th allotment for stone on N.W. by 3rd described road called Lechlade Turnpike Road.

(iii) Ground in High Meadow 7a. or. 34p. exclusive of footway Bounded on N. and N.E. by Windrush on S.E. by 5th allotment for rectorial tithes on S. by Witney Turnpike Road and on N.W. by first allotment to Mary Legg.

(iv) Ground in Batledge Quarter for exchange with Lenthal 39a. 3r. 16p. Bounded on several parts of W. and N. by ancient inclosures in Burford on remaining part of N. by a common Street in Burford on a small part of E. by a Homestall in occupation of Thomas Merrick on rest of E. by Tanner's Lane Road on part of S. and on remaining part of E. by 1st allotment to Lenthal and on rest of S. by 7th public road.

(N.B.—This was not inclosed towards the ' common street ' or towards Tanner's Lane.)

ALLOTMENT TO MARY LEGG, *widow, for rights and interests.* 7 *plots.*

(i) Ground in the West End of High Meadow 2a. 3r. 22p. exclusive of footway Bounded on several parts of N., W., E. and S.E. by the Windrush on remaining part of S.E. by 3rd allotment to Caswall and on S.W. by Witney Turnpike Road.

(Fences to be made next to Caswall and next to Witney Turnpike Road.)

(ii) Ground in East End of High Meadow 6a. 1r. 36p. Bounded on several parts of N. and N.E. by Windrush on E. by an old inclosure in Burford called Long Close and on W. by 3rd allotment for vicarial Tithes.

(iii) Ground in Hell Acre oa. 2r. 36p. Bounded on S.W. by Witney Turnpike Road on N. by 4th public road on E. and S. by old inclosures in Burford called White Hill Ground.

(iv) Ground in the Farther White Hill (*sic*) 19a. 1r. 7p. Bounded on parts of N., W. and S.W. by old inclosures called White Hill ground on other part of N. by 4th public road on N.E. by old inclosures in Widford on S. and on small part of E. by allotment to James Hunt for exchange on other part of E. and rest of N. by 5th allotment to Lenthal for exchange on rest of E. by old inclosures in Widford and on S.W. by Witney Turnpike Road.

(v) Ground in the Homeward Whitehill 47a. 2r. 4p. Bounded on N. and N.E. by Witney Turnpike Road on E. by the 1st allotment for stone· on part of S. by 5th public road called Bird in Hand road on part of N.W. and rest o S. by allotment to Brasenose College and

William Boulter lessee on rest of N.W. by old inclosures in Burford called Spring Grounds.

(vi) Ground in Sturt Quarter 19a. or. 38p. Bounded on N. by 5th public road called Bird in Hand Road on S.E. by old inclosure in Burford called High Park Grounds on S. and W. by 2nd allotment for vicarial tithes.

(vii) Ground in Sturt Down Common for exchange with John Lenthal 6a. 2r. 21p. Bounded on N.E. by 6th allotment to Bishop of Oxford and Caswall by exchange on S.E. by new inclosures of Shilton on part of S.W. by 3rd allotment to Lenthal on rest of S.W. by allotment to Lenthal for manorial rights and on N.W. by 3rd allotment to Lenthal.

ALLOTMENT TO BENJAMIN CUTLER FINCH, MATTHEW FINCH, AND MARY ELEONER TEBBUT *for rights and interests. 3 plots.*

(i) Ground in High Meadow 3a. 2r. 39p. Bounded on N.W., N. and N.E. by Windrush on E. and S.E. by 3rd allotment for vicarial tithes on part of S. by 4th public road on part of W. and rest of S. by an old inclosure in Burford called Bob's Ham on rest of W. by 5th allotment for rectorial tithes.

(ii) Ground in Sturt Quarter and Windsmoor Hedge Quarter 50a. or. 25p. Bounded on part of N. by 5th public road called Bird in Hand road on S.E. by 2nd allotment for vicarial tithes on S.W. by Faringdon Turnpike Road on rest of N. and on N.W. by allotment to Elizabeth Butler.

(iii) Ground in Sturt Quarter and Windsmore Hedge Quarter 27a. 1r. 18p. Bounded on N.E. by 2nd public road called Faringdon Turnpike Road on S. and S.W. by 2nd allotment to Caswall on part of N. by allotment to feoffees for benefit of Bailiffs and Burgesses of Burford and on rest of north by 8th allotment to Lenthal for exchange.

ALLOTMENT TO ELIZABETH PATTEN *in lieu of rights and interests.*

Ground in Windsmore Hedge Quarter 31a. 3r. 0p. Bounded on N. by 5th public road called Bird in Hand road on S.E. and S. by 2nd allotment to Finches and Tebbut on S.W. by 2nd described road called Faringdon Turnpike Road and on N.W. by allotment to Margaret Faulkner.

ALLOTMENT TO MARGARET FAULKNER *for rights and interests.*

Ground in Windsmore Hedge Quarter 28a. 1r. 15p. Bounded on N. by 5th public road called Bird in Hand road on S.E. by allotment to Eliz. Patten   on S.E. by 2nd public road called Faringdon Turnpike Road   on N.W. by 4th allotment for stone.

ALLOTMENT TO BRASENOSE COLLEGE AND WM. BOULTER THEIR LESSEE *for rights and interests.*

Ground in the Homeward White Hill 3a. 3r. 30p.   Bounded on part of N.W. by allotment to Samuel Heath for lands purchased of Robert Woodman   on rest of N.W. and on part of N. by old inclosures in Burford called the Leasows   on rest of N. and on S.E. by 5th allotment to Mary Legg and on S. by 5th public road called Bird in Hand road.

ALLOTMENT TO SAMUEL HEATH *with consent of John Kenn testified by his being made a party to these presents for rights and interests.*

Ground in the Leasows 1a. 2r. 35p.   Bounded on N.W. and N.E. by old inclosures in Burford called the Leasows   on S.E. by allotment to Brasenose College and on S. by 5th public road called Bird in Hand Road.

To THOMAS MINCHIN *in lieu of lands purchased of* MATTHIAS PADBURY.

Ground in Windsmoor Hedge Quarter 3a. 3r. 0p.   Bounded N. and N.E. by 2nd public road called Faringdon Turnpike Road   on S. by allotment to Ann Rich   on N.W. by 2nd allotment to Caswall.

ALLOTMENT TO ANN RICH *for rights and interests.*

Ground in Windsmoor Hedge Quarter 7a. 3r. 8p.   Bounded N. by allotment to Minchin   on N.E. by 2nd public road called Faringdon Turnpike Road   on S. by allotment to feoffees for benefit of Bailiffs and Burgesses of Burford and on W. by 2nd allotment to Caswall.

ALLOTMENT TO FRANCIS KNOLLIS, JOHN LENTHAL, CHARLES FETTIPLACE, THOMAS KIMBER, AND WILLIAM YOUNG, AND ALSO GEORGE DAVIS, *late of Ducklington now of Bensington, Esquire, as feoffees of the land for the benefit of the Bailiffs and Burgesses.*

Ground in Windsmoor Hedge Quarter 15a. 2r. 32p.   Bounded N. by allotment to Ann Rich   on part of N.E. by 2nd public Road called Faringdon Turnpike Road   on parts of S. and rest of N.E. by 7th and 8th allotments to Lenthal for exchange on rest of S. by 3rd allotment to Finches and Tebbut   on W. by 2nd allotment to Caswall.

ALLOTMENT TO CASWALL *as lessee of the Impropriate Rectory and his successors, to* FRANCIS KNOLLIS, *vicar, and his successors,* JOHN LENTHAL, *Lord of the Manor of Burford, and his successors as Trustees for the Poor of Burford and Signet in lieu of the right of the poor to cut furze in Sturt Down.*

Ground in Sturt Quarter 5a. or. 32p. Bounded N. by 4th allotment for rectorial tithes   on E. by 2nd allotment to Lenthal   on S. by 6th allotment to Lenthal for exchange and on W. by Lechlade Turnpike Road.

ALLOTMENT TO THOMAS HUNT AND LOIS HEYES *for rights and interests.*

Ground in Stevens's Ham 0a. 1r. 32p. Bounded on N. by back water course running from Higgins's Mill into the Windrush   on S.E. by allotment to Oriel   on S. by Witney Turnpike Road and on N.W. by an old inclosure in Burford called Chavasse's Paddock.

ALLOTMENT TO ORIEL COLLEGE AND THOMAS SMITH, *lessee for rights and interests.*

Ground in Stevens's Ham 0a. or. 29p. Bounded N. by the same back water course   on S.E. by allotment to feoffees of Church Land   on S. by Witney Turnpike Road   on N.W. by allotment to Hunt and Heyes.

ALLOTMENT TO FRANCIS KNOLLIS, JOHN LENTHAL, CHARLES FETTIPLACE, THOMAS KIMBER, WILLIAM YOUNG, AND GEORGE DAVIS, *Feoffees of Church Land.*

Ground in Stevens's Ham 0a. 1r. 24p. Bounded N. by Windrush   S.E. by allotment to feoffees of School Land   on S. by Witney Turnpike Road   on S.W. by allotment to Oriel.

ALLOTMENT TO THE SAME *as feoffees of the School Land.*

Ground in Stevens's Ham 1a. 3r. 19p. Bounded on several points on N.W., S., N., and N.E. by the Windrush on S.E. by 1st allotment to Richard Weller   on S. by Witney Turnpike Road and on N.W. (? S.W.) by allotment to feoffees of Church Land.

ALLOTMENT TO RICHARD WELLER *for rights and interests. 4 plots.*

(i) Ground in Stevens's Ham and in Chavasse's Ham 1a. or. 6p. Bounded on several parts of N.E., N., and N.W. by the Windrush on S.E. by 11th allotment to Lenthal for exchange   on S. by Witney Turnpike Road and on N.W. by allotment to feoffees of School Land.

(ii) Ground in Kempster's Corner 2a. 2r. 32p. Bounded on W. N., and E. by old inclosure in Upton and on S. by 7th public road from Burford to Cirencester.

(iii) Ground in Upton Inclosures 4a. 1r. 18p. Bounded on N. by said road to Cirencester   on several parts of E. and part of S. by allotment for Glebe   on remaining part of S. by another old inclosure in

Upton and on W. by another old inclosure in Upton called Hunt's Ground and hereinafter exchanged.

(John Kenn)

(iv) Ground in Chavasse's Ham 1a. 1r. 29p. Bounded on E., N. and W. by Windrush on small part of S. and on S.E. by a small meadow called Legg's meadow hereinafter exchanged on S.W. by old inclosures in Burford called Hunt's Closes and on N.W. by 11th allotment to Lenthal for exchange.

Allotments to Hunt and Heyes, Oriel, Church Land, School Land and 1st and 4th to Weller are with the consent of Lenthal, he having received compensation by other allotments.

ALLOTMENT TO JAMES HUNT *for rights and interests.*

Ground in Farther White Hill 1a. 2r. 23p. for exchange with Mary Legg Bounded W. and N. by 4th allotment to Mary Legg on E. and part of S. by an old inclosure in Widford on rest of S. by 5th allotment to Lenthal for exchange.

Clause that these allotments are all in Burford and compensation for all rights and interests in common fields.

Clause reciting authority to authorize exchanges for greater convenience.

EXCHANGES.

To Caswall. 9th allotment to Lenthal.

To Lenthal in Exchange. Pieces of Land called Upton Meadow 3a. 2r. 22p. the Bank called Fernhill Bank 3a. 2r. 16p. Part of meadow adjoining 2a. 3r. 22p. Small piece of land in Ladwell Meadow 0a. 3r. 25p. The Northward Thirty-acre piece 7a. 3r. 19p. the Southward thirty acre piece 9a. 3r. 21p. Two several pieces of inclosed land in Signet called the Down Ground 14a. 1r. 27p. and the Down Bottom 4a. 3r. 10p. Making together 48a. 0r. 2p.

EXCHANGE BETWEEN BISHOP OF OXFORD AND CASWALL AND JOHN LENTHAL.

To Bishop and Caswall. 10th allotment to Lenthal in exchange for piece of ground in Upton Meadow called Glebe Piece 0a. 2r. 20p.

4th allotment to Lenthal in exchange for 6th allotment for rectorial tithes.

JOHN LENTHAL AND MARY LEGG.

To Mary Legg. 5th allotment to Lenthal in exchange for two several closes in Upton called Upston's Withys 2a. 0r. 12p. and Lane's Close 3a. 1r. 16p. Together 5a. 1r. 28p.

JOHN LENTHAL AND TRUSTEES FOR UPTON POOR.

To Trustees. 6th allotment to Lenthal in exchange for Ground in Upton called the Great Downs 8 acres.

JOHN LENTHAL AND FEOFFEES OF FIFTEENS.

To Feoffees. 7th allotment to Lenthal in exchange for ground on west side of the garden ground called Phipps's Garden in Upton 1a. 2r. 21p.

JOHN LENTHAL AND FEOFFEES OF CHURCH LAND.

To Feoffees. 8th allotment to Lenthal in exchange for piece of inclosed ground also on West side of Phipps's Garden in Upton 2r. 21p.

JOHN LENTHAL AND JAMES HUNT.

To Hunt. 11th allotment to Lenthal in exchange for close in Burford called Hallcroft close 0a. 3r. 30p.

CASWALL AND LENTHAL.

To Lenthal. 4th allotment to Caswall (Batledge) in exchange for several pieces of inclosed land at Signet called Hiron's Fatting Close 4a. 0r. 39p. Close and garden called Blacksmith's Close 5a. 1r. 16p. The Pump Ground 12a. 0r. 8p. The Homeward Hollwell Ground 22a. 1r. 5p. Middle Hollwell Ground 13a. 3r. 18p. Further Hollwell Ground 22a. 2r. 16p. and a small part of Hiron's Back Yard being the westward part containing 23p.—together 80a. 2r. 5p.

JAMES HUNT AND MARY LEGG.

To Mary Legg. Hunt's allotment in Further White Hill in exchange for piece of meadow ground called Legg's Ham 2r. 13p.

RICHARD WELLER AND JAMES HUNT.

To Hunt. 4th allotment to Weller in exchange for piece of ground in Upton called Wiggins's Ground 2a. 1r. 1p.

MARY LEGG AND JOHN LENTHAL.

To Lenthal. 7th allotment to Mary Legg in exchange for piece of inclosed ground called Long Close 3a. 3r. 6p.

To the Award is affixed a schedule of the sums due in rectorial and vicarial tithes from messuages, tenements, gardens, old inclosures, &c., for which no compensation had been made in land.

	Quantities.			Rector.			Vicar.	
	a.	r.	p.	£	s.	d.	s.	d.
MATTHIAS PADBURY								
Paper Mill and Premises in occupation of — Ward.	3	0	2		5	3½	5	4¼
The Copse		1	11		—			8½
Warner's Close in occupation of Widow Warner	1	0	6		—		3	8¼
					5	3½	9	9
WILLIAM HIGGINS								
Mill and Premises in occupation of himself		2	25		—		2	3
The Meadow	6	1	36		19	2¼	9	7
		—			19	2¼	11	10
PAUL SILVESTER								
Lady Ham	1	2	8		4	0¼	2	0¼
— SMITH								
Drying Yard in occupation of — Beal		3	32		—		3	2
CHRISTOPHER KEMPSTER								
Picked Close		3	21		1	3½		7¾
Homestead Orchard and Close	7	0	38		9	5	6	8
The Saintfoin Ground	6	0	21	1	0	0	4	0
The Clover Ground	6	3	29	1	3	8½	5	0½
				2	14	5	16	4¼
THOMAS HUNTLEY								
School Ground and Premises	1	2	6		—		5	7¼
Burnet Close		2	16		1	5		8½
Two Cottages and Garden in occupation of Barrett and Green		—			—		1	2
		—			1	5	7	5¾
MR. CHAPMAN								
Houses, Gardens and Premises	1	1	32		1	1	3	8½
THOMAS HUNT AND LOIS HEYES								
Upton Ground in occupation of Chas. Mills	8	3	20	1	4	8¼	5	2¾
Upton Barn Yard and Close	1	0	20		2	0	1	8¾
Upton Close west of ditto	1	1	32		4	0	1	9¾
Houses Yards and Gardens in the Town		—			—			9¾
		—		1	10	8¼	9	7

			s.	d.
Thomas Clare	House Yard & Garden	occ. Chas. Legg		6½
Edward Daniel	Do.	occ. Bunting & Co.	1	7
Jacob James	Do.	own occ.	1	0
Joseph Strafford	Do.	Do.	2	0
Danl. Faulkner	Do.	Do.		4
William Young	Do.	occ. Wm. Hemmings		10
Padbury & Rich	Do.	Jas. Wickins		5
Do.	Do.	Robt. Harris		3
Do.	Do.	Robt. Sperrinck		3
Bucklands Garden		own occ.	1	4
Richard Swancot	Do.	Do.		4
Feoffees of Church	Do.	John Stevens	2	4
John Stevens	House & Yard	own occ.		6
Widow Bun	Do.	Jas. Dyer & Co.		1½
Padbury & Rich	Do.	Wm. Notgrove		1
Do.	Do.	Widow		1½
Do.	Do.	Henry Titcomb		1½
John Wilson	House Yard & Garden	occ. late Stephen Young		10.
Thos. Hunt	Do.	John Mills		1½
Jas. Edgington	House & Yard	Dr. John Nunney		1½
Widow Nicholls	Do.	own occ.		1
Widow Nunny	House Yard & Garden	own occ.		2
Arthur White	Do.	Do.		8
William Reeves	Do.	Do.		10
Stephen Smith	Do.	Dr. Sharp & Co.	2	0
Stphen (sic) Young	Do.	own occ.		10
John Dean	Cottage only	occ. Bunting & Barnes		1
Widow Bun	Cottage & Yard	occ. Wm. Bolt		1
Charity Widows	Land House Yard & Garden	occ. George Sims	2	6
Thos. James	Do.	own occ.		9
Ranchford Strafford	Do.	Do.		8
Widow Woodman	Do.	Chas. Stevens		8
Widows Charity	Do.	own occ.		9
John Mason	House & Yard	own occ.		1½
Widow Bun	Do.	Wm. Miles		1
James Strafford	Do.	James Miles		1
Widow Harman	Do.	own occ.		1½
Widow Chapman	Do.	John James & Co.		1
Widow Nicholls	Do.	Seymour & Waine		1
Do.	Do.	Dan. Mills & Co.		1
Wm. Green	House Yard & Garden	own occ.		4
Widow Chapman	Do.	James Manning		8
Benjamin Waters	Cottage only	Widow Eldridge		1
Widow Chapman	House & Yard	William Cox		1½
Solomon Jeffs	Do.	Widow Beechey		4
Do.	Do.	Moses Smith		2
Do.	Do.	James Spacksman		2
Do.	Do.	own occ.		2
Widow Bun	Do.	Matthias Padbury		1½
Feoffees of Bridge	Do.	Thos. Chavasse		6
Widow Bun	Do.	Saml. Tiptree		6
John Dean	House Yard & Garden	occ. Henry Mander		2
Mary Upston	Do.	own occ.		10
Benjamin Haynes	Do.	Do.	1	2

			s.	d.
Widow Chapman	House Yard & Garden	occ. Saml. Bolt		11
Widow Higgins		own occ.		11
Chas. Yates	Do.	Thos. Clarke	1	6
William Monk	Do.	own occ.	1	6
Feoffees of Church	Do.	John Nunney	1	6
Micl. Wills	Cottage only	Widow Palmer & Co.		
Widow Chapman	Do.	void		
Thomas Humphries	Do.	own occ.		
Feoffees of Workhouse and Alms Houses Yards & Gardens			1	8
	Cottage only	Widow Steer		
Thomas Minchin Butcher			2	0
James Wickin	Do.	Jas. Franklin		
Saml. Parker	Do.	own occ.		
John Arkill	Do.	Wilm. Turner		
Do.	Do.	Thos. Cook & Widow Gillett		
Do.	Do.	John Day		
Do.	Do.	Moses Smith		
Do.	House Yard & Garden	John Turner		3
William Beechey	Do.	own occ.		5
John Smith	Do.	Do.		8
Mr. Lawrence	Do.	Do.		6
Wilm. Bolter	Do.	Do.		3
Miss Bartholomew	Do.	Do.		8
William Clarke	Do.	Wm. Wiggins		4
Fifteens	Do.	void		3
Do.	Do.	Do.		3
Do.	Do.	Rob. Spackman		3
John Hemming	House & Yard	Thos. Holland		1
Matthias Padbury	House Yard & Garden	Jno. Dean & Co.		2
Widow Woodman	Do.	Thos. Large & Co.		2
Thos. Kimber	Do.	own occ.		4
Widow Humphries	Do.	Do.		5
Thos. Badger	Do.	Widow Sessions		4
Widow Chapman	Do.	Thos. Osmond		2
Do.	Do.	John Pankridge		5
Do.	Do.	Joseph Rawlings		2
Ralph Ellis	Do.	own occ.		5
S. & W. Clare	Do.	Do.		2
Widow Chapman	Bruton Orchard	own occ.		9
John Green	House Yard & Garden	Do.		8
Thomas Andrews	Do.	Do.		3
Widow Bun	Do.	Do.		3
John Woodman	Do.	Widow Pocket		3
George Arian	Do.	Thos. Merrick		2
Wm. Bites & Thos. Snowshill	Do.	Widow Miles & Co.		9
Chas. Miles	Do.	John Hitchman		3
John Spurrit junr.	Do.	own occ.		2
Widow Hutton	Do.	Do.		6
S. & W. Clare	Do.	Rev. W. Francis		5
Wm. Beal	Do.	W. Bye & Co.		4
Henry Buckland	Do.	own occ.	1	5
Thos. Randolph	Do.	Do.		10
Richard Tuckwell	Do.	Do.	1	0
Thomas Kempster	Do.	Do.		4

			s.	d.
Thomas Kempster	House Yard & Garden	occ. James Daniel Tenant		4
William Minchin	Do.	Do.		4
William Fry	Do.	Wm. Jeffs		4
William Jeffs	Do.	Widow Wyatt		5
Thos. Clare	Do.	Robert Jacobs		8
William Young	Do.	Mackquirk		2
William Beal	Do.	Himself & Co.	1	0
John Beal	Do.	William Brown		7
Edward Daniel	Do.	own occ.		8
John Turner	Do.	Do.		6
John Brown	Do.	Martin Brown	1	4
Charles Legg	Do.	own occ.		2
James Strafford	Do.	Tilling & Co.		2
Dr. Castle's College	Do.	Thos. Day & Co.		5
Widow Wightwick	Do.	Widow Taylor & Co.		6
Chas. Kimber	Part of Mill & Mill Bank	own occ.	2	0
Mr. Cozens	a small Meadow		1	6

A SECOND SCHEDULE OF MONEYS RECEIVED AND PAID

		£	s.	d.
To cash received for general expenses		1,699	1	0
,, ,, Roads & Surveyor's salary . .		358	11	1
,, ,, Tithe fencing		429	6	2
,, ,, Fencing the poor's allotment & Fifteens		12	14	0
		2,499	12	3
By Cash Paid		2,431	8	5
By Balance in Hand		68	3	10
		2,499	12	3

Note.—The first sheet mentions a plan made by James Jennings of Somerton, Oxon., Land Surveyor, containing open fields, enclosures, &c.

1,300 acres or. 11p.

This plan is *not* with the Award at the Clerk of the Peace Office.

Note also.—First meeting (of which notice given on church door) at house of John Stevens known as the Bull Inn in Burford 27 May, 1794.

H. J. North, Solicitor, was Clerk to the Commissioners.

Clerk of the Peace Office, Oxford.

UPTON ENCLOSURE AWARD

Dated 9th Dec., 14 Geo. III, 1773.

In pursuance of an Act 13 Geo. III for dividing and inclosing the open and common fields of Upton in the Parish of Burford.

Commissioners : Francis Burton of Aynho, Northants, Esq., Thomas Baseley of Friars Marston, Warwick, Gentleman, and Ralph Whitehert of Cirencester, Glos., Gentleman.

Quality Men or Valuers : William Wright and William Ansell. Total area inclosed 803a. 2r. 7p.

Allotment to William Lenthal.

(i) Ground of 706a. 3r. 36p. including Roads and ways Bounded part of E. allotments of Thos. Ansell Thomas Hunt and Richard Heyes and Thomas Castle : Part of S. by allotments of Thomas Castle, Piercy Galliard, and James Hunt : other part of E. Common Fields of Burford and certain old inclosed lands in Upton and allotment of Christopher Kempster : Part of N. certain inclosed meads in parish of Tainton allotment of John Cousins and John Prior and other meads in Tainton : Part of W. and other part of N. by allotment of William Upstone, other part of W. inclosed lands of Little Barrington : other part of S. and W. by certain inclosures in Upton : other part of S. W. and N. by allotment of Furze set out for poor of Upton : other part of S. by inclosed lands of Westwell : other part of E. and S. by allotment for Church Land and another allotment for Land commonly called the Fifteens.

(ii) Ground 2a. 2r. 1p. Bounded on S., E., and N. and W. by old inclosed Lands of Upton.

(iii) Grounds 7a. or. 28p. Bounded E. and part of N. by inclosed land and common field of Fulbrook : on part of W. and other part of N. by allotment to heirs of late Henry Furley : other part of W. inclosed land in parish of Taynton : on S. by Windrush.

Allotment to John Pryor, Lessee of Bishop of Oxford.

(i) Ground oa. 2r. 17p. Bounded S.E. allotment to John Cousins : N. inclosed meadows of Tainton : N.W. 2nd allotment to Pryor : S. allotment of Wm. Lenthal. This in compensation for meadow called Tythe Ham which is to be enclosed and allotted.

(ii) Ground 9a. 2r. 9p. Bounded S.E. by 1st allotment to Pryor : part of N.W. and on E. by inclosed meads of Tainton : W. and S. by allotment to Lenthal.

Allotment to William Upstone.

Ground 2a. or. 21p. Bounded S. and E. by allotment to Lenthal : N. common meadows of Tainton : W. inclosed land of Little Barrington.

Allotment to John Cousins.

Ground oa. 1r. 35p. Bounded N.E. by inclosed meadows of Tainton : N.W. allotment to John Prior : S. allotment to William Lenthal.

Allotment to Robert Fettiplace, Esq.

Ground 4a. 1r. 22p. Bounded E. common fields of Burford and Signet : W. allotment to James Hunt : S. allotment to Thomas Hunt and Richard Heyes.

Allotment to James Hunt.

Ground 2a. 0r. 30p. Bounded E. allotment to Rob. Fettiplace : N. allotment to William Lenthal : W. allotment to Piercy Galliard : S. allotment to Thomas Hunt and Richard Heyes.

Allotment to Piercy Galliard, Esq.

Ground 3a. 0r. 22p. Bounded E. allotment to James Hunt : N. allotment of Wm. Lenthal : W. allotment of Thomas Castle : S. allotment of Thos. Hunt and Richard Heyes.

Allotment to Thomas Castle.

Ground 3a. 0r. 6p. Bounded E. allotment of Piercy Galliard : N. and W. allotment of Wm. Lenthal : S. allotment of Thos. Hunt and Richard Heyes.

Allotment to Thomas Hunt and Richard Heyes.

Ground 8a. 2r. 18p. Bounded E. common fields of Burford : N. by several allotments of Fettiplace, James Hunt, Galliard and Castle : W. allotment of Wm. Lenthal : S. allotment of Thomas Ansell.

Allotment to Thomas Ansell.

Ground 41a. 1r. 27p. Bounded S. and E. by common fields of Burford : N. by allotment of Thomas Hunt and Richard Heyes : W. allotment of Wm. Lenthal and allotment for Church Lands and Fifteens.

Allotment to Wm. Lenthal as surviving Feoffee of Fifteens Land.

Ground 1a. 2r. 21p. Bounded E. Thomas Ansell : N. and W. Wm. Lenthal : S. allotment for Church Land.

Allotment to Wm. Lenthal for Church Land.

Ground oa. 2r. 21p. Bounded E. Thos. Ansell : N. Fifteen Land : W. Wm. Lenthall and S. inclosures of Westwell.

Allotment to Christopher Kempster.

Ground oa. 3r. 0p. Bounded E. old inclosure of Chr. Kempster : N. Public Road from Burford to Cirencester : W. an allotment to Chr. Kempster : N. Public Road from Burford to Cirencester (*sic* repeated) : W. allotment to Lenthal.

Allotment to Heirs of Henry Furley.

Ground oa. 1r. 23p. Bounded S. and E. allotment Wm. Lenthal : N. the Home Close belonging to the late Henry Furley : W. common field of Tainton.

Allotment to Hon. and Rev. Francis Knollis and Wm. Lenthal, Esq., for poor of Upton in lieu of right to cut furze.

Ground 8a. or. op. Bounded S., E. and N. allotment to Lenthal and W. by certain inclosures of Upton.

Roads.

(i) One publick road and highway leading from Burford to Cirencester beginning at N.E. corner of allotment to Chr. Kempster and leading through and over first allotment to Lenthal into inclosure of Westwell.

(ii) Publick road and highway leading from Burford to Gloucester branching out of last named at the Hand and Post in 1st allotment to Lenthal and leading westward in its ancient course or direction to S.W. corner of the said 1st allotment to Lenthal into the inclosures of Little Barrington.

(iii) Publick road and highway branching out of first mentioned road near a certain piece of land called Bunce's Piece and leading from Upton to Little Barrington through and over first allotment to Lenthal in its ancient course or direction to S.W. corner of allotment to Wm. Upstone into the inclosures of Little Barrington.

(iv) Publick road and highway beginning at N.W. corner of allotment to Robt. Fettiplace and leading through and over first allotment to Lenthal into the first mentioned road leading from Burford to Cirencester which road is commonly called the Bird in Hand road.

(v) Publick road and highway branching out of the Turnpike Road leading from Burford to Cirencester at N.E. side of an inn called the Rose and Crown and leading northward through and over the second allotment to W. Lenthal into and through the hamlet of Upton and from there toward the Paper Mill belonging to Edward Baker and several Farms of Wm. Lenthal.

All which roads to be sixty feet broad between and exclusive of the ditches.

(vi) One private road and public bridle road called the Mill Way of breadth of thirty feet branching out of Bird in Hand road at N.W. corner of allotment to Thomas Castle and leading southward through 1st allotment to Lenthal and allotment to Thos. Ansell into Common field of Burford and thence towards Westwell to be used by owners and occupiers of allotments to Thomas Hunt and Richard Heyes, Thomas Ansell, Fifteen and Church Land and Wm. Lenthal.

(vii) Private road and way of 20 feet branching out of publick road from Upton to Little Barrington at E. side of piece of land called Fernhill through 1st allotment to Lenthal into allotment of Pryor to be used by owners and occupiers of Lenthal's and Pryor's allotments.

(viii) Publick footpath of four feet beginning at the E. side of a piece of land called Bunce's Piece and leading along the same through and over 1st allotment to Lenthal into the public road leading from Upton to Little Barrington.

(ix) Private Footpath of four feet branching out of first mentioned road at N.E. corner of the Downs and leading westward along the same to the allotment of Furze.

STATEMENT OF COSTS

Charges allotted as follows :

	£	s.	d.
Wm. Lenthal Esq.	383	1	10
Thos. Ansell	18	9	4½
Mr. John Prior	15	8	10
Mr. Thos. Hunt and Richard Heyes	5	7	1
Robt. Fettiplace Esq.	2	19	7
Mr. Thos. Castle	2	1	11
Piercy Galliard Esq.	2	1	4
Mr. James Hunt	1	8	2
Mr. William Upstone	1	6	0½
Mr. John Cousins		19	1
Heirs of the late Henry Furley		14	4
Mr. Christopher Kempster		11	7
Feoffees of the Fifteens		12	0
The Church Land		4	6
	£435	5	8

Costs as follows :

	£	s.	d.
The several Bills for passing the Act	262	18	6
Francis Burton Esq. one of the Commissioners Bill	29	0	0
Mr. Baseley's	26	0	0
Mr. Whitehert's	8	8	0
The Clerk's	25	7	0
Mr. Pride's Bill for surveying	11	0	6
Mr. Reve's Bill for surveying	25	3	0
Quality Men	6	6	0
Clare's Bills	21	0	0
Labourers	1	14	0
Mr. Smart's	13	3	0
The Servants	2	12	6
The Attorney's Clerk	1	1	0
	£433	13	6
Returned the Ballance	1	12	2
	£435	5	8

INDEXES

I. GENERAL INDEX

II. INDEX OF PERSONS

Glyn, Robert, 212, 213, 457.
Glynn, Rev. Christopher, 123, 129,
 138–9, 327, 346, 352, 353,
 463, 667.
 „ J., 353.
Goddard, Rev. Daniel Ward, 130.
Godfrey, Henry, 453, 454, 461, 463.
 „ John, 463.
 „ Thomas, 397, 514.
Goloffre, John, 611.
Goodenough, John, 397.
 „ Thomas, 524.
Goram, William, 352, 353, 459.
Goring, Lord, 206.
Gossen, Robert, 450, 454.
 „ William, 357.
Gotherd, Captain, 244.
Gough, William, 609, 612.
Goughman, Lambert, 672.
Gower, William, 181, 653.
Granger, John, 95, 96, 319, 365–7,
 400, 424, 425, 426, 438, 439, 592.
Green, John, 359, 390, 400, 512, 672.
 „ John the younger, 100.
 „ Simon, 46, 98, 103, 323,
 339, 342, 417, 428, 442.
 „ Thomas, 331.
Greene, Humphrey, 330.
Greenaway, Charles, 87, 94, 289.
 „ Mrs. Charlotte Sophia,
 87, 94, 289.
Greenhill, Margaret, 330, 356 : see
 also Vincent.
Greenway, John, 465.
Gregory, Edmond, 450.
 „ Francis, 345.
 „ Griffith, 458.
Grene, James, 97.
 „ John, 318, 672.
 „ Thomas, 95.
 „ William, 339, 417, 441.
Grey, Lord, 218.
Griffin, Benjamin, 139.
 „ James, 512.
 „ William, 512.
Griffith, alias Phillips, John, 323,
 324, 325, 339, 341, 363,
 368, 429, 433, 442, 443.
 „ Philip, 322.
Griffiths, Richard, 68 (note), 73, 74,
 317, 332, 390, 396, 399, 418, 436,
 550.
Grimes, 332.
Grove, John, 96, 318, 400, 425, 438,
 670.
Gunn, John, 345.
Gurney, Henry, 360.

Hague, Charles, 330.
 „ Widow, 332.

Hale, William, 623.
Hall, Christopher, 326.
 „ John, 332, 436, 634.
 „ Roger, 420.
 „ Thomas (of Bampton), 452,
 460.
Hambidge, George, 515.
Hamelet, Johanna, 425.
 „ John, 425.
Hamon, 'filius Venfridi', 301.
Hamond, Manwaryng, 390, 484.
Hampson, Francis, 447.
Hanckes, Richard, 325, 326, 343.
Hanne, John, 672.
Hannes (or Hans), John, 34, 97,
 103, 220, 314, 315, 316,
 321, 322, 323, 338, 339,
 363, 368, 400, 401, 410,
 412, 413, 417, 440, 442,
 453, 462, 551, 626–7, 633.
 „ John the younger, 462.
 „ Richard, 34, 96, 97, 103,
 312, 313, 322, 350, 362,
 401, 439, 626, 628, 630,
 631, 639, 661.
 „ Richard the younger, 364,
 463.
 „ William, 328.
Harcourt, Lord, 397.
Harcourt (or Harecourt), Richard,
 424, 425, 426, 438.
 „ Sir Robert, 28, 103, 118,
 362, 424, 425, 426.
 „ Robert, 92, 581.
 „ Symon, 606, 656.
 „ William, 427.
Harding, Abraham, 448.
 „ John, 470.
Hardgrave, John, 621.
Hardinge, Thomas, 341, 403, 433,
 443.
Hardyng, John, 179.
Harleston, Robert, 352.
Harman, Edmund, 42, 53, 86, 92,
 115, 135, 136, 194, 199,
 265–8, 324, 347, 368,
 394, 503, 628, 629, 639,
 641–3, 657, 679.
 „ Mary, 135, 136, 268, 653.
Harper, Francis, 453, 462.
Harris, Caesar, 435.
 „ John, 96, 116, 121, 369, 392,
 396, 399, 486, 489.
 „ John (of Upton), 144.
 „ Jonathan, 479.
 „ Richard, 319, 423.
 „ Robert, 484.
Harrison, Col., 238, 240.
 „ Edmund, 439.
Harrys, John, 96, 336.

III. INDEX OF PLACES